Kid's Box

Teacher's Book 2

Second Edition

Lucy Frino and Melanie Williams
with Caroline Nixon and Michael Tomlinson

CAMBRIDGE
UNIVERSITY PRESS

CAMBRIDGE
UNIVERSITY PRESS

University Printing House, Cambridge CB2 8BS, United Kingdom

One Liberty Plaza, 20th Floor, New York, NY 10006, USA

477 Williamstown Road, Port Melbourne, VIC 3207, Australia

4843/24, 2nd Floor, Ansari Road, Daryaganj, Delhi – 110002, India

79 Anson Road, #06–04/06, Singapore 079906

Cambridge University Press is part of the University of Cambridge.

It furthers the University's mission by disseminating knowledge in the pursuit of education, learning and research at the highest international levels of excellence.

www.cambridge.org
Information on this title: www.cambridge.org/9781107668409

First published 2008
Second edition 2014
Reprinted 2017

Printed in Italy by Rotolito Lombarda S.p.A.

A catalogue record for this publication is available from the British Library

ISBN 978-1-107-66840-9 Teacher's Book 2
ISBN 978-1-107-64497-7 Pupil's Book 2
ISBN 978-1-107-67161-4 Activity Book with Online Resources 2
ISBN 978-1-107-64304-8 Class Audio CDs 2 (4 CDs)
ISBN 978-1-107-68082-1 Teacher's Resource Book with Online Audio 2
ISBN 978-1-107-68044-9 Flashcards 2 (pack of 103)
ISBN 978-1-107-67499-8 Language Portfolio 2
ISBN 978-1-107-63540-1 Interactive DVD with Teacher's Booklet 2
ISBN 978-1-107-65744-1 Presentation Plus 2
ISBN 978-1-107-62900-4 Posters 2
ISBN 978-1-107-65891-2 Tests CD-ROM 1-2
ISBN 978-1-107-65840-0 Monty's Alphabet Book

Additional resources for this publication at www.cambridge.org/kidsbox

Contents

Language summary

	Key vocabulary	Key grammar and functions	Phonics	Revision
1 Hello again! page 4	**Character names:** *Mr Star, Mrs Star, Stella, Simon, Suzy, Grandma Star, Grandpa Star, Marie, Maskman, Monty, Trevor* **Numbers:** *1-10* **Colours:** *red, yellow, pink, green, orange, blue, purple, brown, black, white, grey*	**Greetings:** *Hello, we're the Star family. Who's he/she? This is my brother, Simon. He's seven, and this is my sister, Suzy. She's four.* **Prepositions:** *in, on, under*	*Long vowel sound: 'ay' (play)*	character names from *Kid's Box 1*, numbers *1–10*, colours, prepositions, food
2 Back to school page 10	**Character names:** *Alex, Lenny, Meera* **School:** *bookcase, board, cupboard, computer, desk, ruler, teacher, television, whiteboard* **Numbers:** 11-20	*How many (books) are there? There are / aren't (ten desks). Is there (a ruler) on the (desk)? Yes, there is. / No there isn't. Are there (ten pens) on the (desk)? Yes, there are. / No, there aren't.* **Prepositions:** *next to*	*Long vowel sound: 'ee' (three)*	character names, numbers, *Where are...?* school objects, food, prepositions
Marie's maths Block graphs page 16		**Trevor's values** Be polite page 17		
3 Play time! page 18	**Toys:** *alien, camera, computer game, kite, lorry, robot, watch*	*this, that, these, those Whose is this (bag)? It's Tom's. Whose are these (shoes)? They're Sue's.*	*Long vowel sound: 'i' (five, fly)*	characters, numbers, food, prepositions, toys, adjectives, clothes, face and body
4 At home page 24	**Furniture:** *bath, bed, clock, lamp, mat, mirror, phone, sofa*	*It's mine. It's yours. Is that hat yours? Yes, it is. / No, it isn't. Are those blue socks yours? Yes, they are. / No, they aren't.*	*Long vowel sound: 'oa/o_e' (boat, phone)*	food, prepositions, toys, adjectives, clothes, face and body, house
Marie's art Origami page 30		**Trevor's values** Re-use and recycle page 31		
Review 1 2 3 4 page 32				
5 Meet my family page 34	**Character names:** *Nelson, Anna, Nick, Kim, Ben, Lucy, May, Lenny, Sam, Frank* **Family:** *baby, cousin, mummy, daddy, grandma, grandpa*	*What are you doing? I'm reading. What's Grandpa doing? He's sleeping.* **Verb + -ing spellings:** *hitting, running, sitting, swimming* **Verbs:** *catch, clean, fly, get, hit, jump, kick, run, sit, sleep, talk, throw*	*Long vowel sound: 'oo' (blue, ruler)*	food, prepositions, toys, adjectives, clothes, face and body, house, family, activities, *have got*, question words, present continuous for present actions

Introduction

Kid's Box introduces pupils to the pleasures of learning English and enables them to consistently improve throughout the seven books in the series. All seven levels develop pupils' abilities in the four skills – listening, speaking, reading and writing – as well as challenging them cognitively and helping them to feel a real sense of achievement in learning. As experienced teachers ourselves, we are aware of the demands and difficulties involved in managing a diverse and mixed ability classroom. Teaching younger learners can be at once the most rewarding and the most soul-destroying of pursuits! Sometimes we can have very bad days, but it's the good days that give us an exhilarating sense of achievement, a sense of being part of a child's future development.

Plutarch reminds us that **'The mind is not a vessel to be filled, but a fire to be ignited'** and this concept of learning underpins *Kid's Box*. Pupils learn when they are interested and involved: when they want to find something out, when they are playing a game, when they are listening to a story, when they are doing craft activities. Learning is an active process in every way and *Kid's Box* makes sure that pupils are physically and mentally active and that they are encouraged to make sense of the language themselves. **'The art of teaching is the art of assisting discovery'**, Mark Van Doren.

The language syllabus of *Kid's Box* has been carefully selected and graded to suit the age and level of the pupils. Language is introduced in context and in manageable chunks, giving pupils plenty of opportunities to practise and become familiar with the meanings and the sounds. Language is recycled throughout the units and pupils can practise the language in different contexts. They can also personalise it. Recycling is particularly important for young learners, who tend to forget quite quickly and who do not have the study skills of older learners. For this reason, there is constant revision and recycling throughout the units and course.

The units are based around the Star family and their friends and toys. Characters give pupils a way of contextualising the language and help them to make it meaningful and purposeful. The characters develop throughout the books so as to sustain the pupils' interest and motivation.

Cambridge English: Young Learners (YLE) Tests

In *Kid's Box* we have followed the syllabus for the Young Learners tests so that each cycle of two levels corresponds to one of the tests. Thus the material covered in the first cycle coincides with that which is required for the Starters test, cycle 2 with the Movers test, and cycle 3 with Flyers. *Kid's Box* covers all the relevant language structures, presents and practises the vocabulary and includes examples of the task-types from the tests. Where certain topics include a vocabulary list which is too comprehensive to include all of the lexical items in the Pupil's Book, additional activities have been offered in the Teacher's Resource Book.

Each Young Learners test consists of three papers: Listening, Reading and Writing, and Speaking. These tests are child-friendly and motivating and have been specially written for primary learners. They are taken by pupils all over the world, have international recognition and are backed by the reputation and research of Cambridge Assessment. They provide a gentle introduction to public exams and research shows that children find the tests highly motivating. The tests can act as a stepping stone to other Cambridge English exams, as the highest level test, Flyers, is roughly equivalent in language level to Key (KET) for Schools. The Young Learners tests are an incentive; however, they should at no stage be seen as obligatory. For further information on the component papers for each test, visit: www.cambridgeenglish.org/exams-and-qualifications/

Common European Framework of Reference for Languages – Learning, Teaching, Assessment

Kid's Box has been written taking into account the proposals included in the Common European Framework of Reference (CEFR). The CEFR has been designed for language teachers and material developers to be able to define different levels of competence and performance. These objectives coincide with those of Cambridge English: Young Learners tests.

Flyers	(at around Level A2 of the CEFR)
Movers	(at Level A1)
Starters	(below Level A1)

The framework places emphasis on values such as pupil autonomy, proposing a task-based methodology with functional evaluation criteria. Although large parts of the CEFR are more relevant to older learners and have not been designed specifically for the primary classroom, it includes two particularly useful parts which are the Common Reference Levels and the English Language Portfolio.

The Common Reference Levels offer a description of what a language learner 'can do' at different stages of the learning process. These levels can be consulted separately, but they have been mirrored here in the Self-evaluation sections.

The Language Portfolio is designed as a compendium of skills acquired and work done which incorporates the 'can do' checklists for self-assessment. This is important for pupil motivation and can also be shown to parents to inform them of the syllabus and objectives set for their children.

Course components

Levels one to six of *Kid's Box* include a Pupil's Book, Activity Book, Class Audio CDs, Teacher's Book, Teacher's Resource Book, Presentation Plus, Online Resources, Interactive DVD, Language Portfolio, Tests CD-ROM and Posters. There are also Flashcards for Levels 1 to 4. The new Starter Level offers a Class Book with CD-ROM, Class Audio CDs, Flashcards, Teacher's Book, Teacher's Resource Book, Presentation Plus, Interactive DVD and Posters.

Pupil's Book

This 112-page full-colour book consists of twelve units. Each unit is six pages in length, with each page providing sufficient material for one lesson. After alternate units there is both a Content and Language Integrated Learning (CLIL) page to learn about other subjects through English and a Values page to develop their social awareness. The Review sections cover language from the four previous units. There is a phonics section within every unit. Lessons include a variety of interesting and motivating activities such as pair work, role plays, craft activities, guessing games, songs and chants. The series' strong cast of characters appears throughout the book and their antics are played out in a picture story at the end of each unit. At the end of the book there is a Starters practice test covering the Listening, Reading and Writing parts of the test.

Activity Book

This 96-page book is designed to give pupils further practice with the new language and to help them consolidate their understanding. The pupils will have fun doing the activities and you will find that they stimulate their creativity too. At the early levels there is colouring and matching. As the pupils gain more confidence in reading and writing, more activities to practise these skills are included. The Activity Book materials are designed to be integrated into the lessons and there is guidance in the Teacher's Book as to how this works. This edition also features a full-page Young Learners test practice activity for each unit. At the end of the book there are six coloured stickers for each unit illustrating the six key vocabulary items. This material steadily accumulates into an attractive and useful picture dictionary which they can use for reference and revision.

Class Audio CDs

The Class Audio CDs contain all of the listening material for the Pupil's Book and Activity Book, including all of the songs and stories. The songs are available in both sung and karaoke versions.

Teacher's Resource Book with Online Audio

The Teacher's Resource Book contains a wealth of photocopiable activities to help with mixed ability classes. There are two reinforcement and two extension worksheets for every unit, as well as song and story worksheets for further exploitation. The Teacher's Resource Book also includes extra Young Learners type tests with listening content online. The book also features word cards to reinforce target vocabulary.

Language Portfolio

In accordance with CEFR guidelines, there is a Language Portfolio of individual competencies to lead the pupil to self-evaluation and to record the learning experience of each pupil throughout the primary school years.

Interactive DVD

As you navigate your way through the Star family house on our interactive DVD, you will find animated versions of the stories in Suzy's room, the songs with animation and video in Mr Star's music room, video documentaries in the living room, craft activities and games in the playroom, interactive games in Simon's room and a quiz in Stella's room.

Teacher's Book

This 240-page interleaved Pupil's and Teacher's Book provides teaching notes for each lesson, which include recording scripts for all listening activities and answer keys for all activities, an overview of the syllabus for each level, extra activities, photocopiable pages and evaluation activities.

Teaching notes

The teaching notes provide step-by-step guidelines for each page. Lesson objectives are clearly described and the materials needed for each lesson are specified. Each lesson starts with a *Warmer* and finishes with an *Ending the lesson* activity. Activities from the Activity Book are integrated with the Pupil's Book activities to provide a balanced range of appropriate activities. There are two *Extra activities* provided for each lesson for times when you need even more material. These Extra activities only appear in the Teacher's Book and there are suggestions in the teaching notes as to when each activity should be used in the lesson. They are not designed only for the end of the lesson. Activities which are similar to the task-types in Young Learners tests have the icon 'YLE'.

Photocopiable pages

There is a photocopiable page for each unit in the back of the Teacher's Book. These pages provide you with a range of manual activities to use with your pupils: for example, there are cards, puppets and sentence wheels. There are full instructions in the teaching notes on how to prepare the materials and when and how to use them in class.

Presentation Plus

Presentation Plus includes Interactive Whiteboard tools, a fully interactive Pupil's Book and Activity Book, digital versions of the Teacher's Book and Teacher's Resource Book, a multimedia library including video from the DVD, Class Audio and access to online teacher training support. This pack enables you to plan and deliver your lessons 'paper-free' from a tablet or a computer.

Online Resources

The online platform includes games and extra grammar, vocabulary and writing activities for every single unit, providing plenty of extra practice. All the pupil's online work can be tracked and reviewed by the teacher.

Tests CD-ROM

The Level 1 and 2 Tests CD-ROM and Audio CD allows you to regularly assess your pupils in different ways. You can choose the unit tests, review tests and end-of-level tests, as customisable Microsoft Word documents. If you are preparing pupils for the Young Learners tests you can additionally select the Cambridge English: Young Learners (YLE) style unit tests, review tests and end-of-level tests, as Adobe PDFs.

Posters

These colourful and appealing posters aid revision by giving pupils the chance to practise unit language in a different and fun context. They can be added to the classroom wall as you progress through the course to aid revision. This pack includes twelve posters with clear teaching notes available online.

Flashcards

There are 103 flashcards to accompany level 2. These colourful flashcards illustrate the key vocabulary items of each unit on one side and have the words on the other. They are large enough for all pupils to see and there are numerous ideas of how to use them in the Teacher's Book for each lesson.

What does *Kid's Box* offer?

'To awaken interest and kindle enthusiasm is the sure way to teach easily and successfully', Tyron Edwards.
Once pupils are interested, and ready and eager to learn, then the job of teaching them becomes so much easier. The materials in *Kid's Box* have been designed to do just that. Here's how and why it works:

- **Humour through the characters and the stories**
  'The important thing is not so much that every child should be taught, as that every child should be given the wish to learn', John Lubbock.

  For younger pupils, motivation is vital if the language acquisition process is to be successful. We have tried to include an element of humour in the presentations and, more particularly, in the story which rounds off each of the units. This story is designed to revise what pupils have been studying and galvanise them to study more because they want to follow the adventures of the characters.

- **Creativity and learning through action and activity**
  'I hear and I forget. I see and I remember. I do and I understand', Chinese proverb.

  Young learners need a lot of meaningful, contextualised practice if they are to become successful language learners. In *Kid's Box* there is plenty of 'hands on' practice. Drawing, colouring, 'make and do', songs, games and chants are all activity types which form an integral part of the learning process. These enable pupils to be creative and they help to anchor knowledge more effectively. It's only through repeated practice that skills, awareness and understanding can be developed.
- **Connecting to the world outside the classroom**
  'A child educated only at school is an uneducated child', George Santayana.

  The CLIL sections bring the outside world into the classroom so that pupils learn about the world around them as they learn English. This helps them understand that English is more than a classroom subject and lets them realise ways in which English can be used as a tool for knowledge.

  'I like a teacher who gives you something to take home to think about besides homework', Lilly Tomlin (Edith Ann).
- **Discovery and the development of learner autonomy**
  'The object of teaching a child is to enable him to get along without his teacher', Elbert Hubbard.
  For pupils to be able to learn effectively and to continue to learn, they need to be encouraged and enabled to find things out for themselves. *Kid's Box* includes self-correction and other activities to develop learner autonomy. Communicative activities, such as pair work, group work and role play, give pupils the opportunity to work independently of the teacher. In these types of activities, the teacher's role is as a guide and facilitator. In this instance we should stand back a little from the activity and monitor and assist when necessary.
- **Promoting tolerance and respect**
  'The highest result of Education is tolerance', Helen Keller.
  The material and activities in the book help pupils to appreciate cultural diversity, respect differences and develop human values. Respect for and protection of the natural environment goes hand in hand with the respecting of other human beings. This theme runs throughout the whole of *Kid's Box* and in particular in the Values sections of the Pupil's Book and the Activity Book.

Learning styles / Multiple intelligences

'If a child can't learn the way we teach, maybe we should teach the way they learn', Ignacio Estrada.
We now understand that people learn in different ways. We don't talk about 'intelligence' any more, we talk about 'intelligences'. The activities in *Kid's Box* are designed to stimulate these different intelligences. This means there will always be something to appeal to every learner.

- **Linguistic intelligence:** sensitivity to the written and spoken word and the ability to learn languages.

  It is a core element of any language course, and in *Kid's Box* this is exploited in combination with the other intelligences.
- **Interpersonal intelligence:** effective communication with others.

  Communication activities have been incorporated from the Starter Level onwards. It is a vital aspect of language learning and is essential in making younger learners aware that language is a tool for communication and not just another school subject. Communication activities help interpersonal skills, encouraging children to work together and develop important communication strategies.
- **Intrapersonal intelligence:** expression of inner thoughts and feelings.

  Throughout the course there are various reflective activities, for example 'MY PROGRESS' and the personalisation activities, which help pupils become more aware of themselves.
- **Musical intelligence:** appreciation of rhythm and music.

  This intelligence runs almost parallel to linguistic intelligence, as Howard Gardner points out. Each unit of *Kid's Box* includes a song as well as occasional raps, rhymes and chants.
- **Bodily-kinaesthetic intelligence:** coordination and connection with the whole body.

  This is extremely important for the developing minds and bodies of younger learners, as there is a significant relation between mental and physical activity. In *Kid's Box* there are plenty of action songs and rhymes, which can help develop bodily-kinaesthetic intelligence at the same time as offering a change of rhythm and activity to the ever restless young learner.
- **Logical-mathematical intelligence:** problem solving and logical thought.

  There is a range of different activity types for this intelligence in *Kid's Box*. These activities help develop logical reasoning, problem solving and the detection of patterns. We feel they are vital and extremely motivating.
- **Visual-spatial intelligence:** expression and understanding through the visual world.

  This intelligence is one of the key ways that children learn. In *Kid's Box* there is a range of ways in which pupils' visual-spatial intelligence is supported and developed, such as the full colour illustrations in the Pupil's Books, the flashcards and the drawing and colouring activities.

Tips for teachers

Preparation

- In order to guarantee a positive learning experience, pupils need to be properly prepared before doing any task. Ensure they have the language they need to carry out an activity and that they know exactly how to do it.
- Before starting an activity, demonstrate it. For pair-work activities, choose an individual pupil to help you. Do the first question of the pair-work task with the pupil for the class to get an idea. You can follow this up with an open pair demonstration, choosing two pupils from the class to do another question and answer for the whole class.
- When you divide the class into pairs or groups, point to each pupil and say, for example, *A–B, A–B, A–B* and so on, so they are in no doubt what their role is. You can follow this up with *As, put up your hands. Bs, put up your hands* as a further check. Try to give simple, clear instructions in English. Say, for example, *As ask the question and Bs answer the question: A–B, A–B, A–B. Then Bs ask the question and As answer the question: B–A, B–A, B–A.*

- Always bring a few extra copies of the photocopiable worksheets to avoid tears if any pupils do it wrong and want to start again.

Classroom dynamics

'A good teacher, like a good entertainer, first must hold his audience's attention, then he can teach his lesson', John Henrik Clarke.

- Try to move around the classroom while explaining or doing the activities. Circulating among the pupils enables you more effectively to supervise and monitor those who may need more attention at times.
- In the same way that it is a good idea for teachers to move around, it is also advisable to move the pupils themselves around occasionally. By periodically changing seating arrangements, you can help group dynamics and break up potentially disruptive pupils. For example, weaker pupils could be put next to stronger ones, and more hard-working pupils next to disruptive ones. Pupils might benefit from working with learners they may not usually associate with.
- When forming pairs or groups, we suggest that, whenever possible, pupils just move their chairs. For group work, they can bring chairs around one or two tables, allowing them an easy environment for discussion and written work. For pair work, they can position their two chairs to face each other. This allows a more realistic eye-to-eye communication situation. This change of seating prepares them for the oral work they are about to begin.

Noise

- While speaking activities which involve movement around the classroom can make the class more lively and dynamic, they will also generate a lot of excitement. When pupils are excited, they can become noisy and may even use their first language to talk about or discuss some aspect of the activity. Although it can be difficult to get used to it at first, noise in the classroom is tolerable if it is related directly to the activity and is an expression of interest or enthusiasm for the task in hand. You should ensure, however, that only English is used for the completion of tasks and for correction at the end of the activity.

Teaching and learning

'Mistakes are the portals of discovery', James Joyce.

- Making mistakes is a vital part of the learning process, so when pupils are asked to invent their own sentences, stories, chants, etc. we should not expect these to be perfect. Sometimes accuracy should be forfeited for the sake of creativity, enthusiastic participation and learning.
- Activities that pupils traditionally find engaging include: moving about, singing, playing games, doing puzzles and colouring in. Wherever possible, use these as effective teaching tools. In this way, young learners can use language to practise English, and work very hard, without being conscious of it. By setting them in meaningful contexts, the diverse disciplines of language learning such as grammar, reading, pronunciation and communication can be taught with a dynamic and child-friendly approach.
- The Extra activities for each lesson can be used when you feel that pupils need more practice with some of the language, or when you think you will finish the lesson material before the end of the lesson.
- Try to avoid the immediate repetition of an activity simply because it has worked well in class and your pupils have enjoyed it. If you do this, the novelty will quickly wear off and pupils will become bored. Save it for a later occasion and they will come back to it with fresh enthusiasm.
- When pupils are doing listening activities, it is usual for them to listen to the material twice. After the first listening, it is a good idea for pupils to check their answers with each other. This makes them feel more confident if they have the same answers, and is less intimidating if they don't. This approach also gives them a purpose for listening the second time: to confirm or to check again. When checking answers with the whole class, try to include as many pupils as you can and encourage them to say longer phrases rather than single words.
- Pupils are sometimes shy to speak out. They say the answer quietly to the teacher and then the teacher repeats it for the class. This is effective – but it does not help the pupils develop their speaking or listening skills. Whenever possible, you should encourage pupils to speak loudly and clearly and, if the rest of the class didn't hear what the pupil said, you should ask the pupil to repeat, rather than repeat it yourself.
- **'A teacher is a person who never says anything once'**, Howard Nemerov.
  Recycling is an important part of the learning process. Don't expect pupils to remember everything from a previous lesson in the next one. They will only absorb what attracts or interests them, and what they are ready to learn. *Kid's Box* builds in regular recycling and, as the pupils get older, they will come to realise that they can investigate something further by themselves if it really interests them.
- Be flexible within teaching. It is important to take time to listen to pupils and to connect with them. You should try to familiarise yourself with their likes and dislikes and identify both their learning and their emotional needs. If you can do this, then you will be better able to support them in their learning.

Assessment and evaluation

- With pupils of this age, it is best to use continuous assessment. This means we monitor their progress in the classroom and use this information to help us with our teaching. For example, we may find that we need to review language previously taught, or that we can add more challenging activities because pupils are ready for these.
- Children do not develop at the same rate and they do not learn in the same way. So we need to assess each pupil as an individual and not compare them with the other pupils in the class. We should look for progress and development in every pupil. With young children, we should assess and monitor their social and emotional development, as well as their learning of English. This means we should praise effort, and encourage them to share and to work in pairs and groups, as well as giving them feedback on their English.

Discipline

'No life ever grows great until it is focused, dedicated, disciplined', Harry Emerson Fosdick.

- One of the most challenging aspects of teaching young learners is holding their interest in the classroom. Pupils have limitless energy, combined with an extremely limited attention span. We have to juggle these factors to try to avoid boredom, restlessness and de-motivation, all of which lead to problems with discipline. By channelling pupils' innate energy to the good, we can often avoid unruliness and indiscipline. A lot of discipline problems arise when pupils are underchallenged and bored, or when activities are too repetitive. *Kid's Box* has been written by experienced teachers who at all times have borne in mind the needs and requirements of pupils and have included a variety of activities for them to enjoy.
- It is important that you establish a context of discipline in your class. Make sure pupils know what is acceptable and what is not and make sure you treat all pupils in the same way. Pupils are very aware when we are not 'fair'. Clear and fair discipline parameters create a 'safe' classroom environment in which pupils can work confidently and freely. This makes for an ordered, busy classroom, rather than an anarchic one.

Songs, rhymes and chants

- For the activities based around songs, rhymes and chants, it is not always necessary for pupils to understand every word outside the key words being practised. In these activities, we are more interested in pupils understanding the gist, and we are using the rhyme as a means with which to practise language, rhythm and pronunciation. The visuals that accompany the rhymes, songs and chants, and the actions included in some, should provide pupils with sufficient information to be able to understand the overall concept. It is important then, at this stage, not to spend precious class time on lengthy and complicated explanations of specific words.
- Get pupils to stand up when performing the songs, rhymes or chants. It can make a tremendous difference to their performance and enjoyment.
- Songs, rhymes and chants can be presented in different ways to make them more interesting and challenging. These techniques are especially useful if you want to go back to previously-used material for revision or further exploitation and want to avoid your pupils' reaction of 'We've already done this!'.
  - Whisper the rhyme or phrase while clicking your fingers. Repeat the rhyme, getting gradually louder each time and then reverse the process.
  - Say a rhyme or chant whilst clapping hands and tapping your foot in time to the rhythm.
  - Divide the class into groups and ask them to repeat the rhyme or chant in rounds. To do this, the first group starts to say the rhyme and then, at a suitable point, usually one or two lines into it, the second group starts to say the rhyme from the beginning.
  - With your class audio or video recorder, record the class performing. Be sure to give them a round of applause and encourage the rest of the class to do the same. Let your pupils listen to themselves. If they feel that they could improve on a second attempt, record them again.
- It can be extremely motivating for children to watch their own performances on video, but if you video or photograph your pupils, make sure you get written permission from parents or guardians first.

Competition

- An element of competition can make many pupils try harder. However, while a competition can be a good incentive for an otherwise unenthusiastic pupil, it can sometimes be de-motivating for a less able but ordinarily hard-working one. Before playing a competitive game, it may be useful to explain to pupils that this is only a means of learning. Although they may not win the game, all pupils are 'winners' if they know more English at the end than they knew at the beginning. Help pupils to understand that when they play a game they can practise and learn more English, so they each win a prize and that prize is knowledge.
  Nonetheless, it is always a good idea to balance competitive games with cooperative ones and to include other activities so that you can reward and praise individuals according to their own needs and performance.

Display

- Pupils find it extremely motivating to have their work displayed and will generally work hard to produce work to the best of their ability if they know it is going to be seen by others. So try to arrange to display pupils' work around the classroom or school whenever possible. Don't forget to include work by all the pupils (not in every display, but over a period of time) and to change the displays regularly.

Craft activities: storage of material

- It is useful to keep supplies for craft activities, for example scissors, glue, wool, crayons, in a large box in the classroom. Then when it is time for craft activities, you can put the box on a table and pupils can come and collect what they need.
- Make sure pupils always clear up at the end of craft activities; that they put materials back in the box and that they put rubbish in the bin. You will need to supply each pupil with an envelope for photocopiable activities, such as game cards. At the end of the activity, pupils write their name on their envelope and put their cards inside. With younger pupils, it is best if you look after the envelopes until the next time you want to use the cards.

A final word

We've had a lot of fun writing this course and sincerely hope that you and your pupils have as much fun using it.

Caroline Nixon and Michael Tomlinson, Murcia 2014.

Classroom language

The following language appears at the end of Class Audio CD4.

CD 4, 26

1. Greetings

Hello.
Good morning.
Good afternoon.
Goodbye.
See you tomorrow.

CD 4, 27

2. Classroom activities

Open your Pupil's Book.
Close your Activity Book.
Look at page 1.
Look at the picture.
Look at the flashcard.
Look at the board.
What can you see?
Look at me.
Look at your partner.
Listen to the CD.
Listen to me.
Listen to your partner.

CD 4, 28

3. Songs and chants

Let's sing a song.
Let's say a chant.
Clap your hands.
Click your fingers.
Stamp your feet.
Make a circle.
Watch me, please.
Do the actions.
All together.

CD 4, 29

4. Stories

Let's listen to a story.
Listen to the next part.
Who wants to act out the story?
Who wants to be Maskman?
Can you remember the story?
What happens?

CD 4, 30

5. Crafts and projects

Find your felt tips.
Have you got some paper?
Have you got some glue?
Fold here.
Cut out the picture.
Cut here.
Stick the pictures on the card.

CD 4, 31

6. Classroom management

Sit down, please.
Stand up, please.
Come here, please.
Work in pairs.
Hands up!
Open your books.
Close your books.
Have you got a pen?
Have you got a pencil?
Have you got an eraser?
Have you got a sharpener?
Have you got a ruler?

CD 4, 32

7. Praise

Good.
Very nice.
Well done.
That's lovely.
That's very good.
I'm pleased with you today.
Much better.

CD 4, 33

8. Taking turns

Take it in turns.
It's your turn.
Wait a moment. It isn't your turn.
One at a time.

CD 4, 34

9. Discipline

Quietly, please
Sssshhhh.
There's a lot of noise today.
Be quiet, please.

1 Hello again!

1 CD1 2 Listen and point.

2 CD1 3 Listen and repeat.

OBJECTIVES: By the end of the lesson, pupils will have reviewed greetings and introductions.

• TARGET LANGUAGE

Key language: *Hello, I'm … , We're … , My name's … , Goodbye. What's your/his/her name? How old are you? to be*

Additional language: *look, listen, open/close your books/the door, one, star, pencil*

Revision: numbers *1–10*, character names from *Kid's Box 1*

• MATERIALS REQUIRED

Flashcards: (characters) 1–7

Extra activity 1: ten large pieces of card, with a number in words between *one* and *ten* written on each one, e.g. *five*

Optional: *Kid's Box 2 Language Portfolio* pages 1, 2 and 7

Warmer

- Introduce yourself. Say *Hello. My name's* (your name). Walk up to a pupil and repeat. Add *What's your name?* The pupil responds, e.g. *Hello. My name's* (pupil's name). / *I'm* (pupil's name). Repeat with four or five more pupils.
- Pupils stand up. Clap your hands. They turn to the pupil on their left and take turns to introduce themselves. Clap your hands. They turn to the pupil on their right and introduce themselves. Repeat for the pupils behind and in front.

Presentation

- Display the flashcards of the seven characters. If pupils studied *Kid's Box 1*, elicit the names. If they didn't, hold up each flashcard in turn, say the name and pupils repeat.
- Place the flashcards around the room. Say, e.g. *Point to Suzy.* Pupils point. Repeat with the other characters, saying the instructions quickly one after another.

PB4. ACTIVITY **1.** *Listen and point.*

- Say *Open your Pupil's Books at page 4, please.* Hold up your book and point to the page. Draw a star on the board. Elicit what it is. Say *Find the star in the picture.* Pupils check in pairs. Check with the class (on Mr Star's belt). Pupils say *Here it is.*
- Elicit what pupils can see in the picture (the Star family, their house, garden, dog, cat, etc.).
- Say *Listen and point.* Play the CD. Pupils listen and point to the characters. Set the pre-listening questions: *How old is Stella? How old is Simon? How old is Suzy?* Say *Listen again and answer.* Pupils check in pairs. Check answers (eight, seven, four).

CD 1, 02

STELLA: Hello again! We're the Star family. I'm Stella Star and I'm eight. This is my brother, Simon. He's seven, and this is my sister, Suzy. She's four.
SIMON: This is my grandmother. She's Grandma Star.
GRANDMA: Hello.
SIMON: This is my grandfather. He's Grandpa Star.
SIMON: Grandpa, say hello.
GRANDPA: Oh! Hello, everybody.
MRS STAR: And we're Mr and Mrs Star.
SIMON: What's your name? How old are you?

PB4. ACTIVITY **2.** *Listen and repeat.*

- Say *Look at the picture. Listen and repeat.* Play the CD. Pause after each name for pupils to repeat. Play the CD again. Pupils chorus in time with the recording.

CD 1, 03

Stella, Simon, Suzy, Mr Star, Mrs Star, Grandma Star, Grandpa Star

Practice

- Invite four pupils (boys and girls) to the front. Ask each one *What's your name? How old are you?* Point to each of the pupils in turn and ask the class *What's his/her name? How old is he/she?* Pupils respond, e.g. *She's* (name). *She's* (age). Repeat with another four pupils.
- Weave the questions and answers around the classroom in the same way, gesturing to individual pupils to ask as well as answer.

AB4. ACTIVITY **1.** *Write.*

- Say *Open your Activity Books at page 4, please. Look at Activity 1. Who can you see?* Elicit the characters from the class. Hold up your book and point to the example. Point to each person in turn. Elicit from pupils what they write, e.g. point to *I'm Suzy.* Pupils respond *She's Suzy.*
- Pupils work individually and complete the activity.
- Correct the activity orally with the whole class.

Key: He's Simon. She's Suzy. He's Mr Star. She's Mrs Star. He's Grandpa.

AB4. ACTIVITY **2.** *Draw and write.*

- Say *Look at Activity 2, please.* Point to the frame and say *Whose picture goes here?* The class responds with their own name. Point to each of the questions and elicit the response for a few pupils as an example.
- Pupils draw a picture of themselves and write the answers. Remind them to use *I'm …* and to write their age in words.

Extra activities: see page T114 (if time)

Language Portfolio

- Pupils complete pages 1, 2 and 7 of *Kid's Box 2 Language Portfolio* (*About me, My language skills, English and me*). These materials fit well at the beginning of the lesson. Help with new language as necessary.

Ending the lesson

- Display the character flashcards on the board. Wave and say, e.g. *Goodbye, Suzy.* Invite a pupil to come and take the flashcard of Suzy off the board. Repeat with the other characters. Turn to the class, wave and say *Goodbye, class.* Pupils respond *Goodbye,* (your name).

OBJECTIVES: By the end of the lesson, pupils will have practised greetings and asked and answered questions using *Who's … ?*

• TARGET LANGUAGE

Key language: *Hello. I'm … Goodbye. Who's he/she?* character and toy names (*Monty, Maskman, Marie, Trevor*)

Additional language: *stand up, sit down, point to, pick up, open, close*

Revision: *blue, grey, pink, red, white, purple, yellow, black, brown, orange, green, numbers*

• MATERIALS REQUIRED

Flashcards: (characters) 1–11

Two sets of number cards

Extra activity 1: 11 large pieces of paper, each with one of the colours written on or colour word cards from *Kid's Box 2 Teacher's Resource Book* (page 87)

Extra activity 2: 16 simple sums using numbers 1–10.

Warmer

- Review the Star family, using the flashcards. Flash a card and elicit who it is. Display it on the board. Include Trevor, Marie, Monty and Maskman. If the pupils did not study *Kid's Box 1*, make sure they repeat the new names several times.
- Point to the flashcards in turn. The class says the name. Turn the first one to face the board. Point to each card (including the one facing the board). The class says the names. Repeat, turning one more card to face the board each time. When all flashcards are facing the board, continue the game, turning a flashcard face up each time until all are visible again.

PB5. ACTIVITY 3. *Listen and answer.*

- Say *Open your Pupil's Books at page 5, please. Look at Activity 3.* Say *Who's number nine? Who's number five? Where's Monty?* Say *Listen and answer.* Play the first part of the CD as an example. Check pupils know what to say. Play the rest of the CD. Pupils whisper the response to their partner each time. Play the CD again, pausing after each question. This time invite different pairs to respond each time.

Key: 4 Mr Star, 1 Suzy, 8 Monty, 3 Stella, 6 Grandma Star, 2 Simon, 9 Marie, 10 Maskman, 5 Mrs Star, 7 Grandpa Star

CD 1, 04

TREVOR: Hello. I'm Trevor.
Look at number four. Who's he?
Look at number one. Who's she?
Look at number eight. Who's he?
Look at number three. Who's she?
Look at number six. Who's she?
Look at number two. Who's he?
Look at number nine. Who's she?
Look at number ten. Who's he?
Look at number five. Who's she?
Look at number seven. Who's he?

PB5. ACTIVITY 4. *Ask and answer.*

- Say *Look at number three. Who's she?* The class responds *Stella.* Repeat three or four more times with other questions and answers in open pairs, e.g. Pupil A asks; Pupil B responds; Pupil C asks; Pupil D responds.
- Say *Look at Activity 4. Now you ask and answer in pairs. Take turns.* Put pupils into pairs. Pupils do the activity in pairs. Monitor the pairs as they are working and help where needed.

Team game

- Divide the class into two teams. Hand out the number cards to each team. Ten pupils in each team take and hold up a card. Team members take it in turns to ask and answer, e.g. Team A (about Team B): *Look at number seven. Who's he/she?* Team B: *He's/She's* (name). Award points for correct questions and answers. The team with the most points is the winner.

AB5. ACTIVITY 3. *Colour the stars.*

- Say *Open your Activity Books at page 5, please. Look at Activity 3.* Hold up your book and point to the example. Elicit the sentence from the class (*Colour two stars*). Say *What colour?* Pupils suggest a colour. Repeat for number 2.
- Pupils work individually and colour the correct number of stars in the colours they choose. They can work together. Pupils check in pairs. Check with the class.

AB5. ACTIVITY 4. *Match and join.*

- Do a few simple sums quickly around the class, e.g. say *One and one is …* Wait for the class to respond *two.* Repeat with other simple sums.
- Say *Look at Activity 4, please.* Hold up your book. Read the example sum (*six and one is …*) and elicit the response. With your finger, follow the line in the example to 7 and then *seven.* Say *Now draw the lines for the other sums.*
- Pupils work individually and then check in pairs. Check with the class.

Key: 1. (5); 2. (3); 4. (9); 5. (6); 6. (8); 7. (10)

Extra activities: see page T114 (if time)

Ending the lesson

- Play the Please game. Pupils stand up. Demonstrate the game first. Say, e.g. *Point to your chair.* Pupils don't point. Say, e.g. *Open your Pupil's Books, please.* Pupils open their Pupil's Books. Play the game using the following instructions: *sit down, stand up, close, open, point to / touch a book/pencil/table/chair/pen.* Pupils who respond incorrectly (e.g. do it when you don't say *please*) are out and sit down. Stop when you have a small group of winners.

3 Listen and answer.

CD1 4

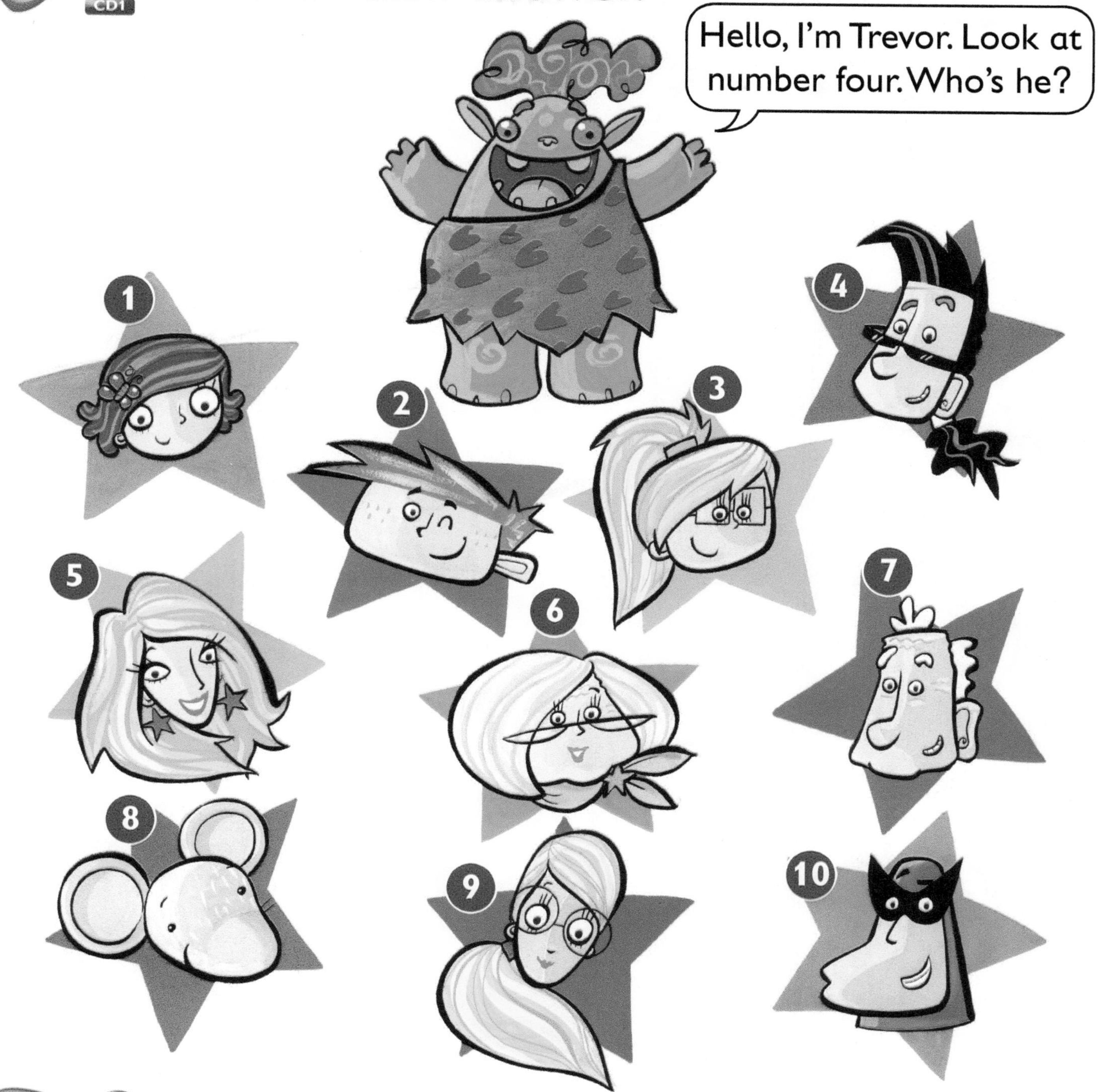
Hello, I'm Trevor. Look at number four. Who's he?
1
2
3
4
5
6
7
8
9
10

4 Ask and answer.

Look at number three. Who's she?

Stella.

Vocabulary

Suzy Simon Stella Mr Star
Mrs Star Grandpa Star Grandma Star

Grammar

What's your name? How old are you?
Who's he / she?

5 CD1 Listen, point and repeat.

6 CD1 Say the chant.

OBJECTIVES: By the end of the lesson, pupils will have learned to say and recognise the letters of the alphabet.

• TARGET LANGUAGE

Key language: the alphabet, *How old are you? Can you spell your name, please?*
Additional language: *his/her*
Revision: *What's your name?*

• MATERIALS REQUIRED

Photocopiable activity 1 (see page T100), copied onto thin card, one copy for each pupil, scissors, an envelope for each pupil
Flashcards: (colours) 12, 13, 15, 18, 20–22; crayons
Optional: *Kid's Box Teacher's Resource Book 2* Unit 1 song worksheet (page 13)

Warmer

- Pupils take out their crayons. Give pupils instructions to follow, e.g. *Hold up the blue crayon. Put it under your Pupil's Book. Put the yellow crayon next to the book. Take the green crayon and put it under your chair.*

Presentation

PB6. ACTIVITY **5.** *Listen, point and repeat.*

- Say *Open your Pupil's Books at page 6*, please. Look at Activity 5.
- Hold up your book and point to the letters. Gesture from left to right along the first row of letters and say the letters aloud. Pupils repeat. Do the same with the rest of the rows. Make sure pupils are reading from left to right, if they do not do this in their first language.
- Display the colour flashcards in a horizontal line on the board. Help pupils to notice the colours of the letters in their books. The letters are coloured to help with pronunciation: grey = /eɪ/ = a, h, j, k; green = /iː/ = b, c, d, e, g, p, t, v; red = /e/ = f, l, m, n, s, x, z; white = /aɪ/ = i, y; yellow = /əʊ/ = o; blue = /uː/ = q, u, w; dark brown = /ɑː/ = r
- Say *Listen, point and repeat.* Play the CD. Pupils listen and point the first time. Play the CD again for pupils to point and repeat the colours and letter names.

CD 1, 05

Grey: a, h, j, k,
Green: b, c, d, e, g, p, t, v
Red: f, l, m, n, s, x, z
White: i, y
Yellow: o
Blue: q, u, w
Brown: r

PB6. ACTIVITY **6.** *Say the chant.*

- Say *Listen to the chant and point to the letters*. Play the CD. Pupils point to the letters. Make sure they are moving from left to right along the rows.
- Play the chant again in sections for the pupils to repeat.

CD 1, 06

a b c d e f g
h i j k l m n o p
q r s t u v
w x y z

Practice

- Ask an able pupil: *What's your name?* When the pupil says it, ask *Can you spell your name, please?* Help the pupil. The class spell the name. Write the name on the board. Repeat. Tell pupils to write their names in their books. They work in pairs. Pupil A asks *Can you spell your name, please?* Pupil B spells it and Pupil A writes it. They swap roles.

Photocopiable 1: see pages T98 and T100

AB6. ACTIVITY **5.** *Listen and colour.*

- Say *Open your Activity Books at page 6, please. Look at Activity 5.* Tell pupils to take out their crayons. Say *Ready? Listen and colour.* Remind pupils to make a dot in the colour the first time they listen. Play the CD. Pupils listen and place a coloured dot on the letter. Play the CD again for pupils to check. Ask, e.g. *What colour is 'p'? What letter is purple?* Pupils colour the letters. Note: These are not the same colours as were used to help with pronunciation. All theses letters have the same pronunciation pattern (/iː/). This phonetic grouping is aimed at pupils who do not use the Roman alphabet in their first language.

Key: g = black, b = orange, v = purple, p = pink, c = yellow, t = brown, e = green, d = blue

CD 1, 07

Colour g black. Colour b orange. Colour v purple. Colour p pink. Colour c yellow. Colour t brown. Colour e green. Colour d blue.

AB6. ACTIVITY **6.** *Listen and point. Write the words.* **[YLE]**

- Say *Look at Activity 6.* Write the two example anagrams on the board: *lealSt, igteh.* Elicit what they are. Tell pupils the first is a name and the second a number. Write them correctly on the board. Don't write the capital letters at the beginning of the name. Encourage pupils to use their letter cards for the other anagrams. They place the cards on their desk and move them around to make the correct spelling. This helps the kinaesthetic learners. Pupils check in pairs. Play the CD for pupils to listen and check.

Key: 2 Simon, seven; 3 Suzy, four

CD 1, 08

1. This is Stella. She's eight. 2. This is Simon. He's seven.
3. This is Suzy. She's four.

Extra activity: see page T114 (if time)

Optional activity

- Hand out copies of the Unit 1 song worksheet from *Teacher's Resource Book 2* and do the rhyming activity (see pages 8 and 13 of the *Teacher's Resource Book*).

Ending the lesson

- Pupils stand up. Do the alphabet chant again together with the CD. Repeat.

OBJECTIVES: By the end of the lesson, pupils will have had more practice with the letters of the alphabet.

• TARGET LANGUAGE

Key language: the alphabet, colours, *Can you spell … , please?*
Additional language: *in alphabetical order*

• MATERIALS REQUIRED

Photocopiable 1 alphabet cards from the previous lesson (page T100), one set for each pupil plus one set of your own.
Optional: *Teacher's Resource Book 2* Unit 1 Reinforcement worksheets 1 and 2 (pages 9 and 10).

Warmer

- Pupils place their alphabet cards on their desks in the same order as on page 6 of the Pupil's Book (alphabetical order). Pupils stand up. Say the alphabet chant with them. They point to the letters on their desks as they say them. Repeat.

PB7. ACTIVITY **7.** *Ask and answer.*

- Say *Open your Pupil's Books at page 7, please.* Say *Point to purple.* Pupils point. Repeat with the other colours. Draw pupils' attention to the speech bubbles on the photograph and elicit the question and answer. Repeat the question with two more colours. Invite a pupil to ask the question about another colour. The class spells it out. Continue until all the colours have been spelt out.
- Pupils work in pairs. They take turns to ask the question and to spell the colours.

Practice

- Hand out all the alphabet cards from your set to different pupils (26 pupils). If you have fewer pupils, give some pupils more than one. Ask pupils to come to the board and to put the letters in order from left to right on the board. Make two lines if you can't get 26 letters in one line. Point to each letter and pupils repeat.
- Ask five pupils, whose names each start with a different letter of the alphabet, to come to the front. Tell them to stand in the order of the alphabet. Help them by pointing to the alphabet on the board. Check with the class if the pupils are in the correct order. Repeat.

PB7. ACTIVITY **8.** *Order the colours.*

- Write the following colours on the board: *Blue, black, brown.* Ask pupils to put them in order. Show them how it's done: point to the first letters and say *B, b, b. They're the same.* Point to the second letters and say *L, l, r. They're different. R comes after l so brown is last.* Point to the third letter and say *U, a. They're different. A comes before u. Can anyone tell me which word is first?* Write them on the board in order: *Black, blue, brown.* Repeat for *green* and *grey*, and *pink* and *purple*.
- Say *Look at Activity 8. Now put all the colours in alphabetical order.* Pupils work in pairs and write the colours in order in their notebooks. Tell them to write them as a list. Monitor pupils as they are working and remind them what is written on the board. Elicit the correct order from the class.

Key: black, blue, brown, green, grey, orange, pink, purple, red, white, yellow

AB7. ACTIVITY **7.** *Read the question. Listen and write a name or a number. There is one example.* **[YLE]**

- Say *Open your Activity Books at page 7, please. Look at Activity 7.*
- Point to the picture of the boy and girl and elicit what the children are doing (*reading*) and what pupils can see (e.g. *books, a library, bags*).
- Say *Listen and write a name or a number. Let's look at and listen to the example.* Point to the example question and read it with the class. Play the example on the CD and pause to indicate the example answer. Ask *Name or number?* Pupils respond (*Name*). Before playing the rest of the CD, encourage pupils to read the rest of the questions and think about whether each answer will be a name or a number.
- Play the CD. Pupils write their answers in pencil. Play the CD again for pupils to check. They can compare answers in pairs. Check as a class or in open pairs.

Key: 1 seven, 2 'Kim', 3 Grace, 4 nine, 4 nine

CD 1, 09

Are you the boy in this classroom?
Yes. My name's Dan.
Can you spell your name?
OK. It's D-a-n.
Can you see the answer? Now you listen and write a name or a number.

1. How old are you, Dan?
   I'm seven.
   Seven! You're very big!
   Yes.
2. What's your favourite book, Dan?
   My favourite book is 'Kim'.
   Can you spell that?
   K-i-m. It's very good.
   Yes, it is. I like the story, too.
3. Is this your friend next to you?
   Yes, it is.
   What's her name?
   Her name's Grace.
   That's nice. How do you spell it?
   G-r-a-c-e.
4. How old is she?
   She's nine today.
   Nine today!
   That's right. It's her birthday.
5. Is Grace in your class at school?
   No, she isn't. She's in class nine.
   Pardon?
   She's in class nine. It's a big class.

Extra activities: see page T114 (if time)

Optional activity

- Unit 1 Reinforcement worksheets 1 and 2 from *Teacher's Resource Book 2* (see pages 8–10 of the *Teacher's Resource Book*).

Ending the lesson

- Teach and do the following chant with the pupils.

Teacher:	Pupils respond:
Give me an o	*o*
Give me an r	*r*
Give me an a	*a*
Give me an n	*n*
Give me a g	*g*
Give me an e	*e*
What does that spell?	*orange*
What does that spell?	*orange*

7 Ask and answer.

pink
grey
green
orange
red
brown
white
blue
yellow
black
purple

8 Order the colours.

Black, blue, brown …

9 10 CD1 Monty's phonics

Four snakes are playing games!

10 Say and answer.

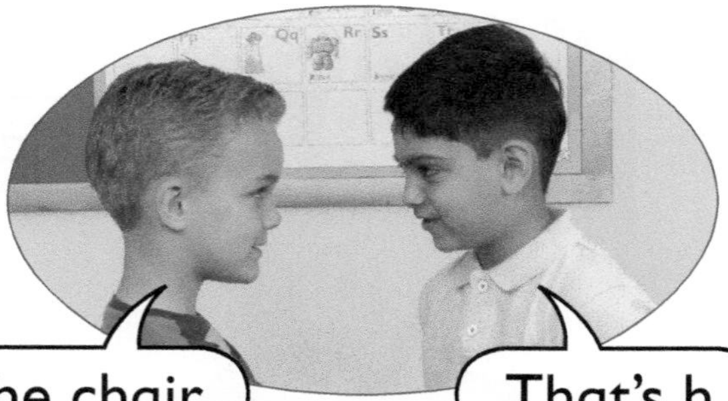

OBJECTIVES: By the end of the lesson, pupils will have learned to identify and say the long ay /eɪ/ vowel sound and to contrast it with the short a /æ/ vowel sound

• TARGET LANGUAGE

Key language: the phoneme /eɪ/ as in *snake, play, game*
Revision: comparison with the short phoneme /æ/ as in black. prepositions, spelling

• MATERIALS REQUIRED

Flashcards: (words with /eɪ/ and /æ/ sound) 19, 21, 91, 94
Extra activity 1: Photocopiable 1 alphabet cards used in the previous two lessons
Extra activity 2: Prepare about 20 questions for Noughts and crosses, e.g. *What's this colour? G–r–e–e–n. What's this animal? T–i–g–e–r.*
Optional: *Teacher's Resource Book 2* Unit 1 Extension worksheet 1 (page 11)

Warmer

- Display the flashcards *cake, paint* and *grey* on the board. Elicit the words and say them for pupils to repeat. Focus on the vowel sound /eɪ/ which all three words have in common. Say *Today's sound is …* Pupils respond by saying /eɪ/. Provide more example words with the sound, if necessary (e.g. *game, play, say, day*).

PB8. ACTIVITY 9. *Monty's phonics*

- Say *Open your Pupil's Books at page 8, please*. Point to the picture of Monty and ask *Who's this?* Pupils respond (*It's Monty*). Elicit the title of the activity. If pupils studied *Kid's Box 1* remind them that the Monty's phonics activities practise different English sounds. Point to the picture of the snake and say snake, emphasising the /eɪ/ sound. Say the word again and draw a snake shape with your finger as you speak. Point to the pictures of the children playing and the game and practise the words in the same way, using mime when you say the words. Say *Now listen to Monty, point and repeat.*
- Play the CD. Pupils listen and repeat the sounds and the words, using the same tone and speed as Monty.
- Say *Four snakes are playing games* several times, getting faster and faster (as a tongue twister). Pupils work in pairs and practise saying the phrase as a tongue twister in the same way.

CD 1, 10

MONTY: Hi, I'm Monty! Repeat after me!
/eɪ/, /eɪ/, snake
/eɪ/, /eɪ/, play
/eɪ/, /eɪ/, game
Four snakes are playing games!
Four snakes are playing games!
Four snakes are playing games!

PB8. ACTIVITY 10. *Say and answer.*

- Pupils work in pairs. Pupil A describes the position of one of the objects in pictures a, h, j or k. Pupil B listens and says the correct letter. Pupils swap roles.

AB8. ACTIVITY 8. *Listen and complete.*

- Say *Open your Activity Books at page 8, please. Look at Activity 8.* Stick the flashcard *black* on the board (or colour a small black blob). Write the word below the picture, with the letter 'a' replaced by a line (as on Activity Book page 8). Say the word and elicit the missing letter. Write it on the line.
- Say *Open your Activity Books at page 8, please*. Play the example and number 2, if necessary.
- Play the CD. Pupils complete the words with the missing letters. They check answers in pairs.
- Play the CD again. Check answers as a class. Elicit the words in the activity which have the /eɪ/ sound (*game, say, play, snake, grey*). Point out that the sound is not always represented with the letter a.
- Play the CD. Pupils listen and complete. They check in pairs. Check with the class.

Key: 2 a, e, 3 a, 4 a, 5 a, 6 a, 7 a, 8 a, e, 9 e, 10, a

CD 1, 11

1. black, 2. game, 3. say, 4. bag, 5. cat, 6. play, 7. hand, 8. snake, 9. grey, 10. apple

AB8. ACTIVITY 9. *Listen and write. Match.*

- Say *Look at Activity 9, please*. Point to the example and play the first item on the CD. Ask *How do you spell 'pen'?* Pupils respond by spelling the word letter by letter, as on the CD. Ask *How do you spell 'look'?* Wait for a pupil to volunteer the answer and see how he/she says the two 'o's in the middle of the word. Explain that we can say double when there are two letters together, e.g. *l - double o - k* to spell *look*. Say *Now listen and write. Use a pencil.*
- Play the rest of the CD, pausing after each item for pupils to write. Repeat the CD and let them check the words in pairs. Elicit answers (the words only) before pupils match.
- Say *Now match the words and the pictures. Write letters.* Show pupils how the example word *pen* has been matched to picture b (the example answer in the small box). Pupils work individually or in pairs to do the matching. Check answers as a class.

Key: 2 eraser c, 3 book e, 4 bag f, 5 pencil g, 6 table a, 7 chair h, 8 door d

CD 1, 12

1. p-e-n, 2. e-r-a-s-e-r, 3. b-o-o-k, 4. b-a-g, 5. p-e-n-c-i-l, 6. t-a-b-l-e, 7. c-h-a-i-r, 8. d-o-o-r

Extra activities: see page T114 (if time)

Optional activity

- Unit 1 Extension worksheet 1 from *Teacher's Resource Book 2* (see pages 8 and 11 of the *Teacher's Resource Book*).

Ending the lesson

- Review the phoneme /eɪ/ with a True/False game. Pupils stand up. Say different words in turn. When pupils hear the sound /eɪ/ in the word, they show thumbs up; when they don't, they show thumbs down. (Alternatively, if more appropriate, they can nod or shake their heads.) Pupils who respond incorrectly sit down. Stop when you have a small group of winners. Use the following words in the game, e.g. *snake, ball, grey, train, apple, play, cat, game, car, day, Grace.*

OBJECTIVES: By the end of the lesson, pupils will have read a story and reviewed language from the unit.

• TARGET LANGUAGE

Key language: language from the unit
Additional language: *toy box, come alive, It's my turn*
Revision: *favourite, toys, Here are … , food, I've only got … , Sorry*

• MATERIALS REQUIRED

Ten simple anagrams of numbers and colours for the Warmer, e.g. *ufor* (four), *edr* (red), written on a large piece of paper
Extra activity 2: two complete sets of the alphabet cards from Photocopiable 1, two pieces of paper
Optional: *Teacher's Resource Book* 2 Unit 1 Extension worksheet 2 (page 12) and/or animated version of the Unit 1 story from *Kid's Box 2 Interactive DVD* (Suzy's room section)

Warmer

- Put the pupils into pairs. Display the simple anagrams of the numbers and colours. Pupils solve the anagrams and write the words correctly on a piece of paper.

Story

PB9. ACTIVITY 11. *Listen to the story.*

- Say *Open your Pupil's Books at page 9, please.* Elicit who they can see (Trevor, Monty, Marie and Maskman). Check pupils remember the sequence of the pictures. Set the pre-listening questions. Divide the class into three groups and give each group one of the questions to listen for: *Who's singing? What is Marie spelling? Is Maskman spelling a colour?* Say *Listen and look.* Play the CD. Pupils listen and look. The groups check in pairs. Check with the class (All four toys, Blue, No, it's a number – four).
- Play the CD again. Pupils listen and repeat.
- Check comprehension, pointing to each picture and asking, e.g. *What are the toys singing?* (The abc song). *What colour's Maskman's car?* (Blue). *How many pencils are there?* (Four). *What's Trevor's favourite food?* (Pencils). *Now there are three pencils. Where's the other pencil?* (Trevor is eating it). Check that pupils understand the meaning of *favourite*. Ask them what their favourite food is.

CD 1, 13

Toys in the toy box,
Come alive.
Walk and talk,
On the count of five.
One, two, three, four, five.

ALL FOUR TOYS *[singing the abc rap from earlier in the unit]*: a, b, c, d, e, f, g, …

MARIE: Let's play a game. What's this colour? B–l–u–e.
MASKMAN: I know. It's blue. My car's blue. Look!

MASKMAN: Now, it's my turn. What's this word? F–o–u–r.
MONTY: I know. That's four. Here are four pencils! My turn.

MONTY: What's this, Trevor? P–u–r–p–l–e.
TREVOR: Er. Is it a pencil? Pencils are my favourite food.
MARIE: No, Trevor. It's purple. Your hair's purple.

MASKMAN: OK, Trevor. It's your turn.
TREVOR: Er … What's this? T–h–r–e–e.

MONTY: Three. I've only got three pencils!

MONTY: Where's the red pencil?
MARIE: Are pencils your favourite food, Trevor?
TREVOR: Er, yes, they are. Sorry, Monty.

PB9. ACTIVITY 12. *Listen and say the number.*

- Say *Listen to the CD and say the number of the picture.* Play the first one as an example. Elicit the number of the frame (Four). Play the rest of the CD. Pupils work in pairs and point to / whisper the number of the frame. Play the CD again. This time stop after each section and elicit the number.

Key: 4, 1, 6, 2, 3, 5

CD 1, 14

MONTY: What's this, Trevor? P–u–r–p–l–e.
ALL FOUR TOYS *[singing the abc rap from earlier in the unit]*: a, b, c, d, e, f, g, …
MARIE: Are pencils your favourite food, Trevor?
MASKMAN: I know. It's blue. My car's blue. Look!
MONTY: I know. That's four. Here are four pencils! My turn.
TREVOR: Er … What's this? T–h–r–e–e.

AB9. MY PICTURE DICTIONARY.

- Say *Open your Activity Books at page 9 please.* Say *What colour is it?* Listen to the spelling. Play number 1 on the CD and elicit the colour. Ask pupils to hold up the correct sticker. They all stick the sticker in the first square. Remind pupils that when there are two of the same letter in a word we say double (e.g. double 'o').
- Play the rest of the CD. Pupils lay the stickers out on their desk in the correct order. Monitor around the class to check before they stick them in their books.
- Point to the example word in square 1. Say *Now write the words.* Pupils write the name of the colour under each sticker. Write the colours on the board in random order if they are having difficulty . Play the CD again if necessary.
- Pupils write the name of the colour under each sticker.

Key: 2 blue, 3 pink, 4 black, 5 yellow, 6 green

CD 1, 15

1. p-u-r-p-l-e, 2. b-l-u-e, 3. p-i-n-k, 4. b-l-a-c-k, 5. y-e-l-l-o-w, 6. g-r-e-e-n

AB9. MY PROGRESS.

- Focus pupils on the activity in their books. Say *Let's read the sentences together.* Read the first sentence. Elicit what it means and count to ten with the pupils. Repeat for the second and the third sentences. Pupils say the words in chorus.
- Pupils work in pairs. They take turns to point to a sentence in their books and do what it says.
- Say *Now ask each other and tick or cross the sentences.* Demonstrate the activity again if necessary. Pupils tick or cross. Encourage pupils to practise so that they can tick all the statements and colour the star.

Extra activities: see page T114 (if time)

Optional activities

- Unit 1 Extension worksheet 2 (see pages 8 and 12 of the *Teacher's Resource Book*).
- The animated version of the story from *Kid's Box 2 Interactive DVD* (Suzy's room section). See pages 41–43 of the Teacher's booklet for the *Interactive DVD.*

Ending the lesson

- Ask pupils which chant/song/game they'd like to do again from the unit. Do it together to end the lesson.

11 13 CD1 Listen to the story.

12 14 CD1 Listen and say the number.

2 Back to school

1 16 CD1 Listen and point.

2 17 CD1 Listen and repeat.

OBJECTIVES: By the end of the lesson, pupils will have learned to talk about objects and people in the classroom.

• TARGET LANGUAGE

Key language: *board, bookcase, cupboard, desk, ruler, teacher, Is this a … ? Yes/No.*

Additional language: *playground, window, look, listen, open/close your books / the door*

Revision: alphabet, colours, school objects: *eraser, pen, pencil, chair, table, bag, book*

• MATERIALS REQUIRED

Flashcards: (Alex, Lenny and Meera) 23–25; (school things) 26–31 and/or school word cards from *Teacher's Resource Book 2* (page 89): a board, a bookcase, a cupboard, a desk, a ruler, a teacher

Warmer

- Greet the class by saying *Hello, I'm … / My name's …* Greet individual pupils for them to respond. Add the greeting *How are you? I'm fine, thank you.* Weave it around the class: Pupil A to Pupil B, Pupil B to Pupil C, Pupil C to Pupil D, etc.

Practice

- Say the Alphabet chant with the class two or three times. Play a quick alphabet game to review words and letters, e.g. *What 'b' is a toy?* (ball). *What 'c' is an animal?* (cat), etc.

Presentation

- Use the flashcards to present the new vocabulary to the class. Display the flashcards (word side) on their objects, where pupils can see them or use the word cards from *Teacher's Resource Book 2* (see page 89). Point to, e.g. the word *board*, point to the board and say *Board.* Say *Point to the board.* Pupils point. Drill the word in chorus, softly and then loudly with the class. Repeat with the other classroom words. Stick the flashcard on yourself too, for *teacher.*
- Play a quick pointing game. Say *Point to the board* (pupils point). *Point to the teacher* (pupils point), etc. Revise other classroom words as part of this activity: *book, bag.*

PB10. ACTIVITY 1. *Listen and point.*

- Say *Open your Pupil's Books at page 10, please. Look at the picture of the classroom.* Say *Find the hidden star. Where is it?* Elicit from pupils where it is, hold up your book and point to it (on the vase). Pupils say *Here it is.*
- Say *Listen and point.* Play the CD. Pupils listen and point to the objects in the picture.
- Set the pre-listening questions: *Is it Meera's classroom? Is Maskman Simon's favourite toy? Where's Lenny's ruler?* Don't accept answers until after the listening. Play the CD again. Pupils listen for the answers. Check with the class (no, yes, on the desk).
- Check comprehension by holding up your book and asking other questions, e.g. *What's this? Who's this? What colour's this? What's in the cupboard? Where's the bookcase?*

CD 1, 16

STELLA: Hello, Alex. Hello, Lenny. How are you?
ALEX AND LENNY: Fine, thanks.
MEERA: Is this your classroom, Simon?
SIMON: Yes.
MEERA: Who's that on the board?
SIMON: That's my favourite toy, Maskman. Look at my Maskman ruler.
LENNY: That's nice. My ruler's on my desk.
STELLA: Are your school books in the bookcase?
SIMON: No, they're in the cupboard. Our teacher's here now.
STELLA AND MEERA: Oops.

PB10. ACTIVITY 2. *Listen and repeat.*

- Say *Let's do Activity 2. Listen and repeat.* Play the CD. Pupils repeat the words in chorus. Listen for correct pronunciation of *cupboard*, and correct word stress of *bookcase, teacher.*

CD 1, 17

Board, bookcase, cupboard, desk, ruler, teacher

AB10. ACTIVITY 1. *Find and write the words.*

- Say *Open your Activity Books at page 10, please.* Elicit what pupils can see (a wordsearch) and check they remember how to do them. Hold up your book and point to the circled word. Elicit what it says (desk). Check pupils understand they have to write the word correctly under the picture.
- Pupils work in pairs and circle all the words, matching them with the pictures. Pupils then write the words under the pictures. Remind them to use Pupil's Book page 10 to help with the spelling (copying from a vertical word can be confusing).
- Check by asking pupils to spell the words for the class.

Key: cupboard, pen, pencil, board, ruler, eraser, chair, bag, classroom, bookcase, teacher

AB10. ACTIVITY 2. *Listen and colour.*

- Say *Look at Activity 2.* Tell pupils to have the following colours ready: *orange, yellow, red, blue, brown, black.* Note: The letters in the puzzle are all part of the same pronunciation group. If you wish, remind pupils that these letters were on the red splodges in the picture for the chant on Pupil's Book page 6.
- Hold up your book and point to the letters. Say *Listen and colour.* Play the CD. Pupils listen and colour the letters appropriately. They compare answers in pairs. Check the colours with the whole class.

CD 1, 18

F is red. L is brown. M is yellow.
N is orange. S is blue. X is black.

Extra activities: see page T115 (if time)

Ending the lesson

- Review the school objects by playing the Please game. Pupils follow your instruction only when you say *please*, e.g. *Put the ruler under the book, please* (pupils do it). *Point to the board* (pupils don't do it).

OBJECTIVES: By the end of the lesson, pupils will have learned to count from *1* to *20* and talk about plural classroom objects.

• TARGET LANGUAGE

Key language: *11–20, eleven–twenty,* plural nouns, *How many … are there?*
Additional language: school language, e.g. *open/close your books*
Revision: numbers *1–10*, the alphabet

• MATERIALS REQUIRED

Flashcards: (school things) 26–31, (numbers 11–20) 32–41
Photocopiable 2 (see page T101), one copy for each pupil, plus one for demonstration
Extra activity 1: two rolled up newspapers
Optional: *Teacher's Resource Book 2* Unit 2 Reinforcement worksheet 1 (page 15)

Warmer

- Go around the classroom sticking the flashcards (word side) onto the wrong objects, e.g. *Bookcase* on the board. Say *OK?* Invite pupils one at a time to come and change over two flashcards so that one is in the right place. Continue until all the flashcards are on the right objects.
- Point to each word and elicit it from the class.

Presentation

- Write the numbers *11–20* in sequence across the board. Above each number, stick the same number flashcard (word side). Point to each number in turn, say it for the class and they repeat in chorus several times. Teach the numbers cumulatively, e.g. teach *11*, teach *12* and review *11, 12*. Teach *13* and review *11, 12, 13*, and so on.
- Write numbers *1–10* above, so that *1* is above *11*, *2* is above *12*, and so on. Encourage pupils to notice the similarities and differences, e.g. *Four/fourteen.* Help them find patterns.

PB11. ACTIVITY 3. *Listen and point. Chant.*

- Point to a desk and elicit the word *desk* and then count desks with the pupils: *One, two, three*, etc. Count to fifteen and then say *Fifteen desks.* Repeat with rulers and count to eighteen.
- Say *Open your Pupil's Books at page 11, please. Look at Activity 3.* Elicit what pupils can see (desk, pen, teacher, etc.). Say *Listen and point to the numbers.* Play the CD. Pupils point to the numbers as they listen. Play the CD again. This time pupils listen and point with two hands: one at the number, and the other at the object in the picture.
- Play the CD again. Encourage pupils to chant.

CD 1, 19

School, school. This is the Numbers School.
Eleven desks,
Twelve erasers,
Thirteen rulers,
Fourteen cupboards,
Fifteen classrooms,
Sixteen teachers,
Seventeen pens,
Eighteen boards,
Nineteen pencils,
Twenty tables.
School, school. This is the Numbers School.

PB11. ACTIVITY 4. *Ask and answer.*

- Pupils work in pairs. Pupil A asks a question about the song lyrics, e.g. *How many desks are there?* Pupil B answers, e.g. *11*. Pupils exchange roles. When pupils have done the activity, ask them to close their books and do it from memory. Award points for correct questions and answers.

Photocopiable 2: see pages T98 and T101

AB11. ACTIVITY 3. *Look at the numbers. Write the words.* **[YLE]**

- Say *Open your Activity Books at page 11, please. Look at Activity 3.* Hold up your book and point to the numeral *11*. Elicit what it is. Point to the anagram *veleen* and then to the example answer *eleven.* Check pupils know what to do. Remind them to check in their Pupil's Books for the spelling.
- Pupils work in pairs, solve the anagrams and write the words correctly in their books.
- Check by asking pupils to come to the board to write the numbers. They can bring their books to help them.

Key: fifteen, eighteen, twelve, twenty, thirteen

AB11. ACTIVITY 4. *Read and colour.*

- Say *Look at Activity 4. Read and tell me the colours you need.* Pupils read and say the colours: *Brown, pink, green, blue, orange.* Point to the first sentence (*Colour number twelve brown*). Say *What do you do here?* Encourage pupils to work out what they have to do and to tell you. Check all pupils understand what to do. Pupils work individually and colour the objects using the correct colours. Monitor pupils as they are working.
- Check with the class by asking, e.g. *What is brown? What colour's the eraser? What colour's number 16?*

Extra activity: see page T115 (if time)

Optional activity

- Unit 2 Reinforcement worksheet 1 from *Teacher's Resource Book 2* (see pages 14–15 of the *Teacher's Resource Book*).

Ending the lesson

- Finish the lesson with a silent activity. Say *Open your Pupil's Books at page 11, please. Look at the numbers. Look and then point. Sshh.* Mouth a number, e.g. *Fourteen*, in an exaggerated way. Pupils look and then point to the number in their books. Make sure everyone is silent and that they don't say the number. Repeat with the other new numbers.

3 Listen and point. Chant.

19 CD1

School, school. This is the Numbers School.
11 Eleven desks,
12 Twelve erasers,
13 Thirteen rulers,
14 Fourteen cupboards,
15 Fifteen classrooms,
16 Sixteen teachers,
17 Seventeen pens,
18 Eighteen boards,
19 Nineteen pencils,
20 Twenty tables.
School, school. This is the Numbers School.

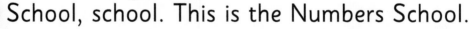

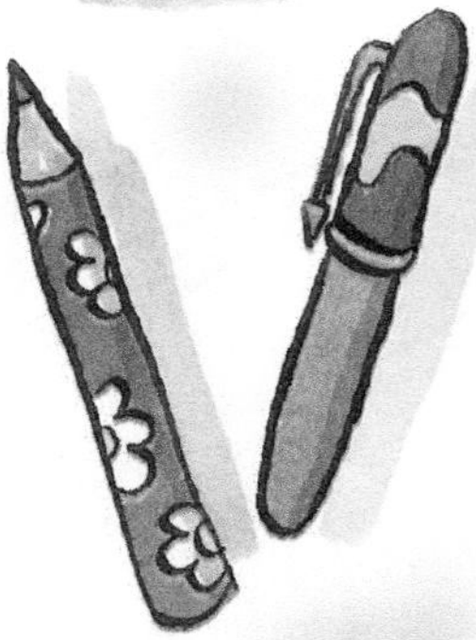

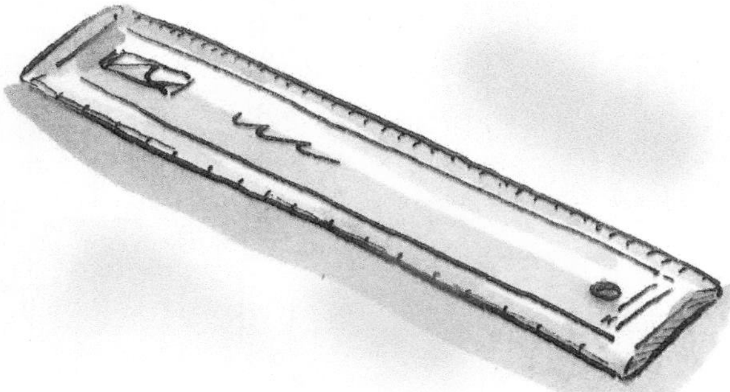

4 Ask and answer.

How many desks are there?

11

Vocabulary

board bookcase cupboard desk ruler teacher

5 Listen and point.

CD1 20

This is my classroom. How many desks are there? There are a lot of desks. That's my desk next to the bookcase. There's a long pink ruler on it. There are a lot of books in the bookcase. There's a big whiteboard on the wall. There's a computer, but there isn't a television.

6 Listen and repeat.

CD1 21

Grammar

How many … are there? There is … There are …

OBJECTIVES: By the end of the lesson, pupils will have learned to ask and answer questions about *How many?*

• TARGET LANGUAGE

Key language: *There is … , There are … , There isn't … , There aren't … , How many … are there? whiteboard, wall*

Additional language: *a lot of, any*

Revision: prepositions, colours, school vocabulary, numbers, *my, long, it, computer, picture, burger, apple, orange, cake, ice cream, banana*

• MATERIALS REQUIRED

Flashcards: (school things) 26–31

Some preparation might be needed for the Warmer (number of pencils/books on your desk).

Extra activity 1: Photocopiable 2 (see page T101), one copy for each pupil, from the previous lesson

Optional: *Teacher's Resource Book 2* Unit 2 Reinforcement worksheet 2 (page 16)

Warmer

- Pupils stand up. Say a true statement, e.g. *In the classroom, there's a board. It's true.* Pupils put their hands on their heads. Say a false statement, e.g. *In the classroom, there are five desks. It's false.* Pupils put their hands by their sides. Continue with true and false statements to review numbers and classroom objects and to raise awareness of *There is … , There isn't … , There are … , There aren't …*

  Note: Don't teach the use of *any* in this lesson, but use it correctly.

PB12. ACTIVITY **5.** *Listen and point.*

- Say *Open your Pupil's Books at page 12. Look at the picture. Tell me … how many chairs are there?* (18). *How many bags are there?* (11). Ask other questions to help pupils focus and review the use of *How many … ?* Elicit the girl's name (Meera).
- Say *Listen to the CD and point to the things in the classroom.* Play the CD. Pupils listen and point. Set pre-listening questions: *Is there a red ruler? Is there a computer?* Play the CD again. Pupils listen for the answers. They check in pairs. Check with the class. (No, there isn't. / Yes, there is.)
- Check comprehension by asking, e.g. *Are there a lot of bags on the chairs?* etc. for pupils to answer *Yes, there are. / No, there aren't. Yes, there is. / No, there isn't.* Check understanding of *whiteboard.* Pupils work in pairs and think of a question to ask the class about the picture, using *Is there … ? / Are there … ?*

CD 1, 20

MEERA: This is my classroom. How many desks are there? There are a lot of desks. That's my desk next to the bookcase. There's a long pink ruler on it. There are a lot of books in the bookcase. There's a big whiteboard on the wall. There's a computer, but there isn't a television.

PB12. ACTIVITY **6.** *Listen and repeat.*

- Say *Now listen to the sentences and repeat.* Play the CD. Pupils repeat. Listen for correct pronunciation and intonation. Repeat the activity.

CD 1, 21

There's a pink ruler on her desk.
There are a lot of books in the bookcase.
There's a big whiteboard on the wall.
There's a computer in the classroom.
There isn't a television.

AB12. ACTIVITY **5.** *Write the sentences.*

- Say *Open your Activity Books at page 12, please.* Hold up your book and point to the example and the words written in the right order on the line underneath. Focus on the capital letters and the punctuation.
- Pupils work in pairs to reorder the words and write sentences. They write them on the lines underneath, carefully copying the capital letters and the punctuation.

Key: 2 There are 12 pencils on the desk. 3 There's a bag under the chair. 4 There are 16 books in the bookcase.

AB12. ACTIVITY **6.** *Look at the picture. Write the answers.*

- Focus pupils on Activity 6. Elicit what they can see (chimps/monkeys, bananas, apples, burgers, oranges, cakes, ice creams). Ask a pupil to read the first question: *How many burgers are there?* and another to read the example response: *There are six.* Pupils work in pairs and take turns to ask and answer about the other items in the picture. They write the sentences following the example. Monitor pupils as they are working.
- Check around the class using open pairs.

Key: 2 There are twelve. 3 There are fifteen. 4 There are fourteen. 5 There are eleven. 6 There are seventeen.

Extra activities: see page T115 (if time)

Optional activity

- Unit 2 Reinforcement worksheet 2 from *Teacher's Resource Book 2* (see pages 14 and 16 of the *Teacher's Resource Book*).

Ending the lesson

- Do the Spelling chant to review the alphabet and the new vocabulary. Repeat with other school objects. More able pairs of pupils can be the 'teacher' and spell out a word for the class to chant.

Teacher:	Pupils respond:
Give me a b	*b*
Give me an o	*o*
Give me an a	*a*
Give me an r	*r*
Give me a d	*d*
What does that spell?	*board*
What does that spell?	*board*

OBJECTIVES: By the end of the lesson, pupils will have sung a song and had more practice in asking and answering questions about *How many … ?*

• TARGET LANGUAGE

Key language: *There is … , There are … , How many are there?* statement/question word order
Revision: school objects, numbers *11–20*, prepositions

• MATERIALS REQUIRED

Flashcards: (school things) 26–31, (numbers 11–20) 32–41
Ten pieces of paper
Extra activity 1: the following sentences written large on strips of paper, cut up as indicated:
There's / a bag / on / the chair.
There are / five books / in / the bookcase.
Is there / a ruler / under / the book?
Are there / twenty pupils / in / our class?
There isn't / a computer / next to / the desk.
There aren't / two teachers / in / our classroom.
Optional: *Teacher's Resource Book 2* Unit 2 song worksheet (page 19)

Warmer

- Play the Disappearing flashcard game. Display the number flashcards on the board in sequence from left to right. Point and elicit the numbers. Place a piece of paper over one of the numbers (not in sequence). Point to each number, including the paper, again to elicit *11–20*. Repeat, covering another number, but not following the sequence, e.g. cover *13*, then *19*, then *16*. Continue until all the numbers are covered.
- Point to pieces of paper (out of sequence) and ask what the number is underneath. When they say it correctly, reveal the number. Repeat until all the numbers are revealed.

PB13. ACTIVITY **7.** *Listen and point. Sing.*

- Say *Open your Pupil's Books at page 13, please. Look at the picture.* Elicit why it's funny, e.g. *The teacher is on the bookcase.* Say *Now listen and point.* Play the CD. Pupils listen and point to the relevant part of the picture. Play the CD again.

CD 1, 22

There are pencils in the classroom, yes there are.
There's a cupboard on the pencils, yes there is.
There's a ruler on the cupboard,
There's a bookcase on the ruler,
There's a teacher on the bookcase, yes there is.
There's a teacher on the bookcase, yes there is.
[Repeat x4]

CD 1, 23

Now sing the song again. (Karaoke version)

PB13. ACTIVITY **8.** *Ask and answer.*

- Pupils work in pairs. Pupil A asks a question about the song, e.g. *Where's the cupboard?* Pupil B answers, e.g. *On the pencils.* Pupils swap roles. Repeat with items in the classroom.

Practice

- Say *Listen* and then say the following words to the pupils: *Pencil, cupboard, bookcase, ruler, teacher.* By beating the rhythm with your hand, show pupils there are two beats (syllables) in these words in the song. Elicit from the class other two-syllable words they could use in the song (they can be silly), e.g. *whiteboard, tiger, jacket, ice cream, burger.*
- Make groups of four. Each group chooses words to write another verse of the song. Monitor and help pupils with the activity. Remind them to use the model in their books.
- Choose groups to perform their versions (with actions).

AB13. ACTIVITY **7.** *Look and read. Write 'yes' or 'no'.* **[YLE]**

- Say *Open your Activity Books at page 13, please.* Read the example statement: *There are two teachers in the classroom.* Say *Look at the picture. Yes or no?* Pupils respond *No.* Point to the example answer *no.* Elicit the correct sentence (*There's one teacher in the classroom.*).
- Pupils work individually and silently read the rest of the statements. They write *yes* or *no* on the lines to the right. Monitor and check they are looking at the picture to find out the answers. Pupils check in pairs. Elicit answers. Choose individuals to correct the false sentences.

Key: 1 yes, 2 yes, 3 no (There are two bookcases under the board.), 4 no (There are some clothes on the bookcases.), 5 no (There are two bags under the desk.)

Extra activities: see page T115 (if time)

Optional activity

- Hand out copies of the Unit 2 song worksheet from *Teacher's Resource Book 2*. Pupils cut out the items and do the *Listen and place* activity while listening to the song (see pages 14 and 19 of *Teacher's Resource Book 2*).

Ending the lesson

- Play a Number bingo game. Pupils draw a 2 x 2 grid in their notebooks and write numbers between *11* and *20* in the squares – one in each. Call out the numbers out of sequence. Pupils cross out the numbers when they hear them. The first pupil to cross out all four numbers shouts *Bingo!* Check the numbers back from them. If they are ones you called, that pupil is the winner. Repeat.

7 22 CD1 Listen and point. Sing.

There are pencils in the classroom, yes there are.
There's a cupboard on the pencils, yes there is.
There's a ruler on the cupboard,
There's a bookcase on the ruler,
There's a teacher on the bookcase, yes there is ...

8 Ask and answer.

Where's the cupboard?

On the pencils.

9 24 CD1 Monty's phonics

3

three

teacher

tree

Three teachers sleeping in a tree!

10 Say and correct.

There are 15 desks in the classroom.

No, there aren't. There are 12 desks.

OBJECTIVES: By the end of the lesson, pupils will have learned to identify and say the long ee /iː/ vowel sound and to contrast it with the short e /e/ vowel sound and had more practice with numbers *11–20*.

• TARGET LANGUAGE

Key language: the phoneme /iː/ as in *three, teacher, tree*
Revision: numbers *1–20*, colours, classroom language, *tree, read, bus, school*

• MATERIALS REQUIRED

Flashcards: red, green (12, 15)
Teacher's Resource Book 2, Unit 2, Extension worksheet 1 (pages 14, 17), *Language Portfolio 2*, page 8

Warmer

- Revise the alphabet with the Alphabet chant on Pupil's Book page 6. Then say *Listen*. Recite the alphabet slowly, missing out a letter. Pupils put their hands up and say the missing letter. Repeat.

PB14. ACTIVITY 9. *Monty's phonics*

- Say *Open your Pupil's Books at page 14, please. Look! It's Monty's Phonics today.* Point to the number three and say *three*, emphasising the /iː/ sound. Say the word again and draw the figure 3 with your finger as you speak. Point to the pictures of the teacher and the tree and practise the words in the same way, emphasising the vowel sound and using mime when you say the words. Say *Now listen to Monty, point and repeat.*
- Play the CD. Pupils listen and repeat the sounds, words, and sentence using the same tone and speed as Monty. Check understanding of the tongue twister by miming as pupils are listening – hold up three fingers for *three*, mime writing on the board for *teacher*, put your hands at the side of your head and close your eyes for *sleeping* and stretch your arms up and out like branches for *tree*. Encourage the pupils to join in with the mime.
- Pupils repeat the tongue twister as a class. Ask small groups to have a go at saying it. Put pupils in pairs. They practise saying the tongue twister quickly to each other. Volunteers say it to the class.
- Write the tongue twister on the board. Focus pupils on the words. Elicit which letters to underline for the sound /iː/.

Key: Three teachers sleeping in a tree!

CD 1, 24

MONTY: Hi, I'm Monty! Repeat after me!
/iː/, /iː/, three
/iː/, /iː/, teacher
/iː/, /iː/, tree
Three teachers sleeping in a tree!
Three teachers sleeping in a tree!
Three teachers sleeping in a tree!

Practice

- Say some true/false statements about the pupils' classroom. Use known vocabulary and numbers between *1* and *20*, e.g. *There are seven pencils on the desk* (False). Prompt the response, e.g. *No, there aren't. There are twelve pencils on the desk.* Continue. Pupils correct your false statements. They say *Yes, there are* to the true ones.
- Pupils work in pairs. They prepare two statements about their classroom. Pupils say their statements for the class to respond.

PB14. ACTIVITY 10. *Say and correct.*

- Focus pupils on Activity 10 and the example speech bubbles. Pupils look at the picture and count the classroom objects. Pupils work in pairs. Pupil A describes something he/she can see in the picture, but says the wrong number. Pupil B listens and corrects the sentence. Pupils swap roles.

AB14. ACTIVITY 8. *Listen and colour red or green.*

- Remind pupils of the way colours matched letter sounds on Pupil's Book page 6. Stick the flashcards red and green on the board and elicit the colour names. Say *Which letters go with red?* Elicit/remind pupils which letters of the alphabet have the same vowel sound as the word red (f, l, m, n, s, x, z). Repeat for green (b, c, d, e, g, p, t, v).
- Say *Open your Activity Books at page 14, please.* Point to Activity 8 and to the first two pictures of the paint pots. Make sure pupils have red and green crayons ready. Say *Listen and colour red* (make the sound /e/) *or green* (make the sound /iː/). Play the first two words on the CD and elicit the colours. Pupils colour in the first two items.
- Play the rest of the CD, pausing after each word for pupils to choose a colour. Remind them to make a dot first. They compare answers in pairs. Play the CD again if necessary. Monitor the activity and make sure pupils are choosing the colour based on sound. Check answers, eliciting phrases, e.g. *a green tree, a red ten.*

Key: 1 red, 2 green, 3 green, 4 red, 5 red, 6 green, 7 red, 8 green, 9 green, 10 red

CD 1, 25

1. red, 2. green, 3. tree, 4. ten, 5. pen, 6. read, 7. twelve, 8. fourteen, 9. teacher, 10. desk

AB14. ACTIVITY 9. *Find the words.*

- Say *Look at Activity 9. What is it?* Pupils answer *A snake.* Hold up your book, point to *bus* and say *What's this word?* Pupils say *Bus.* Check understanding. Say *Find the words, find the pictures and tick.*
- Pupils work individually. They check in pairs. Monitor pupils as they are working. Pupils write the answers to the questions at the bottom of the page. Check with the class.

Key: school, leg, grey, yellow, white, eraser, ruler, red, desk
There are four colours. Grey, yellow, white, red.

Extra activities: see page T115 (if time)

Optional activity

- Unit 2 Extension worksheet 1 from *Teacher's Resource Book 2* (see pages 14 and 17 of the *Teacher's Resource Book*).

Language Portfolio

- Pupils complete page 8 of *Kid's Box 2 Language Portfolio* (My school bag). They write sentences with There's...and There are....'

Ending the lesson

- Do the tongue twister again with the class. Remind pupils of the mimes.
- Pupils stand up and do the tongue twister with the mimes.

OBJECTIVES: By the end of the lesson, pupils will have read a story and reviewed language from the unit.

• TARGET LANGUAGE
Key language: language from the unit
Revision: *beautiful, Can you … , please?*

• MATERIALS REQUIRED
Extra activity 1: Flashcards: (school things) 26–31, (numbers 11–20) 32–41
Ten pieces of paper
Extra activity 2: the following half words on a large piece of paper:

six	*een*	*fourt*	*ve*
cupb	*her*	*twel*	*en*
elev	*ase*	*teac*	*oard*
bookc	*ard*	*bo*	*teen*

Optional: *Teacher's Resource Book 2* Unit 2 Extension worksheet 2 (page 18) and/or animated version of the Unit 2 story from *Kid's Box 2 Interactive DVD* (Suzy's room section)

Warmer

- Play the Please game. Pupils stand up. Say, e.g. *Can you put your hands on your heads, please?* Pupils put their hands on their heads. Say, e.g. *Can you open your book?* Pupils don't respond. Continue practising classroom language (*open, close, sit, stand, put*) and known vocabulary.

Story

PB15. ACTIVITY 11. *Listen to the story.*

- Say *Can you open your Pupil's Books at page 15?* Pupils shouldn't respond. Say *Oh, sorry. Can you open your books at page 15, please?* Elicit who they can see (Trevor, Monty, Marie and Maskman). Set the pre-listening questions. Make groups of three, A, B and C. Each pupil in each group has a different question to listen for: As: *Is there a ruler?* Bs: *Is there an eraser?* Cs: *How many pencils are there in picture 5?* Say *Listen and look.* Play the CD. Pupils listen and look. The groups of three exchange their answers. Check with the class (Yes, there is, Yes, there is, 11).
- Play the CD again. Pupils listen and repeat.
- Check comprehension by asking, e.g. *Is it a school bag?* (Yes). *Who's this?* (Marie). *Is there a ruler?* (Yes, there is). *Is it a Monty ruler?* (No, it isn't. It's a Maskman ruler). *What's this?* (An eraser). *Is the eraser in the bag?* (Yes, it is). *How many pencils are there?* (11). *Where's pencil 12?* (Trevor is eating it). *What's Trevor's favourite food?* (Pencils).

CD 1, 26

Toys in the toy box,
Come alive.
Walk and talk,
On the count of five.
One, two, three, four, five.
MARIE: OK, everybody. This bag is for school. Let's look.
MASKMAN, TREVOR AND MONTY: OK, Marie!

MARIE: Hmm. Is there a ruler?
MASKMAN: Yes, there is. It's a 'Maskman' ruler.

MONTY: Look, Marie. Here's an eraser.
MARIE: Good! Can you put it in the bag, please, Monty?

MONTY: Now there's an eraser in the bag, Marie.
MARIE: Good! Thank you, Monty.

MARIE: Now … how many pencils are there?
MASKMAN: There are 9, 10, 11 pencils.

MONTY: 11 pencils! Where's the pencil? Trevor?!
TREVOR: Sorry. Here you are. Pencils *are* my favourite food.

PB15. ACTIVITY 12. *Listen and say 'yes' or 'no'.*

- Say *Listen. It's about the story. Say 'yes' or 'no'.* Play the first statement on the CD. Pupils put up their hands. Choose a pupil to answer (No). Play the rest of the CD. Pupils point to the picture and do a secret thumbs up or thumbs down to their partner.
- Play the CD again. Pause after each one and elicit the answer. Elicit a correct statement/response for the *Nos*.

Key: No – bag, Yes, No – an eraser, No – Monty, Yes, No – Pencils

CD 1, 27

MARIE: OK, everybody. This book is for school. Let's look.
MASKMAN: Yes, there is. It's a 'Maskman' ruler.
MONTY: Look, Marie. Here's a pencil.
MARIE: Good! Thank you, Trevor.
MASKMAN: There are 9, 10, 11 pencils.
TREVOR: Sorry. Here you are. Erasers *are* my favourite food.

AB15. MY PICTURE DICTIONARY.

- Say *Open your Activity Books at page 15, please.* Point to the scrambled word in the first square and the example answer. Elicit the word (teacher).
- Say *Look at the letters. Unscramble the letters and write words. They are classroom words.* Pupils work individually or in pairs to solve the anagrams. Check answers.
- Pupils prepare the classroom stickers and lay them out on their desks in the correct order. Check around the class before they stick them in their books.

Key: board, ruler, desk, bookcase, cupboard

AB15. MY PROGRESS.

- Say *Let's read the sentences together.* Read the first sentence. Elicit the meaning and point to different objects in the classroom for pupils to name. Repeat for the second sentence. Pupils say the numbers in chorus. Point to a classroom object, e.g. desk and say *What's this?* Pupils reply: *Desk.* Ask: *Can you spell desk?* Repeat with other classroom objects and numbers.
- Pupils work in pairs. They take turns to point to a sentence in their books and do what it says.
- Say *Ask each other and tick or cross the sentences.* Demonstrate the activity again if necessary. Pupils tick and colour the star. Encourage pupils to practise so that they can tick all the statements.

Extra activities: see pages T115–T116 (if time)

Optional activity

- Unit 2 Extension worksheet 2 Teacher's Resource Book 2, pages 14 and 18.
- The animated version of the story from *Kid's Box 2 Interactive DVD* (Suzy's room section). See pages 41–43 of the Teacher's booklet for the *Interactive DVD*.

Ending the lesson

- Ask pupils which chant/song/game they'd like to do again from the unit. Do it together to end the lesson.

11 Listen to the story.

26 CD1

1
OK, everybody. This bag is for school. Let's look.
OK, Marie!
2
Hmm. Is there a ruler?
12 Pencils
Stickers
Notes
Yes, there is. It's a 'Maskman' ruler.
3
Look, Marie. Here's an eraser.
Good! Can you put it in the bag, please, Monty?
4
Now there's an eraser in the bag, Marie.
Good! Thank you, Monty.
5
Now, how many pencils are there?
There are 9, 10, 11 pencils.
6
11 pencils! Where's the pencil? Trevor!
Sorry. Here you are. Pencils are my favourite food.

12 Listen and say 'yes' or 'no'.

27 CD1

Marie's maths Block graphs

1 Listen and point.

CD1 28

orange banana apple pear pineapple lemon

2 Listen and answer.

CD1 29

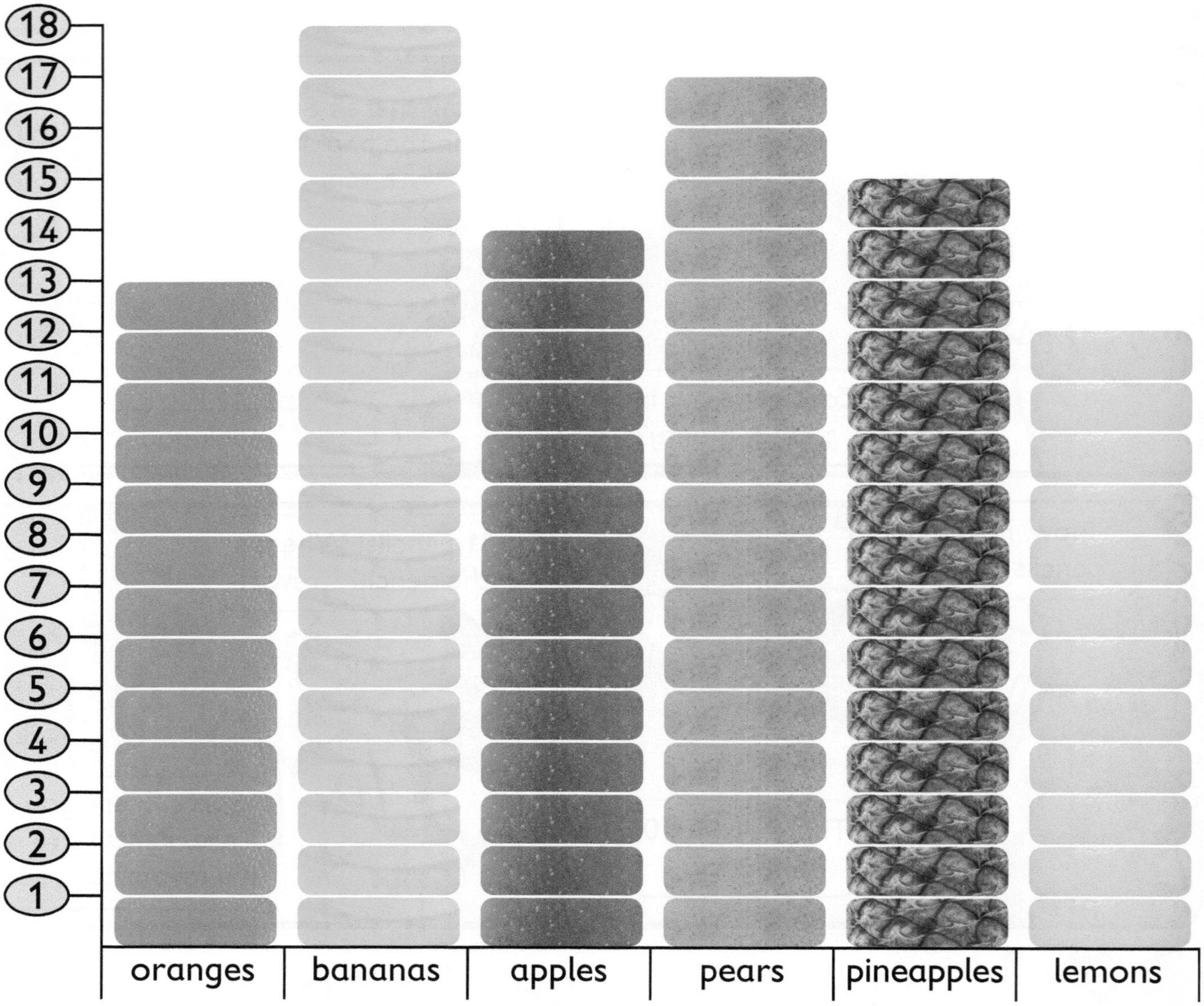

Vocabulary

lemon pear pineapple

Now you!
Activity Book page 16

OBJECTIVES: By the end of the lesson, pupils will have listened to people talking about their favourite fruit, interpreted a block graph and taken part in a class survey.

• TARGET LANGUAGE

Key language: *lemon, pear, pineapple, I like … I don't like … I love …*
Additional language: *This fruit is (yellow). block graph*
Revision: *apple, banana, orange,* colours, numbers 1-20, *horse, hippo, cat, tiger, snake*

• MATERIALS REQUIRED

Pictures of fruit and animals: apple, banana, orange, horse, hippo, cat, tiger, snake; real fruit (an orange, a banana, an apple, a lemon, a pear and a pineapple if possible)

Warmer

- Stick the fruit pictures on the board picture side down. Turn each picture over, point to the fruit and say the name, e.g. *orange.*
- Talk about the fruit, say e.g. *I like oranges, I don't like bananas.* Ask, e.g. *What colour is the banana?* Pupils respond. When all the pictures are face up, point to each one again. Pupils repeat the names of the fruit.

PB16. ACTIVITY 1. *Listen and point.*

- Say *Open your Pupil's Books at page 16, please.* Hold up your book and point to the picture of Marie. Say *Who's this?* Elicit *Marie.* Say *Marie is doing maths today. This lesson is called 'Marie's maths'.*
- Hold up your book. Point and say *Where's the pineapple?* Pupils say *Here it is.* Pupils point to the same fruit in their books. Repeat. Point to the banana and ask *Is this a pineapple?* Choose a confident pupil and elicit the answer *No, it's a banana.* Repeat with the other pictures of fruit. Say *Listen and point.*
- Play the CD. Pupils point to each fruit as they hear the word. Play the CD again. Call volunteers to point to the correct fruit flashcard/picture on the board (or the correct real fruit).

Key: 1 orange, 2 lemon, 3 pear, 4 pineapple, 5 apple, 6 banana

CD 1, 28

1. I love this fruit?
   Is it an apple? I like apples.
   No, it isn't an apple. It's an orange. I don't like apples. But I love oranges!
2. This fruit is yellow.
   That's a banana.
   No, it's a lemon.
3. This fruit is green.
   Oh, that's a pear.
4. What's this?
   It's green.
   Is it a pear?
   No, it's green and brown.
   Oh, that's a pineapple!
5. I like this fruit.
   Is it a pear?
   No, this fruit is red.
   Ah, it's an apple! You like apples!
6. I don't like this fruit.
   Is it a pineapple?
   No, it's a banana!

PB16. ACTIVITY 2. *Listen and answer.*

- Point to the graph. Say *This is a block graph.* Pupils repeat the phrase. Say *A block graph shows us information about numbers.*
- Give pupils time to look at the graph and talk about it in pairs. Ask *How many children like bananas?* Pupils answer (*18*). Repeat for other fruit. Say *17 children like this fruit. What is it?* Pupils answer (*pear*). Make sure pupils understand that the numbers on the vertical axis of the graph represent people who chose each of the fruits listed on the horizontal axis.
- Say *Listen and answer.* Play the CD. Stop after each question. Give pupils time to think and check with each other before eliciting the answer from the class.

Key: 1 apple, 2 17, 3 13, 4 banana, 5 12, 6 pineapple

CD 1, 29

1. 14 children like this fruit. What is it?
2. How many children like pears?
3. How many children like oranges?
4. 18 children like this fruit. What is it?
5. How many children like lemons?
6. 15 children like this fruit. What is it?

AB16. ACTIVITY 1. *Ask and answer. Colour the graph.*

- Review animal vocabulary quickly, using the flashcards from Level 1 or pictures from the Internet. Say *Open your Activity Books at page 16, please. Look at the graph. It's a new graph. Point to the numbers.* (Pupils point to the numbers on the vertical axis.) *Point to the animals.* (Pupils point to the animals on the horizontal axis.) Tell pupils they are going to do their own survey, by asking their classmates about the animals they like.
- Focus pupils on the speech bubble in their books, *Which animals do you like?* Elicit an answer from a confident pupil, e.g. *I like hippos, cats and snakes.* Mime putting a mark on the graph for the hippo, cat and snake columns. Repeat with another pupil.
- Divide the class into small groups. Ask each group to work together.
- Each group chooses other children in the class for their survey. When they have asked everyone in their group/the class, they go back to their seats and colour the graph, using a different colour for each column. Check their graphs while they are colouring.

AB16. ACTIVITY 2. *Answer the questions.*

- Pupils use the information from their graphs to answer the questions. Do the first question with the class as an example if necessary.
- Pupils work in pairs to ask and answer the questions according to the information in their graphs. Check answers in open class.

Extra activities: see page T116 (if time)

Ending the lesson

- Pupils close their books. Choose two confident pupils to come to the front. Give them each a fruit flashcard. They hide their card from the class and describe their fruit without saying what it is, e.g. *I like this fruit. It's green and brown.* The rest of the class ask, e.g. *Is it a (pear)?* Repeat with other pupils and different fruit flashcards.

OBJECTIVES: By the end of the lesson, pupils will have used polite language to act out social situations.

- **TARGET LANGUAGE**

Key language: *After you. Thank you. Can you (open the window/ spell ...), please? Yes, of course. Can we come in? Yes, come in.*
Additional language: *Sorry I'm late. That's OK. Sit down, please. Can I have (a pencil), please? Yes, of course. Here you are.*
Revision: *Thank you.*

- **MATERIALS REQUIRED**

Extra activity 1: The following sentences from dialogues, written on separate pieces of paper (enough for half the pupils in the class to have a piece of paper each):
After you.
Sorry I'm late.
Can you open the window, please?
Can you spell pencil, please?
Can I have a pen, please?
Can I have a ruler, please?
Can we come in, please?
Extra activity 2: Pictures of social situations from the lesson taken from magazines or the Internet.

Warmer

- Pretend to bump into one of the pupils or stand on his/her foot and say *Sorry!* Repeat with another pupil. Brainstorm other polite words and phrases that the pupils know in English and write them on the board (e.g. *Please. Thank you. Excuse me.*).
- Say *We use these words to be polite*. Make sure pupils know the meaning of *polite*. Explain that the words are little, but that British people use them a lot. Get pupils to use some of the language on the board in pairs.

PB17. ACTIVITY 3. *Listen and say the number.*

- Say *Open your Pupil's Books at page 17, please*. Point to the picture of Trevor at the top of the page. Elicit his name. Ask *Is he happy or sad?* Translate the meaning of 'values' so the pupils know that Trevor's pages are about doing the right thing.
- Point to the title of the page and say *Look! This page is about being polite*. Focus pupils on the pictures of children in their classroom. Say *Where's the teacher?* Pupils point. Say *Listen and say the picture number: one, two, three, four, five or six*. Play the CD. Pause after each picture. Give pupils time to think and to check with each other before asking for the answer from the class.

Key: Picture 3, Picture 1, Picture 4, Picture 6, Picture 5, Picture 2

CD 1, 30

Sorry I'm late.
That's okay. Sit down please.

Can we come in, please?
Yes, come in.

Can I have a pencil please?
Yes, of course. Here you are.
Thank you.

Can you spell ruler, please?
Yes, r-u-l-e-r.

Can you open the window, please?
Yes, of course.

After you.
Thank you.

PB17. ACTIVITY 4. *Act it out.*

- Say *Let's act out the first picture*. Demonstrate the activity. Five pupils come to the front. Let each pupil choose a character e.g. the teacher and the other children. Play the CD and help the pupils act out the dialogue. Repeat with another scene.

AB17. ACTIVITY 3. *Read and complete.*

- Say *Open your Activity Books at page 17, please*. Point to the pictures. Point to the gaps in the dialogues and the box of phrases at the top of the page. Go through the example with the class and show them how the words in the box go on the two lines of dialogue 1.
- Say *Read and complete*. Pupils work in pairs to complete the other dialogues. Pairs check with pairs. Check with the class. Pupils say the dialogues in pairs.

Key: 2 After you 3 Can you spell 4 Yes, of course.

AB17. ACTIVITY 4. *Draw a picture of you. Be polite!*

- Pupils visualise themselves in one of the situations from earlier on the page and draw themselves with speech bubbles.
- Check they are either asking a question or responding to a request. Focus pupils on being polite and remembering to say *please, thank you, Can you…?*

Extra activities: see page T116 (if time)

Ending the lesson

- Act out one of the situations from the class but in an impolite way, for example, look sternly at a pupil and say *Give me a pencil!* Pupils put their hands up to correct you and say the polite phrase, e.g. *Can I have a pencil, please?*

3 Listen and say the number.

30 CD1

4 Act it out.

Functions

After you. Thank you. Can you … please? Yes, of course.
Can we come in? Yes, come in.

3 Play time!

1 31 CD1 Listen and point.

2 32 CD1 Listen and repeat.

OBJECTIVES: By the end of the lesson, pupils will have learned to name and talk about toys.

• TARGET LANGUAGE

Key language: *camera, watch, kite, robot, lorry, computer game, alien,* plural nouns

Additional language: *next to, Can you spell … ? What's your favourite toy?*

Revision: *doll, ball, bike, car, train, game, boat, ugly*

• MATERIALS REQUIRED

Flashcards: (toys) 42–48

Extra activity 1: two rolled up newspapers

Optional: *Teacher's Resource Book 2*, pages 20–21, Unit 3 Reinforcement worksheet 1.

Warmer

- Write *Toys* on the board, elicit what it says and draw a large circle around it (to begin a mind map). Play the Spelling game with the class, e.g. *Give me a b,* and spell out the known toy words. As the pupils shout out each one, ask a volunteer to spell it and write it on the mind map. Build up the mind map to include: *doll, ball, bike, car, train, lorry, boat.*

Presentation

- Elicit/teach the new toy vocabulary using the flashcards. Show each flashcard in turn and elicit/say the word. Pupils repeat in chorus and then in groups, loudly, softly, and so on. Stick the flashcards (picture side) around the mind map. Point to each flashcard. As pupils chorus the word, turn the flashcard to show the word side.
- Leave the mind map for Extra activity 1.

PB18. ACTIVITY 1. *Listen and point.*

- Say *Open your Pupil's Books at page 18, please.* Elicit who pupils can see in the picture, to revise the names of the characters. Raise awareness of the plurals of the words by saying, e.g. *Point to the kites. Point to the computer games. Point to the robots.*
- Say *Find the hidden star. Where is it?* Elicit from pupils where it is, hold up your book and point to it (on the kite).
- Say *Listen and point.* Play the CD. Pupils listen and point.
- Set the pre-listening questions: *Where are the kites? What colour is the watch? What is Stella's favourite toy?* Play the CD again. Pupils listen for the answers. Check with the class (Next to the lorries, Yellow, A computer game).
- Check comprehension by asking other questions around the class, e.g. *What are these? Who's this? What colour's this? Where are the watches? What's Suzy looking at?*

CD 1, 31

SUZY: Ooh, kites! Can we look at them, Dad?
MR STAR: OK, Suzy. Where are they?
SUZY: Over there! Next to the lorries.

SIMON: Look at these robots!
STELLA: Ugh! They're ugly.
ALEX: I like this big yellow watch.
MEERA: Look at this camera. It's orange, my favourite colour.
STELLA: Hum! … Look! Computer games! I love computer games!
SIMON: Great! Is there a Maskman Playbox?
STELLA: Yes, there is, and there's a 'Can you spell … ?' game.
MEERA, ALEX, SIMON: Ugh! Stella!

PB18. ACTIVITY 2. *Listen and repeat.*

- Say *Let's do Activity 2. Listen and repeat.* Play the CD. Pupils repeat the words in chorus. Listen for correct pronunciation of *camera* (two syllables) and correct word stress of *computer game.*

CD 1, 32

Camera, watch, kite, robot, lorry, alien, computer game

AB18. ACTIVITY 1. *Read. Circle the toy words. Write.*

- Say *Open your Activity Books at page 18, please.* Copy the first sentence of the text on the board: *Suzy's got a kite.* Circle *kite*, as in the example, and say *What's this word? Is it a colour? A number?* Pupils respond *No, a toy.* Say *That's right. It's a toy word. Read and circle all the toy words.* Say *Can you see a picture of a kite?* Pupils show you. Point to the writing lines with the word *kite.*
- Pupils work individually. They read the text silently and circle the toy words. They check in pairs. They match the word with the picture and then copy the word under the picture. Monitor pupils as they are working.
- Correct as a class. Ask pupils to spell out the words.

Key: Pupils circle robot, train, car, computer game, watch and write (from left to right, top to bottom) computer game, train, robot, car, watch.

AB18. ACTIVITY 2. *Listen and tick (✓) the box.* **[YLE]**

- Say *Look at Activity 2.* Play the example. Elicit the sentence from the class (or play the first one again) to make it clear. Play the rest of the CD. Pupils listen and tick. They check in pairs. Play the CD again and check after each one.

Key: 2 c, 3 b, 4 a

CD 1, 33

1 My computer game's my favourite toy.
2 This is Pat. She's playing with her robot.
3 There's a lorry under the chair.
4 Anna's flying her kite.

Extra activities: see page T116 (if time)

Optional activity

- Unit 3 Reinforcement worksheet 1 from *Teacher's Resource Book 2* pages 20–21.

Ending the lesson

- Display the toy flashcards on the board. Elicit the words. Say *Look and think. What's your favourite toy?* Point to the flashcards. *Now hands up.* Say each toy and write the number of pupil hands under each picture. At the end, announce the class's favourite toy.

OBJECTIVES: By the end of the lesson, pupils will have learned to talk about toys using *this* and *these*.

• TARGET LANGUAGE

Key language: *this, these*

Revision: toy vocabulary, numbers *1–20*, colours, adjectives, adjective order, *There's … , There are … , trousers, kitchen*

• MATERIALS REQUIRED

Flashcards: (toys) 42–48

Photocopiable 3 (see page T102), copied onto thin card, one copy for each pupil, scissors, envelopes

Warmer

- Display the toy flashcards. Elicit the words. Do a simple clapping game to review the plurals: Clap, *One watch,* Clap, clap, *Two watches.* Repeat for the other words (*kite, lorry, robot, camera, computer game, alien*).
- Write the plurals on the board and draw pupils' attention to the spelling.

PB19. ACTIVITY **3.** *Listen and say the number.*

- Say *Open your Pupil's Books at page 19, please. Look at the picture and the examples.* Review the other toy words (*doll, train, ball*) by saying *Point to the doll. Point to the train. Point to the ball.* Play the CD. Pause each time to elicit the number from pupils.

Key: alien 11, train 13, camera 18, lorries 12, watch 20, computer game 16, kite 15, balls 14

CD 1, 34

These are dolls.	These are lorries.
This is a robot.	This is a watch.
This is an alien	This is a computer game.
This is a train.	This is a kite.
This is a camera.	These are balls.

Practice

- Focus on the difference between *this* and *these*, using classroom objects, e.g. put two pencils on the desk near you. Put a pen next to them. Point to the pencils and say *These are pencils.* Point to the pen and say *This is a pen.* Repeat for other objects around the class, giving a clear model each time.
- Point to the objects again in turn and say, e.g. *What are these?* (pencils). *What is this?* (a pen).

PB19. ACTIVITY **4.** *Listen and say 'yes' or 'no'.*

- Say *Look at the picture in your books. Listen.* Play the first sentence on the CD. Pause. Pupils put up their hands. Elicit the answer (no). Play the rest of the CD, pausing after each one to give pupils thinking/processing time. They whisper the answer to their partner. Play the CD again. Stop after each one and check with the class. If the answer is *No*, elicit the correct sentence each time.

Key: No – There's a red lorry and a yellow lorry. Yes. Yes. No – There's an ugly robot with red eyes. No – There's a red camera. Yes. No – There's a dirty orange ball. No – There's one small white ball. No – there are two dolls. No – There's one big yellow watch. Yes.

CD 1, 35

There are two big red lorries.
There's a beautiful pink and purple kite.
There's a Maskman computer game.
There's an ugly robot with green eyes.
There's a small pink camera.
There's a green alien.
There's a clean orange ball.
There are two small white balls.
There are three happy dolls.
There are two big yellow watches.
There's a long brown train.

Photocopiable 3: see pages T98 and T102

AB19. ACTIVITY **3.** *Complete the sentences and colour the pictures.*

- Say *Open your Activity Books at page 19, please. Look at Activity 3.* Point to the picture of the plane and to the first sentence. Say it for the class: *This* (hold up one finger to show it's singular) *is a red plane.* Hold up your finger again to show it's one plane and elicit the colour (red). Pupils colour the plane red. Repeat for the second sentence, holding up three fingers this time to show use of *These/watches* and eliciting the colour (purple).
- Pupils work in pairs. They do the activity orally first. Check with the class. Tell pupils to write the words in the sentences. Monitor pupils as they are working. Help with spelling if asked.

Key: 3 These, 4 This, 5 These, 6 These, 7 These, 8 These

AB19. ACTIVITY **4.** *Match. Write the words.*

- Say *Look at Activity 4.* Point to the two example answers and show how they were made by matching letters on the left and right. Say *Make some more words. These are the beginning of the words* (point to these) *and these are the ends of the words* (point to these). *Do the activity in pairs.* Monitor pupils as they are working and help if necessary.
- Elicit words from pupils. Pupils spell them out and you write them on the board. Check understanding of the words, e.g. *trousers*. If pupils make the word *trane*, don't say it's wrong. Remind them that this is how we say the word, but that we spell it in a different way (*train*).

Key: camera, cake, ruler, robot, doll, dog, trousers, train, please, plane

Extra activity: see page T116 (if time)

Ending the lesson

- Teach the class a simple chant to practise the plurals. Say it softly, then loudly. Divide the class into groups and each group says a line, e.g.
  Lorries, lorries, big red lorries.
  Dolls, dolls, happy dolls.
  Watches, watches, big yellow watches.

3 Listen and say the number.

CD1 34

These are dolls. — 19.

This is a robot. — 17.

4 Listen and say 'yes' or 'no'.

CD1 35

Vocabulary

alien camera computer game kite lorry robot watch

Grammar

this these

5 Listen and point.

36 CD1

6 Listen and repeat.

37 CD1

Grammar

Whose is this? Whose are these?

OBJECTIVES: By the end of the lesson, pupils will have learned to ask and answer questions with *Whose* and the possessive *'s*.

• TARGET LANGUAGE

Key language: *Whose … is this / are these? Whose is it? It's / They're his/hers/Suzy's.*

Additional language: *new, tail, What's that?, Metal Mouth*

Revision: prepositions, adjectives, colours, *can, can't, table, basketball, fly, walk, talk*

• MATERIALS REQUIRED

Flashcards: (toys) 42–48

Extra activity 2: string / elastic bands / safety pins

Optional: *Teacher's Resource Book 2* Unit 3 Reinforcement worksheet 2 (page 22)

Warmer

- Review *this* and *these*. Walk around the classroom and point to / pick up classroom objects. Ask *What's this? What are these?* Pupils respond, e.g. *It's a ruler / They're pencils.*

Presentation

- Hold up a pupil's bag. Ask *What's this?* Pupils respond. Ask *Whose is it? Is it (Juan's) bag?* Point to the pupil (it's NOT his bag). *Is it Paula's bag?* Point to her (it's NOT hers). Repeat for two more pupils (it's NOT theirs). Ask again *Whose it is? Ah, it's Claude's bag* (it IS). Repeat with single objects. Listen for correct use of *'s* at the end of the name. Repeat with plural objects.
- Pupils come to the front in turn and follow the model.

PB20. ACTIVITY 5. *Listen and point.*

- Say *Open your Pupil's Books at page 20, please. Look at the picture. Who can you see? What can you see?* (Monty, Marie, Maskman, a robot, a kite, a table, etc.). Play the CD. Pupils listen and point. Set the pre-listening questions: *Whose is the basketball? Whose is the robot? Whose is the computer game?* Play the CD again. Pupils listen for the answers. Pupils check in pairs. Check with the class (Simon's, Simon's, Stella's). Pupils give complete answers, e.g. *It's Simon's basketball.*

CD 1, 36

Toys in the toy box,
Come alive.
Walk and talk,
On the count of five.
One, two, three, four, five.

MONTY: Look at Suzy's kite! It's beautiful. It's pink and purple with a long tail.
MASKMAN: And it's big, and it can fly. I can fly too. What's that, Marie?
MARIE: It's a 'Can you spell … ?' computer game.
MONTY: Whose is it? Is it Suzy's?
MARIE: No, it isn't. It's Stella's.
MONTY: What's that under the table?
MASKMAN: It's Simon's basketball.
MONTY: No, not that. What's that new toy next to the ball?
MARIE: It's a big robot. It's 'Metal Mouth'.
MASKMAN: Metal Mouth? Hmm, yes. It's an ugly robot.
MONTY: Whose is it?
MASKMAN: It's Simon's.
METAL MOUTH: My name is Metal Mouth. My name is Metal Mouth.
MONTY: Ooh, look! It can walk and talk.
MASKMAN: Yes, but it can't fly. I can fly.
METAL MOUTH: I am a robot.

PB20. ACTIVITY 6. *Listen and repeat.*

- Say *Look at Activity 6. Listen, point and repeat.* Play the CD. Stop after each question or answer for pupils to repeat.

CD 1, 37

Whose is this computer game?	It's Stella's.
Whose is this robot?	It's Simon's.
Whose are these books?	They're Stella's.
Whose are these pencils?	They're Suzy's.

AB20. ACTIVITY 5. *Listen and colour. Then answer.* **[YLE]**

- Pupils put the crayons on their desks: green, purple, orange, yellow, black, pink. Say *Open your Activity Books at page 20, please. Look at Activity 5. Listen and colour the kites.* Play number 1. Say *Whose is the black kite?* Pupils respond *Simon's.* Hold up the black crayon. Follow the line from Simon to his kite. Say *Listen and colour the other kites.* Play the CD. Stop after each one. Pupils check in pairs. Play the CD again. Check with the class, e.g. *Whose is the pink kite?.*
- Point to the question (*Whose is the green kite?*) and the example answer. Write *Stella's* on the board. Focus pupils on the capital letter. Remind them how to write the other capitals (A, L, M) Say *Answer the other questions. Write the names.*

Key: 2 Alex's, 3 Meera's, 4 Simon's, 5 Lenny's, 6 Suzy's

CD 1, 38

Whose is this kite?	It's Simon's. Colour it black.
Whose is this kite?	It's Suzy's. Colour it pink.
Whose is this kite?	It's Lenny's. Colour it orange.
Whose is this kite?	It's Stella's. Colour it green.
Whose is this kite?	It's Meera's. Colour it yellow.
Whose is this kite?	It's Alex's. Colour it purple.

AB20. ACTIVITY 6. *Write the questions.*

- Point to various classroom objects and ask, e.g. *Whose is the red bag?* Pupils respond, e.g. *It's Mark's.*
- Say *Look at Activity 6.* Elicit the objects in the picture (plane, kite, watch, lorry, doll). Go through the example with the class. Say *Write the other questions.*
- Pupils work in pairs. Monitor pupils as they are working.
- Check orally with the class. Write each question on the board.

Key: 2 Whose is the doll? 3 Whose is the plane? 4 Whose is the kite? 5 Whose is the watch?

Extra activities: see page T116 (if time)

Optional activity

- Unit 3 Reinforcement worksheet 2 from *Teacher's Resource Book 2* (pages 20 and 22).

Ending the lesson

- Display the toy flashcards (picture side). Point. Pupils chorus the words. Cover one flashcard with a piece of paper. Pupils chorus the words and hum the covered word, e.g. robot *HHHM hhhm*, to show syllables and word stress. Repeat.

OBJECTIVES: By the end of the lesson, pupils will have sung a song and be able to talk about clothing using *this/these* and *that/those*.

• TARGET LANGUAGE

Key language: *that/those*
Revision: *Whose is this / are these?* possessive 's, clothes, colours, classroom instructions, *Sorry. Can you repeat that, please? Can you say that again?*

• MATERIALS REQUIRED

Extra activity 2: Prepare/find four pictures of children (two boys and two girls) wearing different coloured clothes, e.g. shoes, jacket, shirt, trousers, T-shirt.
Optional: *Teacher's Resource Book 2* Unit 3 Extension worksheet 1 (page 23), *Kid's Box Teacher's Resource Book 2* Unit 3 song worksheet (page 25)

Warmer

- Play a Stella says game to review clothes. Pupils stand up. Say, e.g. *Stella says touch your shoes.* Pupils touch their shoes. *Point to a blue jacket.* Pupils don't point. Continue the game, using known clothes words, colour adjectives and the class instructions *point to, touch.*

PB21. ACTIVITY 7. *Listen and point. Sing.*

- Say *Open your Pupil's Books at page 21, please. Look at the picture. What clothes can you see?* Elicit the clothes and the colours. Elicit/tell pupils the names of the characters (John, Sheila, Sue and Tom are new). Check they know which are the boys' names and which the girls'). Say *Whose clothes are they? Let's listen and see.* Play the CD. Pupils listen and point to the clothes and the owner each time. Elicit the information from the class. Hold up your book and point to, e.g. the black jacket and say *Whose black jacket is this?* Pupils respond *It's John's.*
- Play the CD again. This time pupils follow the text in their books.

CD 1, 39

Whose is this jacket?
Whose is this jacket?
What? That black jacket?
Yes, this black jacket.
Whose is this jacket?
It's John's.
Oh!

Whose are these shoes?
Whose are these shoes?
What? Those blue shoes?
Yes, these blue shoes.
Whose are these shoes?
They're Sheila's.
Oh!

Whose is this skirt?
Whose is this skirt?
What? That purple skirt?
Yes, this purple skirt.
Whose is this skirt?
It's Sue's.
Oh!

Whose are these trousers?
Whose are these trousers?
What? Those brown trousers?
Yes, these brown trousers.
Whose are these trousers?
They're Tom's.
Oh!

CD 1, 40

Now sing the song again. (Karaoke version)

PB21. ACTIVITY 8. *Ask and answer.*

- Pupils work in pairs. Pupil A asks a question about the song lyrics, e.g. *Whose is this jacket?* Pupil B answers, e.g. *It's John's.* Pupils swap roles. Repeat the activity with items in the classroom.

AB21. ACTIVITY 7. *Look and read. Put a tick (✓) or a cross (✗) in the box. There is one example.* **[YLE]**

- Say *Open your Activity Books at page 21.* Point to the picture of the watches and the example sentence. Read aloud: *These are watches* and ask *Is that OK?* Look at the box. Pupils respond *Yes/OK.* Say *Yes. These are watches. There's a tick in the box. Now read the rest of the sentences and tick or cross.*
- Pupils work silently on their own to read and tick or cross. Monitor and check they are reading carefully as well as looking at the pictures. Compare answers in pairs.
- Check answers as a whole class. Elicit the correct sentences for those with a cross (i.e. *This is a computer game. This is a bike. These are planes.*)

Key: These are cameras. ✓, This is a kite. ✗, This is a lorry. ✗, These are trains. ✗, This is a robot. ✓

Extra activities: see page T117 (if time)

Optional activities

- Unit 3 Extension worksheet 1 from *Teacher's Resource Book 2* (see pages 20 and 23 of the *Teacher's Resource Book*).
- Unit 3 song worksheet from *Teacher's Resource Book 2.* Pupils listen and match the characters and clothing (see pages 20 and 25 of the *Teacher's Resource Book*).

Ending the lesson

- Sing the song again from Pupil's Book Activity 7 to end the lesson.

7 39 CD1 Listen and point. Sing.

Whose is this jacket? ...
What? That black jacket?
Yes, this black jacket.
Whose is this jacket?
It's John's.
Oh!

Whose are these shoes? ...
What? Those blue shoes?
Yes, these blue shoes.
Whose are these shoes?
They're Sheila's.
Oh!

Whose is this skirt? ...
What? That purple skirt?
Yes, this purple skirt.
Whose is this skirt?
It's Sue's.
Oh!

Whose are these trousers? ...
What? Those brown trousers?
Yes, these brown trousers.
Whose are these trousers?
They're Tom's.
Oh!

8 Ask and answer.

Whose are these trousers?

They're Tom's.

9 41 CD1 Monty's phonics

fly

five

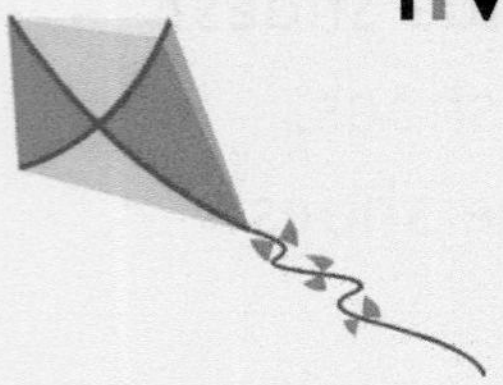

kite

I'm flying my five white kites.

10 Ask and answer.

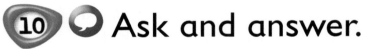

11. Whose is this nose?
It's Simon's.
12. Whose are these eyes?
They're Stella's.

11
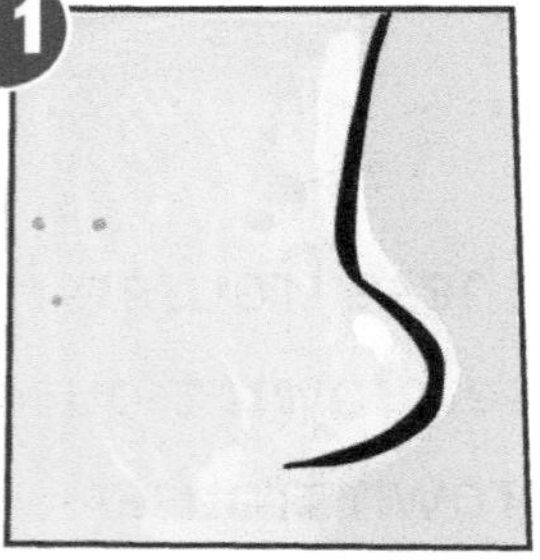

12

13

14

15

16

17

18
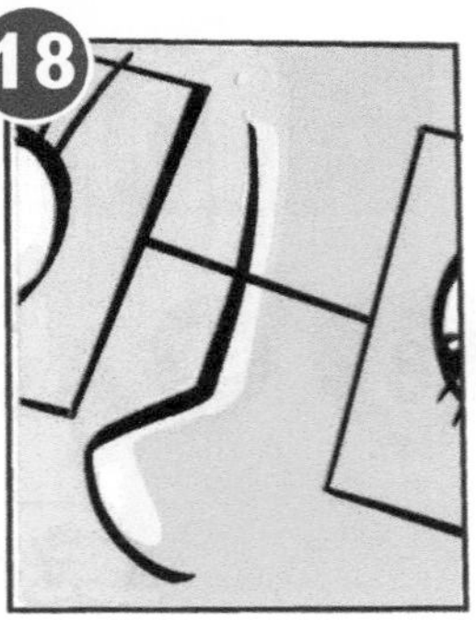

OBJECTIVES: By the end of the lesson, pupils will have learned to recognise the phoneme /aɪ/ and have had more practice with *Whose* and the possessive *'s*.

• TARGET LANGUAGE

Key language: the phoneme /aɪ/ as in *fly, five, kite*

Revision: parts of the face, possessive *'s*, *whose*, numbers *1–20*

• MATERIALS REQUIRED

Extra activity 1: Photocopiable 3 (see page T102), if not previously used copied onto thin card, one copy for each pupil, scissors, envelopes

Extra activity 2: 20 number cards, each with the different number (in words) between *one* and *twenty*

Warmer

- Review the parts of the face by teaching the pupils a quick action song:
  This is my face, my face, my face. (Pupils circle their faces with their hands)
  This is my face. MY FACE. (Pupils point to their faces)
- Repeat for *eyes, nose, mouth, ears, teeth.* Use *These are* for the plural words.

PB22. ACTIVITY **9.** *Monty's phonics*

- Say *Open your Pupil's Books at page 22, please.* Point to the picture of the bird flying and say *fly*, emphasising the /aɪ/ sound. Say the word again and do a flying mime as you speak. Point to the figure 5 and the picture of the kite and practise the words in the same way, emphasising the vowel sound and using mime when you say the words (draw a number 5 in the air with your finger and mime holding the string of a kite on a windy day). Point at the large picture and ask *What's the girl doing? (Flying kites) How many kites? (Five) What colour are they? (White).* Say *Now listen to Monty, point and repeat.*
- Play the CD. Pupils listen and repeat the sounds, words, and sentence using the same tone and speed as Monty.
- Pupils repeat the tongue twister as a class. Do it more and more quickly. Then ask small groups of pupils to have a go at saying it. Go around the class, from group to group. Put pupils into pairs. They take turns to say the tongue twister quickly to each other. Invite volunteers to say it to the class.
- Write the tongue twister on the board. Focus pupils on the words. Elicit from them which letters to underline for the sound /aɪ/.

Key: I'm flying my five white kites.

CD 1, 41

MONTY: Hi, I'm Monty! Repeat after me!
/aɪ/, /aɪ/, fly
/aɪ/, /aɪ/, five
/aɪ/, /aɪ/, kite
I'm flying my five white kites!
I'm flying my five white kites!
I'm flying my five white kites!

PB22. ACTIVITY **10.** *Ask and answer.*

- Say *Look at Activity 10.* Hold up your book and point to the first example (picture 11). Ask the question *Whose is this nose?* Pupils respond using the prompt (or from memory) *It's Simon's.* Repeat with the other example. Practise with one or two other features of different pupils, giving pupils a chance to ask as well to answer. Make sure pupils notice the difference (singular and plural) and remind them to think about the chant from the warmer to help them.
- Pupils work in pairs and take turns to point and ask, and to answer. Remind them to look back in their Pupil's Books if they can't remember the characters.
- Check with the class using open pairs. One pair asks the question across the class. Another pair answers.

Key: 13 Whose is this mouth? It's Suzy's. 14 Whose is this ear? It's Simon's. 15 Whose are these eyes? They're Simon's. 16 Whose is this mouth? It's Stella's. 17 Whose is this ear? It's Suzy's. 18 Whose are these eyes? They're Stella's.

AB22. ACTIVITY **8.** *Listen and write the words.*

- Say *Open your Activity Books at page 22, please.* Point to the large outline pictures in turn and ask *What's this? (A fish, A kite).* Play number 1 on the CD and say *'Fish' has the sound /ɪ/. Look. It's in the fish.* (Point to the example word written on the first line in the fish outline). Play number 2 and say *'Kite' has the sound /aɪ/. Look. It's in the kite. Now listen and think /ɪ/ or /aɪ/? Fish or kite? Write in pencil.*
- Play the rest of the CD, pausing after each word for pupils to consult in pairs and write the word. Play the CD again if necessary. Elicit answers and write the groups of words on the board for pupils to check.

Key: Fish 3 pink, 6 swim, 8 big, 10 sit; Kite 4 five, 5 my, 7 bike, 9 fly

CD 1, 42

1. fish, 2. kite, 3. pink, 4. five, 5. my, 6. swim, 7. bike, 8. big, 9. fly, 10. sit

AB22. ACTIVITY **9.** *Listen and join the dots.*

- Write two or three numbers at random on the board, e.g. *16, 12,* and elicit what they are.
- Say *Look at Activity 9.* Say *Take a pencil. Listen.* Play the CD. Pupils listen and join the numbers in the order they hear them. They check in pairs. Play the CD again. Check with the class. Elicit what the picture is (a lorry).
- Pupils complete the sentence under the picture. Remind them to check on Pupil's Book page 18 for the spelling of the word.

Key: lorry

CD 1, 43

5, 13, 11, 8, 17, 6, 14, 3, 5, 2, 19, 1, 10, 20, 13

Extra activities: see page T117 (if time)

Ending the lesson

- Do the tongue twister again with the class. Pupils stand up. Do it as a class and then invite groups of four to have a go at saying it as fast as they can.

OBJECTIVES: By the end of the lesson, pupils will have read a story and reviewed language from the unit.

- **TARGET LANGUAGE**

Key language: language from the unit
Additional language: *Metal Mouth, I know*
Revision: *can, can't, walk, talk, spell, listen, ugly, stop, sorry, not, nice, superhero, favourite, toy*

- **MATERIALS REQUIRED**

Extra activity 1: Flashcards (toys) 42–48
Optional: *Teacher's Resource Book 2* Unit 3 Extension worksheet 2 (page 24) and/or animated version of the Unit 3 story from *Kid's Box 2 Interactive DVD* (Suzy's room section), *Kid's Box 2 Language Portfolio* page 3

Warmer

- Review *Whose* and use of possessive 's by collecting some objects from pupils, taking them to the front and showing them in turn, asking *Whose is this? Whose are these?*
- Pupils can take turns collecting objects and asking questions.

Story

PB23. ACTIVITY **11.** *Listen to the story.*

- Say *Open your Pupil's Books at page 23, please.* Elicit who they can see (Trevor, Monty, Marie, Maskman and a big ugly robot). Hold up your book to check pupils remember the sequence of the pictures. Set the pre-listening questions. Divide the class into groups of three: A, B and C. Give each pupil in each group a different question to listen for: As: *What's the robot's name?* Bs: *Whose robot is it?* Cs: *Can the robot walk?* Say *Listen and look.* Play the CD. Pupils listen and look. The groups of three exchange their answers. Check with the class (Metal Mouth, Simon's, yes).
- Play the CD again, frame by frame. Pupils listen and repeat. Encourage them to say it with intonation and feeling.
- Check comprehension by pointing to each picture and asking, e.g. *What's this?* (robot). *What colour is it?* (grey). *Is the robot beautiful?* (ugly). *Whose is it?* (Simon's). *Can it talk? Can it walk?* (Yes). *Can it fly?* (No). *Is it a superhero?* (No). *Is it Simon's favourite toy?* (No). *Who is the superhero?* (Maskman). *Who is Simon's favourite toy?* (Maskman).
- Check understanding of *superhero*. Give examples that pupils will know, e.g. *Superman, Spiderman.* Ask pupils who their favourite superhero is.

CD 1, 44

Toys in the toy box,
Come alive.
Walk and talk,
On the count of five.
One, two, three, four, five.
TREVOR: Whose is this robot?
MASKMAN: It's Simon's.

TREVOR: Hello. What's your name?
ROBOT: My name is Metal Mouth.

TREVOR: Oh. Can you walk, Metal Mouth?
ROBOT: I can walk and I can talk.

MASKMAN: Well, *I* can walk. *I* can talk, and *I* can spell. U–g–l–y.
TREVOR: I know! I know! ... It's ugly!
MASKMAN: Yes, it is ... and it can't fly.

MARIE: Maskman! Say 'sorry', please.
MASKMAN: Sorry.
MONTY: It's OK, Maskman. You're a superhero *and* you're Simon's favourite toy.

PB23. ACTIVITY **12.** *Act out the story.*

- Divide the class into groups of five. Pupils decide their roles. Play the CD again. Stop after each frame for the pupils to repeat in role. Groups practise their story. More confident groups of pupils can change some words, e.g. *ugly, walk, talk, fly.* Invite two or three groups to role play their story to the class.

AB23. MY PICTURE DICTIONARY.

- Say *Open your Activity Books at page 23, please.* Pupils prepare the toy stickers. Say *Which toy is it? Listen.*
- Play number 1 on the CD and elicit the toy (kite). Ask pupils to hold up the correct sticker. They all stick the sticker in the first square.
- Play the rest of the CD. Pupils lay the stickers out on their desk in the correct order. Monitor around the class to check before they stick them in their books.
- Point to the example word on the line in square 1 *(kite).* Say *Now write the words.* Pupils write the name of the toy under each sticker. Write the toy names on the board in random order if they are having difficulty. Play the CD again if necessary.
- Elicit where they can find the spelling of the words (Pupil's Book page 18).

Key: 2 camera, 3 computer game, 4 robot, 5 watch, 6 lorry

CD 1, 45

Stick the kite on number 1. Stick the robot on number 4. Stick the lorry on number 6. Stick the computer game on number 3. Stick the watch on number 5. Stick the camera on number 2.

AB23. MY PROGRESS.

- Focus pupils on the activity in their books. Say *Let's read the sentences together.* Read the first sentence. Display the flashcards of the toys and ask different pupils *What's your favourite toy? What colour is it? Is it big?*, etc.
- Read the second sentence. Remind pupils what they did in My picture dictionary, nod and say *You can write 'toy' words.* Pupils work in pairs. They take turns to point to a sentence in their books and do or show what it says.
- Say *Now ask each other and tick or cross the sentences.* Demonstrate the activity again if necessary.

Extra activities: see page T117 (if time)

Optional activities

- Unit 3 Extension worksheet 2 (see pages 20 and 24 of the *Teacher's Resource Book*).
- The animated version of the story from *Kid's Box 2 Interactive DVD* (Suzy's room section). See pages 41–44 of the Teacher's booklet for the *Interactive DVD.*

Language Portfolio

- Pupils complete page 3 of *Kid's Box 2 Language Portfolio (I can ... Units 1–3).*

Ending the lesson

- Ask pupils which chant/song/game they'd like to do again from the unit. Do it together to end the lesson.

11 44 CD1 Listen to the story.

12 Act out the story.

4 At home

1 Listen and point. (46 CD1)

2 Listen and repeat. (47 CD1)

OBJECTIVES: By the end of the lesson, pupils will have learned to name and talk about things in a house.

• TARGET LANGUAGE
Key language: *mat, lamp, clock, phone, sofa, mirror*
Additional language: *bath, bed, armchair, furniture, doll's house*
Revision: *Can I have … ? can/can't, There's a … Where … ? one, bathroom, bedroom, dining room, hall, kitchen, living room, table, under, in, next to, mouse*

• MATERIALS REQUIRED
Flashcards (household objects) 49–54
Kid's Box 1 flashcards (rooms): 85–90 OR pictures of: bathroom, bedroom, dining room, hall, kitchen, living room
Optional: *Teacher's Resource Book 2* Unit 4 Reinforcement worksheet 1 (page 27)

Warmer

- Draw a large, simple cross-section of a house on the board: four rooms downstairs, two upstairs. Display the flashcards/ pictures of bathroom, bedroom, dining room, hall, kitchen, living room. Point to a space in the house. Say *What's this?* Pupils respond. If it's appropriate, a pupil comes and attaches the picture. Repeat for all the rooms. Point and pupils repeat.

Presentation

- Elicit/teach the new vocabulary *mat, lamp, clock, phone, sofa, mirror,* using the flashcards. Pupils repeat in chorus. Check the concept of *mat*. Elicit/discuss which room you can find the objects in, e.g. *Where can I find a mat?* Ask, e.g. *Have you got a phone in your bedroom?*

PB24. ACTIVITY **1.** *Listen and point.*

- Say *Open your books at page 24, please.* Elicit what and who they can see (a house, rooms, Suzy, Stella). Say *It's a doll's house.* Say *Find the hidden star. Where is it?* (on the mirror in the pink bedroom). Pupils say *Here it is.*
- Say *Listen and point.* Play the CD.
- Set the pre-listening questions: *Where are the mirrors? Where's the sofa? Where are the clocks? Where's the bath?* Play the CD again. Pupils listen for the answers. Check with the class (bathroom, Suzy's bedroom, Simon's bedroom; living room; living room, kitchen; bathroom).
- Check comprehension by asking, e.g. *What's this? Whose is the blue bedroom? Where's the phone?* Ask different pupils.

CD 1, 46

STELLA: Can I play, Suzy?
SUZY: OK.
STELLA: Where's my bedroom?
SUZY: It's there, next to the bathroom.
STELLA: OK.
SUZY: Put this blue mat on the floor next to your bed.
STELLA: Can I have a phone in my bedroom?
SUZY: No, you can't. The phone's in the living room next to the sofa.
STELLA: Can I have a lamp, please?
SUZY: OK. You can put the lamp on the table next to your bed.
STELLA: Thanks, Suzy. Where can I put the armchair?
SUZY: Put it in the living room under the clock.
STELLA: Is there a mirror in my bedroom?
SUZY: A mirror in your bedroom? No, there isn't. There are three mirrors. One in the bathroom, one in my bedroom and one in Simon's bedroom.
STELLA: Oh.

PB24. ACTIVITY **2.** *Listen and repeat.*

- Say *Let's do Activity 2. Listen and repeat.* Play the CD. Pupils repeat in chorus.

CD 1, 47

Mat, lamp, clock, phone, mirror, sofa

AB24. ACTIVITY **1.** *Listen and draw lines.*

- Say *Open your Activity Books at page 24, please.* Elicit what pupils can see. Say *Listen. Draw a line in pencil.* Play the first sentence. Point out the example line from the bookcase to the living room. Play the rest of the CD. Pupils draw lines and match. They check in pairs. Play the CD again. Check and elicit a full sentence each time.

CD 1, 48

In the living room there's a bookcase under the window.
There's a clock next to the window in the kitchen.
There are two shoes under the bed.
There's a computer on the desk in the bedroom.
There's a camera on the table in the kitchen.
There's an armchair next to the sofa.
There's a phone on the television.
There's a lamp on the cupboard in the bedroom.
In the bathroom there's a bath under the mirror.
There's a toy duck on the mat in the bathroom.

AB24. ACTIVITY **2.** *Write the words.*

- Say *What can you see in Activity 2?* Elicit *A crossword.* Show pupils the example. Point to the picture of the lamp. Elicit the word (lamp) and the number (2). Say *Where does it go?* Point to 2 in the grid and spell the word aloud with pupils. Pupils complete the crossword in pairs. Check with the class. Elicit the number, the word and the spelling.

Key: Across 4 sofa, 6 mat, 7 bath, 8 mirror
Down 1 clock, 3 phone, 5 armchair, 7 bed

Extra activities: see page T117 (if time)

Optional activities

- Unit 4 Reinforcement worksheet 1 from *Teacher's Resource Book 2* pages 26–27.

Ending the lesson

- Revise the alphabet by playing a game. Say *Listen and put up your hand when you know the word.* Spell out one of the words from Pupil's Book page 24, letter by letter, e.g. *c-l-o-c-k*. When you get to the end of the word, ask the pupil who put his/her hand up first to say the whole word (*Clock*). Repeat with the rest of the words. Pupils can play this game in pairs or in teams.

OBJECTIVES: By the end of the lesson, pupils will have learned to talk about where objects are in a house, using prepositions.

- **TARGET LANGUAGE**

Key language: *mat, lamp, clock, phone, sofa, mirror, next to, in, on*
Revision: *and, There's a … , table, bed, bathroom, hall, wall, bed, bath, boat,* colours, *Yes, there is, No, there isn't.*

- **MATERIALS REQUIRED**

Flashcards (household objects) 49–54
Photocopiable 4 (see page T103), copied onto thin card, a copy for each pupil, scissors, crayons
Optional: *Teacher's Resource Book 2* Unit 4 Reinforcement worksheet 2 and Extension worksheet 1 (pages 28 and 29)

Warmer

- Place the household object flashcards (word side or use the 'At home' word cards from *Teacher's Resource Book 2* page 91) around the room next to / on / in known places, e.g. the mat next to the board, the phone on the desk.
- Say a true or false sentence about each one, e.g. *The mat's on the board* (false). Pupils write *T* or *F* in their notebooks. Check with the class. Pupils correct the incorrect statements.

PB25. ACTIVITY **3.** *Listen and point. Chant.*

- Say *Open your Pupil's Books at page 25, please.* Focus pupils on the pictures and on the text. Play the CD. Pupils listen and point to the pictures. Play the CD again. Teach the chant line by line. Pupils stand up and say it without the CD.

CD 1, 49

There's a mirror in the bathroom,
And a phone in the hall.
A sofa in the living room,
A clock on the wall.
There's a lamp on the table,
And a mat next to the bed.
There's a boat in the bath,
And the boat is red.

PB25. ACTIVITY **4.** *Listen and correct.*

- Play the first sentence on the CD. Pupils look at the picture and say *No, there isn't.* Focus on the corrected sentence in the speech bubble. Play the rest of the CD. Stop after each one. Pupils whisper the correction to their partner. Play the CD again. Check after each one. Elicit corrections.

Key: No, there isn't. There's a boy sitting on the sofa.
No, there isn't. There's a mirror in the bathroom.
No, there isn't. There's a phone in the hall.
No, there isn't. There's a boat in the bath.
No, there isn't. There's a sofa in the living room.
No, there isn't. There's a lamp on the table.
No, there isn't. There's a clock on the wall in the sitting room.
No, there isn't. There's a girl sitting on the bed.

CD 1, 50

There's a girl sitting on the sofa.
There's a mirror in the living room.
There's a phone in the bedroom.
There's a boat on the bed.
There's a sofa in the hall.
There's a lamp under the window.
There's a clock next to the bath.
There's a boy sitting on the bed.

Photocopiable 4: see pages T98 and T103

AB25. ACTIVITY **3.** *Read and write the number. Draw.*

- Say *Open your Activity Books at page 25, please.* Point to the first word *sixteen* and say *Read the word. Write this word as a number.* Show pupils the example answer 16.
- Pupils read the number words and write figures in the spaces. Check answers before going on to the next stage of the activity.

Key: 14, 17, 18, 20, 12, 15, 13, 19

- Pupils use the number code to write the letters in the squares to form words. Then they draw a picture of each word on the right. Pupils check their work in pairs.

Key: 1 mirror, 2 lamp, 3 sofa

AB25. ACTIVITY **4.** *Read and write the words.* **[YLE]**

- Read the first clue aloud and point to the example answer. Pupils work in pairs. They read the sentences silently, find the word and write it. Check with the class.

Key: 2 sofa, 3 phone, 4 armchair, 5 mat

Extra activity: see page T117 (if time)

Optional activity

- Unit 4 Reinforcement worksheet 2 and Extension worksheet 1 from *Teacher's Resource Book 2* pages 26, 28, 29.

Ending the lesson

- Pupils draw and colour a picture of one of the rooms (or a room in their house) including three of the objects, e.g. mat, lamp, phone. They write three sentences about the picture, e.g. *There's a lamp next to the bed.*
- Provide sentence prompts on the board:

There's a	lamp mat phone sofa	next to in on	the bed. the sofa. the TV. the bath.

3 49 CD1 Listen and point. Chant.

There's a mirror in the bathroom,
And a phone in the hall.
A sofa in the living room,
A clock on the wall.
There's a lamp on the table,
And a mat next to the bed.
There's a boat in the bath,
And the boat is red.

4 50 CD1 Listen and correct.

There's a boy sitting on the sofa.

Vocabulary

clock lamp mat mirror phone sofa

5 Listen and point.

51 CD1

6 Listen and repeat.

52 CD1

Grammar
It's mine / yours.

OBJECTIVES: By the end of the lesson, pupils will have learned to talk about possession, using *yours* and *mine*.

• **TARGET LANGUAGE**

Key language: *It's … , They're … , yours, mine, Which … ?*
Additional language: *Which one? The (yellow) one.*
Revision: *Whose is this / are these? his, hers, socks, T-shirt, trousers, skirt, jacket*

• **MATERIALS REQUIRED**

Extra activity 2: Photocopiable 4 (see page T103), if not used in previous lesson copied onto thin card, a copy for each pupil, scissors, crayons
Optional: *Kid's Box 2 Language Portfolio* page 9

Warmer

- Pupils stand up. Review clothes (*socks, T-shirt, trousers, skirt, jacket*) with a pointing game. Say, e.g. *Point to your shirt. Point to your socks.* Pupils follow the instructions.

Presentation

- Pick up a pupil's pencil. Ask the class *Whose is it? Is it hers or his?* Point to two pupils. Pupils respond, e.g. *It's hers.* Repeat with other objects and include *Is it yours?*
- Extend the activity to teach *mine/yours*. Hold up your book. Say *It's not yours* (make a gesture to a pupil). *It's mine.* Repeat for other objects. Pupils hold up objects and say and do the same. Pupils work in pairs. One pupil picks up an object and says *Is it mine or yours?* The other pupil responds, e.g. *It's mine.*

PB26. ACTIVITY 5. *Listen and point.*

- Say *Open your Pupil's Books at page 26, please.* Elicit who pupils can see (Stella, Simon, Grandpa Star). Play the CD. Pupils point to the clothes. Set pre-listening questions: *Whose is the big yellow T-shirt? What colour are Dad's socks?* Play the CD again. Pupils check in pairs. Check with the class (Simon's, Blue).
- Check comprehension, e.g. *Whose is the small yellow T-shirt? What colour are Grandpa's trousers? Which T-shirt is Simon's? The big one or the small one?*

CD 1, 51

GRANDPA: Simon! Stella! Can you take your clothes to your bedrooms, please?
SIMON AND STELLA: OK.
GRANDPA: Whose T-shirt is that?
STELLA: Which T-shirt?
GRANDPA: The yellow one.
STELLA: It's Suzy's.
SIMON: No, it isn't. It's mine!
STELLA: No, Simon. That T-shirt's very small. Yours is the big yellow one over there.
SIMON: Oh! Yes!
GRANDPA: OK. Are those blue socks yours, Simon?
SIMON: No, they aren't mine. They're Dad's.
GRANDPA: What now? Oh, yes! Whose black trousers are those?
STELLA AND SIMON: They're yours, Grandpa.
GRANDPA: Oh, yes! That's right, they are.

PB26. ACTIVITY 6. *Listen and repeat.*

- Say *Look at Activity 6. Listen and repeat.* Play the CD. Pupils repeat each line.

CD 1, 52

GRANDPA: Whose T-shirt is that?
SIMON: It's mine!
GRANDPA: Whose black trousers are those?
STELLA AND SIMON: They're yours, Grandpa.

AB26. ACTIVITY 5. *Write 'yours' or 'mine'.*

- Say *Open your Activity Books at page 26, please.* Focus pupils on the pictures and speech bubbles. Use the example to check they know what to do. Pupils complete the speech bubbles. They check in pairs. Check with the class.

Key: 2 yours, 3 yours, 4 mine

AB26. ACTIVITY 6. *Listen and colour.* **[YLE]**

- Pupils take out their crayons. Play the CD. Pupils don't colour. They listen and look. Play the CD again. Stop after each // below so pupils can colour. They check in pairs. Play the CD again if necessary. Check by asking, e.g. *What colour is the door? What colour are the walls?*

Key: See tapescript.

CD 1, 53

The walls are white and the mirror's grey. // There's a green door next to the mirror. // There are two tables in the living room. The big one's brown and the small one's yellow. // The lamp on the big table's pink and the phone on the small table's black. // The sofa under the window's purple and the mat next to the armchair's red.

Extra activities: see pages T117–T118 (if time)

Language Portfolio

- Pupils complete page 9 of *Kid's Box 2 Language Portfolio (My bedroom).*

Ending the lesson

- Review language from the lesson using a game. Take, e.g. a red crayon from one pupil and a green one from another. Ask *Which one's yours?* Pupils respond, e.g. *The red one.* Repeat for other pupils and other objects. Extend to other questions, e.g. *Look at the two bookcases in the classroom, the big one and the small one. Which one's white?*

OBJECTIVES: By the end of the lesson, pupils will have had more practice talking about possession, using *yours* and *mine*, and sung a song.

• TARGET LANGUAGE

Key language: *Whose are those?*
Additional language: *that, those*
Revision: *yours, mine, his, hers, that one's, this, that,* colours, clothes, toys

• MATERIALS REQUIRED

Flashcards (household objects) 49–54
Extra activity 1: the song from Pupil's Book page 27 Activity 7 written on a large piece of paper, with the following words underlined: *shoes, shoes are Simon's, grey ones are his, shoes are Suzy's, red ones are hers, shoes are those, Grandpa's.*
Optional: *Teacher's Resource Book 2* Unit 4 song worksheet (page 31)

Warmer

- Review school objects, using an open pair activity. Point to, e.g. the computer. Say *What's this?* Pupils respond. Point to, e.g. the books on the bookcase. Say *What are these?* Pupils respond. Pupils take it in turns to walk around the class, point and ask. The class responds.

PB27. ACTIVITY **7.** *Listen and point. Sing.*

- Say *Open your Pupil's Books at page 27, please.* Elicit who they can see (Grandma Star, Stella). Play the CD. Pupils listen and point to the shoes. Play the CD again. Encourage pupils to sing.

CD 1, 54

Look at this! Look at this!

Whose are these shoes? Whose are these shoes?
Stella! Are they yours? Stella! Are they yours?
No, they aren't mine! No, they aren't mine!

Hmm. Which shoes are Simon's? Which shoes are Simon's?
Which, which, which, which?
Which shoes are Simon's?
The grey ones are his. The grey ones are his.

Hmm. Which shoes are Suzy's? Which shoes are Suzy's?
Which, which, which, which?
Which shoes are Suzy's?
The red ones are hers. The red ones are hers.

So! Whose shoes are those? Whose shoes are those?
Whose, whose, whose, whose?
Whose shoes are those?
Those are Grandpa's. Those are Grandpa's.
Grandpa's?

GRANDPA!

CD 1, 55

Now sing the song again. (Karaoke version)

PB27. ACTIVITY **8.** *Ask and answer.*

- Pupils work in groups. They should sit on the floor, in a circle, if possible. Pupils put some of their personal belongings in the middle of the circle. As you monitor, make sure that there are at least two examples of each item. Pupils take it in turns to ask one member of the group a question, e.g. *Which bag is yours?* The pupil answers, e.g. *The red one's mine.* It's now this person's turn to ask a question to another member of the group.

AB27. ACTIVITY **7.** *Listen and draw lines. There is one example.* **[YLE]**

- Say *Open your Activity Books at page 27, please. Look at the pictures. What can you see?* Elicit the names of the things pupils know in two bedrooms (e.g. *armchair, sofa, lamp, clock*) and the toys and other objects at the top and bottom of the page (*ruler, kite, robot, camera, doll, watch, lorry*).
- Say *Listen.* Play the example on the CD (the first four lines). Say *What is it? The ruler? The lorry?* Elicit *The robot.* Ask *Is the robot in the boy's room or the girl's room? (The boy's room).* Ask *Where do I put it?* Elicit *Under the bed.* Hold up the Activity Book page and mime drawing the example line from the robot to the correct position under the bed in the boy's room.
- Say *Listen and draw lines. Use a pencil.* Tell pupils that they will not hear about all the items in the pictures. Play the rest of the CD. Pupils listen and draw lines. They check in pairs. Play the CD again. Check by asking, e.g. *Is the camera in the boy's room or the girl's room? Where is it?* Elicit which item wasn't mentioned (the ruler).

Key: kite – boy's room, next to the clock; camera – girl's room, on the chair; doll – girl's room, on the bed; lorry – girl's room, next to the phone; watch – boy's room in front of the sofa.

CD 1, 56

Can you see the boy?
Yes.
Well, put the robot under his bed.
OK. The robot's under his bed now.

Can you see the line? This is an example. Now you listen and draw lines.

1. OK. Now, put the kite next to his clock.
   Sorry?
   Put the kite next to his clock.
   Right.
2. And what now?
   Can you see the girl? Put the camera on her chair.
   Right. It's on her chair now.
   Good.
3. There's her doll here. Can you see it?
   Yes. It's a beautiful doll.
   Put it on her bed.
   OK. I'm putting it on her bed.
4. Can you see her lorry?
   Yes. Where can I put it?
   Put it next to her phone.
   Right. Her lorry is next to her phone.
5. Now, whose is the watch?
   The watch? It's his. Put it in front of his sofa.
   OK. I'm putting it in front of his sofa.
   Thank you.

Extra activities: see page T118 (if time)

Optional activity

- Pupils complete the Unit 4 song worksheet from *Teacher's Resource Book 2* pages 26, 31.

Ending the lesson

- Six pupils come to the front. Hand each one a household object flashcard. They quickly line up with the objects in alphabetical order. They say their words. The class checks.

7 54 CD1 Listen and point. Sing.

Look at this!
Look at this!

Whose are these shoes? ...
Stella! Are they yours? ...
No, they aren't mine! ...

Hmm. Which shoes are Simon's? ...
Which, which, which, which?
Which shoes are Simon's?
The grey ones are his ...

Hmm. Which shoes are Suzy's? ...
Which, which, which, which?
Which shoes are Suzy's?
The red ones are hers ...

SO! Whose shoes are those? ...
Whose, whose, whose, whose?
Whose shoes are those?
Those are Grandpa's ...
Grandpa's?

GRANDPA!

8 Ask and answer.

Which bag is yours?

The red one's mine.

9 57 CD1 Monty's phonics

phone

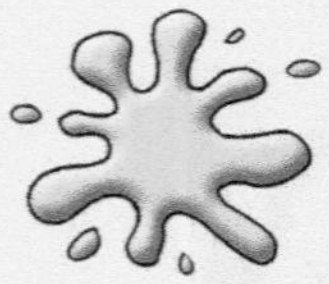

yellow

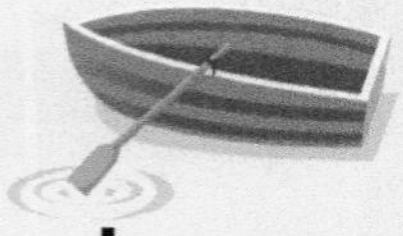

boat

A phone in a yellow boat!

10 Find your partner.

Are these trousers yours or mine?
They're mine.

OBJECTIVES: By the end of the lesson, pupils will have learned to identify and say the long oa /əʊ/ vowel sound and to contrast it with the short o /ɒ/ vowel sound and they will have had more practice with *yours* and *mine*.

• TARGET LANGUAGE

Key language: the phoneme /əʊ/ as in yellow, boat, home
Revision: *yours, mine, Are these … ?, or,* clothes

• MATERIALS REQUIRED

Prepare a worksheet with the following text, cutting along the lines to make 30 cards.

Whose are those lorries?	They're Ben's lorries.
Are those grey trousers yours or mine?	The grey ones are yours.
Whose is that watch?	It's Kim's watch.
Is that red phone yours or mine?	The red one's mine.
Are these dirty shoes Ben's or Tom's?	They're Tom's dirty shoes.
Are these clean jeans Ann's or Sue's?	They're Ann's clean jeans.
Is that brown bag May's or Grace's?	It's May's brown bag.
Is this blue ruler Nick's or Tony's?	It's Nick's blue ruler.
Are those short socks yours or his?	The short ones are mine.
Are those long socks mine or hers?	The long ones are hers.
Is that black phone yours or hers?	The black one's hers.
Are these big books yours or his?	The big ones are mine.
Are those fat white mice his or hers?	The fat white ones are his.
Is this purple T-shirt mine or his?	The purple one's his.
Is that small red camera Jill's or Lucy's?	The small red one's Jill's.

Extra activity 1: three large pieces of paper with one word written at the top of each: *snake, hippo, bee*
Extra activity 2: Photocopiable 4 (see page T103), if not used in previous lesson copied onto thin card, a copy for each pupil, scissors, crayons

Warmer

- Review pets with a mime game. Mime an animal, e.g. *cat*. Elicit from pupils. A pupil comes to the front. Whisper an animal. The pupil mimes. Choose from the word set *pets*, e.g. *cat, dog, horse, fish, mouse, bird*, and any other pets that the class know. Elicit the word for all these animals: *Pets*.

PB28. ACTIVITY **9.** *Monty's phonics*

- Say *Open your Pupil's Books at page 28, please.* Point to the small pictures and say them, emphasise the vowel sound /əʊ/. Pupils practise pronunciation of each word. Point at the large picture and ask *Where's the girl? (In a boat) What colour is the boat? (Yellow) What's in her hand? (A phone).* Say *Now listen to Monty, point and repeat.*
- Play the CD. Pupils listen and repeat the sounds, words, and sentence using the same tone and speed as Monty.
- Pupils repeat the tongue twister as a class. Do it more and more quickly. Then ask small groups of pupils to have a go at saying it. Go around the class from group to group. Put pupils into pairs. They take turns to say the tongue twister quickly to each other. Invite volunteers to say it to the class.
- Write the tongue twister on the board. Focus pupils on the words. Elicit from them which letters to underline for the sound /əʊ/.

Key: A phone in a yellow boat!

CD 1, 57

MONTY: Hi, I'm Monty! Repeat after me!
/əʊ/, /əʊ/, phone
/əʊ/, /əʊ/, yellow
/əʊ/, /əʊ/, boat
A phone in a yellow boat!
A phone in a yellow boat!
A phone in a yellow boat!

PB28. ACTIVITY **10.** *Find your partner.*

- Take out the 30 cards. If you have fewer than 30 pupils, discard the extra cards, ensuring that you have discarded the matching questions and answers. If there is an odd number of pupils in your class, participate in the activity yourself.
- Hand out a card to each pupil. Ask them to read and memorise what is on their card. Ask pupils to stand up, mingle and find their partner by repeating their sentence and listening to the other sentences. Ask pupils to raise their hands when they think they have found their partner so that you can check they are a pair.
- Ask pupils to sit down and work in their new pairs. Give each pair a photocopy of the worksheet already cut into strips of paper. Pupils match the questions and answers. Check answers orally round the class.

AB28. ACTIVITY **8.** *Listen and write the words.*

- Say *Open your Activity Books at page 28, please.* Point to the large outline pictures in turn and ask *What's this? (A box, A boat).* Play number 1 on the CD and say *'Boat' has the sound /əʊ/. Look. It's in the boat.* (Point to the example word written on the first line in the boat outline). Play number 2 and say *'box' has the sound /ɒ/. Look. It's in the box. Now listen and think /əʊ/* or */ɒ/? Boat or box? Write in pencil.*
- Play the rest of the CD, pausing after each word for pupils to consult in pairs and write the word. Elicit answers and write the groups of words on the board for pupils to check.

Key: Box – 3 doll, 5 clock, 8 lorry, 9 socks; Boat – 4 phone, 6 clothes, 7 yellow, 10, sofa

CD 1, 58

1. boat, 2. box, 3. doll, 4. phone, 5. clock, 6. clothes, 7. yellow, 8. lorry, 9. socks, 10. sofa

AB28. ACTIVITY **9.** *Write the words.*

- Quickly review the difference between *this* (near) and *that* (further away) by pointing to objects in the classroom. Focus pupils on the speech bubbles. They work in pairs and choose words from the box at the top. Check with the class.

Key: 2 This, 3 These, 4 That, 5 Those, 6 These.

Extra activities: see page T118 (if time)

Ending the lesson

- Do the tongue twister again with the class. Pupils stand up.

OBJECTIVES: By the end of the lesson, pupils will have read a story and reviewed language from the unit.

• TARGET LANGUAGE

Key language: language from the unit
Additional language: *hide and seek, I'm coming, Whose turn is it now? cupboard, look for us, come out*
Revision: *hair, living room, play, close your eyes, count to … , under, chair, well done, feet, bookcase, sofa, toy, horse*

• MATERIALS REQUIRED

Flashcards: (household objects) 49–54
Extra activity 2: Photocopiable 4 (see page T103), if not used in previous lesson copied onto thin card, a copy for each pupil, scissors, crayons
Optional: *Teacher's Resource Book 2* Unit 4 Extension worksheet 2 (page 30) and/or animated version of the Unit 4 story from *Kid's Box 2 Interactive DVD* (Suzy's room section)

Warmer

- Review the household objects. Display flashcards on the board (picture side). Write a number between *1* and *20* under each one, e.g. *5* under *mat.* Call out the numbers at random. Pupils write the word for the object. Pupils swap papers. Check with the class. Elicit the spelling. Pupils correct each other's work.

Story

PB29. ACTIVITY **11.** *Listen to the story.*

- Say *Open your Pupil's Books at page 29, please.* Elicit who they can see (Maskman, Trevor, Marie, Monty and a toy horse). Set the pre-listening questions: *Where are the toys? Who is next to the bookcase? Is Marie in the cupboard?* Play the CD. Pupils listen and look. They check in pairs. Check with the class (In the living room, Maskman, No, it's a toy horse).
- Play the CD again, frame by frame. Pupils listen and repeat. Encourage them to do so with intonation and feeling.
- Check comprehension by asking, e.g. *What game are they playing? What's Trevor doing? Why? What can Trevor see? What can Monty see?* Ask pupils what their favourite game is.

CD 1, 59

Toys in the toy box,
Come alive.
Walk and talk,
On the count of five.
One, two, three, four, five.
MASKMAN: Let's play hide and seek.
MARIE: Trevor, close your eyes and count to 20.

TREVOR: … 17, 18, 19, 20. I'm coming.

TREVOR: Where are they? Whose is that tail? Ha ha! I can see you, Monty. You're under the armchair.
MONTY: OK. Well done, Trevor.

MONTY: Look. Whose feet are those? Come out, Maskman. We can see you next to the bookcase.

MASKMAN: Now, where's Marie?
MONTY: Marie's in the cupboard. Look! That's her hair.

MASKMAN: Eek! What's that?
MONTY: It's a toy horse.
MARIE: I win!

PB29. ACTIVITY **12.** *Listen and say the number.*

- Focus pupils on the frames of the story again. Say *Listen to the CD and say the number of the picture.* Play the first one as an example. Elicit the number of the frame from the class (Five).
- Play the rest of the CD. Pupils work in pairs and point to/whisper the number of the frame to their partner. Play the CD again. This time stop after each section and elicit the number from a pair of pupils.

Key: 5, 1, 4, 5, 6, 2

CD 1, 60

MONTY: Marie's in the cupboard. Look! That's her hair.
MARIE: Trevor, close your eyes and count to 20.
MONTY: Come out, Maskman. We can see you next to the bookcase.
MASKMAN: Now, where's Marie?
MONTY: It's a toy horse.
TREVOR: … 17, 18, 19, 20. I'm coming.

AB29. MY PICTURE DICTIONARY.

- Say *Open your Activity Books at page 29, please.* Point to the word with missing vowels in the first square and the example answer. Elicit the word (*sofa*). Say *Write the letters to complete the words. They are all things in a room.* Pupils work individually or in pairs to complete the words. Check answers.
- Pupils prepare the stickers and lay them out on their desks in the correct order. Check around the class before they stick them in their books.

Key:
2 mat, 3 clock, 4 phone, 5 mirror, 6 lamp

AB29. MY PROGRESS.

- Focus pupils on the activity in their books. Say *Let's read the sentences together.* Read the first sentence. Elicit what it means. Display the flashcards of the household objects and ask different pupils *What's this? Have you got one in your house? Where is it?*, etc.
- Read the second sentence. Point to various classroom objects, e.g. books, pens, and ask *Whose is this?* for pupils to answer *It's mine.* Pupils work in pairs. They take turns to point to a sentence in their books and do what it says.
- Say *Now ask each other and tick or cross the sentences.* Demonstrate the activity again if necessary. Encourage pupils to practise so that they can tick both statements and colour the star.

Extra activities: see page T118 (if time)

Optional activities

- *Teacher's Resource Book 2* Unit 4 Extension worksheet 2 pages 26 and 30.
- The animated version of the story from *Kid's Box 2 Interactive DVD* (Suzy's room section). See pages 41–44 of the Teacher's booklet for the *Interactive DVD.*

Ending the lesson

- Ask pupils which chant/song/game they'd like to do again from the unit. Do it together to end the lesson.

11 59 CD1 Listen to the story.

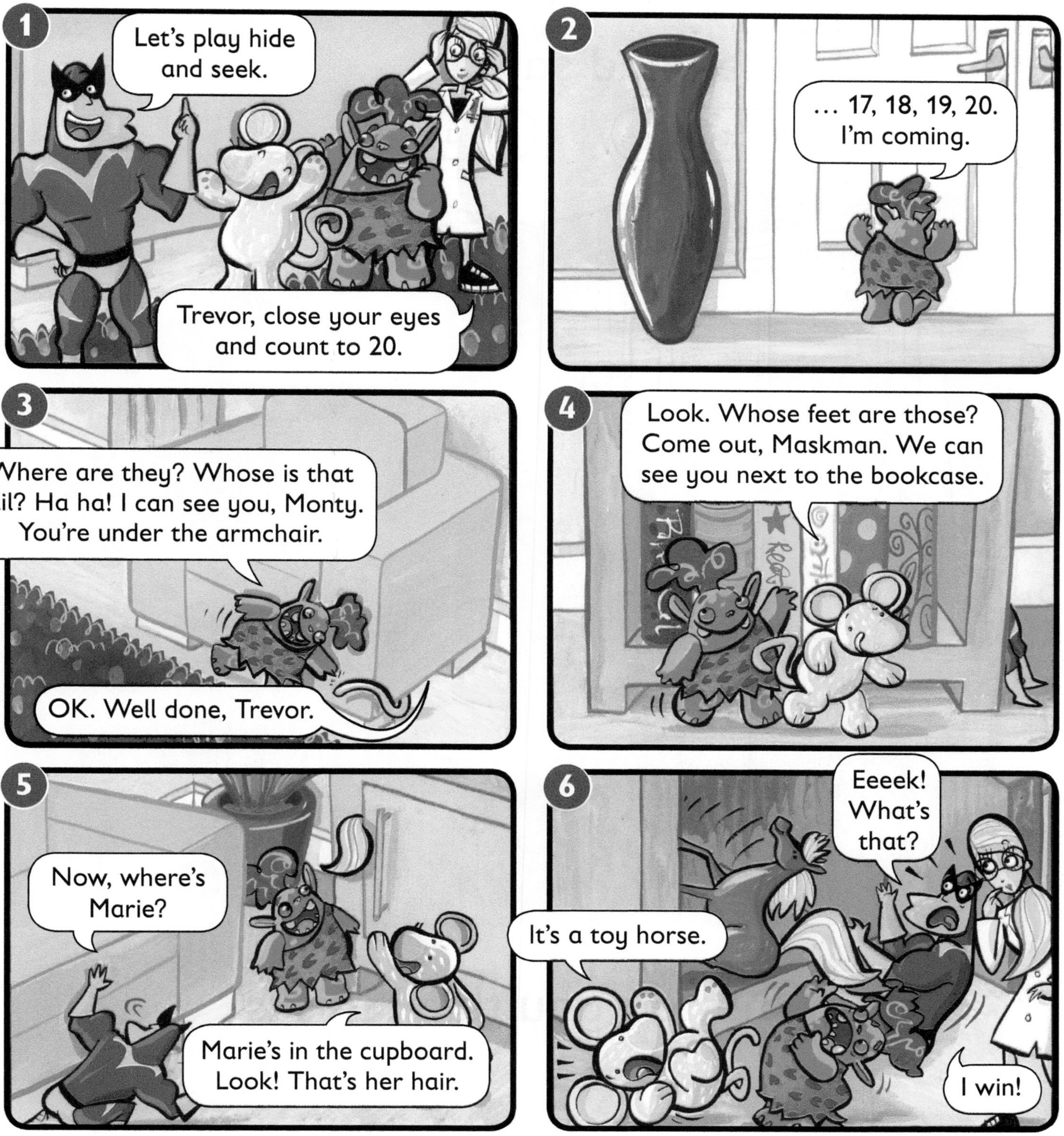

12 60 CD1 Listen and say the number.

1 Listen and say.

CD2

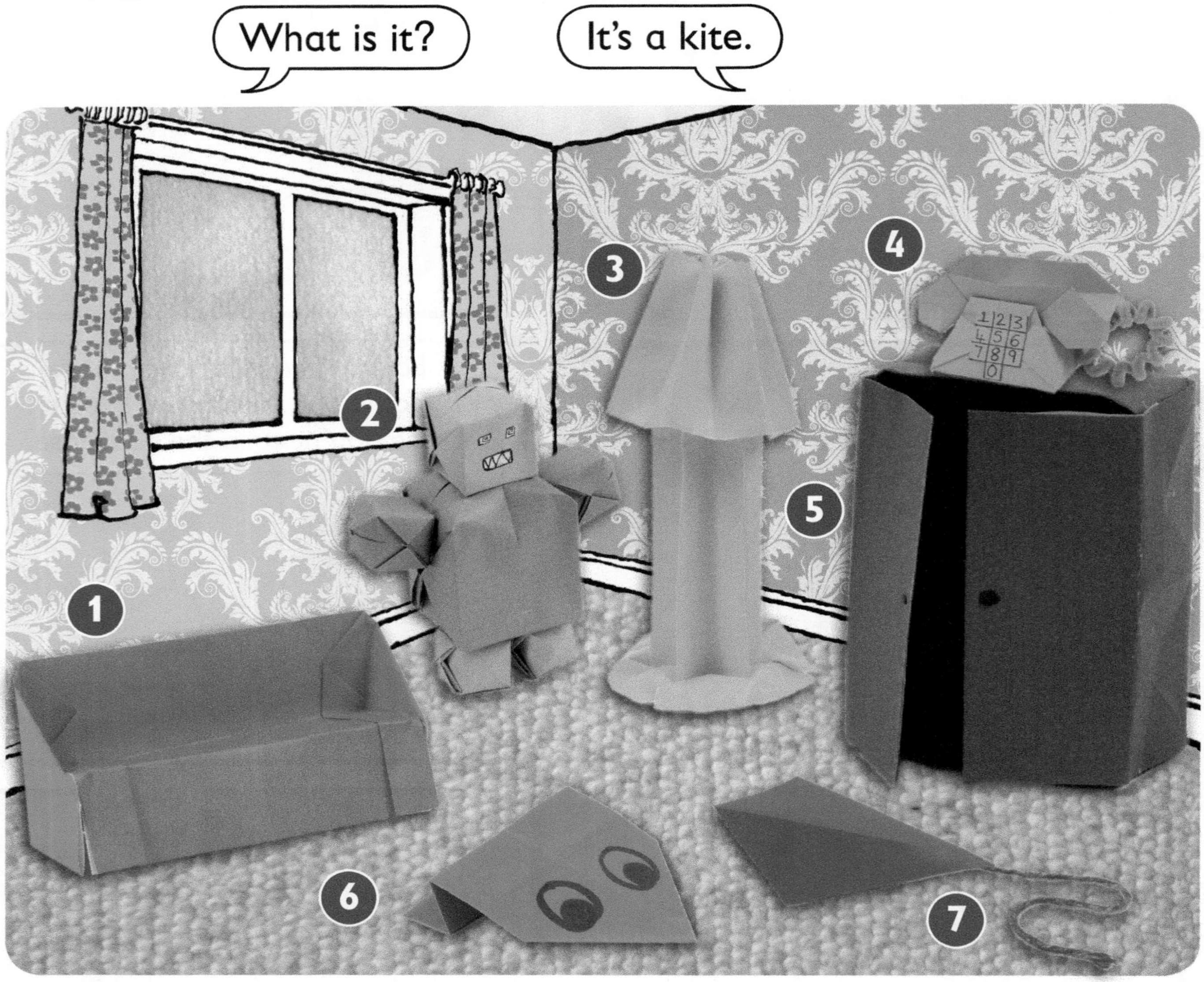

2 What do you think this is?

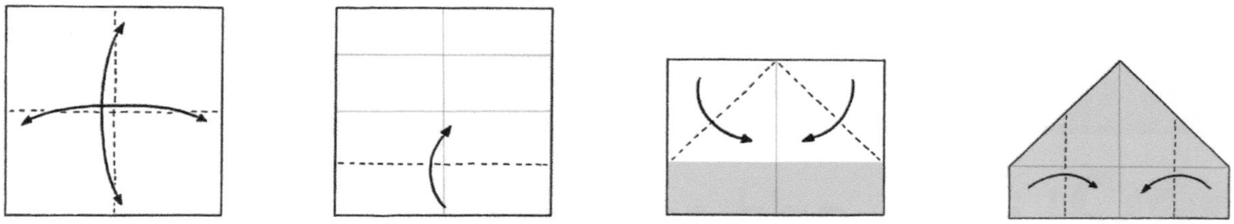

Now you!
Activity Book page 30

OBJECTIVES: By the end of the lesson, pupils will have listened to descriptions of objects, learnt about origami and made a frog from paper.

- **TARGET LANGUAGE**

Key language: *frog, origami*
Additional language: *What is it? What do you think this is?*
Revision: colours, *kite, robot, phone, cupboard, sofa, lamp*

- **MATERIALS REQUIRED**

Flashcards: (colours) 12–22, 28, 45, 46, 50, 52, 54 (kite, robot, phone, cupboard, sofa, lamp)
Make the paper frog (AB page 30, Activity 1) yourself before the lesson, so you are more able to help pupils during this activity and can show it to them as a model.
Squares of thick green paper/card (or regular paper coloured green), each measuring 21 x 21cm or more to make the jumping frog. Make sure you have more squares than pupils in the class (in case of mistakes).
Sticky plastic 'googly' eyes for the frog (if available)

Warmer

- Use the colour flashcards and flashcards of kite, robot, phone, cupboard, sofa and lamp to revise language for the lesson. Stick the flashcards on the board as you point, the pupils say the colour/object.

Presentation

- Say *Open your Pupil's Books at page 30, please*. Point to the picture of Marie and the title of the page and say *This is Marie's art*. Say *Today's lesson is about origami*. Make the short 'o' vowel sound for origami. Pupils repeat.
- Ask pupils if they know what origami is and whether any of them have done it. Say *Origami is art made from paper. It's from Japan. Ori means 'folding'* (fold a piece of paper) and *'kami' means paper* (hold up some paper).

PB30. ACTIVITY **1.** *Listen and say.*

- Point to the speech bubbles at the top of the page and say *What is it?* Point to the kite. Pupils read the other speech bubble out loud *It's a kite*. Elicit the names of the other origami objects in the picture in the same way. Pupils put up their hands when they have the answer. Say *Listen and say.*
- Play the CD. Pupils listen to the descriptions and match them to the objects. Stop the CD after each one to give pupils time to check together in pairs. Pupils say *It's a …*

Key: 1 It's a kite (7)., 2 It's a robot (2)., 3 It's a phone (4)., 4 It's a cupboard (5)., 5 It's a sofa (1)., 6 It's a lamp (3)., 7 It's a frog (6).

CD 2, 02

This can fly. It is beautiful and purple. What is it?
This can walk and talk. It's big and grey. What is it?
This is small and blue. You can talk to your friends with it. What is it?
This is brown. You can put bananas and apples in it. What is it?
You can sit on it and watch TV. It's red. What is it?
This is yellow. You can sit under it and read your books. What is it?
This is green. It jumps. What is it?

PB30. ACTIVITY **2.** *What do you think this is?*

- Focus pupils on Activity 2 and read the question *What do you think this is?* Point at each diagram and run your finger along the shape of the object. Tell pupils to look at the shapes of the objects in the picture in Activity 1 in order to work out which of the origami objects the diagrams show. Pupils put up their hands to answer.

Key: the frog

AB30. ACTIVITY **1.** *Make a jumping frog.*

- Hold up a paper square and say *This is a paper square*. Explain the pupils are going to use these to make their own origami frog. Say *Open your Activity Books at page 30, please*. Say *Make a jumping frog*. Hand out the pieces of paper. Point to the first diagram. Say *Fold the paper like this*. Demonstrate the folding. Pupils copy. Repeat for each diagram so that pupils have their own jumping frog at the end. Pupils draw or stick eyes on their frog and add details e.g. spots/pattern, if time permits.
- Give pupils time to play with the frogs, making them jump, then put them away. If your pupils have problems folding, tell them to work with a partner to make the frogs. Pupils put their hands up when they need help. If you have made a frog yourself, use this to show pupils and help them fold the paper correctly.

AB30. ACTIVITY **2.** *Look and write.*

- Hold up your book. Point to the first picture and the example answer *robot*. Say *Look and write*. Pupils write the correct word from the box to match each picture. Pupils check together in pairs. Check answers in open pairs, using *What is it? It's a …*

Key: 2 kite, 3 lamp, 4 phone, 5 sofa, 6 cupboard

Extra activities: see page T118 (if time)

Ending the lesson

- Make anagrams of words from the lesson and write them on the board e.g. *apcbuodr* (cupboard). Pupils work in pairs to solve the anagrams and put their hands up to answer. Alternatively, this could be a team competition with a time limit – the quickest pupil to work out the word wins a point for their team.

OBJECTIVES: By the end of the lesson, pupils will have listened to interviews of people talking about recycling and talked about recycling for themselves.

• TARGET LANGUAGE

Key language: *What's it made from? It's made from … What have you got? I've got … What are you making? I'm making ... What are you doing? I'm growing …*

Additional language: *plane, re-use, recycle, bottles, paper, ugly, old, computer, keyboard*

Revision: *elephant, robot, flower, shoe, What's this? What's your name?*

• MATERIALS REQUIRED

Objects (or pictures/flashcards of objects) from the lesson which are usually reused (e.g. a plastic bag, an old T-shirt, a plastic toy) or recycled (e.g. an old newspaper, an empty cereal box, a glass jar).

Extra activity 1: a collection of small real-life items that can be re-used/recycled for pupils to make a picture, to include (if possible) cardboard boxes, old socks, buttons and used pencils

Warmer

- Mime drinking from a plastic bottle and then pretend to throw the empty bottle in the bin. Put your thumb up or down as you do so and say *Is that right? Yes or no?* Pupils say *No* (The bottle can be recycled, instead of thrown away.) Teach the words *re-use* and *recycle*. Hold up the objects (or pictures/flashcards) you have brought to class. For each one the pupils say *Re-use* or *Recycle*.

PB31 Activity 3. *Listen and say the number.*

- Say *Open your Pupil's Books at page 31 please*. Remind pupils of the meaning of 'values'. Read the title of the page and say *Trevor's values today are re-using and recycling.* Focus pupils on the photographs by asking *Where's the elephant/plane/old shoe/robot?* Pupils point to the objects. Say *Listen and say the number.* Play the CD.

Key: 2 (plane), 3 (shoe), 1 (elephant), 4 (robot)

CD 2, 03

Ann: Hello.
Interviewer: What's your name?
Ann: I'm Ann.
Interviewer: What have you got?
Ann: I've got some old paper.
Interviewer: And what are you doing?
Ann: I'm making a plane.
Interviewer: Wow! Great!

Grace: Hello.
Interviewer: What's your name?
Grace: I'm Grace.
Interviewer: What have you got?
Grace: I've got an ugly old shoe.
Interviewer: And what are you doing?
Grace: I'm growing a flower in the shoe.
Interviewer: Cool!

Interviewer: Hello
Sam: Hello
Interviewer: What's your name?
Sam: I'm Sam.
Interviewer: What have you got?
Sam: I've got lots of old bottles.
Interviewer: And what are you making?
Sam: I'm making an elephant.
Interviewer: Great!

Tony: Hello
Interviewer: What's your name?
Tony: I'm Tony.
Interviewer: What have you got?
Tony: I've got an old computer and an old keyboard.
Interviewer: And what are you making?
Tony: I'm making a robot.
Interviewer: Wow!

PB31. Activity 4. *Ask and answer.*

- Point to the first speech bubble and read *What's this?* (point to the flower in the old shoe). Pupils answer as in the example *It's a flowerpot.* Point to the next speech bubble and read *What's it made from?* Pupils answer again as in the example *It's made from a shoe.*
- Check comprehension. Say *Ask and answer.* Pupils ask and answer in pairs about the other objects in the same way.

PB31. Activity 5. *What do you re-use at home?*

- Point to the photographs and labels at the bottom of the page. Say the words in the labels. Pupils repeat. Ask *What do you re-use at home?* Choose a confident pupil to read and complete the speech bubble *I re-use …* with what they re-use at home, e.g. *I re-use bottles at home.* Pupils practise in pairs.
- Monitor the activity and help with new vocabulary as necessary.

AB31. Activity 3. *Look, read and match.*

- Say *Open your Activity Books at page 31, please.* Say *Look, read and match.* Focus pupils on the example line drawn from the picture of the sock to phrase b. Pupils complete the activity individually or in pairs. They compare books to check. Elicit answers.

Key: 2 a, 3 d, 4 c

AB31. Activity 4. *You've got four boxes, two socks, a T-shirt and five pencils. Draw a robot.*

- If you have the real-life items, use them to introduce the activity and call two or three volunteers to the front to make a robot. Say *You've got four boxes, two socks, a T-shirt and five pencils. Draw a robot.* Pupils work in pairs to decide how to make the robot.
- Tell pupils they don't have to use all of the items. Go around checking and ask pupils *What have you got?* They say e.g. *I've got four boxes, a T-shirt…* Ask *What are you making?* They answer *I'm making a robot.*

Extra activities: see page T118 (if time)

Ending the lesson

- Books closed. Ask *What do you re-use at home?* Pupils put up their hands to answer e.g. *I re-use old T-shirts at home.* Repeat with other pupils.

3 Listen and say the number.

CD2

1

2

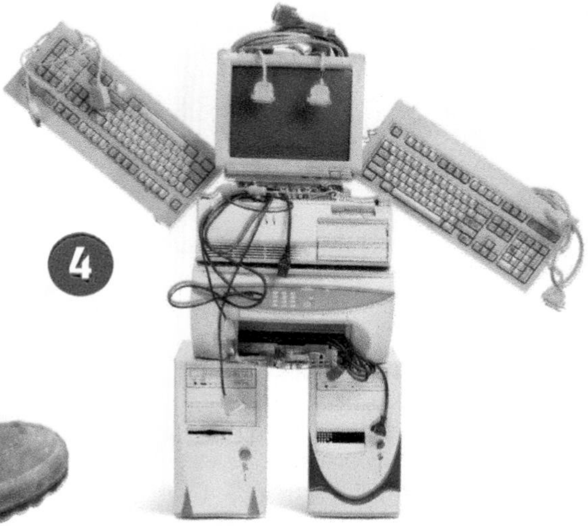

4

3

4 Ask and answer.

What's this?

It's a flowerpot.

What's it made from?

It's made from a shoe.

5 What do you re-use at home?

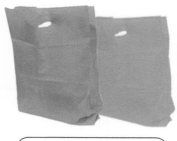

I re-use ... at home.

bottles

paper

plastic bags

Vocabulary

bottle flowerpot keyboard paper plastic bag

Review 1 2 3 4

1 Listen and say the number.

CD2

11 

12 

13 

14 

15 

16 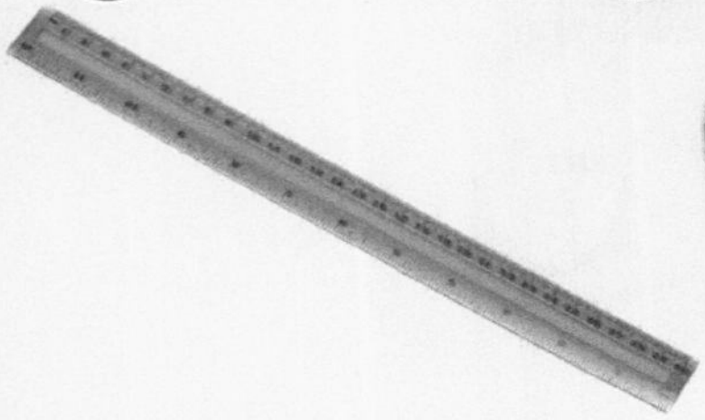

17 

18 

19 

20 

2 Look and say.

In picture one there's a yellow lamp on the table, but in picture two there's a green lamp on the table.

1 

2 

OBJECTIVES: By the end of the lesson, pupils will have reviewed language from Units 1–4.

• TARGET LANGUAGE
Key language: vocabulary and language from Units 1–4
Revision: rooms and objects in a house, numbers, colours

• MATERIALS REQUIRED
A photograph of you and your family OR a picture from a magazine of a family

Warmer

- Review the alphabet by playing a spelling game. Say *Who's this? Listen and look at the class. Point at the right person.* Spell the name of one of the pupils in the class, letter by letter (without looking at the pupil), e.g. *S-o-f-i-a*. Pupils point to the correct person. Repeat with other pupils' names. If you have two pupils with the same first name, spell the pupil's surname, too. Choose a name with a double letter in it if possible, and remind pupils that we use the word *double* before these letters, e.g. *double 'o'*.

PB32. ACTIVITY **1.** *Listen and say the number.*

- Say *Open your Pupil's Books at page 32, please.* Point at each picture in turn and elicit the number and the word (e.g. *eleven, kite*).
- Play the first item on the CD and elicit the correct number (fourteen). Play the rest of the CD. Pupils listen, point and whisper the number to their partner each time. Play the CD again. Stop after each word and elicit the answer.

Key: 14, 11, 20, 17, 13, 18, 16, 19, 15, 12

CD 2, 04

C-l-o-c-k
K-i-t-e
M-i-r-r-o-r
W-a-t-c-h
P-h-o-n-e
B-o-o-k-c-a-s-e
R-u-le-r
R-o-b-o-t
C-a-m-e-r-a
C-u-p-b-o-a-r-d

Pair work game

- Focus pupils on the pictures in Activity 1 again. Say *Listen to the number and spell the word. Put your hand up.* Say one of the numbers (from 11 to 20) from Activity 1, e.g. *Nineteen.* Volunteers put up their hands when they have found the correct picture and are ready to spell the word. Elicit the whole word and the spelling, letter by letter (e.g. *Robot, R-o-b-o-t*).
- Make pairs. Pupils play the game, swapping roles so each one gets the chance to choose the numbers.

PB32. ACTIVITY **2.** *Look and say.*

- Elicit toys, furniture and other objects pupils can see in the two pictures (*bed, lamp, watch, mirror, cupboard, bookcase, robot, chair, car,* etc.).
- Say *Look. Picture 1 and picture 2 are different.* Read the speech bubble with the class. Pupils work in pairs or individually to find the rest of the differences. Elicit the differences and write sentences like the example on page 32 on the board.
- Fast finishers can write sentences about the differences in their notebooks.

Key:
In picture 1, there's a robot on the bed, but in picture 2, there's a robot under the bed.
In picture 1, there's a cupboard, but in picture 2, there's a bookcase.
In picture 1, there's a mirror, but in picture 2, there isn't a mirror.
In picture 1, there's a watch on the table, but in picture 2 there isn't.
In picture 1, there are two lorries under the chair, but in picture 2 there are three lorries under the chair.
In picture 1, the lamp on the table is yellow, but in picture 2, it's green.
In picture 1, there's a purple mat, but in picture 2, there isn't a mat.

AB32. ACTIVITY **1.** *Match the colour.*

- Say *Open your Activity Books at page 32, please. Look at the example.* Point to the first rectangle and say *Read the number.* Elicit *Seven.* Say *It matches the word.* Point to the word. (Pupils point to the other rectangle coloured grey in the bottom row). Make sure they understand that the rectangle has been coloured grey because the word *seven* matches the number 7 in the other rectangle (and that rectangle has grey written in it). Do the next one with the class (nine matches figure 9 – and pupils have to colour both rectangles green).
- Pupils get coloured pencils or crayons ready. Tell them to mark the rectangles with a coloured dot only. They work individually to match and mark the rectangles. Pupils compare their answers in pairs. Check as a class.

AB32. ACTIVITY **2.** *Listen and write the number.* **[YLE]**

- Focus pupils on the pictures in their books. Play the first one on the CD: *The phone's on the table.* Point to the example answer '13' next to the picture of the living room. Play the rest of the CD. Pupils listen and match. Don't check answers. Pupils check in pairs. Play the CD again. Check with the class, playing each one again if necessary.

Key: 14, 17, 15, 13, 16, 18

CD 2, 05

13 The phone's on the table.
14 There are three teachers.
15 Who's that?
My teacher.
16 How many toys are there on the mat?
Four. There are three lorries and a robot.
17 Whose ruler is this?
It's mine.
18 There's an armchair next to the table.

Extra activities: see page T118 (if time)

Ending the lesson

- Show the class the photograph of your family or the family picture from the magazine. Tell pupils about the picture, e.g. *This is my mother and father. This is my brother. This is our house. These are my children.* Show it around the class as you talk about it.
- Tell pupils to bring a picture of their family for the next English class (to prepare for the topic in Unit 5). Pupils write a note about this in their homework books.

OBJECTIVES: By the end of the lesson, pupils will have reviewed language from Units 1–4 and made a book.

• TARGET LANGUAGE

Key language: key vocabulary and language from Units 1–4
Revision: other vocabulary and language from Units 1–4

• MATERIALS REQUIRED

Dice for each group of three or four pupils, counter or small coin for each pupil
A photograph of you and your family OR a picture from a magazine of a family
Extra activity 1: a selection of 12 flashcards from flashcards 26–53, two rolled up newspapers
Optional: *Kid's Box 2 Interactive DVD*: Stella's room Quiz 1

Warmer

- Show pupils your family picture again. Elicit who has brought a picture. Pupils take turns to come to the front, show their picture to the class and talk about it, e.g. *This is my mum. This is my dad. This is my house.*

PB33. ACTIVITY 3. *Play the game. Ask and answer.*

- Say *Open your Pupil's Books at page 33, please.* Point at some of the squares on the board and elicit the words and the numbers. Use the same language as in the speech bubbles at the top of the page (*What's this? A …*).
- Tell pupils they are going to play a game. Demonstrate how to play. Take out a dice (or a spinner, if the pupils studied *Kid's Box 1*) and a counter or coin. Hold up your book and put the counter on the Start square (bottom left). Say *This is the Start. You throw the dice…* Throw the dice and show pupils how to move their counter along the board, e.g. *Look! I've got a four. One …* (moving your counter) *two … three … four. You ask 'What's this?' I say 'Ruler!' I stay on this square. … Then it's Mario's turn. And then it's Emilia's turn. Now it's my turn again.* Throw the dice and move your counter again, e.g. to the square with the robot. Look thoughtful and say *What's this? Oh. I don't know this word. Move your counter back to the ruler square.* Say *I don't know. I move back to where I was … one, two. If you say the word you stay. If you don't say the word, you move back.* Point at the Finish square and say *This red square is the Finish. The first person here is the winner! Hooray!*
- Write a list of useful language for games on the board, e.g. *It's my turn. It's your turn. I've got a (five). Pass me the dice, please. Is this my counter? I'm the winner.* Pupils practise saying the sentences chorally.
- Make groups of three or four pupils. They need one dice per group and a coin or counter for each pupil. Groups play the game. Monitor and check they are saying the words in English and asking each other *What's this?*. If you wish, set a rule that anyone you hear speaking in their own language misses a turn. Encourage pupils to use the language for games. The winner is the first pupil to get to the finish or the pupil who is furthest along the board after a certain amount of time (e.g. ten minutes).

AB33. ACTIVITY 3. *Write the questions. Answer the questions.*

- Pupils use the grid to work out the questions that appear in code. They write the questions and then look at the picture in order to answer the questions.

Key:
1 Where are the lorries? Under the bed.
2 Whose toy is on the bed? Simon's.
3 Are the shoes clean or dirty? Dirty.
4 How many lorries are there? Five.
5 Where is the camera? On the table.
6 What is on the chair? A T-shirt.

Extra activities: see pages T118–T119 (if time)

Optional evaluation:

- Quiz 1 from *Kid's Box 2 Interactive DVD* (Stella's room section). This quiz can be done as a whole-class activity or as a team competition. See pages 39 and 40 of the Teacher's booklet for the *Interactive DVD*.

Ending the lesson

- Pupils work in groups of three. They need one picture dictionary between three. They use a book (or paper) to cover the words from Unit 1. They take turns to say what each picture is. They look and check. They then cover the pictures from Unit 2 and take turns to say the words. They choose which to cover for Units 3 and 4 (words or pictures).
- Talk about the *can do* statements from Units 1–4 with pupils and elicit examples from volunteer pupils for each one.
- Ask pupils which lessons, topics and/or activities were their favourites.

3 Play the game. Ask and answer.

What's this?

A cupboard.

5 Meet my family

1 6 CD2 Listen and point.

2 7 CD2 Listen and repeat.

OBJECTIVES: By the end of the lesson, pupils will have learned to talk about members of their families.

- **TARGET LANGUAGE**

Key language: *family, cousin, mummy, daddy, grandma, grandpa, baby, Frank*
Additional language: *Here you are.*
Revision: *mother, father, brother, sister, grandmother, grandfather, hair, nose, ears, fly a kite, Meera, Lenny, Suzy, Simon, We've/You've got …, Have you got … ? How old is he/she?*

- **MATERIALS REQUIRED**

Flashcards: (characters) 1, 2, 3, 6, 7, 23, 25, 57
Optional: *Kid's Box Teacher's Resource Book 2* Unit 5 Reinforcement worksheet 1 (page 33)

Warmer

- Review the known characters using the flashcards. Flash each one quickly in front of the class. Elicit who the character is and display it on the board. Elicit other known family words, e.g. *grandma, grandpa, mummy, daddy.* Introduce the new characters (Lenny and baby Frank) to the class in the same way.

PB34. ACTIVITY 1. *Listen and point.*

- Say *Open your Pupil's Books at page 34, please.* Elicit who pupils recognise from the Warmer. Say *Find the hidden star.* Pupils check in pairs. Check with the class (on the baby). Pupils say *Here it is.* Say *Listen and point.* Play the CD. Pupils listen and point to the people as they hear them. Set the listening questions: *Who's with Lenny? What's his cousin's name? Who has got the kite?* Play the CD again. Pupils listen and check in pairs. Check with the class (Frank's mum and dad, Frank, Grandpa). Check comprehension by asking, e.g. *Who's that? How many cousins has Meera got? How many cousins has Simon got? How old is Frank? Is Frank Lenny's brother?* Check understanding of new vocabulary.

CD 2, 06

STELLA: Look, Lenny's with Frank's mum and dad.
SIMON: Who's Frank?
STELLA: Frank's Lenny's baby cousin.
MEERA: Oh, how old is he?
STELLA: He's one.
SIMON: How many cousins have you got, Meera?
MEERA: Six: four boys and two girls. How many cousins have you got?
SIMON: None, but we've got a baby. Her name's Suzy.
SUZY: I'm not a baby. I'm a big girl! Grandpa! Simon says I'm a baby.
GRANDPA: Simon, as you're a big boy, you can fly Suzy's kite with her. Here you are!
SIMON: Uh! Thank you.

PB34. ACTIVITY 2. *Listen and repeat.*

- Say *Let's do Activity 2. Listen and repeat.* Play the CD. Pupils repeat the words in chorus.

CD 2, 07

Mummy, daddy, grandma, grandpa, cousin, baby

AB34. ACTIVITY 1. *Read and write the names.*

- Review *hair, nose, ears* by pointing to your hair, etc. and eliciting the words from the class. Say *Open your Activity Books at page 34.* Focus pupils on the text. Say *Read quickly and find the family words. Underline them.* Pupils work in pairs. Check around the class. Pupils then read the descriptions again and write the names in the spaces. They check in pairs. Check with the class.

Key: 1 May, 2 Sam, 3 Lenny, 4 Frank

AB34. ACTIVITY 2. *Write the words.*

- Say *Let's do Activity 2.* Pupils look at the words in the box and write them in the correct shape below. Do the examples with them first. They check in pairs and then as a class.

Key: In the house: bath, mirror, lamp, bed, phone (pupils may also choose desk and ruler). Family: grandma, baby, grandpa, cousin, daddy. Toys: kite, lorry, robot, boat, doll. At school: teacher, desk, playground, board, ruler (pupils may also choose phone and lamp).

Extra activities: see page T119 (if time)

Optional activity

- Unit 5 Reinforcement worksheet 1 *Teacher's Resource Book 2* pages 32–33.

Ending the lesson

- Review the new vocabulary by displaying the flashcards (picture side) around the room. Call out, e.g. *Cousin* and pupils point to the correct flashcard. Repeat. Then point to a flashcard. Pupils supply the word. Point at random to keep pupils active.

OBJECTIVES: By the end of the lesson, pupils will have talked more about families and worked with a family tree.

• TARGET LANGUAGE

Key language: possessive *'s*
Additional language: *family tree*
Revision: family vocabulary, *What's his/her name?*

• MATERIALS REQUIRED

Flashcards: (characters) 1–5
Photocopiable 5 (see page T104), copied onto thin card, one copy for each pupil, scissors, crayons, envelopes
Optional: *Kid's Box Teacher's Resource Book 2* Unit 5 Reinforcement worksheet 2 (page 34)

Warmer

- Elicit the Star family names, using the five flashcards. Display the flashcards on the board like a family tree:

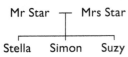

Mr Star — Mrs Star

Stella Simon Suzy

- Ask, e.g. *Who's Stella's father? Who's Suzy's sister?* Elicit/tell pupils that this is called a *family tree*.
  Note: This is a spatial intelligence activity. Don't worry if some of your pupils find the diagrams difficult to interpret.

PB35. ACTIVITY 3. *Listen and answer.*

- Say *Open your Pupil's Books at page 35, please.* Ask what they can see (a family tree). Give pupils a little time to look at the diagram. Check understanding of the oldest generation (grandma/grandpa) and of who are cousins. Say, e.g. *Find May. Find Lenny. Who's May's cousin?* Say all the names for pupils to repeat after you (many of the names are new). Check with pupils the gender of each person. Say *Listen and think.* Play the CD, pausing after each one. Pupils don't answer. They look and think. Play the CD again to give more thinking time. Play the CD a third time. Stop after each one for pupils to check in pairs before you check with the class.

Key: Nick, May, Ben, May, Lucy, Frank, Nelson, Anna

CD 2, 08

He's Lenny's daddy. What's his name?
She's Frank's cousin. What's her name?
He's Kim's brother. What's his name?
She's Lenny's sister. What's her name?
She's Frank's mummy. What's her name?
He's May's cousin. What's his name?
He's Frank's grandpa. What's his name?
She's Sam's grandma. What's her name?

PB35. ACTIVITY 4. *Look and say.*

- Pupils make statements about the family tree for others to respond to. Read out the example speech bubbles. Demonstrate the activity in open pairs around the class. When pupils are more confident, do the activity in closed pairs. Monitor pupils and help with concepts/language where necessary.

Photocopiable 5: see pages T98 and T104 (if time)

AB35. ACTIVITY 3. *Read. Write the name. Colour.*

- Say *Open your Activity Books at page 35, please.* Elicit what they can see (trolls). Focus pupils on the text and do the first part with the class as an example. Pupils write the names and colour the trolls to match the description. Tell pupils to underline the colour words to help them remember the colours to use. Pupils work in pairs. Monitor pupils and then check as a class.

Key: Tricia, Tony, Trudy, Tom

AB35. ACTIVITY 4. *Write the words.* **[YLE]**

- Focus pupils on the anagrams in the book and on the example. Check they know what to do. Pupils work individually and unjumble the family words. They write them on the lines for male and/or female. Check with the class.

Key: Male: grandfather, father, daddy, cousin, brother.
Female: grandmother, mother, sister, cousin, mummy.

Extra activity: see page T119 (if time)

Optional activity

- Unit 5 Reinforcement worksheet 2 *Teacher's Resource Book 2* pages 32 and 34.

Ending the lesson

- Elicit and write the family words on the board: *mother, father, brother, sister, cousin, grandma, grandpa.* Do a quick question and answer around the class. Start the chain by asking a pupil, e.g. *What's your mother's name?* The pupil answers, e.g. *Her name's Teresa* and asks another pupil a question about another family member, e.g. brother. Supply *I haven't got a …* if appropriate.
  Note: Adapt this activity if you have pupils for whom family issues are sensitive.

3 Listen and answer.

CD2 8

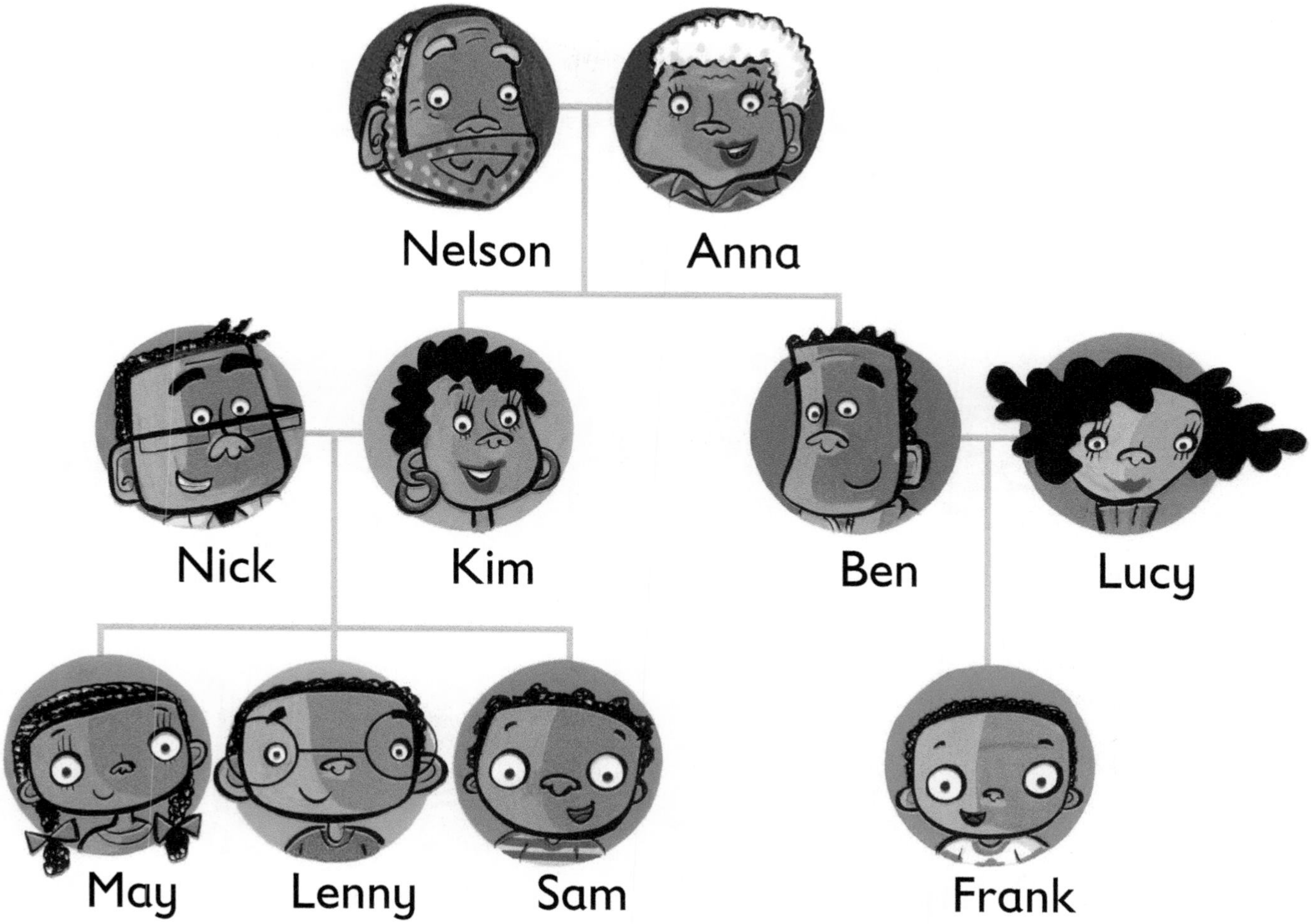

4 Look and say.

He's Lenny's father.
Nick.
She's Ben's mother.
Anna.

Vocabulary

baby cousin mummy daddy grandma grandpa

5 Listen and say the number.

CD2 9

6 Make sentences. Use the words in the box.

The dog's getting the ball.

getting	throwing	catching	flying	talking	jumping
sitting	hitting	cleaning	running	kicking	sleeping

Grammar
He's / She's... ...ing

Vocabulary
catch clean fly get hit jump run sleep throw

OBJECTIVES: By the end of the lesson, pupils will have described actions in the present continuous form.

• TARGET LANGUAGE

Key language: present continuous with present meaning, *I'm/He's/She's/It's running, hitting, jumping, getting, sleeping, throwing, catching, flying, cleaning, talking, kicking*

Additional language: *make sentences with these words*

Revision: present continuous with present meaning, characters, numbers *1–20*

• MATERIALS REQUIRED

Optional: *Kid's Box Teacher's Resource Book 2* Unit 5 Extension worksheet 1 (page 35)

Warmer

- Call out 20 pupils to the front. Whisper a number between *1* and *20* to each one in random order. They line up in number sequence *1* to *20* and call out their numbers starting from *1* for the class to check.

Presentation

- Quickly review the use of the present continuous for actions. Tell a pupil to draw a picture on the board. Ask *What's he doing?* Prompt *He's drawing.* Repeat with other known actions (*writing, opening the door, reading*, etc.) and other pupils. Practise *he* and *she*.

PB36. ACTIVITY 5. *Listen and say the number.*

- Say *Open your Pupil's Books at page 36, please.* Elicit what pupils can see (family members, in the park, playing, etc.). Say *Listen and say the number.* Play the first sentence. Elicit the number from pupils (16). Play the rest of the CD. Pupils write the numbers in order in their notebooks. They check in pairs. Play the CD again. Stop after each sentence to elicit the number from the class and the full sentence, e.g. *The dog's getting the ball.* Play the sentence from the CD again if pupils are unsure of it. They repeat in chorus.
- Check further comprehension of the picture by asking, e.g. *What's Lenny hitting? Who's sitting next to Frank? What's Grandpa doing?*

Key:
16, 19, 14, 11, 15, 18, 12, 17, 13, 20

CD 2, 09

Lenny's hitting the ball.
The dog's getting the ball.
The boy's mother is cleaning his mouth.
The baby's sleeping.
Simon's throwing the ball.
The girl's kicking the football.
Frank's mum and dad are talking.
Meera's catching the ball.
Grandpa's flying a kite.
The cat's jumping.

PB36. ACTIVITY 6. *Make sentences. Use the words in the box.*

- Focus pupils on the words in the box. Call them out at random. Pupils point to the word in the box. Make pairs. Pupils take turns to make sentences about the picture similar to (but not the same as) the ones from Activity 5. Monitor pupils and give prompts if necessary.
- Pairs say one or two sentences to the class. The class decides if they are correct.

AB36. ACTIVITY 5. *Listen and write the number.*

- Say *Open your Activity Books at page 36, please.* Focus pupils on the pictures and elicit the names of the characters and the places, objects and food they can see (e.g. for the first picture: *Suzy, Simon, park, kite*).
- Explain that the characters are talking to each other (each person is saying something – make sure pupils know that the person on the left in each picture speaks first). Tell pupils they are going to listen to the conversations and they need to write the correct number in the boxes at the bottom of each picture.
- Play the CD and pause after the first conversation. Pupils confer in pairs. Elicit the answer. Pupils point to the correct picture. Play the rest of the CD. Pupils write their answers in pencil. Play the CD again. Check answers.

Key: 3, 5, 1, 6, 2, 4

CD 2, 10

1. Whose shoes are you cleaning, Grandpa?
   I'm cleaning Simon's shoes.
2. What are you drawing, Grandma?
   I'm drawing Stella.
3. Whose kite are you flying, Simon?
   I'm flying your kite, Suzy.
4. Which word are you spelling, Stella?
   I'm spelling 'beautiful'.
5. What are you doing, Mum?
   I'm making a cake.
6. What are you eating, Dad?
   I'm eating chocolate ice cream.

AB36. ACTIVITY 6. *Look at the pictures and write the letters.*

- Focus pupils on the speech bubbles and on the pictures. Do the example with the class. Pupils work in pairs and write the letters from the speech bubbles in the correct boxes. Monitor pupils as they are working.

Key: 2: a,b; 3: g,h; 4: e,f; 5: k,l; 6, i,j

Extra activities: see page T119 (if time)

Optional activity

- Unit 5 Extension worksheet 1 *Teacher's Resource Book 2* pages 32 and 35.

Ending the lesson

- Play a mime game, using the verbs from the lesson. In turn, pupils come and mime an action from the lesson to the class. The class give a sentence, e.g. *Miki's hitting a ball.* The pupil responds *Yes, I'm hitting a ball* or *No. Look* and does the mime again.

OBJECTIVES: By the end of the lesson, pupils will have had more practice talking about actions at the moment of speaking and will have sung a song.

• TARGET LANGUAGE

Key language: present continuous with present meaning, *He/She isn't (walking), They're (eating)*

Revision: *walking, playing, cleaning, flying, throwing, sleeping, jumping, sitting,* food, family words, *can, happy, big, grey*

• MATERIALS REQUIRED

Extra activity 1: Pictures or flashcards of an apple, banana, orange, chocolate, ice cream, cake, burger.

Optional: *Kid's Box Teacher's Resource Book 2* Unit 5 song worksheet (page 37)

Warmer

- Review action words by doing a mime game. Whisper an action word to a pupil (e.g. *Flying*) and the pupil mimes for the class. Say, e.g. *He isn't throwing a ball. He's ...* The class completes *flying a kite*. Repeat.

PB37. ACTIVITY 7. *Listen and point. Sing.*

- Say *Open your Pupil's Books at page 37, please.* Focus pupils on the picture and the people. Elicit what/who they can see. Say *Listen and point.* Play the CD. Pupils listen and point to the people. Check understanding of the negative. Say, e.g. *Look at Grandpa. Is he walking?* (No). *What's he doing?* (Flying a kite). Play the CD again in sections. Teach the lines with the actions.

CD 2, 11

My grandpa isn't walking,	*[mime finger waggle and walking]*
He's flying my favourite kite.	*[mime flying kite]*
My grandma's cleaning the table,	*[mime cleaning]*
It's beautiful and white.	
My father's playing baseball,	*[mime hitting ball with baseball bat]*
He can catch and he can hit.	
My cousin's got the ball now,	
And now he's throwing it.	*[mime throwing]*
My baby sister's sleeping,	*[mime baby cradled in arms]*
She is very small.	*[mime small]*
My brother isn't jumping,	*[mime finger waggle and jumping]*
He's kicking his football.	*[mime kicking]*
Hey!	
My grandpa isn't walking,	*[as above]*
He's flying my favourite kite.	
My grandma's cleaning the table,	
It's beautiful and white.	
My mother's sitting reading,	*[mime reading]*
Her book is big and grey.	
And me? I'm very happy,	*[mime big smile]*
I can run and play. *[Repeat x5]*	

CD 2, 12

Now sing the song again. (Karaoke version)

PB37. ACTIVITY 8. *Ask and answer.*

- Pupils work in pairs. Pupil A asks a question about the song lyrics, e.g. *What's Grandpa doing?* Pupil B answers, e.g. *He's flying a kite.* Pupils exchange roles. When pupils have done the activity, ask them to close their books and do it from memory. Award points for correct questions and answers.

AB37. ACTIVITY 7. *Listen and tick (✓) the box. There is one example.* **[YLE]**

- Say *Open your Activity Books at page 37, please.* Elicit the things pupils can see. Read the example and say *Listen. Is it picture 1, 2 or 3?* Play the example on the CD. Elicit the answer and say *He's reading (a book). It's picture 2.* Point to the example tick in the box and say *Look. There's a tick in the box.*
- Play the rest of the CD, pausing to give pupils time to think and tick. Pupils compare answers in pairs. Check as a class.

Key: 1 picture 3, 2 picture 2, 3 picture 3, 4 picture 3

CD 2, 13

Is Dan eating an apple?
No, he isn't. And he isn't sleeping.
What's he doing?
He's reading a book.

Can you see the tick? Now you listen and tick the box.

1. Which is Anna?
   What's Anna doing, Grandpa?
   I don't know. Is she catching a ball?
   No. And she isn't flying her kite.
   Oh, I know! She's playing football.
2. What's Sue doing?
   Is Sue in the kitchen?
   Yes, she is.
   Is she eating?
   No, she's drinking water.
3. What's Grandpa doing?
   Is Grandpa riding a bike?
   No, he's on the bus.
   Oh. Is he listening to music?
   No. He's reading.
   Oh, yes. He likes books.
4. What's Sam drawing?
   Are you drawing a robot, Sam?
   No, Dad. Can't you see?
   I know. Is it a lamp?
   Yes, it is.

Extra activities: see page T119 (if time)

Optional activity

- Pupils complete the Unit 5 song worksheet from *Teacher's Resource Book 2*. (see pages 32 and 37 of the *Teacher's Resource Book*).

Ending the lesson

- Play the Spelling game with pupils. Start as the caller, and then pupils can take over. Use words from the lesson and extend to other words if appropriate.

Teacher:	Class responds:
Give me a k	*k*
Give me an i	*i*
Give me a t	*t*
Give me an e	*e*
What does that spell?	
What does that spell?	

7 Listen and point. Sing.

11 CD2

My grandpa isn't walking,
He's flying my favourite kite.
My grandma's cleaning the table,
It's beautiful and white.
My father's playing baseball,
He can catch and he can hit.
My cousin's got the ball now,
And now he's throwing it.

My baby sister's sleeping,
She is very small.
My brother isn't jumping,
He's kicking his football.
Hey!

My grandpa isn't walking,
He's flying my favourite kite.
My grandma's cleaning the table,
It's beautiful and white.
My mother's sitting reading,
Her book is big and grey.
And me? I'm very happy,
I can run and play ...

8 Ask and answer.

What's Grandpa doing?

He's flying a kite.

9 14 CD2 Monty's phonics

blue

ruler

Sue

Sue's got a big blue ruler!

10 Ask and answer.

What's Simon doing?
He's sleeping.

OBJECTIVES: By the end of the lesson, pupils will be able to identify and say the long oo /uː/ vowel sound and to contrast it with the short u /ʌ/ vowel sound' and will have asked and answered questions about present actions.

• TARGET LANGUAGE

Key language: the phoneme /uː/ as in *blue, ruler, Sue*
Additional language: *finish, egg and spoon race, sweets, Ready, steady, go*
Revision: *Who's … ?, over there, take turns, running*

• MATERIALS REQUIRED

Flashcards: (characters) 2, 3, 4, 5; flashcard *bus* from *Kid's Box 1*
Extra activity 2: ten ping pong balls, ten teaspoons, lots of space
Optional: *Kid's Box 2 Interactive DVD: The living room* 'At the sports centre' episode, *Kid's Box 2 Language Portfolio* page 10

Warmer

- Review the character names and relationships, using the flashcards. Cover each one (picture side) with paper and reveal it slowly. Pupils say *Mrs Star.* Say *Good. She's Simon's …* (mother).

PB38. ACTIVITY **9.** *Monty's phonics*

- Say *Open your Pupil's Books at page 38, please.* Point to the small pictures and say them, emphasising the vowel sound /uː/. Pupils practice pronunciation of each word. Point at the large picture and say *This is Sue. What's that? (A ruler) What colour is the ruler? (Blue)* Say *Now listen to Monty, point and repeat.*
- Play the CD. Pupils listen and repeat the sounds, words, and sentence using the same tone and speed as Monty.
- Pupils repeat the tongue twister as a class. Do it more and more quickly. Then ask small groups of pupils to have a go at saying it. Go around the class from group to group. Put pupils into pairs. They take it in turns to say the tongue twister quickly to each other. Invite volunteers to say it to the class.

CD 2, 14

MONTY: Hi, I'm Monty! Repeat after me!
/uː/, /uː/, blue
/uː/, /uː/, ruler
/uː/, /uː/, Sue
Sue's got a big blue ruler!
Sue's got a big blue ruler!
Sue's got a big blue ruler!

PB38. ACTIVITY **10.** *Ask and answer.*

- Focus pupils on the pictures and on the speech bubbles. Do one or two with the class in open pairs. The first pair repeats the model. The next pair gives another question and answer, e.g. *What's Alex doing? He's hitting a ball.* Pupils work in pairs and take turns to ask and answer questions about the pictures. Monitor pupils and help/prompt where necessary. Check using open pairs.

AB38. ACTIVITY **8.** *Listen and write.*

- Stick the flashcard *bus* on the board (or draw a picture of a bus). Write the word below the picture, with the letter 'u' replaced by a line (as on Activity Book page 38). Say the word and elicit the *missing* letter. Write it on the line.
- Say *Open your Activity Books at page 38, please.* Play the example and number 2, if necessary.
- Play the CD. Pupils complete the words with the missing letters. They check answers in pairs.
- Play the CD again. Check answers as a class. Elicit the words in the activity which have the /uː/ sound (*shoe, Sue, ruler, blue*). Point out that the sound is not always represented with the letter *u*. Elicit the vowel sound in the other words (/ʌ/).

Key: 2 oe, 3 u, 4 ue, 5 u, 6 u, 7 ue, 8 u, 9 u

CD 2, 15

1. bus, 2. shoe, 3. mum, 4. Sue, 5. sun, 6. ruler, 7. blue, 8. run, 9. jump

AB38. ACTIVITY **9.** *Write the letters.*

- Focus pupils on the half sentences. Read *He's kicking …* Wait for pupils to find and respond … *a football.* Check pupils know what to do. They work individually and then check in pairs. Check with the class by eliciting each sentence and asking the pupils to mime the action to check understanding.

Key: c, d, a, g, e, f, b

Extra activities: see page T119 (if time)

Optional activity

- 'At the sports centre' episode from *Kid's Box 2 Interactive DVD* (The living room section). See pages 12–15 of the DVD booklet.

Language Portfolio

- Pupils complete page 10 of *Kid's Box 2 Language Portfolio* (My family). Help with new language as necessary.

Ending the lesson

- Practise recognition of the two phonemes /uː/ and /ʌ/ with a True/False game. Pupils stand up. Say different words in turn. When pupils hear the sound /uː/ (as in *shoe*) in the word, they point to their shoes, when they hear the sound /ʌ/ (as in *run*) in the word, they run on the spot. Pupils who respond incorrectly sit down. Stop when you have a small group of winners. Use words from the lesson in the game, as well as other known words, e.g. *blue, ruler, Sue, computer, you, two, true, mum, jump, bus, sun, one, thumb, fun.*

OBJECTIVES: By the end of the lesson, pupils will have read a story and reviewed language from the unit.

• TARGET LANGUAGE

Key language: language from the unit
Additional language: actions
Revision: *shoes, helicopter, superhero, red, doll's house*

• MATERIALS REQUIRED

Extra activity 2: Photocopiable 5 (see page T104), if not used previously copied onto thin card, one copy for each pupil, scissors, crayons
Optional: *Teacher's Resource Book 2* Unit 5 Extension worksheet 2 (page 36) and/or animated version of the Unit 5 story from *Kid's Box 2 Interactive DVD* (Suzy's room section)

Warmer

- Play a mime game to review action verbs. Whisper an action (flying a plane) to a pupil who mimes it. Say, e.g. *He's driving a car.* Pupils do thumbs up (true) or thumbs down (false). Elicit the sentence from another pupil, e.g. *He isn't driving a car. He's flying a plane.* Repeat with other pupils and other action verbs.

Story

PB39. ACTIVITY 11. *Listen to the story.*

- Say *Open your Pupil's Books at page 39, please.* Elicit who they can see (Grandpa, Trevor, Monty, Marie and Maskman). Set the pre-listening questions: *What's Monty doing? Whose shoes is Marie cleaning?* Say *Listen and look.* Play the CD. Pupils listen and look. They check in pairs. Check with the class (Driving Suzy's yellow lorry, Her shoes).
- Play the CD again. Pupils listen and repeat. Encourage them to say it with intonation and feeling.
- Check comprehension by holding up your book, pointing to each picture in turn and asking, e.g. *What is Grandpa doing?* (cleaning shoes). *What colour are they?* (black). *What's Maskman flying?* (a helicopter). *What's Trevor doing in picture 5?* (cleaning the doll's house).
- Check that pupils remember the meaning of *superhero.* Ask them who their superheroes are.

CD 2, 16

Toys in the toy box,
Come alive.
Walk and talk,
On the count of five.
One, two, three, four, five.
TREVOR: Ooh! What's he doing to those shoes, Marie?
MARIE: He's cleaning them, Trevor.

MONTY: Hello, Trevor! Look at me! I'm driving Suzy's yellow lorry.

TREVOR: Hello, Maskman. What are you doing?
MASKMAN: I'm flying my helicopter. I'm a superhero.

TREVOR: Hello, Marie. What are you doing?
MARIE: I'm cleaning my shoes.

MONTY: What are you doing, Trevor?
TREVOR: I'm cleaning the doll's house.

MARIE: Oh! No!

PB39. ACTIVITY 12. *Listen and say the number.*

- Focus pupils on the frames of the story again. Say *Listen to the CD and say the number of the picture.* Play the first one as an example. Elicit the number of the frame from the class (4). Play the rest of the CD. Pupils work in pairs and point to / whisper the number of the frame to their partner. Play the CD again. This time, stop after each section and elicit the number from a pair of pupils.

Key: 4, 3, 5, 2, 6, 1

CD 2, 17

TREVOR: Hello, Marie. What are you doing?
MASKMAN: I'm flying my helicopter. I'm a superhero.
TREVOR: I'm cleaning the doll's house.
MONTY: Hello, Trevor! Look at me! I'm driving Suzy's yellow lorry.
MARIE: Oh! No!
TREVOR: Ooh! What's he doing to those shoes, Marie?

AB39. MY PICTURE DICTIONARY

- Say *Open your Activity Books at page 39, please.* Pupils prepare the family stickers. Say *Who is it? Listen to the spelling.* Play number 1 on the CD and elicit the family member (*grandma*). Ask pupils to hold up the correct sticker. They all stick the sticker in the first square.
- Remind pupils that when there are two of the same letter next to each other in a word we say *double* (e.g. *double 'm'*). Play the rest of the CD. Pupils lay the stickers out on their desk in the correct order. Monitor around the class to check before they stick them in their books.
- Point to the example word in square 1. Say *Now write the words.* Pupils write the correct family word under each sticker. Write the words on the board in random order if they are having difficulty. Play the CD again if necessary.

Key: 2 grandpa, 3 baby, 4 mummy, 5 daddy, 6 cousin

CD 2, 18

1. g-r-a-n-d-m-a, 2. g-r-a-n-d-p-a, 3. b-a-b-y, 4. m-u-m-m-y, 5. d-a-d-d-y, 6. c-o-u-s-i-n

AB39. MY PROGRESS.

- Focus pupils on the activity in their books. Say *Let's read the sentences together.* Read the first sentence. Elicit some information about a pupil's family and then say to the pupil *Good. You can talk about your family.* Let other pupils do the same. Repeat for the second sentence, using mime prompts if necessary (*actions* is a new word). Pupils work in pairs. They take turns to point to a sentence in their books and do / talk about what it says.
- Say *Now ask each other and tick or cross the sentences.* Demonstrate the activity again if necessary. Encourage pupils to practise so that they can tick both the statements and colour the star.

Extra activities: see page T119 (if time)

Optional activity

- Unit 5 Extension worksheet 2 *Teacher's Resource Book 2* pages 32 and 36.
- The animated version of the story from *Kid's Box 2 Interactive DVD* (Suzy's room section). See pages 41–44 of the Teacher's booklet for the *Interactive DVD.*

Ending the lesson

- Ask pupils which chant/song they'd like to do again from the unit. Do it together to end the lesson.

11 16 CD2 Listen to the story.

1
Ooh! What's he doing to those shoes, Marie?
He's cleaning them, Trevor.
2
Hello, Trevor! Look at me! I'm driving Suzy's yellow lorry.
3
Hello, Maskman. What are you doing?
I'm flying my helicopter. I'm a superhero.
4
Hello, Marie. What are you doing?
I'm cleaning my shoes.
5
What are you doing, Trevor?
I'm cleaning the doll's house.
6
Oh no!

12 17 CD2 Listen and say the number.

6 Dinner time

1 19 CD2 Listen and point.

2 20 Listen and repeat.

OBJECTIVES: By the end of the lesson, pupils will have learned to name and talk about different foods.

• TARGET LANGUAGE

Key language: *bread, water, milk, juice, chicken, eggs, chips, rice, potatoes, carrots, lemons, meat*
Additional language: *breakfast, dinner, lunch, tea, evening, fridge, food, list*
Revision: *kitchen, chocolate cake, table, oranges, bananas, apples, burgers, ice cream, fish, sofa, cupboard, clock, lamp, bath, favourite, school*

• MATERIALS REQUIRED

Flashcards: (food) 58–65, 93, 94, 96
Kids Box 1 Flashcards: (food) 91, 92, 96 or pictures to show: bananas, apples, ice cream
Picture of fish
Extra activity 1: Two rolled up newspapers
Optional: *Kid's Box Teacher's Resource Book 2* Unit 6 Reinforcement worksheet 1 (page 39)

Warmer

- Write *Food* in the centre of the board. Elicit food words from pupils (they will give ones they know) and show the pictures as they say them. Stick the pictures around the word to show they are a word family. Elicit which foods they like.

Presentation

- Elicit/teach the new food vocabulary using the flashcards. Show each flashcard in turn and elicit/teach the word. Pupils repeat in chorus and then in groups. Stick the flashcard (picture side) on the board as part of the food family. Point to each of the new food flashcards in turn. Pupils chorus the word. Turn the flashcard to show the word side. Pupils repeat again.

PB40. ACTIVITY **1.** *Listen and point.*

- Say *Open your Pupil's Books at page 40, please.* Elicit what pupils can see in the picture to review food words and characters. Say *Can you find the hidden star?* Pupils look and check in pairs. Elicit where it is (on the fridge). Pupils say *Here it is.* Teach *fridge* and check understanding. Say *Listen and point to the food.* Play the CD. Pupils listen and point to the food. Set the focus listening questions: *What's Mr Star doing? What's Suzy's favourite drink? What's for dinner?* Play the CD. Pupils listen for the answers. They check in pairs. Check with the class (Making dinner, Milk, Chicken and rice) and encourage pupils to say *Chicken and rice* as it's said on the CD. Check comprehension of the different meals (*dinner, tea, breakfast, lunch*) and the times people eat them. Check what food the Star family say is for different meals. Pupils listen again to check (breakfast: bread and milk, lunch: egg and chips, tea: chocolate cake, dinner: chicken and rice). Elicit if that's what pupils have for their meals.

CD 2, 19

SIMON: What are you doing, Dad?
MR STAR: I'm making dinner. This evening we've got bread and water.
STELLA: No, we can't have bread and water for dinner, Dad. We have bread and milk for breakfast.
SUZY: Hmm. Milk's my favourite drink.
SIMON: Orange juice is my favourite.
SUZY: So, what *is* for dinner, Daddy?
SIMON: Let's have egg and chips.
STELLA: No, Simon! We have egg and chips at school for lunch.
SUZY: Let's have chocolate cake!
MR STAR: No, Suzy. Chocolate cake's for tea.
ALL THREE CHILDREN: So, what's for dinner?
MR STAR: Hmm … for dinner? It's your favourite, it's my favourite, it's our favourite. This evening we've got … Dad's Star dinner! … Chicken and rice!
STELLA, SIMON AND SUZY: Lovely.

PB40. ACTIVITY **2.** *Listen and repeat.*

- Say *Now listen and repeat.* Play the CD. Pupils repeat the words in chorus. Listen for correct pronunciation of the plurals, of *chicken* and of the consonant clusters *-lk, -ggs, -ps.*

CD 2, 20

Bread, water, milk, juice, chicken, eggs, chips, rice

AB40. ACTIVITY **1.** *Read the lists and find the food.*

- Say *Open your Activity Books at page 40, please.* Focus pupils on the two shopping lists on the page and on the grid of pictures. Check understanding of the vocabulary. The following words are new for pupils: *potatoes, carrots, lemons, meat.* Pupils take out a pencil, find 'A Start' on the grid and read the first items on A's shopping list (oranges, bread, rice). They draw a line on the grid from oranges to bread to rice. They work individually, continuing in this way, for lists A and B, until they reach 'A Finish' and 'B Finish'.

Extra activities: see page T119–T120 (if time)

Optional activity

- Unit 6 Reinforcement worksheet 1 from *Teacher's Resource Book 2* pages 38 and 39.

Ending the lesson

- Teach the following chant to pupils. They repeat it softly, loudly, in groups, pairs, going faster and faster each time. Note: The first line is countable nouns; the second uncountable nouns. Don't focus on this, but it will be a useful mnemonic for pupils later on.
  Apples, oranges, bananas, pears
  Water, milk, rice, bread
  Chicken and chips, chicken and chips

OBJECTIVES: By the end of the lesson, pupils will have had more practice talking about food and sung a song.

• TARGET LANGUAGE

Key language: *We're having ... , mum, afternoon, lunch time, morning, garden, our, dad*
Additional language: *with, floats, sinks*
Revision: *friends,* food words, *What's this? What are these?*

• MATERIALS REQUIRED

Flashcards: (food) 58–65, 93, 94, 96
Kids Box 1 Flashcards: (food) 91, 92, 96 or pictures to show: bananas, apples, ice cream
Picture of fish
The following written on a large piece of paper:
My favourite meal is ____________________ .
For __________________ *I like eating* ______________________________ .

Photocopiable 6a (see page T105), one copy for each pupil, crayons, a bucket half full of water and six real food objects, e.g. an egg, a banana, a pear, a lemon, a tomato, a carrot
Optional: *Kid's Box Teacher's Resource Book 2* Unit 6 song worksheet (page 43)

Warmer

- Review the food words and meals. Display the flashcards (picture side). Say *It's breakfast time. I'm having milk.* Pupil 1 continues: *It's breakfast time. I'm having milk and bananas.* Continue with three or four more pupils adding to the list. If the class disagrees with food at that meal, they shout *Change!* Then the game starts again with another meal, e.g. *It's lunch time. I'm having chicken.*

PB41. ACTIVITY 3. *Listen and point. Sing.*

- Say *Open your Pupil's Books at page 41, please.* Elicit what pupils can see in the pictures and encourage them to guess which meal it is: *breakfast, lunch, tea, dinner.*
- Play the CD. Pupils listen and check their guesses. Elicit what the children are eating for each meal and check understanding of *morning, evening, garden, mum, dad.* Play the CD again in sections. Pupils repeat. Continue until pupils have learnt the song. Pupils sing the song without the CD, as a class and in pairs. Divide the class into four, one group for each meal. They sing their part of the song. Swap roles and repeat.

CD 2, 21

It's morning. It's morning.
We're having breakfast with our mum.
Bread and milk, bread and milk.
It's morning. It's morning.

It's lunchtime. It's lunchtime.
We're having lunch with our friends.
Egg and chips, egg and chips.
It's lunchtime. It's lunchtime.

It's afternoon. It's afternoon.
We're having tea in the garden.
Chocolate cake, chocolate cake.
We're having tea in the afternoon.

It's evening. It's evening.
We're having dinner with Mum and Dad.
Chicken and rice, chicken and rice.
It's evening. It's evening. *[Repeat]*

CD 2, 22

Now sing the song again. (Karaoke version)

PB41. ACTIVITY 4. *Point, ask and answer.*

- Point to one of the food flashcards on the board (e.g. rice). Ask *What's this?* Pupils: *It's rice.* Point to the eggs and ask *What are these?* Pupils: *They're eggs.* Say *Look at Activity 4. Ask and answer about the pictures. Work in pairs.* Pupils use the model and ask and answer about the pictures in Activity 3. Monitor pupils and check for use of singular and plural (*'s this / are these*).

Photocopiable 6a: see pages T98 and T105

AB41. ACTIVITY 2. *Find and colour.*

- Say *Open your Activity Books at page 41, please.* Focus pupils on the sentences. Check they understand what to do. They work in pairs and find all the food, e.g. pears, carrots. Check with the class how many there are of each one. Pupils then colour the food according to the instructions.

Key: pears (5) green, carrots (7) orange, tomatoes (4) red, chicken (3) brown, meat (2) slices red, lemons (6) yellow

AB41. ACTIVITY 3. *Draw and write about your favourite food. Ask and answer.*

- Remind pupils of the diagrams they did for Extra activity 2 in the previous lesson (if appropriate). Elicit what their favourite food for breakfast/lunch/dinner is. Pupils draw their favourite food for one of these meals in their books. Display the model text (see Materials required) on the board. Pupils use the model to help them write their text. Monitor and help where necessary. In pairs, pupils ask and answer about their favourite food.

Extra activity: see page T120 (if time)

Optional activity

- Pupils complete the Unit 6 song worksheet from *Teacher's Resource Book 2* pages 38 and 43.

Ending the lesson

- Sing the song again with the class. Pupils only sing the verse which is about their favourite meal. Count the singers for each meal and announce the class's favourite meal.

3 21 CD2 Listen and point. Sing.

It's morning, it's morning.
We're having breakfast with our mum.
Bread and milk, bread and milk.
It's morning, it's morning.

It's lunchtime, it's lunchtime.
We're having lunch with our friends.
Egg and chips, egg and chips.
It's lunchtime, it's lunchtime.

It's afternoon, it's afternoon.
We're having tea in the garden.
Chocolate cake, chocolate cake.
We're having tea in the afternoon.

It's evening, it's evening.
We're having dinner with Mum and Dad.
Chicken and rice, chicken and rice.
It's evening, it's evening ...

4 Point, ask and answer.

What's this? | It's chocolate cake. | What are these? | They're chips.

Vocabulary

bread chicken chips eggs juice milk rice water

5 23 CD2 Listen and answer.

Can I have some brown bread, please?
Here you are.
P
S

6 24 CD2 Listen and repeat.

Grammar

Can I have some … ? Here you are.

OBJECTIVES: By the end of the lesson, pupils will have practised asking politely for different foods.

• TARGET LANGUAGE

Key language: polite request *Can I have … ? Here you are, brown bread*

Additional language: *tonight, after, good, but*

Revision: food vocabulary, *dinner time, some, thank you, please, I'm sorry, favourite*

• MATERIALS REQUIRED

Extra activity 1: CD of lively music

Extra activity 2: a piece of paper for each pupil

Warmer

- Play a Spelling bee game. Write the 15 food words: *bread, water, milk, juice, chicken, eggs, chips, rice, chocolate cake, oranges, bananas, apples, burgers, fish, ice cream* in your notebook and write a number between *1* and *15* next to each one. Divide the class into two teams: A and B. A member from Team A chooses a number between *1* and *15*, e.g. *5*. On your list, word 5 is, e.g. *meat*. Say *Spell meat*. If the pupil spells it correctly, they win two points for their team. If not, a pupil from Team B has a go. If he/she spells it correctly, the team wins one point. Team B then chooses a number. Play continues until all words are spelt. The team with the most points is the winner. Make sure different pupils in each team have a go at spelling out.

PB42. ACTIVITY **5.** *Listen and answer.*

- Say *Open your Pupil's Books at page 42, please.* Elicit what and who pupils can see. Set the pre-listening questions: *What are the Star family doing? What are they drinking? What meal is it?* Play the CD. Pupils listen for the answers. They check in pairs. Check with the class (Eating and drinking, Fruit juice: orange/apple, Dinner). Play the CD again. Stop after // and check comprehension.
  a. *What's Suzy drinking?* (orange juice). Elicit her question *Can I have some fruit juice, please?*
  b. *What's Stella eating?* (brown bread). Elicit her question *Can I have some brown bread, please?* and Mrs Star's answer *Here you are.*
- Play the last part of the CD. Elicit Simon's question *Can I have some egg and chips, please?* and Mr Star's reply *No, Simon. I'm sorry.*

CD 2, 23

MR STAR: Come on, everybody. Sit down. It's dinner time.
ALL THREE CHILDREN: OK, Dad.
SUZY: Can I have some fruit juice, please, Mum?
MRS STAR: Yes, Suzy. Orange juice or apple juice?
SUZY: Orange juice, please.
MRS STAR: Here you are.
SUZY: Thank you. // a.
STELLA: Can I have some brown bread, please?
MRS STAR: Here you are.
STELLA: Thanks. // b.
SIMON: Can I have some egg and chips, please?
MR STAR: No, Simon. I'm sorry. It's chicken and rice for dinner tonight, but, if you're good, you can have chocolate ice cream after.
SIMON: Hmm, great! Chocolate ice cream's my favourite.

PB42. ACTIVITY **6.** *Listen and repeat.*

- Say *Listen to the CD. Repeat what they say.* Play the CD. Pupils listen and repeat in chorus. Divide the class into two. One half says the first line; the other half replies with the second line. Groups change roles. Repeat for lines 3 and 4.

CD 2, 24

SUZY: Can I have some fruit juice, please, Mum?
MRS STAR: Here you are.
STELLA: Can I have some brown bread, please?
MR STAR: Here you are.

AB42. ACTIVITY **4.** *Listen and tick (✓) or cross (✗).* **[YLE]**

- Say *Open your Activity Books at page 42, please.* Elicit what pupils can see in the pictures. Say, *Look at number 1.* Play number 1 on the CD. Elicit from pupils if it's the right question or not (no). Say *No, it isn't the right question. There's a cross in the box. Tick for yes. Cross for no.* Play the CD. Pupils tick or cross. They check in pairs. Play the CD again. Check with the class. Elicit the requests for each one and the corrected requests for the crossed boxes.

Key: 2 ✓, 3 ✗ Juice, please. 4 ✓

CD 2, 25

1. Can I have some carrots, please?
   Here you are.
2. Can I have some bread, please?
   Here you are.
3. Can I have a drink, please?
   Milk, fruit juice or water?
   Water, please.
   Here you are.
4. Can I have some cake, please?
   Here you are.

AB42. ACTIVITY **5.** *Read and write the numbers.*

- Focus pupils on the pictures in Activity 5 and on the text under the pictures. Review/elicit the conversations from Activity Book Activity 4 and Pupil's Book Activity 5. Pupils work individually. They look at the pictures and sequence the two conversations by numbering the sentences in each column. They check in pairs. Check with the class by eliciting the dialogues from pairs. Give different pairs opportunities to repeat the correct dialogues.

Key: 4, 1, 3, 2. 2, 4, 1, 3.

Extra activities: see page T120 (if time)

Ending the lesson

- Review the chant below. Divide the class into two groups. One group asks the questions; the other chants the reply. Divide the class into six groups. Give each group a line. Groups stand up to chant their line and then sit down again. Give groups different lines and repeat.

  What's for breakfast? What's for breakfast?
  Apples, oranges, bananas, pears.
  What's for lunch? What's for lunch?
  Water, milk, rice, bread.
  What's for dinner? What's for dinner?
  Chicken and chips, chicken and chips.

OBJECTIVES: By the end of the lesson, pupils will have had further practice asking and answering politely.

• TARGET LANGUAGE

Additional language: *bingo*

Revision: *Can I have … ? Here you are, favourite, lunch, friend, My name's … , morning, at night, supper,* food vocabulary

• MATERIALS REQUIRED

Flashcards: (food) 58–65, 93, 94, 96

Kid's Box 1 Flashcards (food): 91, 92, 96 or pictures to show: bananas, apples, ice cream

Picture of fish

Small pieces of paper (four per pupil) to cover the bingo squares in Pupil's Book Activity 7

Optional: *Kid's Box Teacher's Resource Book 2* Unit 6 Reinforcement worksheet 2 and Extension worksheet 1 (pages 40 and 41)

Warmer

- Display the food flashcards around the room. Pupils stand up. Say, e.g. *Breakfast.* Pupils point to a food that they eat for breakfast. Repeat for *Lunch* and *Dinner* and then say the words quickly at random. Pupils point each time.

PB43. ACTIVITY 7. *Play bingo.*

- Say *Open your Pupil's Books at page 43, please.* Elicit what foods pupils can see in the pictures. Pupils choose one column of four foods. They cover the others with their notebooks. Hand out four small pieces of paper to each pupil. Call out the foods at random. Pupils cover food in their columns with a piece of paper when they hear it. The first to cover all four shouts *Bingo!* Elicit the foods from the pupil to check. Repeat. Pupils choose other columns each time.
- Pupils play the game in groups of four, one pupil taking turns to be the caller each time.

PB43. ACTIVITY 8. *Read and answer.* **[YLE]**

- Focus pupils on the picture and on the text. Say *This is a story about Alex. Read the story.* Pupils read the story again in pairs, this time working out what the picture words are. Check by going around the class asking pupils to read sections aloud. Don't force pupils to read aloud if they don't want to. Check comprehension using the questions at the bottom of the page.

Key: fish, chips, Fish, chicken, fruit, milk, meat, rice
1 Fruit and milk. 2 Chicken. 3 Meat and rice.

AB43. ACTIVITY 6. *Read and choose a word from the box. Write the word next to numbers 1-5. There is one example.* **[YLE]**

- Say *Open your Activity Books at page 43, please.* Read the instructions at the top of the page and explain that the pupils are going to read a puzzle (or *riddle*) about a thing, person or place. Read the text aloud, pausing at the spaces and talking about what type of word the pupils need to write, but not eliciting answers. Point out that the final line 'What am I? I'm a kitchen.' is the solution to the riddle.
- Make sure pupils know that they have to choose words from the box at the bottom of the page to complete the riddle (and that they don't need to use all the words). Focus on the example answer and show them that it is from the box. Pupils work individually to complete the text. They write in pencil and then compare their answers in pairs. Elicit answers and ask pupils which words they didn't use (*teacher, chairs*).

Key: 1 brother, 2 oranges, 3 milk, 4 banana, 5 egg

Extra activities: see page T120 (if time)

Optional activity

- Unit 6 Reinforcement worksheet 2 and Extension worksheet 1 from *Teacher's Resource Book 2* pages 38, 40, 41.

Ending the lesson

- Display the food flashcards (pictures) around the room. Write ten scrambled food words on the board, e.g. *klim, tame, nasaban, hicckne.* Pupils work in pairs to unscramble them, find the picture and put it next to the right word on the board.

7 Play bingo.

8 Read and answer.

Hello. My name's Alex. I'm Simon's friend. It's lunchtime and I'm having  and  for lunch.  isn't my favourite lunch. My favourite lunch is . In the morning my favourite breakfast is  and , and my favourite dinner is  and .

1. What's his favourite breakfast?
2. What's his favourite lunch?
3. What's his favourite dinner?

9 26 CD2 Monty's phonics

chicken

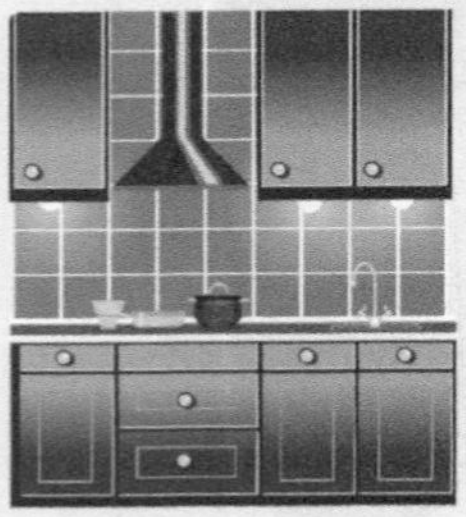

kitchen

flour
sugar

The chickens are cooking in the kitchen!

10 Ask and answer.

Can I have some bread, please?
Here you are.

OBJECTIVES: By the end of the lesson, pupils will be able to identify and say the sound ch /tʃ/ and have had more practice asking and answering questions.

• TARGET LANGUAGE
Key language: the phoneme /tʃ/ as in *chicken, kitchen*
Additional language: *very, only, a lot*
Revision: *Can I have some ..., please? Here you are, cooking, kitchen*

• MATERIALS REQUIRED
Photocopiable 6b, (see T106) one copy for each pair of students, cut in half
Extra activity: Flashcards: (food) 58–65, 93, 94, 96
Kid's Box 1 Flashcards (food): 91, 92, 96 or pictures to show: bananas, apples, ice cream

Warmer

- Sing the chant below. Pupils take turns to ask and answer and to stand up and sit down.
  What's for breakfast? What's for breakfast?
  Apples, oranges, bananas, pears.
  What's for lunch? What's for lunch?
  Water, milk, rice, bread.
  What's for dinner? What's for dinner?
  Chicken and chips, chicken and chips.

PB44. ACTIVITY 9. *Monty's phonics.*

- Say *Open your Pupil's Books at page 44, please.* Point to the small pictures and say them, emphasizing the sound /tʃ/. Pupils practise pronunciation of each word. Point at the large picture and say *Look! Where are the chickens? (In the kitchen.) What are they doing? (Cooking).* Say *Now listen to Monty, point and repeat.*
- Play the CD. Pupils listen and repeat the sounds, words, and sentence using the same tone and speed as Monty.
- Play the CD again. This time pupils repeat in groups and then in pairs. They try saying the tongue twister as fast as they can. Ask volunteers to say it quickly to the class.
- Write the tongue twister on the board and elicit the /tʃ/ sounds. Underline them. Ask pupils if they can think of other words with this sound (chair, chocolate).

Key: The chickens are cooking in the kitchen.

CD 2, 26

MONTY: Hi, I'm Monty! Repeat after me!
/tʃ/, /tʃ/, chicken
/tʃ/, /tʃ/, kitchen
The chickens are cooking in the kitchen!
The chickens are cooking in the kitchen!
The chickens are cooking in the kitchen!

Photocopiable 6b: see below and pages T98 and T106

PB44. ACTIVITY 10. *Ask and answer.*

- Write six food words on the board. Review asking politely for food and drink. Point to, e.g. *apples* and prompt a pupil (1) to ask another pupil (2) *Can I have some apples, please?* Make a thumbs up gesture to Pupil 2. The pupil responds *Here you are* and mimes handing over the apples. Repeat with another two pupils, but pointing to a different food word. After Pupil 1 asks the question, make a thumbs down gesture to Pupil 2 who replies *No, (name). I'm sorry.* Repeat for the other food words for practice.
- Hand out copies of Photocopiable 6b (see page T106); part A to half the class, and part B to the other half. Make sure pupils know if they are A or B. Teach/check the words *customer* and *shopkeeper.* Say Pupil A, *you are the customer.* Pupil B, *you are the shopkeeper.* All the pupils who are 'A' look at the items on their shopping list, while all the pupils who are 'B' look at the items on sale in their shop. Monitor this reading stage and answer any questions.
- Point out the target language in the speech bubbles at the top of each worksheet. Check pupils know which lines are for the customer and which are for the shopkeeper. Drill the target language.
- Pupils work in pairs, A and B. Pupil A asks for the items on his/her shopping list. Pupil B looks at the items on sale in his/her shop. If the item is available, it should be sold. Pupil A ticks or crosses the items on his/her shopping list when he/she knows whether they are available at the shop.
- Pupils exchange roles (Pupil A becomes the shopkeeper and Pupil B is the customer). Pupils compare their worksheets at the end of the activity to check that their answers are correct.

AB44. ACTIVITY 7. *Listen and write the words.*

- Say *Open your Activity Books at page 44, please.* Say *Look at the pictures. All the words have the sound 'ch'. Look and think.* Give pupils time to guess what each word is and how to say it.
- Play the example on the CD and point to the answer on the first line. Play the rest of the CD, pausing for pupils to repeat the word and to write. They check answers in pairs.
- Play the CD again. Correct as a class.

Key: 2 chicken, 3 teacher, 4 chips, 5 watch, 6 lunch, 7 chair, 8 kitchen

CD 2, 27

1. children; 2. chicken; 3. teacher; 4. chips; 5. watch; 6. lunch; 7. chair; 8. kitchen

AB44. ACTIVITY 8. *Write the words and the letters.* **[YLE]**

- Go through the example for Activity 8. Pupils work individually, solve the anagrams and match the words with the pictures. They check in pairs. Check with the class.

Key: 2 milk b, 3 chips a, 4 rice f, 5 water h, 6 chicken d, 7 juice e, 8 bread c

Extra activity: see page T120 (if time)

Ending the lesson

- Do the tongue twister again once with the class. Invite groups of four pupils to come to the front and say it quickly to the other pupils.

OBJECTIVES: By the end of the lesson, pupils will have read a story and reviewed language from the unit.

• TARGET LANGUAGE

Key language: language from the unit
Additional language: *It isn't mine, There isn't … , picnic*
Revision: *yours, mine,* food vocabulary, colours

• MATERIALS REQUIRED

Two rolled up newspapers for the Warmer
Extra activity 2: Flashcards: (food) 58–65
Kid's Box 1 Flashcards (food): 91, 92, 96 or pictures to show: bananas, apples, ice cream
Pictures of oranges and fish
Optional: *Teacher's Resource Book 2* Unit 6 Extension worksheet 2 (page 42) and/or animated version of the Unit 6 story from *Kid's Box 2 Interactive DVD* (Suzy's room section), Test Units 1-6 from *Kid's Box 2 Teacher's Resource Book* (pages 100–114)
Kid's Box 2 Language Portfolio page 4

Warmer

- Display the food flashcards (word side) over the board. Make two teams. Teams line up, pupils one behind another, facing the board. Hand a rolled up newspaper to the two pupils at the front. Say, e.g. *Chicken.* Pupils run to hit the flashcard. The first to hit it takes the flashcard for the team. Repeat. The team with the most flashcards wins.

Story

PB45. ACTIVITY **11.** *Listen to the story.*

- Say *Open your Pupil's Books at page 45, please.* Elicit who they can see (Trevor, Monty, Marie and Maskman) and what they're doing (eating / having a picnic). Set the pre-listening questions: *What's Marie eating? Is there any chocolate cake? Whose is the orange juice? What is Trevor eating?* Say *Listen and look.* Play the CD. Check with the class (Tomatoes and carrots, No, Marie's, A long brown pencil).
- Play the CD again. Pupils listen and repeat.
- Check comprehension by pointing to each picture in turn and asking, e.g. *What are they doing?* (Eating lunch). *What does Monty ask?* (Can I have some apple juice, please?). *Is there chocolate cake or chocolate ice cream?* (Ice cream).
- Ask pupils if they have picnics and what they like to eat.

CD 2, 28

Toys in the toy box,
Come alive.
Walk and talk,
On the count of five.
One, two, three, four, five.
MARIE: I'm having tomatoes and carrots.

MONTY: Can I have some apple juice, please?

MARIE: Here you are.
MASKMAN: Is there any chocolate cake?

TREVOR: No, there isn't, but there's some chocolate ice cream.

MASKMAN: Is this orange juice yours, Monty?
MONTY: No, it isn't mine. It's Marie's.
MASKMAN: What are you eating, Trevor? Is it chicken?
TREVOR: Er, no. It isn't chicken. It's a long brown pencil!
MARIE: Oh, Trevor!

PB45. ACTIVITY **12.** *Listen and say 'yes' or 'no'.*

- Say *Listen to the CD. Are they the same as the story or not?* Play the first one as an example. Play the CD. Pupils whisper the answers to their partner. Play the CD again. Check with the class. Elicit the correct phrase for the 'No' answers.

Key:
No. I'm having tomatoes and carrots.; No. Can I have some apple juice, please?; Yes.; No. No, there isn't.; No. No, it isn't mine. It's Marie's.; Yes.

CD 2, 29

MARIE: I'm having chicken and rice.
MONTY: Can I have some milk, please?
MASKMAN: Is there any chocolate cake?
TREVOR: Yes, there is.
MONTY: No, it isn't mine. It's Trevor's.
TREVOR: Er, no. It isn't chicken. It's a long brown pencil!

AB45. MY PICTURE DICTIONARY.

- Say *Open your Activity Books at page 45, please. Look at the picture dictionary.*
- Point to the scrambled word in the first square and the example answer. Elicit the word (*chicken*). Say *Look at the letters. Unscramble the letters and write words. They are all food words.* Pupils work individually or in pairs to solve the anagrams. Check answers.
- Pupils prepare the classroom stickers and lay them out on their desks in the correct order. Check around the class before they stick them in their books.

Key: eggs, chips, milk, rice, bread

Extra activities: see page T120 (if time)

AB45. MY PROGRESS.

- Say *Let's read the sentences together.* Read the first sentence. Focus pupils on the words they wrote for My picture dictionary. Say *Good, you can write food words.* Read the second sentence and elicit from pupils what their favourite meal is. Repeat for the third sentence. Pupils work in pairs. They take turns to point to a sentence in their books and show each other / talk about what it says.
- Say *Now tick or cross the sentences.* Encourage pupils to practise so that they can tick all the statements and colour the star.

Optional activities

- Unit 6 Extension worksheet 2 (see pages 38 and 42 of *Teacher's Resource Book 2*).
- The animated version of the story from *Kid's Box 2 Interactive DVD* (Suzy's room section). See pages 41–45 of the Teacher's booklet for the *Interactive DVD.*
- The test for Units 1-6 from *Teacher's Resource Book 2.*

Language Portfolio

- Pupils complete page 4 of *Kid's Box 2 Language Portfolio (I can Units 4-6).*

Ending the lesson

- Sing the song from Pupil's Book page 41 again.

11 28 CD2 Listen to the story.

1
I'm having tomatoes and carrots.
milk
2
Can I have some apple juice, please?
3
Here you are.
Is there any chocolate cake?
4
milk
No, there isn't, but there's some chocolate ice cream.
5
Is this orange juice yours, Monty?
milk
No, it isn't mine. It's Marie's.
6
What are you eating, Trevor? Is it chicken?
Er, no. It isn't chicken. It's a long brown pencil.
Oh, Trevor!

12 29 CD2 Listen and say 'yes' or 'no'.

Marie's science Food

1 Look and say.

Where is milk from?

Animals.

2 Listen and correct.

30 CD2

Eggs are from trees.

No, eggs are from animals.

Vocabulary

meat plant tree

Now you!
Activity Book page 46

OBJECTIVES: By the end of the lesson, pupils will have asked and answered about where food comes from.

• TARGET LANGUAGE

Key language: *meat, plant, tree, Where is meat from? Eggs are from animals.*
Additional language: animals
Revision: *eggs, lemons, potatoes, carrots, milk*

• MATERIALS REQUIRED

Photographs/pictures of plants and trees, flashcards 66–71, *Kid's Box 1* Flashcards: animals

Warmer

- Draw or stick some pictures of various plants on the board in a group to teach the word *plants*. Add pictures of trees in a group and elicit/teach *trees*. Stick flashcards of different animals in a third group on the board and say *They are all …* Pupils say *Animals*. Write the three key words under each group of pictures/photos.

Presentation

- Say *Open your Pupil's Books at page 46, please.* Point to the picture of Marie at the top of the page. Say *This is Marie's science.* Say *Today's lesson is about food.*

PB46. ACTIVITY **1.** *Look and say.*

- Hold up your book. Point to e.g. the milk and say *What's this?* Elicit the word. Repeat for the other foods in the photos (also use the apples in the trees in the picture to elicit *apples*).
- Point to and read the question in the speech bubble *Where is milk from?* Pupils respond together *Animals*. Ask about lemons in the same way but emphasise *are* (*Where* ***are*** *lemons from?*). Talk briefly about the singular *is* and plural *are* so that pupils use the verb correctly in their questions. Say *Look and say.*
- Pupils work in pairs and use the labels on the large picture to help them ask and answer the questions.

Key: Where is milk from? Animals. Where is meat from? Animals. Where are eggs from? Animals. Where are carrots from? Plants. Where are potatoes from? Plants. Where are lemons from? Trees.

PB46. ACTIVITY **2.** *Listen and correct.*

- Focus pupils on the photos. Say *Look at the eggs.* Play the CD for number 1. Elicit the answer *No, eggs are from animals.* Make sure the pupils say the verb and the source of the food. Play each one in turn. Pupils whisper the answer to their partner. Don't correct at this stage. Play the CD a second time. Stop after each one and correct as a class.

Key: 1 No, eggs are from animals. 2 No, lemons are from trees. 3 No, milk is from animals. 4 No, carrots are from plants. 5 No, potatoes are from plants. 6 No, meat is from animals.

CD 2, 30

1 Eggs are from trees. 2 Lemons are from animals. 3 Milk is from plants. 4 Carrots are from trees. 5 Potatoes are from animals. 6 Meat is from plants.

AB46. ACTIVITY **1.** *Read and match.*

- Say *Open your Activity Books at page 46, please.* Hold up your book and point to the food words and the large picture. Say *Read and match.* Pupils draw lines from each word to the correct part of the picture (animal, plant or tree), e.g. a line from the word *milk* to a cow in the big picture. Monitor pupils as they are working and help those who are having difficulty.

AB46. ACTIVITY **2.** *Write the words.*

- Hold up your book. Point to the outline of the cow's head and read *From animals.* Point at the word box and elicit a word which fits with the 'From animals' category (e.g. milk). Do the same with the other two categories if necessary. Say *Write the words.* Pupils work in pairs. Check by asking volunteer pairs for the answers.

Key: From animals: milk, eggs, meat, chicken ; From plants: potatoes, carrots, rice, tomatoes ; From trees: apples, bananas, lemons, pears

Extra activities: see page T120 (if time)

Ending the lesson

- End with quick questions from the lesson such as *Where are lemons from?* Pupils put their hands up to answer (*Trees*).

OBJECTIVES: By the end of the lesson, pupils will have listened to people describing different meals. They will have talked about good and bad food and their favourite food.

• TARGET LANGUAGE

Key language: *It's a bad/good breakfast/lunch/dinner, burger, fizzy drink, toast*

Additional language: *(Chicken) is very good for you, Dinner's on the table, Are your hands clean? Can I/we have..? Here you are.*

Revision: *chicken, egg, fruit, fruit juice, chips, carrots, potatoes, apples, tomatoes, oranges*

• MATERIALS REQUIRED

Flashcards/pictures of good and bad foods, e.g. fruits, chocolate, fruit juice, lemonade, a chicken dinner, burgers and chips

Warmer

- Write the word *Food and drink* at the top of the board and then draw two columns with the heading 'good' at the top of one and 'bad' at the top of the other. Elicit food and drink words to write in each column. Teach new vocabulary the pupils can use in the lesson, for example, *fizzy drink* and *burger.*

PB47. ACTIVITY 3. *Listen and say the number.*

- Say *Open your Pupil's Books at page 47, please.* Point to the word breakfast and tell pupils to look at pictures 1 and 2. Ask pupils *What food is there?* Elicit the food pupils know in the pictures (*some chocolate, some toast, a fizzy drink, an egg, some toast, fruit and fruit juice*). Don't worry about new words. Say *Listen and say the number.*
- Play the CD. Stop after the first dialogue. Give pupils time to think which picture is correct before asking for the answer from the class. Repeat for the pictures for lunch (picture 3 shows *chips and a drink*, picture 4 shows *chicken, potatoes, carrots, tomatoes and a drink*) and dinner (picture 5 shows *meat, potatoes, carrots and tomato juice* and picture 6 shows *cake and fizzy drink*).

Key: breakfast number 2, lunch number 4, dinner number 5

CD 2, 31

1.
Hello, Mum.
Hello. How are you this morning?
I'm OK, thanks.
Here's your breakfast: an egg, some toast and orange juice.
Mmm, lovely. Can I have some fruit, please?
Yes, of course.
Thanks, Mum.
That's a good breakfast.
Which breakfast is it?

2.
Hello, Miss Green. What have we got for lunch?
We've got chips; or chicken, potatoes, carrots and tomatoes.
Hmm. I love carrots. Can I have chicken, potatoes, carrots and tomatoes, please?
Yes, of course. Chicken is very good for you!
Yes, it is. And can I have some orange juice and an apple too, please?
Yes. Here you are.
Which lunch is it?

3.
Hello, Dad.
Hello. Dinner's on the table.
Mmm. Good!
Are your hands clean?
Yes, they are.
Good. There you are. Sit down. We've got a good dinner today. We've got meat and potatoes with carrots and tomato juice.
Lovely! Can we have some fruit, too?
Yes. You can have some apples or oranges.
OK. Thanks Dad.
Which dinner is it?

PB47 ACTIVITY 4. *Ask and answer.*

- Hold up the Pupil's Book, point to picture number 1 and read the first speech bubble *What's number 1?* Pupils look at the picture and answer as in the example, *It's a bad breakfast.* Say *Ask and answer.* Pupils work in pairs to ask and answer in the same way for the different meals in the pictures.

Key: 1 It's a bad breakfast, 2 It's a good breakfast, 3 It's a bad lunch, 4 It's a good lunch, 5 It's a good dinner, 6 It's a bad dinner

AB47 ACTIVITY 3. *Draw your favourite food.*

- Draw two circles, one inside the other to look like a plate on the board. Under the plate write *for breakfast.* Then draw your favourite breakfast from the foods in the lesson e.g. *eggs, toast* and *juice*. Also draw some fruit on the plate e.g. *an apple*. Point to the apple, for example and say *What is it?* Pupils answer *apple*. Write the word next to the food or ask confident pupils to come and write the words. (Don't rub the drawing off the board as you may use it in Activity 4.)
- Say *Open your Activity Books at page 47, please.* Point to the circles. Say *Draw your favourite food. Think about your favourite food for breakfast, for lunch and for dinner.* Pupils work individually to draw their favourite food from the box on the three plates. Go around checking the pictures match with the words given. Pupils can also use words from the lesson not in the box, such as *toast.*

AB47. ACTIVITY 4. *Now tell your partner. Draw your friend's food.*

- Read the question in the speech bubble *What's your favourite food for breakfast?* Pupils read the example *I like oranges and apples.* Choose a confident pupil and encourage him/her to ask you about the food you have drawn on your plate on the board. Say *Now tell your partner. Draw your friend's food.*
- Pupils work in pairs to ask and answer in the same way about their drawings from Activity 3. Go around listening to the conversations and helping where necessary. Make sure pupils are speaking English as much as possible.

Extra activities: see page T121 (if time)

Ending the lesson

- Play 'hangman' with food words from the lesson.

3 Listen and say the number.

CD2 31

Breakfast

1

2

Lunch

3

4

Dinner

5

6

4 Ask and answer.

What's number one?

It's a bad breakfast.

What's number four?

It's a good lunch.

7 At the farm

1 32 CD2 Listen and point.

2 33 CD2 Listen and repeat.

OBJECTIVES: By the end of the lesson, pupils will have learned to talk about animals on a farm.

- **TARGET LANGUAGE**

Key language: *farm, cow, duck, frog, goat, lizard, sheep, spider, zoo, tree, give*
Additional language: *Let's ... , nice, shoo, very funny, cages*
Revision: *big, ugly, black, animals, baby, under, on, next to, eat, drink, bag, milk, bread, T-shirt, love, like, hair*

- **MATERIALS REQUIRED**

Flashcards: (animals) 66–72
Kid's Box 1 Flashcards (animals): 47–52, 59–65
Optional: *Kid's Box Teacher's Resource Book 2* Unit 7 Reinforcement worksheet 1 (page 45), *Kid's Box 2 Interactive DVD*: The living room 'Visiting a farm' episode

Warmer

- Review the known animals using the flashcards from *Kid's Box 1*. Elicit each animal and put the flashcards on the board. Elicit the word *Animals* and write it in the centre of the board.

Presentation

- Teach/elicit the new animals (frog, cow, duck, goat, lizard, sheep, spider), using the flashcards. Pupils repeat in chorus and then in groups. Place the flashcards (picture side) on the board. Elicit the names again, then turn the flashcards word side.

PB48. ACTIVITY 1. *Listen and point.*

- Say *Open your Pupil's Books at page 48, please.* Elicit what and who pupils can see in the picture. Say *Can you find the hidden star? Where is it?* Pupils look and respond (on the window). Pupils say *Here it is.* Say *Listen and point to the animals.* Play the CD. Pupils listen and point. Set the focus listening questions: *Where are they? What is under the tree? What is on Stella's T-shirt? Where's the spider?* Play the CD again. Pupils listen. Check with the class (Farm, Cow, A lizard, In Simon's hair). Check understanding of *zoo* and *farm*. Ask, e.g. *Who likes lizards? What's the goat doing? What are the baby sheep doing?* Point out that the plural of *sheep* is *sheep*.

CD 2, 32

SUZY: Look at all those animals. This is a nice zoo.
MR STAR: It isn't a zoo. It's a farm. Look – there's a cow under the tree.
SIMON: Uh oh! Mum! The goat's eating your bag!
MRS STAR: Aaahh! Shoo! Shoo! Stop that!
STELLA: Look, Suzy. The baby sheep are drinking milk.
SUZY: Ahhh.
MR STAR: Let's give the ducks some bread.
SUZY: There's a frog!
SIMON: Look, Stella. There's a lizard on your T-shirt!
STELLA: Ha, ha, Simon. Very funny. I know, and I love lizards. Do you like spiders, Simon?
SIMON: No, I don't.
STELLA: Oh. Well, there's a big, black, ugly spider in your hair.
SIMON: Ahh!

PB48. ACTIVITY 2. *Listen and repeat.*

- Say *Let's do Activity 2. Listen and repeat.* Play the CD. Pupils point to the words on the page and repeat in chorus.

CD 2, 33

Cow, duck, goat, lizard, sheep, spider, frog

AB48. ACTIVITY 1. *Find and write the words.*

- Say *Open your Activity Books at page 48.* Focus pupils on the example (horse). Elicit some of the other animals. Pupils work in pairs. They identify the animals, circle the words and write them under the pictures. Check with the class.

Key: horse, fish, mouse, bird, frog, spider, lizard, chicken, cow, duck, goat, sheep

AB48. ACTIVITY 2. *Read. Draw and write the words.*

- Focus pupils on Activity 2. Elicit that this is a zoo. Read the first two sentences to pupils: *This is the Star zoo. The birds are next to the snakes.* Quickly review *next to*. Elicit which cage is for the birds. Pupils work in pairs, read the sentences and find the cages for the animals. Monitor around the class. Check with the class. Draw the zoo on the board and elicit where the animals are. Write in the names.

Key:

birds,	snakes,	–,	–,	crocodiles
fish,	lizards,	monkeys,	giraffes,	tigers

Extra activities: see page T121 (if time)

Optional activities

- Unit 7 Reinforcement worksheet 1 from *Teacher's Resource Book 2* pages 44–45.
- The 'Visiting a farm' episode from *Kid's Box 2 Interactive DVD* (The living room section). See pages 16–19 of the Teacher's booklet for the *Interactive DVD*.

Ending the lesson

- Play the Spelling game with the plurals of the new animals. Encourage pupils to take turns as callers, e.g.

Give me a c	*c*
Give me an o	*o*
Give me a w	*w*
Give me an s	*s*
What does that spell?	*cows*
What does that spell?	*cows*

OBJECTIVES: By the end of the lesson, pupils will have practised talking about animals and sung a song.

• TARGET LANGUAGE

Key language: *frog, moo, baa, quack, croak, cluck, farmer*
Additional language: *What can we do?*
Revision: animals, *kitchen, bedroom, armchair, bathroom, cupboard, Where's the …? It's in/on/under the …* colours

• MATERIALS REQUIRED

Flashcards: (animals) 66–71
A picture of a chicken (animal, not food)
Extra activity 1: large pieces of paper, one for each group of four
Optional: *Kid's Box Teacher's Resource Book 2* Unit 7 song worksheet (page 49), *Kid's Box 2 Interactive DVD*: The playroom 'Making an animal mask' (plus flashcard of Maskman, paper plates, cardboard, paints, scissors, glue and yarn or string)

Warmer

- Place the flashcards (picture side) around the room. Point to, e.g. the lizard, and say *Spider.* Pupils stand up if it's correct and sit down if it's incorrect. Demonstrate a few times. Pupils take turns to be the callers.

PB49. ACTIVITY 3. *Listen and point. Sing.*

- Say *Open your Pupil's Books at page 49, please.* Focus them on the pictures and elicit that they're funny. Show and display the picture of the chicken. Say *Listen and point.* Play the CD. Pupils point to the animals in the rooms. Check understanding quickly by asking, e.g. *Where are the sheep? What's the man's name?* (In the bedroom, John.). Check understanding of *farmer.* Play each verse in turn. Pupils repeat. Play the CD again for pupils to practise. Repeat the whole song in chorus. Make five groups: cows, sheep, etc. Groups sing their verses.
- Focus pupils on the animal noises. Tell them these are the sounds in English. Elicit the sounds for the animal noises in their language. Which are the same and which are different?

CD 2, 34

Cows in the kitchen, moo moo moo,
Cows in the kitchen,
There are cows in the kitchen, moo moo moo.
What can we do, John Farmer?

Sheep in the bedroom, baa baa baa,
Sheep in the bedroom,
There are sheep in the bedroom, baa baa baa.
What can we do, John Farmer?

Ducks on the armchair,
Ducks on the armchair,
There are ducks on the armchair,
Quack quack quack.

Frogs in the bathroom, croak croak croak,
Frogs in the bathroom,
There are frogs in the bathroom, croak croak croak.
What can we do, John Farmer?

Chickens in the cupboard, cluck cluck cluck,
Chickens in the cupboard,
There are chickens in the cupboard, cluck cluck cluck.
What can we do, John Farmer?

CD 2, 35

Now sing the song again. (Karaoke version)

PB49. ACTIVITY 4. *Ask and answer.*

- Pupils work in pairs. Pupil A asks a question about the song lyrics, e.g. *Where are the cows?* Pupil B answers, e.g. *In the kitchen.* Pupils exchange roles. When pupils have done the activity, ask them to close their books and do it from memory. Award points for correct questions and answers.

AB49. ACTIVITY 3. *Draw lines.*

- Say *Open your Activity Books at page 49, please.* Elicit the animals pupils can see in Activity 3. Point to the example line from the cow to the wardrobe and ask *Where's the cow?* Pupils respond *It's in the cupboard.* Say *Where are the other animals? You choose. Draw lines.* Pupils work individually. Each pupil draws lines from the animals to the pieces of furniture. They choose where to draw the lines. It's a secret.

AB49. ACTIVITY 4. *Now ask your friend and draw lines.*

- Make new pairs. Pupils face one another, holding up their books so they can't see each other's pictures. Pupils take turns to ask and answer, as in the speech bubbles. They draw lines from the animals to the furniture according to their partner's information. Pupils compare their pictures when they have finished. Encourage pupils to use procedural language, e.g. *Can you say that again? Sorry? Your turn.*

Extra activities: see page T121 (if time)

Optional activities

- Pupils complete the Unit 7 song worksheet from *Teacher's Resource Book 2* (see pages 44 and 49).
- Watch the DVD clip 'Making an animal mask' from the 'playroom' section of the *Interactive DVD.* Then make masks with your pupils. See pages 32–33 of the DVD booklet.

Ending the lesson

- Sing the song again with the class and/or make a new song using the verses pupils wrote for Extra activity 1.

3 Listen and point. Sing.

Cows in the kitchen, moo moo moo,
Cows in the kitchen.
There are cows in the kitchen, moo moo moo,
What can we do, John Farmer?

Sheep in the bedroom, baa baa baa ...

Ducks on the armchair, quack quack quack ...

Frogs in the bathroom, croak croak croak ...

Chickens in the cupboard, cluck cluck cluck ...

4 Ask and answer.

Where are the cows?

In the kitchen.

Vocabulary

cow duck frog goat lizard sheep spider

5 36 CD2 Listen and answer.

6 37 CD2 Listen and repeat.

Grammar

I love ... So do I. I don't.

OBJECTIVES: By the end of the lesson, pupils will have talked about likes and expressed agreement.

• TARGET LANGUAGE

Key language: *So do I, I love (goats), I don't, flowers*

Revision: *can, Let's … , Can I have … ? give, put, eat, Here you are, next to, kick,* animals

• MATERIALS REQUIRED

Flashcards: (animals) 66–71

Kid's Box 1 Flashcards: (animals): 47–52, 59–65

Photocopiable 7 (see page T107), copied onto thin card, one for each pair of pupils, crayons, scissors

Optional: *Kid's Box Teacher's Resource Book 2* Unit 7 Reinforcement worksheet 2 (page 46)

Warmer

- Play a Clapping game to review the animals and the noises. Pupils stand and clap as they do the chant below. The chant is cumulative. Groups can take turns to 'invent' and add new verses, using other animals and their noises.

Cows, cows, moo moo moo,
I like cows, yes I do.

Sheep, sheep, baa baa baa,
I like sheep, yes I do.
Cows, cows, moo moo moo,
I like cows, yes I do.
etc.

PB50. ACTIVITY **5.** *Listen and answer.*

- Say *Open your Pupil's Books at page 50.* Elicit who and what they can see. Check pupils realise that the animals in the picture are toy animals. Elicit where the flowers are and check understanding. Set the pre-listening questions: *Who loves sheep? Does Maskman love sheep? Who loves horses? Does Maskman love flowers?* Play the CD. Check with the class (Monty and Trevor, No, Maskman and Marie, Yes). Play the CD again. Pupils listen for what Monty and Trevor say (Monty: Oh, I love sheep. Baa baa. Trevor: So do I.). Pause the CD. Pupils repeat. Do the same for Maskman (Maskman: I don't.). Pause the CD. Pupils repeat. Continue in the same way for Maskman and Marie (ask *Who loves horses?*) and what Maskman says about flowers. Say to a pupil, e.g. *I love ducks.* Prompt the pupil to reply *So do I / I don't.* Practise around the class.

CD 2, 36

Toys in the toy box,
Come alive.
Walk and talk,
On the count of five.
One, two, three, four, five.
MARIE: Trevor, can I have the sheep, please? Let's put it here, next to the cows.
TREVOR: Here you are.
MONTY: Oh, I love sheep. Baa baa.
TREVOR: So do I.
MASKMAN: I don't. I love horses.
MARIE: So do I.
TREVOR: I don't. Horses are very big and they can kick.
MASKMAN: What now?
MONTY: Let's put the goat under the tree.
MARIE: No, Monty. It can eat the flowers and I love flowers.
MASKMAN: So do I.
TREVOR: Flowers, Maskman? Do you love flowers?
MASKMAN: Yes, I do. I can give them to Marie.
MONTY AND TREVOR: Oooohhh!

PB50. ACTIVITY **6.** *Listen and repeat.*

- Pupils listen and repeat in chorus and then in groups. Make sure they use a rising tone for *So do I.*

CD 2, 37

MONTY: Oh, I love sheep. Baa baa.
TREVOR: So do I.
MASKMAN: I love horses.
TREVOR: I don't.

Photocopiable 7: see pages T99 and T107

AB50. ACTIVITY **4.** *Write the words. Listen and check.*

- Say *Open your Activity Books at page 50, please.* Point to the example and tell pupils to complete the dialogues with the words in the box. They can only use the words once. Pupils work in pairs. Check with the class by playing the CD.

CD 2, 38

1. I love spiders.
   So do I.
2. I love fish.
   So do I.
3. I love lizards.
   So do I.
4. I love goats.
   I don't.

AB50. ACTIVITY **5.** *Draw your favourite animal. Ask your friend.*

- Elicit from individuals what their favourite animal is. Pupils draw their animal in the frame, colour it and write, e.g. *I love lizards.* Remind pupils to write the animal name in the plural. Make groups of four. Pupils show the others in their group their animals. They ask and answer, e.g. *What's your favourite animal? I love lizards.* The others respond *So do I / I don't* as appropriate.

Extra activity: see page T121 (if time)

Optional activity

- *Teacher's Resource Book 2* Unit 7 Reinforcement worksheet 2 pages 44 and 46.

Ending the lesson

- Play a Chain game. Start two chains at each end of the class. Stop when the chains meet in the middle. Chain 1: Say *Let's go to the zoo. We can see elephants.* Pupil 1: *Let's go to the zoo. We can see elephants and spiders*, etc. Chain 2: Say *Let's go to the farm. We can see goats.* Pupil 1: *Let's go to the farm. We can see goats and cats.*

OBJECTIVES: By the end of the lesson, pupils will have said a chant and practised talking about likes and expressing agreement.

• TARGET LANGUAGE

Key language: *watermelon, pineapple, mangoes, coconuts, lime, onions, vegetables*

Revision: *fruit, bananas, oranges, lemon, I love ... / So do I / I don't,* colours, prepositions, animals

• MATERIALS REQUIRED

Flashcards: (food) 96, 97

Pictures of: pineapple, mangoes, coconuts, lemon, lime, onions

Kid's Box 1 Flashcards (food): 91, 92

Extra activity 2: 12 food flashcards

Optional: *Kid's Box Teacher's Resource Book 2* Unit 7 Extension worksheet 1 (page 47), *Kid's Box 2 Language Portfolio* page 11

Warmer

- Review the known food vocabulary (orange, banana, apple), using the flashcards. Flash each one quickly (picture side) in front of the class and elicit the word. Teach/elicit *watermelon, pineapple, mango, coconut, lime, onion*, using the other flashcards/pictures in the same way. Pupils repeat the new words in chorus. Give the names *fruit* and *vegetables*. Elicit other vegetables they know: *carrots, potatoes*, etc.

PB51. ACTIVITY **7.** *Listen and point. Chant.*

- Say *Open your Pupil's Books at page 51, please.* Elicit what they can see. Say *Listen and point.* Play the CD. Pupils listen and point to the food. Play the CD again. Pupils join in the chant. Repeat line by line until they are confident. Pupils stand. They chant together in chorus. Divide the class into two groups. One half says the opener *(I love ...)*; the other half replies *(So do I)*. Swap groups. Record pupils if you can and play the recording back to them for enjoyment and feedback.

CD 2, 39

I love watermelon.	So do I.
I love pineapple.	So do I.
I love bananas.	So do I.
I love oranges.	So do I.
I love mangoes.	So do I.
I love coconuts.	So do I.
I love lemon and lime.	Hmm. So do I.
I love onions.	I don't. Goodbye.

PB51. ACTIVITY **8.** *Say and answer.*

- Practise the dialogues from the Pupil's Book page in open pairs. Pupils can change the animals: it's more motivating for them if they speak truthfully.
- Pupils stand up. They walk around the room. Clap. Pupils make pairs and take turns to say, e.g. *I love birds* and to reply *So do I / I don't.* Remind pupils to say what's true. Clap. Pupils move on.

AB51. ACTIVITY **6.** *Listen and colour. There is one example.* **[YLE]**

- Say *Open your Activity Books at page 51, please.* Ask questions about the picture to review the vocabulary. *Where are the animals? (At a farm) Which animals can you see? (Cows, goats, etc.) Where's the white goat? (Next to the sheep./In front of the (farm) house.) Point to the small cow,* etc.
- Pupils take out crayons or pens in green, red, brown, blue, black, yellow and orange. Play the example on the CD. Say *Where's the black goat?* Pupils point and say *Under the tree.* Say *Listen and colour. Make a dot first.*
- Play the CD. Pupils make a coloured dot for each item. They check in pairs. Play the CD again. Check with the class. Pupils colour the objects. Elicit which colour they didn't use (orange).

Key: 1 lizard = brown, 2 frog = green, 3 duck = red, 4 big cow = yellow, 5 sheep in front of the tree = blue

CD 2, 40

Look at the goat.
Which one?
Sorry, the goat under the tree.
Yes.
Can you colour it black, please?
Black. OK.
Can you see the black goat? This is an example. Now you listen and colour.

1. Now, can you see the lizard on the house?
   Yes.
   Colour it brown.
   OK. The lizard on the house is brown. I'm doing it now.
   Great.
2. And there's a frog next to the water.
   Oh yes!
   Colour that frog green, please.
   The frog next to the water? Green?
   Yes, that's right.
   OK.
3. There's a duck on the house. Can you see it?
   Yes, I can. Can I colour it red, please?
   Yes, colour the duck on the house red.
   That's my favourite colour.
   Great.
4. Can you see the two cows?
   Yes, I can.
   Good. Colour the big cow. Colour it yellow please.
   Pardon?
   Colour the big cow yellow.
   OK.
5. Now, look at the sheep in front of the tree. Can you see it?
   Yes.
   Colour it blue.
   The sheep in front of the tree is blue! Great! I love this picture now.
   Good.

Extra activities: see page T121 (if time)

Optional activity

- Unit 7 Extension worksheet 1 from *Teacher's Resource Book 2* (see pages 44 and 47 of the *Teacher's Resource Book*).

Language Portfolio

- Pupils complete page 11 of *Kid's Box 2 Language Portfolio (Things I love)*. Help with new language as necessary.

Ending the lesson

- Pupils repeat the chant from earlier in the lesson OR the chants they did in Extra activity 1.

7 39 CD2 Listen and point. Chant.

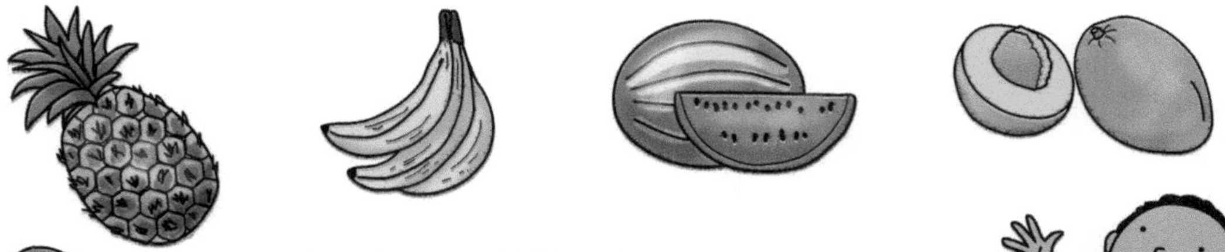

I love watermelon.	So do I.
I love pineapple.	So do I.
I love bananas.	So do I.
I love oranges.	So do I.
I love mangoes.	So do I.
I love coconuts.	So do I.
I love lemon and lime.	Hmm. So do I.
I love onions.	I don't. Goodbye.

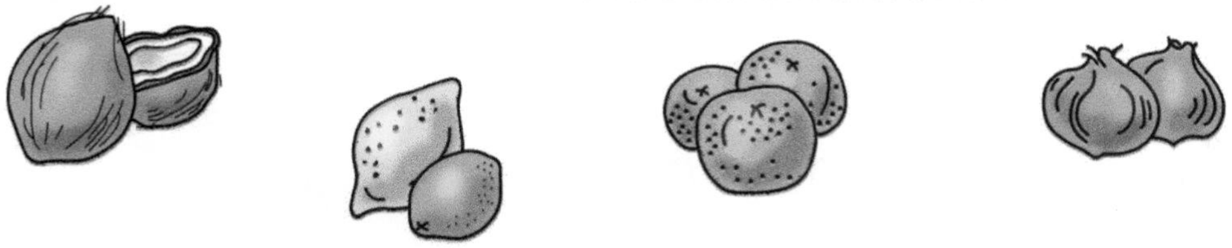

8 Say and answer.

I love cats.
So do I.
I love mice.
I don't.

9 41 CD2 Monty's phonics

spider

sports

star

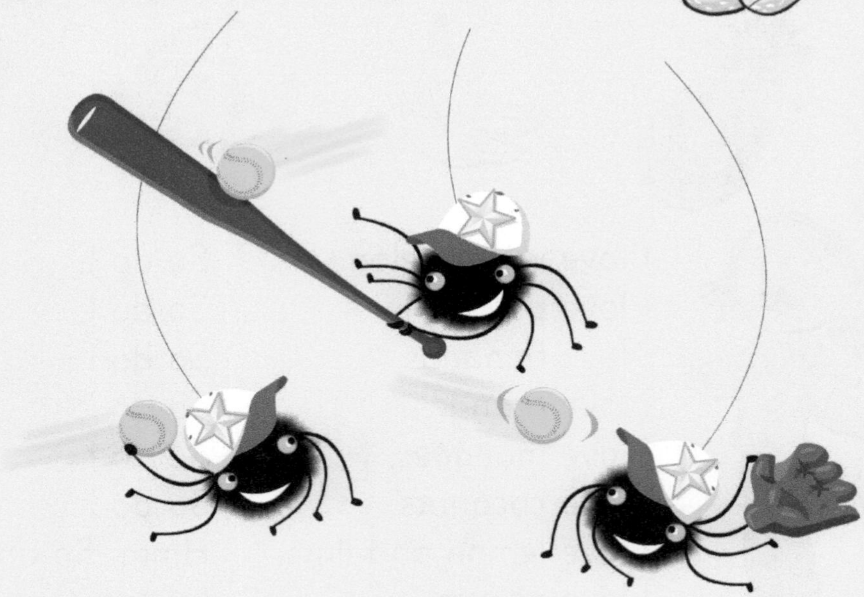

The spiders are sports stars!

10 Say and answer.

They're small and green. They've got short legs and a long tail.

Lizards.

OBJECTIVES: By the end of the lesson, pupils will be able to identify and say consonant clusters with s and will have had more practice with talking about animals.

• TARGET LANGUAGE

Key language: consonant clusters *sp, st, sn, sw, sk* and *sch*
Additional language: *can get (milk/eggs), across/down*
Revision: animals, colours, adjectives, face parts, numbers, *They've got … , swim, jump, clothes, these*

• MATERIALS REQUIRED

Flashcards: (animals) 66–72
Extra activity 2: Photocopiable 7 (see page T107), if not used previously copied onto thin card, one for each pupil, crayons, scissors, glue

Warmer

- Review the animals (*frog, cow, duck, goat, sheep, spider, lizard*), using the flashcards. Say, e.g. *I'm thinking of an animal. It's small. It can swim. It says Quack quack.* Pupils guess (duck). Show the flashcard. Repeat for other animals. Keep the definitions simple.

PB52. ACTIVITY 9. *Monty's phonics*

- Say *Open your Pupil's Books at page 52*. Point to the small pictures and say the words, emphasising the consonant clusters *sp* and *st*. Pupils practise pronunciation of each word. Point at the large picture and say *Look! Point to the spiders. They're playing sport. They're very good. They're sports stars!* Elicit names of some real life sports stars to check comprehension. Say *Now listen to Monty, point and repeat.*
- Play the CD. Pupils listen and repeat the sounds, words, and sentence using the same tone and speed as Monty.
- Pupils try saying the tongue twister as fast as they can. Ask volunteers to say it quickly to the class.

CD 2, 41

MONTY: Hi, I'm Monty! Repeat after me!
/sp/, /sp/, spider
/sp/, /sp/, sports
/st/, /st/, star
The spiders are sports stars!
The spiders are sports stars!
The spiders are sports stars!

PB52. ACTIVITY 10. *Say and answer.*

- Focus pupils on Activity 10 and elicit the animals. Using the pictures, teach *legs, body/bodies, tail, feet.* Say the definitions and pupils guess:
  They're black and white. They're big and they've got four legs. We can get milk from them. (cows)
  You can ride these animals. They've got four legs and a tail. (horses)
  They're small and brown. They've got two legs. We can get eggs from them. (chickens)
  They're small and can be different colours. They've got eight legs. (spiders)
  They're small and green. They've got two big feet, two small feet and big mouths. They can swim. (frogs)
  They have four short legs and a long tail. They are different colours. (lizards)
- Demonstrate the activity with a pupil, using the speech bubbles. Elicit ideas for the other animals. Pupils work in pairs (AA, BB, CC, DD, etc.). They plan definitions for each of the animals. Make new pairs (AB, AB, CD, CD, etc.). Pupils take turns to say their definitions and guess.

AB52. ACTIVITY 7. *Listen and write.*

- Say *Open your Activity Books at page 52, please.* Say *Look at the pictures. All the words start with 's' and different sounds (sw, sp, st, sk and sn). Look and think.* Give pupils time to guess what each word is and how to say it.
- Play the example on the CD and point to the example answer *spider.* Play the rest of the CD, pausing for pupils to repeat the word and to write. Point out that they need to write three letters for number 8. They check answers in pairs.
- Play the CD again. Correct as a class. Check comprehension of *snow.*

Key: 2 st, 3 sn, 4 sw, 5 sk, 6 sn, 7 St, 8 sch

CD 2, 42

1. spider, 2. star, 3. snake, 4. swim, 5. skirt, 6. snow, 7. Stella, 8. school

AB52. ACTIVITY 8. *Write the 'animal' words.* **[YLE]**

- Focus pupils on the crossword and check they understand *down* and *across.* Do the example (1 down) with the class. Read it aloud: *This is small and black. It's got eight legs.* Focus pupils on the example answer *spider* and the tick next to the picture of the spider. Pupils work in pairs. They read the texts together silently and match them with the animals. They write the words in the right places. Monitor as pupils are working. Note: These texts are quite complex and may take pupils some time to work out.

Key: Down 1 spider, 2 chicken, 6 goat. Across 1 sheep, 2 cow, 3 lizard, 4 duck, 5 frog.

Extra activities: see page T121 (if time)

Ending the lesson

- Do the tongue twister from the beginning of the lesson again. Pairs practise saying it quickly and then perform it for the class.

OBJECTIVES: By the end of the lesson, pupils will have read a story and reviewed language from the unit.

• TARGET LANGUAGE

Key language: language from the unit
Additional language: *I'm trying to sleep, talk, be quiet, I know, night-time*
Revision: *sheep, jump, count, can't, Let's talk about … , farms, farm dogs, catch, mice, cows, milk, What are you doing? I'm …- ing.*

• MATERIALS REQUIRED

Flashcards: (animals) 66–72
Kid's Box 1 Flashcards: (animals) 47–52, 59–65
Picture of a chicken (animal, not food)
Optional: *Kid's Box 2 Teacher's Resource Book* Unit 7 Extension worksheet 2 (page 48) and/or animated version of the Unit 7 story from *Kid's Box 2 Interactive DVD* (Suzy's room section), *Kid's Box 2 Interactive DVD: The play room* 'Duck Duck Goose' game.

Warmer

- Write *Farm animals* in the centre of the board. Elicit farm animals from the class, show the flashcard and then write the animal's name on the board to create a mind map. If pupils give you an animal which you don't think is a farm animal, ask them for a reason. They may be right.

Story

PB53. ACTIVITY 11. *Listen to the story.*

- Say *Open your Pupil's Books at page 53, please.* Elicit who pupils can see (Trevor, Monty, Marie, Maskman and some sheep). Elicit what they are doing. Set the pre-listening questions: *What can't they do? What is Maskman counting? Why?* Say *Listen and look.* Play the CD. Pupils listen and look. They check in pairs. Check with the class (Sleep, Sheep, To go to sleep). Note: *Sleep* may be a new word. If pupils say it in L1, then say *Good. In English, it's sleep.*
- Play the CD again. Pupils listen and repeat. Encourage them to say it with intonation and feeling, especially the snoring.
- Check comprehension by pointing to each picture and asking, e.g. *Who is sleeping?* (Trevor). *Is it day or night?* (night). *What are the sheep doing?* (jumping). Ask pupils if they count sheep to help them sleep. Say *Is it a good idea?*

CD 2, 43

Toys in the toy box,
Come alive.
Walk and talk,
On the count of five.
One, two, three, four, five.
MASKMAN: Trevor! Trevor! Pssst! Are you sleeping?

TREVOR: Yes, I am.
MARIE: Trevor! Maskman! Can you be quiet, please? I'm trying to sleep!

MASKMAN: I can't sleep.
TREVOR: Well, count sheep, Maskman.

MASKMAN: 11, 12, 13 … Oh, no! My sheep aren't sleeping. They're jumping! I can't sleep.

MARIE: We can't sleep now.

MARIE: OK. Let's talk about farms. Farm dogs can get sheep. Farm cats can catch mice. And we get milk from cows.
TREVOR: Yes, yes, I know … Maskman!

MARIE: What are you doing, Maskman?
MASKMAN: I'm sleeping, Marie. Goodnight.

PB53. ACTIVITY 12. *Act out the story.*

- Divide the class into groups of four. Pupils decide their roles. Play the CD again. Stop after each frame for the pupils to repeat in role. Pupils practise their story in groups. More confident pupils can change some of the words. Invite two or three groups to perform their role plays to the class.

AB53. MY PICTURE DICTIONARY.

- Say *Open your Activity Books at page 53, please.* Pupils prepare the animal stickers. Say *Which animal is it? Listen.* Play number 1 on the CD and elicit the animal (*spider*). Ask pupils to hold up the correct sticker. They all stick the sticker in the first square.
- Play the rest of the CD. Pupils lay the stickers out on their desk in the correct order. Monitor around the class to check before they stick them in their books.
- Point to the example word on the line in square 1 (*spider*). Say *Now write the words.* Pupils write the name of the animal under each sticker. Write the words on the board in random order if they are having difficulty. Play the CD again if necessary.

Key: 2 lizard, 3 cow, 4 sheep, 5 duck, 6 frog

CD 2, 44

Stick the spider on number 1. Stick the duck on number 5. Stick the frog on number 6. Stick the lizard on number 2. Stick the sheep on number 4. Stick the cow on number 3.

AB53. MY PROGRESS.

- Focus pupils on the activity. Say *Let's read the sentences together.* Read the first sentence. Focus pupils on the words they wrote for My picture dictionary. Say *Good. You can write animal words.* Read the second sentence. Say, e.g. *I love cats.* Elicit a response *So do I / I don't* from different pupils. Encourage pupils to make similar statements for others to respond to.
- Pupils work in pairs. They take turns to point to a sentence in their books and show each other / talk about what it says.
- Say *Now tick or cross the sentences.* Encourage pupils to practise, so they can tick the statements and colour the star.

Extra activities: see page T122 (if time)

Optional activities

- *Teacher's Resource Book 2* Unit 7 Extension worksheet 2 pages 44 and 48.
- The animated version of the story from *Kid's Box 2 Interactive DVD* (Suzy's room section). See pages 41-45 of the Teacher's booklet for the *Interactive DVD*.
- Watch the DVD clip 'Duck Duck Goose' from the 'playroom' section of the *Interactive DVD*. Then play the game with your pupils. See pages 35 and 36 of the DVD booklet.

Ending the lesson

- Ask pupils which chant/song/game they'd like to do again from the unit. Do it together to end the lesson.

11 Listen to the story.

43 CD2

12 Act out the story.

8 My town

1 45 CD2 Listen and point.

2 46 CD2 Listen and repeat.

OBJECTIVES: By the end of the lesson, pupils will be able to name places in a town.

• TARGET LANGUAGE

Key language: *park, shop, street, hospital, café, flat, town*

Revision: *shoe, long, Grandpa, Can you see ... ?, over there, window, look at, What's that? Where is it? those, next to, drink, Oh, sorry, flowers, feet,* colours, adjectives

• MATERIALS REQUIRED

Flashcards: (town) 73–78

Optional: *Kid's Box 2 Interactive DVD: The playroom* 'Hopscotch' (thick chalk and a counter, e.g. a beanbag)

Warmer

- Play a Pointing game to review body and clothes, e.g. *Point to your nose. Point to your eyes. Point to your legs. Point to your feet. Point to your shirt. Point to your shoes.*

Presentation

- Elicit/teach the new words (*park, shop, street, hospital, café, flat*), using the flashcards (picture side). Pupils repeat in chorus and then in groups and pairs. Elicit each word again and place the flashcards in a circle on the board (picture side). Say *these places are all in a town.* Write *Town* in the centre of the circle. Point to each flashcard, elicit the word and then turn it word side.

PB54. ACTIVITY 1. *Listen and point.*

- Say *Open your Pupil's Books at page 54, please.* Elicit who they can see and where the people are (Grandpa and Suzy, Town). Say *Can you find the hidden star?* Pupils look and check in pairs. Check with the class (on the lorry). Pupils say *Here it is.* Say *Listen and point.* Play the CD. Pupils listen and point to the places in the town. Prompt, using the flashcards if necessary. Set the focus listening questions: *Where's Grandpa's flat? Where's the shoe shop?* Play the CD again. Pupils listen for the answers. They check in pairs. Check with the class (Next to the park, Next to the café). Check comprehension by asking, e.g. *Is it a big town or a small town? What colour are Grandpa's windows? What colour shoes does Suzy want?* Ask different pupils. Play the CD again if necessary.

CD 2, 45

SUZY: This is a long street, Grandpa.
GRANDPA: Yes, it is. It's a big city. Can you see my flat?
SUZY: No. Where is it?
GRANDPA: It's over there, next to the park. It's the one with the green windows.
SUZY: Oh, yes. What's this over here, next to the toy shop?
GRANDPA: That's a hospital.
SUZY: Ooh, look! There's a shoe shop! Look at those beautiful red shoes, Grandpa.
GRANDPA: What ... ? Oh, yes.
SUZY: The shoe shop's next to the café, Grandpa.
GRANDPA: Good idea. Let's go to the café for a drink.
SUZY: No, Grandpa. Let's go to the shoe shop for my new red shoes.
GRANDPA: Oh, sorry ... Yes ... Of course.

PB54. ACTIVITY 2. *Listen and repeat.*

- Say *Let's do Activity 2. Listen to the new words and repeat.* Play the CD. Pupils point to the words in the picture and repeat them in chorus. Listen for correct pronunciation.

CD 2, 46

Park, shop, street, hospital, café, flat

AB54. ACTIVITY 1. *Look and read. Tick (✓) or cross (✗) the box.* **[YLE]**

- Say *Open your Activity Books at page 54, please.* Focus pupils on the example. Read the sentence (*This is a flat*), point to the picture (house) and point to the X. Check pupils know what to do. Pupils work individually. They check in pairs. Check with the class. Display the flashcards (picture side) on the board.
  For the sentences with the wrong picture, invite a pupil to go up to the board, point to the house and say, e.g. *This is a house.*

Key: 2 ✓, 3 ✗ This is a school. 4 ✓, 5 ✓, 6 ✗ This is a hospital.

AB54. ACTIVITY 2. *Circle the different word.*

- Say *Look at Activity 2. Read the words in the first line.* Elicit why *shop* is different. Encourage pupils to notice, rather than telling them. Ask *Is a car a kind of transport?* Repeat for *lorry* and *bus*. For *shop*, pupils respond *No, it isn't.*
- Pupils complete the activity in pairs. Pairs check with pairs. Give time for slower readers to finish. Check with the class.

Note: If pupils give you an unexpected answer, ask them why. This activity relies on critical thinking. It's possible for there to be more than one answer. Listen to pupils' reasons for their choice. Be prepared to accept their answer.

Key: 2 goat, 3 bike, 4 park, 5 shop, 6 bedroom, 7 frog, 8 town

Extra activities: see page T122 (if time)

Optional activity

- Watch the DVD clip 'Hopscotch' from the 'playroom' section of the *Interactive DVD.* Then play the game with your pupils. See page 35 of the DVD booklet.

Ending the lesson

- Six pupils come to the front. Hand each one a flashcard (*park, shop, street, hospital, café, flat*). Tell pupils to stand in alphabetical order. Let the class check if they're correct. Use this activity to focus pupils on the second letter of a word when the first letter (s) is the same. Repeat with another six pupils.

OBJECTIVES: By the end of the lesson, pupils will have had more practice reading and talking about places in a town.

• TARGET LANGUAGE

Key language: plurals, *children, men, women, babies, see, buggy*

Additional language: *Spot the difference*

Revision: *How many … ? There are … /There is … park, shop, street, hospital, café, flat, town, woman, pineapple, cat, boy, kite, shoes, lemon, bus, Are there … ? Where … ? pets*

• MATERIALS REQUIRED

Flashcards (town) 73–78

Extra activity 1: The following sentences written on a large piece of paper:

1 *There are five* ________________ *child/children in the park.*
2 *There is one* ________________ *man/men in the shoe shop.*
3 *There are three* ________________ *woman/women in the café.*
4 *There is one* ________________ *child/children on a bike.*
5 *There is one* ________________ *woman/women on the bus.*
6 *There are two* ________________ *baby/babies in the buggy.*
7 *There are four* ________________ *man/men in the pet shop.*
8 *There is one* ________________ *baby/babies with a banana.*

Optional: *Kid's Box Teacher's Resource Book 2* Unit 8 Reinforcement worksheet 2 (page 52)

Warmer

- Revise the town words, using the flashcards. Slowly reveal each one from behind paper (picture side) until pupils say the word correctly.

PB55. ACTIVITY 3. *Read and answer.*

- Say *Open your Pupil's Books at page 55.* Elicit what pupils can see in the picture. Accept their feedback. Make sure you draw out the following words as pupils need them for the reading: *baby, woman, fruit shop, pineapples, lemons, cats, kite, bus.*
- Say *Read the questions. Talk about the answers with your partner.* Pupils work in pairs and answer the questions. Monitor pupils as they are working. Check by asking pupils to read the questions aloud. Other pupils answer. If a pupil doesn't want to read aloud, ask another pupil to volunteer.
- Pupils write the questions and answers in their notebooks.

Key: 1 She's in the park. 2 There are five pineapples. 3 There are four cats (three in the pet shop and one in the tree). 4 He's in the park. 5 The shoes are red. 6 The lemons are in the fruit shop. 7 The bus is yellow.

PB55. ACTIVITY 4. *Ask and answer.*

- Focus pupils on the words in the box. Elicit what they think the following words are: *men, women, babies, children.* Check for correct pronunciation of *women.* Help them to work out that they are plurals of *man, woman, baby, child.* Pupils work in pairs, using the model question and answer and the words in the box. They take turns to ask and answer about the picture in Activity 3. Monitor and help if necessary. Check using open pairs: one pair asks a question, and another answers it.

AB55. ACTIVITY 3. *Spot the differences.*

- Say *Open your Activity Books at page 55, please.* Focus pupils on the pictures. Say *Look. They are different.* Read out the example. Pupils find these differences in the pictures. Say *There are five more differences. Can you find them?* Pupils work in pairs and find the other differences. Monitor and help by pointing to parts of the picture if necessary. Elicit answers from pairs around the class. Write the example sentence on the board and underline the words they change each time: *In A <u>there's one car</u>, but in B <u>there are two cars</u>.* Pupils use the model to complete the other sentences.

Key: (Pupils' answers can be in any order.) 2 In A there's one bus stop, but in B there's no bus stop. 3 In A there's a pet shop, but in B there's a toy shop. 4 In A there's a woman on the bus, but in B there's a man on the bus. 5 In A there are two women in the shop, but in B there are two men on the street. 6 In A there's a café, but in B there's a bookshop.

AB55. ACTIVITY 4. *Write the words.*

- Focus pupils on the shop names: *fruit, toys, pets, furniture.* Point out the examples (pear, ball, dog, chair). Pupils work in groups of four and put the other words into the categories. Monitor and help where necessary. Check by eliciting the words for each category and writing them on the board.

Key:
Fred's Fruit: coconut, apple, pineapple, lemon, orange
Ted's Toys: bike, computer game, train, car, lorry
Pete's Pets: lizard, cat, fish, mouse, bird
Phil's Furniture: armchair, table, mirror, clock, cupboard

Extra activities: see page T122 (if time)

Optional activity

- *Teacher's Resource Book 2* Unit 8 Reinforcement worksheet 2 (see pages 50 and 52).

Ending the lesson

- Play a Chain game of *In the town there are …* Start the chain, e.g. *In the town there are four bookshops.* Pupil 1: *In the town there are four bookshops and two cafés.* Pupil 2: *In the town there are four bookshops, two cafés and …* When the chain is about six places long, shout *Change!* and the next pupil starts another chain. Choose pupils at random to continue the chain to make sure all pupils are listening. Don't do it in seat order.

3 Read and answer.

1. Where's the woman with the baby?
2. How many pineapples are there?
3. How many cats are there?
4. Where's the boy with the kite?
5. What colour are the shoes in the shoe shop?
6. Where are the lemons?
7. What colour's the bus?

4 Ask and answer.

How many cars are there?

There are three cars.

cars	men	women	children	bikes	dogs
babies	pineapples	coconuts	lemons	cats	

Vocabulary

café flat hospital park shop street

5 Listen and point.

47 CD2

6 Ask and answer.

Who's next to Grandma?

Grandpa.

Grammar

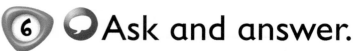

behind between in front of next to

OBJECTIVES: By the end of the lesson, pupils will have asked and answered questions about location.

• TARGET LANGUAGE

Key language: *behind, between, in front of, music*
Additional language: *I can't see, I can't hear, everybody*
Revision: character names, *sitting, Be quiet, very happy, So do I*

• MATERIALS REQUIRED

Photocopiable 8 (see page T108), copied onto thin card, one for each pupil, scissors, crayons
Optional: *Kid's Box Teacher's Resource Book 2* Unit 8 Reinforcement worksheet 1 (page 51)

Warmer

- Revise known prepositions (*in, on, next to*) using classroom objects. Say, e.g. *Pick up a pencil. Put it next to your book. Put your red crayon in the book. Put your ruler on your head. Put your eraser on the ruler.*

Presentation

- Call five pupils to the front of the class. They stand like this:

	P1	
P2	P3	P4
	P5	

- Say *Listen. (Name P1) is behind (name P3). (Name P5) is in front of (name P3). (Name P3) is between (name P2) and (name P4). Who's next to (name P4)?* Repeat several times. Ask questions, e.g. *Where is (name P3)? Where is (name P5)?* Invite five more pupils to the front and give them instructions, e.g. *(Name), stand in front of (name).* They arrange themselves according to your instructions.

PB56. ACTIVITY 5. *Listen and point.*

- Say *Open your Pupil's Books at page 56, please.* Elicit where the people are (At school, in a theatre). Elicit the names of the people. Say *Listen and point.* Play the narrative section of the CD. Pupils point. Repeat. Pre-teach *Music.* Set the focus questions: *Suzy isn't happy. Why? Who's in front of Suzy?* Play the dialogue section of the CD. Pupils listen for the answers. They check in pairs. Play it again. Check with the class (She can't see. Lenny's mum is in front of Suzy.). Say *I love music.* Elicit responses *So do I / I don't.*
- Check comprehension and prepositions by asking about the people in the picture, e.g. *Who is between Mrs Star and Simon? Where is Grandma Star?*

CD 2, 47

NARRATOR: Mr Star is playing his guitar at Simon and Stella's school. Simon's sitting between Stella and Suzy, and Mrs Star's sitting next to Suzy. Lenny's sitting in front of Mrs Star, and Lenny's mum's sitting between Lenny and his dad. Grandpa and Grandma Star are sitting behind Simon and Suzy. Everybody is very happy, but Suzy isn't.
STELLA: I love music.
MRS STAR: So do I.
SUZY: Mum, I can't see.
MRS STAR: Shh, Suzy. Be quiet!
SUZY: But I can't see. Lenny's mum's in front of me.
GRANDMA: Shh, Suzy. Be quiet! I can't hear if you're talking.
SUZY: Can I sit with Stella, please?
MRS STAR: Well, all right, but be quiet.
SUZY: Yes, Mum. Thanks.
SUZY: Oh, this is good. Now I can see.
STELLA: Huh! You can see, but I can't. Mum!

PB56. ACTIVITY 6. *Ask and answer.*

- Pupils work in pairs. They use the model and your examples from the end of the previous activity to take turns to ask and answer about the picture. Monitor pupils and prompt where necessary.

Photocopiable 8: see pages T99 and T108

AB56. ACTIVITY 5. *Listen and colour the stars.*

- Say *Open your Activity Books at page 56, please.* Say *Listen for the colours you need.* Play the CD. Pupils listen and put the right crayons on their desks (grey, red, pink, yellow, purple, orange, blue, green, brown). Play the CD again, pausing after each sentence. Pupils make a dot on the star the first time. They check in pairs. Play the CD again, sentence by sentence. Check with the class. Play the CD again for pupils to colour.

Key: 1 orange, 2 grey, 3 pink, 4 red, 5 purple, 6 yellow, 7 brown, 8 blue, 9 green

CD 2, 48

Colour the star between number 1 and number 3 grey.
Colour the star under number 1 red.
Star number 3 is pink.
Colour the star between number 3 and number 9 yellow.
The star under the grey star is purple.
The star next to number 2 is orange.
Colour the star between 7 and 9 blue.
Colour the star under number 6 green.
The star next to the blue star is brown.

AB56. ACTIVITY 6. *Read and write the names.*

- Do this first as a TPR activity. Arrange six chairs as in the Activity Book activity and invite six pupils to the front. Give each pupil a name: *Tom, Jill,* etc. Read the instructions one by one. Pupils arrange themselves as instructed. The class helps by telling them where to sit.
- Pupils do the activity in the Activity Book. They check in pairs. Check with the class (using the TPR activity again).

Key:
Tom, Ann, Nick
Jill, Sue, Bill

Extra activity: see page T122 (if time)

Optional activity

- *Teacher's Resource Book 2* Unit 8 Reinforcement worksheet 1 pages 50–51.

Ending the lesson

- Ask questions about pupils in the class, e.g. *Who's sitting in front of (name)? Who's sitting between (name) and (name)?* Pupils take turns to ask questions.

OBJECTIVES: By the end of the lesson, pupils will have had more practice with location and will have sung a song.

• **TARGET LANGUAGE**

Key language: *Where's the … ?*
Additional language: *It isn't the one …*
Revision: prepositions, furniture, body parts, school objects, animals

• **MATERIALS REQUIRED**

Extra activity 2: Photocopiable 8 (see page T108), if not used in the previous lesson copied onto thin card, one for each pupil, scissors, crayons
Optional: *Kid's Box Teacher's Resource Book 2* Unit 8 Extension worksheet 1 (page 53) and/or song worksheet (page 55)

Warmer

- Review prepositions (*between, behind, in front of, next to*) by asking questions as in the Ending the lesson activity in the previous lesson.

PB57. ACTIVITY **7.** *Listen and point. Sing.*

- Say *Open your Pupil's Books at page 57, please.* Elicit what pupils can see in the pictures. Say *Listen and point.* Play the CD. They point to the pictures of the actions. Play the CD again in sections with actions. Pupils repeat. Repeat all the sections together with the CD. Pupils take the real objects (books, pencil, etc.) and do the song with the actions. Divide the class into four groups. Each group performs the song. Vote for the best performance.

CD 2, 49

Put two books on the table,
Put two books on the table.
Put a pencil between the books,
Put a pencil between the books.
Put a pencil behind your head,
Put a pencil behind your head.
Put a book in front of your nose,
Put a book in front of your nose.
Put a book under your chair,
Put a book under your chair.
Put a pencil behind your ear,
Put a pencil behind your ear.
Put two books on your head,
Put two books on your head.
Put them all back on the table,
And now, now sit down.

CD 2, 50

Now sing the song again. (Karaoke version)

PB57. ACTIVITY **8.** *Ask and answer.*

- Pupils work in pairs. Pupil A asks a question about the picture and Pupil B answers (as in the example speech bubbles). Pupils swap roles.

AB57. ACTIVITY **7.** *Look at the pictures and read the questions. Write one word answers.* **[YLE]**

- Say *Open your Activity Books at page 57, please.* Point to the first picture and read the example question and answer with the class. Elicit other things pupils can see in both pictures (e.g. *chairs, a dog*).
- Say *Read questions 1 and 2. Look at the picture. Write one word for each answer.* Pupils read the rest of the questions for the first picture individually and write their answers in pencil. Make sure they know they only need to write one word for each gap. They can compare answers in pairs. Copy the questions and answers (with gaps) on the board. Write the missing words on the board for pupils to check their spelling.
- Repeat the process for the second picture and questions 3 to 5.

Key: 1 black, 2 two, 3 boy, 4 between, 5 sleeping

Extra activities: see page T122 (if time)

Optional activities

- *Teacher's Resource Book 2* Unit 8 Extension worksheet 1 (see pages 50 and 53).
- *Teacher's Resource Book 2* Unit 8 song worksheet (see pages 50 and 55).

Ending the lesson

- Select an object or pupil in the classroom. Say, e.g. *I'm thinking of a bag. It's green and it's under a chair. It's next to the window,* for pupils to guess. Repeat. Pupils can take turns to be the callers.

7 Listen and point. Sing.

Put two books on the table ...
Put a pencil between the books ...
Put a pencil behind your head ...
Put a book in front of your nose ...
Put a book under your chair ...
Put a pencil behind your ear ...
Put two books on your head ...
Put them all back on the table,
And now, now, sit down.

8 Ask and answer.

Where's the blue book?

On the sofa.

9 51 CD2 Monty's phonics

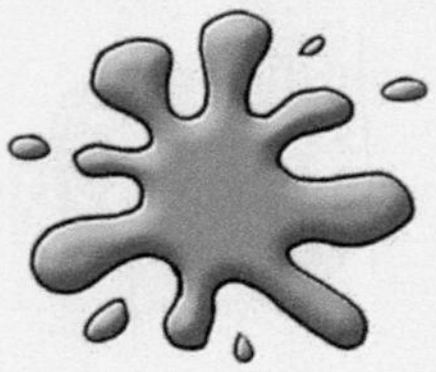

brown

mouse

house

A brown mouse in a town house.

10 Ask and answer.

Where's the car?

It's in front of the toy shop.

OBJECTIVES: By the end of the lesson, pupils will be able to identify and say the long ow / ou /aʊ/ vowel sound and will have had more practice with asking and answering about location.

• TARGET LANGUAGE

Key language: the phoneme /aʊ/ as in *brown, mouse, town, house*

Additional language: *Tom*

Revision: *clock, orange, box, shop,* prepositions, places in a town, *Where's … ? Where are … ? It's … , They're …*

• MATERIALS REQUIRED

Flashcards: (town) 73–78 (household objects) 49–54

Extra activity 1: Photocopiable 8 (see page T108), if not used in the previous lesson copied onto thin card, one for each pupil, scissors, crayons

Optional: *Kid's Box 2 Interactive DVD:* The living room 'The eye test' episode

Warmer

- Revise the town and household objects vocabulary using the 12 flashcards. Flash each one quickly in front of pupils, elicit the word and stick it on the board (picture side).

PB58. ACTIVITY 9. *Monty's phonics*

- Say *Open your Pupil's Books at page 58, please.* Point to the small pictures and say them, emphasising the vowel sound /aʊ/. Pupils practise pronunciation of each word. Point at the large picture and say *What colour is the mouse? (Brown) Where is it? (In a house) Where's the house? (In a town).* Say *Now listen to Monty, point and repeat.*
- Play the CD. Pupils listen and repeat the sounds, words, and sentence using the same tone and speed as Monty.
- Pupils repeat the tongue twister as a class. Do it more and more quickly. Then ask small groups of pupils to have a go at saying it. Go around the class from group to group. Put pupils into pairs. They take it in turns to say the tongue twister quickly to each other. Invite volunteers to say it to the class.

CD 2, 51

MONTY: Hi, I'm Monty! Repeat after me!
/aʊ/, /aʊ/, brown
/aʊ/, /aʊ/, mouse
/aʊ/, /aʊ/, house
A brown mouse in a town house!
A brown mouse in a town house!
A brown mouse in a town house!

PB58. ACTIVITY 10. *Ask and answer.*

- Ask a question about the picture, using the example. Review the meaning of the prepositions they'll need, using gesture: *next to, in front of, between, behind.* Pupils ask and answer first in open pairs. Pupils work in closed pairs, taking turns to ask and answer about the picture.

AB58. ACTIVITY 8. *Listen and write the words.*

- Say *Open your Activity Books at page 58, please.* Say *Look at the pictures. All the words have the sound 'ou' /aʊ/. Look and think.* Give pupils time to guess what each word is and how to say it.
- Play the example on the CD and point to the answer on the first line. Play the rest of the CD, pausing for pupils to repeat the word and to write. They check answers in pairs.
- Play the CD again. Correct as a class.

Key: 2 town, 3 mouse, 4 cow, 5 sit down, 6 house, 7 trousers, 8 mouth

CD 2, 52

1. brown, 2. town, 3. mouse, 4. cow, 5. sit down, 6. house, 7. trousers, 8. mouth

AB58. ACTIVITY 9. *Draw a town. Use these words.*

- Focus pupils on the words in the box and check comprehension.
- Pupils draw a picture of their ideal town to include the places in the box. They write a label next to each feature. Make pairs or groups of four. Pupils compare their pictures and make sentences about what they have drawn, e.g. *There's a pet shop next to the hospital. The bookshop is between the park and the café.*
- Early finishers write sentences about their town in their notebooks.

Extra activities: see page T122 (if time)

Optional activity

- 'The eye test' episode from *Kid's Box 2 Interactive DVD* (The living room section). See pages 8–11 of the Teacher's booklet for the *Interactive DVD.*

Ending the lesson

- Write the six town words in scrambled letter order on the board (*park, shop, street, hospital, café, flat*). Pupils work in pairs and race to unscramble them. Check with the class by asking pupils to spell words out correctly.

OBJECTIVES: By the end of the lesson, pupils will have read a story and revised language from the unit.

• TARGET LANGUAGE

Key language: language from the unit

Additional language: *cinema, Dogzilla, Catzilla, daytime*

Revision: town vocabulary, prepositions, *monster, I'm coming, superhero, run, funny, help, goodbye*

• MATERIALS REQUIRED

Optional: *Kid's Box 2 Teacher's Resource Book* Unit 8 Extension worksheet 2 (page 54) and/or animated version of the Unit 8 story from *Kid's Box 2 Interactive DVD* (Suzy's room section)

Warmer

- Review the prepositions using a TPR game. Invite five pupils to the front and give them instructions, e.g. *(Name) stand in front of (name). (Name) stand behind (name). (Name) stand between (name) and (name). (Name) stand next to (name).* They arrange themselves according to your instructions. Repeat.

Story

PB59. ACTIVITY **11.** *Listen to the story.*

- Say *Open your Pupil's Books at page 59, please.* Elicit who they can see (Monty, Maskman, Simon, Suzy and a dog). Elicit where they are (in the living room). Set the pre-listening questions: *What's Dogzilla? Where's the cat?* Say *Listen and look.* Play the CD. Pupils listen and look. They check in pairs. Check with the class (A monster dog, Behind Monty). Elicit what they think Catzilla is (a monster cat). Play the CD again. Pupils listen and repeat. Encourage them to say it with intonation and feeling, especially the shrieks.
- Check comprehension by holding up your book, pointing to each picture in turn and asking, e.g. *What's the helicopter doing?* (flying). *Is it day or night?* (day). *Does Monty like cats?* (no). *Is there a dog behind Maskman?* (yes). Ask pupils who their superhero is. Ask them if it's Maskman.

CD 2, 53

Toys in the toy box,
Come alive.
Walk and talk,
On the count of five.
One, two, three, four, five.
SIMON: Aaagh! Look behind you! It's behind you!
SUZY: Ooooh! I can't look!

MASKMAN: Oh, no. It's 'Dogzilla', the monster dog.

MASKMAN: I'm coming, children.
CHILDREN: Maskman's our superhero.

MASKMAN: Aaagh! Monty! Look behind you! There's a cat! It's 'Catzilla'.
MONTY: Eeeek! Help! A cat!

MASKMAN: Ha ha ha!
MONTY: It isn't funny.

MONTY: Look! There's a dog. It's behind you.
MASKMAN: Eeeek! Help! There's a dog! It's 'Dogzilla'! Help!

PB59. ACTIVITY **12.** *Listen and say the number.*

- Focus pupils on the frames of the story again. Say *Listen to the CD and say the number of the picture.* Play the first one as an example. Elicit the number of the frame from the class (4). Play the rest of the CD. Pupils work in pairs and point to / whisper the number of the frame to their partner. Play the CD again. This time, stop after each section and elicit the number from a pair of pupils.

Key: 4, 1, 5, 6, 4, 3

CD 2, 54

MONTY: Eeeek! Help! A cat!
SIMON: Aaagh! Look behind you! It's behind you!
MONTY: It isn't funny!
MONTY: Look! There's a dog. It's behind you.
MASKMAN: Aaagh! Monty! Look behind you! There's a cat! It's 'Catzilla'.
MASKMAN: I'm coming, children.

AB59. MY PICTURE DICTIONARY.

- Say *Open your Activity Books at page 59, please.* Point to the word with missing vowels in the first square and the example answer. Elicit the word (*flat*). Say *Write the letters to complete the words. They are all places in a town.* Pupils work individually or in pairs to complete the words. Check answers.
- Pupils prepare the town stickers and lay them out on their desks in the correct order. Check around the class before they stick them in their books.

Key: 2 park, 3 shop, 4 hospital, 5 street, 6 café

Extra activities: see page T122 (if time)

AB59. MY PROGRESS.

- Focus pupils on the activity in their books. Say *Let's read the sentences together.* Read the first sentence. Focus pupils on what they did in Pupil's Book page 58 Activity 10. Elicit some sentences from pupils. Say *Good. You can talk about the town.* Read the second sentence and elicit what they drew and spoke about for Activity Book page 58 Activity 9. Say *Good. You can write about the town, too.*
- Pupils work in pairs. They take turns to point to a sentence in their books and to show each other or talk about what it says.
- Say *Now tick or cross the sentences.* Encourage pupils to practise so that they can tick both the statements and colour the star.

Optional activities

- *Teacher's Resource Book 2* Unit 8 Extension worksheet 2 (see pages 50 and 54).
- The animated version of the story from *Kid's Box 2 Interactive DVD* (Suzy's room section). See pages 41–45 of the Teacher's booklet for the *Interactive DVD.*

Ending the lesson

- Ask pupils which chant/song/game they'd like to do again from the unit. Do it together to end the lesson.

11 53 CD2 Listen to the story.

1
Aaagh! Look behind you. It's behind you!
Ooooh! I can't look!
2
Oh, no. It's 'Dogzilla', the monster dog.
School
3
I'm coming, children.
Maskman's our superhero.
4
Aaagh! Monty! Look behind you. There's a cat. It's 'Catzilla'!
Eeeek! Help! A cat!
5
Ha ha ha.
It isn't funny!
6
Look! There's a dog. It's behind you.
Eeeek! Help! There's a dog. It's 'Dogzilla'! Help!

12 54 CD2 Listen and say the number.

Marie's music — Animals in music

1 Look and say.

What's this?

It's a snake.

a frog	a spider	a fish	a bird	a snake	a horse

2 Listen and say the animal.

CD3 2

Now you!
Activity Book page 60

OBJECTIVES: By the end of the lesson, pupils will have matched animals to music and made a guitar.

• TARGET LANGUAGE
Key language: *They're (cats). It's a (cow).*
Additional language: *What's this? It's a (snake).*
Revision: *horse, frog, fish, bird, snake, spider, cat, cow*

• MATERIALS REQUIRED
Materials to make a guitar. Each pupil will need/need to bring a shoe box, glue, sticky tape, a ruler/length of wood, string/elastic bands (see Activity Book page 60, Activity 2).
Extra activity 2: yogurt pots, cocoa tins, wooden sticks, cotton wool, large paper and small material circles, sticky tape, elastic bands

Warmer

- Review animals using mime. Below are suggestions on how to mime each animal for the lesson. Tell or show these to the pupils and then they mime/copy them. Write the names of the animals on the board as you mime.
- Sheep: Pupils go down on all fours, huddled together with their heads down as if chewing grass quietly. Emphasise that sheep are still and quiet.
- Snakes: Pupils stand with hands joined over their heads. They do a full body sway/wriggle to imitate a snake.
- Spiders: Pupils use five fingers in a creeping movement, then their whole body, arms extended twisting and turning and swooping as though weaving a web.
- Cows: Similar to sheep, but bigger, occasionally making a mooing movement with their mouths, chewing grass slowly with a big jaw movement.
- Birds: Pupils stand with their hands fluttering at shoulder height as wings, nodding their heads with a little chirruping mouth in the shape of a beak.
- Horses: Pupils move their whole body, legs galloping (on the spot). Shoulders rocking backwards and forwards, hands in front of chest, as though holding reins. Heads up, looking at the horizon.
- Frogs: Pupils crouch down, ready to spring, hands between their knees, touching the floor next to their feet. They spring up and down on the spot.
- Cats: Pupils go down on all fours and move their arms and legs slowly and gently, making a meowing shape with their mouths.

Presentation

- Say *Open your Pupil's Books at page 60, please.* Point to the picture of Marie and say *This is Marie's music.* Say *Today's lesson is about Animals in music.* Point to the instruments and notes in the background of the page.

PB60. ACTIVITY 1. *Look and say.*

- Point to the photograph of the snake. Point to the first speech bubble and say *What's this?* Pupils reply as in the example *It's a snake.* Say *Look and say.* Pupils ask and answer about the other animals in the pictures in pairs. Monitor and help as necessary. Practise each question and answer with the whole class.

Key: 2 It's a frog, 3 It's a spider, 4 It's a horse, 5 It's a bird, 6 It's a fish

PB60. ACTIVITY 2. *Listen and say the animal.*

- Explain that pupils are going to listen to some music and they must think of the animal from the photos that it represents. Say *Write numbers 1 to 6 in your notebook. Listen and write the animal.* Play the CD. Pause after each one for pupils to think and write the name of the animal they are reminded of. Tell pupils that there is no 'right' answer. They compare answers in pairs. Play the CD again, pause after each piece of music and elicit ideas.

Key: Possible answers: 1 bird, 2 horse, 3 fish, 4 snake, 5 spider, 6 frog

CD 3, 02

1. Excerpt from *Carnival of the Animals No 10* by Saint Saens (birds)
2. Excerpt from *William Tell* by Rossini (horses)
3. Excerpt from *Carnival of the Animals No 7* by Saint Saens (fish)
4. Excerpt from *Ottoman Sands* by Andreas Panayi (snake)
5. Excerpt from *Spider's Web Smail* by audionetwork (spider)
6. Excerpt from *Jelly and Ice-Cream 3* by Barrie Gleddon (frog)

AB60. ACTIVITY 1. *Listen and say the animal.*

- Say *Open your Activity Books at page 60, please.* Focus pupils on the six photographs and elicit the names of the animals. Say *Listen and say the animal. Look at the examples.* Point to the two speech bubbles *It's a bird.* and *They're cats.* Talk about the singular and plural sentences (remind pupils to use the plural for more than one animal). Play the first item on the CD and elicit the answer to make sure pupils know what they have to do. Play the rest of the CD. Pupils whisper the answer to each other.
- Play the CD again, pausing after each animal noise to elicit the answer. Insist on complete sentences. Play the CD one last time and have pupils do the appropriate animal mimes from the Warmer.

Key: 1 It's an elephant, 2 They're sheep, 3 They're cats, 4 They're cows, 5 They're frogs, 6 They're birds

CD 3, 03

1. [sound effect – elephant]
2. [sound effect – sheep]
3. [sound effect – cat]
4. [sound effect – cow]
5. [sound effect – frog]
6. [sound effect – bird]

AB60. ACTIVITY 2. *Make a guitar.*

- Tell pupils they are going to make a guitar. Point to the photos at the bottom of the page. Make sure that pupils have all the materials they need, as shown in the first photo. If you don't have enough for each pupil, they can make a guitar in pairs or small groups. Tell pupils to look at the photos to see how to make the guitar or make the guitar along with the class.

Extra activities: see page T123 (if time)

Ending the lesson

- Pupils work in pairs. Pupil A mimes an animal and Pupil B guesses, e.g. *It's a snake.* Pupils take turns to mime and guess. Choose confident pupils to come to the front of the class to do their mimes for the rest of the pupils to guess.

OBJECTIVES: By the end of the lesson, pupils will have listened to dialogues with commands and practised giving commands themselves.

• TARGET LANGUAGE

Key language: *balloon, bin, grass, road, traffic lights/lights, rubbish, Stop! Don't… (cross/drop/walk). Listen! We can't (play football on the road).*

Additional language: *Let's (go to the park/play football). This is nice. At the park.*

Revision: *Oh, sorry. Thank you. Oops! OK. Not good. Come on! red, green, man*

• MATERIALS REQUIRED

Large picture of a street showing a road, traffic lights and a litter bin (if available). A picture of a park showing some grass. A balloon.

Extra activity 1: Duplicate photos or flashcards of the following places in a town/features of a street: a park, a street crossing, a bin (one picture each or one for each pair of pupils).

Warmer

- Use photographs, drawings on the board or the pictures on Pupil's Book page 61 to teach *road, grass, traffic lights* and *bin*. Present *balloon* using a real balloon and *rubbish/litter* by throwing some wrappings/paper on the floor. Say each word for pupils to repeat chorally. Choose volunteers to say the words on their own.
- Draw a simple traffic light with red and green lights and elicit what the red light means (stop) and what the green light means (go). Explain that in Britain, pedestrian crossings have lights in the shape of a man walking.

PB61. ACTIVITY 3. *Listen and say the number.*

- Say *Open your Pupil's Books at page 61, please*. Point to Trevor and say *This lesson is about Trevor's values. Today it's 'Your town'.* Hold up your book. Point to picture 1, point to and read the sign *park*. Repeat with the sign in picture 2 *Do not walk on the grass!*
- Say *Listen and say the number.* Stop the CD after each dialogue for pupils to have time to think about their answers. Repeat. Pupils check in pairs. Check answers with the whole class.

Key: 1 Picture 4, 2 Picture 3, 3 Picture 2, 4 Picture 1

CD 3, 04

1.
Don't drop that old balloon there!
Oh, sorry.
Find a bin or take it home. It's not good to drop rubbish.

2.
Stop! Don't cross! The man on the lights is red.
Oh, thank you.
Listen! When there's no green man, you can't cross.

3.
This is nice. Let's sit here and eat our lunch.
Stop! Don't walk on the grass. Look!
Oops! Sorry.

4.
Come on! Let's play football.
No, not here. We can't play football on the road.
OK. Let's go to the park.
OK.

PB61. ACTIVITY 4. *Ask and answer.*

- Focus pupils on Activity 4. Point to the first speech bubble and say *Don't drop rubbish.* Pupils read the answer *Picture 4* and point to the picture in their books. Get a confident pupil to give another example. Use the other language forms e.g. *We/you can't..., It's not good to…* to give examples. Say *Ask and answer.*
- Pupils take turns in pairs to say sentences and match them with the pictures e.g. Pupil A: *Don't walk on the grass!* Pupil B: *Picture 2,* Pupil B: *We can't play football on the road.* Pupil A: *Picture 1.* Ask volunteers to say their sentences for the class. The other pupils point to the correct picture.

AB61. ACTIVITY 3. *Read and circle.*

- Say *Open your Activity Books at page 61, please.* Read the example sentence and say *Which one: red or green?* Pupils say Green. Say *Read and circle.* Pupils work individually to circle the correct option and then check their answers in pairs. Go through the answers with the class.

Key: 2 on the road, 3 Don't walk , 4 rubbish, 5 red

AB61. ACTIVITY 4. *Look and write 'can' or 'can't'.*

- Point to each picture and ask *Where is it? What can you see?* Pupils respond, e.g. *The street. There's a bin.* Say *Look and write 'can' or 'can't* . Nod your head for *can* and shake it for *can't.* Pupils check their answers in pairs. Check with the whole class.

Key: 1 I can put my rubbish here. 2 I can't sit here. 3 I can't cross the road here (the light is showing red). 4 I can play here.

Extra activities: see page T123 (if time)

Ending the lesson

- Pupils come to the front to act out the dialogues from Pupil's Book, Activity 3. Pupils put their hands up to say in which location the dialogue takes place.

3 Listen and say the number.

CD3 4

1

2

3

4

4 Ask and answer.

Don't drop rubbish!

Picture four.

Vocabulary

balloon bin grass road rubbish traffic lights

Review

5 6 7 8

1 Listen and say the letter.

CD3 5

a

b

c

d

e

f

2 Read and answer.

Nick and Tony are at the farm. They're looking at the . Next to the sheep there are three . They're eating 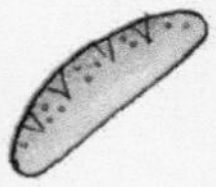. A  is . Tony's very .

1. Where is Nick?
2. What are they looking at?
3. How many ducks are there?
4. What's the frog doing?

OBJECTIVES: By the end of the lesson, pupils will have reviewed language from Units 5–8.

• TARGET LANGUAGE
Key language: vocabulary and language from Units 5–8
Revision: animals, food, family, present continuous

• MATERIALS REQUIRED
Extra activity 1: Flashcards of new words from Units 5–8

Warmer

- Display a selection of eight flashcards of new items from Units 5 to 8 (e.g. *cousin* (Lenny), *milk, eggs, duck, lizard, park, flat, mirror*). Check comprehension by eliciting a sentence for each word (e.g. *My cousin's name is Elena. There's a mirror in my bedroom. I have milk for breakfast.* etc.) Make pairs. Pupils write the words in alphabetical order, as quickly as possible. Elicit the words in the correct order.

PB62. ACTIVITY **1.** *Listen and say the letter.*

- Say *Open your Pupil's Books at page 62, please.* Point at each picture in turn and elicit the letter and what pupils can see (e.g. a – two girls and a goat).
- Play the first item on the CD and elicit the correct letter (d). Play the rest of the CD. Pupils listen, point and whisper the letter to their partner each time. Play the CD again. Stop after each sentence or dialogue and elicit the answer.

Key: d, b, e, c, a, f

CD 3, 05

We're having chicken and chips for dinner.

I love horses.
So do I.

I'm kicking a ball.

We're having fish and chips for dinner.

I love goats.
I don't.

I'm hitting a ball.

PB62. ACTIVITY **2.** *Read and answer.*

- Focus pupils on the picture and on the text. Remind them that they did a similar activity in Unit 6 (refer them to Pupil's Book page 43, Activity 8). Pupils read the story in pairs, working out what the picture words are. Check by going around the class asking pupils to read sections aloud. Don't force pupils to read aloud if they don't want to.
- Check comprehension of the questions. Pupils answer the questions individually in their notebooks in full sentences. Monitor and help as necessary. Check answers in open pairs.
- Ask further questions to check comprehension: *What are the ducks eating? (They're eating bread.) Where are the ducks? (They're in the water.) Where are the sheep? (They're next to the ducks.) Is Tony happy or sad? (He's happy.)*

Key: 1 He's at the farm. 2 They're looking at the sheep. 3 There are three ducks. 4 It's/The frog's jumping.

AB62. ACTIVITY **1.** *Find and write the words.*

- Say *Open your Activity Books at page 62. Look at the word search.* Focus pupils on the two examples and the columns of writing lines to the left and right of the puzzle. Make sure pupils understand they need to write the words they find in the two categories. Pupils work in pairs. They find and circle the words and then copy them into the appropriate columns. Monitor pupils and help or guide where necessary. Check with the class.

Key: 'food' words: breakfast, eggs, juice, dinner, chips; 'family' words: grandmother, mummy, daddy, sister, grandfather

AB62. ACTIVITY **2.** *Listen and write the number.* **[YLE]**

- Focus pupils on the pictures and elicit what they can see (the Star family, animals, shops). Play number 1 on the CD and point out the example answer. Play the rest of the CD. Pupils write the numbers to match what they hear with the pictures. They check in pairs. Play the CD again. Check with the class.

Key:
3, 1, 6
5, 4, 2

CD 3, 06

1. Are you Stella's mum?
   No, I'm her grandma.
2. Dad, can I have some orange juice, please?
   Yes, here you are.
3. What's Stella's mum doing?
   She's sleeping.
4. Which animals can you see?
   I can see two ducks and a chicken.
5. The café is between the park and the pet shop.
6. The lizard is in front of the ducks.

Extra activities: see page T123 (if time)

Ending the lesson

- Pupils close their books. Play a Memory game. Pupils say what they can remember about the picture in Pupil's Book page 62 Activity 2. Elicit sentences from different pupils.

OBJECTIVES: By the end of the lesson, pupils will have reviewed language from Units 5–8 and learnt a chant.

• TARGET LANGUAGE

Key language: vocabulary and language from Units 5–8
Revision: question words, prepositions

• MATERIALS REQUIRED

Dice for each group of three or four pupils, counter or small coin for each pupil
Extra activity 1: a selection of 12 flashcards from the new words in Units 5–8, two rolled up newspapers
Optional: *Kid's Box 2 Interactive DVD*: Stella's room Quiz 2

Warmer

- Review prepositions by hiding five or six soft toy animals (or flashcards of animals) around the classroom (make sure the position of each animal can be described with known language), e.g. put a cat under a table, a dog in the cupboard (leave the door open), a mouse between two of the pupils' bags. Pupils put their hands up when they can say a sentence about where one of the animals is. Write the sentences on the board.
- Move the toys and repeat the activity. This time pupils write all the sentences in their notebook. Check with the class.

PB63. ACTIVITY 3. *Play the game. Answer the question.*

- Say *Open your Pupil's Books at page 63, please.* Tell pupils they are going to play a game, similar to the one on Pupil's Book page 33.
- Read the question and answer at the top of the page and say *In this game you answer the question 'Where's the star?'* Point at some of the squares on the board and ask individual pupils *Where's the star?* They respond, e.g. *It's on the table, next to the pineapple.*
- Demonstrate how to play the game. Take out a dice (or a spinner, if the pupils studied *Kid's Box 1*) and a counter or coin. Hold up your book and put the counter on the Start square (bottom left). Say *This is the Start. You throw the dice…* Throw the dice and show pupils how to move their counter along the board, e.g. *Look! I've got a five. One … (moving your counter) two … three … four… five. You ask 'Where's the star?' I say 'It's on the hospital!' I stay on this square. … Then it's Yana's turn. And then it's Thomas's turn. Now it's my turn again.* Throw the dice and move your counter again, e.g. to the square with the star on the table. Look thoughtful and say *Where's the star? Oh. I don't know.* Move your counter back to the square you were on before. Say *I don't know. I move back to where I was … one, two.* If you say the word you stay. If you don't say the word, you move back. If you land on an arrow square you can stay where you are without saying where the star is. Point at the Finish square and say *This is the Finish. The first person here is the winner! Hooray!*
- Review the useful language for games and write it on the board, if necessary, e.g. *It's my turn. It's your turn. I've got a (five). Pass me the dice, please. Is this my counter? I'm the winner.* Pupils practise saying the sentences chorally.
- Make groups of three or four pupils. They need one dice per group and a coin or counter for each pupil. Groups play the game. Monitor and check they are speaking English and asking each other *Where's the star?*. If you wish, set a rule that anyone you hear speaking in their own language misses a turn. Encourage pupils to use the language for games. The winner is the first pupil to get to the finish or the pupil who is furthest along the board after a certain amount of time (e.g. ten minutes

AB63. ACTIVITY 3. *Read and draw lines.*

- Say *Open your Activity Books at page 63, please.* Elicit what pupils can see (bedroom lamp, clock, goat, spider, baby, mother). Focus pupils on the first sentence: *The baby is behind the door.* Pupils look at the example line from the picture of the baby to the right place in the bedroom. They work in pairs. They read the sentences (silently) and draw lines to position the things correctly. Monitor pupils and prompt where necessary. Correct as a class.

AB63. ACTIVITY 4. *Listen and complete. Chant.*

- Focus pupils on the picture and elicit what some of the children are doing and what pupils can see in the picture. Play the CD. Pupils listen and point to the children in the picture. Pupils work in pairs and try and put the right question words in the sentences. Play the CD again for pupils to check. Check using open pairs around the class (Pupil 1 asks, Pupil 2 answers). Teach the chant. Pupils stand and say it as a class.

Key: 2 What, 3 Whose, 4 How old, 5 Where, 6 What, 7 How many, 8 Which, 9 who

CD 3, 07

Who is that?
That's my brother, Paul.
What's he doing?
He's catching a ball.
Whose ball is it?
It's my cousin Nick's.
How old is he?
He's very young.
He's only six.
Where is he now?
He's in the hall.
What's he doing?
He's throwing his ball.
How many balls have you got?
I don't know! We've got a lot!
Which one's your favourite, red or blue?
I don't know!
And who are you?

Extra activities: see page T123 (if time)

Optional evaluation:

- Quiz 2 from *Kid's Box 2 Interactive DVD* (Stella's room section). This quiz can be done as a whole-class activity or as a team competition. See pages 39 and 40 of the Teacher's booklet for the *Interactive DVD.*

Ending the lesson

- Pupils work in groups of three. They need one picture dictionary between three. They use a book (or paper) to cover the words from Unit 5. They take turns to say what each picture is. They look and check. They then cover the pictures from Unit 6 and take turns to say the words. They choose which to cover for Units 7 and 8 (words or pictures).
- Talk about the *can do* statements from Units 5–8 with pupils and elicit examples from volunteer pupils for each one.
- Ask pupils which lessons, topics and/or activities were their favourites.

3 Play the game. Answer the question.

Where's the star?

It's in front of the pet shop.

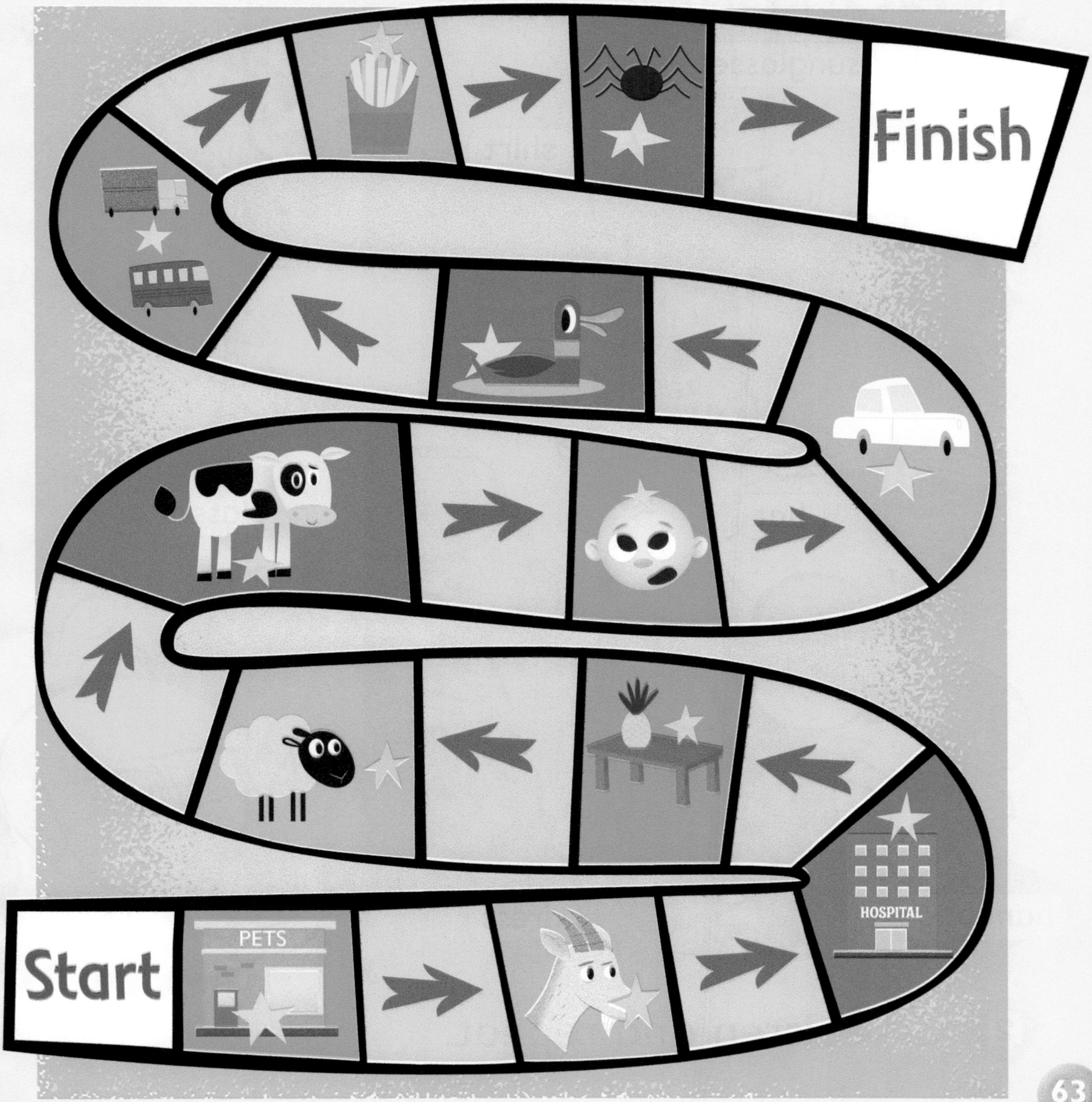

9 Our clothes

1 8 CD3 Listen and answer.

2 9 CD3 Listen and repeat.

OBJECTIVES: By the end of the lesson, pupils will have learned to talk about what they are wearing.

• TARGET LANGUAGE

Key language: *dress, handbag, sunglasses/glasses, hat, shirt, jeans, watch, gold*

Additional language: *fashion show*

Revision: clothes, colours, adjectives, *wearing, lizard*

• MATERIALS REQUIRED

Flashcards: (clothes) 79–84

Kid's Box 1 Flashcards: (clothes) 66–71 (or pictures): a jacket, shoes, a skirt, socks, trousers, a T-shirt

Extra activity 1: One section of the text from the Pupil's Book activity written on a large piece of paper or on the board. *Now here's Meera. She's wearing a short brown skirt and an orange jacket. She's wearing long yellow socks and green shoes. Thank you, Meera.*

Optional: *Kid's Box Teacher's Resource Book 2* Unit 9 Reinforcement worksheet 1 (page 57)

Warmer

- Review the clothes (*jacket, shoes, skirt, socks, trousers, T-shirt*), using pictures or the flashcards. Show each one and elicit the name. Display the flashcards around the edge of the board. Make a circling gesture with your hands and say *These are all …* Wait for pupils to say *Clothes.* Check for correct pronunciation. Write *Clothes* in the centre of the board.

Presentation

- Elicit/teach the new clothes vocabulary, using the flashcards. Show each flashcard in turn and elicit/say the word. Pupils repeat in chorus and then in groups, loudly, softly and so on. Stick the flashcards on the board (picture side) around the mind map to show they are also clothes, apart from *handbag* and *sunglasses.* Put these at the side of the board. Point to each new flashcard in turn. Pupils chorus the word. Turn the flashcard to show the word side. Pupils chorus the word again.

PB64. ACTIVITY 1. *Listen and answer.*

- Set the scene, but pupils don't open their books. Say *Listen. The Star children and their friends are wearing different clothes.* Set the pre-listening questions: *What are Simon and Alex wearing? What's Meera wearing? What's Suzy wearing? What's Lenny wearing?* Play the CD. Pupils listen for the answers. They check in pairs. Say *Open your Pupil's Books at page 64, please. Listen again and check.* Play the CD again as pupils are checking. Use the picture to teach *watch, sunglasses.* Elicit the difference between *glasses* and *sunglasses.* Check comprehension by asking, e.g. *What colour is Suzy's hat? Who's got grey trousers?*
- Say *Can you find the hidden star? Show your partner.* Check with the class (on Suzy's shoe). Pupils say *Here it is.*

CD 3, 08

STELLA: Hello and welcome to the Star Fashion show. Here are Simon and Alex. They're wearing black shirts, blue jeans and white shoes. Simon's got small black sunglasses on his head. Alex is wearing a new yellow watch. Thank you, Simon. Thank you, Alex.

Now here's Meera. She's wearing a short brown skirt and an orange jacket. She's wearing long yellow socks and green shoes. Thank you, Meera.

Now we've got Suzy, the star of the show. She's wearing a long purple dress and big pink shoes. She's wearing a nice big red hat and she's got a beautiful gold handbag. Thank you, Suzy.

Now here's Lenny. He's wearing grey trousers, black shoes, and a red T-shirt with a green lizard on. What a beautiful T-shirt! Thank you, Lenny.

PB64. ACTIVITY 2. *Listen and repeat.*

- Say *Now let's do Activity 2. Listen, point to the clothes and repeat.* Play the CD. Pupils repeat the words in chorus, in groups and then individually (choose pupils at random).

CD 3, 09

Dress, sunglasses, handbag, hat, shirt, jeans

AB64. ACTIVITY 1. *Listen and join the dots.*

- Say *Open your Activity Books at page 64, please.* Say *Listen for the words. Join the dots to make a picture.* Play the CD. Pupils join the words. They check in pairs. Check with the class (A dress).

CD 3, 10

Shirt, handbag, glasses, watch, skirt, hat, sock, T-shirt, jeans, shoe, dress, shirt

AB64. ACTIVITY 2. *Follow the 'clothes' words.*

- Pupils work in pairs and draw a line through the clothes words. Pairs check with pairs. Check with the class. Pupils answer the questions.

Key: Clothes (13): watch, shoes, glasses, socks, jeans, T-shirt, hat, trousers, dress, skirt, jacket, shirt, handbag. Animals: lizard, frog, sheep, goat, cow, spider. Food: cake, meat, burger, carrots, ice cream, bread.

Extra activities: see page T123 (if time)

Optional activity

- *Teacher's Resource Book 2* Unit 9 Reinforcement worksheet 1 pages 56–57.

Ending the lesson

- Display the clothes flashcards, plus *handbag* and *glasses* (word side). Pupils stand up. Say, e.g. *Stella says Point to the handbag.* Pupils point. Say *Point to the shirt.* Pupils don't point. Continue repeating some of the clothes quickly, one after another, to keep pupils active.

OBJECTIVES: By the end of the lesson, pupils will have practised talking about things they wear and learnt a chant.

- **TARGET LANGUAGE**

Key language: *I'm/You're/He's/She's/They're wearing ..., put (it/them) on, take (it/them) off*
Additional language: *code*
Revision: clothes vocabulary, *handbag, watch, glasses, wear, with,* adjectives, colours

- **MATERIALS REQUIRED**

Photocopiable 9 (see page T109), one for each pupil, scissors, crayons, a hat and a pair of sunglasses
Optional: *Kid's Box Teacher's Resource Book 2* Unit 9 Reinforcement worksheet 2 (page 58)

Warmer

- Pupils stand up. They look at each other's clothes for 30 seconds. Then they stand back to back and take turns to say what the other is wearing. Demonstrate the activity with a pupil, using *You're wearing …*

PB65. ACTIVITY 3. *Listen and point. Chant.*

- Say *Open your Pupil's Books at page 65, please.* Elicit the clothes they can see. Say *Listen and point.* Play the CD. Pupils listen and point to the clothes in the pictures (or the words). Play the CD again in sections. Pupils repeat, pointing to clothes or touching theirs as they say the words. Pupils stand and do the chant as a class without the CD. Divide the class into three groups. Groups take turns to do the chant. Vote for the best one.

CD 3, 11

Handbags, glasses,
Jackets and shirts.
T-shirts, trousers,
Dresses and skirts.
Hats, jeans,
Shoes and socks.
Put them on,
They're in the box.

PRACTICE

- Show pupils the hat you have brought to class and say, e.g. *This is my new hat.* Put it on and while you are doing so say *I'm putting on my hat. I'm putting it on.* Take the hat off and say or elicit *I'm taking off my hat.* Say *I'm taking …* and elicit the pronoun *it*. Complete the sentence by saying *off*. Repeat this process with the sunglasses. (*These are my new sunglasses. I'm putting on my sunglasses. I'm putting them on. etc.*).
- Get the class to give you instructions in chorus, as follows: *Put your hat on. Take your hat off. Put your sunglasses on. Take your sunglasses off.* Repeat several times until pupils are confident with the language. Every time they tell you to do something make a sentence in the present continuous with a pronoun (e.g. for the hat: *I'm putting it on. I'm taking it off.* For the sunglasses: *I'm putting them on. I'm taking them off.*)
- Pupils stand up. They mime putting on and taking off various items of clothing, as you give the instructions below. Encourage pupils to say the sentences on the right chorally as they mime. They can then repeat the drill in pairs (one gives instructions, the other mimes and makes a sentence with *it* or *them*, as appropriate).

Put your hat on.	*I'm putting it on.*
Take your shoes off.	*I'm taking them off.*
Put your dress on.	*I'm putting it on.*
Take your socks off.	*I'm taking them off.*
Take your jacket off.	*I'm taking it off.*
Put your glasses on.	*I'm putting them on.*
Take your shirt off.	*I'm taking it off.*
Put your jeans on.	*I'm putting them on.*
Take your watch off.	*I'm taking it off.*
Put your skirt on.	*I'm putting it on.*

PB65. ACTIVITY 4. *Listen and correct.*

- Focus pupils on the example statements in the speech bubbles. Say *Listen.* Play number 1 on the CD (the first false statement). Check pupils know what to do. Play each sentence in turn. Pupils whisper the response to their partner. Play the CD again. This time, pause before asking the class to respond as a group. Elicit the response from smaller groups and individuals too.

Key: 2 No, one boy is wearing jeans. 3 No, one girl is wearing red shoes. 4 No, four children are wearing glasses. 5 No, three girls are wearing a dress. 6 No, there are four handbags. 7 No, one boy is wearing short trousers. 8 No, there are four hats.

CD 3, 12

1. There's a big box with toys.
2. Three boys are wearing jeans.
3. Two girls are wearing red shoes.
4. Five children are wearing glasses.
5. One girl's wearing a dress.
6. There are six handbags.
7. Two boys are wearing short trousers.
8. There are five hats.

Photocopiable 9: see pages T99 and T109

AB65. ACTIVITY 3. *Write the words and colour the picture.*

- Say *Open your Activity Books at page 65, please.* Elicit what pupils can see (a code). Check pupils know what to do using the example word (I'm). Pupils work individually and complete the writing, using the code. They check in pairs. Check with the class by asking different pupils to read out sections of the sentence. Check understanding of *new*. Pupils colour the picture according to the instructions.

Key: I'm wearing blue jeans, a yellow shirt, grey socks, black shoes and a new red hat.

AB65. ACTIVITY 4. *Describe your clothes.*

- Pupils work in pairs and take turns to orally describe their clothes to their partner. Pupils then individually write a description of their clothes. Monitor and help where needed.

Extra activity: see page T123 (if time)

Optional activity

- *Teacher's Resource Book 2* Unit 9 Reinforcement worksheet 2 pages 56 and 58.

Ending the lesson

- Do the chant again. This time pupils mime putting the clothes on as they say them (rather than just pointing to them).

3 Listen and point. Chant.

11 CD3

Handbags, glasses,
Jackets and shirts.
T-shirts, trousers,
Dresses and skirts.
Hats, jeans,
Shoes and socks.
Put them on,
They're in the box.

4 Listen and correct.

12 CD3

There's a big box with toys.

No, there's a big box with clothes.

Vocabulary

dress glasses handbag hat jeans shirt

5 Listen and point.

CD3 13

6 Listen and repeat.

CD3 14

Grammar

Have you got … ? Yes, I have. No, I haven't.
Has he/she got … ? Yes, he/she has. No, he/she hasn't.

OBJECTIVES: By the end of the lesson, pupils will have asked and answered about ownership using *have got.*

• TARGET LANGUAGE

Key language: *Have you got … ? Has he/she got … ? Yes, I have. No, I haven't. I've got/We've got … Yes, he/she has. No, he/she hasn't.*

Additional language: *a good life*

Revision: *family, friends, garden, flowers, trees, animals, car, bus, cake, milk, So do I, can't drive, superhero*

• MATERIALS REQUIRED

School objects

Optional: *Kid's Box Teacher's Resource Book 2* Unit 9 Extension worksheet 1 (page 59),

Kid's Box 2 Language Portfolio page 12

Warmer

- Revise *have got.* Ask a pupil, e.g. *Have you got a blue crayon?* Prompt the pupil to respond truthfully, e.g. *No, I haven't.* If it's *Yes, I have*, the pupil gives it to you. Continue around the class, sometimes asking for objects you know pupils don't have. After asking a pupil and the pupil's response, turn to the class and say, e.g. *Has he got a bag?* The class responds, e.g. *No, he hasn't.* Continue, making sure pupils get practice of *I/she/he* and positive and negative.

PB66. ACTIVITY 5. *Listen and point.*

- Say *Open your Pupil's Books at page 66, please.* Elicit who and what they can see. Elicit *garden, flowers, trees.* Say *Listen and point to what the toys have got.* Check it's only what they've got (ownership). Play the CD. Pupils listen and point. Play the CD again for pupils to make sure. Play the CD, stopping where indicated below // for pupils to respond. Personalise the activity. Ask pupils, e.g. *Have you got a garden? Have you got a dog? Have you got a car?* Encourage pupils to ask you questions as well.

Key: nice family, friends (Trevor), house, garden, big car, superhero clothes (Maskman), jacket and glasses (Marie), black glasses (Maskman), dog (Trevor).

CD 3, 13

Toys in the toy box,
Come alive.
Walk and talk,
On the count of five.
One, two, three, four, five.

TREVOR: You know, Maskman, we've got a good life. We've got a nice family and we've got a lot of friends. //

MASKMAN: I know, Trevor, and we've got a house and a garden with lots of trees and beautiful flowers. //

MARIE: Yes, a lot of toys haven't got a house or a garden …

MASKMAN: Or a car. I've got a big car. Have you got a car, Trevor? //

TREVOR: No, I haven't got a car. I can't drive.

MASKMAN: I've got superhero clothes. Have you got superhero clothes, Trevor? //

TREVOR: No, I haven't. I'm not a superhero.

MONTY: Marie's a doctor. She's got a long white jacket and glasses. //

MASKMAN: Yes, I've got black glasses, too. //

TREVOR: Yes, Maskman, we've got a good life. We've got a nice dog too. Look, there she is. //

MASKMAN: Aaaghh!! … And she's got a big mouth.

OTHERS: Ha ha ha!

PB66. ACTIVITY 6. *Listen and repeat.*

- Say *Now, let's listen and repeat the words.* Play the CD. Pupils repeat in chorus and then in groups and pairs.

CD 3, 14

TREVOR: We've got a nice family and we've got a lot of friends.

MASKMAN: Have you got superhero clothes, Trevor?

TREVOR: No, I haven't. I'm not a superhero.

MONTY: Marie's a doctor. She's got a long white jacket and glasses.

AB66. ACTIVITY 5. *Look and write.*

- Say *Open your Activity Books at page 66, please.* Focus pupils on the example. Follow the line through the maze to find what the first child has got. Point to the completed sentence. Pupils work individually to follow the lines from the children to the objects. They check in pairs. Check with the class. Pupils then complete the sentences at the bottom of the page. Monitor to help if necessary.

Key: I've got a robot, a dress and a bird. I've got a camera, a shirt and a phone. I've got a doll, a handbag and a duck.

Extra activities: see page T123 (if time)

Optional activity

- *Teacher's Resource Book 2* Unit 9 Extension worksheet 1 (see pages 56 and 59).

Language Portfolio

- Pupils complete page 12 of *Kid's Box 2 Language Portfolio (My favourite clothes).* Help with new language as necessary.

Ending the lesson

- Choose eight classroom objects: ruler, pencil, bag, book, etc. Hold them up in turn, saying *I've got a book, a bag, a ruler, a pencil …* Hide them from the class. In pairs, pupils try and remember the objects you had and anything else about them. Elicit from pairs, e.g. *You've got a ruler. It's blue.* Show objects as they are mentioned.

OBJECTIVES: By the end of the lesson, pupils will have had more practice talking about ownership and will have sung a song.

• TARGET LANGUAGE
Key language: I've got/I haven't got ... Have you got?
Revision: colours, clothes, adjectives, *garden, house, toy, mouse, car, glasses, superhero, hair, nose*

• MATERIALS REQUIRED
Extra activity 1: Flashcards: (clothes) 79–84
Kid's Box 1 Flashcards (clothes): 66–71 (or pictures): a jacket, shoes, a skirt, socks, trousers, a T-shirt
Optional: *Kid's Box Teacher's Resource Book 2* Unit 9 song worksheet (page 61)

Warmer

- Review colours and adjectives. Say, e.g. *I can see something in the classroom. It's small, blue and beautiful and it's under a chair.* Pupils guess (a bag). Continue with other objects, including clothes.

PB67. ACTIVITY 7. *Listen and point. Sing.*

- Say *Open your Pupil's Books at page 67, please.* Elicit what pupils can see. Say *Listen and point.* Play the CD. Pupils point to the objects in the song. Play the CD again. Encourage pupils to sing.

CD 3, 15

MARIE: I've got a big garden.
I've got a big house.
I've got a good friend,
A small toy mouse.
I've got you, Monty.
I've got you.
MONTY: Oh, Marie!

MASKMAN: I've got a black mask,
And a big blue car.
I've got black glasses,
I'm the Maskman star,
And I've got you, Monty.
I've got you.
MONTY: Oh, Maskman!

TREVOR: I haven't got
Superhero clothes.
I've got purple hair,
And a big, green nose,
And I've got you, Monty.
I've got you.
MONTY: Oh, Trevor!
MARIE, MASKMAN, TREVOR: I've got you, Monty.
I've got you.

CD 3, 16

Now sing the song again. (Karaoke version)

PB67. ACTIVITY 8. *Ask and answer.*

- Pupils work in groups. They take it in turns to ask each other *have got* questions, like the ones in the speech bubbles. Monitor and make sure pupils answer Yes, *I have. / No, I haven't.*

AB67. ACTIVITY 6. *Look at the pictures. Look at the letters. Write the words.* **[YLE]**

- Say *Open your Activity Books at page 67, please.* Point to the picture of the T-shirt and to the scrambled letters inside the clothes hanger on the right. Ask a volunteer to read the example answer. Say *Look at the pictures. Move the letters in the hangers.* Copy the letters in the order they appear inside the first hanger on the board and show pupils how they make the word *T-shirt*, by crossing out each letter as you write the word with the letters in the correct order below.
- Pupils work individually to solve the rest of the anagrams. Elicit the answers and call volunteers to write the words on the board. Check spelling carefully.

Key: 1 hat, 2 dress, 3 handbag, 4 jeans, 5 glasses

Extra activities: see page T123–T124 (if time)

Optional activity

- Pupils complete the Unit 9 song worksheet from *Teacher's Resource Book 2* (see pages 56 and 61 of the *Teacher's Resource Book*).

Ending the lesson

- Sing the song again with pupils. They mime the actions as they sing.

7 Listen and point. Sing.

CD3 15

I've got a big garden,
I've got a big house.
I've got a good friend,
A small toy mouse.
I've got you, Monty.
I've got you.

Oh, Marie!

I've got a black mask,
And a big blue car.
I've got black glasses,
I'm the Maskman star,
And I've got you, Monty.
I've got you.

Oh, Maskman!

I haven't got
Superhero clothes.
I've got purple hair,
And a big green nose,
And I've got you, Monty.
I've got you.

Oh, Trevor!

I've got you, Monty.
I've got you.

8 Ask and answer.

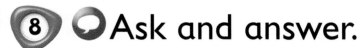

Have you got a garden?

Yes, I have.

9 17 CD3 Monty's phonics

seven

sheep

shop

Seven sheep are sleeping in a shop!

10 Ask and answer.

Ben

Has Ben got a small black cat?

No, he hasn't.

OBJECTIVES: By the end of the lesson, pupils will have learned to identify and say the phonemes s /s/ and sh /ʃ/ at the beginning, middle and end of words and had more practice with listening.

• TARGET LANGUAGE

Key language: the phonemes /s/ and /ʃ/ as in *seven, sleep, sheep, shop*

Revision: colours, adjectives, family

• MATERIALS REQUIRED

Flashcards: (clothes) 79–84

Kid's Box 1 Flashcards: (clothes) 66–71 (or pictures): a jacket, shoes, a skirt, socks, trousers, a T-shirt

Extra activity 2: Dark bag with eight classroom objects inside, e.g. ruler, eraser

Optional: *Kid's Box 2 Interactive DVD: The living room* 'The eye test' episode (if not used in Unit 8)

Warmer

- Elicit the clothes, using the flashcards. Reveal each one slowly (word side). When pupils say it, stick it on the board. Display them at random.

PB68. ACTIVITY **9.** *Monty's phonics*

- Say *Open your Pupil's Books at page 68, please.* Point to the small pictures and say them, emphasizing the sounds /s/ and /ʃ/. Pupils practise pronunciation of each word. Remind pupils that the plural of *sheep* is *sheep*. Point at the large picture and say *How many sheep are there? (Seven) Where are the sheep? (In a shop) What are they doing? (Sleeping)*. Say *Now listen to Monty, point and repeat.*
- Play the CD. Pupils listen and repeat the sounds, words, and sentence using the same tone and speed as Monty.
- Pupils repeat the tongue twister as a class. Do it more and more quickly. Pupils try saying the tongue twister as fast as they can. Invite volunteers to say it to the class.
  Write the tongue twister on the board and elicit the /ʃ/ sounds. Underline them. Focus pupils on the flashcards on the board and ask which words have the /ʃ/ sound (shirt, shoes, T-shirt) and which have the /s/ sound (dress, glasses, jeans, skirt, socks, trousers).

Key: Seven sheep are sleeping in a shop.

CD 3, 17

MONTY: Hi, I'm Monty! Repeat after me!
/s/, /s/, seven
/ʃ/, /ʃ/, sheep
/ʃ/, /ʃ/, shop
Seven sheep are sleeping in a shop!
Seven sheep are sleeping in a shop!
Seven sheep are sleeping in a shop!

PB68. ACTIVITY **10.** *Ask and answer.*

- Say *Look at Activity 10.* Demonstrate the activity for the pupils. Choose one of the pictures and write the letter (a, b, c or d) on a piece of paper, keeping it hidden from the class. Don't say which picture you have chosen. Tell the class they have to ask you questions to find out which of the four pictures you are thinking of. The questions can only be the type with yes or no answers (e.g. *Is …? Has … got …?* or *Is/Are there…?*). If necessary, write some questions on the board to get pupils started, e.g. *Has Ben got 2 brothers? Has Ben got a big brown dog? Has Ben got a house?* When pupils guess the correct picture, show them the letter you wrote on the piece of paper (e.g. *Yes, that's right. It's picture c*).
- Make pairs. Pupil A chooses a picture for Pupil B to identify by asking questions. Monitor and help as necessary. Pupils swap roles once Pupil B has guessed the answer. They can play a number of times.

AB68. ACTIVITY **7.** *Listen and write.*

- Say *Open your Activity Books at page 68, please.* Say *Look at the pictures. All the words have the sound 's' or 'sh'. Look and think.* Give pupils time to guess what each word is, how to say it and which letter(s) to write.
- Play the example on the CD and point to the answer on the first line. Play the rest of the CD, pausing for pupils to repeat the word and to write. They check answers in pairs.
- Play the CD again. Correct as a class.

Key: 2 sh, 3 s, 4 s, 5 sh, 6 s, 7 sh, 8 ss, 9 s, 10 sh

CD 3, 18

1 sheep, 2 shoe, 3 seven, 4 chips, 5 shirt, 6 desk, 7 fish, 8 dress, 9 sleep, 10 shop

AB68. ACTIVITY **8.** *Cross out five objects. Ask your friend.*

- Elicit the objects in the picture. Pupils use a pencil and secretly put a cross through five objects. They work in pairs, but they don't look at each other's books. They take turns to ask *Have you got a … ?* and to answer. They say *No, I haven't* if they have put a cross through it. Again in pencil, pupils write ticks or crosses in the boxes about their partner's objects. The first in each pair to find all the objects crossed out is the winner. Pupils erase their crosses and ticks and repeat the game.

Extra activities: see page T124 (if time)

Optional activity

- 'The eye test' episode from *Kid's Box 2 Interactive DVD* (The living room section), if not used in Unit 8.
  See pages 8-11 of the Teacher's booklet for the *Interactive DVD.*

Ending the lesson

- Do the tongue twister again with the class. Pupils stand up. Do it as a class and then invite groups or pairs to have a go at saying it as fast as they can.

OBJECTIVES: By the end of the lesson, pupils will have read a story and reviewed language from the unit.

- **TARGET LANGUAGE**

Key language: language from the unit
Additional language: *Trollman, Masktroll, arms*
Revision: adjectives, clothes, colours, *wearing, mask, sing, dance, can't, can, look at, legs, pencil, eating, spell, fly, nice, friends*

- **MATERIALS REQUIRED**

Flashcards: (clothes) 79–84
Kid's Box 1 Flashcards: (clothes) 66–71 (or pictures): a jacket, shoes, a skirt, socks, trousers, a T-shirt
Optional: *Teacher's Resource Book 2* Unit 9 Extension worksheet 2 (page 60) and/or animated version of the Unit 9 story from *Kid's Box 2 Interactive DVD* (Suzy's room section), *Kid's Box 2 Language Portfolio* page 5

Warmer

- Review the 12 clothes words, using the flashcards. Hold one behind your back. Pupils guess, asking *Have you got a dress?* etc. Answer *Yes, I have. / No, I haven't.* The pupil who guesses comes and hides a flashcard and the class asks him/her questions. Re-use flashcards to make it more challenging.

Story

PB69. ACTIVITY 11. *Listen to the story.*

- Say *Open your Pupil's Books at page 69, please.* Elicit who they can see (Trevor, Monty, Maskman, Marie). Elicit where they are (in the house). Set the pre-listening questions: *Can Trevor fly? What colour's Maskman's hair? Can Maskman spell?* Say *Listen and look.* Play the CD. Check with the class (Yes, Purple, No). Check pupils understand that Trevor and Maskman have changed roles. Play the CD again. Pupils listen and repeat. Encourage them to say it with intonation and feeling.
- Check comprehension by holding up your book, pointing to each picture in turn and asking, e.g. *What's Monty wearing?* (Marie's long white jacket and glasses). *What's Trevor wearing?* (blue trousers, shirt and hat and a black mask). *What's Trevor's name?* (Masktroll). *What's Maskman eating?* (a pencil).

CD 3, 19

Toys in the toy box,
Come alive.
Walk and talk,
On the count of five.
One, two, three, four, five.
MARIE: Monty! Are you wearing my long white jacket and my glasses?
MONTY: Yes, I am. I'm Marie mouse.

MARIE: Trevor! What *are* you wearing?
TREVOR: I'm wearing blue trousers, a blue shirt, a blue hat and a black mask … Who am I?

TREVOR: I can swim and fly, but I can't sing or dance. I'm … Masktroll!

MONTY: Look at Maskman!

TREVOR: Maskman! Are you eating a pencil?
MASKMAN: Yes, I am. Who am I?

MONTY: You're … Trollman!
MASKMAN: That's right! I can't swim and I can't spell.
TREVOR: No, you can't, Trollman, but you've got a lot of friends.

PB69. ACTIVITY 12. *Listen and say the number.*

- Say *Now listen and look. Say the number of the picture.* Play the CD. Pupils point to the picture and whisper the number to their partner. Play the CD again. Check with the class.

Key: 5, 2, 4, 3, 1, 6.

CD 3, 20

TREVOR: Maskman! Are you eating a pencil?
TREVOR: I'm wearing blue trousers, a blue shirt, a blue hat and a black mask … Who am I?
MONTY: Look at Maskman!
TREVOR: I can swim and fly, but I can't sing or dance. I'm … Masktroll!
MARIE: Monty! Are you wearing my long white jacket and my glasses?
MASKMAN: That's right! I can't swim and I can't spell.

AB69. MY PICTURE DICTIONARY.

- Say *Open your Activity Books at page 69, please.* Pupils prepare the clothes stickers. Say *Which word is it? Listen to the spelling.* Play number 1 on the CD and elicit the word (handbag). Ask pupils to hold up the correct sticker. They all stick the sticker in the first square. Remind pupils that when there are two of the same letter in a word we say *double* (e.g. *double 'l'*).
- Play the rest of the CD. Pupils lay the stickers out on their desk in the correct order. Monitor around the class to check before they stick them in their books.
- Point to the example word in square 1. Say *Now write the words.* Pupils write the name of the clothes item under each sticker.

Key: 2 hat, 3 dress, 4 jeans, 5 shirt, 6 glasses

CD 3, 21

1. h-a-n-d-b-a-g, 2. h-a-t, 3. d-r-e-s-s, 4. j-e-a-n-s, 5. s-h-i-r-t, 6. g-l-a-s-s-e-s

AB69. MY PROGRESS.

- Say *Let's read the sentences together.* Read the first sentence. Refer pupils back to Activity Book page 65. They describe their clothes again. Say *Good, you can talk about your clothes.* Pupils look back at Activity Book page 66 and say which of the items they have got. Say *Good, you can talk about the things you have got.*
- Pupils work in pairs. They take turns to point to a sentence in their books and show each other / talk about what it says.
- Say *Now tick or cross the sentences.* Encourage pupils to practise, so they can tick the statements and colour the star.

Extra activities: see page T124 (if time)

Optional activities

- *Teacher's Resource Book 2* Unit 9 Extension worksheet 2 (see pages 56 and 60).
- The animated version of the story from *Kid's Box 2 Interactive DVD* (Suzy's room section). See pages 41–45 of the Teacher's booklet for the *Interactive DVD.*

Language Portfolio

- Pupils complete page 5 of *Kid's Box 2 Language Portfolio* (*I can … Units 7–9*).

Ending the lesson

- Ask pupils which chant/song/game they'd like to do again from the unit. Do it together to end the lesson.

11 19 CD3 Listen to the story.

1
Monty! Are you wearing my long white jacket and my glasses?
Yes, I am. I'm Marie Mouse.
2
Trevor! What are you wearing?
I'm wearing blue trousers, a blue shirt, a blue hat and a black mask. Who am I?
3
I can swim and fly, but I can't sing or dance. I'm … Masktroll!
4
Look at Maskman!
5
Maskman! Are you eating a pencil?
Yes, I am. Who am I?
6
You're … Trollman!
That's right! I can't swim and I can't spell.
No, you can't, Trollman, but you've got a lot of friends.

12 20 CD3 Listen and say the number.

10 Our hobbies

1 Listen and answer.

2 Listen and repeat.

OBJECTIVES: By the end of the lesson, pupils will be able to name and talk about hobbies.

• TARGET LANGUAGE

Key language: *hobby/hobbies, paint, sports, play hockey, table tennis, baseball, badminton, basketball*

Additional language: *take a photo, about, And yours?*

Revision: characters, *favourite, book, reading, talking, man, hat, hit, ball, play football, play the guitar*

• MATERIALS REQUIRED

Flashcards: (sports/hobbies) 85–91

A picture of a camera

Kid's Box 1 Flashcards: (activities) 74–78: play tennis, play the guitar, play the piano, swim, ride a bike

Extra activity 2: two rolled up newspapers

Optional: *Kid's Box Teacher's Resource Book 2* Unit 10 Reinforcement worksheet 1 (page 63)

Warmer

- Mime a known action in turn (playing football, playing basketball, playing tennis, playing the guitar, playing the piano, swimming, riding a bike). Pupils guess, e.g. *You're swimming.* Show each flashcard, elicit the word and stick it on the board.

Presentation

- Show each sports/hobbies flashcard in turn and elicit/say the word. Pupils repeat in chorus and then in groups. Stick the flashcards on the board (picture side) to make a mind map. Elicit from pupils what the word in the middle is. Don't write anything yet.
- Point to each new flashcard in turn. Pupils chorus the word. Turn the flashcard word side. Pupils chorus the word.

PB70. ACTIVITY **1.** *Listen and answer.*

- Set the scene, but pupils don't open their books. Say *Listen. Suzy and Stella are talking about some of these things* (point to the board). Set the pre-listening questions: *What are Lenny and Simon doing? What's Grandma doing? What are the words for all these activities?* (gesture to the board). Play the CD. Pupils listen for the answers. They check in pairs. Say *Open your Pupil's Books at page 70, please. Listen again and check* (Playing hockey, Painting, Sports and hobbies). Play the CD again as pupils are checking. Write the words *Sports and hobbies* in the centre of the mind map on the board.
- Say *Can you find the hidden star? Show your partner.* Check with the class (in Suzy's hair). Pupils say *Here it is.*

CD 3, 22

SUZY: Stella, I've got a book about sports. What are these sports?

STELLA: The man with the hat's hitting the ball. He's playing baseball, and this man here's playing basketball. He's bouncing the ball.

SUZY: What are Lenny and Simon doing?

STELLA: They're playing hockey.

SUZY: Are Grandpa and Alex playing tennis?

STELLA: No, they're playing badminton.

SUZY: Grandma's painting. Is painting a sport?

STELLA: No, it isn't, Suzy. It's a hobby.

SUZY: Meera's taking a photo. Is that a sport or a hobby?

STELLA: It's a hobby, Suzy.

SUZY: What's your favourite hobby, Stella?

STELLA: It's reading, ... and yours?

SUZY: My favourite hobby? ... Er ... It's, er ... talking.

STELLA: Yes, it is.

PB70. ACTIVITY **2.** *Listen and repeat.*

- Say *Now listen and repeat.* Play the CD. Pupils repeat in chorus as a class, then in groups and pairs.

CD 3, 23

Painting, badminton, table tennis, hockey, baseball, basketball

AB70. ACTIVITY **1.** *Write the words and the numbers.*

- Say *Open your Activity Books at page 70, please.* Focus pupils on the pictures and elicit what they can see. Pupils work in pairs. They unscramble the words and match each one with a picture. Check with the class.

Key: guitar 3, badminton 5, table tennis 1, hockey 6, baseball 2

AB70. ACTIVITY **2.** *Listen and colour.* **[YLE]**

- Focus pupils on the pictures. Say *Listen and choose the right colours for each picture. Don't colour this time.* Pupils listen and choose. Play the CD again. Pupils listen and mark the item with a coloured dot. They check in pairs. Play the CD again. Pause after each one to check. Pupils colour the clothes.

CD 3, 24

1 Look at the boy playing badminton. / Oh, yes. Can I colour his trousers? / Yes, colour them black. / OK. What colour is his T-shirt? / It's orange.

2 Find the boy taking a photo. / OK. I can see him. / Can you colour his trousers blue? / Yes, he's got blue trousers. What colour's his T-shirt? / It's purple.

3 What's this girl doing? / She's playing basketball. Colour her T-shirt yellow. / OK. She's wearing a yellow T-shirt. Now what? / Colour her trousers green.

4 Now, find the girl playing badminton. / OK. Here she is. / Good. She's wearing a pink T-shirt and red trousers. / A pink T-shirt and red trousers? / Yes, that's right.

Extra activities: see page T124 (if time)

Optional activity

- *Teacher's Resource Book 2* Unit 10 Reinforcement worksheet 1 (see pages 62 and 63).

Ending the lesson

- Display the sports/hobbies flashcards (picture side) around the room. Call out the sports/hobbies. Pupils point to the right card.

OBJECTIVES: By the end of the lesson, pupils will have talked and read further about sports and hobbies.

• **TARGET LANGUAGE**

Key language: *player, goalkeeper*

Additional language: *In this picture ...*

Revision: sports and hobbies, colours, clothes, *can, has got, see, catch, kick, ball, run, hands, children, wear, fishing,* present continuous

• **MATERIALS REQUIRED**

Flashcards: (sports/hobbies) 85–91

A picture of a camera

Activities flashcards from *Kid's Box 1* 72–78: play football, play basketball, play tennis, play the guitar, play the piano, swim, ride a bike

Optional: *Kid's Box 2 Interactive DVD: The living room* 'Let's go climbing!' episode

Warmer

- Review the sports and hobbies using flashcards. Hold one behind your back. Pupils take turns to guess, e.g. *Is it basketball?* Respond *Yes, it is. / No, it isn't.* The pupil to guess chooses a flashcard and becomes the caller.

PB71. ACTIVITY 3. *Listen and match. Say the hobby.*

- Say *Open your Pupil's Book at page 71, please.* Focus pupils on the pictures. Say *Listen and look.* Play number 1 on the CD. Pause. Point to the example (f basketball). Play the rest of the CD. Pupils point to the answer and confirm silently with their partner. Play the CD again for pupils to check. Elicit answers by playing the CD a third time. Pause after each one and elicit the sport/hobby. Elicit a description of the character in each one (clothes, colours, etc.).

Key: c baseball, d table tennis, a badminton, e football, b hockey

CD 3, 25

1. She's bouncing the big ball. Now she's throwing it to her friend.
2. He's throwing the small ball to his friend … Yes, she's hitting it. Oh! Yes … now she's catching the ball.
3. They're playing with a small ball. They've got a big table between them and the ball's bouncing on the table.
4. They aren't playing with a ball. They're hitting a small white object. It isn't bouncing and they aren't catching it.
5. She's running and kicking the ball. The ball isn't bouncing and they aren't catching it.
6. They're running with a small ball. He's hitting it with a long stick.

PB71. ACTIVITY 4. *Read and answer.* **[YLE]**

- Focus pupils on the picture in Activity 4. Elicit what the sport/hobby is (football). Say *Quickly read the text* (point to the text) *and find the name for the girl with the orange T-shirt.* Pupils read and check (goalkeeper). Ask more questions about the picture to review vocabulary, e.g. *Is she kicking the ball? Is she bouncing it? Can you touch the ball in football?* Make sure you involve the girls and the boys when asking questions. Say *Now read the text again and answer the questions.* Pupils work individually and write their answers in their notebooks. They check in pairs. Give pairs time to check and review their answers. Check with the class. Check understanding and pronunciation of *players* and *goalkeeper.*

Key: 1c, 2a, 3c

AB71. ACTIVITY 3. *Write the words.*

- Say *Open your Activity Books at page 71, please.* Elicit what they can see (a crossword). Elicit the directions (down and across) and elicit the example from pupils (1 down: table tennis). Pupils work in pairs. They work through the clues. Remind pupils to check spelling of the words (it's not a test). Monitor pupils as they are working. Check with the class.

Key: Down 2 tennis, 3 badminton, 5 reading, 7 piano, 8 guitar. Across 3 basketball, 4 swimming, 6 football, 7 painting, 9 fishing, 10 hockey.

AB71. ACTIVITY 4. *Complete the sentences.*

- Focus pupils on the sentences and on the example. They work individually and complete the sentences, using the information from the crossword. Check with the class.

Key: 4 across They're swimming. 5 down She's reading. 6 across They're playing football. 7 across She's painting. 9 across He's fishing.

Extra activities: see page T124 (if time)

Optional activity

- The 'Let's go climbing!' episode from *Kid's Box 2 Interactive DVD* (The living room section). See pages 20–23 of the Teacher's booklet for the *Interactive DVD.*

Ending the lesson

- Divide the class into groups according to their favourite sport: hockey or football or tennis. Each group decides the mime for their sport. Teach the chant. Groups say their chant in turn, doing the actions as they chant.

Hockey, hockey, I like hockey.
Hockey is the sport for me!

Football, football, I like football.
Football is the sport for me!

Tennis, tennis, I like tennis.
Tennis is the sport for me!

3 Listen and match. Say the hobby.

25 CD3

It's f. It's basketball.

a

b

c
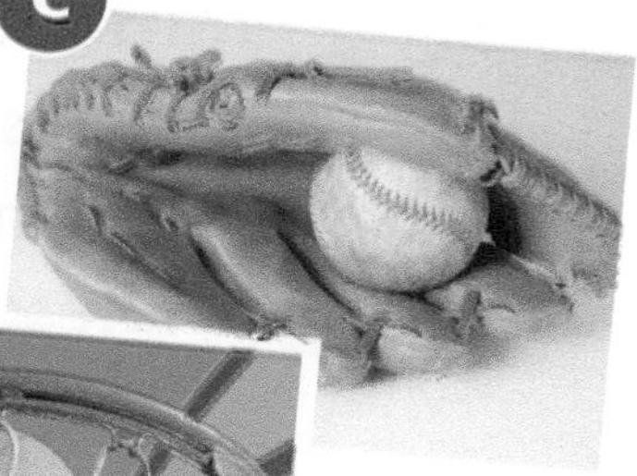

d

e

f

4 Read and answer.

These children are playing football. This sport has got two names: football and soccer. In a football team, there are ten players who can run and kick the ball, and one player who can kick and catch the ball. This player is the goalkeeper. Can you see the goalkeeper in this picture? She's wearing an orange T-shirt and black trousers.

1. The children are playing
   a) badminton.
   b) basketball.
   c) football.
2. Eleven players can
   a) kick the ball.
   b) catch the ball.
   c) bounce the ball.
3. One player can
   a) run.
   b) hit the ball.
   c) catch the ball.

Vocabulary

paint   play badminton/baseball/basketball/hockey/table tennis

5 (26, CD3) Listen and say the number.

Number three.

1

Name: Grandpa Star
Likes: fishing and badminton
Dislikes: cleaning his shoes

2

Name: Lenny
Likes: swimming and football
Dislikes: table tennis

3

Name: Mr Star
Likes: the guitar and cooking
Dislikes: horses

4

Name: Grandma Star
Likes: painting and driving
Dislikes: gardening

5

Name: Meera
Likes: bikes and photos
Dislikes: TV

6

Name: Alex
Likes: badminton and the piano
Dislikes: baseball

7

Name: Simon
Likes: basketball and hockey
Dislikes: cleaning his room

8

Name: Mrs Star
Likes: horses and reading
Dislikes: cooking

9

Name: Suzy
Likes: singing and drawing
Dislikes: soccer

10

Name: Stella
Likes: the piano and reading
Dislikes: doing sport

Grammar

I like / love ...ing. I don't like ...ing.

OBJECTIVES: By the end of the lesson, pupils will have talked about likes and dislikes.

- **TARGET LANGUAGE**

Key language: *I like … / I love … / I don't like … + ing, cooking, gardening, driving, reading about … , likes, dislikes*
Additional language: *ID card*
Revision: characters, sports and hobbies, *riding horses, fishing, cleaning shoes, watching TV, name*

- **MATERIALS REQUIRED**

Flashcards: (sports/hobbies) 85–91
Pictures of driving, gardening, cooking, riding horses, singing
A picture of a camera
Kid's Box 1 Flashcards: (activities) 72–78: play football, play basketball, play tennis, play the guitar, play the piano, swim, ride a bike
Photocopiable 10 (see page T110), copied onto thin card, one for each pupil, scissors, crayons
Optional: *Kid's Box Teacher's Resource Book 2* Unit 10 Extension worksheet 1 (page 65)

Warmer

- Review sports and hobbies, using the flashcards. Show a flashcard. Pupils stand up if it's a sport, and sit if it's a hobby. Repeat. Display the flashcards on the board. Point to one, do thumbs up and say, e.g. *I love playing soccer.* Point to another, make a positive (but less than for *love*) gesture with your hand and say, e.g. *I like painting.* Point to another, do thumbs down and say, e.g. *I don't like swimming.* Elicit some sentences from pupils.

PB72. ACTIVITY 5. *Listen and say the number.*

- Say *Open your Pupil's Books at page 72, please.* Focus pupils on the ID cards and elicit/teach/check *ID cards.* Use the pictures to pre-teach *driving, gardening, cooking* and to review *riding horses, singing.* Play the first item on the CD. Point out the example answer in the speech bubble. Play the rest of the CD. Pupils listen and look the first time. They check in pairs. Play the CD again. Pause after each one and elicit the answer. Wait for most of the class to put up their hands before eliciting the answers. For each one, say *Good, tell me about him/her. What does he/she like doing? What does he/she dislike doing? Does he/she like gardening?* etc. Pupils ask and answer about the characters in pairs in the same way.

Key: 3, 8, 1, 4, 10, 7, 9, 6, 2, 5

CD 3, 26

MR STAR: Hi. My name's Bruce Star. I like playing the guitar and I love cooking, but I don't like riding horses.
MRS STAR: Hi. I'm Angelina Star. I love riding horses and reading, but I don't like cooking.
GRANDPA: Hello. I'm Grandpa Star. I like fishing and playing badminton, but I don't like cleaning my shoes.
GRANDMA: Hello. I'm Grandma Star. I love painting and driving. I don't like gardening.
STELLA: Hi. I'm Stella. I love playing the piano and I like reading about sports, but I don't like doing sport.
SIMON: Hello. My name's Simon. I like playing basketball and hockey, but I don't like cleaning my room.
SUZY: Hi. I'm Suzy. I love singing and drawing, but I don't like playing soccer.
ALEX: Hello. I'm Alex. I like playing badminton and I love playing the piano, but I don't like playing baseball.
LENNY: Hi. My name's Lenny. I like swimming and playing football, but I don't like playing table tennis.
MEERA: Hi. I'm Meera. I like riding my bike and I love taking photos, but I don't like watching TV.

Photocopiable 10: see pages T99 and T110

AB72. ACTIVITY 5. *Listen and tick (✓) or cross (✗).* **[YLE]**

- Say *Open your Activity Books at page 72, please.* Focus pupils on the pictures. Say *Listen. Tick what they like. Cross what they don't like.* Make a tick and a cross on the board. Play the first item on the CD. Point out the example answer. Play the rest of the CD. Pupils listen and tick and cross. They check in pairs. Play the CD again. Check with the class.

Key: 1 b ✓, c ✓. 2 a ✗, b ✓, c ✗. 3 a ✗, b ✗, c ✓. 4 a ✓, b ✗, c ✓.

CD 3, 27

1 She likes carrots, ice cream and cake.
2 He doesn't like taking photos or riding bikes. He likes swimming.
3 He likes playing hockey. He doesn't like playing table tennis or badminton.
4 She likes painting and reading. She doesn't like playing the guitar.

AB72. ACTIVITY 6. *Draw and write about you.*

- Focus pupils on the sentence prompts and the frame for drawing. Elicit sentences from pupils, using all the prompts. Review necessary language in this way. Pupils work individually. They complete the sentences first and then draw a picture of themselves. Monitor pupils as they are working. Encourage pupils to write true sentences and supply new vocabulary as appropriate.

Extra activity: see page T124 (if time)

Optional activity

- *Teacher's Resource Book 2* Unit 10 Extension worksheet 1 (see pages 62 and 65).

Ending the lesson

- Call out sports and hobbies from Pupil's Book Activity 5. Pupils do thumbs up if they love it, thumbs wiggling up then down if they like it and thumbs down if they don't like it.

OBJECTIVES: By the end of the lesson, pupils will have had more practice talking about likes and dislikes and sung a song.

• TARGET LANGUAGE

Key language: *Does he/she like …- ing? Yes, he/she does. / No, he/she doesn't.*

Revision: colours, hobbies, sports, *love/like/don't like …-ing, fly a plane, flying kites, running, train, cleaning, shoes, cooking*

• MATERIALS REQUIRED

Extra activity 2: Flashcards: (sports/hobbies) 85–91

A picture of a camera

Kid's Box 1 Flashcards (activities) 72–78: play basketball, play tennis, play the guitar, play the piano, swim, ride a bike

Optional: *Kid's Box Teacher's Resource Book 2* Unit 10 song worksheet (page 67)

Warmer

- Say *I'm thinking of a sport or hobby. It's something I love doing.* Pupils try and guess by asking, e.g. *Swimming?* When the pupils guess correctly, say *Yes, I love*, e.g. *cooking*. Repeat for *like/don't like*. Pupils take turns to come and be the callers.

PB73. ACTIVITY 6. *Listen and point. Sing.*

- Say *Open your Pupil's Books at page 73, please.* Elicit what pupils can see in the pictures, e.g. *fishing*. Focus them on the symbols, e.g. ♥♥ and elicit what they think they mean. Play the CD. Pupils listen and check (two hearts = love, one heart = like, crossed heart = don't like). Play the CD again. Pupils listen to the verses and point to the people and the actions. Check understanding by asking, e.g. *This person loves swimming. Who is it?* (Simon).
- Play the CD again, this time in sections. Pupils repeat the section. Teach the whole song in this way. Pupils stand up. They sing the song again in chorus. Divide the class into two. One half is Simon, the other Grandpa. The groups take turns to sing their parts. Swap roles. You can record pupils and let them see/hear themselves singing the song.

CD 3, 28

GRANDPA: I love fishing,
I love flying kites.
I like taking photos,
I like riding bikes.
I love fishing!
Bedum … bedoo.

SIMON: I love swimming,
Playing hockey too,
And I love painting,
With the colour blue.
I love swimming!
Bedum … bedoo.

GRANDPA: I don't like driving,
Or flying in a plane,
I don't like cleaning shoes,
I don't like running for a train.
Bedum bedum bedoo.

SIMON: I don't like cooking,
Or playing the guitar,
I don't like badminton,
Or cleaning my dad's car.
I don't like it!
Bedum … bedoo. Yeh!

CD 3, 29

Now sing the song again. (Karaoke version)

PB73. ACTIVITY 7. *Ask and answer.*

- In pairs, pupils ask questions about the characters in the song, following the model. They work in open and then closed pairs.

AB73. ACTIVITY 7. *Look and read. Write 'yes' or 'no'.* **[YLE]**

- Say *Open your Activity Books at page 73, please.* Read the example statement: Two girls are playing hockey. Say *Look at the picture. Yes or no?* Pupils respond *No*. Point to the example answer *no*. Elicit the correct sentence (*Two boys are playing hockey.*).
- Pupils work individually and silently read the rest of the statements. They write yes or no on the lines to the right. Monitor and check they are looking at the picture to find out the answers. Pupils check in pairs. Elicit answers. Choose individuals to correct the false sentences.

Key: 1 yes, 2 yes, 3 yes, 4 no (He's painting.), 5 no (The girl in a black skirt is playing badminton./She's wearing a black skirt.)

Extra activities: see page T124 (if time)

Optional activity

- Hand out copies of the Unit 10 song worksheet from *Teacher's Resource Book 2*. Pupils do the matching activity and then personalise by writing 'So do I' or 'I don't'. (See pages 62 and 67 of the *Teacher's Resource Book*.)

Ending the lesson

- Invite a group of eight pupils to the front. Each of the eight pupils says one thing they like, e.g. *I like playing football.* Ask the class, e.g. *Does Pablo like riding bikes?* The class answer from memory *Yes, he does. / No, he doesn't.* Ask further questions about the group, e.g. *Who likes riding bikes? What does Pablo like doing?*

6 Listen and point. Sing.

28 CD3

I ♥♥ fishing,
I ♥♥ flying kites,
I ♥ taking photos,
I ♥ riding bikes.
I ♥♥ fishing!
Bedum ... bedoo.

I ♥♥ swimming,
Playing hockey too,
And I ♥♥ painting,
With the colour blue.
I ♥♥ swimming!
Bedum ... bedoo.

I ~~♥~~ driving,
Or flying in a plane,
I ~~♥~~ cleaning shoes,
I ~~♥~~ running for a train!
Bedum ... bedoo.

I ~~♥~~ cooking,
Or playing the guitar,
I ~~♥~~ badminton,
Or cleaning my dad's car.
I ~~♥~~ it!
Bedum ... bedoo.

7 Ask and answer.

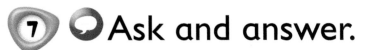

Does Simon like painting?

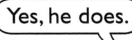

Yes, he does.

8 Monty's phonics

king

sing

morning

The king sings in the morning.

9 Ask your friend.

1. Do you like playing basketball?
2. Do you like reading?
3. Do you like fishing?
4. Do you like playing table tennis?
5. Do you like painting?
6. What's your favourite hobby?

OBJECTIVES: By the end of the lesson, pupils will have learned to identify and say the phoneme ng /ŋ/ and have practised asking and answering questions.

• TARGET LANGUAGE

Key language: the phoneme /ŋ/ as in *king, sing, morning, Do you like ...- ing? Yes, I do. No, I don't.*

Revision: sports and hobbies, *long*, clothes, food

• MATERIALS REQUIRED

Picture of a king (with crown)

Extra activity 1: Write the following chant on a large piece of paper before the lesson:

Do you like mice?
Mice are .... nice/big.
They've got big heads,
And little .... legs/feet.
My mouse lives next door,
At number .... six/four.
His windows are blue,
And there are .... three/two.

Optional: *Kid's Box Teacher's Resource Book* 2 Unit 10 Reinforcement worksheet 2 (page 64),
Kid's Box 2 Interactive DVD: The play room 'Skipping games' (plus a long skipping rope and a short skipping rope)

Warmer

- Show a picture of a king or draw a simple king's head on the board (with a crown on it). Present *king*. Say the word for pupils to listen and repeat. Say *Listen*. Then say the following list of words, emphasising the /ŋ/ sound at the end of each one: *king, sing, song, long*. Say *Hmm. What do you think today's sound is?* Pupils respond ng (/ŋ/).

PB74. ACTIVITY **8.** *Monty's phonics*

- Say *Open your Pupil's Books at page 74, please*. Point to the small pictures and say them, emphasizing the sound /ŋ/. Pupils practise pronunciation of each word. Point at the large picture and say *What's the king doing? (Singing) Is it night time? (No) When is it? (Morning)*. Say *Now listen to Monty, point and repeat.*
- Play the CD. Pupils listen and repeat in chorus. Play the CD again. This time, pupils repeat in groups and then in pairs. They try saying the tongue twister as fast as they can. Ask volunteers to say it quickly to the class. Write the tongue twister on the board and elicit the /ŋ/ sounds. Underline them.

Key: The king sings in the morning!

CD 3, 30

MONTY: Hi, I'm Monty! Repeat after me!
/ŋ/, /ŋ/, king
/ŋ/, /ŋ/, sing
/ŋ/, /ŋ/, morning
The king sings in the morning!
The king sings in the morning!
The king sings in the morning!

PB74. ACTIVITY **9.** *Ask your friend.*

- Focus pupils on Activity 9 and elicit/explain that the children in the photograph are doing a survey (asking each other the questions on the left).
- Choose six volunteers to read the questions on the clipboard aloud (*1 Do you like playing basketball?* etc). Check comprehension by asking individual pupils (a different pupil for each question).
- Make pairs (Pupil A and Pupil B). Pupil A asks the questions on the clipboard, pupil B answers. Pupil A writes the answers in his/her notebook. Then they swap roles.
- Pupils use the answers in their notebook to write a short report about their partner's likes and dislikes. Write the following example on the board before they write, explaining the use of *and, but* and *or. Ben doesn't like playing basketball, fishing or painting, but he likes reading and playing table tennis. His favourite hobby is swimming.* Monitor and help as pupils write.
- Make groups of four. Pupils read their reports to the other members of their group.

AB74. ACTIVITY **8.** *Listen and match.*

- Say *Open your Activity Books at page 74, please. Listen and match.* Point to the first phrase and play the first item on the CD. Pupils repeat. Say *Now look at the pictures. A long dog. It's picture c!* (Point to the picture of the dog and the example letter 'c'.) Make sure pupils know that they have to listen and repeat first, then match each of the rest of the sentences with a picture.
- Say *Listen and say. Don't match.* Play the rest of the CD, pausing after each item for pupils to repeat the first time.
- Say *Now match.* Pupils work individually or in pairs to do the matching. Check answers as a class.

Key: 2 b, 3 d, 4 a, 5 e

CD 3, 31

1 A long dog. 2 The boy's eating. 3 She's singing a song. 4 The king's reading. 5 She's painting.

AB74. ACTIVITY **9.** *Read. Write the words.*

- Focus pupils on the pictures. Elicit some of the words. Set the task. Pupils read the text and complete it with the appropriate words from the pictures. They work individually. They tick the pictures and then write the words in the right place. They can check with their partner as they work. Monitor pupils as they are working. Check with the class. Pupils take turns to read out parts of the text.

Key: hockey, T-shirt, trousers, chicken, apple

Extra activities: see page T125 (if time)

Optional activities

- Unit 10 Reinforcement worksheet 2 from *Teacher's Resource Book 2* (see pages 62 and 64 of the *Teacher's Resource Book*).
- Watch the DVD clip 'Skipping games' from the 'playroom' section of the *Interactive DVD*. Then play the game with your pupils. See page 36 of the DVD booklet.

Ending the lesson

- Do the tongue twister again with the class. Pupils stand up. Do it together as quickly as you can. Pairs then practise saying it fast. Invite pairs to come to the front and say it as fast as they can.

OBJECTIVES: By the end of the lesson, pupils will have read a story and reviewed language from the unit.

• TARGET LANGUAGE

Key language: language from the unit
Additional language: *What a great game! It's your turn.*
Revision: numbers, present continuous, *kick, sports, run, fly, hit, eat, ball, head, Come and play*

• MATERIALS REQUIRED

Flashcards: (sports/hobbies) 85–91
A picture of a camera
Kid's Box 1 Flashcards: (activities) 72–78: play football, play basketball, play tennis, play the guitar, play the piano, swim, ride a bike
Extra activity 2: Photocopiable 10 (see page T110), if not used in a previous lesson, copied onto thin card, one for each pupil, scissors, crayons
Optional: *Kid's Box 2 Teacher's Resource Book* Unit 10 Extension worksheet 2 (page 66) and/or animated version of the Unit 10 story from *Kid's Box 2 Interactive DVD* (Suzy's room section)

Warmer

- Review the sports and hobbies, using the flashcards. Secretly hand the flashcards out to 13 pupils. They don't show them to their friends. The rest of the class tries to remember the sports and hobbies. When one of the 13 pupils hears his/her sport/hobby, they hold up their flashcard.

Story

PB75. ACTIVITY 10. *Listen to the story.*

- Say *Open your Pupil's Books at page 75, please.* Elicit who they can see (Trevor, Monty, Maskman, Marie) and what they're doing (playing football). Set the pre-listening questions: *Who's kicking the ball in picture 2? Who's number 18? Who's number 15?* Play the CD. Pupils listen and look. They check in pairs. Check with the class (18/Maskman, Maskman, Trevor). Elicit the other word used in the story to talk about football (soccer). Say *Does Marie like playing football?* (No, she likes reading about it). Play the CD again. Pupils listen and repeat. Encourage them to say it with intonation and feeling.
- Check comprehension by holding up your book, pointing to each picture in turn and asking, e.g. *1 What's Monty doing?* (taking a photo). *2 What's number 15 doing?* (hitting the ball with his head). *3 What's Maskman doing?* (touching the ball with his hands). *4 Who's running with the ball?* (15/Trevor).

CD 3, 32

Toys in the toy box,
Come alive.
Walk and talk,
On the count of five.
One, two, three, four, five.

MONTY: What a great game of soccer! Yes! What a great goal!

MONTY: Number 18 is kicking the ball. Now number 15 is hitting the ball with his head.

MASKMAN: Ouch! My hands!
MARIE: No, Maskman! You can't touch the ball with your hands!

MONTY: Now number 15 is running with the ball.

MARIE: Trevor! Are you eating the ball?
TREVOR: No, I'm not.

MASKMAN: Come and play football with us, Marie!
MARIE: Oh, no, boys! I love reading about soccer, but I *don't* like playing it.

PB75. ACTIVITY 11. *Listen and say 'yes' or 'no'.*

- Say *Now listen. Is it the same as the pictures or not?* Do the first one as an example (yes). Play the rest of the CD. Pause after each one. Pupils check in pairs. Play the CD again, stopping after each one to elicit the response. Elicit corrections for the 'no' answers.

Key: 1 yes, 2 no – 18 and 15, 3 no – hands, 4 yes, 5 no – ball, 6 no – football

CD 3, 33

1 What a great game of soccer. Yes! What a great goal!
2 Number 8 is kicking the ball. Now number 5 is hitting the ball with his head.
3 No, Maskman! You can't touch the ball with your head!
4 Now number 15 is running with the ball.
5 Trevor! Are you eating the book?
6 Come and play badminton with us, Marie!

AB75. MY PICTURE DICTIONARY.

- Say *Open your Activity Books at page 75, please.* Point to the scrambled word in the first square and the example answer. Elicit the word (*badminton*). Say *Look at the letters. Unscramble the letters and write words. They are all sports or hobbies.* Pupils work individually or in pairs to solve the anagrams. Check answers.
- Pupils prepare the hobbies stickers and lay them out on their desks in the correct order. Check around the class before they stick them in their books.

Key: badminton, table tennis, baseball, basketball, painting, hockey

Extra activities: see page T125 (if time)

AB75. MY PROGRESS.

- Focus pupils on the activity. Say *Let's read the sentences together.* Read the first sentence. Focus pupils on what they wrote for My picture dictionary activity and then say to the pupils *Good. You can write sport and hobby words.* Draw ♥♥,

  ♥, and ✗♥ on the board. Elicit what these mean. Elicit sentences from pupils, e.g. *I like playing the piano. I love reading. I don't like cleaning my room.* Pupils work in pairs. They take turns to read out a *can do* sentence from their books and show/talk about what it says.
- Say *Now tick or cross the sentences.* Demonstrate the activity again if necessary. Encourage pupils to practise, so that they can tick both the statements and colour the star.

Optional activities

- *Teacher's Resource Book 2* Unit 10 Extension worksheet 2 (see pages 62 and 66).
- The animated version of the story from *Kid's Box 2 Interactive DVD* (Suzy's room section). See pages 41–46 of the Teacher's booklet for the *Interactive DVD.*

Ending the lesson

- Ask pupils which chant/song/game they'd like to do again from the unit. Do it together to end the lesson.

10 32 CD3 Listen to the story.

11 33 CD3 Listen and say 'yes' or 'no'.

1 Ask and answer.

What's this?

It's a sheep.

2 Listen and say.

34 CD3

It's wool. It's a toy. What is it?

It's a doll.

Vocabulary

wool

Now you!
Activity Book page 76

OBJECTIVES: By the end of the lesson, pupils will have learnt to identify and describe items in a Venn diagram. They will be able to write sentences about their Venn diagrams.

• **TARGET LANGUAGE**

Key language: *wool, In my classroom there are … We wear it/them.*

Additional language: *What is it/are they? You can put your feet on it.*

Revision: *It's/They're … sheep, jeans, skirt, jacket, hat, socks, shirt, rug, doll, colours*

• **MATERIALS REQUIRED**

Items made of wool – e.g. a ball of a wool, a woollen jumper, a scarf and gloves made of wool. Make sure two or more of these items are the same colour (e.g. a green wool jumper and a green ball of wool). Other items that are the same colours as the woollen items, e.g. a green book. Red items, e.g. a red pencil, a red table tennis bat, a red hat. Items of clothing of various colours, including red (e.g. socks, jeans, skirt, T-shirt, hat).

Large plastic hoops (for example those used for hoola-hooping or in football training).

Warmer

- Place the woollen items and other red and green items around the classroom. Tell pupils that they need to look very carefully in today's lesson. Teach *wool* using a ball of wool.
- Say *Find something green.* Pupils go and stand next to something green (or point at a green object). Say *Find something made of wool.* Pupils stand next to it or point, as before. Say *Find something green and made of wool.* Pupils race to find something in the classroom made from that material/colour.

Presentation

- Say *Open your Pupil's Books at page 76, please.* Point to the picture of Marie at the top of the page. Remind pupils that Marie's lessons are about different school subjects. Say *This is Marie's maths. The lesson is about Venn diagrams.* If pupils are unsure what a Venn diagram is, explain that a Venn is used to sort things into 3 categories, the middle category having the characteristics of the other two.
- Use the items from the warmer activity to make a physical Venn diagram. Place two plastic hoops on the floor, overlapping so there are three sections (as in the Venn diagram on page 76). Put all the items made of wool in the left hand hoop. Put the green items in the right hand hoop. Now ask pupils to help you move the items which are both green and made of wool into the central section, where the two hoops meet (e.g. the green jumper and the green ball of wool). If you cannot do this physical activity, draw or write the items on the board.

PB76. ACTIVITY 1. *Ask and answer.*

- Hold up your book and point to the speech bubbles at the top of the page. Point to each item in turn in the diagram and say *What's this?* Pupils answer in chorus *It's a…(sheep).* Say *Ask and answer.* Pupils work in pairs to ask and answer about the items in the diagram.
- Ask pupils to work on the part of the diagram labelled 'wool' then the part labelled 'clothes'. Pupils finally ask and answer about the clothes in the middle section. Monitor and help as necessary with this part and elicit the word *wool* in their answers. Check by choosing pairs to ask and answer about the objects in front of the class.

Key: *What's this?* Answers: *It's a doll/a rug/a sheep/some wool/a shirt/a skirt/(a pair of) jeans/a wool jacket/a wool hat. They're wool socks.*

PB76. ACTIVITY 2. *Listen and say.*

- Hold up your book. Point to the speech bubble and play the first clue on the CD *It's wool. It's a toy. What is it?* Pupils respond as in the book *It's a toy doll.* Play the second item on the CD. Pupils listen. Pupils whisper their answers in pairs.
- Play the rest of the CD, pausing to give pupils time to think between each item. Pupils check in pairs and put up their hands when they have the answer.

Key: 2 They're socks, 3 It's a shirt, 4 It's a hat, 5 It's a rug, 6 They're jeans

CD 3, 34

It's wool. We don't wear it. It's a toy. What is it?
We wear them and they're wool. We wear them on our feet. What are they?
We wear it but it's not wool. We wear it on our body and arms. What is it?
It's wool and we wear it. We wear it on our heads. What is it?
It's wool. We don't wear it. You can put your feet on it. What is it?
They're not wool. We wear them on our legs. What are they?

AB76. ACTIVITY 1. *Find, draw and write.*

- Say *Open your Activity Books at page 76, please.* Point to the Venn diagram. Read the labels in the boxes and tell the pupils that there are these things around the classroom for them to find and draw.
- Say *Find, draw and write.* Pupils work individually to find the items around the classroom. They draw a picture of each item in the correct part of the Venn diagram (on the left if it is an item of clothing, but not red, on the right if it is red, but not an item of clothing and in the centre if it is both red and an item of clothing). Pupils label each item with the correct word.
- They compare answers in pairs. Check by copying the blank diagram on the board. Say one of the items (e.g. *Pencil*). Call a volunteer to draw the item/write the word on the correct part of the diagram. Leave the completed diagram on the board.

Key: Answers will depend on the items supplied by the teacher.

AB76. ACTIVITY 2. *Write about your Venn diagram.*

- Point to the completed diagram on the board from Activity 1. Ask pupils to count the red things with you as you point with your finger. Read the first sentence in Activity 2 aloud and elicit the missing word (the number of things: *In my classroom there are (number) red things).* Pupils complete the sentences according to the items in the diagram in their books/on the board.

Key: Answers will depend on the number of items supplied by the teacher.

Extra activities: see page T125 (if time)

Ending the lesson

- Guessing game: think of an object from the lesson and describe it/them e.g. *They're wool, we wear them on our feet. What are they?* Pupils put up their hands to answer (socks). Volunteers make up their own clues for the class to guess.

OBJECTIVES: By the end of the lesson, pupils will have listened to rules about different sports and described how to play some sports.

• TARGET LANGUAGE

Key language: *bounce, stick*
Additional language: *with/in your hands*
Revision: *You can/can't (play, hit, kick, run),* sports words

• MATERIALS REQUIRED

Flashcards: (sports) 85–90;
Kid's Box 1 Flashcards: (sports) 72–78 a ball and a table tennis bat or tennis racket

Warmer

- Use the sports flashcards to elicit the different sports and write the words on the board. Mime/elicit verbs to do with the sports when you show the flashcards *run, play, kick, hit, bounce*. Use a ball and a racket to elicit *kick, bounce* and *hit*. Pupils stand up. Give simple instructions to practise the verbs, e.g. *Bounce a ball. Play tennis. Kick a ball.* Pupils mime.

PB77. ACTIVITY 3. *Listen and say the number.*

- Say *Open your Pupil's Book at page 77, please.* Point to Trevor at the top of the page and the title *Sports rules*. Elicit/Explain the meaning of *rules* (say that they are things you *can* and *can't* do in a sport to play it properly). Hold up your book, pointing to picture 1 and ask pupils *What's the sport?* Pupils respond *Table tennis.* Repeat for the other pictures. Use picture 2 to present *stick*. Say *Listen and say the number.* Play the CD, pausing after each statement to give pupils time to think. Pupils put their hands up to answer.

Key: football, basketball, hockey, table tennis

CD 3, 35

You can kick the ball. You can't hit the ball with your hands.

You can throw and catch the ball. You can bounce the ball. You can't run with the ball in your hands.

You hit the ball with a stick. You can run and hit the ball with the stick.

You play this game on a big green table. You can't hit the ball with your hands.

PB77. ACTIVITY 4. *Ask and answer.*

- Point to the speech bubbles and read the examples together *You can kick the ball. Which sport is it? Football.* Pupils work in pairs. Pupil A says a sentence about a sport and asks *Which sport is it?* Pupil B guesses. Then they swap roles. Ask confident pupils to say their clues for the class to guess the sport.

Key: Example clues and answers: You can hit the ball with a stick (hockey). You can bounce the ball (basketball). You can throw and catch the ball (basketball). You can play this game on a green table (table tennis).

AB77. ACTIVITY 3. *Look and tick (✓) or cross (✗).*

- Say *Open your Activity Books at page 77, please.* Point to picture 1 and read the sentence about the sport. Pupils think whether this is the *right* (nod your head) or *wrong* (shake your head) rule for that sport. Pupils put a tick or cross in the box which shows the correct answer. Pupils check answers in pairs and put their hands up to answer.

Key: 1 Wrong rule, 2 Right rule, 3 Wrong rule, 4 Wrong rule

AB77. ACTIVITY 4. *Listen and say the sport.*

- Say *Listen and say the sport.* Play the first sound on the CD and get a confident pair of pupils to read the example in the speech bubble. Pupils work in pairs. Pause the CD after each sound effect to give pupils time to think about which sport is being played.
- Elicit the names of the sports and say what the sport is. Check as a class.

Key: (spoken responses) 2 *They're kicking a ball. It's football.* 3 *They're hitting the ball. It's table tennis.* 4 *They're hitting the ball (with a stick). It's hockey.* (written responses) 1 basketball, 2 football, 3 table tennis, 4 hockey

CD 3, 36

1.
[sound effects of basketball]

2.
[sound effects of a football match]

3.
[sound effects of table tennis]

4.
[sound effects of hockey]

Extra activities: see page T125 (if time)

Ending the lesson

- Make two teams. Reveal the sports flashcards slowly for pupils to say which sport it is. The first pupil to say the word gets a point for their team. If they can say a correct rule for the sport, they get an extra point.

3 Listen and say the number.

35 CD3

4 Ask and answer.

You can kick the ball. Which sport is it?

Football.

Vocabulary

bounce stick

11 My birthday

1 CD3 37 Listen and answer.

2 CD3 38 Listen and repeat.

OBJECTIVES: By the end of the lesson, pupils will have learned to name and talk about foods.

• TARGET LANGUAGE
Key language: *sausage, lemonade, Happy birthday*
Additional language: *party, any, don't, fries/chips*
Revision: food, *We've got … , taking a photo, kitchen, stand, ugly, cook,* present continuous, prepositions

• MATERIALS REQUIRED
Flashcards: (food) 92–97
Kid's Box 1 Flashcards: (food) 91, 92, 95, 96
Optional: *Teacher's Resource Book 2* Unit 11 Reinforcement worksheet 1 (page 69)

Warmer

- Review the known foods, using the flashcards. Flash each one quickly. Give the pupil who says it correctly the flashcard. When pupils have all the flashcards, each pupil holds it up, says the word and comes and sticks the flashcard on the board (word side). Arrange the flashcards around the edge of the board to make a mind map. Elicit the word for the centre (Food) and write it.

Presentation

- Elicit/teach the new food words, using the flashcards. Pupils repeat in chorus, in groups, in pairs. Check pronunciation of *sausages, oranges.* Say *Which are your favourite foods?* Stick the flashcards on the board around the food mind map.

PB78. ACTIVITY **1.** *Listen and answer.*

- Books closed. Say *Listen. The children are talking about some of these things* (point to the board). Set the pre-listening questions: *What is Mr Star cooking? What have they got to drink? What is Meera doing? Where are they?* Play the CD. Pupils listen for the answers. They check in pairs. Say *Open your Pupil's Books at page 78, please. Listen again and check.* (Burgers and sausages, Lemonade and fruit juice, Taking a photo, A party). Play the CD again. Check understanding of *party, birthday, chips/fries.*
- Say *Can you find the hidden star? Show your partner.* Check with the class (on the present). Pupils say *Here it is.*

CD 3, 37

SIMON: What are you cooking?
MR STAR: I'm cooking burgers and sausages.
SIMON: Are we having chips too?
MR STAR: Yes, we're having fries. Grandma's getting them from the kitchen. Grandpa's helping her.
SIMON: Yum, yum. And we've got lemonade to drink.

SUZY: Mummy, is there any fruit juice?
MRS STAR: Yes, I can get it for you.
SUZY: Thanks.

STELLA: What are you doing, Meera?
MEERA: I'm trying to take a photo of Simon.
ALEX: Yoo hoo, Meera! We're in front of you. Take a photo of us.
STELLA: No, don't take a photo of them. Take one of Simon.
MEERA: I'm trying to take a photo of him. Alex, Lenny, can you stand behind me, please? I don't like taking ugly photos.

PB78. ACTIVITY **2.** *Listen and repeat.*

- Say *Now listen, point to the picture and repeat.* Play the CD. Pupils repeat in chorus. Listen for correct pronunciation.

CD 3, 38

Sausages, burgers, cake, watermelon, oranges, lemonade

AB78. ACTIVITY **1.** *Write the letters and the words.* **[YLE]**

- Say *Open your Activity Books at page 78, please.* Focus pupils on the example in the left circle. Point to the picture of *under,* elicit *under* and say *What's the first letter?* Pupils respond *u.* Show them the example *u.* Say *Do the same for the other pictures. Write the food word here.* Pupils work in pairs. They write the first letter of each picture inside the circle, then put all the letters in order to make a food word. Then they do the same for the second circle. Monitor and help/prompt where necessary. Pairs check with pairs. Check with the class.

Key: armchair, arm, shoe, under, sock, ear, glasses – sausage; milk, apple, dress, eye, nose, egg, lizard, orange – lemonade

AB78. ACTIVITY **2.** *Circle the different words.*

- Focus pupils on Activity 2 and on the example. Elicit why *car* is different (the others are alive). Pupils complete the activity in pairs. Check with the class. Listen for pupils' reasons if they have chosen another word from the one you expected.

Key: 2 shoe (the others are toys), 3 armchair (the others are food), 4 orange (the others are drinks), 5 bus (the others are sports), 6 desk (the others are in a town), 7 kitchen (the others are household objects), 8 mirror (the others are rooms).

Extra activities: see page T125 (if time)

Optional activity

- *Teacher's Resource Book 2* Unit 11 Reinforcement worksheet 1 (see pages 68, 69).

Ending the lesson

- Play a word game. Say *It's my birthday party. I'm having burgers.* Pupil 1: *It's my birthday party. I'm having burgers and lemonade.* Pupil 2: *It's my birthday party. I'm having burgers, lemonade and watermelon.* Start another chain at the back of the class. Choose pupils at random to continue the chains. Listen for correct use of plurals/uncountables.

OBJECTIVES: By the end of the lesson, pupils will have talked and read more about birthdays.

- **TARGET LANGUAGE**

Key language: *Look at them/her/him/us/me/you*
Additional language: *at the bus stop, playground, Smile at me*
Revision: *Happy birthday, party, cook, taking photos, nice, new, bike, number,* colours, *bus, shoe, skirt, swim, can, tree*

- **MATERIALS REQUIRED**

Photocopiable 11 (see page T111), copied onto thin card, one copy for each pupil, scissors, glue, coloured tissue paper, crayons, glitter, a birthday card
Optional: *Teacher's Resource Book 2* Unit 11 Reinforcement worksheet 2 (page 70)

Warmer

- Review the object pronouns: *us, me, them, you, him, her.* Say, e.g. *Look at Juan. Look at him.* Repeat for other pupils in the class. Invite a group of pupils to the front to practise *Look at them.* Include yourself for *Look at us.* Point clearly at each person/group of people referred to by the pronoun to make the meaning clear.

PB79. ACTIVITY 3. *Listen and point. Chant.*

- Say *Open your Pupil's Book at page 79, please.* Elicit what pupils can see in the pictures. Revise *bus, skirt, shoe, tree, swim.* Say *Listen and point.* Play the CD. Pupils point to the pictures. Elicit the letter for each section of the chant. Check understanding, e.g. *Look at him. What can he do? Look at her. What's she wearing?* Play the CD again. Pupils repeat the chant in sections. Pupils stand up. They repeat it in chorus. Pupils practise. You can record pupils and play the chant for them to listen to / watch.

Key: d, e, a, f, b, c

CD 3, 39

Look at them,
Five young men.
Look at him,
He can swim.
Look at her,
In her new skirt.
Look at you,
And your nice clean shoe.
Look at us,
On a big red bus.
Look at me,
I'm under a tree.

PB79. ACTIVITY 4. *Read and answer.* **[YLE]**

- Focus pupils on the picture in Activity 4. Elicit what it's a picture of (a birthday party). Say *Quickly read the text* (point to the text) *and find out what they are drinking at the party.* Pupils read and check (Lemonade and orange juice). Pupils read the text again, working out what the pictures are. Ask more questions to check comprehension, e.g. *What are they having to eat? Who's cooking?* Make sure you involve all pupils when asking questions. Say *Now read the text again and answer the questions.* Pupils work individually and write their answers in their notebooks. They check in pairs. Give pairs time to check and review their answers. Check with the class.

Key: 1 Simon's 2 He's cooking burgers and sausages. 3 Meera's taking photos. 4 He's got a nice new bike.

Photocopiable 11: see pages T99 and T111

AB79. ACTIVITY 3. *Listen and draw.*

- Say *Open your Activity Books at page 79, please.* Elicit what pupils can see. Say *Listen and look. Don't draw.* Play the CD. Pupils listen, look and point. They don't draw the pictures. Play the CD again. Pause after each one for pupils to draw the picture as directed. Limit the time for the drawing each time: allow the same time for each one, e.g. 30 seconds. Pairs check with pairs.

CD 3, 40

A girl's standing under a tree. Draw two flowers next to her.
A boy's standing at the bus stop. Draw a bike in front of him.
Some children are playing in the park. Draw a ball between them.
I'm standing in the playground. Draw a school behind me.

AB79. ACTIVITY 4. *Write the words.*

- Focus pupils on Activity 4. Elicit the example. Check understanding with a quick pointing game, as in the Warmer. Pupils work in pairs. They complete the sentences with words from the box. Monitor pupils as they are working. Encourage pairs to ask other pairs. Check with the class. Get pupils to point each time to check the concept.

Key: 2 you, 3 me, 4 her, 5 us, 6 it

Extra activity: see page T125 (if time)

Optional activity

- *Teacher's Resource Book 2* Unit 11 Reinforcement worksheet 2 (see pages 68 and 70).

Ending the lesson

- Say the chant again from Pupil's Book page 79 Activity 3. Select: five boys (look at them), one boy (look at him), one girl (look at her), one girl (look at you), four boys and girls (look at us), one girl (look at me). The rest of the class say the first four verses of the chant and point to the groups as they say it. The groups/individuals mime as necessary. The last two groups do the last two verses of the chant themselves and mime.

3 Listen and point. Chant.

39 CD3

Look at them
Five young men.
Look at him
He can swim.
Look at her
In her new skirt.
Look at you
And your nice clean shoe.
Look at us
On a big red bus.
Look at me
I'm under a tree.

4 Read and answer.

This is 's birthday party. His friends are at his house. 's cooking and for them. They're having and to drink. 's taking photos with her . 's very . He's got a nice new for his birthday.

1. Whose is the birthday party?
2. What's Mr Star cooking?
3. Who's taking photos?
4. What has Simon got for his birthday?

Vocabulary

burger cake lemonade orange sausage watermelon

5 Listen and answer.

Would you like some fries?
Yes, I'd love some.
Juice
Lemonade
Lemonade

6 Listen and repeat.

Grammar

Would you like …? Can I have …? Here you are.

OBJECTIVES: By the end of the lesson, pupils will be able to make offers, using *Would you like ... ?* and respond appropriately.

• TARGET LANGUAGE

Key language: *Would you like some/a ... or some/a ... ? Yes, I'd love some/one. I'd like a/some ... What would you like to drink/eat?*
Additional language: *It's not your turn, lots, too, Wait a moment*
Revision: *Can I have ... ? Here you are. Oh, sorry, favourite, please,* food

• MATERIALS REQUIRED

Flashcards: (food) 92–97 and 64
Kid's Box 1 Flashcards: (food) 91, 92, 95, 96
Optional: *Kid's Box Teacher's Resource Book 2* Unit 11 Extension worksheet 1 (page 71)

Warmer

- Elicit the food, using the flashcards. Hold out a flashcard, e.g. *watermelon*, to a pupil. Say *Would you like some watermelon?* Pupils respond *Yes, please* or *No, thanks*, as they wish. Offer the other foods to pupils in this way. Pupils with flashcards then make offers to others in the class, using the model. Help pupils notice when to use *Would you like some ... ?* and when *Would you like a ... ?* Display the flashcards on the board. Remind pupils that another word for *chips* is *fries*.

PB80. ACTIVITY 5. *Listen and answer.*

- Books closed. Say *Listen. The toys are talking about food.* Set the pre-listening question: *What would Maskman like to eat and drink? (Four things.)* Point to the board. Play the CD. Pupils listen for the answers. They check in pairs. Say *Open your Pupil's Books at page 80, please. Listen again and check* (sausage, burger, fries, lemonade). Play the CD again. Check comprehension by asking, e.g. *Who would like some fruit juice? What would Monty like to eat? What does he say?* Elicit the key language, e.g. *Would you like a burger or a sausage? I'd like a sausage, please.*

CD 3, 41

Toys in the toy box,
Come alive.
Walk and talk,
On the count of five.
One, two, three, four, five.
TREVOR: Monty, what would you like to eat? Would you like a burger or a sausage?
MONTY: I'd like a sausage, please, Trevor.
TREVOR: Here you are.
MONTY: Thanks.
MASKMAN: Can I have a sausage and a burger, please?
MARIE: One moment, please, Maskman. It's not your turn.
MONTY: Er, here you are, Maskman. Would you like some fries too?
MASKMAN: Yes, I'd love some. Lots, please, Monty.
TREVOR: Marie, what would you like to drink?
MARIE: I'd like some fruit juice, please, Trevor.
MASKMAN: Can I have some lemonade, please?
TREVOR: Maskman, please would you like to wait a moment. It's not your turn.
MASKMAN: Oh, sorry.
MONTY: Would you like some fries too, Trevor? ... Please.
TREVOR: Er ... Well ... OK, Monty. Fries aren't my favourite food, but ... for you.

PB80. ACTIVITY 6. *Listen and repeat.*

- Say *Now listen and repeat.* Play the CD. Pupils repeat in chorus, then in groups. Listen for correct pronunciation and for a rise/fall in the question. Make pairs. Pupils take turns making offers and responding, using the model.

CD 3, 42

TREVOR: Would you like a burger or a sausage?
MONTY: I'd like a sausage, please, Trevor.
TREVOR: Here you are.
MASKMAN: Can I have some lemonade, please?

AB80. ACTIVITY 5. *Write the sentences.*

- Say *Open your Activity Books at page 80, please.* Elicit what pupils have to do (write the words in the right order). They work in pairs, saying the offers and responses before writing. Check with the class.

Key: 2 I'd like some cake, please. 3 Would you like to play with us? 4 I'd like to play table tennis.

AB80. ACTIVITY 6. *Read and write the information.*

- Focus pupils on the first sentence (*May ...*) Say *What would she like to eat? What would she like to drink?* (Chicken and chips, Orange juice). Elicit where pupils write this in the grid. They work in pairs, read the sentences and complete the grid. Check by drawing the grid on the board and eliciting what to write where.

Key:

Name	Food	Drink	Game
May	chicken and chips	orange juice	badminton
Sam	sausages and tomatoes	water	hockey
Ben	burgers and potatoes	lemonade	hockey
Anna	carrots and rice	lemonade	badminton

Extra activities: see page T126 (if time)

Optional activity

- *Teacher's Resource Book 2* Unit 11 Extension worksheet 1 (see pages 68 and 71).

Ending the lesson

- Revise the spelling of food vocabulary. Say, e.g.

	Class responds:
Give me a b	*b*
Give me an r	*r*
Give me an e	*e*
Give me an a	*a*
Give me a d	*d*
What does that spell?	*bread*
What does that spell?	*bread*

OBJECTIVES: By the end of the lesson, pupils will have had more practice making and responding to offers and have sung a song.

• TARGET LANGUAGE

Additional language: *great big, Don't give any to me, coconut*
Revision: *Would you like … or … ? I'd like … , pencils,* food, adjectives, *Can you say that again, please? Sorry?*

• MATERIALS REQUIRED

Flashcards: (food) 92–97 and 64
Kid's Box 1 Flashcards: (food) 91, 92, 95, 96
Optional: *Kid's Box Teacher's Resource Book 2* Unit 11 song worksheet (page 73)

Warmer

- Prompt pupils to make offers and respond, using the flashcards. Hold up two food flashcards, picture side, e.g. *bananas* and *apples*. Say *Question? Would … ?* Elicit the question from a pupil: *Would you like bananas or apples?* Elicit the response from another pupil, e.g. *I'd like apples, please.* Using other pairs of food or drink flashcards, elicit more offers and responses from pupils in the class.

PB81. ACTIVITY 7. *Listen and point. Sing.*

- Say *Open your Pupil's Books at page 81, please.* Elicit who they can see and what food and drink they can see. Say *Listen and point to the toys and the food they'd like.* Play the CD. Pupils listen and point. Play the CD again. Check with the class. Repeat lines 1, 3, 5, 7, 9 of the song. Pupils put up their hands if they'd like this too. Count which is the most popular. Play the CD again. Encourage pupils to sing.

CD 3, 43

I'd like a great big chocolate cake,
And I'd like one for me.
I'd like a nice long sausage,
And I'd like one for me.

I'd like a burger and some fries,
And I'd like some for me.
I'd like a drink of lemonade,
And I'd like some for me.

I'd like coloured pencils,
I'd like coloured pencils,
I'd like a box of coloured pencils,
Don't give any to me!
[Repeat verses 2 and 3]

CD 3, 44

Now sing the song again. (Karaoke version)

PB81. ACTIVITY 8. *Ask and answer.*

- Pupils work in pairs. They take it in turns to ask each other *would like* questions, like the ones in the speech bubbles.

AB81. ACTIVITY 7. *Listen and draw lines. There is one example.* **[YLE]**

- Say *Open your Activity Books at page 81, please. Look at the pictures. What can you see?* Elicit the names of the things pupils know in the large picture (e.g. *kitchen, table, window, chair, clock, book, water, lorries,* etc) and teach *coconut* (point to the coconut on the table). Elicit the vocabulary at the top and bottom of the page (*sausages, burgers, cake, watermelon, juice, ball, chips*).
- Say *Listen.* Play the example on the CD (the first four lines). Say *What is it?* Elicit *The cake.* Ask *Where's the cake? Where do I put it?* Elicit *On the table, behind the coconut.* Hold up the Activity Book page and mime drawing the example line from the cake to the correct position in the picture of the kitchen.
- Say *Listen and draw lines. Use a pencil.* Tell pupils that they will not hear about all the items in the pictures. Play the rest of the CD. Pupils listen and draw lines. They check in pairs. Play the CD again. Check by asking, e.g. *Where are the chips? Where's the watermelon?* Elicit which item wasn't mentioned (the sausages).

Key: burgers – under the window; ball – between the lorries; juice – next to the book under the window; watermelon – on the table next to the coconut, chips – under the clock, between the book and the water

CD 3, 45

Put the cake on the table.
Where? On the table?
Yes, behind the coconut.
Right.

Can you see the line? This is an example. Now you listen and draw lines.

1. Put the burgers under the window.
   Pardon? Where do I put the burgers?
   Put them under the window.
   Fine.
2. Put the ball between the two lorries.
   Between the lorries?
   Yes, that's right.
   Good.
3. Put the juice next to the book.
   Which book? There are two.
   Sorry, next to the book under the window.
   OK. The juice is next to the book.
4. Now, put the watermelon on the table, next to the coconut.
   Sorry? Put the watermelon where?
   Next to the coconut.
   OK.
5. Put the chips under the clock, between the book and the water.
   The chips? Where?
   Between the book and the water.
   OK. I can do that.

Extra activities: see page T126 (if time)

Optional activity

- Hand out copies of the Unit 11 song worksheet from *Teacher's Resource Book 2*. Play the song again for pupils to complete the lyrics (see pages 68 and 73 of the *Teacher's Resource Book*).

Ending the lesson

- Sing the song again from Pupil's Book Activity 7. Divide the class into two groups: A and B. A sings the odd lines and B the even ones (the responses). Pupils only sing if they would like the food, drink or pencils. If they don't want them, they don't sing. Groups swap roles and repeat.

7 Listen and point. Sing.

43 CD3

I'd like a great big chocolate cake,
And I'd like one for me.
I'd like a nice long sausage,
And I'd like one for me.

I'd like a burger and some fries,
And I'd like some for me.
I'd like a drink of lemonade,
And I'd like some for me.

I'd like coloured pencils, ...
I'd like a box of coloured pencils,

Don't give any to me!

8 Ask and answer.

Would you like a burger?

Yes, please.

No, thank you.

9 Monty's phonics

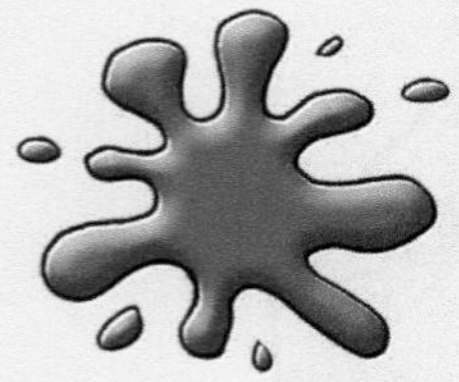

purple

bird

girl

A purple bird for the birthday girl!

10 Look at the menu. Ask and answer.

Menu

Food

- burger
- sausages
- chicken
- fish
- fries
- tomatoes
- carrots

Drinks

- lemonade
- orange juice
- milk
- water

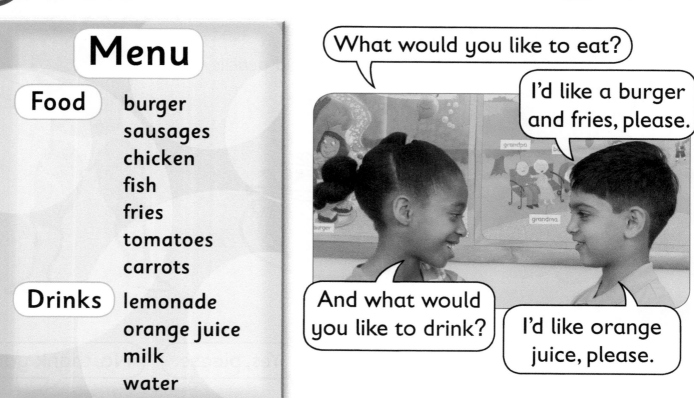

What would you like to eat?
I'd like a burger and fries, please.
And what would you like to drink?
I'd like orange juice, please.

OBJECTIVES: By the end of the lesson, pupils will have learned to identify and say the long ir / ur /ɜː/ vowel sound and have done a menu role play.

• TARGET LANGUAGE

Key language: the phoneme /ɜː/ as in *purple, bird, girl*
Additional language: *menu*
Revision: *thirteen, skirt, shirt, burger, What would you like to eat/drink? I'd like … , please.* food and drink, *young*

• MATERIALS REQUIRED

Extra activity 1: card, one piece for each pair of pupils, coloured felt tips / crayons, samples of menus
Optional: *Kid's Box 2 Interactive DVD: The playroom* 'The Hokey Cokey' and 'Duck Duck Goose'

Warmer

- Elicit the following words from pupils (point/mime): *bird, skirt, shirt, burger.* Write them on the board. Repeat the four words and then say *Today's sound is …* Wait for pupils to say /ɜː/.

PB82. ACTIVITY 9. *Monty's phonics.*

- Say *Open your Pupil's Books at page 82, please.* Point to the small pictures and say them, emphasising the vowel sound /ɜː/. Pupils practise pronunciation of each word. Point at the large picture and say *What colour is the bird? (Purple) Whose birthday is it? (The girl's).* Say *Now listen to Monty, point and repeat.*
- Play the CD again. This time pupils repeat in groups and then in pairs. They try saying the tongue twister as fast as they can. Ask volunteers to say it quickly to the class. Write the tongue twister on the board and elicit the /ɜː/ sounds. Underline them. Point out that the sound /ɜː/ is usually represented by the letters *ir* or *ur* (and less often by *er* (e.g. *were*)).

Key: A purple bird for the birthday girl!

CD 3, 46

MONTY: Hi, I'm Monty! Repeat after me!
/ɜː/, /ɜː/, purple
/ɜː/, /ɜː/, bird
/ɜː/, /ɜː/, girl
A purple bird for the birthday girl!
A purple bird for the birthday girl!
A purple bird for the birthday girl!

PB82. ACTIVITY 10. *Look at the menu. Ask and answer.*

- Focus pupils on Activity 10. Elicit/teach *Menu.* Invite two pupils to read out the speech bubbles from the page. Repeat with other pairs of pupils in open pairs: pupils choose items from the menu. When the class understands what to do, pupils do the activity in closed pairs, taking turns to ask and answer. Monitor and give ideas. Invite pairs to do their dialogues to the class.

AB82. ACTIVITY 8. *Listen and write the words.*

- Say *Open your Activity Books at page 82, please.* Say *Look at the pictures. All the words have the sound /ɜː/. Look and think.* Give pupils time to guess what each word is and how to say it.
- Play the example on the CD and point to the answer on the first line. Play the rest of the CD, pausing for pupils to repeat the word and to write. They check answers in pairs.
- Play the CD again. Correct as a class.

Key: 2 girl, 3 birthday, 4 skirt, 5 bird, 6 shirt, 7 thirteen, 8 burger

CD 3, 47

1. purple
2. girl
3. birthday
4. skirt
5. bird
6. shirt
7. thirteen
8. burger

AB82. ACTIVITY 9. *Look at the letters. Write words.*

- Write *Happy birthday, Simon. It's your garden party* on the board. Point to the letters *y–o–u–n–g* and point to the example word *young* underneath. Say *Can you make another word from the letters?* Let pupils talk together and suggest other words. Say *Look at Activity 9. Write the words you can think of there.* Pupils work in pairs and make as many words as they can. Give a time limit. Check with the class.
Note: If you have mostly kinaesthetic learners, then let them write each letter of the sentences on a separate piece of paper and move them around to make words. They will find this much easier.

Extra activities: see page T126 (if time)

Optional activity

- Watch the DVD clips 'The Hokey Cokey' and 'Duck Duck Goose' from the 'playroom' section of the *Interactive DVD.* Play one or both games with your pupils. They are commonly played at birthday parties in Britain. See pages 33, 35 and 36 of the DVD booklet.

Ending the lesson

- Do the tongue twister with the class again. Pupils stand up and say it in chorus. Invite pairs of pupils to say it as fast as they can. Go around the class.

OBJECTIVES: By the end of the lesson, pupils will have read a story and reviewed language from the unit.

• TARGET LANGUAGE

Key language: language from the unit

Revision: food, pronouns, present continuous, *Let's make …, I'd like …, Happy birthday, Can you get me … ? favourite, today, can*

• MATERIALS REQUIRED

Flashcards: (food) 92–97 and 64

Kid's Box 1 Flashcards: (food) 91, 92, 95, 96: an apple, a banana, chocolate, ice cream

Optional: *Kid's Box 2 Teacher's Resource Book* Unit 11 Extension worksheet 2 (page 72) and/or animated version of the Unit 11 story from *Kid's Box 2 Interactive DVD* (Suzy's room section)

Warmer

- Revise the food words, using the flashcards. Look at one in secret. Say, e.g. *You can eat this.* Pupils take turns to guess. Repeat, including food and drink. Pupils take turns to come and choose a flashcard and the class guesses.

Story

PB83. ACTIVITY 11. *Listen to the story.*

- Say *Open your Pupil's Books at page 83, please.* Elicit who they can see (Trevor, Monty, Maskman, Marie) and what they're doing (making a cake). Elicit why they're making a cake (for someone's birthday). Set the pre-listening questions: *Whose birthday is it? What cake is Monty making? What does Marie say?* Play the CD. Pupils listen and look. They check in pairs. Check with the class (Marie's, lemon cake, 'Would you like to come to the café with me?'). Play the CD again. Pupils listen and repeat. Encourage them to say it with intonation and feeling.
- Check comprehension by holding up your book, pointing to pictures in turn and asking, e.g. *What cake would Trevor like?* (pencil cake). *What would Maskman like to eat?* (burgers and fries). *Who's coming?* (Marie).

CD 3, 48

Toys in the toy box,
Come alive.
Walk and talk,
On the count of five.
One, two, three, four, five.

NARRATOR: It's Marie's birthday today.

TREVOR: Let's have a party for Marie! Let's make her a pencil cake!

MONTY: No, Trevor. *Marie* would like a lemon cake.

MASKMAN: Let's have burgers and fries to eat!

MONTY: No, Maskman. It isn't your birthday.

MONTY: Now, let's make the cake!

MASKMAN: Shh! Marie's coming!

MONTY: Now we can't make her a cake.

MONTY, TREVOR AND MASKMAN: Happy birthday, Marie! Happy birthday, Marie!

MARIE: Thanks, boys! Would you like to come to the café with me?

TREVOR: Can I have some pencil cake, please?

PB83. ACTIVITY 12. *Act out the story.*

- Divide the class into groups of four. Pupils decide their roles (Trevor, Monty, Maskman, Marie). Play the CD again. Stop after each frame for pupils to repeat in role. Pupils practise their story in groups with mime. More confident groups of pupils can change some of the words, e.g. *chocolate cake.* Invite one or two groups to role play their story to the class.

AB83. MY PICTURE DICTIONARY.

- Say *Open your Activity Books at page 83, please.* Pupils prepare the food and drink stickers. Say *Which food or drink is it? Listen.* Play number 1 on the CD and elicit the food (*cake*). Ask pupils to hold up the correct sticker. They all stick the sticker in the first square.
- Play the rest of the CD. Pupils lay the stickers out on their desk in the correct order. Monitor around the class to check before they stick them in their books.
- Point to the example word on the line in square 1 (*cake*). Say *Now write the words.* Pupils write the food or drink under each sticker. Write the words on the board in random order if they are having difficulty. Play the CD again if necessary.

Key: 2 sausage, 3 lemonade, 4 watermelon, 5 burger, 6 orange

CD 3, 49

Stick the cake on number 1. Stick the orange on number 6. Stick the lemonade on number 3. Stick the sausage on number 2. Stick the burger on number 5. Stick the watermelon on number 4.

AB83. MY PROGRESS.

- Focus pupils on the activity. Say *Let's read the sentences together.* Read the first sentence. Focus pupils on Pupil's Book page 82 Activity 10. Elicit some of the dialogues. Say *Good, you can ask for food and drink.* Focus pupils on the words in My picture dictionary. Say *What kind of food and drink is it? Do we eat it every day?* Elicit that it's party/birthday food. Say *You can talk about this.* Pupils work in pairs. They take turns to read out a *can do* sentence from their books and do/talk about what it says.
- Say *Now tick or cross the sentences.* Demonstrate the activity again if necessary. Encourage pupils to practise so that they can tick both the statements and colour the star.

Extra activities: see page T126 (if time)

Optional activities

- Unit 11 Extension worksheet 2 (see pages 68 and 72 of the *Teacher's Resource Book*).
- The animated version of the story from *Kid's Box 2 Interactive DVD* (Suzy's room section). See pages 41–46 of the Teacher's booklet for the *Interactive DVD.*

Ending the lesson

- Ask pupils which chant/song/game they'd like to do again from the unit. Do it together to end the lesson.

11 48 CD3 Listen to the story.

1
It's Marie's birthday today.
Let's have a party for Marie! Let's make her a pencil cake.
Pencils
Lemon cake mix
No, Trevor. Marie would like a lemon cake.
2
Let's have burgers and fries to eat.
No, Maskman. It isn't your birthday.
3
Now let's make the cake.
4
Ssh. Marie's coming!
Now we can't make her a cake.
5
Happy birthday, Marie!
6
Thanks, boys! Would you like to come to the café with me?
Can I have some pencil cake, please?

12 Act out the story.

12 On holiday!

1 CD4 2 Listen and point.

2 CD4 3 Listen and repeat.

OBJECTIVES: By the end of the lesson, pupils will have learned to talk about holiday activities.

• TARGET LANGUAGE

Key language: *mountain, sea, sand, beach, sun, shell, on holiday, pick up*

Revision: *lots of, flowers, trees, fishing, walking, sitting, reading, love, So do I, can't, clean, colours, animals, I love playing*

• MATERIALS REQUIRED

Flashcards: (holiday) 98–103

Example of a picture postcard.

Extra activity 1: three rolled up newspapers

Optional: *Kid's Box Teacher's Resource Book 2* Unit 12 Reinforcement worksheet 1 (page 75)

Warmer

- Review sports/hobbies, using mime. As pupils say each one, write it at the side of the board and say, e.g. *I love swimming.* Elicit a response from pupils, e.g. *So do I. / I don't.* Sports/hobbies: *playing table tennis, painting, riding a bike, swimming, fishing, reading, walking, playing the guitar, taking photos.*

Presentation

- Elicit/teach the new holiday vocabulary, using the flashcards (picture side). Pupils repeat in chorus, in groups, in pairs. Display the flashcards on the board (picture side), point, and pupils repeat. Turn each flashcard over (word side). Pupils chorus each one again. Make a circling motion with your hands and say *These are holiday words.* Check the concept of *holiday*, using the picture postcard. Point to the words from the Warmer. Say, e.g. *Do you go fishing on holiday?* Ask questions about the other sports/hobbies in the same way.

PB84. ACTIVITY **1.** *Listen and point.*

- Set the scene, books closed. Say *Listen. Lenny and Simon are talking about their holidays.* Set the pre-listening questions: *What does Simon love doing? (Three things.) What does Lenny love doing? What does Suzy like doing? What does Stella like doing?* Make groups of four. Each pupil in the group listens for the answer to one question. Play the CD. Pupils listen for the answers. They tell the others in their group. Say *Open your Pupil's Books at page 84, please.* Play the CD again for pupils to check. (Playing on the beach, swimming in the sea, fishing with Grandpa; Walking in the mountains; Picking up shells from the beach; Sitting in the sun and reading). Check comprehension by asking, e.g. *Can Simon fish in the city?*
- Say *Can you find the hidden star? Show your partner.* Check with the class (on the sand). Pupils say *Here it is.*

CD 4, 02

LENNY: We're on holiday! Great!

SIMON: I love holidays.

LENNY: So do I.

SIMON: I love playing on the beach. The clean, yellow sand, the big sun, the beautiful, blue sea. I love swimming in the sea!

LENNY: Er, the beach is OK, but I love walking in the mountains. There are lots of green trees and beautiful flowers.

SIMON: What! Flowers, Lenny?

LENNY: Well, yes, er … flowers and animals, big animals.

SIMON: Hmm. I like fishing with my grandpa. We can't fish in the city.

LENNY: Do Stella and Suzy like fishing?

SIMON: Oh, no. Suzy likes picking up shells from the beach and Stella loves sitting in the sun and reading.

LENNY: Come on, Simon. Let's go! We're on holiday!

SIMON: Yeh!

PB84. ACTIVITY **2.** *Listen and repeat.*

- Say *Now let's listen and repeat.* Play the CD. Pupils chorus the words. Listen for correct pronunciation.

CD 4, 03

Beach, sand, sea, shell, sun, mountain

AB84. ACTIVITY **1.** *Listen and tick (✓). Find the words.*

- Say *Open your Activity Books at page 84, please.* Do the first one as an example. Play the CD. Elicit the word (sea) and show pupils the tick. Play the CD. Pupils tick the words. They check in pairs. Play the CD again. Check with the class. Pupils then find the words in the wordsearch. Elicit answers.

CD 4, 04

1. sea	4. shell	7. flowers	10. fish
2. sun	5. mountain	8. bird	11. holiday
3. sand	6. tree	9. animals	

AB84. ACTIVITY **2.** *Match. Write the words.*

- Focus pupils on the example. Check they know what to do. Remind them that the letters on the left match with two sets of letters on the right. Pupils work individually and write the words. They check in pairs. Check with the class.

Key: beautiful, beach, mountain, mouse, sand, sun, shell, shirt, train, trees

Extra activities: see page T126 (if time)

Optional activity

- *Teacher's Resource Book 2* Unit 12 Reinforcement worksheet 1 (see pages 74, 75).

Ending the lesson

- Make four teams. They line up facing the board. Whisper a different word from the lesson to the first member of each group. They whisper it back along the line. The pupil at the back then runs to the front and writes the word on the board. The first to do it correctly wins two points for their team. The other teams win one point if they do it correctly. The pupils from the back of the lines come to the front. Repeat with different words.

OBJECTIVES: By the end of the lesson, pupils will have talked more about holiday activities and sung a song.

• TARGET LANGUAGE

Key language: *What's he/she doing? What's (name) doing?*
Additional language: *a new song*
Revision: present continuous, holiday vocabulary, character names, *lots of, at the beach, sleeping, walking, swimming, getting, writing*

• MATERIALS REQUIRED

Flashcards: (holiday) 98–103
Extra activity 2: a holiday postcard, one piece of card for each pupil
Optional: *Teacher's Resource Book 2* Unit 12 song worksheet (page 79),
Kid's Box 2 Interactive DVD: The living room 'At the seaside' episode

Warmer

- Review the holiday words using the flashcards. Flash each one (picture side) in front of the class and elicit the word. Display them word side around the room. Call them out quickly one after another. Pupils point to the correct word each time.

PB85. ACTIVITY 3. *Listen and point. Sing.*

- Say *Open your Pupil's Books at page 85, please.* Elicit what and who pupils can see and what they're doing. Play the CD. Pupils listen and point to the people in the picture. Play the CD again. Check understanding by asking, e.g. *Who's singing? What's she doing? What's Suzy doing?*
- Play the CD in sections. Pupils repeat. Teach the song in this way. Pupils repeat the whole song in chorus with the CD. Pupils stand up. They sing the song as a class. Make five groups (Stella, Suzy, Simon, etc.). Everyone sings and the groups mime their action during the whole song (so the pupils are miming different actions at the same time). Change roles and repeat. You could record pupils and they could watch / listen to their performance for added motivation.

CD 4, 05

STELLA: I'm writing a new song,
I'm writing a new song.
At the beach. At the beach.

Suzy's getting lots of shells,
She's getting lots of shells.
At the beach. At the beach.

Simon's swimming in the sea,
Simon's swimming in the sea.
At the beach. At the beach.

Dad's walking on the sand,
Dad's walking on the sand.
At the beach. At the beach.

Mum's reading in the sun,
Mum's reading in the sun.
At the beach. At the beach. *[Repeat x3]*

CD 4, 06

Now sing the song again. (Karaoke version)

PB85. ACTIVITY 4. *Ask and answer.*

- Pupils work in pairs. Pupil A asks a question about the song lyrics, Pupil B answers. Read the example speech bubbles before they begin. Pupils exchange roles. When pupils have done the activity, ask them to close their books and do it from memory. Award points for correct questions and answers.

AB85. ACTIVITY 3. *Look at the picture and answer the questions.*

- Say *Open your Activity Books at page 85, please.* Focus pupils on the picture and say *Tell me about the picture. What can you see?* Elicit some of the things in the picture.
- Focus pupils on the example question and answer. Pupils work in pairs. They take turns to ask one of the questions and to answer it. They do the activity orally first. Pupils then write the answers in their books.
- Monitor and help with spelling. Check with the class using open pairs. Write the sentences on the board for pupils to check their work.

Key: 2 He's drinking lemonade. 3 She's sleeping. 4 No, it's running. 5 He's swimming in the sea. 6 She's picking up shells. 7 There are three birds. 8 They're flying.

AB85. ACTIVITY 4. *Look at the letters and write the words.*

- Point to the clouds with the scrambled letters inside. Ask a volunteer to read the example answer. Say *Move the letters to make words.* Copy the letters in the order they appear inside the first cloud on the board and show pupils how they make the word sand by crossing out each letter as you write the word with the letters in the correct order below.
- Pupils work individually to solve the rest of the anagrams. Elicit the answers and call volunteers to write the words on the board. Check spelling carefully. Early finishers can draw a picture for each word in their notebooks.

Key: 2 shell, 3 flower, 4 beach, 5 tree, 6 mountain

Extra activities: see page T126 (if time)

Optional activities

- Pupils do the gap-fill activity and make the dice on the Unit 12 song worksheet from *Teacher's Resource Book 2* (see pages 74 and 79 of *Teacher's Resource Book 2*).
- The 'At the seaside' episode from *Kid's Box 2 Interactive DVD* (*The living room* section). See pages 24–27 of the Teacher's booklet for the Interactive DVD.

Ending the lesson

- Pupils sing the song again from memory. They all do the actions for each verse as they sing it.

3 Listen and point. Sing.

CD4 5

I'm writing a new song,
I'm writing a new song.
At the beach, at the beach.

Suzy's getting lots of shells,
She's getting lots of shells.
At the beach, at the beach.

Simon's swimming in the sea,
Simon's swimming in the sea.
At the beach, at the beach.

Dad's walking on the sand,
Dad's walking on the sand.
At the beach, at the beach.

Mum's reading in the sun,
Mum's reading in the sun.
At the beach, at the beach ...

4 Ask and answer.

What's Stella doing?

She's writing a song.

Vocabulary

beach mountain sand sea shell sun

5 7 CD4 Listen and answer.

Grammar

Do you want to …? I want to … I don't want to …

OBJECTIVES: By the end of the lesson, pupils will have learned to ask and answer questions using *want*.

• TARGET LANGUAGE

Key language: *Where do you want to go on holiday? I want to … Do you want … ?*

Additional language: *end of school, this year, watch, notebook, sunhat, all*

Revision: holiday words, adjectives, *draw, birds, trees, animals, pencils, town, sunglasses, Let's go, walk, sit*

• MATERIALS REQUIRED

Flashcards: (holiday) 98–103

Photocopiable 12a (see page T112), enlarged and copied onto card, one copy for each group of four pupils, coloured counters, coins

Extra activity: a CD of holiday-type music

Optional: *Teacher's Resource Book 2* Unit 12 Reinforcement worksheet 2 (page 76)

Warmer

- Teach a mime for each of the new holiday words:

– *sun*: shading your eyes from the bright sun
– *sea*: swimming action
– *shells*: looking at a tiny shell in the palm of your hand
– *beach*: spreading arms wide
– *mountains*: hand making shape of mountains
– *sand*: sand running through fingers

- Say the words quickly one after another at random. Pupils do the mimes. Pupils take turns to be the callers.

PB86. ACTIVITY **5.** *Listen and answer.*

- Keep books closed. Say *Listen. The Star family are talking about their holidays.* Set the pre-listening questions: *Who likes beach holidays? Who likes mountain holidays? Where are they going? The mountains or the beach?* Play the CD. Pupils listen for the answers. They check in pairs. Say *Open your Pupil's Books at page 86, please. Listen again and check.* (Simon, Stella, Mountains). Play the CD again. Check comprehension and focus on the target structure. Say *Where does Simon want to go? Where does Stella want to go? Who wants some sunglasses? What does he say? Who wants a sunhat? What does she say?*

CD 4, 07

MRS STAR: Well, children. It's the end of school. Where do you want to go on holiday?
SIMON: Let's go to the beach.
STELLA: Oh, I want to go to the mountains this year. I want to draw birds and trees and I want to watch small animals. I'd like a new notebook and pencils, please.
SUZY: Are there shells in the mountains, Stella?
STELLA: No, there aren't, but you can get lots of beautiful flowers.
MR STAR: Do you want to go to a big city? We can walk in the streets and sit in cafés.
ALL: Oh, no! We don't want to go to a city.
SIMON: OK, let's go to the mountains. Can we swim there, Mum?
MRS STAR: Yes, you can.
MR STAR: OK, that's good. We're all happy to go to the mountains for our holiday.
STELLA: So can I have a new notebook and pencils, then?
SIMON: Well, I want some new sunglasses, please.
SUZY: And I want a new sunhat, please.
GRANDPA: Hmm, and now I want my dinner.

Practice

- Display the flashcards on the board. Say *Where do you want to go on holiday?* Point to the flashcards on the board. Elicit/prompt a response from a pupil: *I want to go to the (beach).* Elicit other responses from pupils. Practise in open pairs.

Photocopiable 12a: see pages T99 and T112

AB86. ACTIVITY **5.** *Listen and tick (✓) the box.* **[YLE]**

- Say *Open your Activity Books at page 86, please.* Play number 1 and point to the ticked box. Play the rest of the CD. Pupils listen and tick. They check in pairs. Play the CD again. Check with the class.

Key: 2 a, 3 c, 4 b, 5 b, 6 c

CD 4, 08

1. Nick's sitting on the sofa. He wants to watch his favourite programme on television.
2. What do you want for lunch, Mary?
   Can I have some chicken and carrots, please?
3. Mum, please can I have a camera for my birthday?
4. What do you want to drink, Susan?
   Please can I have some milk?
5. Sally, let's play football.
   OK. I love playing football.
6. Come on, John. Let's go to the café for some lemonade.
   Er … I don't want to go to the café. I want to go to the park.

AB86. ACTIVITY **6.** *Read. Write 'Yes, he does' or 'No, he doesn't'.*

- Elicit the meaning of *birthday list.* Elicit the things on Daniel's list. Go through the example. Pupils work in pairs and write the answers on the lines as appropriate. Check with the class. Elicit the corrections, e.g. *2 He wants a long ruler.*

Key: 2 No, he doesn't. 3 No, he doesn't. 4 Yes, he does. 5 Yes, he does. 6 No, he doesn't.

Extra activity: see page T126 (if time)

Optional activity

- *Teacher's Resource Book 2* Unit 12 Reinforcement worksheet 2 (see pages 74 and 76).

Ending the lesson

- Brainstorm a class birthday list (ten items). Pupils individually choose four items and write their own list. They swap lists with their partner. Ask questions of A about B, using the words on the board, e.g. *Does (Sue) want a new computer?* A: *Yes, she does / No, she doesn't*, according to what's in the list. Pupils continue the activity in pairs.

OBJECTIVES: By the end of the lesson, pupils will have had more practice using *want* and done a chant.

• TARGET LANGUAGE
Revision: *wants, that/this one,* clothes, animals, toys, food, town, colours, household objects, question words

• MATERIALS REQUIRED
A selection of flashcards from *Kid's Box 2*, e.g. six clothes, six foods, six animals
Extra activity 2: Six true/false sentences about the picture in Pupil's Book Activity 7, e.g. *The shoe shop is next to the fruit shop. There are two frogs in the toy shop.*
Optional: *Kid's Box Teacher's Resource Book 2* Unit 12 Extension worksheet 1 (page 77)

Warmer

- Display a selection of flashcards, e.g. six clothes, six foods, six animals, on the board. Ask a pupil *Which one do you want?* The pupil responds *I want the (dog), please.* Give the pupil the flashcard. Repeat with the other flashcards and other pupils.

PB87. ACTIVITY **6.** *Listen and point. Chant.*

- Say *Open your Pupil's Books at page 87, please.* Focus pupils on the words and pictures. Play the CD. They don't add the words at this stage. Play the CD again. Pupils add the words for each picture to complete the chant. Pupils stand up. Make two groups. One group says the chant (the words written on the page). The other group mimes and supplies the word, e.g. *hat* (putting a hat on their heads). Pupils swap roles.

Key: hat, jeans, potatoes, beans, sheep, goat, lorry, boat

CD 4, 09

I want a *[pause]*,
And you want some *[pause]*.
She wants some *[pause]*,
And he wants some *[pause]*.

They want a *[pause]*,
And we want a *[pause]*.
She wants a *[pause]*,
And he wants a *[pause]*.

PB87. ACTIVITY **7.** *Listen and say the letter.*

- Focus pupils on the picture and on the letters (a, b, etc.). Elicit what they can see in the picture (the shops, the street, etc.). Say *Listen. Don't speak, but point with your partner.* Play the CD. Pupils listen and point. Play the CD again. Stop after each one to elicit the letter. Elicit the names of the shops / the word family for each one.
- Pupils do the activity in pairs. They take turns to ask, e.g. *Which shoes do you want?* and respond, e.g. *I want the red ones.*

Key: 1 m, 2 l, 3 e, 4 a, 5 p, 6 h, 7 d, 8 j

CD 4, 10

1. Which melon do you want?
   I want the big green one.
2. Which shoes do you want?
   I want the red ones.
3. Which monster do you want?
   I want the ugly one.
4. Which ice cream do you want?
   I want the lemon one.
5. Which apples do you want?
   I want the green ones.
6. Which doll do you want?
   I want the happy one.
7. Which cake do you want?
   I want the small one.
8. Which shoes do you want?
   I want the white ones.

AB87. ACTIVITY **7.** *Listen and colour. There is one example.* **[YLE]**

- Say *Open your Activity Books at page 87, please.* Ask questions about the picture to review the vocabulary.
- Pupils take out crayons or pens in green, pink, blue, red, black, yellow and orange. Play the example on the CD. Say *Where's the black shell?* Pupils point and say *Under the tree.* Say *Listen and colour. Make a dot first.*
- Play the CD. Pupils make a coloured dot for each item. They check in pairs. Play the CD again. Check with the class. Pupils colour the objects. Elicit which colour they didn't use (blue).

Key: 1 ball in the sea = pink, 2 sun on the boy's T-shirt = yellow, 3 shell in the girl's hand = green, 4 hat on the beach = red, 5 mountain = orange

CD 4, 11

Look. Here's a picture of the beach.
Great! Can I colour it, please?
Yes. Can you see the shell under the tree?
Yes, I can.
Well, colour it black.
OK. The shell under the tree is black.
Can you see the black shell under the tree? This is an example.
Now you listen and colour.

1. One boy is in the sea. He's playing with a ball. Can you see it?
   Oh yes.
   Well, colour the ball pink.
   OK. The ball in the sea is pink now.
2. Now look at the boy on the beach.
   There he is. There's a sun on his T-shirt.
   Yes. Colour it yellow.
   OK. The sun on the boy's T-shirt is yellow.
3. The girl is holding a shell.
   Oh, yes.
   Colour her shell green, please.
   Right. The girl's shell is green now.
4. Can you see the hat on the beach?
   On the beach? Yes, there it is.
   Well, colour that hat red.
   Red? OK.
5. Now, what's your favourite colour?
   Oh, it's orange.
   Then colour the mountain orange.
   Right. The mountain is orange.
   Good. I like this picture now.

Extra activities: see page T127 (if time)

Optional activity

- Unit 12 Extension worksheet 1 from *Teacher's Resource Book 2* (see pages 74 and 77).

Ending the lesson

- Write *sea, sand, mountain, shell, beach, sun, holiday,* plus three other related words, e.g. *swimming, sunglasses, ice cream* on the board, each with jumbled letters. Pupils work in pairs and race to unjumble them. Elicit correct spellings from pairs.

6 CD4 9 Listen and point. Chant.

I want a 

And you want some .

She wants some 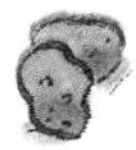

And he wants some .

They want a 

And we want a .

She wants a 

And he wants a .

7 CD4 10 Listen and say the letter.

Which melon do you want?

I want the big green one.

That's m.

8 Monty's phonics

Mum Dad

Ben Jill

Tom

Mum, Dad, Ben, Jill, and Tom are on the bus.

9 Ask and answer.

Do you like fishing?
No, I don't.

OBJECTIVES: By the end of the lesson, pupils will be able to identify and say all the short vowel sounds which have appeared in the course (a /æ/, e /e/, i /ɪ/, o /ɒ/ and u /ʌ/) and will have practised asking and answering questions.

• TARGET LANGUAGE

Key language: the phonemes /æ/ as in *Dad*, /e/ as in *Ben*, /ɪ/ as in *Jill*, /ɒ/ as in *Tom* and /ʌ/ as in *Mum*

Revision: *Do you like …- ing? Yes, I do, No, I don't,* food, hobbies, holidays, adjectives, animals

• MATERIALS REQUIRED

Photocopiable 12b (see page T113) copied onto thin card, cut into dominoes, one set for each group of three or four pupils. Extra activity 1: three rolled up newspapers

Warmer

Draw a simple family tree showing grandpa (Lewis), grandma (Ellen), mum (Beth) and dad (James), their two children (Ben and Jill), an uncle and aunt (Steve and Ann) and a cousin to Ben and Jill (Tom), as shown below.

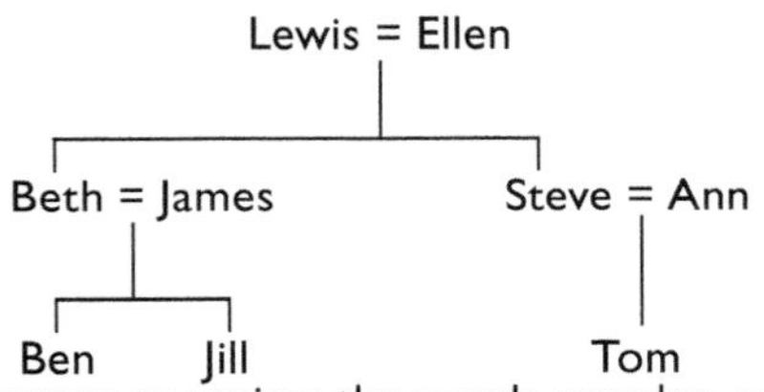

Use the family tree to review the words grandpa, grandma, mum, dad, etc. to start the focus on the short vowel sounds (all the names in the tree have short vowel sounds).

PB88. ACTIVITY **8.** *Monty's phonics*

- Say *Open your Pupil's Books at page 88, please.* Point to the small pictures and say the names, emphasizing the vowel sounds. Pupils practise pronunciation of each one. Point at the large picture and say *Look! Who's in the picture? (Mum, Dad, Ben, Jill, Tom)? Where are they? (On a bus) What animals can you see? (A cat and a dog).* Say *Now listen to Monty, point and repeat.*
- Play the CD. Pupils listen and repeat the sounds, words, and sentence using the same tone and speed as Monty.
- Pupils repeat the tongue twister as a class. Do it more and more quickly. Pupils try saying the tongue twister as fast as they can. Invite volunteers to say it to the class.

CD 4, 12

MONTY: Hi, I'm Monty! Repeat after me!
/ʌ/, /ʌ/, Mum
/æ/, /æ/, Dad
/e/, /e/, Ben
/ɪ/, /ɪ/, Jill
/ɒ/, /ɒ/, Tom
Mum, Dad, Ben, Jill and Tom are on the bus!
Mum, Dad, Ben, Jill and Tom are on the bus!
Mum, Dad, Ben, Jill and Tom are on the bus!

Photocopiable 12b: see below and page T113

PB88. ACTIVITY **9.** *Ask and answer.*

- Tell the class that they are going to play dominoes. Ask pupils to gather around one table and teach/check the rules with a set of cards from Photocopiable 12b (page T113). Each player has an equal number of dominoes. One domino is placed facing upward on the table. The first player matches the picture or word(s) on one of their dominoes with the same word(s) or picture already placed on the table. Play continues round the table in this way until one player uses all his/her dominoes. He/She is the winner.
- Divide the class into groups of three or four pupils. Hand out a set of domino cards from Photocopiable 12b to each group. Teach the verb *to deal.* Ask one member of each group to deal the cards. Pupils take it in turns to lay a card face up on the table. The player to the left asks, e.g. *Do you like fishing?* The player answers truthfully *Yes, I do. / No, I don't.* Play continues. The first player to get rid of all their cards is the winner.
- You could extend the activity by asking each group to prepare a set of domino cards based on their favourite words from *Kid's Box 2.*

AB88. ACTIVITY **8.** *Listen and match.*

- Say *Open your Activity Books at page 88, please. Listen and say.* Point to the first incomplete sentence and play the first item on the CD. Pupils repeat. Mime drawing a line from *Dad catches his* to *hat.* Make sure pupils know that they have to listen and repeat first, then match the sentence halves.
- Say *Listen and say. Don't match.* Play the rest of the CD, pausing after each item for pupils to repeat the first time.
- Say *Now match.* Pupils work individually or in pairs to do the matching (only the sentences at this stage). Check answers as a class.

Key: See audioscript

- Say *Now look at the pictures.* Point to picture a and say *Look! Ben gets shells. It's number 2.* Point to the example number 2 on the line.
- Pupils look and match the rest of the pictures to sentences 1 to 5 by writing numbers. Check as a class.

Key: b 5, c 1, d 3, e 4

CD 4, 13

1. Dad catches his hat. 2. Ben gets shells. 3. Jill swims with the fish. 4. Tom stops the dog. 5. Mum runs in the sun.

AB88. ACTIVITY **9.** *Complete the questions. Then answer.*

- Focus pupils on the words in the box and on the example. Ask a pupil to read it out: *Is your kitchen big or small?* Elicit how they know the word to write is *small.* Check understanding of the concept of *opposite*. Pupils work in pairs. They complete the questions first. Check with the class and check understanding of each question.
- Pupils then work individually and answer the questions about themselves. Monitor and help where necessary.

Key: 2 ugly, 3 short, 4 dirty, 5 new

Extra activities: see page T127 (if time)

Ending the lesson

- Do the tongue twister again with the class. Pupils stand up and say it in chorus. Then invite groups or pairs to have a go at saying it quickly.

OBJECTIVES: By the end of the lesson, pupils will have read a story and reviewed language from the unit.

• TARGET LANGUAGE
Key language: language from the unit
Additional language: *postcard*
Revision: holiday, clothes, food, adjectives, *haven't got, got, Let's go, sunhat, sunglasses*

• MATERIALS REQUIRED
Flashcards: (holiday) 98–103
Extra activity 2: Photocopiable 12a (see page T112), enlarged and copied onto card, one copy for each group of four pupils, coloured counters, coins
Optional: *Teacher's Resource Book 2* Unit 12 Extension worksheet 2 (page 78) and/or animated version of the Unit 12 story from *Kid's Box 2 Interactive DVD* (Suzy's room section), *Kid's Box 2 Language Portfolio* pages 6 and 13

Warmer

- Revise the holiday words, using the flashcards. Display the flashcards (picture side) on the board and write a number between *1* and 6 under each one. Write a tiny number on the corner of the board and cover it with your hand. Elicit guesses, e.g. *Is it sand?* until a pupil guesses the right one. The pupil then comes up and repeats the activity.

Story

PB89. ACTIVITY **10.** *Listen to the story.*

- Say *Open your Pupil's Books at page 89, please.* Elicit who they can see (Trevor, Monty, Maskman, Marie). Set the pre-listening questions: *Where are they? What does Marie want? What's Maskman got on his eyes?* Play the CD. Pupils listen and look. They check in pairs. Check with the class (Mountains; Dress, shoes, sunhat, sunglasses; Shells). Play the CD again. Pupils listen and repeat.
- Check comprehension by asking questions, e.g. *Is Trevor happy? Is Marie's bag small? Where is Maskman?*

CD 4, 14

Toys in the toy box,
Come alive.
Walk and talk,
On the count of five.
One, two, three, four, five.

MARIE: Here we are in the mountains.
TREVOR: Look, I've got a postcard from Maskman.

TREVOR: Listen. 'Hello. I'm at the beach. It's beautiful. I love sleeping in the sun and drinking lemonade.'

TREVOR: I want to go to 'Star Beach' and see Maskman.
MARIE: OK, Trevor. We can go and find Maskman.

MARIE: Hmm … I want my new dress, my new shoes and my new sunhat and sunglasses.

MASKMAN: I'm on holiday. Can you get me some lemonade, please, Metal Mouth?

MARIE: Maskman! Is this 'Star Beach'?
MASKMAN: Hello. Er, yes, it is.

TREVOR AND MONTY: Ha ha ha!

PB89. ACTIVITY **11.** *Listen and say the number.*

- Say *Now listen and look at the pictures. Say the number of the picture to your partner.* Play the CD. Pupils point to the picture and whisper the number to their partner. Play the CD again. Check with the class.

Key: 3, 5, 1, 4, 2, 6

CD 4, 15

TREVOR: I want to go to 'Star Beach' and see Maskman.

MASKMAN: I'm on holiday. Can you get me some lemonade, please, Metal Mouth?

MARIE: Here we are in the mountains.
TREVOR: Look, I've got a postcard from Maskman.

MARIE: Hmm … I want my new dress, my new shoes and my new sunhat and sunglasses.

TREVOR: Listen. 'Hello. I'm at the beach. It's beautiful. I love sleeping in the sun and drinking lemonade.'

MARIE: Maskman! Is this 'Star beach'?
MASKMAN: Hello. Er, yes, it is.

AB89. MY PICTURE DICTIONARY.

- Say *Open your Activity Books at page 89, please.* Point to the word with missing vowels in the first square and the example answer. Elicit the word (*beach*). Say *Write the letters to complete the words. They are all holiday words.* Pupils work individually or in pairs to complete the words. Check answers.
- Pupils prepare the holiday stickers and lay them out on their desks in the correct order. Check around the class before they stick them in their books.

Key: 2 shell, 3 sun, 4 mountain, 5 sand, 6 sea

Extra activities: see page T127 (if time)

AB89. MY PROGRESS.

- Read the first sentence. Focus pupils on Pupil's Book page 88 Activity 9. Elicit some of the dialogues. Say *Good. You can talk about your holidays.* Focus pupils on the words on Pupil's Book page 87. Say *Remember the chant.* Say *You can talk about this.* Pupils work in pairs to read out a *can do* sentence and talk about what it says.
- Say *Now tick or cross the sentences.* Encourage pupils to practise, so that they can tick both the statements and colour the star.

Optional activities

- Unit 12 Extension worksheet 2 (see pages 74 and 78 of *Teacher's Resource Book 2*).
- The animated version of the story from *Kid's Box 2 Interactive DVD* (Suzy's room section). See pages 41–46 of the DVD booklet.

Language Portfolio

- Pupils complete page 6 of *Kid's Box 2 Language Portfolio* (*I can … Units 10–12*) and page 13 (*A holiday*).

Ending the lesson

- Ask pupils which chant/song/game they'd like to do again from the unit. Do it together to end the lesson.

10 14 CD4 Listen to the story.

1
Here we are in the mountains.
Look, I've got a postcard from Maskman.
2
Listen. 'Hello. I'm at the beach. It's beautiful. I love sleeping in the sun and drinking lemonade …
3
I want to go to 'Star Beach' and see Maskman.
OK, Trevor. We can go and find Maskman.
4
Hmm … I want my new dress, my new shoes … and my new sunhat and sunglasses.
5
I'm on holiday. Can you get me some lemonade, please, Metal Mouth?
6
Maskman! Is this 'Star Beach'?
Hello. Er, yes, it is.
Ha ha ha.

11 15 CD4 Listen and say the number.

1 Listen and answer.

CD4 16

Look at D1. What can you see?

I can see mountains.

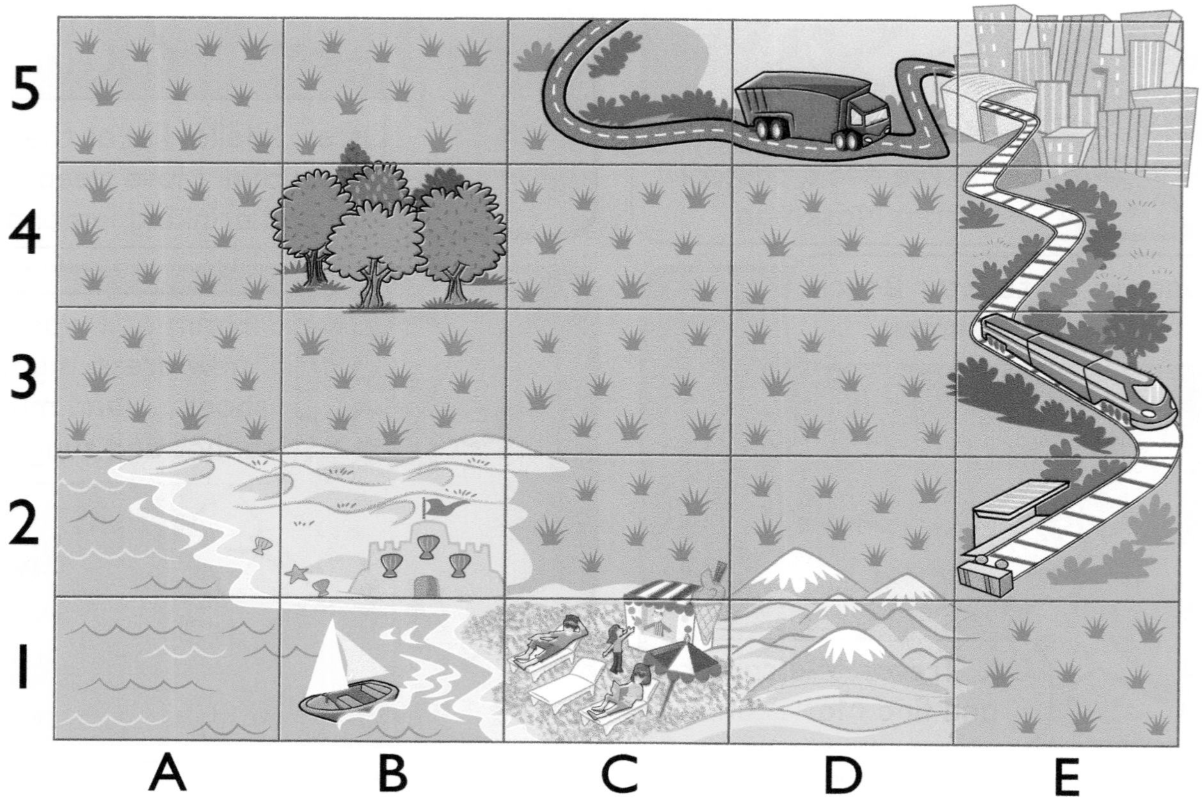

2 Play the game with a friend.

Now you! Activity Book page 90

OBJECTIVES: By the end of the lesson, pupils will have practised interpreting maps.

• TARGET LANGUAGE

Key language: letters *A-E*, numbers *1-5*, *map, What can you see? I can see …*

Additional language: *Where is the …? Draw a … Colour it … Where am I?*

Revision: colours, *house, flower, car*

• MATERIALS REQUIRED

A map, preferably of your pupils' home town or city, which has large grid squares

Coloured pens or pencils

Extra activity 1: large paper map you have/have made with items drawn on it

Extra activity 2: Paper with a photocopied map grid or squared paper (one piece for each pupil)

Warmer

- Review the alphabet in English. Write the capital letters on the board or refer to an alphabet poster. Say the names of the letters (not the sounds). Focus particularly on the first few letters A-E. Also revise numbers 1-10 and practise pronunciation.
- Write the numbers on the board for pupils to say chorally – from 1 to 10 and backwards from 10 to 1, slowly, quickly, softly, loudly, etc.

Presentation

- Point to the picture of Marie and say *This is Marie's Geography and today's lesson is about maps.* Show pupils a real map (preferably of their own town or city) and say *This is a map of* (name of the town/city). Show pupils that the map has grid squares and point to the numbers and letters used at the side and along the top/bottom.

PB90. ACTIVITY **1.** *Listen and answer.*

- Say *Open your Pupil's Books at page 90, please.* Say *Look at the map. What can you see?* Elicit the names of things on the map, e.g. *a road, the sea, the beach, the mountains, the trees, the city.* Say *Listen and answer.* Pupils listen to the first grid reference. Pause the CD so that pupils have time to find the correct point on the map.
- Show them how to follow column D and row 1 to find the answer. Focus on the speech bubbles at the top of the page. Do the same for number 2. Pupils whisper the answer in pairs to check and then put up their hands to answer. Play the rest of the CD in the same way, pausing to elicit answers.

Key: 2 I can see the sea, 3 I can see some/the trees, 4 I can see a/the city, 5 I can see a boat/the beach, 6 I can see the road/a truck

CD 4, 16

1. Look at D1. What can you see?
2. Look at A1. What can you see?
3. Look at B4. What can you see?
4. Look at E5. What can you see?
5. Look at B1. What can you see?
6. Look at D5. What can you see?

PB90. ACTIVITY **2.** *Play the game with a friend.*

- Focus on the photograph of the children looking at the map. Say *Play the game with a friend.* Pupils work in pairs to ask and answer as in the example speech bubbles. Pupils swap roles so that they have a chance to practise asking the questions and saying the grid references. Go around the class to check and help any pupils who may be confused by the grid references.

AB90. ACTIVITY **1.** *Read, draw and colour.*

- Say *Open your Activity Books at page 90, please. What can you see?* Elicit *A map. Some roads.* Point to the sentences under the map. Say *Read, draw and colour. Choose any square.* Read the first sentence aloud and mime thinking about where to draw a car. Point to a square on the map and say *I'm going to draw my car here. I'm colouring it blue.* Mime drawing.
- Pupils work individually to draw the items in the grid above. Make sure that they draw each item within the lines of a square so that it is clear which grid reference the item is in. Monitor and help as necessary. Pupils colour the items as directed in the sentences.

AB90. ACTIVITY **2.** *Ask and answer. Draw.*

- Pupils work in pairs to ask and answer about the map they have drawn in Activity 1 using the speech bubbles to help. They keep their pictures hidden from each other. Pupil A asks, e.g. *Where's the car?* Pupil B answers, e.g. *B3.* Pupil A draws a car in B3. Pupil A continues asking until he/she has drawn all five items.
- Then pupils swap roles and Pupil B asks and draws, with Pupil A answering about his/her picture. At the end they compare their pictures to make sure they have drawn the items in the correct squares.

Extra activities: see page T127 (if time)

Ending the lesson

- Write letters from the alphabet on the board and pupils say them (with correct pronunciation) as you write.

OBJECTIVES: By the end of the lesson, pupils will have read about 'helping' holidays and written about their own experiences helping someone.

• TARGET LANGUAGE

Key language: *helping holidays, teaching, speak* (with their hands), *dirty, be on holiday*

Additional language: *clean, don't have, give, love, Where's (Ben) on holiday? helping*

Revision: *elephant, bird, children, beach, teacher, food, park, family, mountains, green, beautiful, hands, happy, black, sea, fly, swim*

• MATERIALS REQUIRED

Extra activities: Photos from magazines/newspapers/internet showing people helping others or helping injured or sick animals (at least five – with numbers written on the back).

Warmer

- Mime talking with your hands to the pupils (if possible learn one or two signs, e.g. those for *Hello* and *How are you?*). Ask whether any of the pupils know any sign language to demonstrate. Make up your own signs to mime to the class and they guess what you are saying e.g. *open your books* (pretend to open a book with your hands, point to the pupils and a book). Let the pupils have a go in pairs. Say *Speak with your hands.*

PB91. ACTIVITY **3.** *Read and match.*

- Say *Open your Pupil's Books at page 91, please.* Read the title for Trevor's Values 'Helping holidays' and use the photographs to explain that some people go on holidays where they help others/animals. Point to each photo in turn. Say *What/who can you see?* Elicit some of the things in the pictures (*bird, elephant, beach, children, teacher*).
- Say *Read and match. Point to the emails below the photographs.* Tell pupils they must find the key words to help them match the messages to the photos. They don't need to read and understand all of the text to be able to answer. Give pupils a time limit to 'scan read' the paragraphs and match them to the photos.
- Pupils put up their hands to answer. Ask pupils to read each text again and ask questions for further comprehension and to help prepare pupils for the listening in Activity 4 e.g. *Who is Miss Jones? (A teacher), What animal is Ben helping? (An elephant), Where's Grace on holiday? (The beach).*

Key: 1 C, 2 B, 3 A

PB91. ACTIVITY **4.** *Listen and say 'yes' or 'no'.*

- Read the speech bubble at the bottom of the page. Say *Read the email from Grace, Yes or No?* Point to the example answer (No). Play the CD. Pause after each statement to give pupils time to decide whether the statement is correct or incorrect according to the emails in Activity 3. Pupils check together in pairs and say '*yes*' for correct and '*no*' for incorrect. They correct the false sentences.

Key: No (Grace is on holiday at the beach), No (The beach is black and dirty), Yes, Yes, No (Sue's on holiday in the mountains), Yes, No (Ben's ten), No (Ben's helping some elephants), Yes

CD 4, 17

Grace is on holiday in the mountains.
The beach is beautiful and clean.
The sea birds can't fly.
Sue's a teacher.
Sue's on holiday at the beach.
Sue's teaching children to speak with their hands.
Ben's nine.
Ben's helping some tigers.
Ben loves animals.

AB91. ACTIVITY **3.** *Listen and write the number.*

- Say *Open your Activity Books at page 91, please.* Point to the first picture and say *Look. They're cleaning.* Point to the other pictures and ask pupils *What's he/she doing?* Elicit *cleaning the bird/helping the boy/giving the dogs water.* Say *Listen and write the number.* Play the CD and pause after each number to give pupils time to think.
- Pupils work in pairs to number the pictures according to the information on the CD. Check the order as a class.

Key: 1 the second picture (with the dogs), 2 the first picture (with the trees), 3 the third picture (with the book), 4 the fourth picture (with the bird)

CD 4, 18

1. Alex is helping at the dogs' home. He's giving them water.
2. The children are in the mountains. They're cleaning.
3. Tony's reading with his hand. Ann's helping him.
4. The bird can't fly and it's very sad. Nick's cleaning it.

AB91. ACTIVITY **4.** *Write and draw.*

- Pupils use the blank square on the left to draw a picture of them helping somebody or something. This could be something they have actually done or something they would like to do in the future. If possible, show a photo of you or someone else helping someone or an animal. Write some sentences as in Activity 3 of the Pupil's book to describe your picture, using *I'm*. Pupils write about their pictures in their notebooks and then copy into their Activity Books. Say *Write and draw.* Go around the class checking and helping as necessary.

Extra activities see T127 (if time)

Ending the lesson

- Pupils take the Activity Book home for the holidays and write a postcard. They could find/take a photo of themselves to stick on the postcard to write about.

3 Read and match.

1

2

3
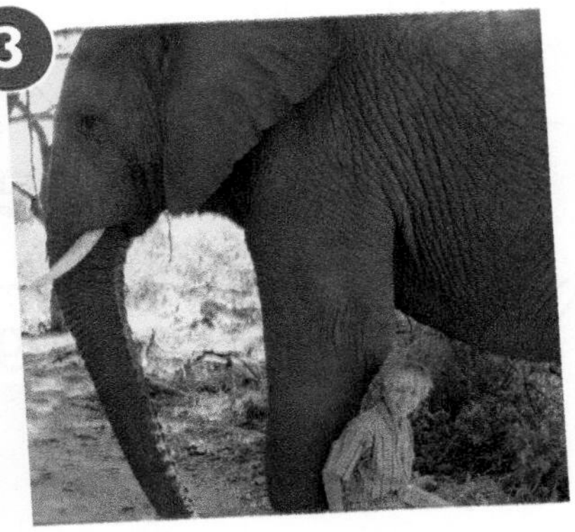

a

Hello
I'm Ben and I'm ten. I'm on holiday at an elephant park. These elephants don't have a family. I clean the baby elephants and give them food.
I love animals!
Ben

b

Hello
I'm Miss Jones. I'm a teacher and I'm on holiday in the mountains. The mountains are beautiful and green. I'm teaching these children to speak with their hands.
We are very happy!
Miss Jones

c

Hello
I'm Grace. I'm on holiday at the beach. The beach is black and dirty. The sea birds can't fly or swim. I'm cleaning the beach and the birds on the beach.
Grace

4 Listen and say 'yes' or 'no'.

17 CD4

Grace's on holiday in the mountains.

No.

Review

9 10 11 12

1 Listen and correct.

CD4 19

The boy's wearing a green shirt.

No, he's wearing a red shirt.

2 Look and say with a friend.

In picture one the woman's reading, but in picture two she's writing.

OBJECTIVES: By the end of the lesson, pupils will have reviewed language from Units 9–12 and will have talked about the differences between two pictures.

• TARGET LANGUAGE

Key language: vocabulary and language from Units 9–12
Revision: sports, clothes, holidays, adjectives, hobbies, food

• MATERIALS REQUIRED

Flashcards of new words from Units 9–12
Extra activity 1: any of Photocopiable activities 1–12b

Warmer

- Display a selection of eight flashcards of new items from Units 9 to 12 (e.g. *glasses, watch, table tennis, paint, lemonade, watermelon, shell, mountain*). Check comprehension by eliciting a sentence for each word (e.g. *My glasses are on my head. I don't like table tennis.* etc.) Make pairs. Pupils write the words in alphabetical order, as quickly as possible. Elicit the words in the correct order (*glasses, lemonade, mountain, paint, shell, table tennis, watch, watermelon*).

PB92. ACTIVITY **1.** *Listen and correct.*

- Say *Open your Pupil's Books at page 92, please.* Elicit known items in the picture by asking *What can you see?* (e.g. *sausages, a cake, lemonade, jeans, mountains,* etc). Present *pineapple*.
- Play the first item on the CD and point to the example speech bubbles. Make sure pupils know that they need to listen and look carefully at the picture in order to correct the sentence. Play the rest of the CD. Pupils listen, point and whisper the correct sentence to their partner each time. Play the CD again. Stop after each sentence and elicit the answer.

Key: No, she's eating a pineapple. No, there are three trees. No, there are some sausages on the table. No, he's painting a picture. No, there are five yellow flowers. No, there's some lemonade on the table. No, she's wearing a blue shirt and jeans. No, she hasn't got a handbag.

CD 4, 19

The boy's wearing a green shirt.
The girl's eating a watermelon.
There are six trees.
There are some burgers on the table.
The boy's taking a photo.
There are five purple flowers.
There's some orange juice on the table.
The woman's wearing an orange dress.
The woman's got a handbag.

PB92. ACTIVITY **2.** *Look and say with a friend.*

- Focus pupils on the two pictures in Activity 2. Elicit sports, hobbies, fruit, items of clothing and other objects pupils can see in the two pictures (*badminton, baseball, reading, writing, watermelon, pineapple, sunglasses, hat,* etc.).
- Say *Look. Picture 1 and picture 2 are different.* Read the speech bubble with the class. Pupils work in pairs or individually to find the rest of the differences (tell them there are four more). Elicit the differences and write sentences like the example on page 92 on the board.
- Fast finishers can write sentences about the differences in their notebooks.

Key: In picture 1, there's a watermelon on the table, but in picture 2, there's a pineapple on the table.
In picture 1, there are 3 shells under the table, but in picture 2, there are 2 shells under the table.
In picture 1, the boy making a sandcastle is wearing a big hat (a sunhat), but in picture 2, he's wearing a small hat.
In picture 1, the children are playing badminton, but in picture 2 they're playing baseball.

AB92. ACTIVITY **1.** *Listen and join the dots.*

- Say *Open your Activity Books at page 92, please.* Check that pupils know what they have to do. Say *Join the dots. Look. Start at letter 'd'. Listen for the next letter. Let's listen and follow first.* Play the CD while pupils trace the route with their fingers (pencils down, without drawing).
- Play the CD again for pupils to join the dots. Elicit the name of the object. Read the question *What's this?* below the picture. Pupils complete the answer. Pupils can colour the picture if there is time.

CD 4, 20

Can you see the letter d? Put your pencil on d. Now listen and draw.
d, y, a, m, x, b, z, c, h, o, q, e, l, p, w, v, s, g, i, f, j, d

AB92. ACTIVITY **2.** *Listen and colour.* **[YLE]**

- Focus pupils on the picture and elicit what they can see (a beach). Play the CD. The first time pupils choose the colours they need and look at the pictures. Play the CD again. Pupils colour the objects in the picture. Check with the class.

CD 4, 21

1. Find the boat.
   OK. It's in the water.
   Can you colour the ball on the boat black?
2. Can you see the ball in the sea?
   The one in front of the boat?
   That's right. Colour it red.
3. Look at the ball behind the tree.
   OK. Is it the big one?
   Yes, it is. Colour it blue.
4. Find the chair.
   Here it is.
   There's a ball next to it. Colour it yellow.
   OK, a yellow ball next to the chair.
5. Can you see the ball between the shoes?
   Yes, I can.
   OK. Colour it purple, please.

Extra activities: see page T127 (if time)

Ending the lesson

- Play a memory game using the flashcards. Stick a selection of flashcards with the word facing outwards on the board. Ask the pupils to close their eyes and then take one away. Ask pupils to remember which word has gone.

OBJECTIVES: By the end of the lesson, pupils will have reviewed language from Units 9–12 and played a game.

• **TARGET LANGUAGE**

Key language: vocabulary and language from Units 9–12
Additional language: procedural language
Revision: question words, present continuous

• **MATERIALS REQUIRED**

Flashcards: (holiday) 98–103
Extra activity 1: a selection of 12 flashcards from the new words in Units 9–12, three rolled up newspapers
Optional: *Kid's Box 2 Interactive DVD*: Stella's room Quiz 3, Test Units 7–12 from *Kid's Box 2 Teacher's Resource Book* (pages 115–129)

Warmer

- Review the holiday vocabulary, using the flashcards. Cover each one and slowly reveal it (picture side). Pupils say the word. Ask *Do you want to go there? What can you do there?* Pupils respond.

PB93. ACTIVITY **3.** *Play the game.*

- Say *Open your Pupil's Books at page 93, please.* Tell pupils they are going to play a game, similar to the one on Pupil's Book pages 33 and 63.
- Read the white box at the top of the page and say *In this game you do different things on the red, blue and green squares. On a red square you follow the instructions.* Read some examples of the instructions on the red squares. Say *On a blue square you answer the question 'What's this?'* Do some examples of blue squares. Then say *On a green square you have to say what the person in the picture is doing. Look!* Point at one of the green squares (e.g. the boy playing baseball) and ask *What's he doing?* Pupils respond, e.g. *He's playing baseball.*
- Demonstrate how to play the game. Hold up your book and put the counter on the Start square (bottom right). Say *This is the Start. You move forward one square at a time. One* ... (moving your counter) *Red. I follow the instruction. 'The sea's clean. Go forward 2 squares'* Move your counter forward and stay on the square you land on. Say *OK, I was right. I stay where I am. Now it's Hilaria's turn. Now it's my turn again. I'm on a green square. I have to say He's playing basketball. I can move one square.* Point at the Finish square and say *This is the Finish. The first person here is the winner! Hooray!*
- Review the useful language for games and write it on the board, if necessary, e.g. *It's my turn. It's your turn. Is this my counter? I'm the winner.* Pupils practise saying the sentences chorally.
- Make pairs. Each pupil needs a coin or counter. Pupils play the game. Monitor and check they are speaking English and following the colour key for each square. If you wish, set a rule that anyone you hear speaking in their own language misses a turn. Encourage pupils to use the language for games. The winner is the first pupil to get to the finish or the pupil who is furthest along the board after a certain amount of time (e.g. ten minutes).

AB93. ACTIVITY **3.** *Match the questions and answers.*

- Say *Open your Activity Books at page 93, please.* Read the example question *How many sausages have you got?* and point at the example letter 'f' in the box on the right. Elicit the answer *I've got two.*
- Say *Read and match.* Pupils work individually or in pairs to match by writing letters.
- Check answers in open pairs (one pupil asks a question and chooses another pupil in the class to answer).

Key: 2 b, 3 e, 4 d, 5 a, 6 c

AB93. ACTIVITY **4.** *Read and complete.*

- Focus pupils on Activity 4. Explain that this is a puzzle they need to complete by writing a word on each card. Point out the arrows, which show the direction they follow. Point to the example answer and say *Look at the picture. It's 'eat'. Write the word. Follow the arrow down to the next card.* Point at the picture on the second card and elicit *ear*. Ask a volunteer to spell it aloud. Explain/elicit that *eat* and *ear* are spelt in the same way, apart from one different letter. Say that all the words in the puzzle will be like that – with just one letter different from one to the next.
- Demonstrate with two or three more cards if necessary. Pupils complete the puzzle in pairs. Monitor and help as necessary.
- Check answers by eliciting the words in order and writing them on the board so pupils can check their spelling.

Key: ear, car, cat, hat, mat, man, men, ten, pen, pea, sea

Extra activities: see page T127 (if time)

Optional evaluations:

- Quiz 3 from *Kid's Box 2 Interactive DVD* (Stella's room section). This quiz can be done as a whole-class activity or as a team competition. See pages 39 and 40 of the Teacher's booklet for the *Interactive DVD*.
- The test for Units 7–12 from *Teacher's Resource Book 2* (see pages 115–129).

Ending the lesson

- Pupils work in groups of three. They need one picture dictionary between three. They use a book (or paper) to cover the words from Unit 9. They take turns to say what each picture is. They look and check. They then cover the pictures from Unit 10 and take turns to say the words. They choose which to cover for Units 11 and 12 (words or pictures).
- Talk about the *can do* statements from Units 9–12 with pupils and elicit examples from volunteer pupils for each one.
- Ask pupils which lessons, topics and/or activities were their favourites.

3 Play the game.

Red square – read and do
Blue square – What's this?
Green square – What's he / she doing?

Finish
You've got your sunhat. Go forward 2 squares.
You haven't got your sunhat. Go back 2 squares.
Your kite hasn't got a tail. Go back 1 square.
The sea's dirty. Go back 2 squares.
The sea's clean. Go forward 2 squares.
Start

Grammar reference

Pupil's Book

1
Who's he?
This is my brother, Simon. **He's** seven.
Who's she?
This is my sister, Suzy. **She's** four.
Who's he? = Who is he?
he's = he is
she's = she is

2
How many desks **are there**?
There are a lot of desks.
Is there a whiteboard **on** the wall?
Yes, **there is**. / No, **there isn't**.
Are there 10 desks **in** the classroom?
Yes, **there are**. / No, **there aren't**.
there's = there is
there aren't = there are not

3
Whose is this camera?
It's Simon**'s**.
Whose are these books?
They're Suzy**'s**.
It's Simon's. = It's Simon's camera.
They're Suzy's. = They're Suzy's books.

4
Whose is that green T-shirt?
It**'s mine**.
Whose socks **are those**?
They**'re yours**.
Is that dress **yours**, Suzy?
Yes, **it is**. / No, **it isn't**.
Are **those** socks **yours**, Simon?
Yes, **they are**. / No, **they aren't**.
It's mine. = It's my T-shirt.
No, they aren't. = No, they are not.

5
I**'m**
He**'s** / She**'s**
You**'re** / They**'re** / We**'re**
sing**ing**.
not fly**ing**.
What **are** you do**ing**, Suzy?
What**'s** Grandpa do**ing**?

6
Can I have some chicken, **please**?
Here you are.

7
I love horses. **So do I**. / **I don't**.

8
Where's the park?
It's behind / **in front of** / **next to** the shops.
Where are the flats?
They're behind / **in front of** / **next to** the shops.
Where's the school?
It's **between** the café and the park.
Where are the shops?
They're **between** the café and the park.

9
He**'s** / She**'s**
wear**ing** blue jeans and white shoes.
They**'re**
wear**ing** sunglasses and big hats.
Have you
Has he / she
got a watch?
Yes, I **have**. / No, I **haven't**.
Yes, he / she **has**.
No, he / she **hasn't**.
haven't got = have not got
hasn't got = has not got

10
I
love / **like** / **don't like**
He / She
loves / **likes** / **doesn't like**
swimming.
playing table tennis.
Do you **like** reading? Yes, **I do**. / No, **I don't**.
doesn't = does not

11
Would you like a burger?
Would you like some lemonade?
Yes, please.
No, thank you. I'd like some juice.
I'd like = I would like

12
Where do you want to go on holiday?
Do you want to go to a big city?
I **want** to go to the mountains.
I **don't want** to go to the beach.

Grammar reference

Activity Book

AB94. ACTIVITY 1. *Order the words.*
Key: 1 What's his name? He's Tom. 2 Who's she? She's my teacher, Mrs Brown.

AB94. ACTIVITY 2. *Look and write.*
Key: 1 Yes, there is. 2 No, there aren't. 3 Yes, there are.

AB94. ACTIVITY 3. *Circle the question and the answer.*
Key: Whose is this robot? It's Lenny's.

AB94. ACTIVITY 4. *Match the questions and answers.*
Key: 1 Whose is that red dress? It's mine. 2 Whose blue trousers are those? They're Dad's. 3 Are those blue socks yours? Yes, they are.

AB95. ACTIVITY 5. *Look and complete.*
Key: 1 I'm singing. 2 I'm not dancing. 3 You're reading. 4 He's not running. 5 She's playing tennis. 6 We're not painting.

AB95. ACTIVITY 6. *Circle the question and the answer.*
Key: Can I have some fish, please? Here you are.

AB95. ACTIVITY 7. *Look and write.*
Key: 1 So do I. 2 So do I. 3 I don't.

AB95. ACTIVITY 8. *Look and complete.*
Key: 1 It's behind the school. 2 It's in front of the hospital. 3 It's between the park and the flats.

AB96. ACTIVITY 9. *Write the answers.*
Key: 1 Yes, I have. 2 No, he hasn't. 3 Yes, she has. 4 No, I haven't.

AB96. ACTIVITY 10. *Look and complete.*
Key: 1 I love reading. 2 He likes playing badminton. 3 She doesn't like singing. 4 I don't like cooking.

AB96: ACTIVITY 11. *Look and complete.*
Key: 1 Yes, please. 2 No, thank you.

AB96: ACTIVITY 12. *Look and complete.*
Key: 1 I want to go to the beach. 2 I don't want to go to a big city.

Starters practice test key

LISTENING

Part 1 – 5 marks

Lines should be drawn between:

1 T-shirt and under table
2 Elephant and in box
3 Giraffe and boy's hand
4 Jeans and on bed, next to girl
5 Hippo and between mat and chair

Part 2 – 5 marks

1 4//four; 2 WHITE; 3 PARK; 4 8//eight; 5 6//six

Part 3 – 5 marks

1 C; 2 B; 3 A; 4 A; 5 C

Part 4 – 5 marks

1 Colour ball next to woman – yellow
2 Colour ball on girl's head – purple
3 Colour ball on boat – pink
4 Colour ball man is throwing – orange
5 Colour ball behind boy – green

READING AND WRITING

Part 1 – 5 marks

1 ✓; 2 ✗; 3 ✓; 4 ✗; 5 ✓

Part 2 – 5 marks

1 yes; 2 yes; 3 no; 4 no; 5 yes

Part 3 – 5 marks

1 onion; 2 bread; 3 burger; 4 tomato; 5 chicken

Part 4 – 5 marks

1 arms; 2 tail; 3 tree; 4 fruit; 5 cats

Part 5 – 5 marks

1 clock; 2 running; 3 bus; 4 sleeping; 5 teacher

Starters practice test audio script

The following audio appears at the end of the Class Audio CD4.

CD 4, 22 Pupil's Book. Starters practice test. Page 99. Listening. Part 1.

Now look at the picture. Listen and look. There is one example.
Put the sock in the cupboard.
Sorry?
Please put the sock in the cupboard.
All right.

Can you see the line? This is an example. Now you listen and draw lines.

1 Can you see the T-shirt?
Yes, I can see it.
Put the T-shirt under the table.
OK. I'm putting it under the table now.

2 Now the elephant. Put it in the box.
In the box?
That's right. Put the elephant there.
OK.

3 Look at the giraffe.
Yes. Can I put it in the boy's hand?
Yes. Put the giraffe in the boy's hand.
Good.

4 Can you put the jeans next to the girl, on the bed?
Put the jeans where?
Next to the girl.
All right.

5 Right. What now?
Well, can you see the hippo?
Yes. I like the hippo. Can I put it between the mat and the chair?
Yes. Please put it between the mat and the chair. Good! Well done!

CD 4, 22 Now listen again.

See audio script above.

CD 4, 23 Pupil's Book. Starters practice test. Pages 100 and 101. Listening. Part 2.

Look at the picture. Listen and write a name or a number. There are two examples.
Hello! This is your new classroom. What's your name?
My name's Tony.
And how do you spell that?
T-O-N-Y.
Good! Now, how old are you, Tony?
I'm nine.
Sorry, how old?
Nine.

Can you see the answers? Now you listen and write a name or a number.

1 You're in class four now, Tony.
Class four?
That's right.
So, are you our new teacher?
Yes, I am.

2 Can I ask you a question, please?
All right.
What's your name?
I'm Mrs White.
Oh. How do you spell White?
It's W-H-I-T-E.

3 Where do you live, Tony?
We live in Park Street.
And can you spell Park?
Yes. It's P-A-R-K.
Good. I know that street. I live there, too!

4 What number is your house?
It's number eight.
Pardon? Is it eight?
Yes, that's right.

5 How many people live in your house, Tony?
There are six of us.
Six?
Yes. There's me, Mum, Dad, my brother, my sister and Grandma. That's my family!

CD 4, 23 Now listen again.

See audio script above.

CD 4, 24 Pupil's Book. Starters practice test. Pages 102 and 103. Listening. Part 3.

Look at the pictures. Now listen and look. There is one example.
What can Sam have?
Can I have an ice cream, Mum?
No, not now, Sam.
Oh. Well, can I have a cake?
No. You can have a carrot. Here you are!

Can you see the tick? Now you listen and tick the box.

1 **What does Anna want?**
Look, Anna. You can wear these trousers today.
Oh, no! They're old. I don't like them.
OK, then. Let's find a clean skirt for you.
No, Mum. I want my new dress!

2 **What's Ben drawing?**
What are you drawing, Ben? Is it a sheep?
No, it isn't. Try again!
Oh, dear! Um, is it a cow?
No! It's a funny old goat!

3 **What's Mum doing?**
Where's Alex? Is he playing on the computer?
No. He's watching TV.
Is Mum with him?
No. Mum's listening to the radio.

4 **What's Mr Gray's favourite game?**
Have you got a hobby, Mr Gray?
Well, Lucy, I like a lot of sports.
So do I. I love tennis and badminton.
I like them too, but basketball is my favourite game.

5 **Which girl is Kim?**
Is your friend Kim in this photo?
Yes, she is. She's got long brown hair and blue eyes.
Is this her?
No! That girl's got short hair and blue eyes.
This is Kim.

CD 4, 24 Now listen again.

See audio script above.

CD 4, 25 Pupil's Book. Starters practice test. Page 104. Listening. Part 4.

Look at the picture. Listen and look. There is one example.
Here's a nice picture for you. Would you like to colour it?
Yes. I like colouring.
OK. Find the ball in the sea, and colour it red.
Red?
That's right. Colour the ball in the sea red.

Can you see the red ball in the sea? This is an example. Now you listen and colour.

1 Can you see the ball next to the woman?
Yes, I can.
Well, colour it yellow.
OK. The ball next to the woman. I'm colouring it yellow now.

2 Look at the girl.
I can see her! She's funny! She's got a big ball on her head!
That's right.
Can I colour the ball on the girl's head purple?
Yes. Make it purple. That looks good. Well done!

3 Now find the ball on the boat.
OK. I can see it.
Let's make it pink.
Pink? The ball on the boat?
That's right.
OK. I'm doing that now.

4 Look, the man's got a ball.
Yes. He's throwing it.
Right. Now, colour that ball orange.
OK. The man's throwing an orange ball.

5 There's a ball behind the boy.
That's right. It's on the beach, behind the boy.
Good. Now, what's your favourite colour?
Green.
OK. Make that ball green, then.
Great! I like this picture now!

CD 4, 25 Now listen again.

See audio script above.

Starters practice test
Listening
Reading & writing

Starters practice test Listening

Part 1 5 questions

22 CD4 Listen and draw lines. There is one example.

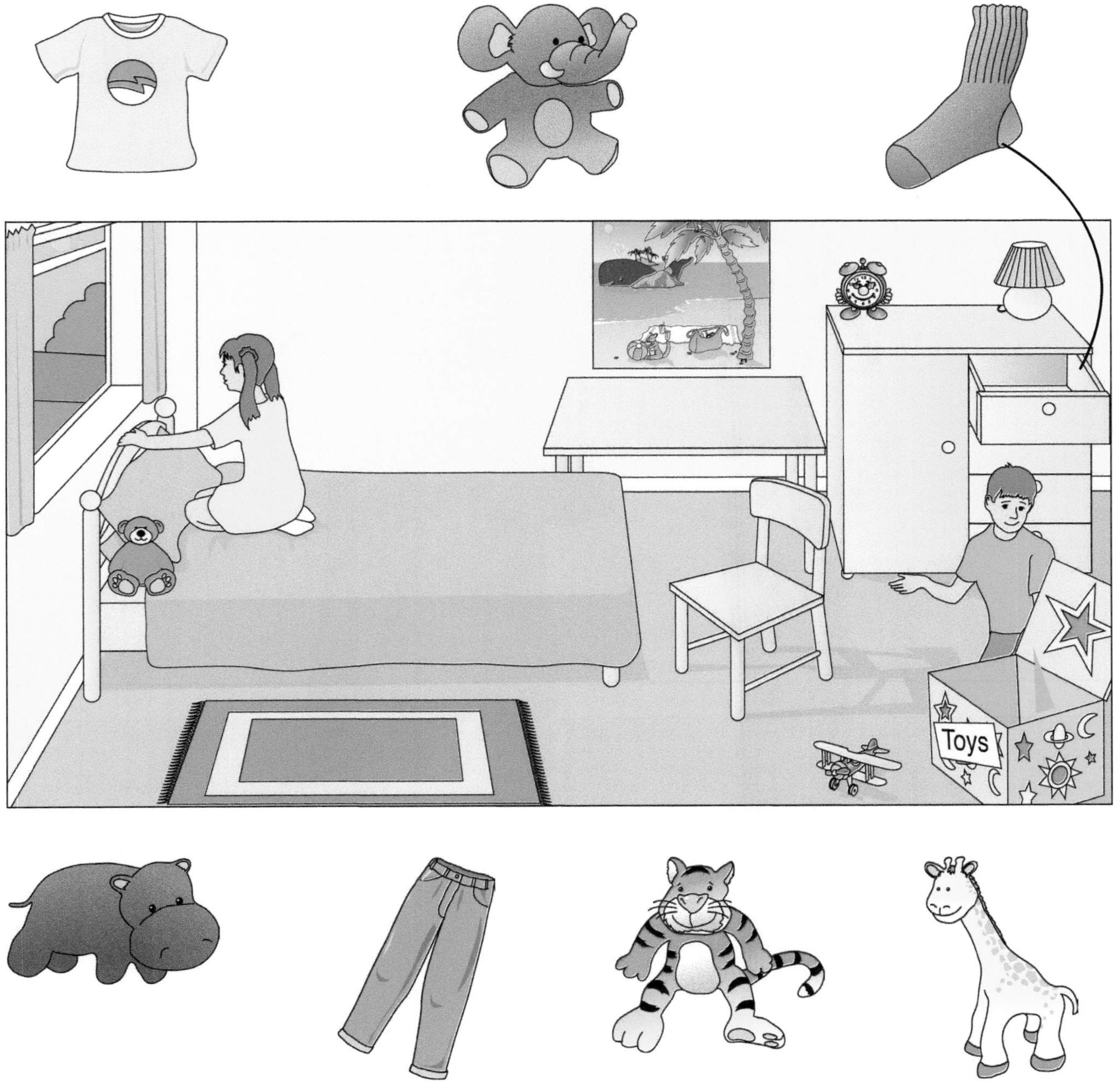

Part 2 5 questions

23 CD4 Read the question. Listen and write a name or a number.

There are two examples.

Examples

What is the boy's name? ....Tony........

How old is he? ....9........

Questions

1. Which class is Tony in now? ____________

2. What's the teacher's name? Mrs ____________

3. Where does Tony live? ____________ Street

4. What number is the teacher's house? ____________

5. How many people live in Tony's house? ____________

Part 3 5 questions

Listen and tick (✓) the box. There is one example.
What can Sam have?

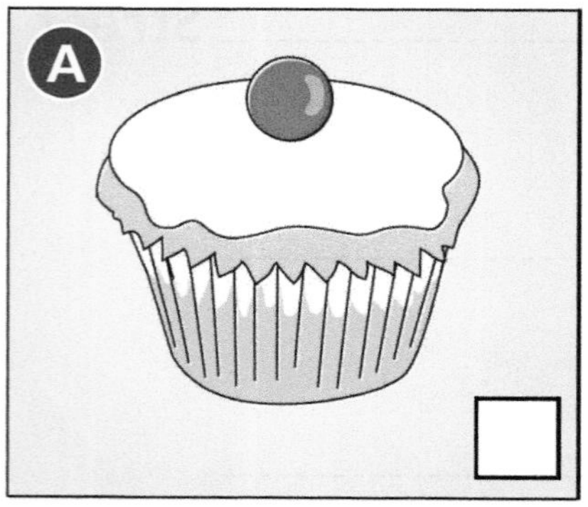

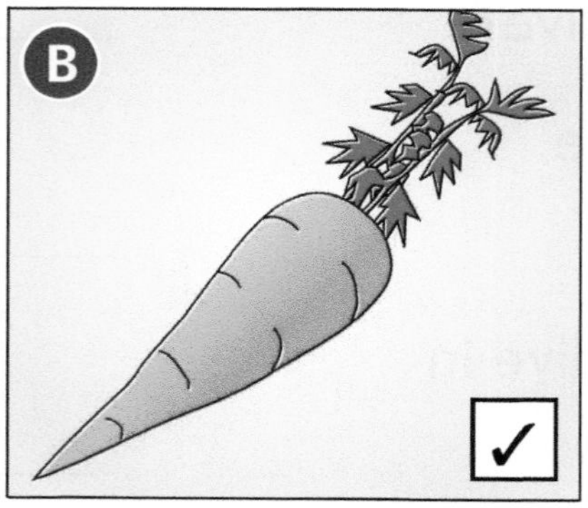

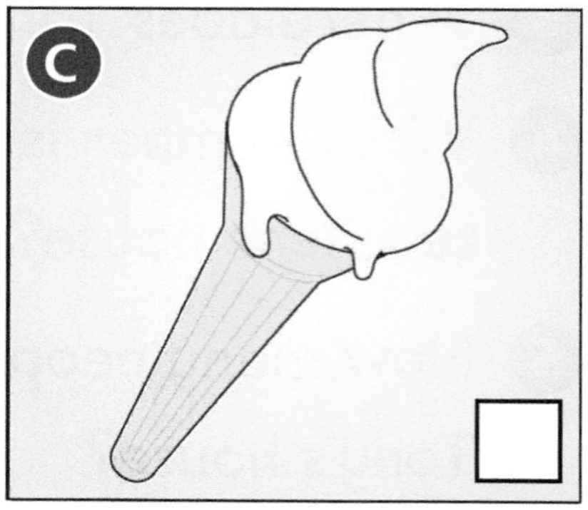

1 What does Anna want?

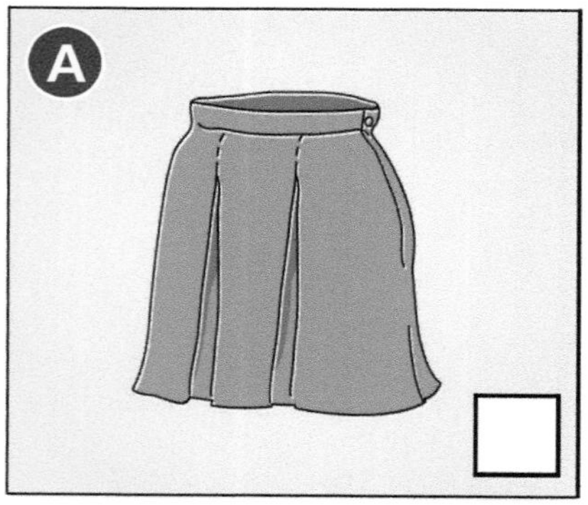

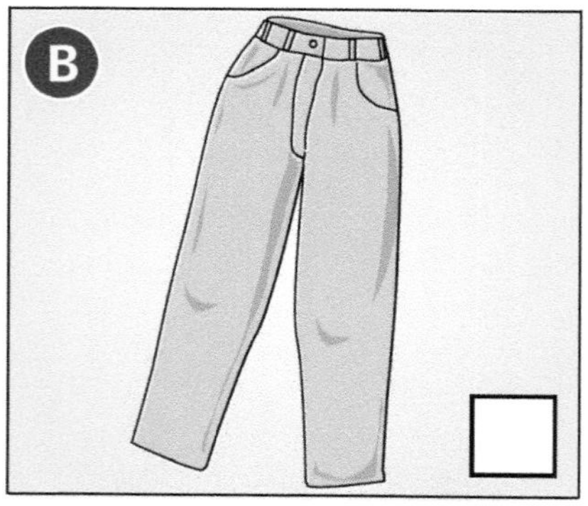

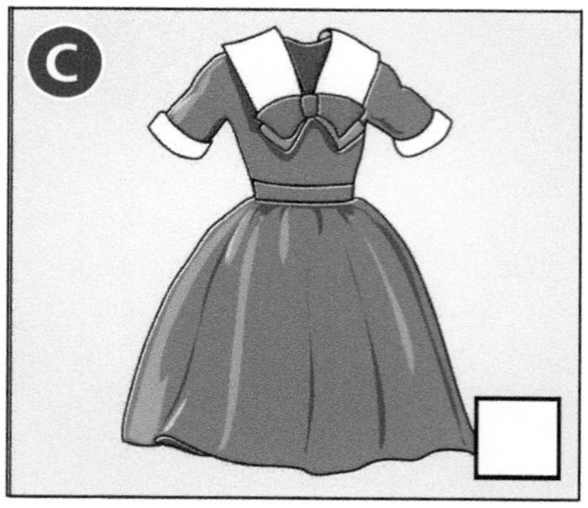

2 What's Ben drawing?

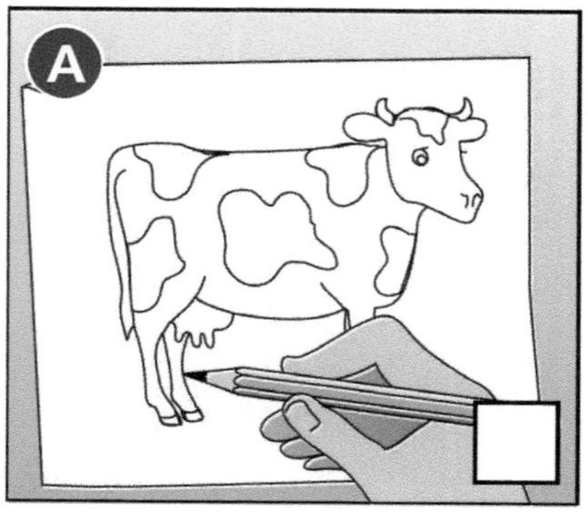

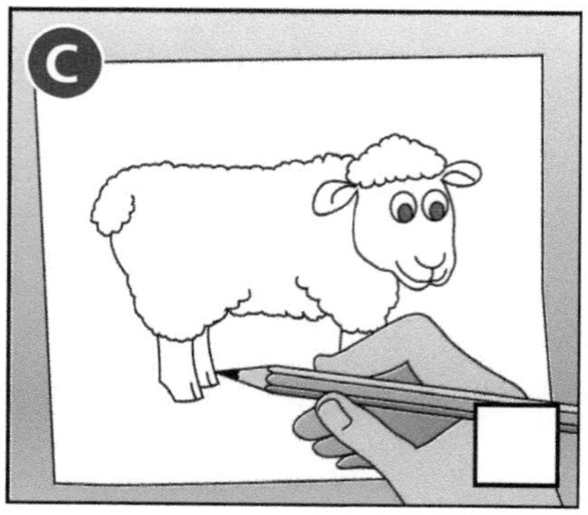

3 What's Mum doing?

4 What's Mr Gray's favourite game?

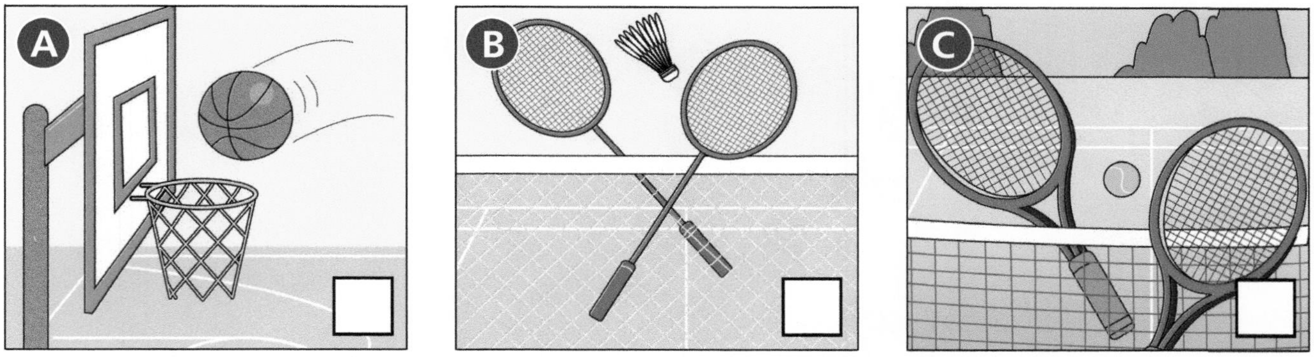

5 Which girl is Kim?

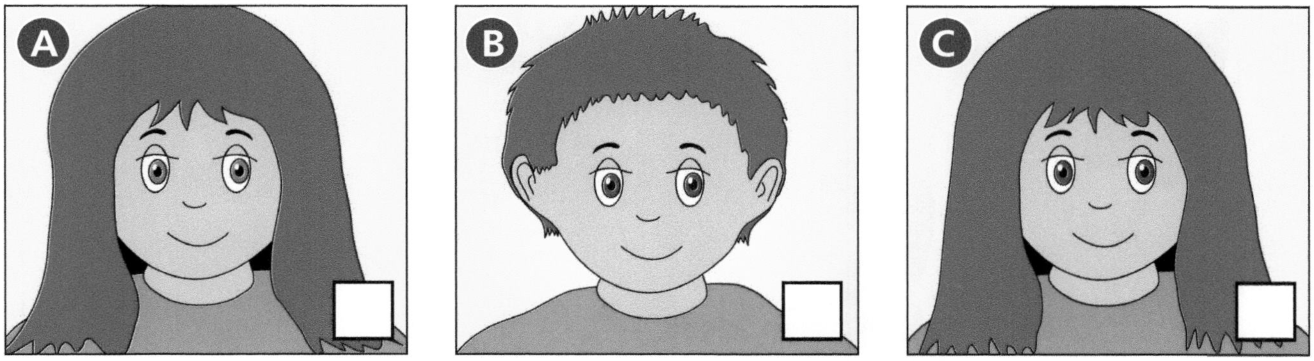

Part 4 5 questions

25 CD4 Listen and colour. There is one example.

Part 1 5 questions

Look and read. Put a tick (✓) or a cross (✗) in the box.

There are two examples.

Examples

This is a car. ✓

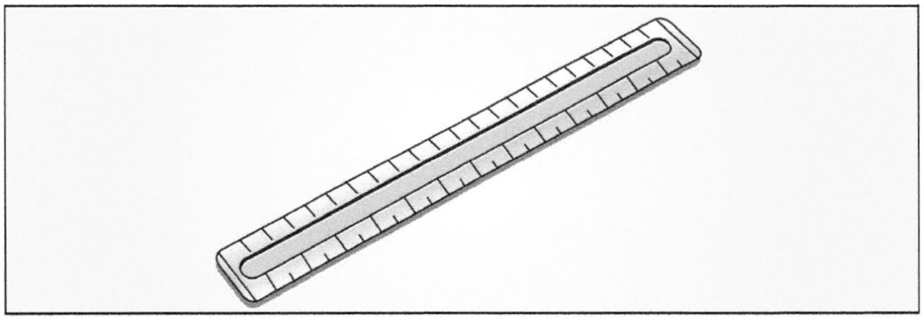

This is a pencil. ✗

Questions

1

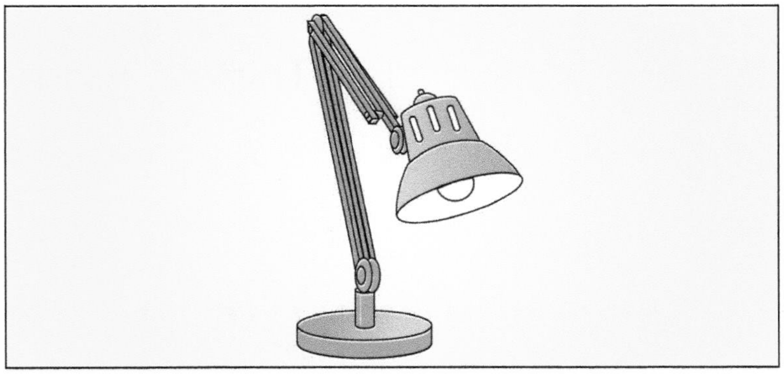

This is a lamp. ☐

2

This is a mango. ☐

3

This is a jacket. ☐

4

This is a piano. ☐

5

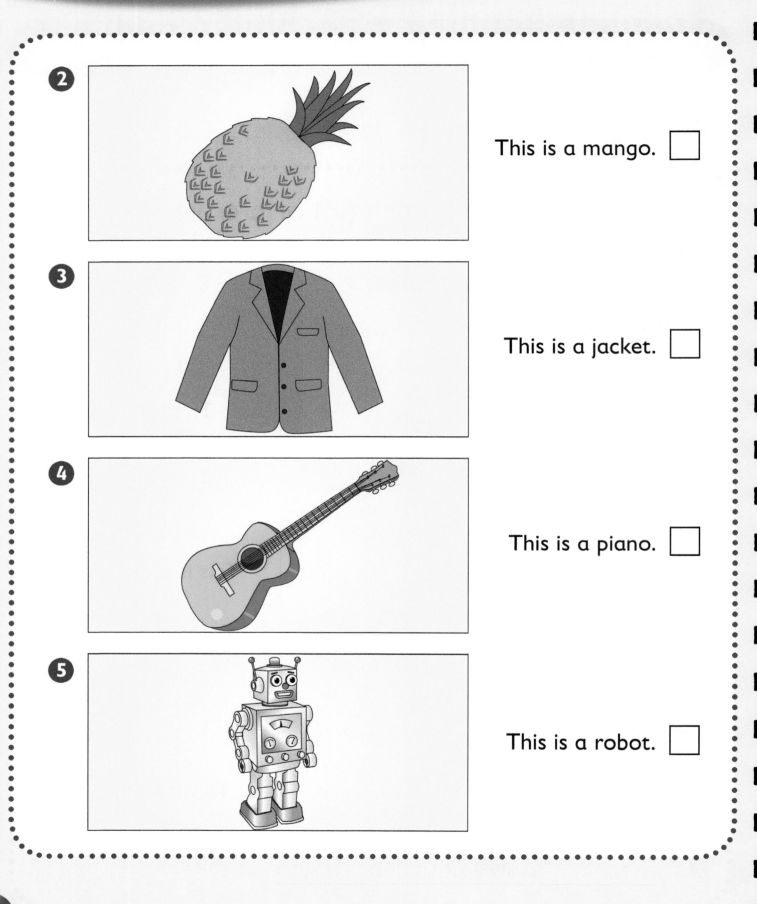

This is a robot. ☐

Part 2 5 questions

Look and read. Write **yes** or **no**.

Examples

A girl is kicking a football. ______yes______

Two children have got kites. ______no______

Questions

1. The boys are riding bikes. ____________
2. There are two ducks in the water. ____________
3. The woman is painting a picture. ____________
4. The baby is playing with a doll. ____________
5. The man has got a black dog. ____________

Part 3 5 questions

Look at the pictures. Look at the letters.
Write the words.

Example

f i s h

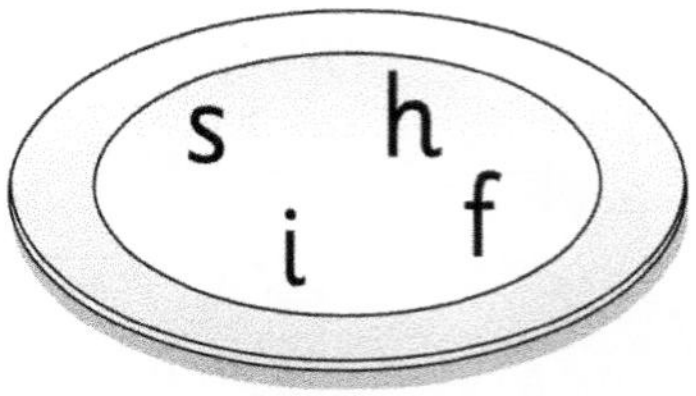

Questions

1

_ _ _ _ _

2

_ _ _ _ _

3

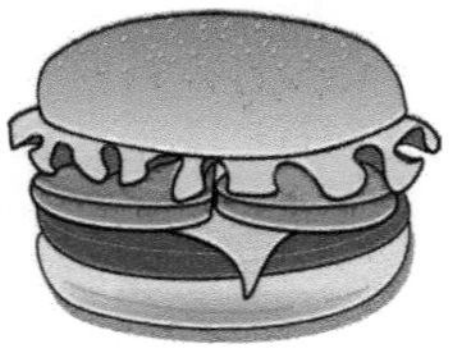

_ _ _ _ _ _

4

_ _ _ _ _ _

5

_ _ _ _ _ _ _

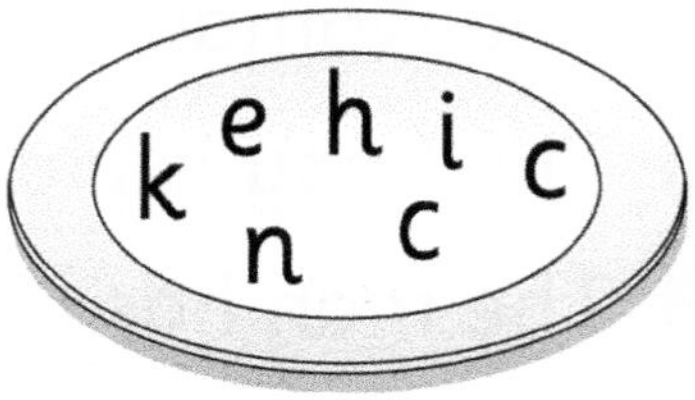

Part 4 5 questions

Read this. Choose a word from the box. Write the correct word next to numbers 1–5. There is one example.

A bird

I'm a small animal. I've got two
_____legs_____ , but I haven't got
(1) ________________ . I've got a
(2) ________________ . I can fly and
I live in a (3) ________________ in a
garden. In the morning I sing beautiful
songs. I like eating (4) ________________
and small animals like spiders. I don't like
(5) ________________ .
What am I? I am a bird.

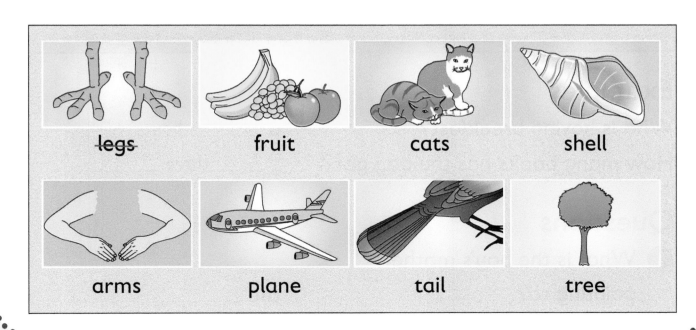

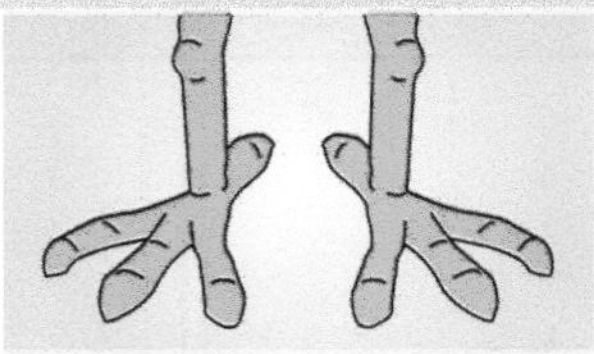

~~legs~~

fruit

cats

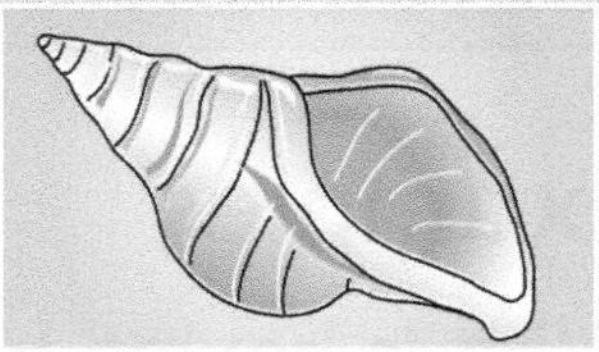

shell

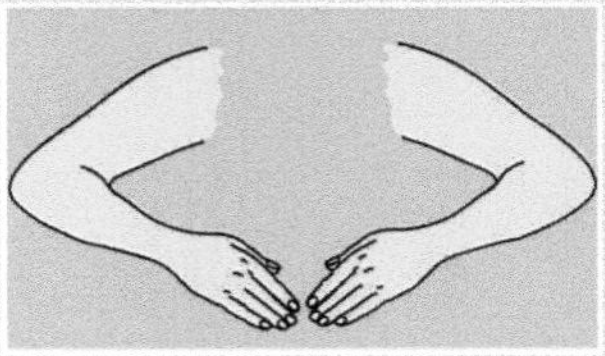

arms

plane

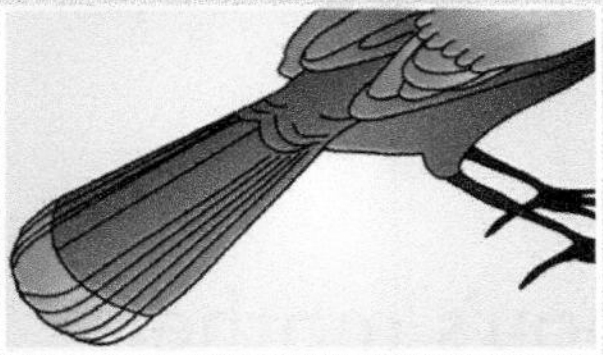

tail

tree

Part 5 5 questions

Look at the pictures and read the questions. Write one-word answers.

Examples

Who is having breakfast? a ____boy____

How many books has the boy got? ____three____

Questions

1 What is the boy's mother pointing to? the ______________

❷ What is the boy doing? ______________________

❸ Where are the girls? on the ______________________

❹ What is the boy doing now? ______________________

❺ Who looks angry? the ______________________

Teaching notes for Photocopiables

Photocopiable 1 (Unit 1 page 6)

- Hand out copies of Photocopiable 1 (page T100), one for each pupil.
- Pupils cut the 26 letter cards out and spread them on their desks.
- Spell out some simple words for pupils to spell using the letters, e.g. say *C–a–t*. Pupils find the letters and make the word. Elicit the word *Cat*.
- Continue with other short, known words, e.g. *pen, dog, chair, eight*. Avoid words which have the same letter twice, e.g. *book*.

Photocopiable 2 (Unit 2 page 11)

- Hand out copies of Photocopiable 2 (page T101), one for each pupil.
- Hold up your copy and show pupils where to fold the paper. Fold back the section where they write the numbers (they will do this in another lesson).
- Show pupils what they have to do. Each pupil decides on the colours for the objects and writes the name of the different colours on each line. The pupils then colour the objects in the right colour.
  Note: There are 12 colours. One of the colours can be, e.g. dark blue / dark brown / dark red.
  In pairs, pupils then take turns to ask each other how many of each item their partner can see. Start them off with an example, e.g. *How many desks are there?*
  Pupils write their names at the top of the photocopies.
- Collect the photocopies to hand out in the next lesson.

Photocopiable 3 (Unit 3 page 19)

- Hand out copies of Photocopiable 3 (page T102) on thin card, one for each pupil.
- Pupils cut out and colour the cards. Make pairs. Pupils put the cards face down on the desk. They take it in turns to turn over two cards at random. If the cards are different, they say, e.g. *This is a brown lorry. This is an orange kite.* If the cards are the same, they say, e.g. *These are watches. This is blue and this is yellow.*
- If the two cards show the same object, the pupil keeps them. If not, the pupil turns them face down again and it's the other pupil's turn. Play continues until all the cards have been matched. The winner is the pupil with the most pairs at the end of the game.
- When they have finished playing, pupils take their own cards and put them in an envelope with their name on.

Photocopiable 4 (Unit 4 page 25) [YLE]

- Hand out copies of Photocopiable 4 (see page T103), one for each pupil.
- Pupils cut along the cutting line to separate the two sections. They colour the objects at the bottom of the page and then cut out the six cards.
- They work in pairs, facing one another. Pupil A places the cards anywhere in the house without Pupil B seeing. Pupil A gives instructions to Pupil B, e.g. *Put the lamp in the living room next to the TV.* When Pupil B has placed all the cards in his/her house, they look and check that the items are in the same positions. They swap roles.
- When they have finished playing, pupils take their materials and put them in an envelope with their name on.

Photocopiable 5 (Unit 5 page 35)

- Hand out copies of Photocopiable 5 (see page T104), one for each pupil. Elicit what the diagram at the top is (a family tree) and what the faces are (the people to put on the tree).
- Pupils cut out the faces and colour them in as they wish.
- Make pairs. Pupils position the faces as follows: Top line: Anna, Nelson. Middle line: Nick, Kim, Ben, Lucy. Bottom line: May, Lenny, Sam, Frank. Looking at the family trees together the children ask each other questions, e.g. Who is Lenny's sister? Who is May's Grandma?
- Collect the materials and put them in named envelopes at the end of the activity.

Photocopiable 6a (Unit 6 page 41)

Note: You will need a large bucket half full of water for this activity and six real foods, e.g. an egg, a banana, a pear, a lemon, a tomato and a carrot.

- Hand out copies of Photocopiable 6a (see page T105), one for each pupil.
- Show the class the foods you have, one at a time, and elicit the word. Say, e.g. *Number 1. An egg.* Pupils write egg in the top left of the table, marked *1*, on the writing line. Repeat for the other five foods. Pupils write the words in each of the numbered squares in the left column (*Foods*). Make sure all the pupils write the same word for each number. Pupils draw a picture of each food in the square and colour it.
- Show pupils the bucket of water. Demonstrate *float* and *sink*, using a ruler and an eraser.
- Pupils predict what will happen to each of the six foods. They write *Yes* or *No* in the middle column (Guesses: Yes or no?) for each food.
- Invite pupils in turn to come and place one of the food objects in the water. Elicit what happens each time. Pupils write the result (*floats/ sinks*) in the right-hand column (*What happens?*).
- Pupils complete the sentences at the bottom of the page. Do the first one as an example (e.g. *When you put an egg in water, it floats*).

Photocopiable 6b (Unit 6 page 44 – see also page T44)

- Write six food words on the board. Review asking politely for food and drink. Point to, e.g. *apples* and prompt a pupil (1) to ask another pupil (2) *Can I have some apples, please?* Make a thumbs up gesture to Pupil 2. The pupil responds *Here you are* and mimes handing over the apples. Repeat with another two pupils, but pointing to a different food word. After Pupil 1 asks the question, make a thumbs down gesture to Pupil 2 who replies *No, (name). I'm sorry.* Repeat for the other food words for practice.
- Hand out copies of Photocopiable 6b (see page T106); part A to half the class, and part B to the other half. Make sure pupils know if they are A or B. Teach/check the words *customer* and *shopkeeper*. Say *Pupil A, you are the customer. Pupil B, you are the shopkeeper.* All the pupils who are 'A' look at the items on their shopping list, while all the pupils who are 'B' look at the items on sale in their shop. Monitor this reading stage and answer any questions.
- Point out the target language in the speech bubbles at the top of each worksheet. Check pupils know which lines are for the customer and which are for the shopkeeper. Drill the target language.
- Pupils work in pairs, A and B. Pupil A asks for the items on his/her shopping list. Pupil B looks at the items on sale in his/her shop. If the item is available, it should be sold. Pupil A ticks or crosses the items on his/her shopping list when he/she knows whether they are available at the shop.

- Pupils exchange roles (Pupil A becomes the shopkeeper and Pupil B is the customer). Pupils compare their worksheets at the end of the activity to check that their answers are correct.
- You could extend the activity by asking pupils in their pairs to think of the shop of their choice. The customer writes their shopping list and the shopkeeper decides what's available. Help with vocabulary as necessary. Pupils could perform their dialogues to the rest of the class, who listen and guess the type of shop that the dialogue is happening in.

Photocopiable 7 (Unit 7 page 50)

- Write the dialogue below on the board, with words and phrases underlined as shown (these are the parts of the dialogue which pupils can change).
  A: Can I have the <u>sheep</u>, please? Let's put them here, next to the <u>cows</u>.
  B: Here you are.
  A: I love <u>sheep</u>. <u>Baa baa</u>.
  B: <u>So do I. / I don't</u>.
  B: Can I have the <u>ducks</u>, please? Let's put them here, next to the <u>lizards</u>.
  A: Here you are.
  B: I love <u>ducks</u>. <u>Quack quack</u>.
  A: <u>So do I. / I don't</u>
  Do one or two practice dialogues in open pairs, with pupils changing the underlined words and phrases. Leave the dialogue on the board.
- Hand out copies of Photocopiable 7 (see page T107), one to each pair of pupils. They cut along the dotted line to separate the page into two sections. They also cut out the pictures at the bottom of the page and colour them.
- Pupils put the cards and the plan face up in front of them. Remind them of the dialogue on the board. They take turns to pick up an animal card and start the dialogue (e.g. *Can I have the frogs, please?*). Stress that they can make true responses/sentences about likes/dislikes (e.g. *A: I love frogs. B: I don't.*)
- Pairs can perform dialogues to the class.
- Collect the materials at the end of the activity.

Photocopiable 8 (Unit 8, page 56)

- Hand out copies of Photocopiable 8 (see page T108), one for each pupil. They cut along the dotted lines to separate the three sections. They cut out the small pictures at the bottom of the page and colour them.
- Elicit the names of the items in the pictures. Pupils point.
- Pupils put the town map on their desks. Say *Listen and put the places in the right position.*
  Read out the eight sentences on the worksheet.
- Pupils check in pairs. Read the sentences again. Check with the class by drawing the answer key quickly on the board:

Flats				
Shoe shop	Furniture shop	Hospital	Toy shop	Park
Bus				
Pet shop	Café	Fruit shop	Flower shop	Café
		Flats	Grandpa's flat	

Photocopiable 9 (Unit 9, page 65)

- Hand out copies of Photocopiable 9 (see page T109), one for each pupil. They cut the page into two. Then they carefully cut out the boy and the girl and put them to one side.
- Pupils take out their crayons. Say *Listen.* Read the instructions to the class:
  Colour the dress pink. Colour the shirt yellow.
  Colour the skirt purple. Colour the T-shirt orange.
  Colour the jeans blue. Colour the hat white.
  Colour the trousers green. Colour one jacket red.
  Colour two shoes brown. Colour one jacket grey.
  Colour two shoes black.
  Give pupils time to finish the colouring. They cut out the clothes, including the tabs. They dress the girl and the boy as they wish.
- In pairs, pupils take turns to describe what the boy and girl are wearing, e.g. *Look! She's wearing a purple skirt, brown shoes, a yellow shirt and a grey jacket.*

Photocopiable 10 (Unit 10, page 72)

- Hand out copies of Photocopiable 10 (see page T110), one for each pupil. They cut to separate parts A and B.
- Focus pupils on A. Elicit the three questions at the bottom: *What's your name?* etc. Pupils work in pairs. They take turns to ask each other the questions and to complete the information in the table.
- Pupils then cut out the ID card in B and make one for their friend. They write the information (as on Pupil's Book page 72) and decorate it as they wish. They hand the ID card to the pupil they have written about. Pupils display their ID cards on their desks.

Photocopiable 11 (Unit 11, page 79)

- Hand out a copies of Photocopiable 11 (see page T111), one for each pupil. They either make a card for Simon's birthday, for someone in the class (if you have pupils with birthdays that week/month) or for someone in their family.
- Pupils cut out the birthday card. They complete the text (*To* (name) *Love from* (name)) and then fold the card down the dotted line at the centre. They decorate the outside of the card, using coloured tissue paper, glitter, etc. More confident pupils can write on the front of the card as well.
- Display the birthday cards. If appropriate, pupils give their card to the person they made it for.

Photocopiable 12a (Unit 12, page 86)

- Make groups of four. Hand out copies of Photocopiable 12a (see page T112), one for each group, plus four different coloured counters and a coin.
- Explain the game. Pupils take turns to spin the coin. If the coin lands on 'heads' they move one space, if it is 'tails' they move two. They do what the prompts require on the square on the game board: spell / make a question (on the squares with a question mark and a reply) / make a sentence (on the squares with words and picture clues) / complete a sentence or phrase (on the squares with dotted lines). Check understanding of *Miss a turn, Go forward two spaces*.
- Pupils play the game in their groups. They decide if their friends' answers are correct. Monitor and help check answers and resolve any disputes. The first pupil in each group to reach the 'Finish' square is the winner. If they have time, pupils can colour the game board.

Photocopiable 12b (Unit 12, page 88)

- Tell the class that they are going to play dominoes. Ask pupils to gather around one table and teach/check the rules with a set of cards from Photocopiable 12b (page T113). Each player has an equal number of dominoes. One domino is placed facing upward on the table. The first player matches the picture or word(s) on one of their dominoes with the same word(s) or picture already placed on the table. Play continues round the table in this way until one player uses all his/her dominoes. He/She is the winner.
- Divide the class into groups of three or four pupils. Hand out a set of domino cards from Photocopiable 12b to each group. Teach the verb *to deal*. Ask one member of each group to deal the cards. Pupils take it in turns to lay a card face up on the table. The player to the left asks, e.g. *Do you like fishing?* The player answers truthfully *Yes, I do. / No, I don't.* Play continues. The first player to get rid of all their cards is the winner.
- You could extend the activity by asking each group to prepare a set of domino cards based on their favourite words from *Kid's Box 2*.

Photocopiable 1

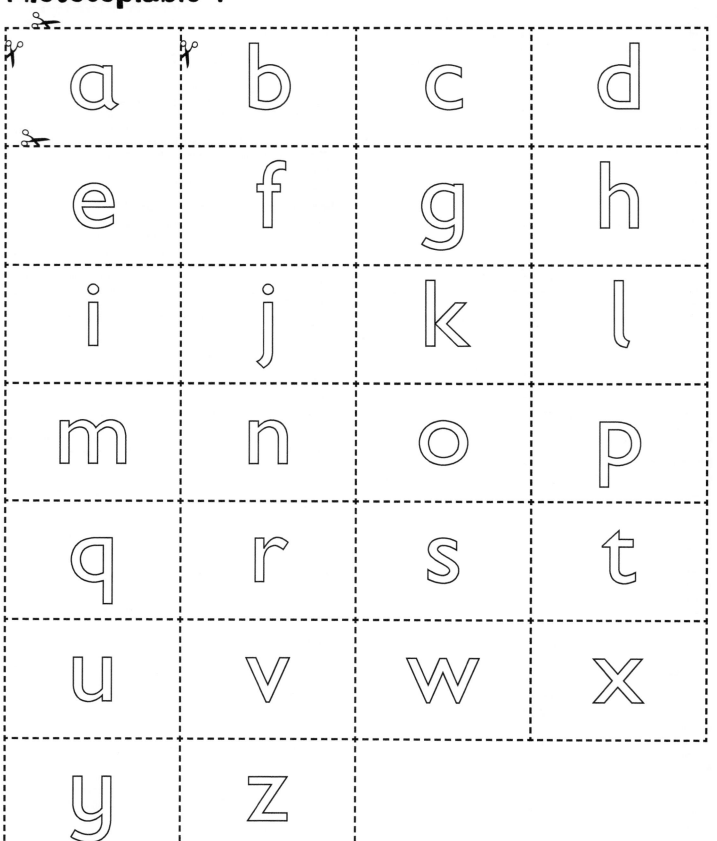

a	b	c	d
e	f	g	h
i	j	k	l
m	n	o	p
q	r	s	t
u	v	w	x
y	z		

Photocopiable 2

Name: ....

Choose, write and colour.

Colour the desks ....
Colour the chairs ....
Colour the windows ....
Colour the rulers ....
Colour the bags ....
Colour the cupboards ....
Colour the pictures ....
Colour the bookcases ....
Colour the erasers ....
Colour the pens ....
Colour the pencils ....
Colour the stars ....

Fold here

Fold here

Now ask and write. How many?

....eighteen.... desks
.... chairs
.... windows
.... rulers
.... bags
.... cupboards
.... pictures
.... bookcases
.... erasers
.... pens
.... pencils
.... stars

Photocopiable 3

Name: ______________________

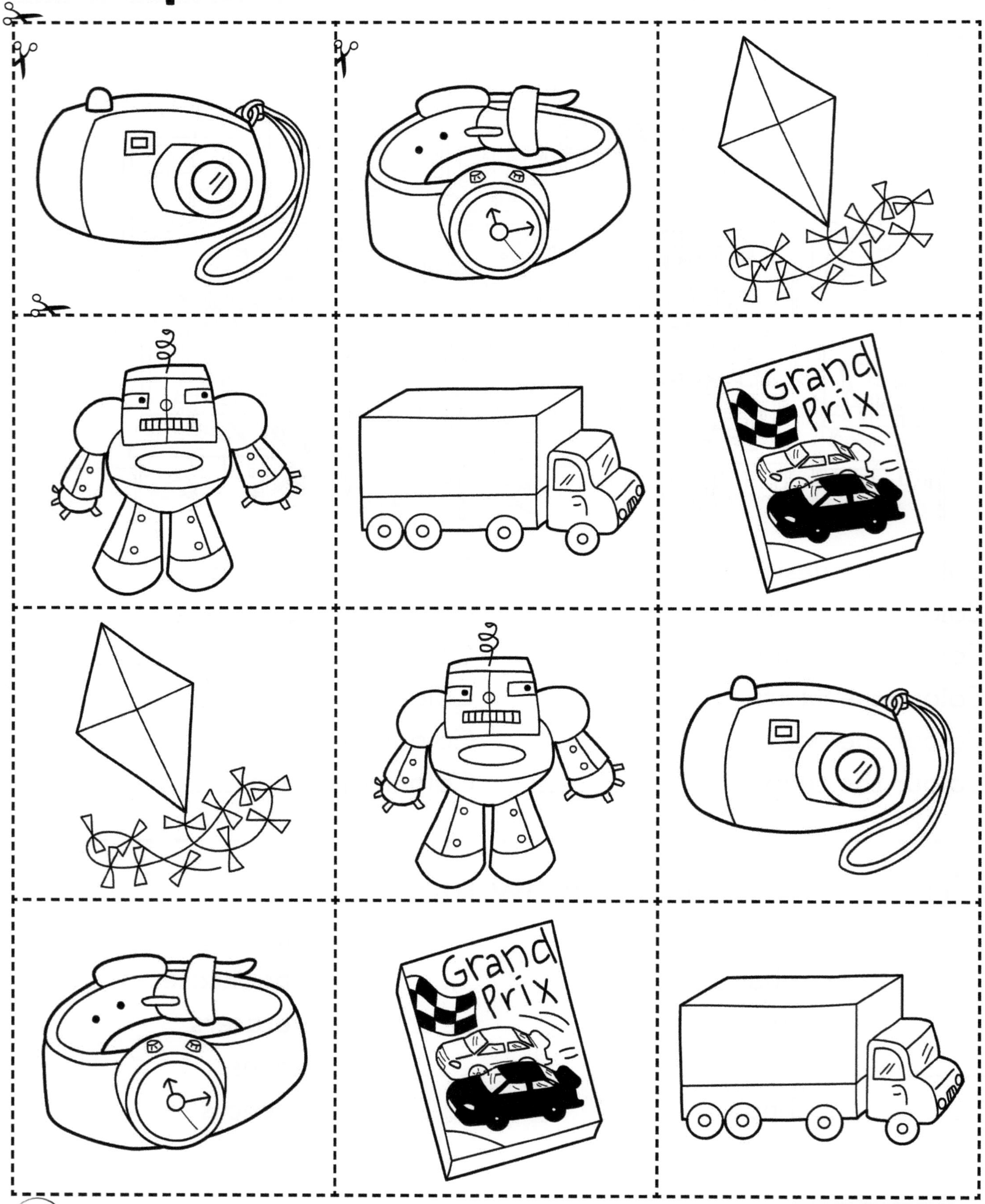

Photocopiable 4

Name: ____________________________

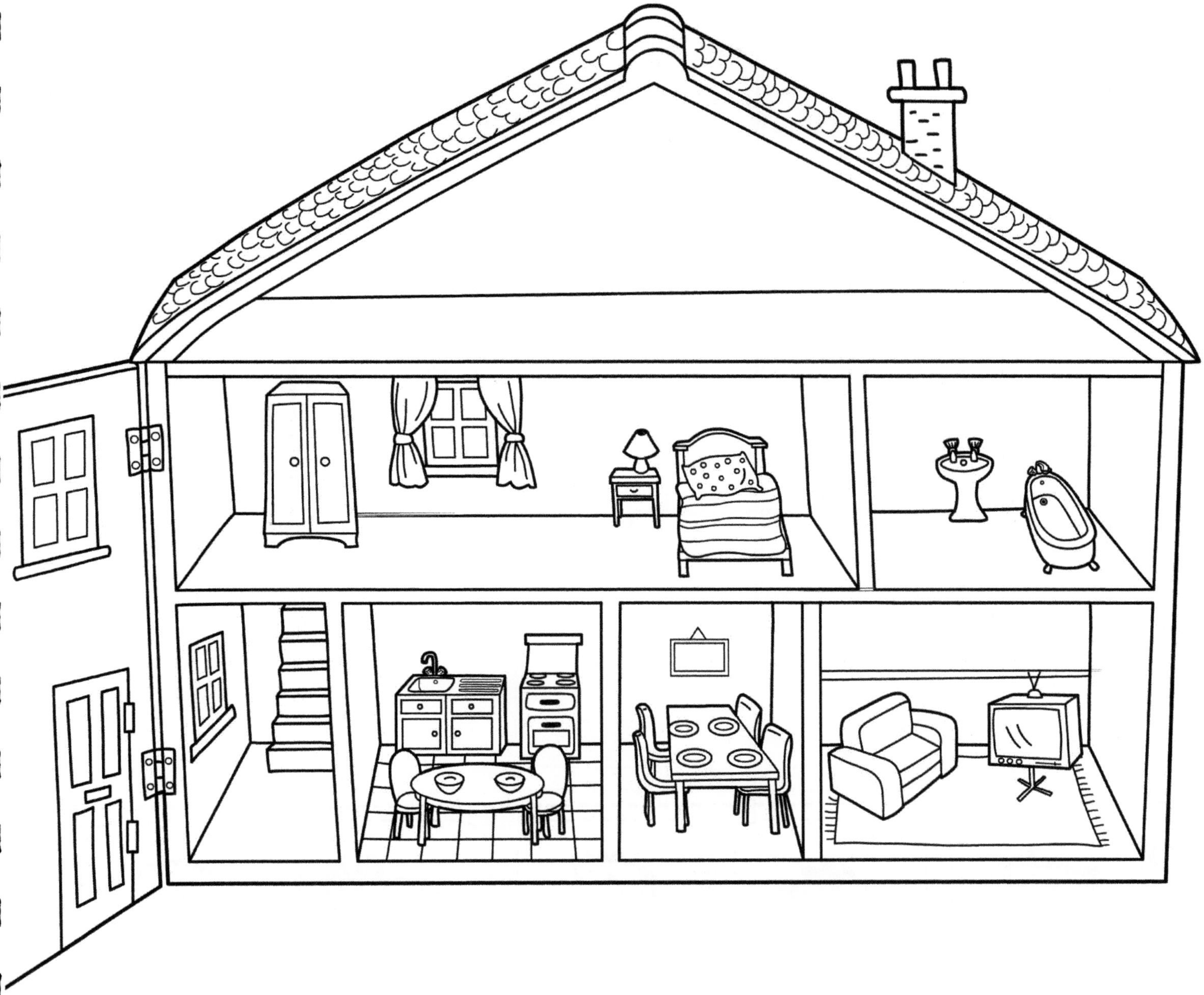

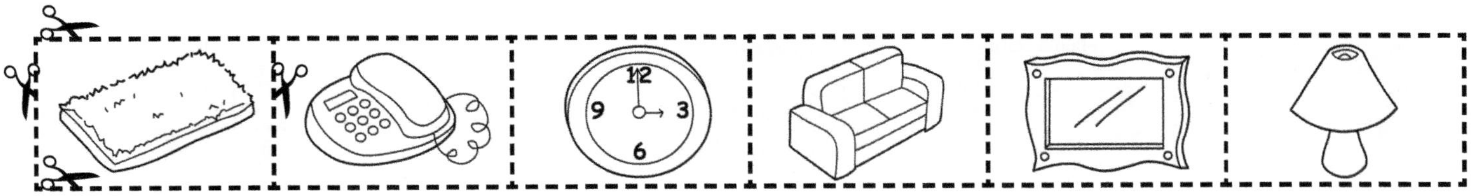

Photocopiable 5

Name: ______________________

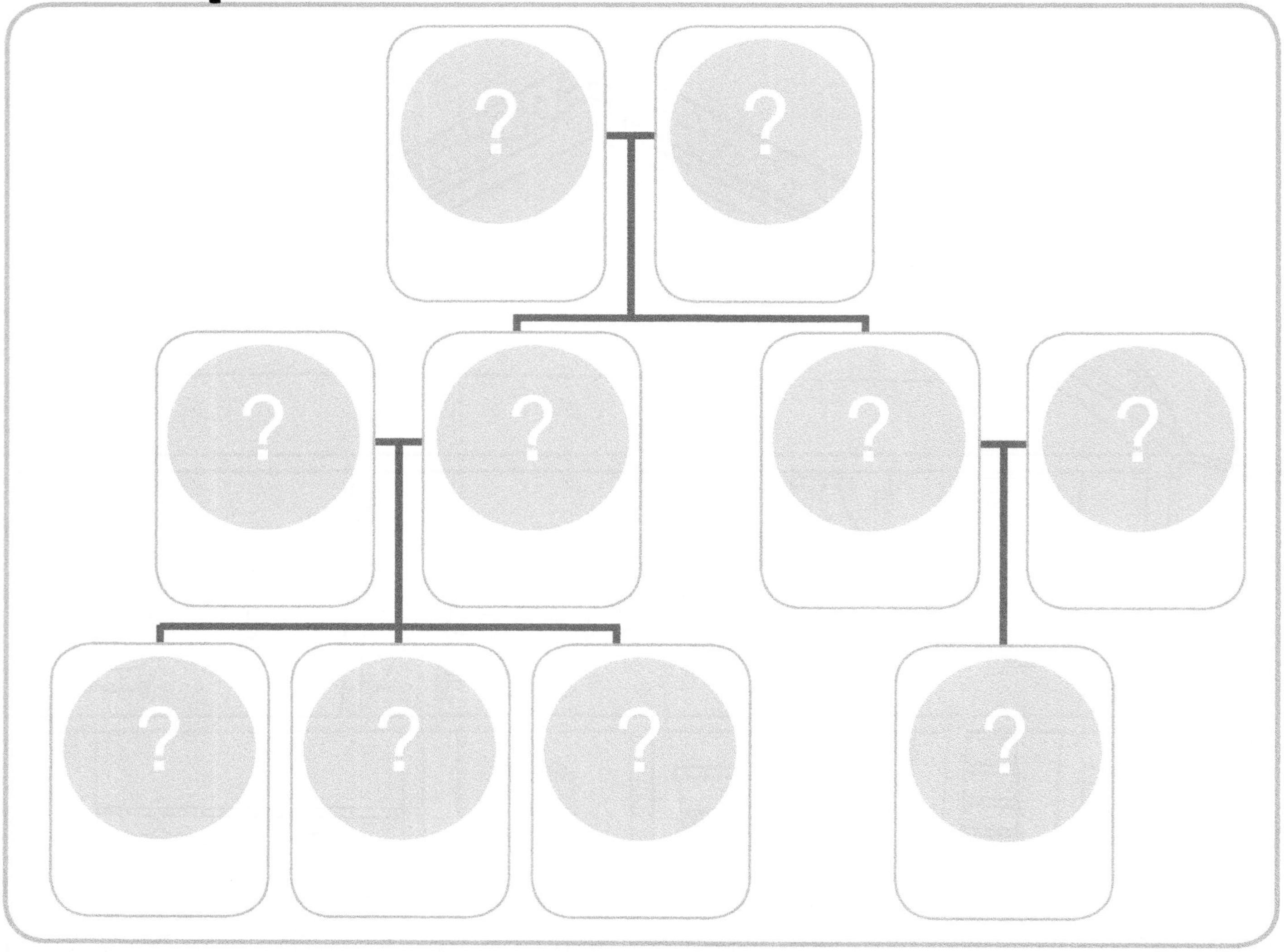

Photocopiable 6a

Name: ____________

Floating and sinking

Foods	Guesses: Yes or no?	What happens?
1 ____________	____________	____________
2 ____________	____________	____________
3 ____________	____________	____________
4 ____________	____________	____________
5 ____________	____________	____________
6 ____________	____________	____________

Floats or sinks?

1 When you put ____________ in water, it ____________ .
2 When you put ____________ in water, it ____________ .
3 When you put ____________ in water, it ____________ .
4 When you put ____________ in water, it ____________ .
5 When you put ____________ in water, it ____________ .
6 When you put ____________ in water, it ____________ .

Photocopiable 6b

Name: ____________________

A

Can I have some bread, please?

Here you are.

Can I have some lemons, please?

No, I'm sorry.

Your shopping list

- bread ☐
- lemons ☐
- apples ☐
- meat ☐
- oranges ☐
- potatoes ☐
- carrots ☐

Your shop

B

Can I have some bread, please?

Here you are.

Can I have some lemons, please?

No, I'm sorry.

Your shop

Your shopping list

- bread ☐
- lemons ☐
- milk ☐
- egg ☐
- pears ☐
- chicken ☐
- rice ☐

Photocopiable 7

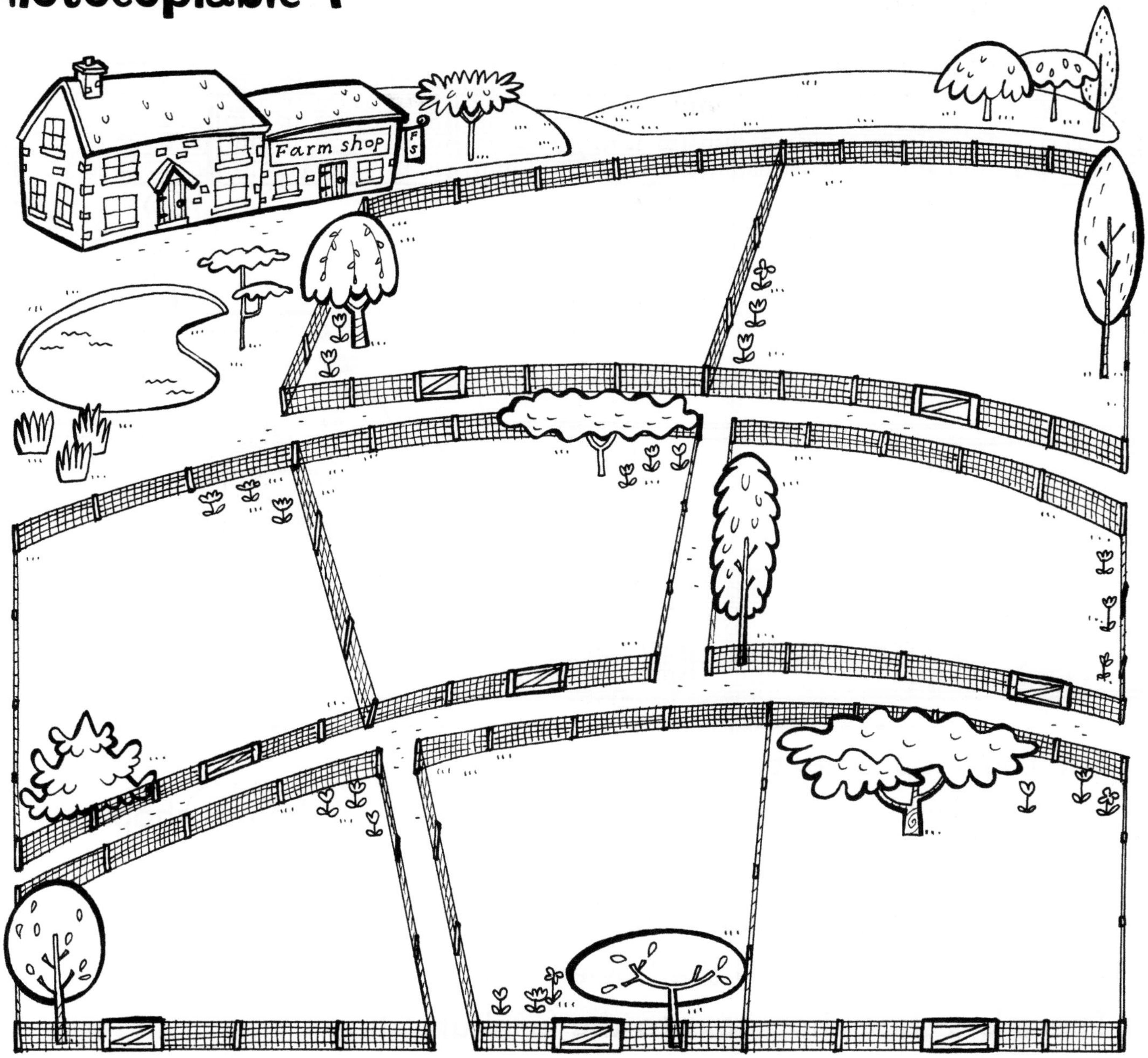

Photocopiable 8

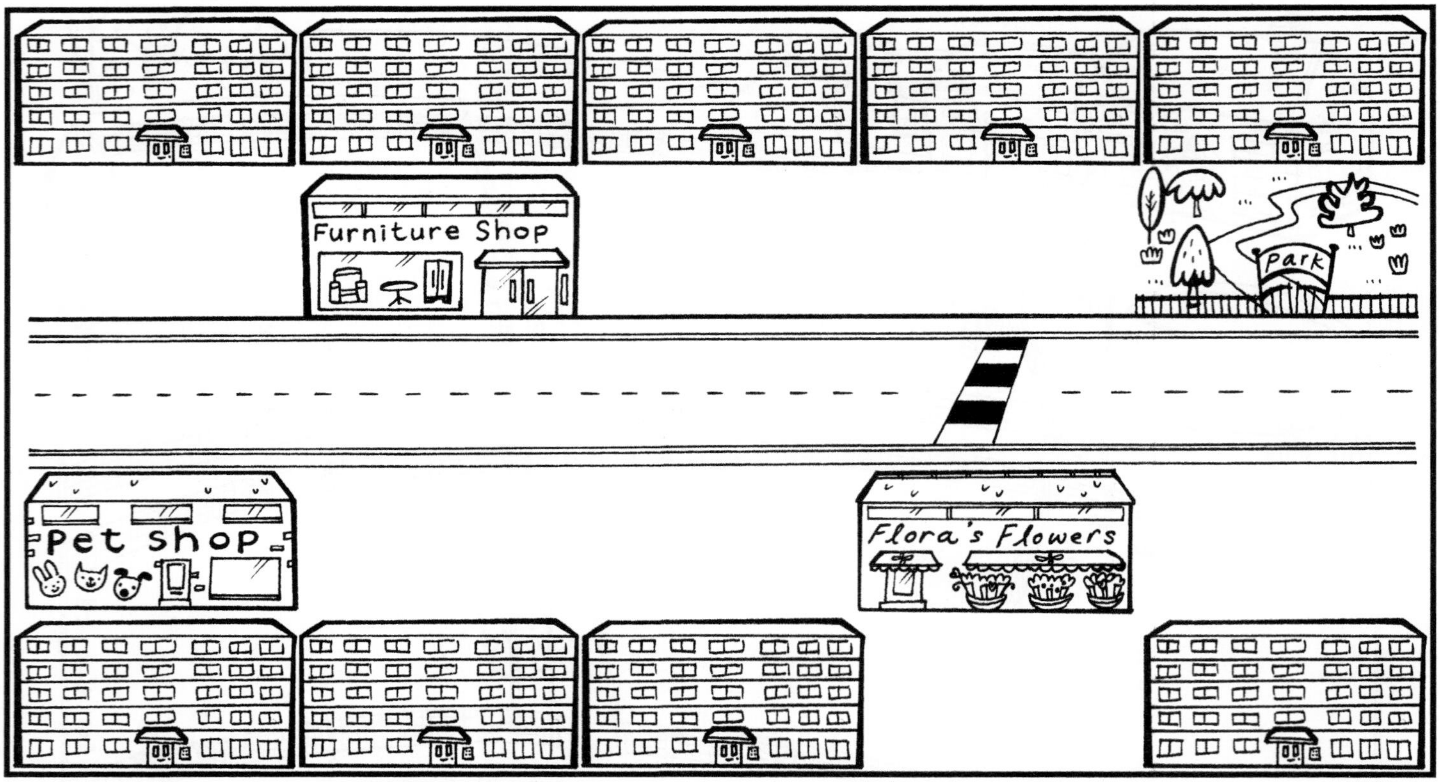

1 The toy shop is next to the park.
2 The hospital is between the furniture shop and the toy shop.
3 There is one café next to the pet shop.
4 The fruit shop is between the café and the flower shop.
5 There is a café next to the flower shop.
6 There is a shoe shop next to the furniture shop.
7 There is a bus in front of the hospital.
8 Grandpa's flat is behind the flower shop.

Photocopiable 9

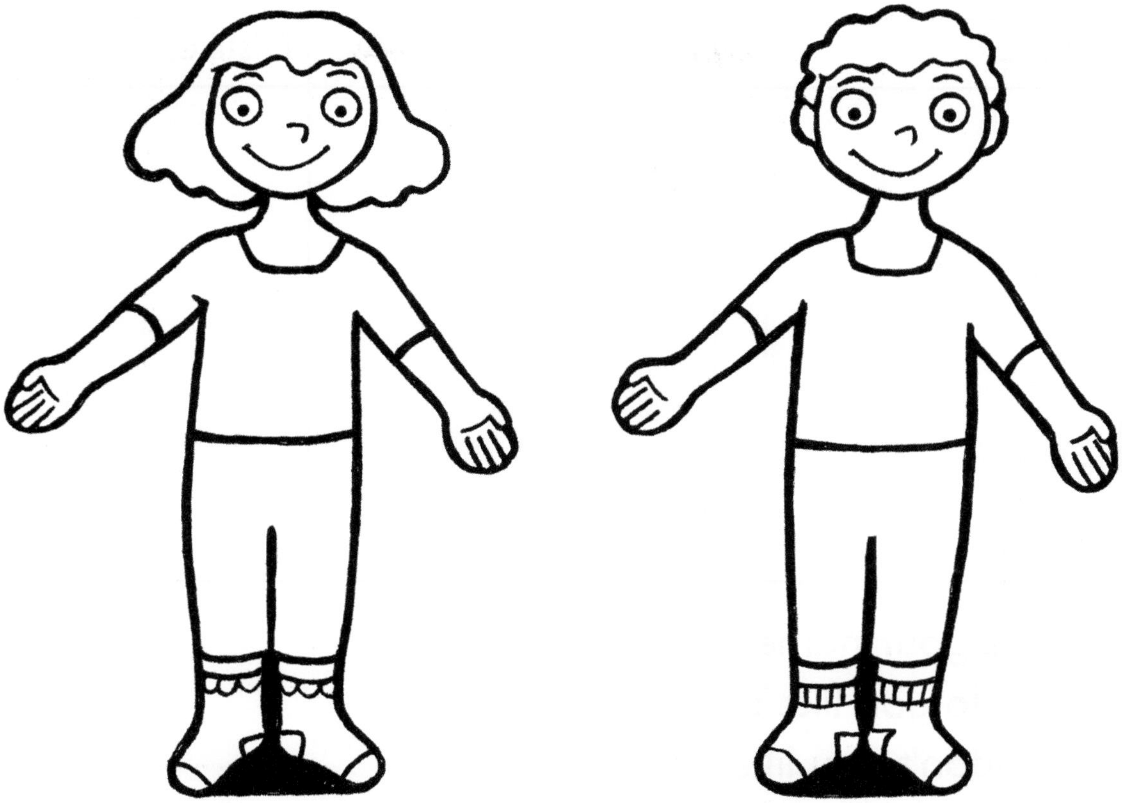

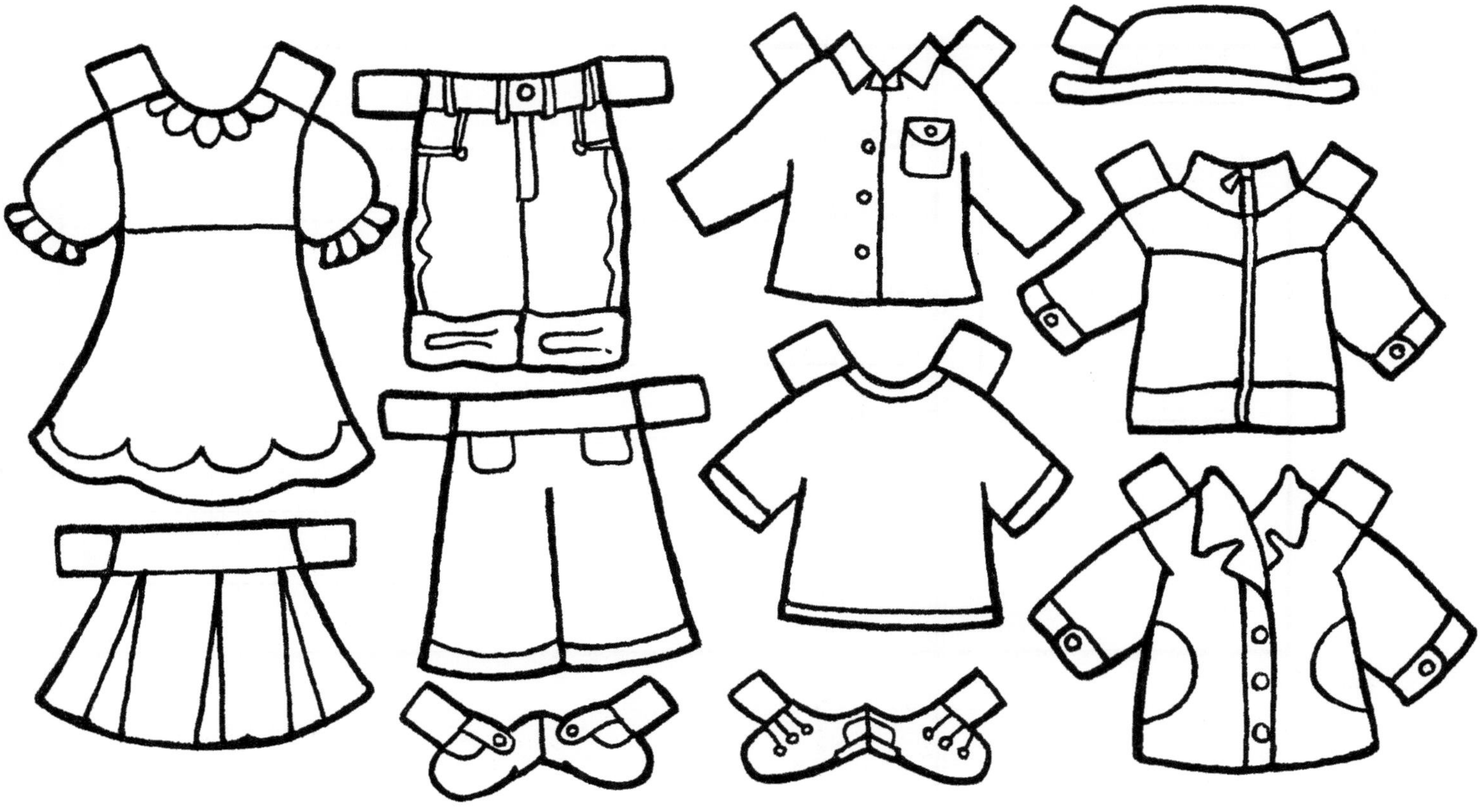

Photocopiable 10

A

Name	Likes	Dislikes

What's your name?
What do you like doing?
What don't you like doing?

B

Name: ____________________

Likes: ____________________

____

____

Dislikes: ____________________

____

____

Photocopiable 11

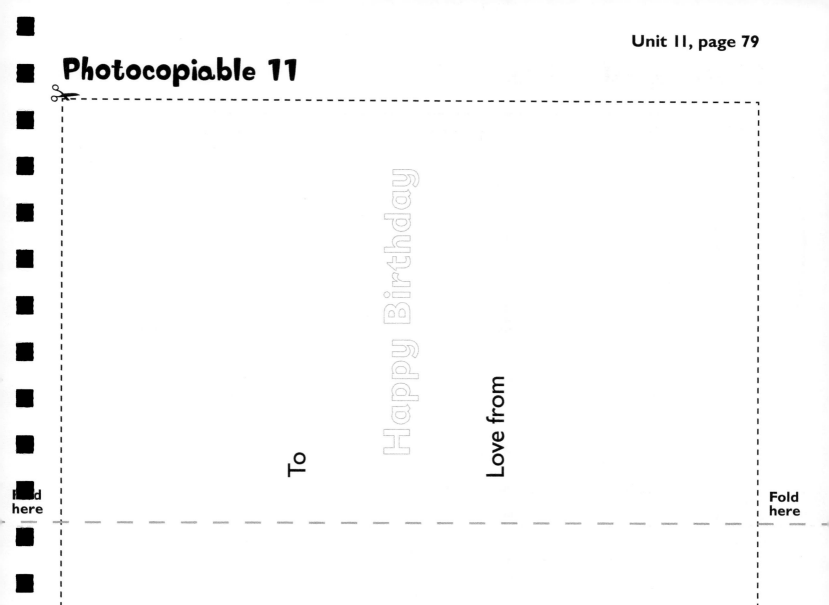

To

Happy Birthday

Love from

Fold here

Fold here

Photocopiable 12a

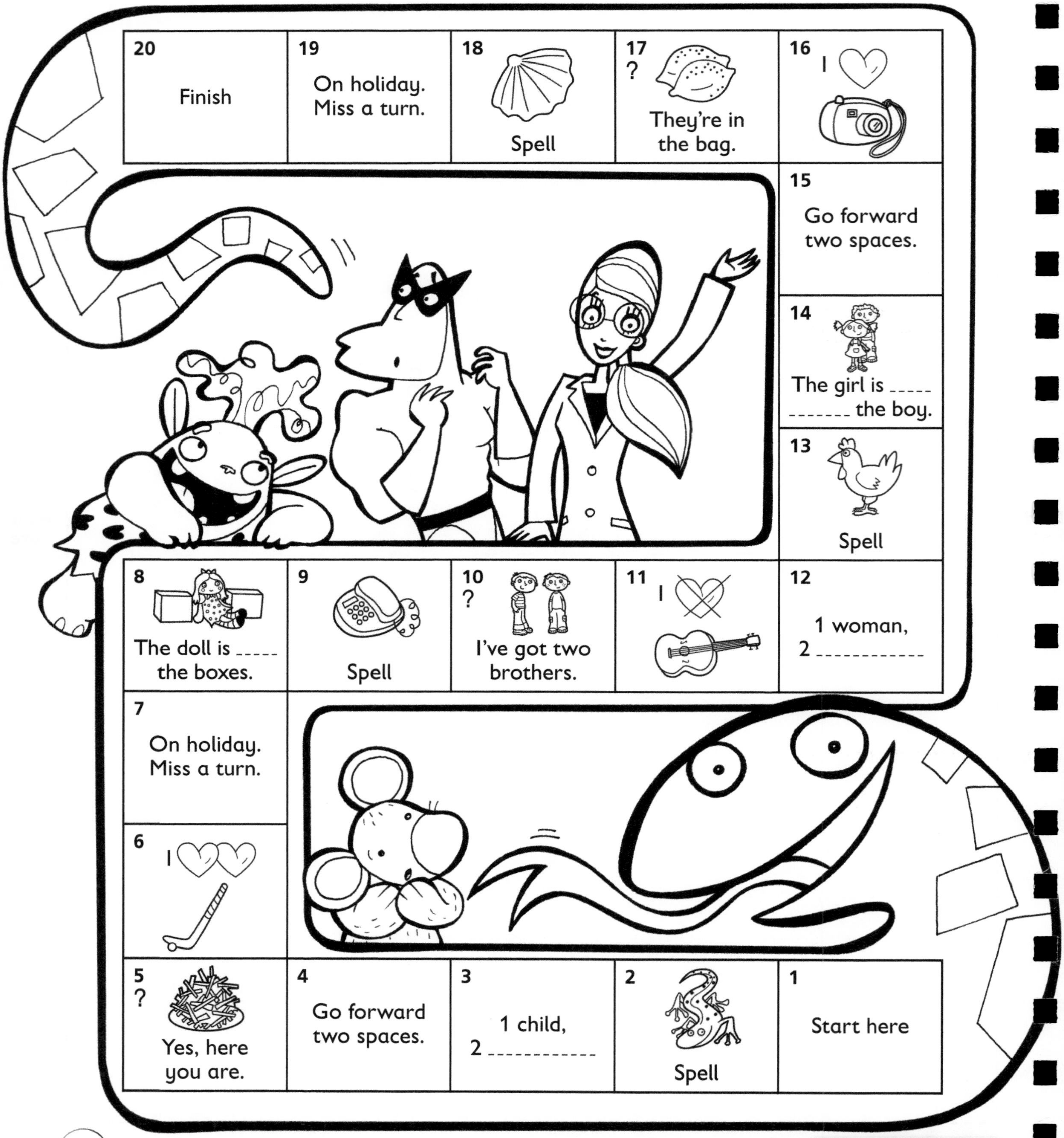
1
Start here
2
Spell
3
1 child,
2 ___________
4
Go forward two spaces.
5
?
Yes, here you are.
6
I
7
On holiday. Miss a turn.
8
The doll is _____ the boxes.
9
Spell
10
?
I've got two brothers.
11
I
12
1 woman,
2 ___________
13
Spell
14
The girl is _____ _______ the boy.
15
Go forward two spaces.
16
I
17
?
They're in the bag.
18
Spell
19
On holiday. Miss a turn.
20
Finish

Photocopiable 12b

	taking photos		horse-riding		painting
	playing the guitar		fishing		playing baseball
	mountains		the sea		the sun
	beaches		shells		cities
	sausages		fries		burgers
	lemonade		water		milk

Extra activities

Unit 1

Page 4

- **Extra activity 1: Numbers game**

Invite ten pupils to come to the front. Hand each one a card with a number on. Say *Ready, steady, go.* Pupils quickly get in a line showing the correct number sequence. Check with the class. The class counts aloud and the pupils hold up their cards in turn. Repeat two or three times.

Invite nine pupils up and hand out nine numbers. Pupils get in line and the class checks. They say which number is missing. Repeat, with a different missing number each time.

- **Extra activity 2: Name chant**

Teach the following chant to the class. Display the flashcard of Suzy Star. Point to it and chant:

What's your name? What's your name?
What's your name? How old are you?
My name's Suzy, Suzy, Suzy.
My name's Suzy and I'm four.

Practise two or three times with the whole class. Throw a ball of paper to a pupil for them to answer their name and age. The next time, the pupil throws the ball to another pupil, and so on. If appropriate, divide the class into three or four groups. They make large circles and repeat the chant.

Page 5

- **Extra activity 1: Colour game**

You will need space for this game. Display the 11 large pieces of paper with different colours written on or word cards from *Teacher's Resource Book 2* around the room. Pupils stand in the middle. Divide pupils into four groups. Group 1 are all 1s, Group 2 all 2s, and so on. Mix the groups up again. Say, e.g. *1s to red.* 1s run to the red piece of paper. Repeat for other numbers and other colours, repeating numbers and colours to keep pupils active.

- **Extra activity 2: Sums bingo**

Pupils draw a 2 x 2 grid in their notebooks. They write a different number between *1* and *10* in each square. Do a practice game first. Say, e.g. *Three and four is …* Pupils don't say the answer, but if they have *7* in their grids, they cross it out. Read out more of your sums until a pupil has crossed out all their numbers and shouts *Bingo!* Read out the sums again to check they are correct. Repeat. Reuse some of the sums. Pupils draw a new grid with different numbers each time.

Page 6

- **Extra activity: Matching game**

Pupils colour the individual letters from Photocopiable 1 (see page T100) in the correct colour (as in Pupil's Book page 6). They cut out their cards.

Pupils then play a matching game. They use one set of cards for each group of four. They take turns to turn over the cards and say the letters. If the letters have the same sound, e.g. /e/, then the pupil takes the pair. If not, then the pupil turns them face down again and it's the next pupil's turn. Play continues until most cards are matched. Pupils put their alphabet cards into envelopes for use in other lessons.

Page 7

- **Extra activity 1: Spell it**

Pupils take out their alphabet cards from Photocopiable 1. Tell pupils to choose colour and number words. Pupils work in pairs. Make sure pupils can't see their partner's word. Pupil A 'writes' a word using his/her alphabet cards, e.g. *Blue*. Pupil A then spells out the word for Pupil B, e.g. *B–l–u–e*. Pupil B 'writes' the word using his/her letters and then says the word. Pupil A says *Correct* or *Not correct.* Pupils look and check. Pupils swap roles.

- **Extra activity 2: I spy …**

Say, e.g. *I spy with my little eye something beginning with 'b'. It's green.* (A green book.) Pupils take turns to guess. Help them with ideas if they are stuck. Repeat with two or three more known classroom items. If pupils find the game easy, then don't give the colour. More able pupils can come to the front, whisper the word to you and then say the prompt to the class.

Page 8

- **Extra activity 1: Spell the words and find the sounds**

Pupils take out their alphabet cards from Photocopiable 1. Pupils work in pairs and make the words below, using the letters as you spell them. After they make each word, they write it in their notebooks. Check understanding of each one by gesture, sound, etc.

1 sn<u>a</u>ke, 2 h<u>a</u>nd, 3 f<u>a</u>ce, 4 pl<u>a</u>y, 5 ball, 6 star, 7 car, 8 g<u>a</u>me

- **Extra activity 2: Noughts and crosses**

Draw a 3 x 3 noughts and crosses grid on the board. In each square write a different number in letters, e.g. *Five*. Divide the class into two teams, A and B. One team is 0 and the other X. Teams take turns to choose a number. Ask them one of your 20 questions, e.g. *What's this colour?* If the team member says the word correctly (G–r–e–e–n), then erase the number in the square and draw a *X* or a *0*. If they aren't correct, leave the number in the square. Teams can choose this number later (but ask a different question). The object of the game is for a team to complete a line of *0* or *X* diagonally, vertically or horizontally. The first team to do this is the winner. If neither team does it, then it's a draw. Repeat.

Page 9

- **Extra activity 1: Roleplay**

Pupils work in groups of four, each one taking on one of the roles in the story on Pupil's Book page 9. Pupils practise their story in groups. More confident pupils can change some of the questions in their groups. Invite two or three groups to roleplay their story to the class.

- **Extra activity 2: Team game**

Place a desk or table on either side of the room. Put a piece of paper on each table and divide each one into seven columns. Write a colour at the top of each column. Do a quick demonstration with the whole class on the board. Hold up one letter card, e.g. *k*, and elicit where it goes (in the grey column). Divide the class into two teams. Hand out a set of cards to members of each team (some will have more than one card). They take it in turns to go and place their cards in the right columns on their paper. The team who correctly completes the columns first is the winner. Check with the class by putting the cards in the correct places on the board.

Unit 2

Page 10

• Extra activity 1: Team game

Divide the class into two teams. They line up facing the board. The pupils at the front of each team take turns to ask and answer questions. They win a point for their team if their question is correct and a point if their answer is correct. The pupil at the front of Team A goes to the board, points to it and says *What's this?* The pupil at the front of Team B answers *The board* (or *A board*). Both teams win a point. The two pupils go to the back of the team and then the pupil at the front of Team B asks a question and the pupil from Team A answers. Questions can be: *What colour is it? What is it? Where is the teacher?*, etc.

At the end of the game, the team with the most points is the winner.

• Extra activity 2: Classroom chant

Teach the following chant to the pupils. Add other verses for other new words. Divide the class into groups, one group for each verse, and say the chant around the class. Pupils can also suggest other words to include in the chant.

Where's the window? Where is it? [look questioning]
There, there, there. [pointing]

Where's the bookcase? Where is it? [look questioning]
There, there, there. [pointing]

Where's the cupboard? Where is it? [look questioning]
There, there, there. [pointing]

Where's the board? Where is it? [look questioning]
There, there, there. [pointing]

Where's the teacher? Where is he/she? [look questioning]
There, there, there. [pointing]

Page 11

• Extra activity 1: Numbers and words

Divide the class into two teams. Display the number flashcards 11–20 (32–41) on the board (word side). Teams line up facing the board. Hand a rolled up newspaper to the first pupil in each team. Say a number. Pupils race to hit the correct word with their newspaper. The first to do it wins a point for their team. The two pupils go to the back of the team. Hand the newspapers to the two pupils at the front and continue. Repeat numbers to make it more challenging. When all pupils have had a go, the team with the most points is the winner.

Page 12

• Extra activity 1: How many?

Hand out Photocopiable 2 to the pupils. Give them their own copies if you used them in the previous lesson. Focus pupils on the section at the bottom where they write the numbers. Pupils work in pairs and take turns to ask and answer about the objects in the picture, e.g. *How many desks are there? There are eighteen desks.* They write the numbers in words on the lines.

Check with the class by asking pupils to spell out the numbers.

Key: sixteen chairs, four windows, fourteen rulers, seventeen bags, five cupboards, three pictures, three bookcases, twelve erasers, fourteen pens, eleven pencils, twelve stars

• Extra activity 2: I spy ...

Play a game of I spy to review the letters of the alphabet and the school objects. Divide the class into four teams. Start the game like this: *I spy with my little eye something beginning with 'b'.* Pupils take turns to guess. The pupil who guesses correctly wins a point for their team. Repeat with other classroom words.

Page 13

• Extra activity 1: Crazy sentences

Divide the class into six groups. Hand out the sentence parts (see page T13 Materials required), one sentence to each group. Each group works quickly to make their sentence/question. Check around the class. Collect the sentence parts and pass them on to the next group. Continue until all the groups have done all the sentences/questions. Ask the last group to come and stick their sentence/question on the board. Check with the class if they agree. Focus on the capital letters and the full stops and question marks.

• Extra activity 2: Our classroom

Pupils work in pairs. Each pair writes two sentences about their classroom on a piece of paper, using the model from Activity Book page 13 Activity 7. The sentences can both be true, both be false or be one of each. They write the answer after each one (*yes* or *no*). They write their names on the paper.

Collect the sentences and play a class game. Read out statements at random. Pupils put up their hands to say *Yes* or *No*. Pupils who wrote the statements can't answer.

Page 14

• Extra activity 1: Spelling game

Play the Spelling game with pupils. A pupil is the caller and the class responds. Use it as a way of revising vocabulary from the unit. e.g.

Pupil:	Class responds:
Give me a b	*b*
Give me an o	*o*
Give me an o	*o*
Give me a k	*k*
What does that spell?	*book*
What does that spell?	*book*

• Extra activity 2: Wordsnakes

Write the wordsnake from Activity Book page 14 on the board. Review with pupils how it works.

Pupils look back through the unit and choose six new words. They put their words into a wordsnake. They draw simple pictures around the snake and draw writing lines under each picture. Pupils swap wordsnakes with another pupil, complete them and return them. Review with pupils the words in their snakes, e.g. *How many pupils have got 'sixteen' in their snakes?* Pupils put their hands up.

Page 15

• Extra activity 1: Bingo

Display the school flashcards (26–31) and the number flashcards 11–20 (32–41), word and numeral side on the board. Write a number between *1* and *16* under each one. Pupils draw a 2 x 2 grid in their books. They choose four items and write the corresponding number in their grids, e.g. *Board* has the number *4* under it. A pupil chooses *Board* and writes the number *4* in one square of the grid.

Call out the words at random. Pupils cross out numbers which correspond to the words. The first pupil to cross out all four shouts *Bingo!* Ask the pupil to say each word. If they are the correct words, he/she is the winner. Repeat.

• Extra activity 2: Spelling game

Demonstrate the activity, using the following words: *ruler, eraser.* Write them like this on the board:

rul	*ser*
era	*er*

Pupils match the words. Elicit the spelling of each one.

Put pupils into pairs. Set a time limit, e.g. five minutes. Display the paper with the half words on it (see page T15 Materials required). Pupils match and then write the eight words. Stop pupils after the time limit and check the answers by asking pupils to spell the words to you.

Key: sixteen, cupboard, eleven, bookcase, fourteen, twelve, teacher, board

Page 16

• Extra activity 1: Guess the fruit

Pupils work in pairs using their notebooks and pens. They take turns to draw pictures of fruit/animals for their partners to guess. They must guess as their partner is drawing. The quickest to guess is the winner.

• Extra activity 2: Favourite fruit

Pupils work in small groups and do a survey of their group's favourite fruit. They draw a simple blank graph, with pictures of five or six types of fruit along the horizontal axis and numbers on the vertical axis (draw the graph on the board for pupils to copy if necessary). They ask questions as for Activity Book Activity 1 and colour the graph. Monitor and ask groups about their results as they colour, e.g. *How many children like apples? How many children like lemons?*

Page 17

• Extra activity 1: Conversation starter

Pupils work in pairs, A and B. Give one of the opening gambits from a dialogue to all the Pupil As (i.e. to half the class). Pupil A reads out the phrase, e.g. *Sorry I'm late.* Pupil B has to reply with the correct polite response, e.g *That's OK. Sit down.*

Collect the pieces of paper, mix them up and give them out to Pupil Bs. Repeat the activity – this time Pupil Bs read the phrases and Pupil As respond.

• Extra activity 2: Guess the situation

Give pupils pictures cut from magazines or printed from the internet with the same social situations as the ones featured in the lesson. Pupils practise dialogues to match the pictures in pairs. Stick all the pictures on the board.

Call a pair of pupils to the front. They choose one picture (secretly) to act out in front of the class. The other pupils have to identify which picture the pair is acting out.

Unit 3

Page 18

• Extra activity 1: Run and touch

Divide the class into two teams. They line up, facing the board. Hand the pupils at the front of each team a rolled up newspaper. Put two columns, one for each team, at the side of the board. Call out one of the words on the Toys mind map from the Warmer on page T18. The two pupils race to hit the word with their newspaper. The first to do it wins the word for their team. Erase the word and then ask the pupil to spell it for you so you can write it in their column at the side of the board. If they spell it correctly, they win 2 points (1 for the touch and 1 for the spelling). If they don't spell it correctly, they only win 1 point for the touch. In this case, elicit the spelling from another pupil. The two pupils go to the back of the lines. Continue the game, using the two pupils at the front until all the words have been won. The team with the most points is the winner.

• Extra activity 2: Toy chant

Teach the following clapping chant to the pupils. Divide the class into two groups. The first group says the first verse, and the second group replies. Change group roles and repeat. Change toys by pointing to flashcards (picture side) of the new toys.

Play time! Play time!
Yes, it's play time!
Where's my robot? Where's my ball?

Play time! Play time!
Yes, it's play time!
Here's your robot! Here's your ball!

Page 19

• Extra activity: Picture dictation

Demonstrate the activity first on the board. Draw a 5 x 5 grid, write numbers and letters for the axes and then draw some objects in the squares. For example, three kites (A3, B4, D2), one doll (A5), and so on. 'Hide' 12 objects in this way. Pupils work in pairs to tell each other where their objects are.

Pupils draw two 5 x 5 grids in their books, one at the top of the page and one at the bottom, and number and letter the axes. Tell them all to draw and colour 12 objects in the top grid. Remind them to keep it secret from their partner. Pupils then face one another, holding up their grids so their partner can't see them. Pupil A starts and says, e.g. *There are four watches.* Pupil B says *Where are they?* Pupil A says, e.g. *In B4, D2, E1 and E2.* Pupil B says *What colour are they?* Pupil A answers. Pupil B then draws and colours them in the grid at the bottom of their page. Pupil A continues to give information about the grid until Pupil B has drawn and coloured all the objects. Then they change roles. Pupil B describes his/her top grid and Pupil A draws and colours in his/her bottom grid.

Pupils look at the grids and check.

Page 20

• Extra activity 1: True or false

Look around the classroom and quickly prepare ten statements about pupils and their classroom objects/clothes (use known words), e.g. *Paul's jacket's blue. Fiona's bag's pink and white.* Make some of the statements true and some false. All the sentences should follow the model: possessive *'s* followed by contracted *'s*.

Say each sentence twice, e.g. *1. Paul's jacket's blue.* Pupils write the number and then *T* for true or *F* for false. Say the sentences again. Pupils swap papers with a partner for the checking phase. Check with the class. Ask pupils to correct the false statements. Pupils award their friends a mark out of 10 and return the papers.

• Extra activity 2: The *Whose?* game

Tell pupils to choose something for the game. It can be a single object (pencil) or multiple objects (pencils). If it's multiple objects, they need to put them together with string/elastic bands. Go around the class and make sure pupils are following instructions. Hand out the necessary string, etc.

Divide the class into two teams. Invite half of Team A to come and give you their objects. Hold up each one in turn and say *Whose is this / are these?* The pupil responds *It's / They're mine* each time. Play the game with Team B. Hold up or point to each of the objects in turn and say *Whose is this / are these?* Ask members of Team B in turn to answer, e.g. *It's / They're Jack's.* Team A must keep silent. Award points for correct answers (1 for the right pupil, and 1 for the correct use of the *'s*).

Repeat with half of Team B's objects and, if time, with the remaining objects from both teams. The team with the most points is the winner.

Page 21

• Extra activity 1: Writing a new song

Pupils use the model of the song on CD 1, 39 to work in groups and write new verses for the song. Write one verse on the board and, with the help of the pupils, underline the words that they can change for their verse, e.g.

Whose are these shoes?
Whose are these shoes?
What? Those blue shoes?
Yes, these blue shoes.
Whose are these shoes?
They're Sheila's.
Oh!

Do a similar example for a singular object and elicit from pupils what the difference between the two verses is.

In their groups, pupils compose two new verses, one singular and one plural. Some groups perform their verses with actions for the class.

• Extra activity 2: Who is it?

Put the four pictures of children wearing different coloured clothes on the board, elicit names for each one and write the names below the pictures.
Play simple games with the pictures, e.g.

a) Start to describe a picture until pupils put up their hands to answer, e.g. *This pupil's got blue shoes, a red skirt, a yellow T-shirt …*
b) Say true/false statements, e.g. *Sally's got a yellow and purple T-shirt.*
c) Ask, e.g. *Whose jacket is blue?* for pupils to respond with *'s*.

Page 22

• Extra activity 1: Whose is this toy?

Give pupils their envelopes with the Photocopiable 3 cards in. If not previously used, hand out the photocopies to each pupil. They cut and prepare the cards.

Pupils write the names of the characters from Pupil's Book page 22 Activity 10 on small pieces of paper. Put pupils into pairs. Pupil A places the objects next to the characters as he/she wishes. The pupil keeps it a secret from their partner by placing a book over their work. Pupil B then holds up a card, e.g. a lorry, and says *Whose is it?* Pupil A looks at the allocation and tells B, e.g. *It's Stella's.* Pupil B places the lorry next to Stella. Pupil B continues to ask until all the cards are next to the characters. Pupil A reveals the correct information and they check. Pupils swap roles.

• Extra activity 2: Number game

Invite eight pupils to come to the front. Hand out eight of the 20 number cards at random. The pupils look at the numbers and stand in the right order, facing the class, holding their number cards up, e.g. *One, three, seven, eight, twelve, fourteen, seventeen, twenty.* The class checks the pupils are right by chanting the numbers, filling in the missing ones, e.g. *One, two, three, four, five, …* Repeat.

Page 23

• Extra activity 1: My favourite toy

Write the words *My favourite toy* on the board. Draw a circle around them to make them the centre of a mind map. Display the toy flashcards (42–48) at the bottom of the board. Work with the class to think of the information / key words and write *What? Colour? Big/small? Where?* around the centre of the mind map, drawing lines from the words to the centre. Together with the class, brainstorm the questions: *What's your favourite toy? What colour is it? Is it big? Is it small? Where is it?*

Demonstrate the activity to the class. Choose a more confident pupil. Don't ask the pupil the questions: the pupil uses the questions as a prompt, e.g. *My favourite toy is my lorry. It's red and yellow. It's small. It's in the cupboard in my bedroom.* Congratulate the pupil and invite another pupil to talk about their favourite toy. Repeat.

Divide the class into groups of three. Pupils take it in turns to talk to their group about their favourite toys. Monitor pupils as they are working and choose four or five to talk about their toys to the class at the end of the activity.

• Extra activity 2: Dictation

Say *Let's do a spelling game. Open your notebooks. Listen and write.* Dictate the new toy words to the class. They write them in their notebooks. Pupils swap books and correct each other's work. Ask pupils to spell out the words for the class to check.

Unit 4

Page 24

• Extra activity 1: Anagrams

Write the following words as anagrams on the board: *Shoes, computer, camera, bookcase*, plus four of the new words from the lesson and two rooms. Pupils work in pairs. They race to unscramble the words and write them correctly. Check by asking one pair to spell a word out and another to write it on the board.

• Extra activity 2: Action song

Teach the class the following nursery rhyme with actions:

Hickory dickory dock,	
The mouse ran up the clock.	(fingers of right hand running up left arm)
The clock struck one – DONG!	(nod head forward)
The mouse ran down.	(fingers of right hand running down left arm)
Hickory dickory dock.	
Tick tock, tick tock.	(move head from left to right)

Do the song as a round. Divide the class into three groups. Group 1 starts. When they start the third line, Group 2 starts the first line. When they start the third line, Group 3 starts the first line.

Page 25

• Extra activity 1: True or false

Pupils work in pairs. They use the model from Pupil's Book page 25 Activity 4 and take turns to say sentences about the pictures which are true or false. Their partner says either *True* or *False*. If it's false, the partner corrects the sentence. Elicit sentences from the class.

Page 26

• Extra activity 1: Mine or yours?

Pupils use CD 1, 52 dialogue to create mini roleplays. Write the dialogue on the board and underline the words they can change, e.g.

Whose T-shirt is that?
It's mine!
Whose black trousers are those?
They're yours, Grandpa.

Elicit possible options. Pairs prepare their roleplays and volunteers perform them for the class.

• **Extra activity 2: Which one? [YLE]**
Hand out Photocopiable 4 (page T103) to each pupil. If not used in the previous lesson, pupils cut along the cutting line to separate the two sections. They colour the objects at the bottom of the page and then cut out the six cards.

Make pairs. Each pair needs one copy of the house and two sets of cards. Pupils place the objects in pairs (two lamps, two mats, etc.). They take turns to give instructions and to carry them out, e.g. Pupil A points to the lamps and says *Put the blue one in the sitting room. Put the red one in the bedroom.* They continue until all the objects are in the rooms.

Collect the materials at the end of the activity.

Page 27

• **Extra activity 1: Creating a class song**
Display the large piece of paper with the words of the song from Pupil's Book page 27 Activity 7. Elicit why words are underlined (pupils can change these words to make their own song). Make groups of four. Pupils work in groups and create a verse for the song. Select four groups to perform their verses with mime one after another for the class. Repeat with another four groups.

• **Extra activity 2: Initial letters**
Write the following words at random over the board: *Bag, shoes, ruler, jacket, bookcase, pencil, mat, lamp, mirror, sofa.* Pupils work in pairs to write the list in their books in alphabetical order. Elicit and check with the class. Repeat with another ten words if appropriate.

Page 28

• **Extra activity 1: Word sounds**
Display the three pieces of paper with the words written at the top (*hippo, snake, bee*) and number them *1, 2, 3.* Divide the class into three groups. Each group (pupils can sub-divide into pairs) focuses on one sound/paper for two minutes. They think of as many words as they can with that sound. They can use their books for reference. Say *Stop.* Groups move on to the next sound. Repeat until all three groups have brainstormed words for all three sounds. Elicit words from all three groups for each sound and write the correct ones on the papers. Congratulate the groups who got the most correct words for each sound.

• **Extra activity 2: This one or that one?**
Hand out Photocopiable 4 to each pupil. If not used in the previous lessons, pupils cut along the cutting line to separate the two sections. They colour the objects at the bottom of the page and then cut out the six cards.

Make pairs. Pupils will only need the cards (12 for each pair). Pupils place them face down on the desk, taking one card out and hiding it under a book. Some of the cards are near them and some further away. Pupils take turns to turn over one card and say (if it's their partner's), e.g. *It's a lamp. This one's yours.* Pupils say *mine* if it's their own. The pupil either hands the card to the partner or keeps it, depending on whose it is. Play continues until all the cards are turned over. Pupils then say which card is missing and whose it is.

Page 29

• **Extra activity 1: Noughts and crosses**
Draw a 3 x 3 grid on the board and write numbers *1–9* at random in the grid. Make two teams: A and B. Pupils close all their books. Team A choose a number. Ask them a question about the story on Pupil's Book page 29 Activity 12. If they answer correctly, draw a *0* in the square. Repeat for Team B and draw a *X* if they give a correct answer. Continue, with teams taking turns to choose and answer. The first team to make a row of *0* or *X* is the winner.

• **Extra activity 2: My house**
Hand out Photocopiable 4 to each pupil. If not used in the previous lessons, pupils cut along the cutting line to separate the two sections. They colour the objects at the bottom of the page and then cut out the six cards.

Pupils work individually. They stick the house in their notebooks and then stick each card in or next to one of the rooms. They write a sentence about each card, e.g. *There's a blue lamp next to the TV in the living room.* Monitor pupils as they are working. They say each sentence to you before they write it.

Page 30

• **Extra activity 1: Guessing game**
Play a guessing game. Describe one of the objects from the lesson or a different known object in the classroom. Pupils have to guess what it is e.g. *This is small and blue. You talk to your friends with it. What is it?* Pupils put their hands up to answer (*phone*). Pupils work in pairs to play the guessing game or alternatively volunteers describe objects for the class to guess.

• **Extra activity 2: Origami model**
Find a different origami pattern for your pupils to make another simple object. Alternatively, pupils have a go at making one of the objects from Pupil's Book page 30 Activity 1, e.g. the kite or the sofa.

Page 31

• **Extra activity 1: Recycled model**
Pupils work in pairs to make an object of their choosing from recycled/re-used materials. They can draw the object or make it using real-life everyday objects. Ask the questions from the lesson *What have you got? What are you making/doing?* Pupils say the materials they have got and what they are making.

• **Extra activity 2: Memory chain**
Start a chain by saying *I recycle plastic bottles.* A pupil continues by saying *I recycle plastic bottles and paper.* The chain goes on around the class. When pupils run out of ideas, start a new chain with *I don't recycle …*

Page 32

• **Extra activity 1: Spelling game**
Pupils play in groups of three or four. They choose someone to write for the group. Display a selection of flashcards from Units 1 to 4 (picture side). In their groups, pupils decide how the words are spelled and the chosen pupil writes them on a piece of paper. Set a time limit if you wish. Elicit the words, letter by letter, and write them on the board for groups to check their work. The group with the most correctly spelled words wins.

• **Extra activity 2: Play a game**
Play one of the games from Units 1–4 with the class.

Page 33

• **Extra activity 1: Board slap**
Display the 12 flashcards you've chosen from flashcards 26–53 (word side) on the board. Make two teams. Teams line up behind each other. Hand each pupil at the front of the teams a rolled up newspaper. Call out one of the words on a flashcard. Pupils run to hit it with the newspaper. The first to do so wins a point for their team. The pupils go to the back. Hand the newspapers to the new pupils at the front and repeat, calling another word. Make the game more fun by occasionally calling words that aren't on the board. Award points to the pupil who doesn't run.

- **Extra activity 2: Sing a song or do a chant**

Sing one of the songs or do a chant from Units 1–4 with the class.

Unit 5

Page 34

- **Extra activity 1: Family webs**

Draw a circle in the middle of the board and write the word *Family* in the middle. Draw eight lines coming from the web. Pupils suggest words to add to the web. Accept correct ones and write them around the mind map: *cousin, brother, sister, mother/mummy, father/ daddy, baby, grandfather/grandpa, grandmother/ grandma*. Pupils copy the mind map into their notebooks.

- **Extra activity 2: Family song**

Teach the Family song to pupils, e.g. to the tune of *Frère Jacques*. They repeat as a class. Divide the class into two groups. Groups take turns to say each verse. Divide the class into three groups and sing the song as a round (Group 1 starts; Group 2 starts when Group 1 starts line 3; Group 3 starts when group 2 starts line 3).

Brother, sister,
Mother, father.
There they are, there they are.

Grandma and grandpa,
Baby, cousin Frank.
They're all here. They're all here.

Page 35

- **Extra activity: My family tree**

Note: Only use this activity if you are sure it won't be distressing for any of your pupils.

Using the family tree on Pupil's Book page 35 as a model, pupils draw their own family tree in their notebooks and label it.

In pairs, they talk about their families, e.g. *This is my mother. This is my cousin, Juan. He's a baby.*

Page 36

- **Extra activity 1: Match the words**

Write the following words across the board in one colour: *Running, hitting, jumping, getting, sleeping, throwing, catching, flying, cleaning.* Write these in another colour: *Run, hit, jump, get, sleep, throw, catch, fly, clean.* Make sure the verbs, e.g. *hit/hitting* are not next to each other. Pupils come in turn and draw a line to match the verbs (*run–running*). If appropriate, invite pupils to notice the spelling (double letters for *running, hitting, getting*).

- **Extra activity 2: Draw and write**

Pupils choose one of the verbs from Pupil's Book page 36 Activity 6. They draw a picture in their notebooks of themselves doing something and label it, e.g. flying a kite and write underneath *I'm flying a kite.*

Page 37

- **Extra activity 1: Silent bingo**

Review the seven food words: *Orange, banana, apple, chocolate, ice cream, cake, burger,* using the flashcards or the pictures. Display them (picture side) on the board. Elicit the spelling of the food words and write them in a list down the side of the board, not next to the right pictures. Pupils draw a 2 x 2 grid in their books. They choose four foods and write one food word in each square. Hold up a picture in turn. Don't say the word. If it's the food a pupil has, he/she crosses out the word. The first pupil to cross out all four is the winner. Check the words and spelling back from the pupil. Repeat.

- **Extra activity 2: Song roleplay**

Make groups of eight. If there are extra pupils, spread them over the other groups. Review the song from Pupil's Book page 37 Activity 7 with the class. Groups decide who is who (there are eight characters). Choose a confident pupil to be the singer in each group (the boy). Groups practise the song: 'the boy' sings and the others in the group mime as he/she says the lines about them. Invite more confident groups to come and perform their song roleplay to the class.

Page 38

- **Extra activity 1: Odd one out**

Write the following on the board:

mother, brother, father, sister
ball, chair, small, board
hit, eat, sit, kick
throw, run, fun, sun
catch, watch, lamp, mat

Pupils work in pairs to find the word that has a different sound each time. Check with the class by asking pairs to say the words clearly.

Key: sister, chair, eat, throw, watch

- **Extra activity 2: Egg and spoon race**

You will need space for this activity. Ten pupils take part in the first race. Mark out a starting line and a finishing line. The ten pupils line up at the start with their ping pong balls on their spoons. Say *Ready, steady, go!* Pupils race to get to the finish without dropping their ping pong ball and without holding it on the spoon. The first three to finish go to the next round. Repeat in groups of ten for the other pupils, choosing the first three each time. Repeat the race with the three best from each 'heat'. This time, the first to reach the finishing line (without dropping or holding) is the winner.

Page 39

- **Extra activity 1: Roleplay**

Pupils work in groups of five, each one taking on one of the roles in the story from CD 2, 16. Pupils practise their story in groups. More confident pupils can change some of the actions in their groups. Invite two or three groups to roleplay their story to the class.

- **Extra activity 2: Make the family**

Pupils play the Family game again. See the instructions for Photocopiable 5 (pages T98 and T104).

Unit 6

Page 40

- **Extra activity 1: Run and touch**

Display all the food flashcards (word side) over the board: *bread, water, milk, juice, chicken, eggs, chips, rice, chocolate cake, oranges, bananas, apples, burgers, fish, ice cream.* Make two teams. They line up, facing the board. Hand a rolled up newspaper to one member of each team. Call out, e.g. *Eggs*. Pupils race to hit the egg word with their papers. The first to do so wins a point for their team. Repeat.

- **Extra activity 2: Food diagram**

Write the words *Breakfast, lunch, dinner* on the board. Elicit what the Star family have for each one (breakfast – bread and milk, lunch – egg and chips, dinner – chicken and rice) and elicit what pupils have. Some of the words can be in L1.

Write all the known food words on the board: *Bread, water, milk, juice, chicken, eggs, chips, rice, potatoes, carrots, pears, lemons, meat, chocolate cake, oranges, bananas, apples, burgers, ice cream, fish.* Draw three large interlocking circles like this:

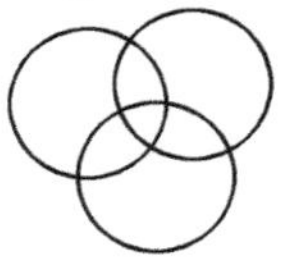

Label one *Breakfast*, one *Lunch* and one *Dinner*. Do an example with the class. Say *When do we have milk?* Pupils respond (e.g. breakfast, lunch and dinner). Write *milk* in the space where the three circles meet. Repeat for two or three other words.

Pupils work in groups of four. They draw a large diagram on a large piece of paper and write the foods for the different meals. Display, discuss and compare the diagrams.

Page 41

- **Extra activity: Class songs**

Pupils work in groups, each group taking a meal from the song in CD 2, 21. They create a verse for the song, based on other foods for the meal. They use the structure of the song to help them, e.g.

It's morning. It's morning.
We're having breakfast with our mum.
Eggs and milk, eggs and milk.
It's morning. It's morning.

Pupils perform their new verses for the class. Vote for the one the class likes best.

Page 42

- **Extra activity 1: Can I have ...?**

Pupils each draw small pictures of the following: bread, milk, juice, chips. They cut them out.

Pupils stand up, holding their pictures. Play the CD of lively music. Pupils move around the room. Stop the CD. Pupils find partners and take turns to ask for one of the four foods, e.g. *Can I have some milk, please?* They reply *Here you are* and hand the paper to their friend. Play the music. Pupils move on. Stop the music and repeat. Pupils ask a new partner. If their partner does not have the food picture any more, they say *No,* (name). *I'm sorry.* Repeat.

- **Extra activity 2: Consequences**

Review the sequence of the conversations from Activity Book page 42 Activity 5:

1 Can I have ______________________________?
2 Which _____________ – apple or orange / bananas or pears / milk or water?
3 _____________, please.
4 Here you are.

Pupils work in groups of four. Each pupil takes a piece of paper. They keep it secret from their group. Say *1*. Pupils each write a request at the top of their paper. They fold the paper down to hide the request and pass it to the left. Say *2*. Pupils each write a question for line 2. They fold the paper down and pass it to the left. Repeat for 3 and 4. Pupils take back the paper they started with. Pupils unfold their conversations and read them. Groups read out the best/silliest ones to the class.

Page 43

- **Extra activity 1: Creating stories**

Pupils use the model story from Pupil's Book page 43 Activity 8 to write their own texts. Pupils can copy the same text and just change the pictures and the names. Stronger pupils can change the meal and more of the text if they wish. Pupils swap texts in groups and 'read' each other's to the rest of the group.

- **Extra activity 2: My favourite school meal**

Pupils draw a picture of their favourite meal from the school canteen and label it. Display the drawings on the walls.

Page 44

- **Extra activity: Anagram game**

Display the food flashcards 58–65 and 94 and Flashcards 92–96 from Level 1 (picture side). Pupils work individually. They choose a word and write its anagram on a small piece of paper. They fold the paper. Collect the papers. Redistribute the papers to other pupils. They solve the anagrams and put the paper next to its picture. Count which word most pupils chose.

Page 45

- **Extra activity 1: Spelling**

Say *Listen and then write.* Dictate the new food words: *Bread, water, milk, juice, chicken, eggs, chips, rice*, one after another, saying each one twice. Pupils write the words. They swap papers. Check with the class by eliciting the spelling for each one and writing them on the board. Pupils correct each other's work.

- **Extra activity 2: What's for lunch?**

Pupils each write what they want for lunch on a piece of paper, e.g. *Some chicken and chips and some milk.* They write the food and the drink (they can look at the story on Pupil's Book page 45 to help them). Make groups of four. Give a pupil in each group a list of food they can have, e.g. write *Milk, orange juice, carrots, meat, chocolate cake* on a piece of paper. Write different menus for each group. The other pupils in a group take turns to ask about one of the foods they want for lunch, e.g. *Can I have some milk, please?* The pupil with the paper says *Yes, here you are* if they can (i.e. it's on their menu) and *No, I'm sorry* if they can't (it's not on the menu). Pupils take turns to ask and find out what they can have.

Page 46

- **Extra activity 1: Food diagram**

Make teams of four to six pupils. Draw three circles on the board and start writing the names of food from plants in the first one. The first pupil to say the correct category (*plants*) gets a point for his/her team. Teams write as many other foods as they can to add to the 'plants' category. Teams get a point for every correct word and whichever team writes the most correct words gets an extra point.

Repeat the activity with food from animals. Count up the points to find a winning team. Do the last category (food from trees) together. Encourage pupils to come to the board and write the words themselves.

- **Extra activity 2: True or false**

Pupils work in pairs. One pupil writes down/says incorrect sentences about food e.g. *Eggs are from trees.* Their partner corrects the sentences as in the lesson e.g. *No, eggs are from animals.* Go around the class checking. Choose confident individuals to come to the front and say their sentences, which the class can correct together.

Page 47

• Extra activity 1: Make a dialogue

Pupils work in small groups to make up a dialogue between e.g. a child and his/her mum about a meal (as in the listening activity in the Pupil's Book). Pupils use language such as *Can I have…? Here's your breakfast/lunch/dinner. Are your hands clean? That's a good (dinner).* While pupils are writing the dialogue down, go around checking and correcting. Make sure the language sounds natural.

Two pupils from each group come to the front to act out their dialogue and the class says which meal it is or you draw the meal on the board as they speak.

• Extra activity 2: Your favourite meal

Pupils draw three blank plates in their notebook and ask a different pupil about their favourite food for breakfast, lunch and dinner e.g *What's your favourite food for breakfast?* They draw the food described. Go around checking the pairs.

Unit 7

Page 48

• Extra activity 1: Farms and zoos

Divide the board in half horizontally. Display all the animal flashcards at the top (word side) at random. Divide the bottom half vertically and write *Zoo* on one side and *Farm* on the other. Elicit from pupils one animal for the zoo and one for the farm, e.g. *Tiger* and *Duck*. Make pairs. Give pupils thinking time to decide on where to put the other animals. Tell them that some can go in both. Pairs take turns to come and take a flashcard and put it in the right column. They check with the class if it's correct. Add your feedback if necessary.

Pupils copy the two columns of words into their books, complete with headings.

Key: Farm: cow, duck, goat, sheep, spider, cat, dog, horse, mouse, bird
Zoo: lizard, spider, fish, bird, crocodile, elephant, hippo, giraffe, snake, tiger, monkey

• Extra activity 2: Where is it?

A pupil goes out of the room. Hide an animal flashcard, e.g. tiger, under the table. The pupil comes back. Say *Where's the tiger?* The pupil says, e.g. *Is the tiger in the desk?* The class answers *No*. Prompt the pupil by saying, e.g. *Bookcase, table*. When the pupil guesses correctly, another pupil goes out and the class hides another animal flashcard. Make sure the class practises *on, in, next to, under.*

Page 49

• Extra activity 1: Write a verse for the song

Pupils work in groups of about four. They choose an animal (which makes a noise) and a room and write a verse for it, following the model of the song in CD 2, 34. Monitor and help or advise. Groups perform their verses to the class. Pupils write their verse on large paper and draw a group picture to illustrate it. Display the pictures on the wall.

• Extra activity 2: Jumbled words

Choose eight animals (ones from the lesson and ones from the previous lessons) and write their names in jumbled letters on the board. Pupils work in pairs and unjumble the words. Elicit the spelling and write the words correctly. Each pair then chooses another animal word and writes it in jumbled letters in their notebook. Pairs take turns to come to the board and write their jumbled word. The pair to guess first then takes a turn.

Page 50

• Extra activity: Guessing game

Use the animal flashcards for a guessing game. Secretly look at one flashcard. Give the class one clue about it, e.g. *You can find it in a zoo.* Pupils take turns to guess, e.g. *Is it a tiger?* Answer *No, it isn't.* The pupil who guesses becomes the caller. Repeat as a whole class or make three groups and divide the flashcards into three.

Page 51

• Extra activity 1: Class chant

Display the pictures/flashcards for the foods in Pupil's Book page 51 Activity 7 on the board. Divide the class into eight groups by their favourite food. The groups will be of different sizes. Number the groups *1–8*. Say *Group 1* (they chose *watermelon*). They stand and say in chorus *I love watermelon.* They sit. Other pupils in the class who like it too stand up together and say *So do I.* They sit. Pupils in the class who don't like it stand and say *But I don't* and sit. Continue group by group by calling out *Group 2 … Group 3 …* etc. Make sure you 'conduct' the pupils so that all stand/speak/sit at the same time.

• Extra activity 2: Whispering game

Display about 12 food flashcards (word side) on the board (or use word cards from *Teacher's Resource Book 2*). Make two teams. They line up, one behind the other, facing the board. Whisper a different food word to each pupil at the front of the teams. Pupils whisper the word one to another until it reaches the back. The pupil at the back runs to the front and takes the flashcard. If the flashcard matches the word whispered, the team wins a point. Replace the flashcard. The pupil from the back comes to the front of the line. Repeat.

Page 52

• Extra activity 1: Ten little frogs

Do a finger rhyme and teach the chant below. Pupils hold up both hands to show the ten frogs (ten fingers). Each time a frog runs away, they hide a finger, until all are hidden. As the frogs come back, they show their fingers again.

There are ten green frogs on the farm today.
One jumps up and runs away.
There are nine green frogs on the farm today.
One jumps up and runs away.
There are eight …

etc. until …

There is one green frog on the farm today.
It jumps up and runs away.
There are no green frogs on the farm today.
But wait … Look … Ah! A frog!
One frog, two frogs, three frogs (etc.), *nine frogs, ten frogs!*
There are ten green frogs on the farm today.
And they're here to stay. Hooray!

• Extra activity 2: Animals on the farm

Hand out Photocopiable 7 to each pupil (see pages T99 and T107). If not used previously, pupils cut to separate the two sections and then cut out and colour the eight cards at the bottom of the page. If used previously, hand pairs one set to prepare as above. When they have prepared the set, hand them another set which was prepared in the previous lesson.

Pupils glue their animals where they want in the picture. They stick the picture to a piece of paper and write ten sentences about the animals (depending on how they coloured them), e.g. *There are seven green and blue lizards. They've got long tails.*

Page 53

• Extra activity 1: Finger rhyme

Teach pupils a finger rhyme:

This little girl is going to bed,	(place right forefinger in left hand)
Down, down, down she puts her head.	
Wraps herself in the covers tight,	(fold left hand over right forefinger)
This is how she sleeps all night.	
Morning time! She opens her eyes,	(blink eyes as if just opening)
Throws the covers to the side.	(unfold left hand from right forefinger)
She jumps up to start the day,	
Ready for school, ready for play.	(open left fist and quickly raise right forefinger, wiggle it and move hand as if walking)

Extra activity 2: Wordsnakes

Display all the animal flashcards on the board (word side). Pairs choose six animal words from the board to make a wordsnake. They write it on paper. Pairs swap wordsnakes with pairs. They solve each other's wordsnakes and write the words under the snakes.

Unit 8

Page 54

• Extra activity 1: Memory game

Pupils look at the picture on Pupil's Book page 54 for one minute. They close their books. Make ten statements about the picture, e.g. *Grandpa's jacket is red.* Pupils write *Yes* or *No* in their notebooks from memory. Pupils look and check. Check with the class. They correct the incorrect statements.

• Extra activity 2: Mime story

You will need space for this activity. Pupils walk around the room. Say, e.g. *You're in the town. You're in the street. Look at the shops.* (Pupils mime looking around.) *There's a shoe shop. Oh! Some beautiful shoes!* (Pupils look excited.) *Oh, look! There's Suzy with Grandpa. Say Hi.* (Pupils say *Hi.*) *They're in the café. Sit down.* (Pupils sit down.) *Have a drink of milk.* (Pupils mime drinking.)

Page 55

• Extra activity 1: How many?

Display the large piece of paper with the eight sentences (see page T55 Materials required). Pupils copy the sentences into their notebooks, completing them with the correct word. They check in pairs. Check with the class. Pupils take turns to read the sentences aloud.

Key: 1 children, 2 man, 3 women, 4 child, 5 woman, 6 babies, 7 men, 8 baby

• Extra activity 2: Corner game

You will need space for this activity. Whisper one of the words from the box in Activity Book page 55 Activity 4 to each pupil. If you have more than 24 pupils, whisper the same word to two pupils (in different parts of the classroom). Make sure pupils understand and remember their words. Demonstrate the game first for practice. Point to each corner of the room in turn. Say *This is the red corner. This is the blue corner. This is the yellow corner. And this is the green corner.* Say *Fruit to the red corner.* The pupils who are fruit run to the red corner. Say, e.g. *Toys to the yellow corner.* The 'toy' pupils go there. Continue, moving groups from corner to corner, repeating groups to make the game more fun.

Page 56

• Extra activity: Giving instructions

Pupils work in groups of six. They write instructions for another group as in Activity Book page 56 Activity 6 (*You're Jill. You're sitting behind Tom*). Groups take turns to give instructions to other groups and the groups sit as instructed.

Page 57

• Extra activity 1: Action songs

Pupils work in groups of four and use the song from CD 2, 49 to generate one of their own. They practise the song together. Groups take turns to sing their songs and do the actions for the class.

• Extra activity 2: My town

Hand out a copy of Photocopiable 8 (see page T108) to each pupil. If not used in the previous lesson, pupils cut along the cutting lines to separate the three sections. They cut out the places at the bottom of the page and colour them. Elicit the names of the places. Pupils stick the places where they choose and write sentences using the prepositions to describe where they are, e.g. *The fruit shop's between the hospital and the park.*

Page 58

• Extra activity 1: Talking about my town

Pupils take out Photocopiable 8 (page T108), if they stuck the shops in place in the previous lesson. If not, hand out a copy of Photocopiable 8 to each pupil. Pupils cut along the cutting lines to separate the three sections. They cut out the places at the bottom of the page and colour them. Elicit the names of the places. Pupils stick the places where they choose.

Pupils work in groups of four. They take turns to talk about their towns, describing where the places are. They don't show each other their towns. If another pupil has a place in the same position, they say *Snap!* Then that pupil starts to describe his/her town until another pupil says *Snap!* They continue until all four have described their towns. Then they look and compare.

• Extra activity 2: Town chant

Teach the following chant to pupils. They stand and point when saying *Look, there it is. Right there!* Divide the class into two groups. Each group says a verse to the other group. They swap roles.

There's a park in my town. It's next to the shops.
Look, there it is. Right there!
Where's the park? Where's the park?
There it is. Right there!

There's a café in my town. It's between the shops.
Look, there it is. Right there!
Where's the café? Where's the café?
There it is. Right there!

Page 59

• Extra activity 1: Roleplay

Divide the class into groups of six (Maskman, Monty, Suzy, Simon, two children). Pupils decide their roles. Play the story from CD 2, 53 again. Stop after each frame for pupils to repeat in role. Pupils practise their story in groups. More confident groups of pupils can change some of the words, e.g. *Frogzilla.* Invite one or two groups to roleplay their story to the class.

• Extra activity 2: Play a chain game

Start the chain: *In my town there are three cafés.* Pupil 1: *In my town there are three cafés and a hospital.* Pupil 2: *In my town there are three cafés, a hospital and a park.* After Pupil 6, start another chain. Select pupils at random to continue the chain, to make sure all are listening.

Page 60

• Extra activity 1: Guess the animal

Pupils work in pairs. Pupil A makes an animal noise for Pupil B to guess the animal. Pupil B says, for example, *It's a cat.*

• Extra activity 2: Make a drum

Pupils make a drum using a tin, covered with paper at the open end, held in place with an elastic band. They make drumsticks out of wooden sticks with cotton wool on the ends held on with small round pieces of material and elastic bands.

Alternatively, pupils make shakers using yogurt pots with dried pasta inside. Again the open end is covered with a paper circle held on with sticky tape. Pupils decorate the instruments and play them to accompany one of the pieces of music from the lesson.

Page 61

• Extra activity 1: Park rules

Pupils work in pairs or individually. Give each pair/pupil a photo of a park with grass, a road with a bin or a street crossing with a traffic light. Pupils write one or two sentences about their picture with *Don't* ..., similar to the examples from the lesson (e.g. Park: *Don't walk on the grass. I can eat my lunch here.* Street: *Don't drop rubbish. Don't play here. Traffic lights: Don't cross. The man is red.*)

Pupils work with other pairs/individuals who have a different picture. Keeping their picture hidden, they say their sentence(s). The other pair/pupil guesses which place is in the picture (park, street, traffic lights).

• Extra activity 2: School rules

Pupils work individually to think of some instructions which could be used around their school e.g. *Don't run in the corridors! Listen in class! You can't play football indoors.* Help with new vocabulary. Pupils give examples to the class. Alternatively, ask pupils to write one true and one false instruction. The class correct the false sentences.

Page 62

• Extra activity 1: Reading pictures

Copy the text from Pupil's Book page 62 Activity 2 on the board, but replace the pictures with flashcards of different animals/items (e.g. replace the picture of the sheep with a picture of a cat). The class read the text aloud chorally. Invite volunteers to read it. Repeat with different flashcards.

• Extra activity 2: Play a game

Play one of the games from Units 5–8 with the class.

Page 63

• Extra activity 1: Board slap

Display 12 flashcards from the new words in Units 5–8 (word side) on the board. Make two teams. Teams line up behind each other. Hand each pupil at the front of the teams a rolled up newspaper. Call out one of the words on a flashcard. Pupils run to hit it with the newspaper. The first to do so wins a point for their team. The pupils go to the back. Hand the newspapers to the new pupils at the front and repeat, calling another word. Make the game more fun by occasionally calling words that aren't on the board. Award points to the pupil who doesn't run.

• Extra activity 2: Sing a song or do a chant

Sing one of the songs or do a chant from Units 5–8 with the class.

Unit 9

Page 64

• Extra activity 1: Fashion show

Display or write the text (see page T64 Materials required). Elicit from pupils suggestions for changing the words underlined, to talk about a pupil in the class. Demonstrate with one or two pupils. Pupils work in groups and create a short text about one of them for the fashion show. They don't write it. Groups take it in turns to give the commentary and for one (or more) of them to parade in front of the class.

• Extra activity 2: Mime and sing

Teach the chant below with actions to the tune of *Head, shoulders, knees and toes.* As pupils say the words, they point to the relevant part of their body where they wear/carry the clothes/items. Each time pupils repeat the song, they hum one of the words, e.g. *Hat.* They still do the action (point to their head). After seven goes, they are humming everything and still pointing. They continue, bringing back a word each time until they are singing the whole song again.

Hat, glasses, shirt and jeans,
Shirt and jeans.
Hat, glasses, shirt and jeans,
Shirt and jeans.
Dress and watch and gold handbag.
Hat, glasses, shirt and jeans,
Shirt and jeans.

Page 65

• Extra activity: Secret messages

Pupils work individually and write a description of clothes, using the symbols as in Activity Book page 65 Activity 3. They write the correct version on another piece of paper. They swap descriptions with their partner and each works out the other's message. They check, using the correct versions of each.

Page 66

• Extra activity 1: Game

You will need space for this activity. Brainstorm school objects with pupils, e.g. *Pencil, eraser, crayons, book, ruler, pencil case.* Pupils choose four objects and put them in their pocket/bag. Pupils walk around the room. Clap and say, e.g. *Eraser.* Pupils make pairs and take turns to ask each other *Have you got an eraser?* They answer truthfully, showing the object if they have it. Repeat with other words from the brainstorm.

• Extra activity 2: I've got ...

Pupils think of three things they have at home (e.g. dog, cat, garden). Elicit ideas to make sure pupils are using the structure *I've got* ... correctly. Pupils draw a picture of the three things in their notebooks and write a sentence underneath as in the model in Activity Book page 66 Activity 5.

Page 67

• Extra activity 1: Spelling bee

In your notebook, allocate numbers to the clothes that appear on the 12 flashcards, e.g. *1 = dress, 2 = hat.* Don't tell the pupils. Make two teams: A and B. Team A chooses a number between *1* and *12.* Check what clothes word the number corresponds with in your notebook, e.g. *5 = jeans,* and say *Spell jeans.* A pupil from Team A spells it. If it's correct, award two points to Team A. If it's not, let Team B have a try. If a pupil spells it correctly, award Team B one point. Continue until all the words are spelt. If a team chooses a number that's 'gone', they miss a turn. Congratulate the winners.

• Extra activity 2: Anagrams

Pupils write anagrams for their partner to solve, as on Activity Book page 67, Activity 6.

Page 68

• Extra activity 1: Same or different?

Dictate the pairs of words below to pupils. They write a tick if they have the same sound and a cross if they don't. Dictate the words again. Stop after each pair to check with the class. If they are different, elicit one which has the same sound as the first.
Words: 1 box, Monty (✓), 2 mouse, house (✓), 3 fly, play (✗) – my, 4 jacket, giraffe (✓), 5 swim, hair (✗) – thin, 6 hat, cake (✗) – mat, 7 brown, down (✓), 8 clothes, nose (✓).

• Extra activity 2: What's in my bag?

Show pupils a dark bag with eight classroom objects inside. Shake it so they can hear there are things in it. Say *What have I got? Can you guess?* Pupils take turns to guess, asking, e.g. *Have you got a ruler?* When they guess correctly, take the object out and put it on the desk. Continue until they guess all the objects. Put the objects back in the bag. Pupils work in pairs and write a list of the objects from memory. Check by eliciting the objects from pupils. The winners are the pairs who remembered them all.

Page 69

• Extra activity 1: Roleplay

Divide the class into groups of four (Maskman, Monty, Trevor, Marie). Pupils decide their roles. Play the story on CD 3, 19 again. Stop after each frame for pupils to repeat in role. Pupils practise their story in groups. More confident groups of pupils can change some of the words. Invite one or two groups to roleplay their story to the class.

• Extra activity 2: Fashion show

You will need space for this activity. Pupils walk around the room. Tell them they are at a fashion show. Speak as if giving a commentary. They mime and show off their clothes.
Commentary: *Today is the fashion show. You're wearing a beautiful hat with a big red flower on it. Your T-shirt is green and it has got a yellow lizard on the front. Your jeans are small, but they look great! On your feet you've got pink shoes. Oh, and your hair. It's a lovely … purple!*

Unit 10

Page 70

• Extra activity 1: How do you spell it?

Write the following on the board:

_ _ d _ _ n _ o _ / t _ _ _ _   _ e _ _ i _ / _ o _ k _ y / _ _ i _ _ i _ _ /
_ a _ _ e _ b _ _ _ / _ a _ e _ a _ _

Pupils work in pairs to remember the spelling of the hobby words. They don't look in their books at first. Encourage them to try, using the sounds to help them. Elicit from the class. Pairs help other pairs. Complete the words as they spell them out.

Key: badminton, table tennis, hockey, painting, basketball, baseball

• Extra activity 2: Slap the sports and the hobbies

Display the following flashcards on the board (picture side): *badminton, table tennis, hockey, painting, basketball, baseball, football, tennis, the guitar, the piano, swim, ride a bike*, plus the picture of the camera. Say *Some are sports and some are hobbies and some are both. Talk to your friend and decide.* Make two teams. They line up one behind the other, facing the board. Give a rolled up newspaper to the pupils at the front of each team. Say, e.g. *Sport.* The pupils run to touch a sport. Elicit from the class if they are correct (they don't have to touch the same one). If they are, award a point to each team. Remove the two flashcards and repeat for *Hobby.* Continue calling *Sport/Hobby* at random.

Key: Sports: badminton, table tennis, hockey, basketball, baseball, football, tennis
Hobbies: painting, playing the guitar, playing the piano, taking photos
Both: swimming, riding a bike

Page 71

• Extra activity 1: Describing the picture

Display the flashcards for *hockey, baseball, basketball, table tennis, badminton* on the board. Pupils choose a sport, draw one or two players and colour their kit. Monitor pupils as they are working and supply words, e.g. *bat, stick, racket, net*, as necessary. Write them on the board. Supply prompts on the board for the speaking part of the activity: *In this picture this player is wearing … and this player is wearing … They are holding …* Pupils work in groups of four and describe their pictures to their friends. Pupils write a description under their pictures, using the prompts on the board.

• Extra activity 2: Freeze!

You will need space for this activity. Pupils move around the room. Say *Painting. Freeze!* Pupils stand still in a painting pose. Walk around and look at the pupils. They mustn't move. Clap. Pupils move around again. Repeat for other sports and hobbies.

Page 72

• Extra activity: Categories

Write the following words in random order over the board: *red, blue, purple, green, brown, dog, cat, fish, mouse, dress, shirt, shoes, jeans, painting, taking photos, playing the piano, cooking, swimming.*

Pupils work in pairs and put the words into categories and then give you the word for each set (e.g. colours). Check with the class.
Key: Sets are *colours, pets, clothes, hobbies.*

Page 73

• Extra activity 1: Write and draw

Pupils use the model in Pupil's Book page 73 Activity 6 to write a verse about themselves, using hearts, etc. instead of the words. They don't have to make it rhyme. They illustrate their texts as in the Pupil's Book. Display them on the wall.

• Extra activity 2: Bingo game

Display the hobby/sport flashcards (picture side) on the board. Write a number under each one (*1–13*). Pupils draw a 2 x 2 grid in their notebooks, choose four hobbies/sports and write the corresponding number in the grid. Call out the hobbies/sports at random. If pupils have the corresponding number, they cross it out. The first pupil to cross out all four and to say the four hobbies/sports correctly is the winner.

Page 74

• Extra activity 1: Read, choose and chant

Display the chant on page T74 (Materials required) written on a large piece of paper. Pupils read it in pairs and decide which words to choose. Cross out the wrong word on the paper. Elicit from them why they choose the words (they rhyme). Teach actions to go with the rhyme, e.g.

Do you like mice?	(shape of a mouse with hands)
Mice are nice.	(stroking mouse)
They've got big heads,	(one hand each side of head, wide apart)
And little legs.	(hands close one above the other)
My mouse lives next door,	(pointing next door)
At number four.	(drawing four in the air)
His windows are blue,	(drawing shape of windows with hands)
And there are two.	(mime counting one, two)

• Extra activity 2: Draw and write

Pupils use the model in Activity Book page 74 Activity 9 to write a text about themselves. In place of the pictures in the box, they draw a picture on the line to represent the word, e.g. *Hello. I'm Geraldo. Now, I'm at* (picture of school). *I'm ...*

Pupils swap texts and 'read' each other's.

Page 75

• Extra activity 1: Roleplay

Divide the class into groups of four (Maskman, Monty, Trevor, Marie). Pupils decide their roles. Play the story on CD 3, 32 again. Stop after each frame for pupils to repeat in role. Pupils practise their story in groups. More confident groups of pupils can change some of the actions in the story. Invite one or two groups to roleplay their story to the class.

• Extra activity 2: ID cards

Hand out a copy of Photocopiable 10 to each pupil (see page T110).

If they didn't make the ID cards before, they cut to separate A and B. Focus pupils on A. Elicit the three questions at the bottom: *What's your name?*, etc. Pupils work in pairs. They take turns to ask each other the questions and to complete the information in the table. Pupils then cut out the ID card and make one for their friend. They write the information and decorate it as they wish. They hand the ID card to the owner.

Make groups of six. Pupils hold their ID cards so that the others can't see. The first pupil says a sentence using *like* or *don't like*, e.g. *I like riding horses.* The other pupils guess if it's true or false (i.e. if it's on their ID card or not). The pupil to the left then makes a statement (*I like / don't like ...*). Play continues around the circle. Encourage pupils to say true as well as false things, and to say silly things too.

Page 76

• Extra activity 1: Your own Venn diagram

Pupils work in pairs to draw their own Venn diagrams. They can use their own ideas for the categories but suggest topics which use vocabulary from the book such as Animals/Brown things (the Venn diagram categories would be: brown things/brown animals/animals) or Food/Green things (the Venn diagram categories would be: green things/food/green food).

Pupils write sentences about their diagram as in Activity Book, Activity 2. Go around the class checking. A confident pair then draw their Venn diagram on the board and the rest of the class write some sentences about it. Pupils read their sentences to the class to check.

• Extra activity 2: Language diagram

Say *Draw a Venn diagram.* The two categories are English words, [your pupils' language] words. Say some known English words, some of which are different from your pupils' language and some of which are the same. Pupils write the words from their own language in one section of the diagram, the different English words on the other side of the diagram and words which are common to both languages in the central section (some examples which might be the same in your pupils' language are: *leader, star, football, jeans, robot, computer*).

Pupils check in pairs and work together to write the English words correctly. Correct as a class, making a diagram on the board, and adding more words to each category.

Page 77

• Extra activity 1: Miming game

Pupils work in pairs. Pupil A mimes playing a sport. Pupil B guesses which sport it is and says a rule associated with the sport, e.g. *Football. You can kick the ball.* Then pupils swap roles. When they are confident with this game, volunteers can come to the front to mime for the class to guess.

• Extra activity 2: Sport anagrams

Write anagrams of words from the lesson on the board for pupils to solve, e.g. bounce = ueobnc.

Unit 11

Page 78

• Extra activity 1: Noughts and crosses

Draw a 3 x 3 grid on the board. Write a number in each square. Write numbers 1–9 in your notebook and write a food word next to each one. It's a secret. Make two teams: A and B. A are 0s and B are Xs. A starts. They choose a square and say the number in it, e.g. *5, please.* Hold up the food flashcard (picture side), but don't say the word. A pupil from Team A spells the word. If it's correct, put a 0 in the square. If it's not, Team B has a turn. If they spell it correctly, put a X in the square. Then it's Team B's turn. Continue until one team has a line of 0s or Xs or the grid is full.

• Extra activity 2: Odd one out

Write the following vocabulary sets on the board: *toys, food, furniture, drinks, sports, town, household objects, rooms.* Pupils work in pairs. They create five odd-one-out lines like those in Activity Book page 78 Activity 2. Remind them to use other words in the sets, not just the ones already used. Encourage pupils to be creative. Pairs swap with pairs and find the different word in each line. They check with each other. Monitor and sort out any disputes.

Page 79

• Extra activity: Follow the instructions

Invite a group of nine pupils to the front. Set out nine chairs in a 3 x 3 grid. Sit Pupils 7 and 6 in their chairs (see Key below). Give instructions to pupils on where to sit, using *next to, between, in front of, behind.* The first time they listen only. When you finish the instructions, they sit in the right place. Read the instructions again and check with the class. Repeat.

Text:

P1 / name is behind P7 / name.
P3 / name is behind P6 / name.
P3 / name is in front of P8 / name.
P5 / name is next to P1 / name.
P9 / name is in front of P5 / name.
P2 / name is between P4 / name and P6 / name.

Key:

P5	P1	P8
P9	P7	P3
P4	P2	P6

Page 80

• Extra activity 1: Would you like ...?

Write dialogue prompts on the board, like this:

A: *What would you like to eat? Would you like a burger or a sausage?*
B: *I'd like a sausage, please.*
A: *Here you are.*
B: *Thanks.*
C: *Can I have a sausage and a burger, please?*
B: *Here you are. Would you like some fries too?*
C: *Yes, I'd love some. Lots, please.*
C: *Can I have a drink, please?*
B: *What would you like?*
C: *Some lemonade, please.*
B: *Here you are.*

Elicit from pupils how to change the words underlined (other foods/drinks). Invite three confident pupils to demonstrate the roleplay to the class. Make groups of three. Pupils take the roles of A, B or C. They change the dialogue as they wish and practise it. More confident pupils can swap roles and repeat the dialogue. Pupils perform their dialogues to the class.

• Extra activity 2: Birthday parties

Tell pupils it's their birthday party and they can choose the food they'd like. Brainstorm ideas with pupils, making sure they use *I'd like* ... Pupils each draw a party table and then write sentences underneath, e.g. *For my birthday party I'd like to eat sausages and rice and I'd like to drink water.*

Page 81

• Extra activity 1: Our song

Pupils work in groups of five. Using the information from Extra activity 2 in the previous lesson, if appropriate, they create their own song, each pupil contributing one line. They use the model in CD 3, 43. Display the food flashcards on the walls to give pupils ideas. Groups take turns to perform their own songs to the class.

• Extra activity 2: Spelling

Choose ten food words for pupils to write down in their notebooks. Say each word twice. Pupils swap notebooks and correct each other's. Check spelling by eliciting from pupils and writing the words on the board as they spell them out.

Page 82

• Extra activity 1: Making menus

Show some sample menus. Elicit foods and drinks there are in cafés. Hand out some card, one piece for each pair of pupils. They decide on the foods and drinks (set a limit, e.g. six foods and four drinks). They draw lines in pencil on the menu card to help them with writing the food and drink. They add design to the menus, e.g. flowers, plates, knives and forks. Display the menus around the class and vote for the yummiest.

• Extra activity 2: Using menus

Make groups of four. Groups use one menu from Extra activity 1. One person is the waiter, and the others are the customers. The waiter takes all the orders. They change roles and repeat.

Page 83

• Extra activity 1: Who said it?

Read out the following sentences from the story on Pupil's Book page 83. Pupils call out who said which one.

Let's make her a pencil cake! (Trevor)
Let's have burgers and fries to eat! (Maskman)
Now, let's make the cake. (Monty)
Happy birthday, Marie! (Trevor, Maskman, Monty)
Would you like to come to the café with me? (Marie)

• Extra activity 2: Chant

Teach the chant below to the class. Divide the class into four groups. Groups take turns to sing a verse. Still in groups, pupils write a verse for a pupil in the group. They perform it for the class. If it's one pupil's birthday that day, the class create and perform a verse for him/her.

It's Marie's birthday, hoorah, hoorah!
Let's have cake and ice cream,
Hoorah, hoorah, hoorah!

It's Trevor's birthday, hoorah, hoorah!
Let's have pens and pencils,
Hoorah, hoorah, hoorah!

It's Maskman's birthday, hoorah, hoorah!
Let's have fries and burgers,
Hoorah, hoorah, hoorah!

It's Monty's birthday, hoorah, hoorah!
Let's have sausages and lemonade,
Hoorah, hoorah, hoorah!

Unit 12

Page 84

• Extra activity 1: Board slap

Write the words from Activity Book page 84 Activity 1 on the board. Write them at random (not next to each other as in the Activity Book). Make three teams. They line up, one behind the other, facing the board. Hand a rolled up newspaper to the first pupil in each team. Call out one of the pairs of words, e.g. *shell, she*. Pupils run to hit both words. The first to do so wins a point for their team. The pupils at the front go to the back of the teams. Repeat for the other words (11 goes in all).

• Extra activity 2: Wordsnakes

Pupils use the words from the Warmer on page T84 and the new holiday words to make a wordsnake. They work in pairs and choose at least eight words. They swap wordsnakes with another pair and find the words. Pairs check with each other.

Page 85

• Extra activity 1: Listen and mime

You will need space for this activity. Pupils move around the room. Say *Ah, you're picking up shells. They are very small and pretty. Put them in your bag. Now you're swimming in the sea*, etc. Add other activities from the lesson for pupils to mime.

• Extra activity 2: Make a postcard

Talk about holidays with pupils. Elicit where they like going and what they like doing. Show a holiday postcard and elicit what the picture is. Hand out the pieces of card. Pupils draw a picture for the front of their postcard. Monitor and help pupils, making sure it's not too complicated. Make groups of four. Pupils talk to their friends about their pictures.

Page 86

• Extra activity: Mingling activity

You will need a big space for this activity.
Play a CD of holiday-type music. Pupils walk/skip/run around the room. Pause the CD. Pupils make pairs and take turns to ask and answer, using the model: *Where do you want to go on holiday? I want to go to* ... Start the music again. Pupils move on. Repeat.

Page 87

• Extra activity 1: Picture chants

Pupils work in groups of four and write a chant on a large piece of paper, using the model in Pupil's Book page 87 Activity 6. They write the words and then draw pictures. Display the chants on the wall. Groups stand next to their chant. Say, e.g. *Everyone move two chants to the left.* Groups move to the left. They look at the new chant. Ask one or two groups to say the new chant. Repeat. Elicit two more chants from groups.

• Extra activity 2: True or false

Pupils look at the picture in Pupil's Book page 87 Activity 7 for 30 seconds. They close their books and stand up. Say six true/false sentences about the picture, one by one, e.g. *The shoe shop is next to the fruit shop. There are two frogs in the toy shop.* If the sentence is false, pupils put their hand over their mouth. If it's true, they nod their heads. Pupils who respond incorrectly sit down for the rest of the game. Congratulate the group of winners at the end.

Page 88

• Extra activity 1: Big or small?

Write the following words at random over the board, not in pairs: *big, small, beautiful, ugly, clean, dirty, old, young, old, new.* Make three teams. They line up, one pupil behind the other, facing the board. Hand a rolled up newspaper to the first pupil in each team. Call out, e.g. *Clean.* Pupils run to hit the opposite (dirty). The first one to hit it wins a point for their team. The pupils go to the back of the lines. Continue with the other words, repeating some to make it more fun.

• Extra activity 2: About me

Pupils choose three or more answers from Activity Book page 88 Activity 9. They draw pictures to illustrate them in their notebooks and write the relevant sentences underneath, e.g. *My kitchen is small.*

Page 89

• Extra activity 1: Roleplay

Divide the class into groups of four. Pupils decide their roles (Marie, Trevor, Maskman, Monty). Play the story on CD 4, 14. Stop after each frame for pupils to repeat in role. Pupils practise the story in groups. More confident groups can change some of the words/dialogues. Invite one or two groups to perform their roleplays to the class.

• Extra activity 2: Revision game

Pupils play the Revision game again. See Photocopiable 12a (page T112).

Page 90

• Extra activity 1: Map questions

Stick a very large map with grid lines on the board with features such as mountains, trees, beach, etc. drawn on. Pupils write questions about the map to ask a partner. Go around listening and checking the questions and answers.

• Extra activity 2: Make a map

Hand out squared paper. Pupils make their own maps for a guessing game. Give them a list of items to place on their maps. Then ask about the maps e.g. *Where is the beach? Where are the mountains?* Pupils compare their maps in pairs or small groups.

Page 91

• Extra activity 1: Write a postcard

Pupils imagine a 'helping' holiday they would like to go on and write and draw a postcard. Use the photos from magazines/the internet to give pupils ideas and help them with vocabulary.

• Extra activity 2: Write about it

Show 5 or 6 pictures of people helping others/animals and pass them around the class for pupils to look at them carefully. Pupils work in pairs to write sentences about the pictures, similar to the ones in the lesson (e.g. *They're in the mountains. They're helping a snake.*). Stick the pictures on the board in numerical order. Confident pupils come to the front and read one of their sentences. Pupils say the number of the picture/photo which matches the sentence.

Page 92

• Extra activity 1: Do an activity

Pupils do any one of Photocopiable activities 1–12b.

• Extra activity 2: Play a game

Play one of the games from Units 9–12 with the class.

Page 93

• Extra activity 1: Board slap

Display 12 flashcards from the new words in Units 9–12 (word side) on the board. Make three teams. Teams line up behind each other. Hand each pupil at the front of the teams a rolled up newspaper. Call out one of the words on a flashcard. Pupils run to hit it with the newspaper. The first to do so wins a point for their team. The pupils go to the back. Hand the newspapers to the new pupils at the front and repeat, calling another word.

• Extra activity 2: Sing a song or do a chant

Sing one of the songs or do a chant from Units 9–12 with the class.

Thanks and Acknowledgements

The authors and publishers acknowledge the following sources of copyright material and are grateful for the permissions granted. While every effort has been made, it has not always been possible to identify the sources of all the material used, or to trace all copyright holders. If any omissions are brought to our notice, we will be happy to include the appropriate acknowledgements on reprinting.

t = top, c = centre, b = below, l = left, r = right

p.16 (orange): Shutterstock/Maks Narodenko; p.16 (banana): Shutterstock/brulove; p.16 (apple): Shutterstock/Roman Samokhin; p.16 (pear): Shutterstock/Andrey Eremin; p.16 (pineapple): Shutterstock/Alex Staroseltsev; p.16 (lemon): Shutterstock/topseller; p.17 (t): Thinkstock; p.31 (t): Thinkstock; p.31 (1): Thinkstock/iStockphoto; p.31 (2): Shutterstock/Sergey Karpov; p.31 (3): Shutterstock/Aron Brand; p.31 (4): Shutterstock/Feng Yu; p.31 (bl): Shutterstock/Picsfive; p.31 (bc): Shutterstock/Skylines; p.31 (br): Shutterstock/Quang Ho; p.32 (11): Shutterstock/Iwona Grodzka; p.32 (12): Shutterstock/K. Miri Photography; p.32 (13): Shutterstock/DenisNata; p.32 (14): Shutterstock/Luis Carlos Torres; p.32 (15): Shutterstock/Masalski Maksim; p.32 (16): Shutterstock/terekhov igor; p.32 (17): Shutterstock/Nikuwka; p.32 (18): Alamy/Graham Morley; p.32 (19): Alamy/Mike Stone; p.32 (20): Shutterstock/Mostphotos; p.46 (tl): Alamy/Christine Whitehead; p.46 (tc): Shutterstock/Paul Cowan; p.46 (tr): Shutterstock/Nattika; p.46 (bl): Shutterstock/Diana Taliun; p.46 (bc): Shutterstock/Nattika; p.46 (br): Shutterstock/Maks Narodenko; p.47 (t): Thinkstock; p.60 (1): Shutterstock/agrosse; p.60 (2): Shutterstock/IbajaUsap; p.60 (3): Shutterstock/ Aleksandr Kurganov; p.60 (4): Shutterstock/Eduard Kyslynskyy; p.60 (5): Shutterstock/Menno Schaefer; p.60 (6): Shutterstock/ mexrix; p.61 (t): Thinkstock; p.71 (a): iStockphoto/valda; p.71 (b): istockphoto/RapidEye; p.71 (c): istockphoto/TAPshooter; p.71 (d): istockphoto/valdecasas; p.71 (e): istockphoto/padnpen; p.71 (f): istockphoto/Oksana Struk; p.76 (wool): Shutterstock/OlyaSenko; p.76 (tl): Shutterstock/Againstar; p.76 (tc): Shutterstock/Karkas; p.76 (tr): Shutterstock/tarasov; p.76 (cl): Shutterstock/Eric Isselee; p.76 (c): Shutterstock/Mitrofanova; p.76 (cr): Shutterstock/Ruslan Kudrin; p.76 (bl): Shutterstock/LeshaBu; p.76 (bc): Shutterstock/Maksym Bondarchuk ; p.76 (br): Shutterstock/Chiyacat; p.77 (t): Thinkstock; p.91 (t): Thinkstock; p.91 (1): Getty Images/Ben Osborne/Stone; p.91 (2): Corbis/Richard T. Nowitz; p.91 (3): Corbis/Ariel Skelley.

Commissioned photography on pages 7, 8, 14, 22, 28, 30, 35, 38, 44, 52, 58, 74, 82, 88, 90 by Trevor Clifford Photography.

The authors and publishers are grateful to the following illustrators:

Andrew Hennessey; Beatrice Costamagna, c/o Pickled ink; Chris Garbutt, c/o Arena; Lucía Serrano Guerroro; Andrew Hennessey; Kelly Kennedy, c/o Syvlie Poggio; Rob McKlurkan, c/o The Bright Agency; Melanie Sharp, c/o Syvlie Poggio; Marie Simpson, c/o Pickled ink; Emily Skinner, c/o Graham-Cameron Illustration; Lisa Smith; Gary Swift; Lisa Williams, c/o Sylvie Poggio;

The publishers are grateful to the following contributors:

Carrie Lewis: editor
Louise Edgeworth: picture research and art direction
Wild Apple Design Ltd: page design
Blooberry: additional design
Lon Chan: cover design
John Green and Tim Woolf, TEFL Audio: audio recordings
Songs written and produced by Robert Lee, Dib Dib Dub Studios.

Br
Top
Attractions

CADOGAN

Cadogan Guides
West End House
11 Hillls Place
London W1R 1AH
guides@cadogan.demon.co.uk

The Globe Pequot Press
6 Business Park Road, PO Box 833,
Old Saybrook, Connecticut 06475-0833

Conceived and produced for Cadogan Guides by
The Jacket Front Ltd
postmaster@bookprodservices.demon.co uk
Book design by Ann Burnham
Cover design by Fielding Rowinski

Written and edited by Joseph Fullman
Research: Joanne Taborn, J.A.Fullman, Caroline Taborn

ISBN 1-86011-703-1

A catalogue record for this book is available from the
British Library

Colour reproduction by
The Setting Studio, Newcastle upon Tyne
Printed in China by
Leo Paper Products Ltd

Photo Credits

Beaulieu: © The National Motor Museum, Beaulieu. Blackpool Pleasure Beach: © Blackpool Pleasure Beach. Blackpool Tower: Blackpool Tourism Deparment. Brighton Pavilion: © Royal Pavilion, Brighton. Burrel Collection: © Glasgow Museums. Canterbury Cathedral: © The Dean and Chapter of Canterbury. Chester Cathedral: © Chester Cathedral. Group Edinburgh: © Crown Copyright: Reproduced by Permission of Historic Scotland. Flagship Portsmouth: © Flagship Portsmouth Trust. Glasgow Art Gallery & Museum: © Glasgow Museums. Hampton Court: © Crown Copyright: Historic Royal Palaces 1998. Hampton Court Palace Gardens: © Crown Copyright: Historic Royal Palaces 1998. Jorvik Viking Centre: © York Archaeological Trust.Knowsley Safari Park: © Jarrold Publishing. Leeds Castle: © Leeds Castle Foundation. National Railway Museum: © National Railway Museum. Roman Baths and Pump Room: © Simon McBride. Royal Academy: © Royal Academy of Arts. Science Museum: © Science Museum. Shakespeare: © The Shakespeare Birthplace Trust, Stratford Upon Avon. Snowdonia National Park: © Kevin J. Richardson. Stonehenge: © English Heritage Photographic Library. St Paul's: © John Buckler. Strathclyde Country Park: © Greater Glasgow & Clyde Valley Tourist Board. Tate Gallery: The Gardener Vallier Cézanne, © Tate Gallery, London. Tate Gallery of Modern Art: © Hayes Davidson. Westminster Abbey: © Dean & Chapter of Westminster. Windermere Lake Cruises: © Windermere Lake Cruises Ltd. Windsor Castle: © Her Majesty Queen Elizabeth II. Wisley Gardens: © Michael C. Sleigh. York Minster:

Contents

ALTON TOWERS

LOCATION:
Alton, Staffordshire
ST10 4DB
TEL: 0990 20 40 60
OPENING TIMES:
Mid Mar–early Nov
9.30–dusk
ADM: Adult £19.50, Child £15.50, Family £59
GETTING THERE:
Road: From North: M6 J16; M1 J28. From South: M6 J15; M1 J23A
Train: Alton, Luton & Stafford stations
FACILITIES: On-site hotel, various fast food restaurants
DISABLED:
Wheelchair access to park, all rides and facilities, adapted toilets
WEBSITE: www.alton-towers.co.uk

Have you ever wanted to plummet 60ft into a pitch-black hole at 110mph? You have? Well, Alton Towers may just be able to help. The recent trend for theme parks to build larger, faster, more regurgitatingly scary rides reached its peak in 1998 when Alton Towers unleashed 'Oblivion', the world's first vertical drop rollercoaster, on an innocent public. Billed as 'the ultimate in psychological and physical endurance', the ride, during the drop stage, exerts a force of 4.5G on its passengers—by way of comparison, astronauts experience 3G on take-off.

If this doesn't leave you a gibbering wreck, fear not—there are dozens of other rides designed to test your powers of digestion to the very limit, including Ripsaw which has three 360° loops and Blackhole, a rollercoaster ride in total darkness.

Although they're not really the reason why you're here, Alton Towers does have its more sedate attractions. Once the largest private residence in Europe, much of the house has, after a century of neglect, been restored and reopened to the public. There are also some delightful gardens with a conservatory and pagoda where you can wander whilst you wait for your heartbeat to come back down under 200.

BEAULIEU

LOCATION:
Beaulieu, Hampshire
SO42 7ZN
TEL: 01590 612 345
OPENING TIMES:
10–5, open until
6pm during Easter
ADM: Adult £8.75,
Child £6.25, Conc's
£7.50, Family £28.50
GETTING THERE:
Road: M3,
M27, A236
Train: Brockenhurst
station
FACILITIES:
Restaurant,
bar (seasonal),
several gift shops,
guided tours
available

There are two distinct sides to Beaulieu. A quiet serene side, as represented by the 16th-century Beaulieu Palace and its beautiful lakeside park; and the noisier, more exuberant side of the world-famous Motor Museum with its thousands of clanking, clunking, whirring exhibits. Here at this temple to all things mechanical you will find exquisitely preserved cars from throughout the history of the motoring age, from late 19th-century prototypes to ultra-modern speed machines. Priceless luxury cars—a 1909 Rolls Royce Silver Ghost or a 1962 E Type Jaguar—sit alongside archetypal people carriers: Volkswagen Beetles, Minis and, of course, the original people's car, the Ford Model T.

The record breakers of yesteryear are also here, including the 1927 Sunbeam 1,000hp, the first car to break the 200mph barrier, its once unbelievable feats long since surpassed.

DISABLED:
Access to all except 2 abbey buildings, free wheelchair hire, toilets
WEBSITE:
www.beaulieu.uk

Elsewhere, you can find an historic garage and an interactive gallery where children can unravel the mysteries of the internal combustion engine before sampling the museum's radio-controlled cars and hi-tech arcade driving games. A jaunty little monorail makes a regular tour of the palace grounds.

The museum's showpiece is its 'Wheels' ride, which takes you past seven motorised tableaux designed to tell the story of motoring in the 20th century.

BIRMINGHAM CITY ART GALLERY & MUSEUM

LOCATION:
Chamberlain Square, Birmingham B3 3DH
TEL: 0121 303 2834
OPENING TIMES:
Mon–Thu & Sat 10–5, Fri 10.30–5, Sun 12.30–5
ADM: Free (contributions welcome)
GETTING THERE:
Road: M5 J1 & 3; M6 J6
Train: New Street and Moor Street stations
FACILITIES: Lots of car parking space, Edwardian tea room and gift shop
DISABLED:
Wheelchair access, loop system for hard of hearing, wheelchair hire, adapted toilets
WEBSITE:
www.brillsummer.org.uk

Birmingham City Art Gallery and Museum is both a collection of art and artefacts from around the world and a proud promoter of Birmingham's own artistic and industrial heritage. It is home to one of the finest collections of pre-Raphaelite paintings in the world, with works by Rossetti, Holman Hunt, Millais and Madox-Brown, and also dedicates an entire room to the romantic paintings of local artist Sir Edward Burne-Jones. A close friend of William Morris, Burne-Jones also turned his hand to stained glass and tapestry design and is credited with influencing the young Pablo Picasso who, perversely and typically, regarded Burne-Jones as a modernist. Particular prominence is also given, in the gallery's collection of British art from the 18th to the 20th century, to the watercolour landscapes of David Cox, a Birmingham contemporary of Constable. The gallery also holds some of William Morris' original wallpaper designs.

In the museum section, in amongst the silverware, jewellery and sculptures, is a gallery dedicated to Birmingham's industrial history, with various black and oily exhibits from the age of steam. Elsewhere, you can find galleries devoted to natural and social history and a new science gallery which will form part of a Discovery Centre due to open in 2001.

BLACKPOOL PLEASURE BEACH

LOCATION:
Ocean Boulevard, Blackpool FY4 1E2
TEL: 01253 341 033
OPENING TIMES:
April–Nov 9.30–dusk
ADM: Free, individual prices for rides, or book of tickets £20
GETTING THERE:
Road: M6 J32; M55
Train: Blackpool North & Blackpool Pleasure Beach stations, change at Preston
FACILITIES:
Car parks, shops, various fast food restaurants
DISABLED: Parking spaces in all car parks, wheelchair access to most of park, wheelchair hire available
WEBSITE:
www.bpbltd.com

Here, size matters. The BPB is the current Big Daddy of British tourist attractions; its every vital statistic requiring an 'in Britain', 'in Europe' or 'in the world' suffix. It attracts over 7,000,000 visitors a year, which makes it the most popular tourist attraction in Britain, the 4th most popular in Europe and the 9th most popular in the world. In fact, if you discount all attractions which charge an admission fee, the BPB *is* the most popular in the world.

It has the greatest number of rides, 145, of any theme park in Britain and its showpiece ride, the Pepsi Max Big One, is, at a height of 235ft, not only the tallest rollercoaster in the world but also the fastest, capable of travelling at speeds of up to 87mph.

It has the only ride in Britain, the Playstation ride, designed to recreate the effects of being ejected from a fighter plane, as well as 10 rollercoasters, a log flume, 45 restaurants and a cabaret lounge—again that's a variety unmatched anywhere else in Britain.

Its success has given rise to some astounding statistics: each year BPB visitors consume 1,000,000 ice cream cones, 550,000 burgers and 2.5 million plates of

It has the greatest number of rides of any theme park in Britain.

chips, and, perhaps as a result, use 20,000 packets of toilet roll.

This love of extremes is perhaps best exemplified by the American Richard Rodriguez who in August 1998 spent 1,013 continuous hours on a BPB rollercoaster, the longest time ever spent riding a rollercoaster, anywhere in the world.

BLACKPOOL TOWER

LOCATION: Bank-Hey Street, Blackpool, Lancashire FY1 4BJ
TEL: 01253 622 242
OPENING TIMES:
Easter–early Nov 10–11 daily;
Nov–Easter Sat 10–11, Sun 10–6
ADM: £5
GETTING THERE:
Road: M6 J32, M55
Train: Blackpool North & Blackpool Pleasure Beach stations, change at Preston
FACILITIES:
Shops, bar, various restaurants
DISABLED:
Limited wheelchair access

In a little over two centuries, Blackpool has grown from a small hamlet built next to a 'black pool' into the most popular resort in Britain, the heart and symbol of which is its world-famous Tower. Built in 1895 and modelled on the Eiffel Tower, it stands 518ft high and is a truly awesome sight. You can take a lift to the top from where you can enjoy fantastic panoramic views of the coast and Irish Sea.

Following a £13 million face-lift, the Tower now has seven floors stuffed full of attractions including a circus, an aquarium (home to Britain's only giant sea turtles), Jungle Jim's Adventure Playground, a dinosaur theme ride and the beautiful Edwardian Tower Ballroom, as seen on countless editions of 'Come Dancing'. Thrill-seekers can try the Walk of Faith, a 5cm-thick glass floor, 385ft above the ground.

The Tower is perhaps at its most resplendent in September when it becomes the glittering focal point of Blackpool's famous Golden Mile of illuminations.

Built in 1895, and modelled on the Eiffel Tower, Blackpool Tower stands 518ft high and is a truly awesome sight.

BRIGHTON PALACE PIER

LOCATION:
Off Madeira Drive, Brighton BN2 1TW
TEL: 01273 609 361
OPENING TIMES:
Summer 9–2, winter 10–12
ADM: Free, rides are individually charged
GETTING THERE:
Road:
From London: M23
Train: Brighton station. London Victoria–Brighton 49 mins
FACILITIES:
3 bars, various fast food outlets
DISABLED:
Wheelchair access, toilets

Vaguely reminiscent of an ocean liner on stilts, this beautiful snow-white pier, stretching 1,722ft out to sea, was constructed in the 1890s after the original 'chain' pier was destroyed in a storm. Much of the filigree ironwork remains, as well as some kiosks and a signal cannon from the original pier. In 1931 the pier's first, rather small, Ferris wheel was installed, since when (other than a brief period during World War II when a section was dismantled to prevent enemy landings) the number and size of the pier's attractions have increased year on year.

Today the Pier manages to combine an old-world style and elegance with a more modern knees-up sensibility. There is a rollercoaster, a waltzer, a Ferris wheel, three bars, a 250-seat fish and chip restaurant and an amusement arcade; plus an inexhaustible supply of such timeless seaside essentials as candy floss, winkles and mussels.

Today the Pier manages to combine an old-world style and elegance with a more modern knees-up sensibility.

THE BRIGHTON PAVILION

LOCATION: North Street, Brighton BN1 1EE
TEL: 01273 290 900
Infoline: 0990 20 40 60
OPENING TIMES: Oct–May 10–5, June–Sept 10–6
ADM: £3.75
GETTING THERE:
Road: From London: M23
Train: Brighton station
FACILITIES: Two parking areas on Church Street; Queen Adelaide tearoom, book and gift shop
DISABLED: Wheelchair access, signed tours by appointment, Seinheiser for hard of hearing, adapted toilets
WEBSITE: www.brighton.co.uk/tourist

In 1810, when George III finally succumbed to the madness which had blighted his life and reign for over thirty years, Britain's architecture was dominated by two main schools, neoclassicism and neogothic. The Prince Regent, later to become George IV, decided to ignore both when he commissioned a new seaside residence to be built in Brighton. Designed by John Nash in the Indian style with a Chinese interior, the result was described by Stanley Smith thus: 'it's as if St Paul's had travelled to the seaside and pupped'.

Neither the Prince Regent nor his chosen architect were great believers in the maxim 'less is more' and together they produced a glorious icing-sugar concoction of domes, turrets and cast-iron palm trees. Recently restored, the sheer opulence of the Pavilion, with its gilded ceilings, vast crystal chandeliers and extravagant frescoes, can at times be a little overwhelming. It's so over-the-top as to be beyond questions of taste and style. Just come and rejoice in the excess: pad softly across the music room's hand-knotted carpet, gaze at the banqueting room's chandelier held aloft by a silver dragon before enjoying a Regency tea in the Queen Adelaide tearoom overlooking the majestic sweep of the newly restored gardens.

THE BRITISH MUSEUM

LOCATION: Great Russell Street, London WC1B 3DG
TEL: 0171 636 1555
OPENING TIMES: Mon–Sat 10–5, Sun 12–6

London's great free museum has been delighting and educating the public since 1753. It was then and is now easily the most popular museum in Britain, with perhaps the greatest range of archaeological exhibits of any museum in Europe. Its vital statistics alone give some idea of the scope and importance of its collection: the site covers 13½ acres of prime Bloomsbury real estate topped with 7½ acres of roof; there are over

ADM: Free, but some temporary exhibitions make a small charge
GETTING THERE: *Underground:* Holborn, Russell Square
Bus: 7, 10, 24, 29, 73, 134
FACILITIES: Museum Tavern, book and souvenir shop
DISABLED: Wheelchair access, adapted toilets
WEBSITE: www.british-museum.ac.uk

90 permanent and temporary exhibitions which, if you walked around them all, would take you on a trip 2 miles 721 yards long. On your travels you would find perhaps the largest and most comprehensive collection of Egyptian antiquities outside Cairo; a superb Greek and Roman exhibition; a gallery of Japanese decorative art; a priceless collection of medieval illuminated manuscripts; as well as such singular attractions as the Rosetta Stone, with which scholars finally broke the Egyptian hieroglyphic code; Lindow Man (or Pete Bog as he is affectionately known), the leathery remains of a 2,000-year-old Briton and the Elgin Marbles. The famous neoclassical building which houses this grand collection of global historical memorabilia was designed by Sir Sidney Smirke and constructed in the mid-19th century.

THE BRITISH MUSEUM GREAT COURT PROJECT

The museum's central courtyard, closed to the public for nearly 150 years, is to be re-opened following a thorough architectural transformation

In 2003 the British Museum will be 250 years old. It has decided to celebrate this milestone, and the forthcoming millennium, by commissioning one of the largest development projects in its history. The museum's central courtyard, closed to the public for nearly 150 years, is to be re-opened following a thorough architectural transformation. The circular reading room at its centre, which used to house the British Library (recently moved to new multi-million pound premises at St Pancras), will now hold a public reference library and exhibition galleries, whilst the surrounding two acres of courtyard are to be landscaped and rebuilt to contain an education centre and various areas where people can sit, relax and have a bite to eat. The classical façades that border the court will also be restored. The whole will be covered by a 6,000 square metre glass roof (comprised of 3,312 unique triangular panels and weighing 1,000 tonnes), making it the first covered public square in London. The museum will be further enhanced by the renovation of the main forecourt and the return of its ethnographic collection housed since 1970 at the Museum of Mankind in Burlington Gardens.

It will cost around £100 million and is due to open at the end of 2000.

THE BURRELL COLLECTION

LOCATION: 2060 Pollokshaws Road, Glasgow G43 1AT
TEL: 0141 649 7151
OPENING TIMES: Mon–Sat 10–5, Sun 11–5
ADM: Free

William Burrell, the great Glasgow shipping magnate, began collecting works of art in 1866 when he was just 15 years old and continued right up until his death in 1958, by which time he had amassed some 8,000 treasures—or roughly two a week.

The collection, housed in a purpose-built building in lovely Pollok Park, is both

GETTING THERE:
Road: From South: M8 J22, M77 J2; from North: M8 J24
Train: Pollokshaws West station
Bus: 25,45,48,57,57A from Union Street
FACILITIES:
Car and coach parking available (charges may apply), gift shop, restaurant, free guided tours
DISABLED:
Wheelchair access, adapted toilets

hugely varied and deeply traditional. Burrell had little time for the avant-garde or experimental side of art; he liked classic lines and timeless designs: jewellery from ancient Greece and Egypt, silverware and porcelain from Renaissance Europe and paintings by the great masters. He had a particular penchant for traditional oriental art—Chinese ceramics from the Yuan, Ming and Tang dynasties make up around a quarter of the collection. His most prized items, however, were his medieval tapestries, many of which are over 500 years old.

Burrell's tastes may have been catholic but they were often as not inspired. There are paintings by Cézanne, Bellini, Monet and Rembrandt as well as a bronze cast of Rodin's 'The Thinker'. A glimpse into the private life of this most avid of collectors is provided by a reconstruction of the hall and drawing room of the Burrell family home at Hutton Castle, the place where, almost 150 years ago, Burrell's father had attempted to warn his son away from pursuing an 'unmanly' interest in art.

CABINET WAR ROOMS

LOCATION: King Charles Street, London SW1A 2AQ
TEL: 0171 930 6961
OPENING TIMES: April–Sep 9.30–6, Oct–Mar 10–6
ADM: Adult £4.60, Child £2.30, Conc's £3.40, half-price entry for disabled visitors
GETTING THERE: *Underground:* Westminster, St James's Park
Bus: 3, 109, 159

Down below London's streets in a former government storage basement are 21 cramped, low ceilinged rooms which, for the six years of World War II, were the headquarters of the British war effort. To visit these rooms today is to take a step into the past; they have remained untouched since the final days of the conflict. They are wonderfully evocative; their very smallness (Churchill's office was a converted broom cupboard) giving some sense of the desperate pressure which must have been felt by the men and women who worked here. Each individual detail, so ordinary in itself, becomes, in the context, charged with significance: coloured drawing pins still stuck into faded maps of Europe, papers laid

FACILITIES: Free audio guide, education service and lectures available
DISABLED: Wheelchair access, lift to museum ground floor, adapted toilets
WEBSITE: www.iwm.org.uk

out in the Cabinet Room as if for an imminent briefing, and the desk in Churchill's bedroom from where he made his legendary radio broadcasts. In this small, subterranean patch of London, decisions were made which not only affected the lives of thousands of people but changed the course of history forever.

These rooms have remained untouched since the final days of the conflict.

CAERNARFON CASTLE

LOCATION: Caernarfon, Gwynedd
TEL: 01286 677 617
OPENING TIMES: Apr–Oct 9.30–6.30 daily, Nov–Mar Mon–Sat 9.30–4, Sun 11–4
ADM: Adult £4, Conc's £3, Family £11
GETTING THERE:
Road: A405, A487(T), B4366
Train: Bangor station is 9 miles away
Bus: Buses stop at the castle itself, call 0891 910 910
FACILITIES: Car and coach parking, souvenir and gift shop
DISABLED: Some wheelchair access, call in advance
WEBSITE: www. caernarfon.com

Inscribed on the World Heritage list, the majestic Caernarfon is Wales' best known castle. Construction began in 1283, on the orders of Edward I, following his defeat of Llywelyn ap Gruffydd, the last Welsh Prince of Wales. Conceived as a military stronghold, seat of government and royal palace, Edward wanted his castle to imitate the intimidating walls of Constantinople, the imperial power of Rome and the dream-castle of Welsh myth and legend—no small feat for his chosen architect, James of St George. In military terms, he performed his task ably; the fortress, which towers over the walled town of Caernarfon, also founded by Edward, withstood two sieges in the 15th century with a complement of just 28 men-at-arms. Its most striking landmark is the King's Tower, adorned with eagle sculptures and affording an eagle's-eye view over the surrounding countryside. The Queen's Tower holds the Museum of the Royal Welsh Fusiliers, Wales' oldest regiment. In 1969 the castle was the focus of worldwide attention when the investiture ceremony for Charles, Prince of Wales, was held there.

CANTERBURY CATHEDRAL

LOCATION: Canterbury, Kent CT1 2EH
TEL: 01227 762 862
OPENING TIMES: Apr–Sep Mon–Sat 8.45–7, Sun 12.30–2.30 & 4.30–5.30; Oct–Mar Mon–Sat 8.45–5, Sun 12.30–2.30

Canterbury, as befits the administrative, spiritual and theological capital of the English Church, is home to one of the country's most beautiful cathedrals. It looks particularly magical at night when spotlights pick out the detail in the exterior carving.

Most of the building was constructed in the 15th century although parts, including the crypt and some of the stained glass (amongst the very oldest in Britain), date

ADM: Adult £3, Child & Conc's £2, Under 5's free, guided tours £3 per person—minimum charge £30
GETTING THERE: *Road:* A2, A28 *Train:* Canterbury West & Canterbury East stations
FACILITIES: Welcome Information Centre; audio-visual presentations on 'Story of Cathedral': Adult £1, Child & Conc's 70p; permit required to take photos in cathedral: Adult £1.25, Child & Conc's 70p
DISABLED: Advance notice of wheelchair visits needed

back to the 12th century. Other, later examples of stained glass feature representations of Thomas à Becket, murdered here in 1170 at the wish, if not the order, of Henry II. After the saint's death, Canterbury became a centre of pilgrimage and catering for the needs of pilgrims became the principal activity of most of the town's inns and taverns, a process described in Chaucer's 'Canterbury Tales'. Becket's shrine was destroyed in the 16th century on the orders of Henry VIII following the English church's break with Rome, and his tomb can now be found in Trinity Chapel near the high altar.

During World War II Canterbury was targeted for bombing by Germany as part of its Baedeker Campaign—an attempt to break Britain's will by destroying its most precious religious and cultural landmarks (picked out of a Baedeker guide). Miraculously, however, the cathedral and its beautiful stained glass managed to survive the war unscathed.

CHESSINGTON WORLD OF ADVENTURE

LOCATION:
Chessington,
Surrey KT9 2NE
TEL: 01372 727227
OPENING TIMES:
Mar–Nov 10–5.15.
Last admission 3pm.
Later closing for
Family Fright Nights
ADM: Adult £19,
Child £15,
Conc's £8.50,
Disabled/Helper
£7.50
GETTING THERE:
Road: Just off A243;
two miles from A3 &
M25 (J9 from North,
J10 from South)
Train: Chessington
South station,
regular services from
Waterloo, Clapham
Junction and
Wimbledon
FACILITIES:
Free parking;
various fast food
outlets including
McDonalds, KFC
& Pizza Hut
DISABLED:
Safety restrictions
apply on some
rides—a leaflet gives
details. A limited
number of
wheelchairs are
available on request
WEBSITE:
Information on
Chessington is
available on Thorpe
Park's website:
www.thorpepark.co.
uk

Chessington World of Adventure began its life as a zoo and there are still a few animals, including lions, gorillas and meerkats, to be found in amongst all the hi-tech gadgetry. These are best viewed from the unusual vantage point provided by the monorail that trundles along above the enclosures. These days, however, natural attractions take second place to mechanical ones. The most intense ride on offer is the 60mph loop-the-looping Rameses Revenge, followed closely by the Vampire, which takes its passengers on a harum-scarum ride over the park's rooftops. A much gentler excursion is provided by the new Mexican-themed Rattlesnake with its serpent shaped cars. At the end of each season on 'Family Fright Night' there is an opportunity to sample all these rides in the dark.

Younger children, and those of a less brave disposition, are well catered for at Toytown, the Dragon River log flume and Professor Burp's Bubble Works. There is also a small circus with regular performances featuring trapeze artists and clowns.

Reminders of the park's origins are provided at set times during the day by sea lion and penguin displays, and the newly opened Creepy Cave is home to a collection of spiders, insects and other crawling horrors.

CHESTER CATHEDRAL

LOCATION:
St Werburgh Street, Chester CH1 2HU
TEL: 01244 324 756
OPENING TIMES:
9.30–6 daily

Chester is not a purpose-built cathedral but rather a huge monastic complex which was converted into a cathedral after the dissolution of the monasteries in the mid-16th century. The genesis of the building was slow, organic even. The first Chester

GETTING THERE:
Road: M56, follow signs to Chester
Train: Chester station is a 10-minute walk away
FACILITIES:
Cathedral shop; restaurant in 13th-century Refectory (sells cathedral's own-label wine)
DISABLED:
Wheelchair access, adapted toilets
WEBSITE: www.chestercathedral.org.uk

church was probably built some time in the 7th century and may have been rebuilt several times over the next few centuries—little evidence from this period survives. What is known is that in 1092 Hugh D'Avranches, the second Norman Earl of Chester (known, not particularly affectionately, as Hugh Lupus, 'The Wolf'), began construction of a Benedictine monastic complex.

Building continued for the next 130 years, adapting all the time to changing architectural fashions. The early parts of the complex were classically Romanesque, whilst the later sections are Gothic. Almost as soon as the last building was completed in 1220, the decision was made to rebuild the now stylistically outdated monastic church. This second phase of construction lasted until 1500 and most of the cathedral we see today dates from this period. Despite the huge variety of its architecture, Chester Cathedral hangs together perfectly. It is a wonderfully serene place where visitors can stop and reflect in the quiet ambience of its delightful arcaded cloisters.

EDINBURGH CASTLE

LOCATION: Old Town, Edinburgh
TEL: 0131 225 9846
OPENING TIMES: Apr–Sept 9.30–6, Oct–Mar 9.30–5
ADM: Adult £6, Child £1.50, Conc's £4.50
GETTING THERE: *Road:* M8, A1, A70, A71, A90 *Train:* Waverley station is a 5-minute walk away
FACILITIES: Car and coach parking; self-service restaurant, souvenir & gift shops
DISABLED: Reasonable wheelchair access, courtesy vehicle from esplanade, adapted toilets
WEBSITE: www.historic-scotland.gov.uk

The heart of Scotland's defensive system

Built on a volcanic outcrop 443ft above sea level, Edinburgh Castle has loomed over the city and surrounding countryside for 900 years, defending Scotland and Scottishness from southern encroachments. Architecturally, the fortress is something of a hotch-potch; the tower and ramparts are of 18th-century origin but there are remains and remnants from every stage of its development, including the beautifully preserved 11th-century chapel of St Margaret.

For centuries the heart of Scotland's defensive system, the castle is home to some of the country's greatest historical and military relics including the Scottish Crown Jewels (much older than their English counterparts), the Stone of Destiny and the medieval siege gun Mons Meg. The castle also houses the Scottish United Services Museum.

As you walk around the castle, you will notice various gruesome landmarks to its murky past, including a spot where over 300 witches were burned and a memorial stone to Sir William Kirkcaldy, whose distinguished career saw him assisting in the murder of Cardinal Beaton and Rizzio, secretary to Mary Queen of Scots (you can visit the Queen's newly restored apartments). Alternatively, should you desire more serene pleasures, you could stand on the battlements and admire the magnificent views over the Firth of Forth.

FLAGSHIP PORTSMOUTH

LOCATION:
Historic Dockyard, Portsmouth Harbour
Main Office: Porter's Lodge Building, 1–7 College Road, HM Naval Base, Portsmouth PO1 3LJ
TEL: 01705 861 512
OPENING TIMES:
Mar–Oct 10–5.30, Nov–Feb 10–5
ADM: Ticket to all attractions: Adult £14, Child £10, Conc's £12, Family £33; Single ship tickets: Adult £5.75, Child £4.25, Conc's £5
GETTING THERE:
Road: M27 & M275 then follow brown Historic Ships signs through Portsmouth
Train: Portsmouth Harbour station is a 2-minute walk away
FACILITIES:
Car park, gift shops, restaurant, adapted toilets, baby changing facilities
WEBSITE: www.flagship.org.uk

Flagship Portsmouth is the umbrella organisation which runs Portsmouth's four main naval attractions.

HMS VICTORY

It was aboard this ship that Vice Admiral Nelson commanded the British naval victory at Trafalgar over the combined Franco-Spanish fleet. Fatally wounded in the battle, he spent his final hours here before being brought home, preserved in a barrel of brandy, to a hero's funeral.

The ship, commissioned in 1759, was the most awesome fighting machine of its day. It carried 100 cannons and was manned by 821 officers and crew including 153 Royal Marines 'to provide accurate musket fire in battle'. It has been beautifully restored to look exactly as it would have done on that fateful day in 1805. Both Nelson's and Hardy's quarters are particularly rich in period detail.

ROYAL NAVAL MUSEUM

Housed in an 18th-century dockside building, this museum tells the story of the Royal Navy from its beginnings to the Falklands War. As you would expect, there is a good deal of Nelson memorabilia, including his uniform, the furniture from his cabin on HMS Victory, his watch and a miniature of Emma Hamilton. There is also a delightful exhibition tracing the evolution of the sailor's uniform—from frogging and ribands to bell-bottom pants.

A genuine Tudor time capsule...

THE MARY ROSE

In 1982, when the Mary Rose was raised from the Solent silt in one of the greatest recovery operations in archaeological history, it turned out to be a genuine Tudor time capsule laden with hundreds of unique artefacts. It was built in 1509 on the orders of Henry VIII and was the flagship of the King's fleet in his wars against the French. In 1545 it sank in the Solent during a skirmish and there it lay until rediscovered in 1965. Between 1978 and 1982 many of its contents were recovered; some 19,000 objects made up of a mixture of the ship's military hardware, including heavy guns and longbows (the only examples to survive from Tudor times); and sailors' personal effects: painted pocket sundials, embroidered pouches, rosary beads and lice combs.

HMS WARRIOR

When completed in 1861, HMS Warrior was the fastest, most heavily armed, most heavily armoured warship in the world. It was the first to be fitted with an iron hull and the first to carry 110lb guns. Overnight, it made all other warships obsolete and was described by Napoleon III, whose naval threat it had been designed to curb, as 'a black snake amongst rabbits'. Just fifteen years later, however, and without ever having been used in battle, it too was obsolete, surpassed by faster, nastier craft. For much of the 20th century it languished in a state of disrepair and, for a while, even suffered the indignity of becoming a floating pontoon. It was restored to its former splendour in the early Eighties and, in 1987, returned to Portsmouth.

Overnight, it made all other warships obsolete.

FLAMINGO LAND

LOCATION: Kirby Misperton, Malton, North Yorkshire YO17 0UX
TEL: 01653 668 287
OPENING TIMES: April–Sept opens 10am, closing times vary according to season, Oct–Mar open weekends and half term only

In a little over 20 years, Flamingo Land has been transformed from a small provincial zoo into one of the most popular tourist attractions in Britain. The zoo is still there, larger than ever, with over 180 animal species on display, including Siberian tigers, baboons, zebras, penguins and, of course, flamingoes—although today they share the site with a large fully-equipped theme park.

Flamingo Land is home to some truly terrifying rides known collectively as the

Flamingo 5. These are: the Corkscrew, a 100ft-high loop the looper; Wild Mouse, which travels at 28mph along a series of near right-angle bends; the Terrorizer, which is best described as a cross between a roller-coaster and a waltzer; Topgun, a hyper-realistic flight simulator ride; and, top of the heap, the Bullet. Flamingo Land has developed its own classification system to describe the scariness of its rides. There are five categories: 'Challenging', 'Teeth Chattering', 'Stomach Churning', 'Brain Scrambling' and 'Bone Crunching'. The Bullet, with its unique propulsion system and near vertical descents, is all five.

A rival for the Bullet's crown will open in 1999. The Para Tower will lift its passengers 105ft in the air only to release them again for a seriously scary gravity-defying fall to earth.

Younger children, and adults feeling the need to recover from their exertions, can visit Captain Fortune's Square which offers the gentler pleasures of carousels, a pirate ship boat ride and a haunted castle railway.

ADM: Adult or Child £9.95, Under 4's free, Conc's £5, Family £34
GETTING THERE: *Road:* From South A1, A64, A169; From North A19, A169, A170, *Train:* Nearest station is Malton *Bus:* Yorkshire Coastliner from Leeds and Whitby tel 01653 692 556
FACILITIES: Parking, fish and chip shop, Indian takeaway, donuts & ices shop, bar, gift shop
DISABLED: Wheelchair access to park but rides subject to operator's discretion

FRONTIERLAND

LOCATION:
Marine Road West, Morecambe Bay, LA4 4DG
TEL: 01524 410 024
OPENING TIMES:
Mar–Oct, actual times vary but usually opens at 10am and closes between 4pm and 10pm
ADM: Day Pass High Season (July–Sept) £8.95, Low Season £7.50; Junior Day Pass High Season £6.95, Low Season £5.95; Family Day Pass High Season £29.95, Low Season £25.95; Yippee Night (selected Fridays through season) £2.95; Full Evening Pass (High Season only) £5; Junior Evening Pass £4; Family Evening Pass £15
GETTING THERE:
Road: From South: M6 J35, then A5105; From North: M6 J34, then A589
Train: Morecambe station is 10 minutes away
FACILITIES:
Free coach parking, baby changing facilities, over a dozen catering outlets including 2 licensed restaurants
DISABLED:
Wheelchair access to park and adapted toilets. Access to rides is at the discretion of the ride operators

Brush off your spurs, slip on your stetson and utter a loud 'Yee-hah!' in preparation for a trip to this small piece of pioneer-era America transported to north-west England.

There are over 40 rides, each with its own wild west theme: the Texas Tornado, Runaway Mine Train and Stampede are the white-knuckle show-pieces, whilst gentler entertainment is provided by the El Paso railroad and crazy-golf course. High steppin' fun is on offer at the Country Show in the

Crazy Horse Saloon and Frontier Fred's Family show—the park is inhabited by various Deputy-Dawgesque rubber-suited characters.

The most striking landmark at Frontierland, however, is strangely out of character with the rest of the park. The Polo Tower, which has been designed to look like an enormous tube of mints, affords some spectacular views over Morecambe Bay and the surrounding countryside.

GLASGOW MUSEUM & ART GALLERY

LOCATION:
Kelvingrove,
Glasgow G3 8AG
TEL: 0141 287 2699
OPENING TIMES:
Mon–Sat 10–5,
Sun 11–5
ADM: Free
GETTING THERE:
Train:
Nearest station is Exhibition Centre
Underground:
Nearest station is Kelvinhall
Bus: 6, 6A, 8, 8C from George Square; 62, 62B, 62D, 64, 64A from Argyle Street
FACILITIES:
Car and coach parking available (charges may apply), gift shop, restaurant, free guided tours
DISABLED:
Wheelchair access, adapted toilets
WEBSITE: www.biggarnet.co.uk/tour/glasgow/museums.htm

Housed in the magnificent red brick Kelvingrove mansion, this is one of the world's best city art galleries, with paintings by Botticelli (including his Annunciation), Rembrandt, Monet and Van Gogh; sculptures by Rodin and Epstein; and furniture designed by the great Scottish architect, Charles Rennie Mackintosh.

It is neatly complemented by a pleasant little museum where you can find, in the prehistory section, a fabulously detailed reconstruction of the Antonine wall and some beautifully preserved Bronze Age cists. There is also a large natural history section as well as hordes of silver, silver plate, porcelain, and a number of suits of armour.

The Kelvingrove mansion itself was built in 1901 with proceeds received from an exhibition held in Kelvingrove Park. Today, visitors to the museum can wander through the gorgeous 85 acres of parkland down to the River Kelvin where, in summer, concerts are held in the amphitheatre.

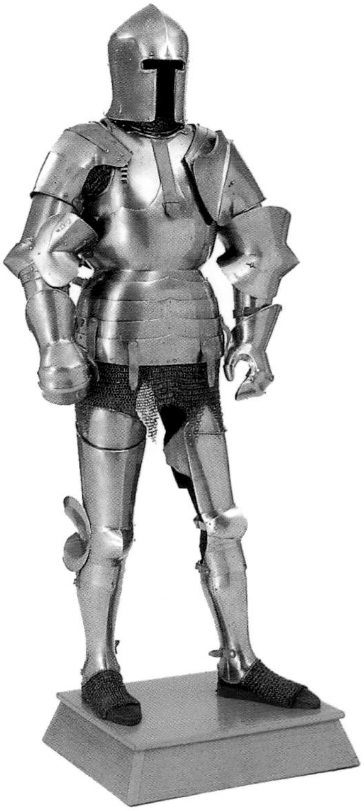

HAMPTON COURT PALACE

LOCATION:
Surrey, KT8 9AU
TEL: 0181 781 9500
OPENING TIMES:
Oct–Mar Mon 10.15–4.30, Tue–Sun 9.30–4.30, Mar–Oct Mon 10.15–6, Tue–Sun 9.30–6
ADM: Adult £10, Child £6.60, Under 5's free, Conc's £7.60, Family ticket £29.90

Hampton Court, one of the most famous and best loved of all royal palaces, hasn't actually had a royal in residence for over 250 years. Despite its undoubted magnificence, the typical regal attitude towards it has been at best ambiguous and at times downright hostile. The construction of the palace began when Henry VIII seized the Hampton estate from his chief advisor, Cardinal Wolsey, having earlier refused it when offered to him as a gift.

Over the next ten years, Henry spent more than £62,000 (that's around £18 million in today's money) on rebuilding work. By the

GETTING THERE:
Road: From London: A3, A309 to Esher/Staines, then follow signs. From M25: Exit 12 for M3 towards London, Exit J1, A308 to Kingston, then follow signs
Train: Hampton Court station
FACILITIES:
Car park (£3 charge), shops, restaurant, café, guided tours available
DISABLED:
Wheelchair access, disabled parking, adapted toilets

time he had finished, he had created the most modern, sophisticated palace in England with a real tennis court, a bowling alley, a vast 36,000 sq ft kitchen (staffed by 200 people), pleasure gardens and, perhaps its greatest feature, a multiple lavatory which could seat 28 people at a time and was known as 'The Great House of Easement'. The next monarch to take an interest in the palace was William III, 150 years later. He instigated further rebuilding work, this time costing a mere £131,000 (today £9.5 million), the most important element of which was the planting of new gardens and a maze. Of subsequent monarchs, only George II made use of the palace and in 1838 it was opened to the public.

Today, visitors can wander around the vast 50-room Tudor kitchen, the wonderfully elaborate King's staircase, the fountain court (the centrepiece of William III's palace reconstruction) and a Renaissance picture gallery containing works by Brueghel and Mantegna.

HAMPTON COURT GARDENS

ADM: Free when visiting the gardens on their own.

It contains many wonders: a 1,000-year-old oak tree, the oldest and longest vine in the world and, of course, the maze.

Hampton Court's superb landscaped gardens were started by Henry VIII back in the early 16th century. Their current form and layout, however, is mostly the result of work undertaken during the reign of William III and modifications made by the great royal gardener Lancelot 'Capability' Brown in the 18th century. It contains many wonders: a 1,000-year-old oak tree, the oldest and longest vine in the world, planted in 1768 (in the early part of this century the grapes were harvested in baskets made by soldiers blinded in World War I), 100,000 rose bushes, 250,000 flowering bulbs and, of course, the most famous maze in the world. It was planted in 1690 for William III and lures in around 300,000 people a year (and lets roughly the same number out again, give or take a few). It takes about twenty minutes to reach the centre of the maze and at least double that to negotiate your way back through the 1/3 acre of yew-lined paths. No wonder, then, that this is the most popular garden in Britain, attracting around 1.3 million people a year.

IMPERIAL WAR MUSEUM

LOCATION:
Lambeth Road,
London SE1 6HZ
TEL: Enquiries 0171 416 5320, Infoline 0891 600 140
OPENING TIMES:
10–6 daily
ADM: Adult £5, Child £2.50, Conc's £4, Family ticket £13; free entry after 4.30pm

This museum, dedicated to tracing the history of civilisation's great madness, is housed, appropriately enough, in what was formerly the Bedlam lunatic asylum.

The museum makes no attempt to treat conflict as some sort of great Boys Own adventure. Instead, the displays tend to focus on the human experience of war as illustrated by two excellent exhibitions: the Trench Experience, a vivid recreation of the life of an ordinary footsoldier holed up beneath the Flanders mud; and the Blitz Experience which, with the aid of some special sound and visual effects, goes some way towards illustrating the terrors and privations of an aerial siege.

There is, of course, plenty of hardware on display, from zeppelins and Lancaster bombers to cruise missile launchers, which, shorn of their movement and function, now seem rather innocuous and tasteful.

In the basement is a clock counting the number of lives lost to war in the 20th century. By 1999, it is estimated that the figure will reach 100,000,000.

the human experience of war...

GETTING THERE:
Underground: Lambeth North, Elephant & Castle
Train: Waterloo, Elephant & Castle
Bus: 1, 3, 12, 45, 53, 63, 68, 159, 168, 171, 172, 176, 188, 344 & C10
FACILITIES:
Café, gift/bookshop
DISABLED:
Wheelchair access, the cinema has infra-red audio enhancement
WEBSITE:
www.iwm.org.uk

JORVIK VIKING CENTRE

LOCATION:
Coppergate,
York YO1 1NT
TEL: 01904 643 211
OPENING TIMES:
1 Jan–12 Feb 9–3.30, 13 Feb–21 Feb 9–5.30, 22 Feb–26 Mar 9–3.30, 27 Mar–31 Oct 9–5.30, 1 Nov–31 Dec 10–4.30
ADM: Adult £4.99, Child £3.99, Conc's £4.59, Under 5's free, Family £16.50
GETTING THERE:
Road: A1036, A1079
Train: York station
FACILITIES:
Gift shop and café
DISABLED:
Wheelchair access
WEBSITE: www.jorvik-viking-centre.co.uk

The Jorvik Viking Centre is a unique archaeological experience where visitors have the opportunity to ride through a time tunnel to see the sights, hear the sounds and even smell the smells of a 10th-century Viking village. Between 1976 and 1981 the York Archaeological Trust unearthed, in the centre of York, the greatest collection of Viking remains ever found in Britain—a find so large that it merited the construction of a museum all to itself. This was to be no ordinary museum, however, with rows of glass cases stuffed full of dusty fragments and indeterminate relics. Instead, it would hold a full-scale recreation of a Viking settlement, painstakingly designed to look exactly as it would have done 1,000 years ago. Thatched huts, workshops, alleys and wharfs inhabited by accurately rendered models of the Vikings themselves: tradesmen, craftsmen, fishermen and their families arranged in a series of everyday tableaux. To complete the

picture, authentic sound and smell effects were added. The result is an intense, hyper-real Viking universe. 'Time cars' carry the visitors through the recreated village along a magnetic track.

There is also a reproduction of the laboratory where the scientific research for the project was carried out and a more traditional gallery where, in rows of glass cases, you can see some of the dig's better preserved items, including examples of Viking jewellery.

KEW GARDENS

LOCATION:
Kew, Richmond, Surrey TW9 3AB
TEL: 0181 332 5622
Infoline 0181 940 1171
OPENING TIMES:
9.30–dusk
ADM: Adult £5, Child £2.50, Under 5's free, Conc's £3.50, Family ticket £13, blind, partially sighted and wheelchair users free

It's the middle of December, there's a chill in the air, snow on the ground and dark grey clouds overhead, but without the time or money to take that trip to the Caribbean there's precious little to do except wrap up warm and pray for spring. Alternatively, you could pay a visit to the one part of London where tropical weather is guaranteed 365 days a year. And after ten minutes spent in the sweltering heat of the Palm House, a huge Victorian conservatory where the conditions are designed to mimic those of a tropical rainforest, you'll never complain about a British winter again.

The Royal Botanic Gardens, spread over a 300-acre site on the south bank of the Thames, have grown over the course of their 200-year history into the largest and most comprehensive collection of living plants in the world, containing representatives of more than 1 in 8 of all flowering plants. All year round, these beautifully manicured parks provide a dazzling display of blooms, from crocuses, camellias and bluebells in spring to strawberry trees and witch hazel in winter. There are three enormous conservatories: the above mentioned Palm House (the most important surviving 19th-century glass and iron structure in the world), the late Victorian Temperate House, and the Princess of Wales Conservatory, built in the 1980s and home to both the giant Amazonian water lily and *Titan Arum*, the largest, and quite possibly the smelliest, flower in the world. There is also a ten-storey, 165ft-high 18th-century pagoda.

GETTING THERE:
Train: Kew Bridge, Kew Gardens
Underground: Kew Gardens
Bus: 65, 391, 267, R68 (Sun only)
FACILITIES:
Baby changing facilities; 2 gift shops, 2 self-service restaurants, coffee bar, bakery, snack shop
DISABLED:
Wheelchair access, adapted toilets
WEBSITE:
www.kew.org

KNOWSLEY SAFARI PARK

LOCATION:
Prescot, Merseyside, L34 4AN
TEL: 0151 430 9009
OPENING TIMES:
Mar–Oct 10–4
ADM: £12 per car regardless of no. of passengers
GETTING THERE:
Road: M62 exit 6, M57 exit 2
Train: The nearest station is Lime Street in Liverpool

Opened in 1971 by the eighteenth Earl of Derby, this was the first safari park in Britain to be built near a major city—just eight miles from the centre of Liverpool. A series of moats and electric fences prevents the animals from putting in any unexpected appearances in the high street.

In the mid 19th-century the thirteenth Earl of Derby kept one of the largest private collections of animals in the world on this site. Members of the public could visit, in groups of no more than six, only with the written permission of the Earl. Today the park's authorities are much more accommodating. The full 'Safari' experience takes you on a five-mile ride through the park's enclosures, home to the largest herd of elephants in Europe, wildebeest, buffalo, zebra and rhinos—known collectively, rather appropriately, as a 'crash'. The park is one of only a handful in the world to have successfully reintroduced rhinos bred in captivity into the wild, as well as ostriches, camels and a troop of baboons. You are allowed to travel past but not through the lion and tiger enclosures.

Elsewhere in the park is a children's funpark, a small steam railway and a show area for daily sea lion performances.

FACILITIES:
Coach and car parking available on site, baby changing rooms, fairground, restaurant, souvenir and gift shop
DISABLED:
Adapted toilets
WEBSITE:
www.merseyworld.com/safari

LEEDS CASTLE

LOCATION: Maidstone, Kent ME17 1PL
TEL: 01622 765 400
OPENING TIMES: Castle: Mar–Oct 11–5.30, Nov–Feb 10.15–3.30; Park & Gardens Mar–Oct 10–5, Nov–Feb 10–3
ADM: Adult £9.30, Child £6, Conc's £7.30; Park & Gardens only: Adult £7.30, Child £4.50, Conc's £5.80

Henry VIII's favourite royal residence, Leeds is one of Britain's great castles. Set on two islands in the middle of a lake in 500 acres of beautifully sculpted Kent countryside, the castle provides an architectural summary of the last 1,000 years. The cellar dates from the 11th century, the Gatehouse from the 12th (within is a collection of dog collars, some over 400 years old), the Maiden's Tower is Tudor whilst the main residential quarters were built in the last century.

There was a manor on this site back in the 9th century but it wasn't until 1119, following the Norman invasion, that the construction of a stone castle began. Both Edward I and Edward III left their mark, but it took the largesse of Henry VIII, who spent a fortune on enlarging the castle and beautifying the grounds, to turn the castle into one of the most splendid fortresses in Europe. Today, visitors can get some sense of the castle's former opulent glory in Henry's 72ft Banqueting Hall with its ebony wood floors and carved oak ceiling and in the Queen's bedroom, furnished to look as it would have done when occupied by Catherine de Valois, Henry V's wife.

Within the enchanting grounds are a maze, a grotto, a duckery, a vineyard, greenhouses and even a golf course. Throughout the year, the grounds play host to various special events including wine festivals and open air concerts.

GETTING THERE:
Road: M20 J8
Train: Nearest station is Bearsted, Eurostar stops at Ashford International, 20 minutes away
FACILITIES: Gift, clothing and plant shops, restaurant, picnic area, golf course
DISABLED: Some wheelchair access, disabled car parking spaces
WEBSITE: www.se-eng-tourist-board.org.uk/seetb/

LEGOLAND

LOCATION: Windsor, Berkshire SL4 4AY
TEL: 01753 626 111
Tickets: 0990 04 04 04
OPENING TIMES: 10–6 daily, park closes 8pm between mid Jul–Aug
ADM: Adult £16.50, Child £13.50, Conc's £10.50
GETTING THERE: *Road:* 2 miles from Windsor on the Windsor to Ascot Road, close to M4, M3, M25
Train: Riverside, Windsor Central
FACILITIES: 7 restaurants/cafés and 11 catering stalls
DISABLED: Wheelchair access, wheelchair hire available, adapted toilets
WEBSITE: www.lego.com/world

Legoland is fast becoming one of the country's top family attractions and is perhaps best described as a cross between a theme park and an activity centre. It has some great thrill rides including a dragon themed rollercoaster which jets its way over the park's roofs and treetops. The most popular attractions, however, those designed to get the under twelves jumping with joy, are of a more interactive nature, like Lego Traffic, where children have the chance to drive electrically powered Lego cars through a model town, negotiating traffic lights, pedestrian crossings and roundabouts on the way—the most skilful drivers are awarded their own special Legoland Driving Licence. In 1999 Legoland hopes to complement this ride with a Flying School where children and adults will test their flying skills aboard a tethered balloon as it flies high above the centre of the park. More hands-on fun is provided at the Imagination Centre, where children are encouraged to indulge in 'creative play', which translates as erecting model buildings and then destroying them on the special Earthquake Table. Older children can create robotic models, using the rather eerie concept of 'intelligent' Lego bricks at the Mindstorm Centre, whilst their younger siblings run riot in the Duplo Gardens.

Perhaps the most intriguing section, for children and adults alike, is Miniland with its beautifully rendered model cities—London, Amsterdam, Paris, Brussels et al. It took 100 model makers three years to complete and is made up of no less than 20,000,000 Lego blocks.

LONDON PLANETARIUM

LOCATION: Marylebone Road, London NW1 5LR
TEL: 0171 935 6861
OPENING TIMES: Shows run every 40 mins from 12.20–5; weekends and school holidays from 10.20am
ADM: Adult £5.85, Child £3.85, Conc's £4.50; combined Planetarium, Madame Tussaud's ticket: Adult £11.50, Child £7.55, Conc's £8.75
GETTING THERE: *Underground:* Baker Street *Bus*: 18, 27, 30, 74, 159
FACILITIES: Gift shop
DISABLED: Wheelchair access, induction loop for the hard of hearing

The Planetarium has been using state-of-the-art technology to explain the mysteries of the cosmos for over 40 years now: interactive demonstrations, live satellite weather transmissions, images from space telescopes and an enormous spinning globe provide a tasty hors d'oeuvre for the celestial main course, the £1 million Planetary Quest 3D extravaganza in the world-famous dome which takes you on a whizz-bang tour of the galaxy. As you hurtle past exploding supernovas, whirling starfields and crashing asteroid belts, it is sometimes difficult to remember that you are sitting in an auditorium on the Marylebone Road and not aboard a careering space shuttle. There are also a number of video and audio displays where you can hear such astral luminaries as Neil Armstrong, Stephen Hawking and Patrick Moore giving their opinions on the great beyond. In addition, the planetarium provides regular live programmes throughout the year with a range of guest speakers.

the world-famous dome takes you on a whizz-bang tour of the galaxy...past exploding supernovas and whirling starfields.

LONDON ZOO

LOCATION: Regent's Park, London NW1 4RY
TEL: 0171 722 3333
OPENING TIMES: Summer 10–5.30 (last admission 4.30pm); winter 10–4 (last admission 3pm)
ADM: Adult £8.50, Child £6.50, Conc's £7.50, Under 4's free, Family ticket £26

Did you know that the elephant has 60,000 muscles in its trunk? Or that the sparrow has twice as many bones in its neck (14) as a giraffe? Or that the swan has more feathers (25,000) than any other species of bird? If you did, it's probably because you've recently paid a visit to London Zoo, still the best place for people to come and learn about the creatures that share their planet.

These days, the zoo is careful how it promotes itself; gawping at the animals for gawping's sake is no longer the done thing. The modern London Zoo is first and foremost a scientific institute and conservator of endangered species. Nonetheless, it still makes the majority of its revenue through turnstile receipts, which means it must continue to display its animals in a way that is both attractive to the public and consistent with its remit. Thankfully, this is exactly what it does. The zoo is home to a huge collection of animals, from elephants and rhinos to gibbons and pythons, each provided with as much space as they need to live and interact in as natural a way as possible. Nowhere is this better illustrated than in the Reptile House, where part of the fun lies in trying to spot the wonderfully camouflaged snakes and lizards, and the Moonlight World where, in simulated night-time conditions, you can observe animals never normally seen in daylight.

GETTING THERE:
Train: Camden Road
Underground: Regent's Park, Camden Town, Mornington Crescent, Baker Street
Bus: 274, C2.
Waterbus also runs along Regent's Canal (hourly 10–5 every day).
FACILITIES: Parking, baby changing facilities, café, various fast food outlets, gift shop
DISABLED: Some wheelchair access, adapted toilets
WEBSITE: www.york.biosis.org/zrdocs/zsl.htm

MADAME TUSSAUD'S

LOCATION:
Marylebone Road, London NW1 5LR
TEL: 0171 935 6861
OPENING TIMES:
Mon–Fri 10–5.30, Sat–Sun 9.30–5.30; earlier opening during summer
ADM:
Adult £9.75, Child £6.60, Conc's £6.95; Combined ticket with Planetarium: Adult £12, Child £8.05, Conc's £8.75
GETTING THERE:
Underground: Baker Street
Bus: 18, 27, 30, 74, 159
FACILITIES:
Gift shop, café, Thomas Cook Bureau de Change
DISABLED:
Wheelchair access

Set amongst the stuccoed terraces that surround Regent's Park, this is the grand temple of waxwork kitsch. The two and half million visitors who pass through its doors each year get to explore four floors stuffed full of ersatz celebrities, featuring everyone from Dr Crippen to Princess Anne.

The museum itself is divided into eight themed areas including the Garden Party, the Grand Hall, the Spirit of London—a sort of tableaux funfair in which you are carried in a mock-up London taxi through representations of London history from Elizabethan times to the present day—

and, of course, the Chamber of Horrors with its collection of gruesomely rendered murderous favourites.

Madame Tussaud made her reputation in the late 17th century making wax portraits of the French aristocracy. Thrown in jail during the Revolution (the 1780s were not a good time to start cosying up to the nobility), she was released on the condition that she sculpted the death masks of the Revolution's more celebrated victims.

In 1902 she moved to England where she spent the next 33 years touring her models around the country until, in 1835, a permanent site was found for them in Baker Street—the museum moved to its present location in 1885. She died in 1850 aged 89. Her last work, a rather eerie self-portrait, is still on display in the Grand Hall.

MUSEUM OF WELSH LIFE

LOCATION: St Fagans, Cardiff CF5 6XB
TEL: 01222 573 500
OPENING TIMES: July–Sep 10–6; Oct–Jun 10–5
ADM: Adult £4.25, Child & Conc's £2.50, Under 5's free, Family £9.75
GETTING THERE: *Road:* M4 J33, A4232
Train: Cardiff Central station
FACILITIES: Free car park, restaurant, tea rooms
DISABLED: Wheelchair access to most areas but upper floors of some cottages inaccessible, adapted toilets, tactile maps for the visually impaired, disabled car parking
WEBSITE: www.nmgw.ac.uk

pretend to be a time-traveller wending your way through the mud and thatch huts of a primitive Celtic village - tending to the animals in a 19th-century farmyard.

Croeso i Amgueddfa Werin Cymru, or Welcome to the Museum of Welsh Life, one of the largest open air museums in Europe. Spread across 100 acres of beautiful countryside are various recreated environments from the last 2,000 years of Welsh history.

The emphasis here is on interaction; you can pretend to be a time-traveller wending your way through the mud and thatch huts of a primitive Celtic village, tending to the animals in a 19th-century farmyard, learning your lessons in a Victorian schoolroom or doing the weekly shop in a 1920s grocery. There are festivals, theatre performances, storytellings and craft demonstrations by

blacksmiths, skilled wood turners and potters as well as opportunities to try some of the crafts for yourself. Children in particular, are always eager to be let loose with a ball of clay and a potter's wheel. Afterwards you can take a ride in a horse-drawn carriage travelling in style past the medieval farmhouse and Tudor Manor.

NATIONAL GALLERY

LOCATION: Trafalgar Square, London WC2N 5DN
TEL: 0171 747 2885
OPENING TIMES: Mon–Sat 10–6, Sun 2–6
ADM: Free, charges apply for some temporary exhibitions
GETTING THERE: *Underground:* Charing Cross, Leicester Square, Embankment
Bus: 3, 6, 9, 11, 12, 13, 15, 23, 24, 29, 53, 88, 91, 109, 139, 159, 176, 184, 196
FACILITIES: Gift shop, café, restaurant
DISABLED: Wheelchair access, Loop system for hard of hearing
WEBSITE: www.national-gallery.org.uk

NATIONAL PORTRAIT GALLERY
LOCATION: St Martin's Place, London WC2H 0HE
TEL: 0171 306 0055
OPENING TIMES: As above
ADM: Free, charges apply for some temporary exhibitions
GETTING THERE: *Underground:* As above
Bus: As above
FACILITIES: Restaurant, café, shop, audio tour available
DISABLED: Wheelchair access
WEBSITE: www.npg.org.uk

On Trafalgar Square facing Nelson's Column, in the heart of the capital, this collection of some 2,000-plus pictures is one of the country's most splendid national treasures. All the greats from the history of western European painting are here: Cézanne, Constable, Leonardo da Vinci, Monet, Picasso, Raphael, Rembrandt, Rubens, Titian, Turner, Van Eyck, Van Gogh...the list is endless. It has been internationally acclaimed as one of the world's great art galleries and yet has attracted its fair share of controversy. When it opened in 1838, the building was widely criticised for its lack of grace and symmetry. This was nothing, however, to the furore aroused by the proposed Sainsbury's extension in the early Eighties. The original glass and steel design was described by Prince Charles as a 'monstrous carbuncle' and promptly dropped for the more traditional, conservative design we see today.

NATIONAL PORTRAIT GALLERY

If history is, as Thomas Carlyle once claimed, merely the 'biographies of great men', then the National Portrait Gallery is its picture album. Arranged in chronological order from the 13th century (top floor) to the present day (ground floor) are 2,000 pictures of Britain's greatest national figures—kings, queens, statesmen, politicians, scientists and writers—rendered in a variety of styles. In the collection are Holbein's wonderful Renaissance portraits of Henrys VII and VIII, a cubist T.S. Eliot by Jacob Epstein and Annigoni's famous film star treatment of Elizabeth II.

NATIONAL MUSEUM OF SCOTLAND

LOCATION: Chambers Street, Edinburgh EH1 1JF
TEL: 0131 247 4422
Textphone: 0131 247 4027
OPENING TIMES: Mon–Sat 10–5, Sun 12-5, late night opening Tues until 8pm
ADM: Adult £3, Child free, Conc's £1.50 (ticket includes entry to Royal Museum of Scotland), free entry Tues 4.30–8pm
GETTING THERE:
Road: A1, A703
Train: Waverley station
Bus: Most buses from Prince's Street go past the museum
FACILITIES: Museum shop, 2 restaurants and a café. Guided tours available
DISABLED: Wheelchair access to all parts of museum, adapted toilets
WEBSITE: http://www.nms.ac.uk

Opened by the Queen on 1 December 1998, this is the only museum in Scotland devoted to the history of Scotland itself. The six sections within this beautiful, specially constructed sandstone building tell the story of Scotland and the Scottish people from prehistory to the present day; from volcano-ravaged landscape to industrial power. It contains some of the country's most precious artefacts, including the Monymusk Reliquary, a tiny shrine made in around AD 750 containing the relics of St Columba, which was carried at the head of Robert the Bruce's army at the Battle of Bannockburn. There's also a brooch belonging to Mary Queen of Scots, James VI's stirrup cup and Bonnie Prince Charlie's canteen. Perhaps the most impressive exhibits, however, are those relating to Scotland's Industrial Revolution—in particular, the vast, 40ft-high, iron and wood Newcombe Atmospheric Engine, one of the world's first steam engines, which seems to dominate the entire museum.

The exhibits on display in the Twentieth Century Gallery have been chosen in a particularly novel way. Rather than rely on the whims of curators and administrators, the gallery asked members of the public, as well as political and national figures, to nominate those items which, for them, best represented the 20th century. The 800 exhibits make a strange and eclectic display. There's a washing machine, a typewriter, a video game player, a packet of contraceptive pills, an NHS card and, of course, a bottle of Irn Bru 'made in Scotland, from girders'.

the only museum in Scotland devoted to the history of Scotland itself.

NATIONAL RAILWAY MUSEUM

LOCATION:
Leeman Road,
York YO26 4XJ
TEL: 01904 621 261
OPENING TIMES:
10–6 daily
ADM: Adult £4.95,
Child £3.15,
Family £14.50

This is the largest railway museum in the world with artefacts, memorabilia and rolling stock from the entire railway age—from Stephenson's Rocket (which will be on display here during 1999 before returning to the Science Museum in 2000) to the Eurostar. Its pride and joy, however, is its huge collection of classic steam engines arranged around a 1955 turntable in the

GETTING THERE:
Road: A59, A64, A1079, then signposted from York's ring road
Train: York station is 500yds away
Bus: Special bus service runs from York Minster every 30 mins Apr–Oct, call no. above for details
FACILITIES: Long stay parking available on-site (charges apply), gift shop, restaurant, café, barbecue during summer, reference library
DISABLED:
Wheelchair access to most parts of the museum, wheelchair loan available, special parking at the City entrance
WEBSITE:
www.nmsi.ac.uk/nrm/

Great Hall. You can go inside most, including the Mallard which, capable of reaching speeds of up to 126mph, is the fastest steam locomotive in the world.

The royal family has travelled on trains since the late 19th century. You can see the privations they have had to endure at the 'Palace on Wheels' exhibition—sumptuous bedrooms, reading rooms and salons, as well as Queen Victoria's gold plated toilet. The Queen, it seemed, never fully embraced the capabilities of the new technology and would not allow her train to travel above 40mph.

Children are well catered for with Play 'n' Picnic areas, an interactive learning centre and regular visits from Thomas the Tank Engine.

A new £4 million wing is currently under construction and will open sometime early in the millennium. It will contain more locomotives as well as a workshop where visitors will be able to watch trains being restored from a viewing gallery.

THE NATURAL HISTORY MUSEUM

LOCATION:
Cromwell Road, London SW7 5BD
TEL: 0171 938 9123
OPENING TIMES:
Mon–Sat 10–5.50, Sun 11–5.50
ADM: Adult £6, Child £3, Under 5's free, Conc's £3.20, Family £16, Joint Museum season tickets (National History Museum, Science Museum and the Victoria and Albert Museum) Adult £22, Child £12, Conc's £12, Family £45. Free entry after 4.30pm Mon–Fri and after 5pm Sat, Sun & Bank Holidays

Which, as every child knows, means dinosaurs. These 65 million-year-old attractions have always been the museum's biggest draw. Until recently, the nation's youth was happy to marvel at fossils in cases and plaster cast reconstructions, particularly the enormous diplodocus in the vast cathedral-like central hall. In the wake of the worldwide success of Jurassic Park, however, the dinosaur section was revamped and now features a rather gruesome (and thus extremely popular) animatronic display.

Although children often forget it, the Natural History Museum does have more to offer besides monsters from the past. It is divided into two sections, the Life Galleries and the Earth Galleries. Highlights from the Life Galleries include a section cut from a 1,300-year-old giant sequoia tree and an awesome life-size model of a blue whale, suspended from the Mammal Gallery ceiling. The Earth Galleries are reached via one of the largest escalators in the world which wends its way around a massive suspended globe. Here you can experience a virtual earthquake in a reconstructed Japanese supermarket and see the eerie lava casts of people killed as they attempted to flee the Pompeii volcanic eruption.

These days the museum is very keen on promoting interaction; there are buttons to press, levers to pull and videos to see. Nonetheless, it remains one of the best places in the country simply to stand and marvel.

GETTING THERE:
Underground: South Kensington
Bus: 14, 49, 70, 345, C1
FACILITIES:
Restaurant, café, coffee bar, snack bar, gallery shop, bookshop, souvenir and gift shop, baby changing facilities
DISABLED:
Wheelchair access, adapted toilets
WEBSITE:
www.nhm.ac.uk

experience a virtual earthquake in a reconstructed Japanese supermarket ...

PLEASURE BEACH, GREAT YARMOUTH

LOCATION: South Beach Parade, Great Yarmouth NR30 3EH
TEL: 01493 844 585
OPENING TIMES: Mar–Sept, dates and times vary.
ADM: Free entry; rides can be paid for either with tokens, 50p each or wristbands £8
GETTING THERE: *Road:* From South: M11 J6, A11, A14, A143, A146. From North: A17, A47, A12. *Train:* Great Yarmouth station *Bus*: First Blue Service from Norwich
FACILITIES: Sweet shops, inn, tea room
DISABLED: Most rides accessible, adapted toilets
WEBSITE: www.pleasure-beach.co.uk

This nine-acre sea-front site, encompassing over 70 rides, is East Anglia's most popular tourist attraction. Its flagship ride, the Ejector Seat, is an ingenious variation on the traditional bungee jump. Passengers start the ride at ground level in a tethered two-seater cage. Once released, the 'mother of all elastic bands' flings its victims into the air to a height of 160ft, going from 0–70mph in just under a second, before returning them back down to earth at 125mph. Alternatively, there's the Terminator or Top Spin, a large 360° spinning gondola which can terrify a staggering 900 people an hour, or Sheer Terror, a walk-through attraction where performing arts students from Great Yarmouth College dress up in scary costumes (mad axe man, Hannibal Lecter etc.) and try to terrify those who enter. The choice is huge: there's a go-cart track, a log flume, a waltzer, an adventure golf course as well as various rollercoasters.

Great Yarmouth developed into a popular seaside resort between 1800 and 1860, and the seafront centre was born in 1909. The original Pleasure Beach had a scenic railway and little else until, in 1911, it acquired a Joywheel; its collection of attractions has been expanding ever since. A reminder of this earlier, gentler era is provided by Gallopers, a merry-go-round built in 1915, still with its original hand-carved horses.

PLEASURELAND, SOUTHPORT

LOCATION:
Marine Drive,
Southport PR8 1RX
TEL: 01704 532 717
OPENING TIMES:
Early Mar–early Nov weekends only; open daily during school holidays. Hours of opening vary–call in advance
ADM: Free entry; wristband for 10 rides Adult £12, Child £7, Under 1.2m £5
GETTING THERE:
By car: From north: M6 J31, follow A59 through Preston, take A565 and follow signs. From south: M6 J26 onto M58, exit J3 onto A570, follow signs
Parking: Ample car and coach parking facilities; charges apply
By rail: Southport station
By bus: A shuttle operates during the summer between Southport Station and Pleasureland, Stagecoach service no.X59 also stops at the park.
FACILITIES:
Restaurants and gift shops.
DISABLED:
Wheelchair access, adapted toilets, access to rides at the discretion of the park.
WEBSITE: www.
pleasureland.uk.com

Whilst other big name theme parks concentrate on building faster, nastier rides designed to flip you as they spin you as they send you to the bottom of the ocean/into outer space, Pleasureland gives you the opportunity to keep in touch with the spirit of fairgrounds past.

There are a couple of modern-style rides with plans afoot to open a new suspended rollercoaster in the spring of 1999, which, it is promised, will compete in terms of terror value with anything currently available in the country. Until then, however, enjoy the park as it is, a reminder of how things used to be.

The park's pride and joy is Cyclone, an old wooden rollercoaster built in 1937, the speed of which depends on how many people it carries. When full, it can be quite hairy but, although it doesn't exactly slow to a crawl when empty, the ride is still gentle enough to allow you to take a pleasant elevated look at the local area.

Further trips down memory lane are provided by Gulliver, a 1954 carousel; the River Boat journey, built in 1923; and the park's oldest rollercoaster which first saw action in 1914—don't panic, it was fully renovated in 1996.

The park also contains a log flume, 3 go-cart tracks and the Sultan Towers, a children's play area with a bouncy castle, mini rollercoaster and junior Ferris wheel.

ROCK CIRCUS

LOCATION:
The London Pavilion,
1 Piccadilly Circus,
London W1V 9LA
TEL: 0171 734 8025
OPENING TIMES:
Mon, Wed, Thurs, Sun 11–9; Fri–Sat 11–10; Tues 12–9
ADM: Adult £7.95, Child £6, Conc's £6.95
GETTING THERE:
Underground: Piccadilly Circus
Bus: 3, 6, 9, 12, 13, 14, 15, 19, 22, 23, 38, 53, 88, 94, 139, 159
FACILITIES:
Rock & pop shop, hot snacks, sweets bar
DISABLED:
Adapted toilets

Three floors of designer doppelgängers sing you through the history of popular music. In the New Music Revolving Show, in Europe's largest revolving auditorium, animatronic stars from Bruce Springsteen to Phil Collins belt out their biggest hits—the sound is relayed through individual infra-red headsets. There's also a horde of priceless rock memorabilia, including a shirt that once belonged to Elvis Presley, and the jacket worn by Ringo Starr in 'A Hard Day's Night' as well as various signed gold and platinum records.

Animatronic stars from Bruce Springsteen to Phil Collins belt out their biggest hits—the sound is relayed through individual infra-red headsets.

ROMAN BATHS & PUMP ROOM

LOCATION: Stall Street, Bath, BA1 1LZ
TEL: 01225 477 782/6
OPENING TIMES: Daily Apr–Sept 9–6, also opens 8pm–10pm in Aug; Oct–Mar Mon–Sat 9.30–5, Sun 10.30–5
ADM: £6, Child £3.60, Conc's £5.60, Family £15.60

Here in Bath you will find an elegant 18th-century tearoom built over some of the best preserved Roman remains in Britain. In AD 75 the Romans erected a small shrine to the Goddess Sulis Minerva next to a natural hot spring (which produces 250,000 gallons of water a day at a temperature of 45.6°C or 116°F), where pilgrims would come to worship and throw curses written on sheets of lead into the sacred water. Inveterate bathers that they were, however, the Romans soon put the water to less spiritual use at a huge bathing complex where the great and good of Roman society would go to socialise, chat about the day's business and, of course, bathe.

The baths were only rediscovered in the 18th century when the prevailing health fashion for 'taking the waters' led to a new spate of construction near the spring. Remarkably, the baths had remained largely intact. Indeed, the Great Bath still receives its daily water from pipes laid down by the Romans. In summer, at night, the complex is beautifully floodlit.

GETTING THERE:
Road: M4, then A4
Train: Bath station
FACILITIES: Free audio tour of baths; museum, gift shop, restaurant and coffee room in Pump Room, glass of spring water 45p
DISABLED: No wheelchair access to Baths, Pump Room is fully accessible
WEBSITE: www.romanbaths.co.uk

The Pump Room, an exquisitely tasteful tea and coffee house, fulfilled much the same function for the 18th-century social élite as the baths had done for their Roman forebears. It was primarily a meeting place, somewhere to see and be seen, as described in the novels of Jane Austen. Today visitors to the Pump Room can enjoy a traditional pot of tea or sample a glass of spa water from the pump fountain.

ROYAL ACADEMY OF ARTS

LOCATION: Piccadilly, London W1V 0DS
TEL: 0171 300 8000
ADM: Prices vary per exhibition, usually between £3–£9
OPENING TIMES: Daily 10–6, late night Friday until 8.30pm; individual exhibition times vary
GETTING THERE: *Underground:* Piccadilly Circus, Green Park
Bus: 9, 14, 19, 22, 38 stop at the Academy's gate, 3, 6, 12, 13, 88, 159 stop at Piccadilly Circus
FACILITIES: Restaurant, café, shop
DISABLED: Wheelchair access to all areas, wheelchair hire available in advance
WEBSITE: www.royalacademy.org.uk

The list of former Royal Academicians reads like a Who's Who of British art.

The Royal Academy of Arts was founded by George III in 1768 and was the first institution in Britain to be devoted solely to the promotion of the visual arts. It's unique in that it is governed and run by artists rather than academics or government appointees. The list of former Royal Academicians reads like a Who's Who of British art—Sir Joshua Reynolds, Constable, Gainsborough, Turner and Stanley Spencer among them—all of whom have donated work to the Academy's permanent exhibition. Current members of the academy include Peter Blake and David Hockney.

The great joy of the Royal Academy is that you are guaranteed to see something different every time you visit. Most of the gallery space is devoted to loans and temporary exhibitions. The proposed 1999 programme will include an exhibition of 'Monet in the Twentieth Century', featuring some 80 works including one never before seen in public; a selection of Kandinsky watercolours; and, to commemorate the 400th anniversary of the birth of Van Dyck, the great portraitist of royals past, an exhibition of his work held under the patronage of royals present: Her Majesty the Queen and King Albert II and Queen Paulo of Belgium.

ROYAL MUSEUM OF SCOTLAND

LOCATION: Chambers Street, Edinburgh EH1 1JF
TEL: 0131 225 7534
OPENING TIMES: Mon, Wed–Sat 10–5, Tues 10–8, Sun 12–5
ADM: Adults £3, Child free, Conc's £1.50 (ticket includes entry to National Museum of Scotland); Season ticket £5, Conc's £2.50, free entry on Tues 4.30–8
GETTING THERE: *Road:* A1, A703
Train: Waverley station
Bus: Most buses from Princes Street go past the museum
FACILITIES: Café and tearoom, museum shop, free guided tours, metered parking in streets around the museum
DISABLED: Museum is fully accessible with lifts to all floors and adapted toilets
WEBSITE: www.nms.ac.uk

There's a wonderfully eclectic range of exhibits on display in this Crystal Palace-like iron and glass building.

On Chambers Street, next to the memorial to Greyfriars Bobby, stands the Royal Museum of Scotland which, along with the new National Museum of Scotland next door, represents Edinburgh's answer to London's Kensington museum complex. There's a wonderfully eclectic range of exhibits on display in this Crystal Palace-like iron and glass building, including some exquisite French silverware from the reign of Louis XIV; ceramics from ancient Greece, sculptures from Rome and Assyria, and even a native American totem pole. There's also an interactive technology section where, in amongst the steam behemoths of industrial Britain, you can find the 1896 Hawk Glider, Britain's first flying machine. There are also sections devoted to oriental art, geology, fossils, ethnology and natural history—the last a veritable temple to taxidermy with cases and cases full of stuffed animals and birds.

SCIENCE MUSEUM

LOCATION:
Exhibition Road,
London SW7 2DD
TEL: 0171 938 8008
OPENING TIMES:
10–6 daily
ADM: Adult £6.50,
Child £3.50,
Conc's £3.50
GETTING THERE:
Underground:
South Kensington
Bus: 9, 10, 14, 49,
52, 74, 345, C1
FACILITIES:
Museum shop,
Dillons Bookstore,
post office,
Bureau de Change,
cash machine

Children's affection for this collection of whirring gizmos and gadgets is such that the museum has recently started letting them spend the night. At these evening campnights mini science nuts are treated to an after-hours tour of the building, workshops and bedtime stories. The rest of the population, who must visit this most fun of museums in daylight, can only look on with envy.

On the ground floor, dedicated to industrial and technological progress, you will find steam engines (including Stephenson's 'Puffing Billy'), a model reworking of Foucault's Pendulum (the device which first illustrated the turning of the earth), a World War II V2 rocket and the Apollo 10 space capsule. The Launch Pad, on the first floor, is full of flashing beeping interactive displays and as a result is permanently inhabited by

DISABLED:
An 'Access and Facilities Guide' is available. Disabled Person's Enquiry Line 0171 938 9788
WEBSITE:
www.nmsi.ac.uk

throngs of wide-eyed kids. Adults wearing a similar expression can be found in the Science of Sport gallery, where pride of place is given to a £2 million Formula 1 McLaren.

In 2000 the museum will open a new £47 million 10,000 square metre wing, which will increase the available floor area of the museum by a third. It will be dedicated to explaining the most modern of scientific and technological breakthroughs, such as the Internet and genetic engineering. It will also hold an IMAX (large screen) 3D film theatre.

THE SHAKESPEARE HOUSES

LOCATION: The Shakespeare Centre, Henley Street, Stratford-upon-Avon CV37 6QW
TEL: 01789 204 016
OPENING TIMES: Times vary per house and according to season, but usually open daily between 9.30/10–4/5
ADM: Joint ticket for all 5 houses £10, for 3 houses £7, otherwise each house £4.50, tour bus with commentary linking 5 houses £8

The Shakespeare Houses is a tour around the five buildings in Stratford-upon-Avon where the bard spent much of his early and later life. He was born in 1562 in a small house on Henley Street, where today you can find some beautiful period furniture and a small interactive display on his life. Nearby, at the home of his mother, Mary Arden, there are daily falconry displays. In 1582 the 20-year-old William married Anne Hathaway, the daughter of a local farmer. Her house, the next on the tour, is a beautifully preserved thatched Tudor farmhouse. Soon after, he moved to London, where his plays enjoyed such success that by the time he returned to Stratford in 1611 he was the shareholder in a new theatre, the Globe, on the south bank of the River Thames, and had been granted royal patronage by

GETTING THERE: Call no. above for details of individual houses
FACILITIES: Teashops at Mary Arden and Hall's Croft
DISABLED: Wheelchair access to Hall's Croft only
WEBSITE: www.shakespeare.org.uk

James I. With his new-found wealth he bought New Place, one of the largest houses in Stratford, where he would spend his final years. It was destroyed in the 18th century although the Elizabethan knot garden remains. He also spent much of his later life at Hall's Croft, a lovely gabled property and the home of Dr John Hall, who married Shakespeare's daughter.

SNOWDONIA NATIONAL PARK

SNOWDONIA NATIONAL PARK
LOCATION: National Park Office, Penrhydendraeth, Gwynedd LL48 6LP
TEL: 01766 770 274
GETTING THERE:
Road: A55, A470, A487, A5, A494, A458
Train: Harlech, Barmouth, Betws-y-Coed, Bangor, Llanfayrfechan stations
FACILITIES: Lots of visitor centres dotted around, some village shops and post offices operate as tourist information points, giving free literature. Recognisable from blue 'i' logo
DISABLED: No specific facilities

HARLECH CASTLE
LOCATION: Castle Square, Harlech, Gwynedd LL46 2YH
TEL: 01766 780 552
OPENING TIMES: April–Oct 9.30–6.30 daily, Nov–Mar Mon–Sat 9.30–4, Sun 11–4
ADM: Adult £3, Child & Conc's £2, Family £8
GETTING THERE:
Road: A496
Train: Barmouth, Port Madoc stations
FACILITIES: Limited parking, souvenir shop
DISABLED: No wheelchair access

The Snowdonia National Park covers an area of 840 square miles in north-west Wales, a vast swathe of countryside made up of a myriad different landscapes: woodlands of ash, oak and hazel, steep glacial valleys, waterfalls and lakes. The latter includes Llyn Tegid, Wales' largest freshwater lake, which, according to local legends, was either formed when the keeper of Gaver's Well forgot to replace the lid one night or was the result of a flood sent to punish a cruel local ruler; rowing boats, sailboards and fishing permits are available from the lake warden. This is a walker's paradise with literally hundreds of well marked routes of varying degrees of difficulty—some more or less flat, others practically vertical. There are castles, such as the beautifully preserved 13th-century Harlech with its commanding views

over Cardigan Bay and Caernarfon (*see* p.15), manor houses, farmhouses and cottages as well as caravan and picnic sites. The whole area is brimming with wildlife, including fish, wild fowl and otters. In fact, there are more nature reserves in Snowdonia than in any other national park in Britain. The park is also home, of course, to the snow-capped splendour of Mount Snowdon which, at 3,560ft, is the tallest peak in England or Wales. A steam railway chugs its way from Llanberis to the summit in a little under two and a half hours, where you can take refreshment in the café and bar, write a postcard and pop it into the highest postbox in the UK.

ST PAUL'S CATHEDRAL

LOCATION: Ludgate Hill, London EC4M 8AD
TEL: 0171 236 4128
OPENING TIMES: Mon–Sat 8.30–4
ADM: Cathedral only: Adult £4, Child £2, Conc's £3.50; Charge for Galleries Adult £3.50, Child £1.50, Conc's £3

GETTING THERE: *Underground:* St Paul's, Mansion House *Train:* City Thameslink *Bus*: 4, 8, 11, 15, 17, 23, 25, 26, 56, 76, 172, 242, 501, 521
FACILITIES: Cathedral shop, guided tours available
DISABLED: No wheelchair access to Galleries, access all other areas
WEBSITE: www.stpauls.london.anglican.org

St Paul's Cathedral is one of London's greatest landmarks, an icon of the city itself, as familiar as Tower Bridge or Big Ben. Prior to the creation of Sir Christopher Wren's masterpiece, the site was occupied by a Gothic cathedral topped with a massive 500ft spire. It burned down in the Great Fire of London with only a single statue of John Donne surviving. Wren's plans for a replacement cathedral initially met with considerable resistance. Intriguingly, it was the notion of a dome which particularly aroused

the Church authorities' hostility—'too Popish'. Twice Sir Christopher submitted plans for a domed cathedral and twice they were rejected. Wren, convinced of the merits of a dome, persevered and was rewarded with a warrant of approval from the King allowing him to overule the church's objections. Nonetheless, the construction of the cathedral was carried out in as secret a manner as possible, with whole sections under wraps, to prevent further interference.

Time has proved the worth of Wren's vision. Interior highlights include the Whispering Gallery, 100ft up (so named because it is possible to whisper something on one side and have it heard on the other, 107ft away) and the beautiful carved choir stalls of Grinling Gibbons. There are fantastic views across the City of London from the Golden Gallery, 365ft up, just below the cathedral's topmost ball and cross.

STONEHENGE

LOCATION: Salisbury Plain, Wiltshire
TEL: 01980 624 715
OPENING TIMES: 16 Mar–31 May 9.30–6, 1 Jun–31 Aug 9–7, 1 Sep–15 Oct 9.30–6, 16 Oct–15 Mar 9.30–4
ADM: Adult £3.90, Child £2.90, Conc's £2, Family £9.80
GETTING THERE: *Road:* 2 miles west of Amesbury on the junction of the A303 & A344/A360
Train: Salisbury station is 9.5m away
Bus: Call 01722 336 855 for details
FACILITIES: Parking available, gift shop, refreshments
DISABLED: Wheelchair access
WEBSITE: www.english-heritage.org.uk

As one of the world's most famous prehistoric monuments, Stonehenge has been much studied and yet is still only partially understood. What was the precise purpose of the stones? The significance of their astronomical alignments? The reason why the great blocks had to be transported all the way from south Wales? There are many questions still unanswered.

In the Sixties, the henge was adopted by many as a symbol of peace and renewal. However, clues hinting at a more grisly purpose have been found at nearby Wood Henge, a similar, albeit organic, monument where, in the centre of a circle of wooden posts, archaeologists have found the remains of a little girl axed to death as part of an ancient ceremony. It should be remembered that when they were first erected, sometime between 3000 and 1600 BC, the stones would have stood, not as they do now in splendid isolation, but rather as part of an extensive network of similar ceremonial monuments.

What isn't in doubt is the skill of the builders, who managed not only to transport the huge stones vast distances, but also, working with only very basic tools, erected and connected them using mortice and tenon and tongue and groove joints. Their expertise is evident in the fact that, 4000 years after they finished the job, around half of the structure is still standing.

STRATHCLYDE COUNTRY PARK

LOCATION:
Hamilton Road,
Motherwell ML1 3EA
TEL: 01698 266 155
OPENING TIMES:
Park, 9.30–dusk;
M&D's Theme Park, call 01698 333 777 for details
ADM: Entry to the park is free. M&D's Theme Park is also free entry, unlimited rides pass Adult £9.95, Child £6.75, Family £30, individual rides from 50p

Set in the industrial heart of Scotland, these 1,100 acres of mature woodland, rough wetland, wildlife refuges and neat open parkland constitute Britain's most popular country park. Over 4 million people visit the area each year to fish, go horse-riding or just sit and enjoy the spectacular rolling views. The focal point of the park is its loch, a great stretch of water home to cormorants, coots, mute swans and black swans as well as otters, water voles and even the odd osprey. Should you feel inspired to examine the wildlife more closely, you can hire rowing boats and canoes from the Watersports Centre. Fishing permits are also available; the loch is well stocked with bream, roach, carp and tench.

GETTING THERE:
Road: From South: M74 J5 or 6, from North & West: M8, M74, J5 or 6, from East: M8, A725
Train: Nearest station is Motherwell
FACILITIES:
Free car parking, on-site Holiday Inn, picnic sites, cafés, restaurants, water sports centre, mountain bike hire, pub, caravan & camping site, guided walks
DISABLED:
Wheelchair access to theme park

Other activities catered for within the confines of the park include horseriding—there are seven miles of bridle paths—and mountain biking.

A less strenuous alternative might involve a leisurely stroll through some of the park's 250 acres of mixed deciduous woodland, passing through the remains of a Roman fort and bathhouse on the way, before finishing up in the excellent loch-side restaurant.

As the sun sets, bathing the tree tops in a soft golden light, it's time to break the tranquillity and take a trip on the Tornado, Scotland's largest rollercoaster in M&D's, the park's very own theme park.

The focal point of the park is its loch, a great stretch of water home to cormorants, coots, mute swans and black swans.

THE TATE GALLERY

LOCATION: Millbank, London SW1P 4RG
TEL: 0171 887 8008
OPENING TIMES: 10–5.50 daily
ADM: Free, charges apply for some temporary exhibitions
GETTING THERE: *Underground:* Pimlico, Vauxhall *Train*: Vauxhall *Bus*: 2, 3, 36, 77A, 88, 159, 185, 507, C10
FACILITIES: Restaurant, café, shop
DISABLED: Wheelchair access, disabled parking spaces in the Clore car park can be booked on 0171 887 8813/4
WEBSITE: www.tate.org.uk

The Tate Gallery was founded in 1897 by Sir Henry Tate as a showcase for British art. Over the succeeding century, however, it built up such a collection of international art, including works by Dalí, Matisse, Picasso and Warhol, that the amount of space given over to domestic product was necessarily reduced. That interest in a gallery devoted to British art still exists is demonstrated by the public's attendance of the Turner Prize; the gallery recently had to take the unprecedented step of closing the entrance doors early to prevent overcrowding. The need for a more coherent and structured approach to the bulging collection has led to two radical plans. A new £130 million Tate Gallery of Modern Art (*see* p.54) is to be opened in May 2000 at Bankside, liberating much-needed space at the Tate, which, in turn, is to have its own rebirth in 2001 as the Tate Gallery of British Art, renewing Sir Henry Tate's vision and concentrating on the history, evolution and future of British art. The £32.3 million development project will provide a chronological display of British art since 1500 and three major exhibitions a year will be held, augmented by smaller shows. The Tate's renowned education programmes will be improved with a new education centre and advanced facilities, including the British Art Information Project, which will allow access to the Tate's collection via the Internet.

THE TATE GALLERY OF MODERN ART

LOCATION:
Gallery: Bankside, London SE1 9JU, Visitor Centre: 25 Summer Street, London SE1 9JU
TEL: Visitor Centre 0171 401 7302 (information point until the Gallery's opening in May 2000)
OPENING TIMES:
Centre open by appointment Mon–Fri 10–5
ADM: Free
GETTING THERE:
To the Visitor Centre: *Underground:* London Bridge, Blackfriars
Train: London Bridge
To the Gallery: Proposed new transport links include the new Jubilee line station, the extension of Blackfriars station south of the river and a jetty stop for a river boat service
WEBSITE:
www.tate.org.uk

The new Tate Gallery of Modern Art is due to open in May 2000, as one of the Millennium Commission's landmark projects. This revamped power station opposite St Paul's Cathedral will, it is confidently predicted, become one of the most important museums of modern art in the world, rivalling such big names as the Guggenheim and Centre Pompidou. A huge glass structure will span the length of the 8.5-acre roof, beneath which will be three enormous levels where fine art, architecture, design, film and the decorative arts will all have their own dedicated sections. Three big loan exhibitions a year are planned and there will also be a 'projects programme' which will invite artists to create works for specific sites around the building. The Tate is taking its responsibilities as a good neighbour seriously and plans to take an active role in the much-needed regeneration of the borough of Southwark by operating 'outreach projects' with the local community and collaborating closely with schools and community groups. It is expected that around two million people a year will visit the new £130 million state-of-the-art Gallery.

One of the most important museums of modern art in the world, rivalling such big names as the Centre Pompidou.

THORPE PARK

LOCATION: Staines Road, Chertsey, Surrey KT16 8PN
TEL: 01932 562 633
OPENING TIMES: Mar–Oct, times vary but usually opens at 9.30 or 10am and closes between 5pm and 7.30pm
ADM: Adult £16.50, Child £13, Under 1m free, Conc's £13, Disabled Adult £13, Disabled Child £10

All theme parks need a show-piece ride, a glittering piece of terror-inducing hardware to set against the competition. Thorpe Park's champion is the bizarrely titled 'X:/ No Way Out', which, although not the first rollercoaster to operate in pitch darkness, is certainly the first to force its passengers to travel at speeds of around 65 mph in the dark…backwards.

This concession to modern super-thrill-seeking trends aside, most of the attractions at Thorpe Park have clearly been designed to cater for families rather than adrenalin junkies. Children are particularly well provided for, with various cutesily–named

GETTING THERE:
Road: M25 J11 or 13 (no access from J12), A320
Train: Chertsey station
FACILITIES: Parking, various fast food outlets, gift shop, baby changing facilities
DISABLED: Wheelchair access, adapted toilets
WEBSITE: www.thorpepark.co.uk

theme areas such as Mrs Hippo's Jungle Safari and Mr Monkey's Banana Ride, as well as Model World, which features miniature versions of the Eiffel Tower, the Pyramids and Stonehenge. They can also take a boat ride to the Thorpe Farm to bond with the resident goats, sheep and rabbits. Swimwear is a must, however, unless you want to return home with a car full of bedraggled children; there are more water-themed attractions here than at most parks, including the tallest log flume in the country; Thunder River, an ersatz white-water rafting adventure; and several pools and water chutes.

THE TOWER OF LONDON

LOCATION: Tower Hill, London EC3N 4AB
TEL: 0171 709 0765
OPENING TIMES: Mar–Oct Mon–Sat 9–5, Sun 10–5; Nov–Feb Tue–Sat 9–4, Sun–Mon 10–4
ADM: Adult £10.50, Child £6.90, Conc's £7.90, Family £31
GETTING THERE: *Underground:* Tower Hill
Bus: 15, 25, 42, 78, 100, D1
FACILITIES: Car park, 4 shops, restaurant, coffee stall
DISABLED: Very limited wheelchair access, call 0171 403 1115 for access guide
WEBSITE: www.tower-of-london.com/

Keeping guard over Tower Bridge, this is one of the best preserved medieval castles in the world. Built during the reign of William I, it has been used in its time as a stronghold for fugitive princes, as a jail for traitors and as the setting for some of British history's most notorious executions. Lady Jane Grey, Anne Boleyn and Walter Raleigh all ate their final meals here.

Today, the Tower's principal purpose is somewhat less dramatic. It is a Royal Museum dedicated to the preservation of all things monarchical. The Crown Jewels are here as are various suits of armour including Henry VIII's bespoke model. The continued presence of the Tower's resident raven population is supposedly a prerequisite for the continued survival of the monarchy.

The Tower, previously rather hard on the legs, has in recent years become more user–friendly: there is a moving walkway to take you past the Crown Jewels, and the Tower Hill Pageant is a sort of underground ghost train ride past tableaux of famous historical episodes, with regular battle re-enactments by members of the English Civil War Society. And, of course, there are always the Yeoman Guards, or Beefeaters, to guide you around the principal sights.

THE VICTORIA & ALBERT MUSEUM

LOCATION:
Cromwell Road,
London SW7 2RL
TEL: 0171 938 8500
OPENING TIMES:
Mon 12–5.50,
Tue–Sun 10–5.50,
Wed Late View
6.30–9.30 (seasonal)
ADM: Adult £5, Child, Disabled and their Helpers free, OAP's £3; free entry after 4.30pm

Perhaps the V&A's most impressive feature is the sheer scope of its collection. These seven miles of galleries are stuffed to bursting with accumulated treasures: silverware, suits of armour, tapestries, paintings, sculptures, plaster casts, shoes, wallpaper—almost anything, in fact, which could possibly be categorised under the heading Art and Design. The variety is quite mind-boggling: there's a wonderful dress gallery where you can trace the evolution of fashion from the 17th century to the present day, from corsets, bodices and other forms of elaborate bondage to flapper dresses,

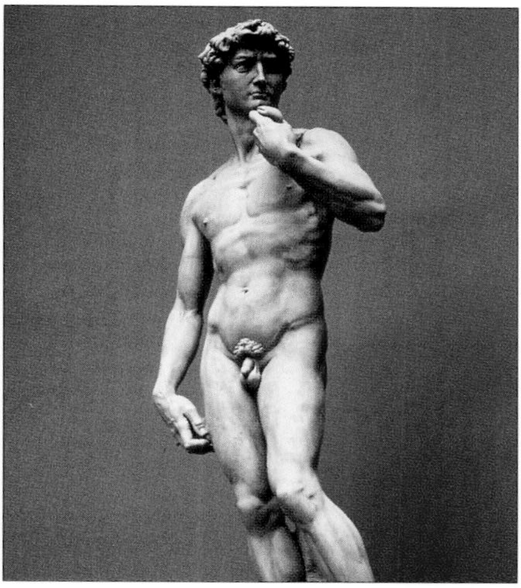

Huge plaster cast models of the world's great sculptures—from Trajan's column (in two pieces) through Ghiberti's Gates of Paradise to Michelangelo's David

GETTING THERE:
Underground: South Kensington
Bus: C1, 14 and 74
FACILITIES:
Licensed restaurant, gift/book shops
DISABLED:
Wheelchair access to most of the museum. Use Exhibition Road entrance or call 0171 938 8638 to book an escort in advance
WEBSITE:
www.vam.ac.uk

miniskirts and stilettos; a gallery devoted to William Morris, the high priest of wallpaper; an oriental art section; a medieval tapestry section; a collection of Raphael cartoons; the greatest collection of Renaissance sculpture outside Italy; the greatest collection of Constables in the world; and the plaster cast room which, above all the other galleries, perhaps best encapsulates the essence of this temple of artifice and decoration—it is both the most impressive gallery in the museum and the one place without a single original artefact. Huge plaster cast models of the world's great sculptures, from Trajan's column (in two pieces) through Ghiberti's Gates of Paradise to Michelangelo's David, are on display in a vast hall. In part, it is the display's lack of design, with the casts placed seemingly quite at random, which gives it its great charm.

WARWICK CASTLE

LOCATION: Warwick, Warwickshire CV34 4QU
TEL: 01926 495 421
OPENING TIMES: Apr–Oct 10–6, Nov–Mar 10–5
ADM: Adult £9.25, Child £5.60, Under 4's free, Conc's £6.65, Family £26
GETTING THERE: *Road:* M40 J15 *Train:* Warwick station

Warwick is one of the oldest and most evocative castles in England. Most of the present structure was built in the 14th and 15th centuries, although parts date back to the 10th century when it was home to Ethelfleda, daughter of Alfred the Great. In the Middle Ages the castle provided the backdrop for some of England's greatest intrigues and scandals. In the 14th century it was owned by Richard Neville, the Earl of Warwick, known as 'The Kingmaker', the man who deposed both Henry VI and Edward IV. The Kingmaker exhibition in the castle's undercroft is an atmospheric tableau which aims, with the help of some suitably spooky lighting and sound effects, to bring to life the preparations for the Earl's final battle. Visitors to the castle are also told the tale of Fulke Greville, a private landowner who converted the castle into a private mansion at the beginning of the 17th century and was brutally murdered by his manservant in 1628.

In the armoury you can try on medieval helmets and chain mail and practise a few thrusts and parries with a medieval sword.

The magnificent grounds were laid out in the 18th century by Lancelot 'Capability' Brown and in summer play host to re-enactments of jousts and knights' combat.

FACILITIES: Free car park, 2 restaurants, café, gift shop
DISABLED: Wheelchair access to ground floor only, adapted toilets, disabled parking
WEBSITE: www. warwick-castle.uk

WESTMINSTER ABBEY

LOCATION:
Parliament Square, London SW1P 3PA
TEL: 0171 222 7110
OPENING TIMES:
Mon–Fri 9–4.45, Sat 9–2.45pm
ADM: Adult £5, Child £2, Conc's £3, Family £10
GETTING THERE:
Underground: Westminster station
Bus: 3, 11, 12, 24, 53, 88, 109, 159, X53, 211
FACILITIES:
Museum, brass-rubbing centre, audio tour, book and souvenir shop
DISABLED:
Wheelchair access
WEBSITE: www.westminster-abbey.org

Westminster Abbey has, for a thousand years, been the focal point of England's royal, political and cultural life, the epicentre of Englishness, where every king and queen is crowned and buried, where every great statesman has a memorial plaque and where every great scientist, artist and writer is remembered. In recent decades, views of the abbey have been beamed around the world at times of great national significance. Two of the most watched TV events in history, the coronation of Elizabeth II and the funeral of Princess Diana, took place here, when the huge vaulted interior became the image of England for the whole world.

The construction of the abbey required an effort of suitably regal proportions. Begun in the 13th century by Henry III, the nave wasn't finished until 1532 whilst the towers were only added in 1745. Recently the similarly mammoth task of cleaning the exterior was completed, the grime and grit of centuries stripped away to reveal the beautiful sandy–coloured stone beneath—regular hawk patrols are in operation to stop nesting pigeons from restarting the deterioration process.

The abbey has the tallest nave in England at 103ft and around it are the collected reminders and relics of the great and the good from the last 1,000 years of English history.

WHIPSNADE WILD ANIMAL PARK

LOCATION:
Dunstable, Bedfordshire LU6 2LF
TEL: 0990 200 123
OPENING TIMES:
10–4 daily
ADM: Adult £9.50, Child £7, Conc's £7,

Disabled/Helper free
GETTING THERE:
Road: 20 mins from M25 J21; signposted from M1 J9 & 12. Just 'follow the elephants'
Train:
Luton and Hemel Hempstead stations
Bus: Shires Services from Luton and Dunstable, call 0345 788 788, Green Line buses from London Victoria (summer only), call 0181 688 7261
FACILITIES:
Gift/book shops, cafés around park, free bus around park
DISABLED:
Wheelchair access to most of the park, wheelchair hire available
WEBSITE:
www.york.biosis.org/zrdocs/zsl.htm

The opening of Whipsnade Wild Animal Park in 1931 was a landmark event in the history of wildlife conservation. It was Britain's first 'open' wildlife park, the first to house its animals in large open paddocks (rather than cages) designed to mimic as closely as possible the animal's natural environment. Today, spread over 6,000 acres of Bedfordshire countryside, Whipsnade is home to over 2,500 animals ranging from elephants, giraffes and rhinos to penguins, sea lions and chimps. Most inhabit large fenced enclosures although there are also some 'free' areas where peacocks, deer and wallabies can roam more or less at will. Staring benignly down upon the park is the famous Whipsnade lion, a 460ft-wide chalk picture cut into the Chiltern hillside in 1932.

Visitors to the park can choose to explore its attractions in one of four ways: by car, following the marked one-way route; by open-top tour bus; aboard the park's steam railway, which gently chugs its way around two miles of track; or even, in the free areas, on foot.

Not all of the park's residents live outdoors. Displayed in the Discovery Centre, in

a series of controlled environments, are animals from some of the world's most inhospitable regions. Many of the reptiles here have been bequeathed to the park by Her Majesty's Customs officials, having been seized from people attempting to smuggle them into the country. For younger visitors there are daily demonstrations of bird handling and animal talks.

WINDERMERE LAKE CRUISES

LOCATION: Launches: Bowness on Windermere, Cumbria LA23 3HQ. Steamers: Lakeside, Newby Bridge, Ulverston, Cumbria LA12 8AS
TEL: Launches 01539 531 188. Steamers 01539 443 360
OPENING TIMES: Open most of the year; earliest departures 9.05, latest 6.35
ADM: Two fare brackets available: boat only and boat & train/aquarium. Boat only returns Adult £5.50, Child £2.75. Boat & train/aquarium Adult £8.35, Child £4.25. Freedom of the Lake ticket Adult £9, Child £4.50, Family £24.50. Half-lake cruise ticket Adult £5.70, Child £2.85. Under 5's and 'well-behaved dogs' travel free
GETTING THERE: *Road:* M6 J36, A590 Newby Bridge Road *Train:* Windermere, Oxenholme stations
FACILITIES: 300 parking spaces, coach parking, restaurants, cafés, licensed bars on boats. Gift shops on some steamers
DISABLED: Steamers suitable for wheelchair users but toilet facilities only access by stairs. Adapted toilets at Lakeside and Ambleside
WEBSITE: www.marketsite.co.uk/lakes

Imagine yourself leaning against the rail of a classic 1930s steamer, glass of wine in hand, gazing out at some of England's most beautiful scenery as the sun begins to dip below the snowy mountain-peaked horizon. This, or something very like it, is what Windermere Lake Cruises hopes to offer. It's by far the most popular boating excursion in Britain, probably because of the great variety of cruises on offer. You can take a full three-hour jaunt around England's largest lake, all 21 miles of it, a half–length version (1½ hours) or opt for one of their wide variety of themed cruises. There's an island cruise, a wine cruise, a lunch cruise (which stops off at some of the elegant waterfront hotel restaurants), an evening buffet cruise and even a submarine dive to the lake's shipwreck-laden bottom.

A 'Freedom of the Lakes' pass provides 24 hours unlimited travel on all the company's boats—there are launches as well as steamers allowing you to stop off at whichever of the lakeside attractions take your fancy. You can choose from the Windermere Steamboat Museum, the Beatrix Potter museum, the Lake District National Park Visitor Centre with its 30 acres of terraced gardens, or the Aquarium of the lakes, home to the largest collection of freshwater fish in England. You might even like to recreate a day-trip from yesteryear with a steam cruise to Lakeside and then a jaunty ride along the Old Furness Steam Railway Line through the Lake District's beautiful poet-inspiring countryside.

WINDSOR CASTLE

LOCATION:
Windsor, Berkshire
SL4 1NJ
TEL: 01753 868286
0171 839 1377,
Infoline
01753 831118
OPENING TIMES:
Mar–Oct 10–5.30
(last admissions
5pm), Nov–Feb 10–4
(last admissions
3pm)
ADM: Mon–Sat Adult
£10, Child £5, Conc's
£7.50; Sun Adult
£8.50, Child £4,
Conc's £6.50
GETTING THERE:
Road: M4 exit 6;
M3 exit 3.
Train: London
Waterloo direct to
Windsor (every
30mins Mon–Fri).
London Paddington
via Slough (every
30mins Mon–Sun).
Coach: Victoria
coach station at
regular intervals
throughout day,
call 0181 668 7261
for details
FACILITIES: Coach
parking available
10 mins from castle
DISABLED:
Wheelchair access
to most areas of
castle
WEBSITE:
www.royal.gov.uk

from the top on a clear day, you can see no less than 12 counties

This splendid concoction of towers, ramparts and pinnacles is today the official residence of the Queen and the setting for innumerable state banquets and functions. The first wooden castle, built by William the Conqueror some 900 years ago to protect the western approach to the capital, was replaced with a stone version by Henry II 100 years later. A survivor from this time is the famous Round Tower, from the top of which, on a clear day, you can see no less

than 12 counties. Later architectural highlights include St George's Chapel, founded in 1475 by Edward IV and finished by Henry VIII, with its amazing fan-vaulted ceiling, and the Queen Mary Doll's House, built by Edward Lutyens in the 1920s with perfectly scaled furniture and decorations.

In 1992, the State Apartments were ravaged by fire although, following £37 million worth of restoration work, you would be hard-pressed to tell. They are today as opulent as they ever were, and decorated with hundreds of priceless paintings from the royal collection, including Van Eycks and Rembrandts, as well as porcelain, armour, fine furniture and the carvings of Grinling Gibbons.

WISLEY GARDENS

LOCATION: Wisley, Woking, Surrey GU23 6QB
TEL: 01483 224 234
OPENING TIMES: Mon–Fri 10–sunset, Sat–Sun 9–sunset. Members only on Sun
ADM: Adult £5, Child £2, under 6's free, disabled/helpers free
GETTING THERE: *Road:* M25 Exit 10; follow brown tourist signs with flower symbol
Train: West Byfleet station 3 miles away; Woking station 5 miles away.
Bus: Call Guildford bus station for details 01483 572 137
FACILITIES: Free parking, restaurant, café, plant centre, book & gift shop
DISABLED: Free map showing best route around garden for wheelchair users. Shop, café & plant centre accessible. Adapted toilets
WEBSITE: www.rhs.org.uk

Set up by the Royal Horticultural Association in 1904, Wisley has become, over the course of the century, one of the country's best loved gardens. Although most people come to enjoy the beautiful planted borders, delightful rose gardens and glasshouses, there is a more prosaic side to Wisley. It is also a valuable and well respected agricultural institute where cultivation techniques such as composting and pleaching are tried and tested and experimental model gardens are grown. The Gardens' Temperate Glass House was re-landscaped in the summer of 1998 and now contains a waterfall and pool. Elsewhere in this 240-acre site, you can find a traditional country garden, a farm, an orchard, some delightful woodland and the new Garden of the Senses where a major collection of bonsai is displayed. Every August there is a popular flower show. Living souvenirs can be picked up from the nursery.

Beautiful planted borders, delightful rose gardens and glasshouses...

YORK MINSTER

LOCATION:
Deangate,
York YO1 2HG
Visitor's Department:
St Williams College,
5 College Street,
York YO1 7JF
TEL: 01904 639 347
OPENING TIMES:
Summer 7–8.30pm;
Winter 7–6.
No sightseeing permitted before 1pm on Sundays
ADM: Free, donations welcome
GETTING THERE:
Road: From South M18 J2, A1, A64, follow signs to York. From North A68, A1, A59, follow signs to York
Train: Served by GNER, Regional Railways, Virgin Cross Country, North Western
Coach: National Express provides regular services to York from all major cities in the UK
FACILITIES: Gift shop, conference centre, restaurant and catering facilities
DISABLED:
Some areas not accessible for wheelchairs, various facilities available for the visually impaired and hard of hearing
WEBSITE: www.yorkminster.org

The largest Gothic cathedral in northern Europe, York Minster is a supreme example of English medieval architecture. Its builders took a long time making sure they got it just so—begun in 1220, it was finally completed 250 years later.

Despite a couple of inflammatory episodes—fires in 1829 and 1984, started respectively by an arsonist and a lightning bolt, destroyed much of the original roof—today York Minster contains more medieval glass than any other church in England; approximately half, in fact, of all the medieval glass known to exist. After the latest fire the roof was rebuilt at a cost of £2 million using, where possible, the traditional methods and materials of medieval builders.

The inside of the minster is dominated by the fantastic stained glass east window which tells the stories of Genesis and Revelations, the top and tail of the Bible, in 27 exquisitely rendered panels. Other highlights include the wonderfully ornate ceiling of the Chapter House and the choir screen, decorated with sculptures of every king from William the Conqueror to Henry VI. You can also climb the tower for some fabulous views over the city of York.

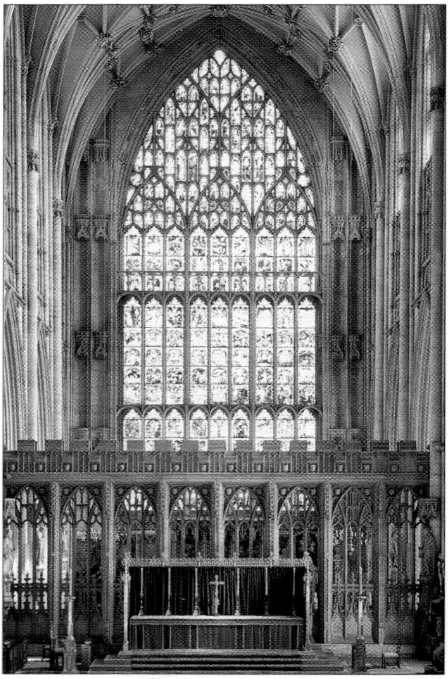

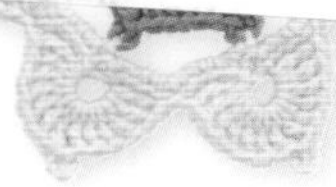

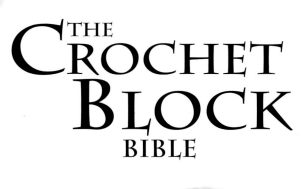

THE CROCHET BLOCK BIBLE

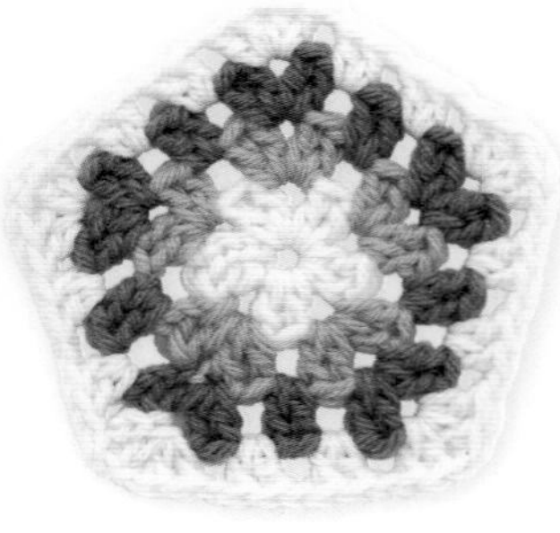

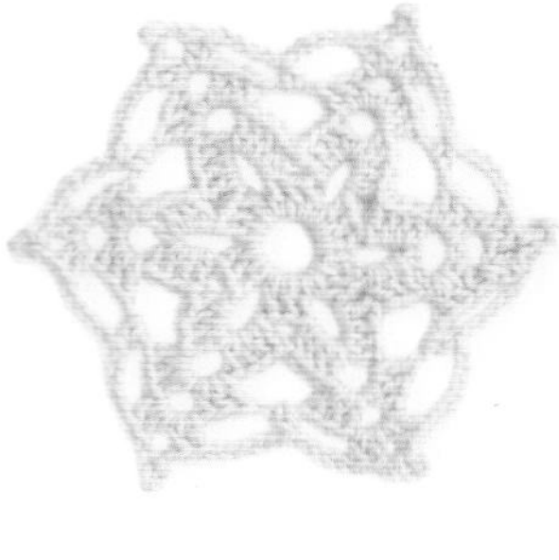

THE CROCHET BLOCK BIBLE

Luise Roberts and Heather Lodinsky

Search Press

A QUARTO BOOK

Published in 2015 by
Search Press Ltd
Wellwood
North Farm Road
Tunbridge Wells
Kent TN2 3DR

ISBN: 978-1-78221-373-4

Conceived, designed and produced by
Quarto Publishing plc
The Old Brewery
6 Blundell Street
London N7 9BH

QUAR.CBLB

Technical consultant: Leonie Morgan
Illustrators: Kuo Kang Chen, Coral Mula, Luise Roberts
Photographers: Paul Forrester, Phil Wilkins
Art director: Caroline Guest
Creative director: Moira Clinch
Publisher: Paul Carslake

The material in this book previously appeared in *150 Knit & Crochet Motifs* by Heather Lodinsky and *Crochet Blocks in a Box* by Luise Roberts.

Colour separation by
Cypress Colours (HK) Ltd, Hong Kong
Printed by
Midas Printing International Ltd, China

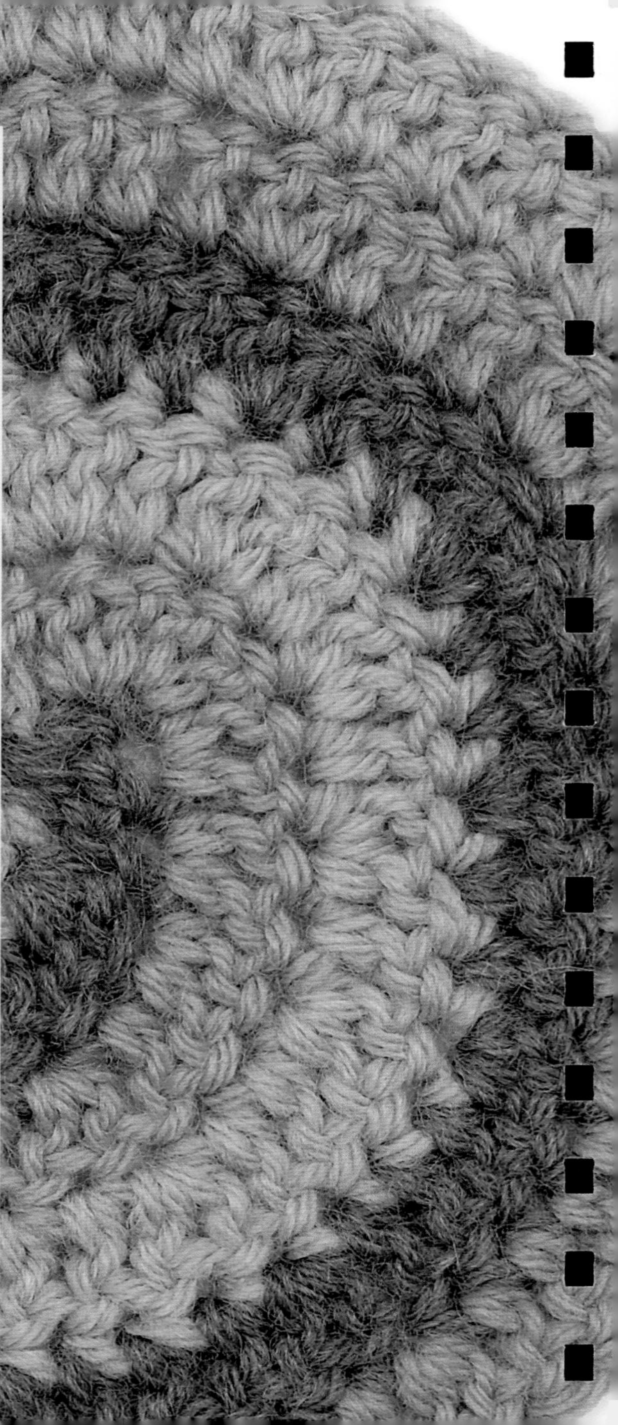

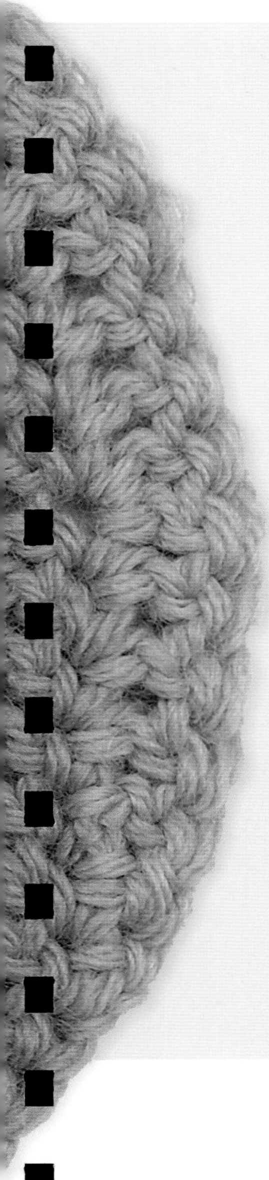

Contents

About This Book

This book features 100 fabulous crochet blocks, in a range of shapes and sizes, that can be mixed and matched and made into all sorts of projects, from throws and cushions to bags, scarves and even toys.

Block designs (pages 8–207)

In the main section of the book you will find instructions on how to create 100 different crochet blocks. Organised by shape, and by skill level within each shape, this section contains full instructions, a photograph and a chart to aid you in the creation of your chosen design.

Techniques (pages 208–223)

This section explains how to fit the different shaped blocks together for your particular project. There is a handy stitch reminder of all the basic crochet stitches used in the book, details of blocking and joining methods, and tips on choosing yarn and calculating how much to buy. At the end you will find a list of the pattern abbreviations and chart symbols.

SKILL LEVEL

You don't need advanced crochet skills to make any of the blocks in this book but some require more concentration than others.

Beginner

Some experience required

More challenging

SIZE OF BLOCKS

The blocks fall into four size categories:

1 Small: 9–12cm ($3\frac{1}{2}$–$4\frac{3}{4}$in)
2 Medium: 12–15cm ($4\frac{3}{4}$–6in)
3 Large: 15–18cm (6–7in)
4 Extra large: 18–21cm (7–$8\frac{1}{4}$in)

All of the blocks shown in the photographs have been made using either DK-weight yarn on a 4.5mm hook or Aran-weight yarn on a 5.5mm hook. This information is provided beside the photograph of the block.

The size of the blocks you make yourself will depend on the type of yarn you select and the tension at which you crochet. See Choosing Yarn (page 209) and Tension (page 219) for further details.

DIRECTION OF WORK

Worked in rows: This symbol shows that the block has been worked backwards and forwards in rows.

Worked in rounds: This symbol is used for blocks worked in the round from the centre outwards.

Some blocks are accompanied by both symbols because part of the pattern is worked in rows and part in rounds.

Block number

Block name

Additional materials such as beads

Shape/pattern category

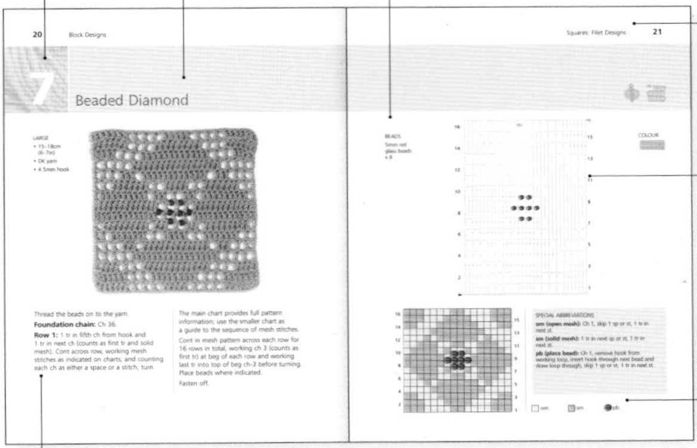

Charts amplify the written instructions. They are colour-coded to match the yarns used in the sample. Some blocks have more than one chart.

Key to chart where needed

Skill level

Written pattern instructions

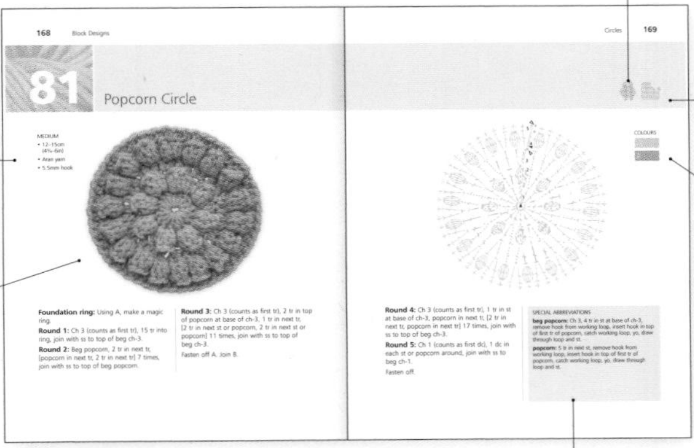

Direction of working

Size guide when worked using stated yarn and hook size

Yarn colours used

Photograph of block

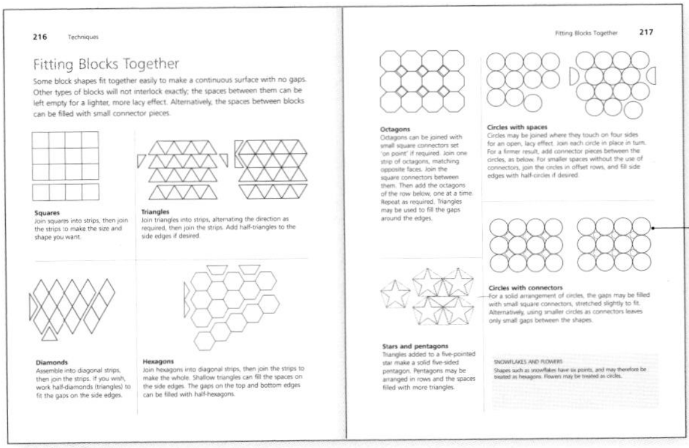

216 Techniques
Fitting Blocks Together
Some block shapes fit together easily to make a continuous surface with no gaps. Other types of blocks will not interlock exactly; the spaces between them can be left empty for a lighter, more lacy effect. Alternatively, the spaces between blocks can be filled with small connector pieces.
Squares
Join squares into strips, then join the strips to make the size and shape you want.
Triangles
Join triangles into strips, alternating the direction as required, then join the strips. Add half-triangles to the side edges if desired.
Diamonds
Assemble into diagonal strips, then join the strips. If you wish, work half-diamonds (triangles) to fit the gaps on the side edges.
Hexagons
Join hexagons into diagonal strips, then join the strips to make the whole. Shallow triangles can fill the spaces on the side edges. The gaps on the top and bottom edges can be filled with half-hexagons.
Fitting Blocks Together 217
Octagons
Octagons can be joined with small square connectors set "on point" if required. Join one strip of octagons, matching opposite faces. Join the square connectors between them. Then add the octagons of the row below, one at a time. Repeat as required. Triangles may be used to fill the gaps around the edges.
Circles with spaces
Circles may be joined where they touch on four sides for an open, lacy effect. Join each circle in place in turn. For a firmer result, add connector pieces between the circles, as below. For smaller spaces without the use of connectors, join the circles in offset rows, and fill side edges with half-circles if desired.
Circles with connectors
For a solid arrangement of circles, the gaps may be filled with small square connectors, stretched slightly to fit. Alternatively, using smaller circles as connectors leaves only small gaps between the shapes.
Stars and pentagons
Triangles added to a five-pointed star make a solid five-sided pentagon. Pentagons may be arranged in rows and the spaces filled with more triangles.
SNOWFLAKES AND FLOWERS
Shapes such as snowflakes have six points, and may therefore be treated as hexagons. Flowers may be treated as circles.

Special abbreviations, instructions, additional notes or tips

The techniques section features concise explanations of how to work crochet stitches plus advice on turning the blocks into projects, including how to fit different shapes together.

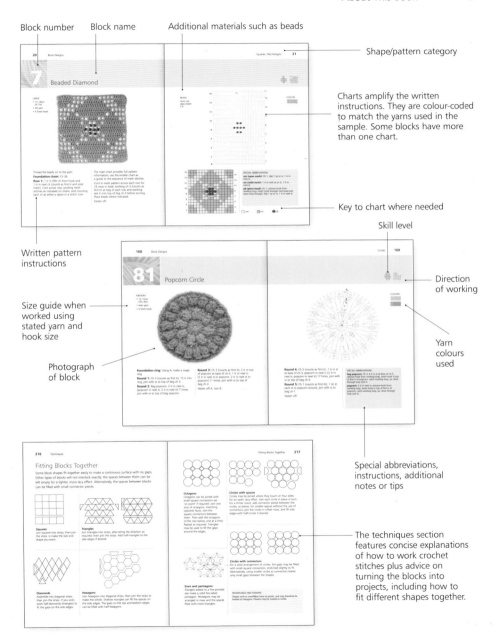

1 Concentric Squares

LARGE
- 15–18cm (6–7in)
- DK yarn
- 4.5mm hook

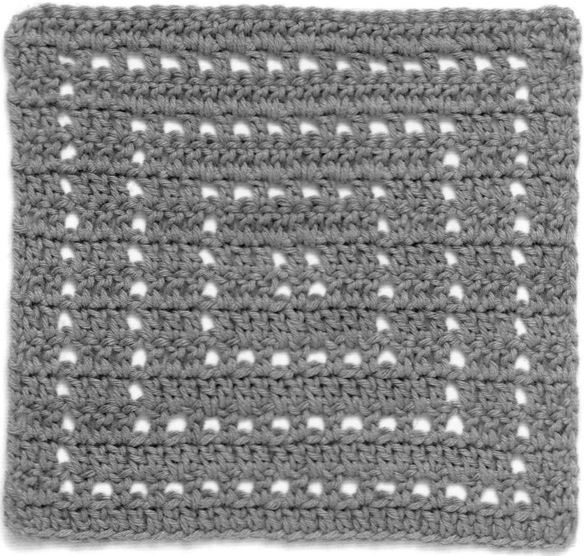

Foundation chain: Ch 36.

Row 1: 1 tr in fifth ch from hook and 1 tr in next ch (counts as first tr and solid mesh). Cont across row, working mesh stitches as indicated on charts, and counting each ch as either a space or a stitch, turn.

The main chart provides full pattern information; use the smaller chart as a guide to the sequence of mesh stitches.

Cont in mesh pattern across each row for 16 rows in total, working ch 3 (counts as first tr) at beg of each row and working last tr into top of beg ch-3 before turning.

Fasten off.

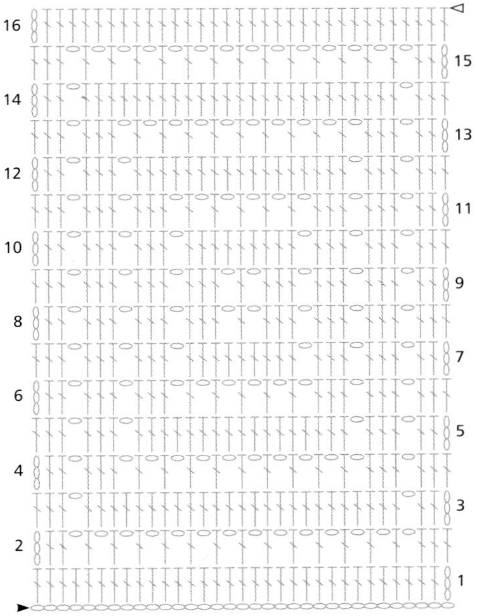

COLOUR

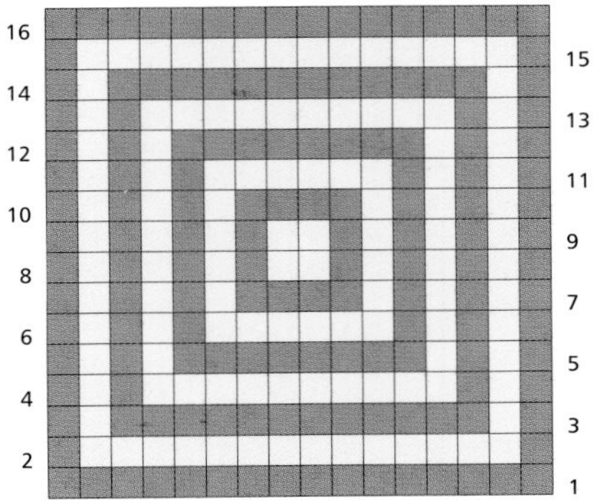

SPECIAL ABBREVIATIONS

om (open mesh): Ch 1, skip 1 sp or st, 1 tr in next st.

sm (solid mesh): 1 tr in next sp or st, 1 tr in next st.

om sm

2 Spiral Blocks

LARGE

- 15–18cm (6–7in)
- DK yarn
- 4.5mm hook

Foundation chain: Ch 36.

Row 1: 1 tr in fifth ch from hook and 1 tr in next ch (counts as first tr and solid mesh). Cont across row, working mesh stitches as indicated on charts, and counting each ch as either a space or a stitch, turn.

The main chart provides full pattern information; use the smaller chart as a guide to the sequence of mesh stitches.

Cont in mesh pattern across each row for 16 rows in total, working ch 3 (counts as first tr) at beg of each row and working last tr into top of beg ch-3 before turning.

Fasten off.

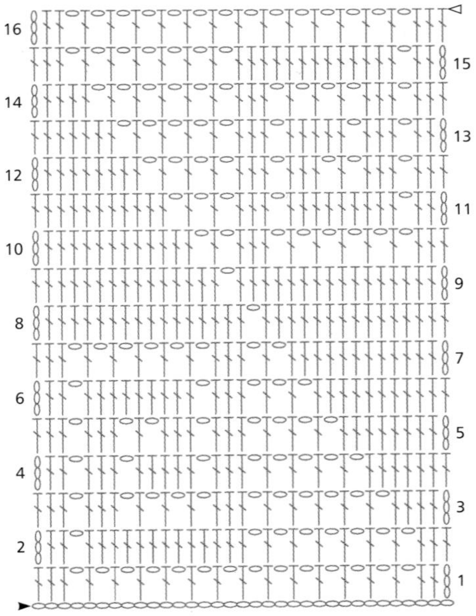

COLOUR

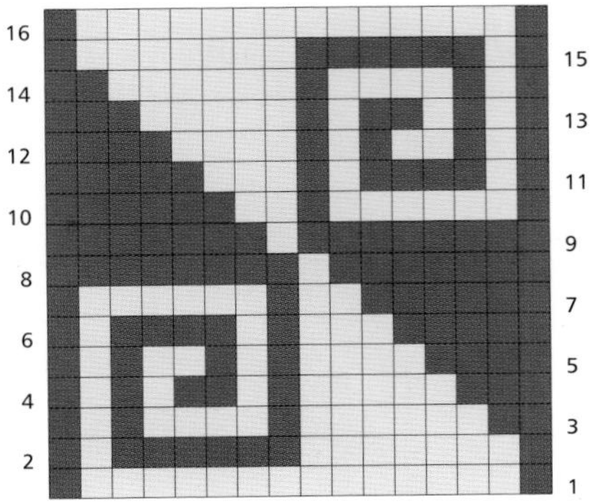

SPECIAL ABBREVIATIONS

om (open mesh): Ch 1, skip 1 sp or st, 1 tr in next st.

sm (solid mesh): 1 tr in next sp or st, 1 tr in next st.

om

sm

3 Octagon Rose

LARGE

- 15–18cm (6–7in)
- DK yarn
- 4.5mm hook

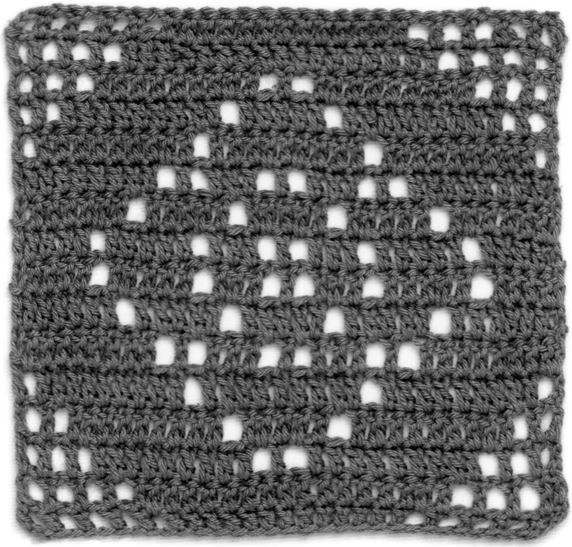

Foundation chain: Ch 37.

Row 1: 1 tr in seventh ch from hook (counts as first tr and open mesh). Cont across row, working mesh stitches as indicated on charts, and counting each ch as either a space or a stitch, turn.

The main chart provides full pattern information; use the smaller chart as a guide to the sequence of mesh stitches.

Cont in mesh pattern across each row for 16 rows in total, working ch 3 (counts as first tr) at beg of each row and working last tr into top of beg ch-3 before turning.

Fasten off.

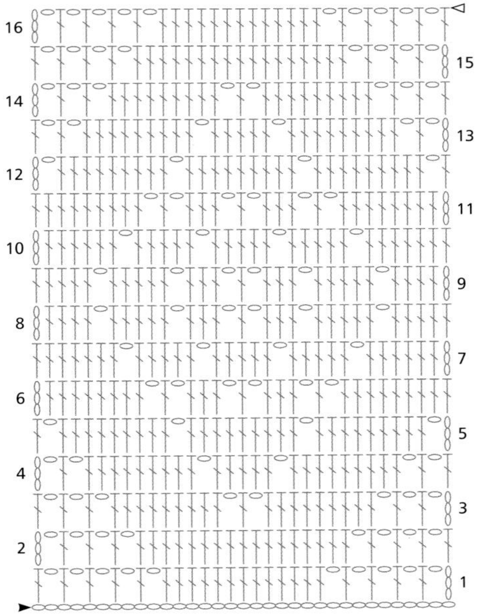

COLOUR

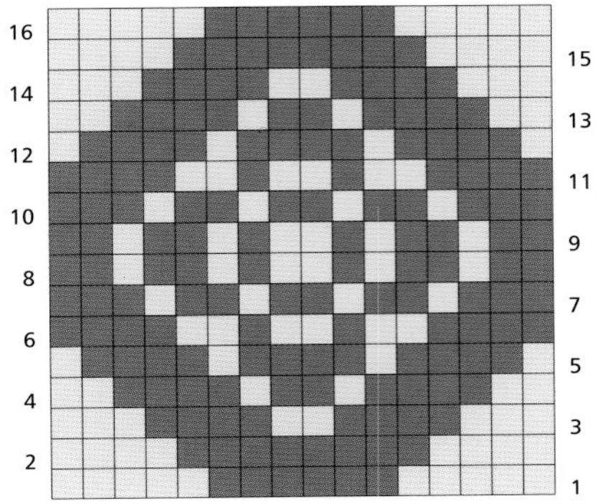

SPECIAL ABBREVIATIONS

om (open mesh): Ch 1, skip 1 sp or st, 1 tr in next st.

sm (solid mesh): 1 tr in next sp or st, 1 tr in next st.

om

sm

4 Runway

LARGE
- 15–18cm (6–7in)
- DK yarn
- 4.5mm hook

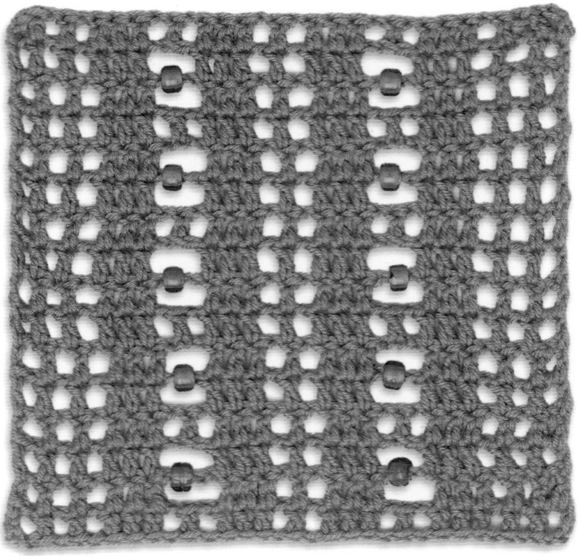

Thread the beads on to the yarn.

Foundation chain: Ch 37.

Row 1: 1 tr in seventh ch from hook (counts as first tr and open mesh). Cont across row, working mesh stitches as indicated on charts, and counting each ch as either a space or a stitch, turn.

The main chart provides full pattern information; use the smaller chart as a guide to the sequence of mesh stitches.

Cont in mesh pattern across each row for 16 rows in total, working ch 3 (counts as first tr) at beg of each row and working last tr into top of beg ch-3 before turning. Place beads where indicated.

Fasten off.

BEADS

6mm turquoise glass beads x 10

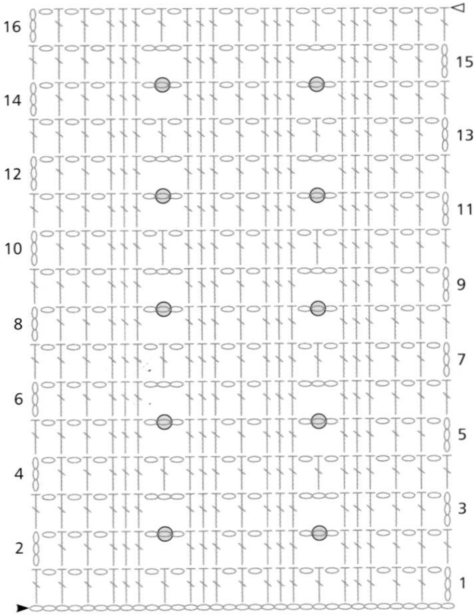

COLOUR

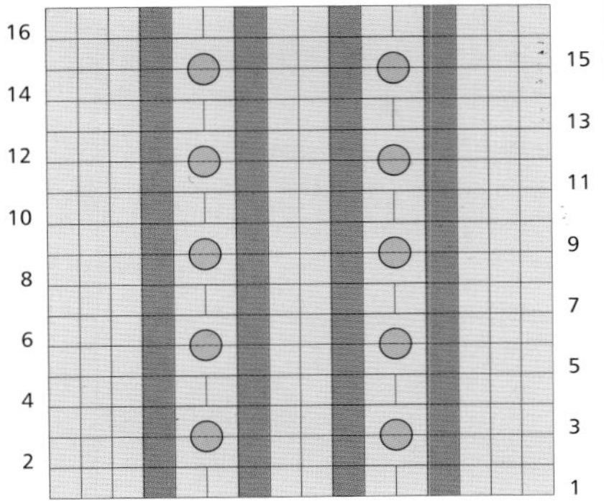

SPECIAL ABBREVIATIONS

om (open mesh): Ch 1, skip 1 sp or st, 1 tr in next st.

sm (solid mesh): 1 tr in next sp or st, 1 tr in next st.

dom (double open mesh): Ch 3, skip 3 ch, 1 tr in next st.

pb (place bead): Ch 3, remove hook from working loop, insert hook through next bead and draw loop through, skip 1 tr, 1 tr in next st.

om sm pb dom

5 Lacy Heart

LARGE
- 15–18cm (6–7in)
- DK yarn
- 4.5mm hook

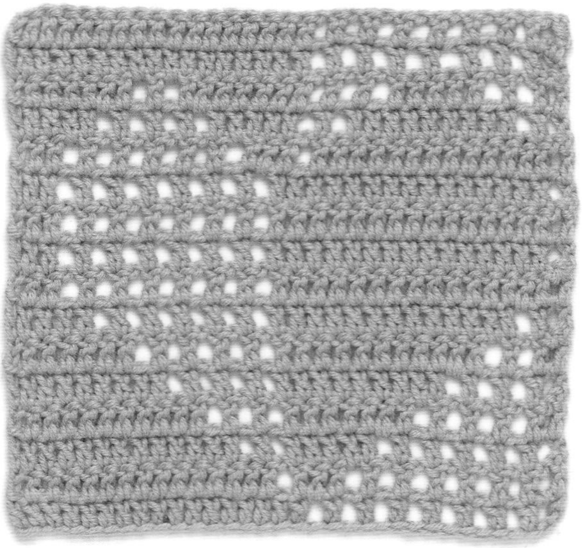

Foundation chain: Ch 37.

Row 1: 1 tr in seventh ch from hook (counts as first tr and open mesh). Cont across row, working mesh stitches as indicated on charts, and counting each ch as either a space or a stitch, turn.

The main chart provides full pattern information; use the smaller chart as a guide to the sequence of mesh stitches.

Cont in mesh pattern across each row for 16 rows in total, working ch 3 (counts as first tr) at beg of each row and working last tr into top of beg ch-3 before turning.

Fasten off.

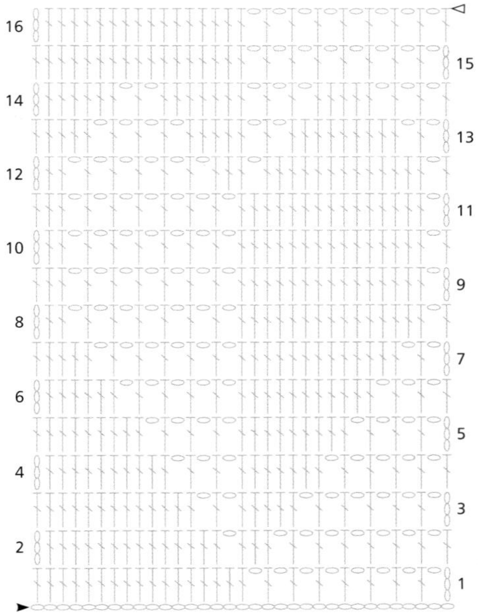

COLOUR

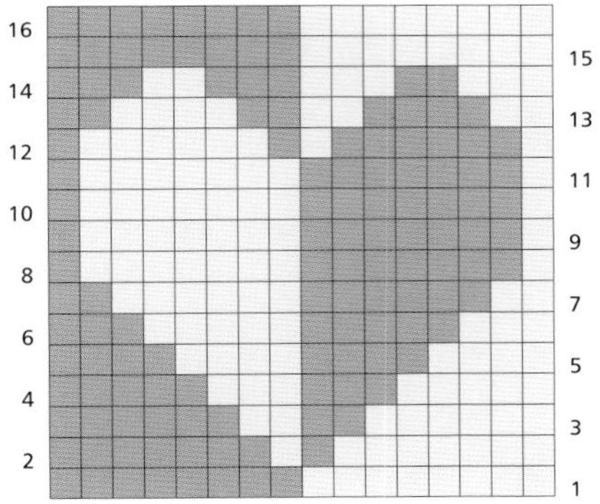

SPECIAL ABBREVIATIONS

om (open mesh): Ch 1, skip 1 sp or st, 1 tr in next st.

sm (solid mesh): 1 tr in next sp or st, 1 tr in next st.

om sm

6 Lacy Eight-pointed Star

LARGE

- 15–18cm (6–7in)
- DK yarn
- 4.5mm hook

Foundation chain: Ch 37.

Row 1: 1 tr in seventh ch from hook (counts as first tr and open mesh). Cont across row, working mesh stitches as indicated on charts, and counting each ch as either a space or a stitch, turn.

The main chart provides full pattern information; use the smaller chart as a guide to the sequence of mesh stitches.

Cont in mesh pattern across each row for 16 rows in total, working ch 3 (counts as first tr) at beg of each row and working last tr into top of beg ch-3 before turning.

Fasten off.

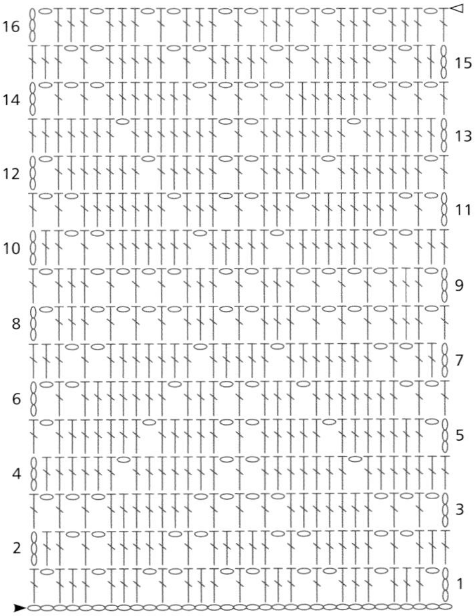

COLOUR

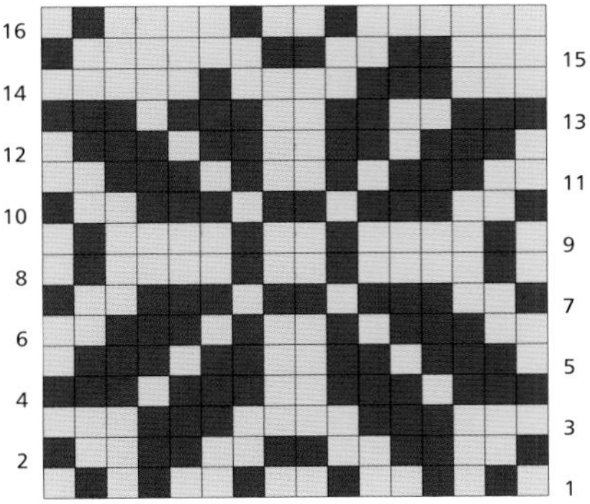

SPECIAL ABBREVIATIONS

om (open mesh): Ch 1, skip 1 sp or st, 1 tr in next st.

sm (solid mesh): 1 tr in next sp or st, 1 tr in next st.

om sm

7 Beaded Diamond

LARGE
- 15–18cm (6–7in)
- DK yarn
- 4.5mm hook

Thread the beads on to the yarn.

Foundation chain: Ch 36.

Row 1: 1 tr in fifth ch from hook and 1 tr in next ch (counts as first tr and solid mesh). Cont across row, working mesh stitches as indicated on charts, and counting each ch as either a space or a stitch, turn.

The main chart provides full pattern information; use the smaller chart as a guide to the sequence of mesh stitches.

Cont in mesh pattern across each row for 16 rows in total, working ch 3 (counts as first tr) at beg of each row and working last tr into top of beg ch-3 before turning. Place beads where indicated.

Fasten off.

BEADS

5mm red glass beads x 8

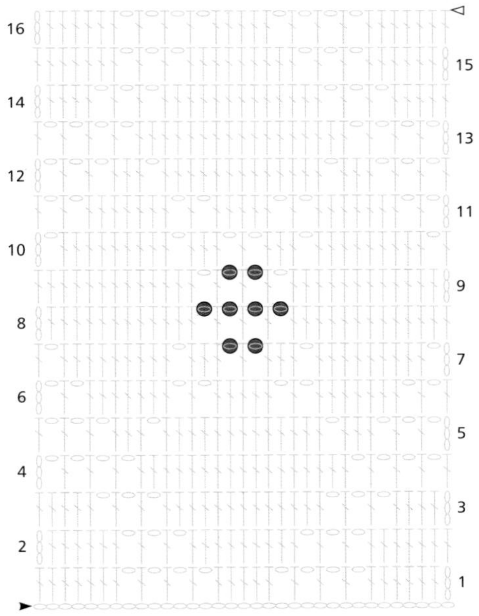

COLOUR

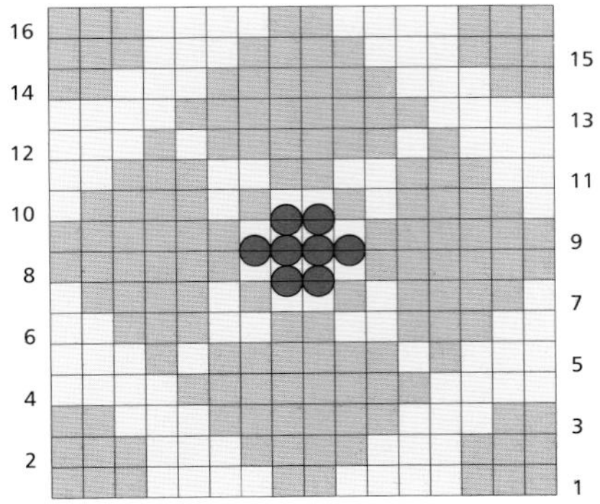

SPECIAL ABBREVIATIONS

om (open mesh): Ch 1, skip 1 sp or st, 1 tr in next st.

sm (solid mesh): 1 tr in next sp or st, 1 tr in next st.

pb (place bead): Ch 1, remove hook from working loop, insert hook through next bead and draw loop through, skip 1 sp or st, 1 tr in next st.

om sm pb

8 Gerbera

LARGE

- 15–18cm (6–7in)
- DK yarn
- 4.5mm hook

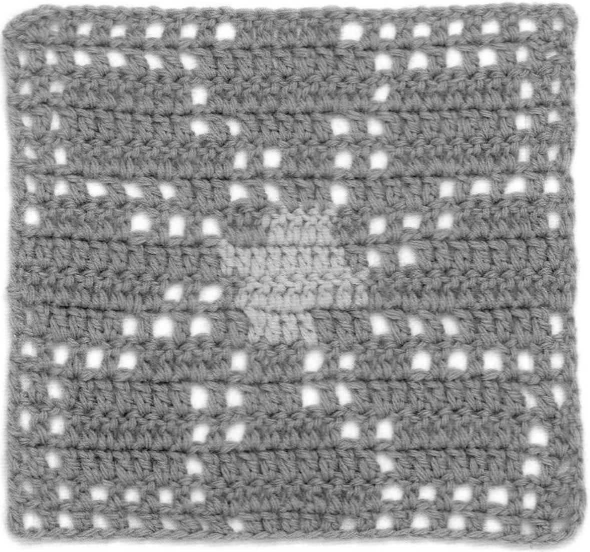

Foundation chain: Using A, ch 37.

Row 1: 1 tr in seventh ch from hook (counts as first tr and open mesh). Cont across row, working mesh stitches as indicated on charts, and counting each ch as either a space or a stitch, turn.

The main chart provides full pattern information; use the smaller chart as a guide to the sequence of mesh stitches.

Cont in mesh pattern across each row for 16 rows in total, working ch 3 (counts as first tr) at beg of each row and working last tr into top of beg ch-3 before turning. Change colours where indicated, weaving in A on reverse of each st worked in B (see page 101).

Fasten off.

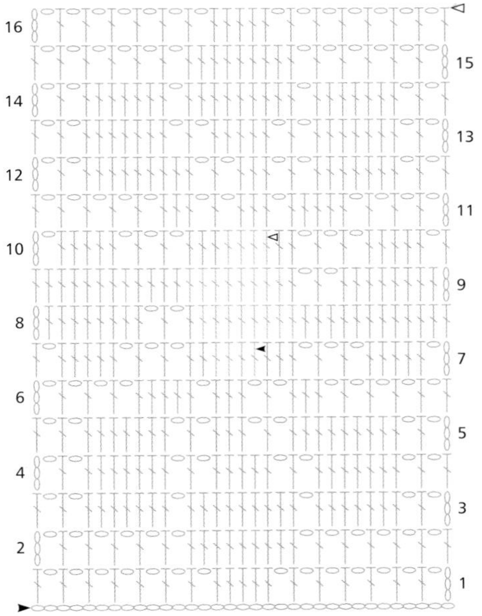

COLOURS

A

B

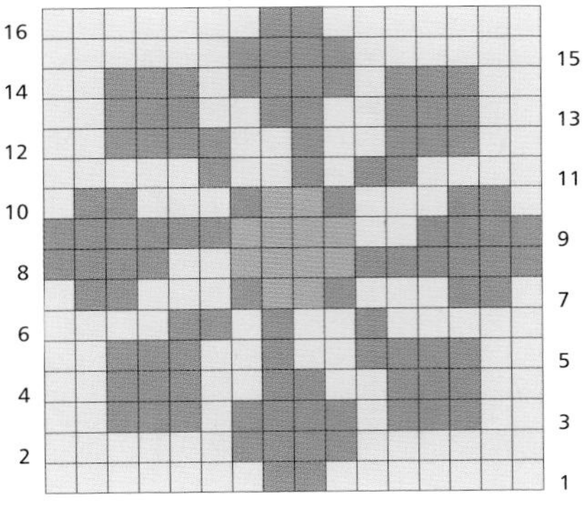

SPECIAL ABBREVIATIONS

om (open mesh): Ch 1, skip 1 sp or st, 1 tr in next st.

sm (solid mesh): 1 tr in next sp or st, 1 tr in next st.

om in A

sm in A

sm in B

9 Large Leaf

LARGE

- 15–18cm (6–7in)
- DK yarn
- 4.5mm hook

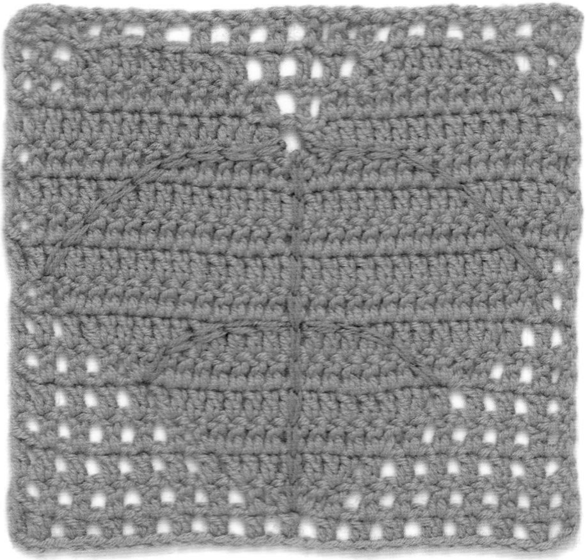

Foundation chain: Using A, ch 37.

Row 1: 1 tr in seventh ch from hook (counts as first tr and open mesh). Cont across row, working mesh stitches as indicated on charts, and counting each ch as either a space or a stitch, turn.

The main chart provides full pattern information; use the smaller chart as a guide to the sequence of mesh stitches.

Cont in mesh pattern across each row for 16 rows in total, working ch 3 (counts as first tr) at beg of each row and working last tr into top of beg ch-3 before turning. The heart is shaped by working increases and decreases leaning to the left or right.

Surface crochet

Using B and referring to main chart and photograph as a guide, work surface chain sts for the leaf veins. Fasten off.

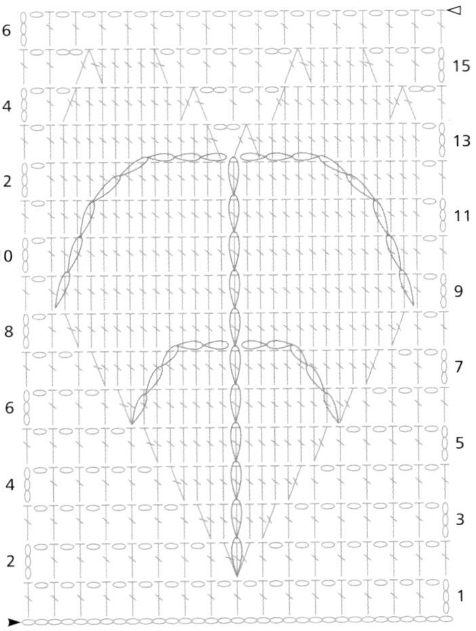

COLOURS

A

B

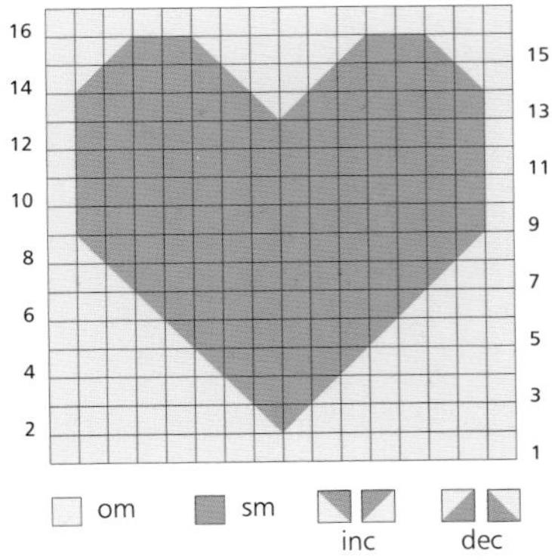

SPECIAL ABBREVIATIONS

om (open mesh): Ch 1, skip 1 sp or st, 1 tr in next st.

sm (solid mesh): 1 tr in next sp or st, 1 tr in next st.

inc (increase): For right-leaning increase, skip 1 sp or st, 2 tr in next tr. For left-leaning increase, 1 tr in same st as last tr, skip 1 sp or st, 1 tr in next st.

dec (decrease): For right-leaning decrease, tr2tog working in last st, skip 1 sp or st, and in next st, ch 1. For left-leaning decrease, ch 1, tr2tog over next 2 sts.

Note: The chart on the left shows the right side. Reverse the shaping on wrong-side rows – e.g., a left-leaning increase on the front becomes a right-leaning increase on the reverse.

10 Little Gems

LARGE
- 15–18cm (6–7in)
- DK yarn
- 4.5mm hook

Foundation chain: Using A, ch 37.

Row 1: 1 tr in seventh ch from hook (counts as first tr and open mesh). Cont across row, working mesh stitches as indicated on charts, and counting each ch as either a space or a stitch, turn.

The main chart provides full pattern information; use the smaller chart as a guide to the sequence of mesh stitches.

Cont in mesh pattern across each row for 16 rows in total, working ch 3 (counts as first tr) at beg of each row and working last tr into top of beg ch-3 before turning. Change colours to work bobbles where indicated.

Fasten off.

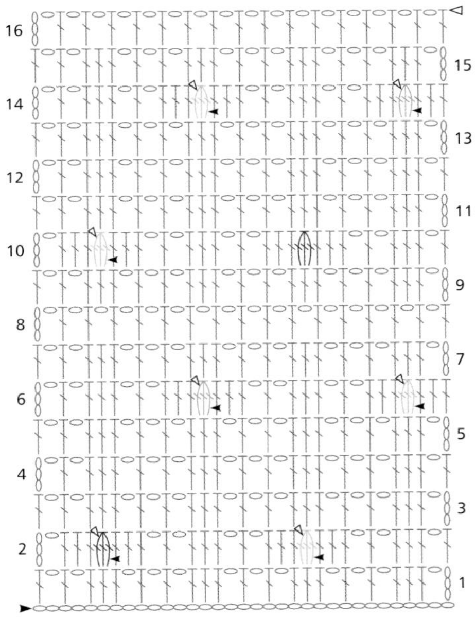

COLOURS

A

B

C

D

E

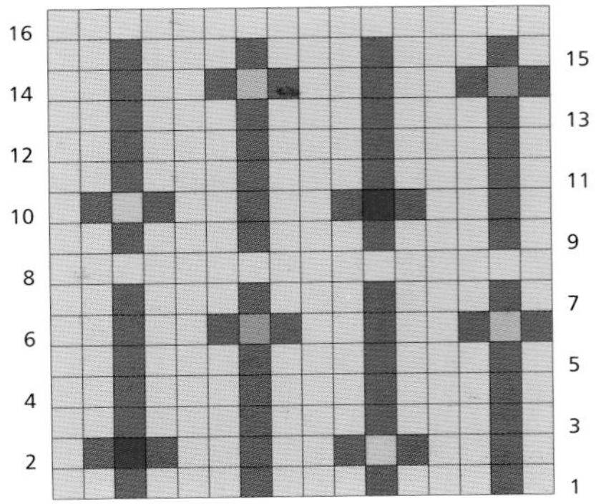

SPECIAL ABBREVIATIONS

om (open mesh): Ch 1, skip 1 sp or st, 1 tr in next st.

sm (solid mesh): 1 tr in next sp or st, 1 tr in next st.

bm (bobble mesh): Using bobble colour, *insert hook in next st, yo, draw loop through, yo, draw yarn through 2 loops on hook; rep from * twice more into same st, yo, draw yarn through all 3 loops, fasten off bobble colour; using A, 1 tr in next st to complete mesh.

om in A

sm in A

bm in colour indicated

11 Bamboo

LARGE
- 15–18cm (6–7in)
- DK yarn
- 4.5mm hook

Foundation chain: Ch 37.

Row 1: 1 tr in seventh ch from hook (counts as first tr and open mesh). Cont across row, working mesh stitches as indicated on charts, and counting each ch as either a space or a stitch, turn.

The main chart provides full pattern information; use the smaller chart as a guide to the sequence of mesh stitches.

Cont in mesh pattern across each row for 16 rows in total, working ch 3 (counts as first tr) at beg of each row and working last tr into top of beg ch-3 before turning. Work leaves where indicated.

Fasten off.

COLOUR

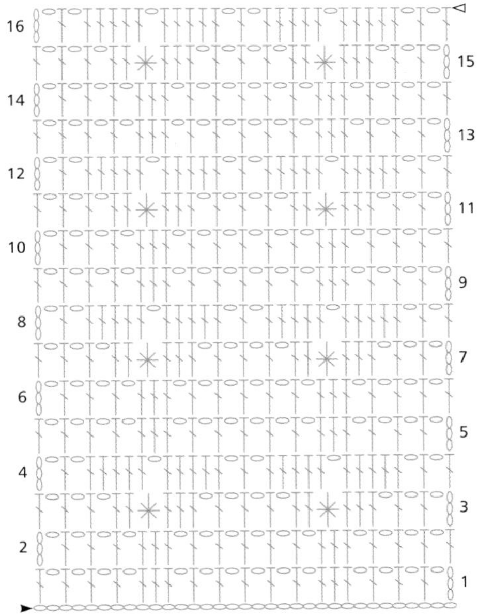

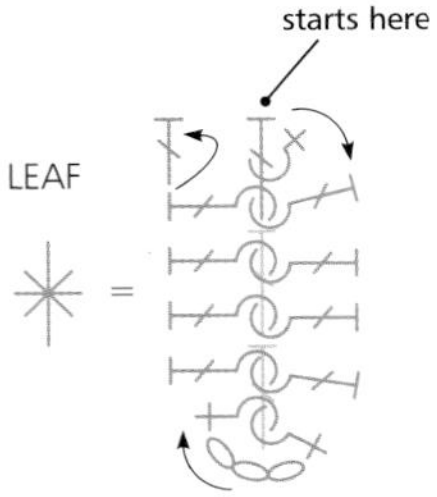

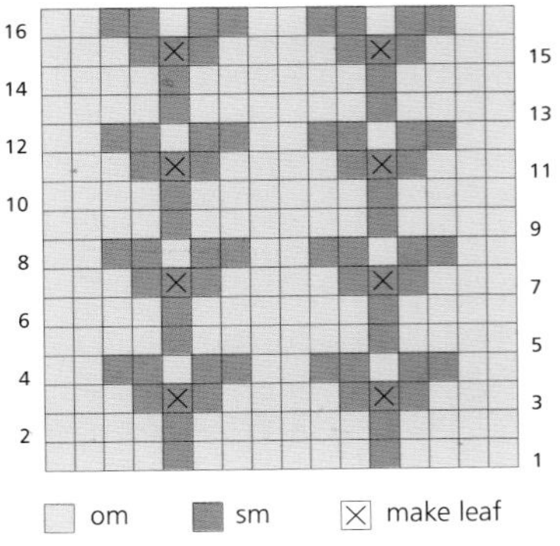

SPECIAL ABBREVIATIONS

om (open mesh): Ch 1, skip 1 sp or st, 1 tr in next st.

sm (solid mesh): 1 tr in next sp or st, 1 tr in next st.

make leaf: 1 tr in next st, 1 FPdc and 1 FPtr around same st, 2 FPtr around st on row below, 1 FPtr and 1 FPdc around st on row below that, ch 3. Working around sts just worked, 1 FPdc between dc and tr, 1 FPtr above tr, 1 FPtr between 2 tr on next row, 1 FPtr above tr, 1 FPtr between tr and dc on next row. Working along row in original direction, 1 tr in next st to complete mesh.

12 Layered Spiral

LARGE

- 15–18cm (6–7in)
- DK yarn
- 4.5mm hook

Foundation chain: Using A, ch 36.

Row 1: 1 tr in fifth ch from hook and 1 tr in next ch (counts as first tr and solid mesh). Cont across row, working mesh stitches as indicated on charts, and counting each ch as either a space or a stitch, turn.

The main chart provides full pattern information; use the smaller chart as a guide to the sequence of mesh stitches. Cont in mesh pattern across each row for 16 rows in total, working ch 3 (counts as first tr) at beg of each row and working last tr into top of beg ch-3 before turning. Fasten off.

Surface crochet

Surface chain: Using B and starting from centre, surface crochet around the open mesh spiral, working 2 chains in each open mesh space to end of spiral, turn.

Row 1: Working into surface chain, ch 3 (counts as first tr), 1 tr in next ch, *1 htr in next ch, 1 dc in next ch, ss in each of next 2 ch, 1 dc in next ch, 1 htr in next ch, 1 tr in each of next 2 ch; rep from * to end, turn.

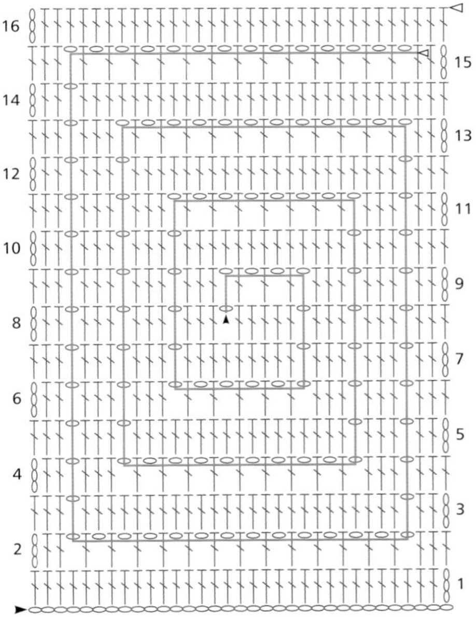

COLOURS

A

B

SURFACE CROCHET

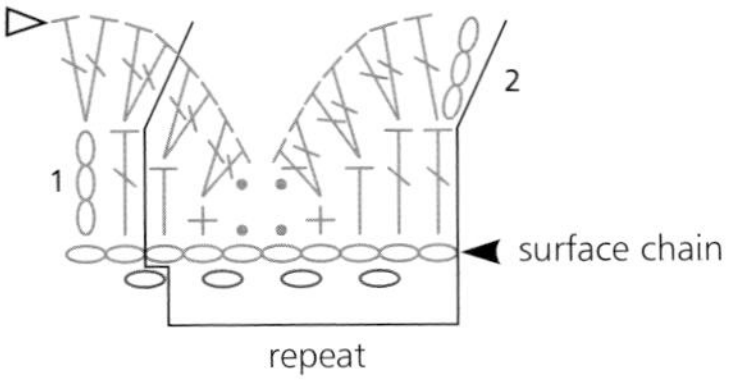

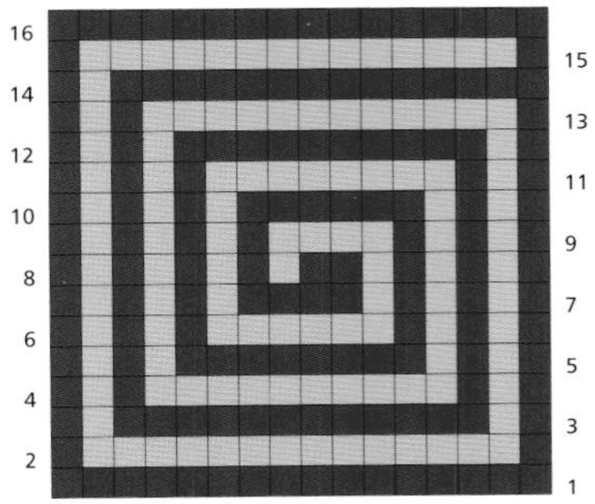

om sm

Row 2: Ch 3 (counts as first tr), 1 tr in st at base of ch-3, then work 2 tr in each st and 1 ss in each ss of previous row.

Fasten off.

SPECIAL ABBREVIATIONS

om (open mesh): Ch 1, skip 1 sp or st, 1 tr in next st.

sm (solid mesh): 1 tr in next sp or st, 1 tr in next st.

13 Colour Dot Square

MEDIUM

- 12–15cm (4¾–6in)
- Aran yarn
- 5.5mm hook

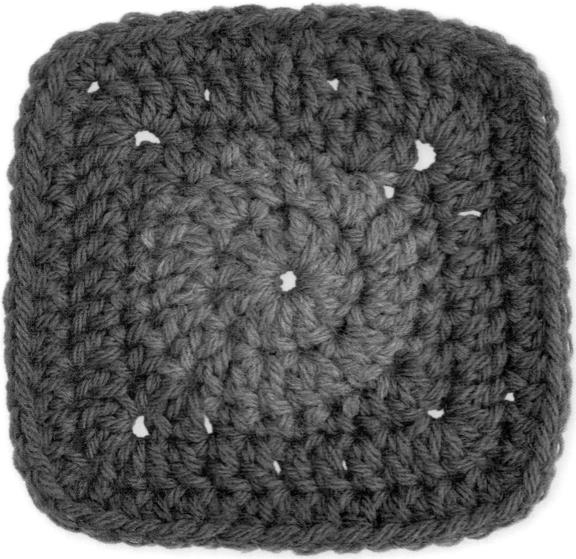

Foundation ring: Using A, ch 4, join with ss to form a ring.

Round 1: Ch 3 (counts as first tr), 11 tr into ring, join with ss to top of beg ch-3. (12 sts)

Round 2: Ch 3 (counts as first tr), 1 tr in st at base of ch-3, 2 tr in each tr around, join with ss to top of beg ch-3. (24 sts)

Fasten off A. Join B.

Round 3: Ch 1, 1 dc in st at base of ch-1, 1 dc in next st, 1 htr in next st, *3 tr in next st, 1 htr in next st, 1 dc in each of next 3 sts, 1 htr in next st; rep from * twice more, 3 tr in next st, 1 htr in next st, 1 dc in next st, join with ss to first dc. (32 sts)

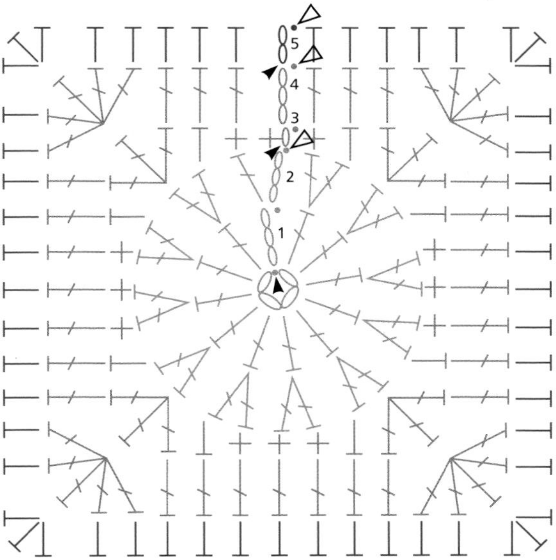

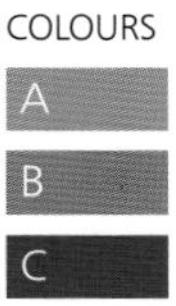

Round 4: Ch 3 (counts as first tr), 1 tr in each of next 3 sts, *5 tr in next st, 1 tr in each of next 7 sts; rep from * twice more, 5 tr in next st, 1 tr in each of next 3 sts, join with ss to top of beg ch-3. (48 sts)

Fasten off B. Join C.

Round 5: Ch 2 (counts as first htr), 1 htr in each of next 5 sts, *3 htr in next st, 1 htr in each of next 11 sts; rep from * twice more, 3 htr in next st, 1 htr in each of next 5 sts, join with ss to top of beg ch-2. (56 sts)

Fasten off.

14 Treble Crochet Square

MEDIUM

- 12–15cm (4¾–6in)
- Aran yarn
- 5.5mm hook

Foundation ring: Ch 4, join with ss to form a ring.

Round 1: Ch 5 (counts as first tr and ch 2), [3 tr into ring, ch 2] 3 times, 2 tr into ring, join with ss to third ch of beg ch-5.

Round 2: Ss in next ch-2 sp, ch 7 (counts as first tr and ch 4), 2 tr in sp at base of ch-7, *1 tr in each of next 3 tr, [2 tr, ch 4, 2 tr] in next ch-2 sp; rep from * twice more, 1 tr in each of next 3 tr, 1 tr in same sp as ch-7, join with ss to third ch of beg ch-7.

COLOUR

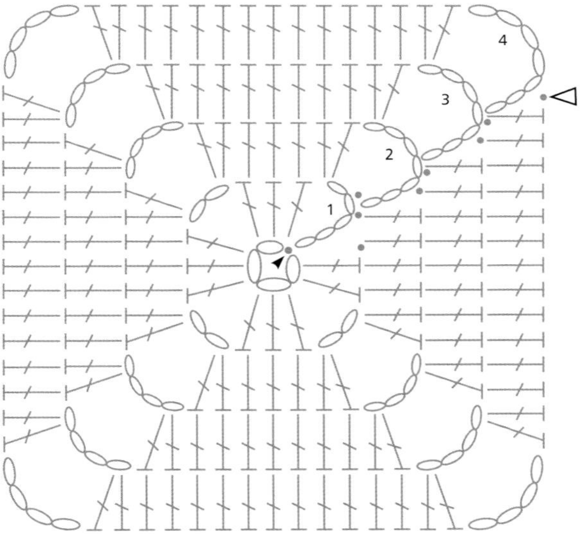

Round 3: Ss in next ch-4 sp, ch 7 (counts as first tr and ch 4), 2 tr in sp at base of ch-7, *1 tr in each of next 7 tr, [2 tr, ch 4, 2 tr] in next ch-4 sp; rep from * twice more, 1 tr in each of next 7 tr, 1 tr in same sp as ch-7, join with ss to third ch of beg ch-7.

Round 4: Ss in next ch-4 sp, ch 7 (counts as first tr and ch 4), 2 tr in sp at base of ch-7, *1 tr in each of next 11 tr, [2 tr, ch 4, 2 tr] in next ch-4 sp; rep from * twice more, 1 tr in each of next 11 tr, 1 tr in same sp as ch-7, join with ss to third ch of beg ch-7.

Fasten off.

15 Woven Stripes

LARGE

- 15–18cm (6–7in)
- DK yarn
- 4.5mm hook

Foundation chain: Using A, ch 31.

Row 1 (RS): Weaving B, 1 tr in fifth ch from hook (counts as first 2 tr), 1 tr in each ch to end, turn. (28 sts)

Row 2: Ch 3 (counts as first tr), weaving B, 1 tr in each st to end, turn.

Rows 3–4: Rep row 2 twice more.

Fasten off B.

Weaving yarns across each row as indicated, continue in tr across each row for 16 rows in total, working ch 3 (counts as first tr) at beg of each row and working last tr into top of beg ch-3 before turning.

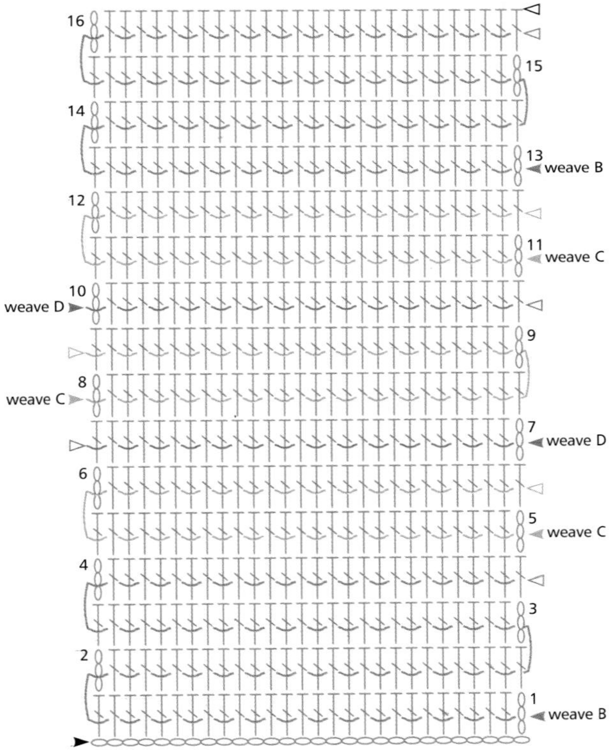

COLOURS

A

B

C

D

Weave yarns across each row as follows: Rows 5–6C, 7D, 8–9C, 10D, 11–12C, 13–16B.

Fasten off.

SPECIAL ABBREVIATION

Weaving: *Bring weaving yarn from back to front, 1 tr in next st, take weaving yarn from front to back, 1 tr in next st; rep from * to end of row, with weaving yarn at front, work last tr in top of beg ch-3.

16 Textured Quarters

LARGE

- 15–18cm (6–7in)
- DK yarn
- 4.5mm hook

Foundation chain: Ch 26.

Row 1: 1 dc in fourth ch from hook (counts as first 2 dc), 1 dc in each of next 10 ch, *MB in next ch, 1 dc in next ch; rep from * 5 times more, turn.

Row 2: Ch 2 (counts as first dc), 1 dc in each of next 11 sts, *MB in next st, 1 dc in next st; rep from * 5 times more, turn.

Rep row 2, 12 times more.

Row 15: Ch 2 (counts as first dc), 1 dc in each st to end, turn.

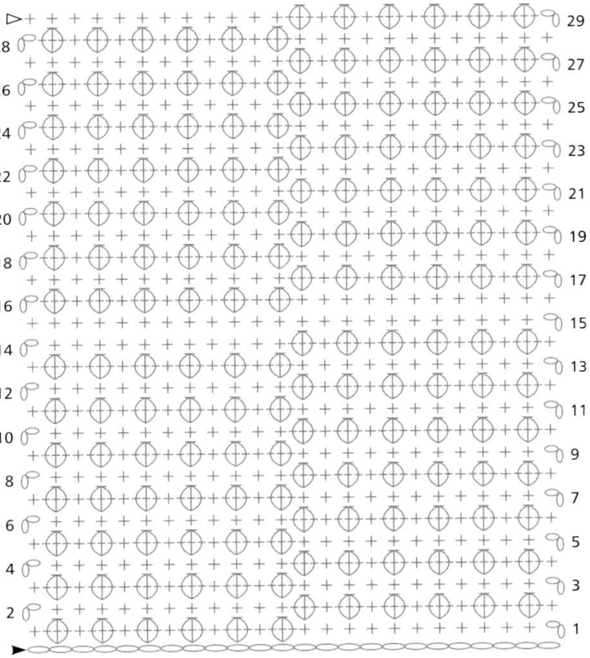

COLOUR

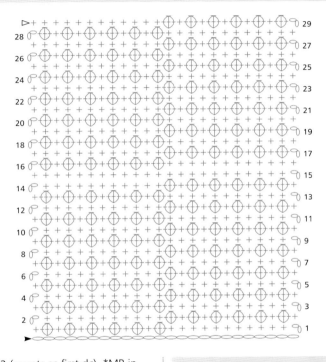

Row 16: Ch 2 (counts as first dc), *MB in next st, 1 dc in next st; rep from * 5 times more, 1 dc in each st to end, turn.

Rep row 16, 13 times more.

Fasten off.

SPECIAL ABBREVIATION

MB (make bobble): *Insert hook in next ch or st, yo, draw yarn through, yo, draw through last loop on hook; rep from * twice more in same ch or st, yo, draw through all 4 loops on hook.

17 Textured Stripes

LARGE
- 15–18cm (6–7in)
- DK yarn
- 4.5mm hook

Foundation chain: Ch 29.

Row 1: 1 dc in fourth ch from hook (counts as first 2 dc), 1 dc in each ch to end, turn. (27 sts)

Row 2: Ch 2 (counts as first dc), 1 dc in each st to end, turn.

Row 3: Ch 2 (counts as first dc), 1 dc in each of next 2 sts, *1 dc in foundation ch below next st, 1 dc in each of next 3 sts; rep from * 5 times more, turn.

Rows 4–5: Rep row 2 twice more.

Row 6: Ch 2 (counts as first dc), 1 dc in each of next 2 sts, *1 dc in next st 3 rows down, 1 dc in each of next 3 sts; rep from * 5 times more, turn.

Rows 7–12: Rep rows 4–6 twice more.

Row 13: Ch 2 (counts as first dc), 1 dc in each st to end, turn.

Row 14: Ch 3 (counts as first tr), 1 tr in each st to end, turn.

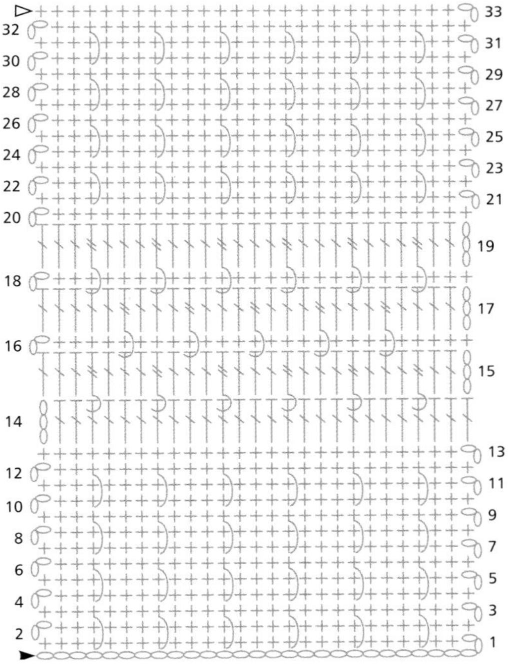

COLOUR

Row 15: Ch 3 (counts as first tr), 1 tr in each of next 2 sts, *FPdtr around next st, 1 tr in each of next 3 sts; rep from * 5 times more, turn.

Row 16: Rep row 13.

Row 17: Ch 3 (counts as first tr), 1 tr in each of next 4 sts, *FPdtr around next st 2 rows down, 1 tr in each of next 3 sts; rep from * 4 times more, 1 tr in each of next 2 sts, turn.

Row 18: Rep row 13.

Row 19: Ch 3 (counts as first tr), 1 tr in each of next 2 sts, *FPdtr around next st 2 rows down, 1 tr in each of next 3 sts; rep from * 5 times more, turn.

Row 20: Rep row 13.

Rows 21–33: Rep rows 4–6, 4 times more, then row 4 again. Fasten off.

18 Tri-colour Wheel in Square

LARGE
- 15–18cm (6–7in)
- Aran yarn
- 5.5mm hook

Foundation ring: Using A, ch 4, join with ss to form a ring.

Round 1: Ch 5 (counts as first tr and ch 2), [1 tr into ring, ch 2] 7 times, join with ss to third ch of beg ch-5.

Round 2: Ss in next ch-2 sp, ch 3 (counts as first tr), 2 tr in sp at base of ch-3, ch 1, [3 tr in next ch-2 sp, ch 1] 7 times, join with ss to top of beg ch-3.

Fasten off A. Join B to next ch-1 sp.

Round 3: Ch 3 (counts as first tr), 2 tr in sp at base of ch-3, ch 1, 3 tr in next ch-1 sp, ch 5, [3 tr in next ch-1 sp, ch 1, 3 tr in next ch-1 sp, ch 5] 3 times, join with ss to top of beg ch 3.

Round 4: Ss between next 2 tr, ch 3 (counts as first tr), 1 tr in next st-sp, 3 tr in next ch-1 sp, 1 tr in each of next 2 st-sp, [3 tr, ch 2, 3 tr] in next ch-5 sp, *1 tr in each of next 2 st-sp, 3 tr in next ch-1 sp, 1 tr in each of next 2 st-sp, [3 tr, ch 2, 3 tr] in next ch-5 sp; rep from * twice more, join with ss to top of beg ch-3.

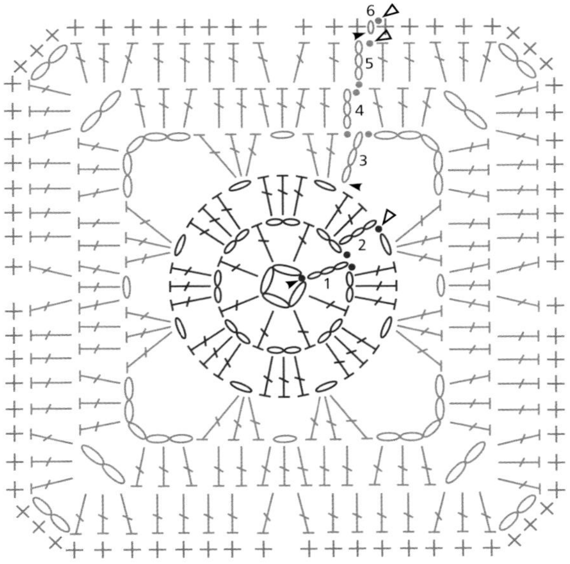

COLOURS

A

B

C

Round 5: Ss between last 2 tr, ch 3 (counts as first tr), 1 tr in next st-sp, skip 1 st-sp, 1 tr in each of next 2 st-sp, skip 1 st-sp, 1 tr in each of next 4 st-sp, *[3 tr, ch 2, 3 tr] in next ch-2 sp, 1 tr in each of next 4 st-sp, skip 1 st-sp, 1 tr in each of next 2 st-sp, skip 1 st-sp, 1 tr in each of next 4 st-sp; rep from * twice more, [3 tr, ch 2, 3 tr] in next ch-2 sp, 1 tr in each of next 2 st-sp, join with ss to top of beg ch-3.

Fasten off B. Join C.

Round 6: Ch 1, 1 dc in each tr and 3 dc in each ch-2 sp around, join with ss to first dc.

Fasten off.

SPECIAL ABBREVIATION

St-sp: The space between the posts of 2 sts.

19 Tri-colour Granny Square

SMALL

- 9–12cm ($3\frac{1}{2}$–$4\frac{3}{4}$in)
- Aran yarn
- 5.5mm hook

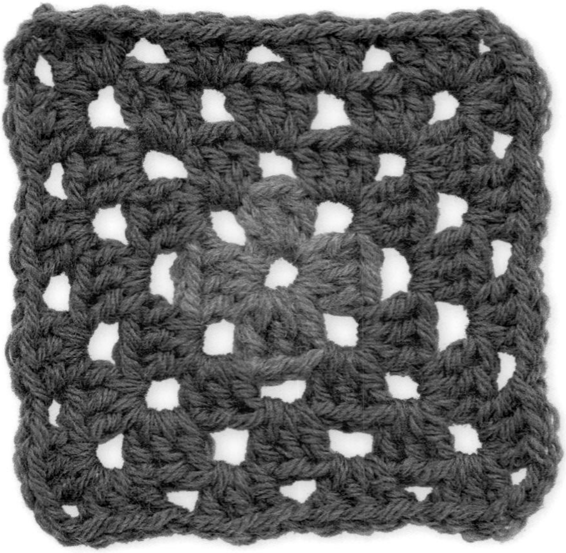

Foundation ring: Using A, ch 4, join with ss to form a ring.

Round 1: Ch 5 (counts as first tr and ch 2), [3 tr into ring, ch 2] 3 times, 2 tr into ring, join with ss to third ch of beg ch-5.

Fasten off A. Join B to any ch-2 sp.

Round 2: Ch 5 (counts as first tr and ch 2), 3 tr in sp at base of ch-5, *ch 1, skip 3 tr, [3 tr, ch 2, 3 tr] in next ch-2 sp; rep from * twice more, ch 1, skip 3 sts, 2 tr in same sp as ch-5, join with ss to third ch of beg ch-5.

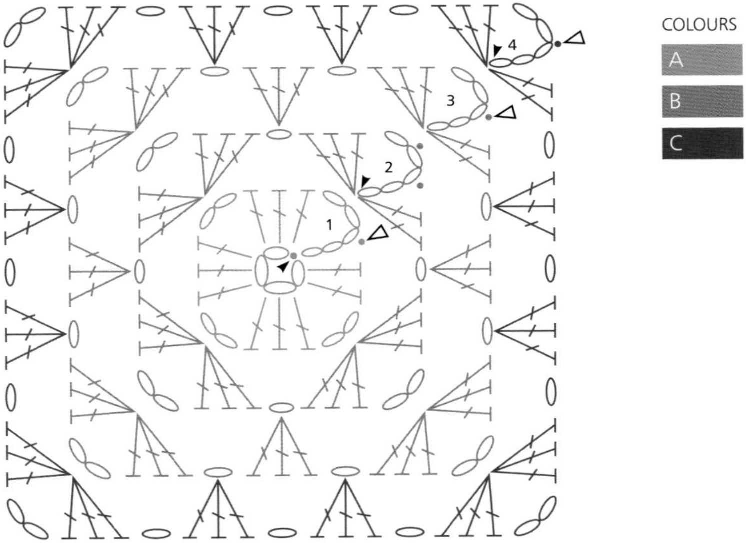

Round 3: Ss in next ch-2 sp, ch 5 (counts as first tr and ch 2), 3 tr in sp at base of ch-5, *ch 1, skip 3 tr, 3 tr in next ch-1 sp, ch 1, skip 3 tr, [3 tr, ch 2, 3 tr] in next ch-2 sp; rep from * twice more, ch 1, skip 3 tr, 3 tr in next ch-1 sp, ch 1, skip 3 tr, 2 tr in same sp as ch-5, join with ss to third ch of beg ch-5.

Fasten off B. Join C to any ch-2 sp.

Round 4: Ch 5 (counts as first tr and ch 2), 3 tr in sp at base of ch-5, *[ch 1, skip 3 tr, 3 tr in next ch-1 sp] twice, ch 1, skip 3 tr, [3 tr, ch 2, 3 tr] in next ch-2 sp; rep from * twice more, [ch 1, skip 3 tr, 3 tr in next ch-1 sp] twice, ch 1, skip 3 tr, 2 tr in same sp as ch-5, join with ss to third ch of beg ch-5.

Fasten off.

20 Blue and White Check

LARGE
- 15–18cm (6–7in)
- DK yarn
- 4.5mm hook

Foundation chain: Using A, ch 17. Without fastening off A, join B and ch 20.

Row 1: 1 tr in fifth ch from hook (counts as first 2 tr), 1 tr in each of next 5 ch, ch 1, skip 1 ch, 1 tr in next ch, ch 1, skip 1 ch, 1 tr in each of next 7 ch, change to A, 1 tr in each of next 7 ch, ch 1, skip 1 ch, 1 tr in next ch, ch 1, skip 1 ch, 1 tr in each ch to end, turn.

Row 2: Ch 3 (counts as first tr), 1 tr in each of next 6 sts, ch 1, skip 1 ch, 1 tr in next st, ch 1, skip 1 ch, 1 tr in each of next 7 sts, change to B, 1 tr in each of next 7 sts, ch 1, skip 1 ch, 1 tr in next st, ch 1, skip 1 ch, 1 tr in each st to end, turn.

Row 3: Ch 3 (counts as first tr), 1 tr in each of next 6 sts, ch 1, skip 1 ch, 1 tr in next st, ch 1, skip 1 ch, 1 tr in each of next 7 sts, change to A, 1 tr in each of next 7 sts, ch 1, skip 1 ch, 1 tr in next st, ch 1, skip 1 ch, 1 tr in each st to end, turn.

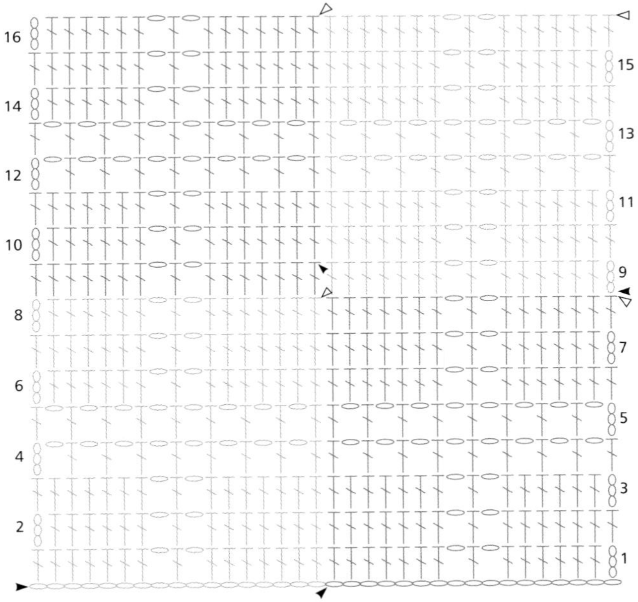

COLOURS

A

B

Row 4: Ch 4 (counts as first tr and ch 1), skip 1 st, 1 tr in next st, [ch 1, skip 1 st or ch, 1 tr in next st] 7 times, change to B, 1 tr in next st, [ch 1, skip 1 st or ch, 1 tr in next st] 8 times, turn.

Row 5: Ch 4 (counts as first tr and ch 1), skip first st or ch, 1 tr in next st, [ch 1, skip 1 st or ch, 1 tr in next st] 7 times, change to A, 1 tr in next st, [ch 1, skip 1 st or ch, 1 tr in next st] 8 times, turn.

Rows 6–7: Rep rows 2–3.

Row 8: Rep row 2 but fasten off A and B after completing each section.

Rows 9–16: Continue pattern as set for rows 1–8, alternating A and B to create checked design.

21 Heart Check

LARGE
- 15–18cm (6–7in)
- DK yarn
- 4.5mm hook

Thread 62 beads on to each yarn.

Foundation chain: Using A, ch 30.

Row 1: 1 dc in fourth ch from hook (counts as first 2 dc), 1 dc in each of next 12 ch. Without breaking off A, join B. Using B, 1 dc in each ch to end, turn. (28 sts)

Row 2: Ch 2 (counts as first dc), 1 dc in each of next 13 sts, change to A, 1 dc in each st to end, turn.

BEADS

4mm red glass beads x 124

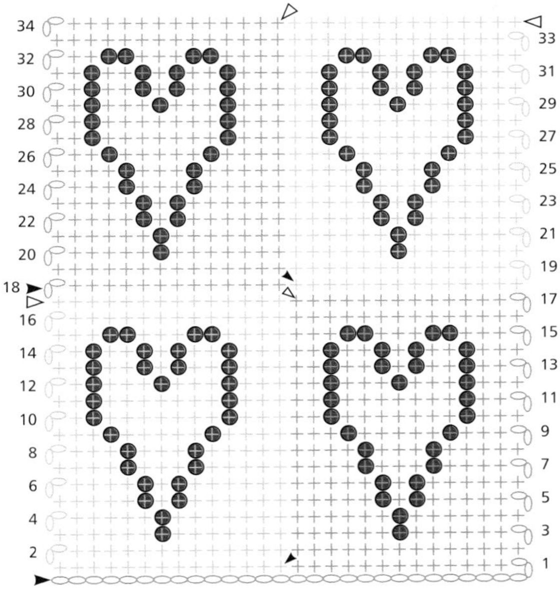

COLOURS

A

B

Continue in dc across each row for 34 rows in total, working ch 2 (counts as first dc) at beg of each row and working last dc into top of beg ch-2 before turning. Change colours and place beads as indicated on chart.

Fasten off.

SPECIAL ABBREVIATION

Place beads: On even-numbered (wrong-side) rows, slide bead along yarn to base of hook and then dc into next st. On odd-numbered (right-side) rows, slide bead along yarn to base of hook, insert hook into next st, yo, draw yarn and bead through st, and then complete the dc.

22 Flower Square

EXTRA LARGE
- 18–21cm (7–8¼in)
- Aran yarn
- 5.5mm hook

Foundation ring: Ch 4, join with ss to form a ring.

Round 1: Ch 1, 12 dc into ring, join with ss to first dc.

Round 2: Beg 2-dtr cl, ch 3, 3-dtr cl in st at base of beg 2-dtr cl, *ch 4, skip 2 sts, [3-dtr cl, ch 3, 3-dtr cl] in next st; rep from * twice more, ch 4, join with ss to top of beg 2-dtr cl.

Round 3: Ch 3 (counts as first tr) *1 tr in top of next cl, [3-tr cl, ch 3, 3-tr cl] in next ch-3 sp, 1 tr in top of next cl, 4 tr in next ch-4 sp; rep from * 3 times more, omitting last tr, join with ss to top of beg ch-3.

Round 4: Ch 3 (counts as first tr), 1 tr in next tr, *1 tr in top of next cl, [3-tr cl, ch 3, 3-tr cl] in next ch-3 sp, 1 tr in top of next cl, 1 tr in each of next 6 sts; rep from * twice more, 1 tr in top of next cl, [3-tr cl, ch 3, 3-tr cl] in next ch-3 sp, 1 tr in top of next cl, 1 tr in each of next 4 sts, join with ss to top of beg ch-3.

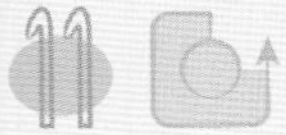

COLOUR

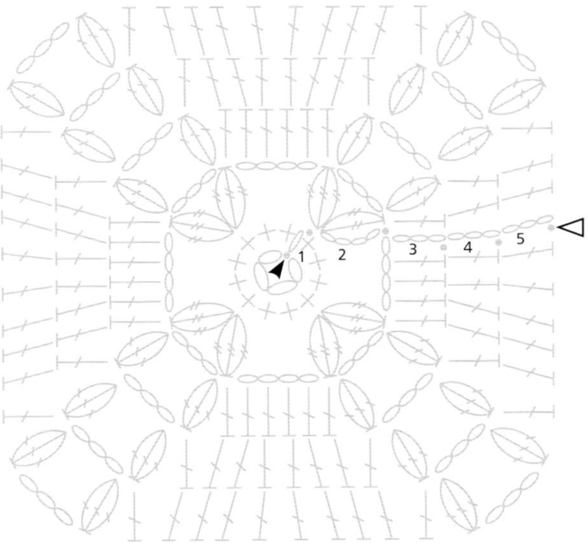

Round 5: Ch 3 (counts as first tr), 1 tr in each of next 2 tr, *1 tr in top of next cl, [3-tr cl, ch 3, 3-tr cl] in next ch-3 sp, 1 tr in top of next cl, 1 tr in each of next 8 sts; rep from * twice more, 1 tr in top of next cl, [3-tr cl, ch 3, 3-tr cl] in next ch-3 sp, 1 tr in top of next cl, 1 tr in each of next 5 sts, join with ss to top of beg ch-3.

Fasten off.

SPECIAL ABBREVIATIONS

beg 2-dtr cl (beginning 2 double treble crochet cluster): Ch 4, *[yo] twice, insert hook in next st, yo, draw yarn through, [yo, draw through 2 loops on hook] twice; rep from * once more working in same st, yo, draw through all 3 loops on hook.

3-dtr cl (3 double treble crochet cluster): Work as above from *, but rep from * twice more working in same st, yo, draw through all 4 loops on hook.

3-tr cl (3 treble crochet cluster): [Yo, insert hook in next st, yo, draw yarn through, yo, draw through 2 loops on hook] 3 times, yo, draw through all 4 loops on hook.

23 Popcorn Square

MEDIUM

- 12–15cm (4¾–6in)
- Aran yarn
- 5.5mm hook

Foundation ring: Ch 8, join with ss to form a ring.

Round 1: Beg popcorn into ring, [ch 5, popcorn into ring] 3 times, ch 5, join with ss to top of beg popcorn.

Round 2: Ch 3 (counts as first tr), *[2 tr, ch 2, popcorn, ch 2, 2 tr] in next ch-5 sp, 1 tr in top of next popcorn; rep from * twice more, [2 tr, ch 2, popcorn, ch 2, 2 tr] in next ch-5 sp, join with ss to top of beg ch-3.

Round 3: Ch 3 (counts as first tr), 1 tr in each of next 2 tr, *2 tr in next ch-2 sp, ch 2, popcorn in top of next popcorn, ch 2, 2 tr in next ch-2 sp, 1 tr in each of next 5 tr; rep from * twice more, 2 tr in next ch-2 sp, ch 2, popcorn in top of next popcorn, ch 2, 2 tr in next ch-2 sp, 1 tr in each of next 2 tr, join with ss to top of beg ch-3.

Round 4: Ch 3 (counts as first tr), 1 tr in each of next 4 tr, *2 tr in next ch-2 sp, ch 2, popcorn in top of next popcorn, ch 2, 2 tr in next ch-2 sp, 1 tr in each of next 9 tr; rep from * twice more, 2 tr in next ch-2 sp, ch 2,

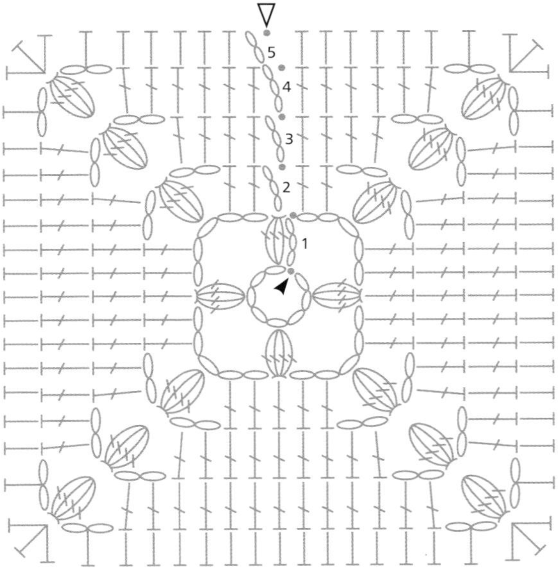

COLOUR

popcorn in top of next popcorn, ch 2, 2 tr in next ch-2 sp, 1 tr in each of next 4 tr, join with ss to top of beg ch-3.

Round 5: Ch 2 (counts as first htr), 1 htr in each of next 5 sts, *1 htr in next ch-2 sp, 3 htr in top of next popcorn, 1 htr in next ch-2 sp, 1 htr in each of next 13 sts; rep from * twice more, 1 htr in next ch-2 sp, 3 htr in top of next popcorn, 1 htr in next ch-2 sp, 1 htr in each of next 6 sts, join with ss to top of beg ch-2.

Fasten off.

SPECIAL ABBREVIATIONS

beg popcorn: Ch 3, 4 tr into ring, remove hook from working loop, insert hook in top of beg ch-3, catch working loop, yo, draw through loop and st.

popcorn: 5 tr in place indicated, remove hook from working loop, insert hook in top of first tr of popcorn, catch working loop, yo, draw through loop and st.

24 Off-centred Granny

MEDIUM

- 12–15cm (4¾–6in)
- Aran yarn
- 5.5mm hook

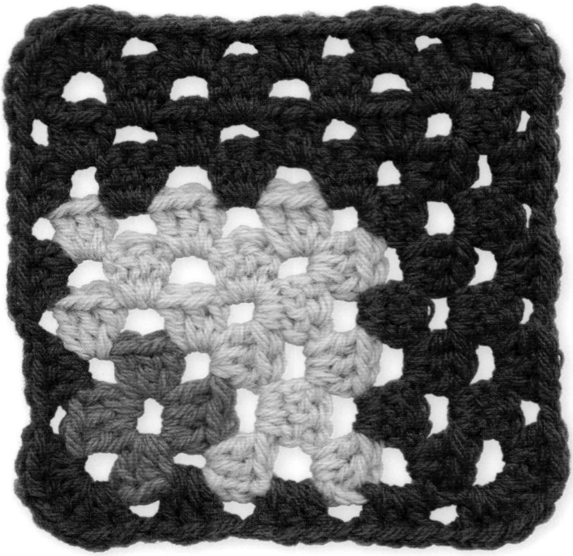

Foundation ring: Using A, ch 4, join with ss to form a ring.

Round 1: Ch 5 (counts as first tr and ch 2), [3 tr into ring, ch 2] 3 times, 2 tr into ring, join with ss to third ch of beg ch-5.

Only two sides of original round are worked until last round. Fasten off A. Join B to any ch-2 sp.

Row 2: Ch 2 (counts as first tr), 2 tr in sp at base of ch-2, ch 1, [3 tr, ch 2, 3 tr] in next ch-2 sp, ch 1, 3 tr in next ch-2 sp, turn.

Row 3: Ch 3 (counts as first tr and ch 1), 3 tr in next ch-1 sp, ch 1, [3 tr, ch 2, 3 tr] in corner ch-2 sp, ch 1, 3 tr in next ch-1 sp, ch 1, 1 tr in last st, turn.

Row 4: Ch 2 (counts as first tr), 2 tr in next ch-1 sp, ch 1, 3 tr in next ch-1 sp, ch 1, [3 tr, ch 2, 3 tr] in corner ch-2 sp, [ch 1, 3 tr in next ch-1 sp] twice.

Fasten off B. Join C.

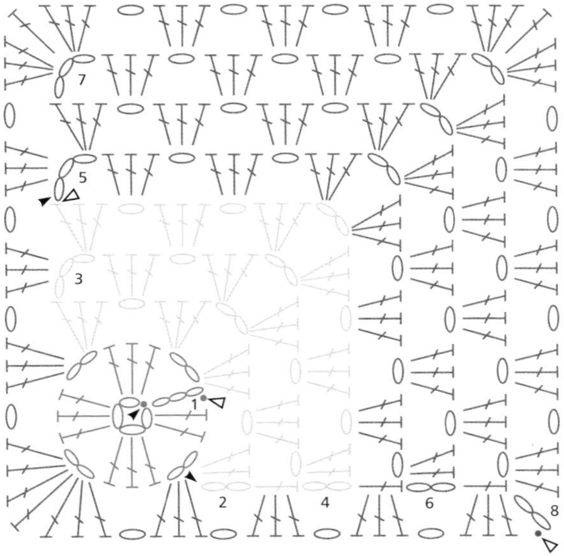

COLOURS
A
B
C

Row 5: Ch 3 (counts as first tr and ch 1), [3 tr in next ch-1 sp, ch 1] twice, [3 tr, ch 2, 3 tr] in corner ch-2 sp, [ch 1, 3 tr in next ch-1 sp] twice, ch 1, 1 tr in last st, turn.

Row 6: Ch 2 (counts as first tr), 2 tr in next ch-1 sp, ch 1, [3 tr in next ch-1 sp, ch 1] twice, [3 tr, ch 2, 3 tr] in corner ch-2 sp, [ch 1, 3 tr in next ch-1 sp] 3 times, turn.

Row 7: Ch 3 (counts as first tr and ch 1), [3 tr in next ch-1 sp, ch 1] 3 times, [3 tr, ch 2, 3 tr] in corner ch-2 sp, [ch 1, 3 tr in next ch-1 sp] 3 times, ch 1, 1 tr in last st, turn.

Round 8: Ch 2 (counts as first tr), 3 tr in next ch-1 sp, *[ch 1, 3 tr in next ch-1 sp] 3 times, ch 1, 7 tr in corner ch-2 sp; rep from * once more, [ch 1, 3 tr in beg ch-3 at start of row] twice, ch 1, 3 tr in ch-2 sp of round 1, ch 1, 7 tr in next ch-2 sp, ch 1, 3 tr in next ch-2 sp, [ch 1, 3 tr around post of tr at end of row] 3 times, join with ss to top of beg ch-2.

Fasten off.

25 Raised Squares

LARGE
- 15–18cm (6–7in)
- DK yarn
- 4.5mm hook

Foundation chain: Using A, ch 31.

Row 1 (RS): 1 tr in fifth ch from hook (counts as first 2 tr), 1 tr in each ch to end, turn. (28 sts)

Row 2: Ch 3 (counts as first tr), 1 tr in each st to end, turn.

Row 3: Ch 3 (counts as first tr), 1 tr in each of next 5 sts, 1 tr tbl in each of next 6 sts, 1 tr in each of next 4 sts, 1 tr tbl in each of next 6 sts, 1 tr in each st to end, turn.

Rows 4–5: Rep row 2 twice more.

Row 6: Ch 3 (counts as first tr), 1 tr in each of next 5 sts, 1 tr tfl in each of next 6 sts, 1 tr in each of next 4 sts, 1 tr tfl in each of next 6 sts, 1 tr in each st to end, turn.

Rows 7–8: Rep row 2 twice more.

Row 9: Rep row 3.

Rows 10–15: Rep rows 4–9.

Row 16: Rep row 2.

Fasten off.

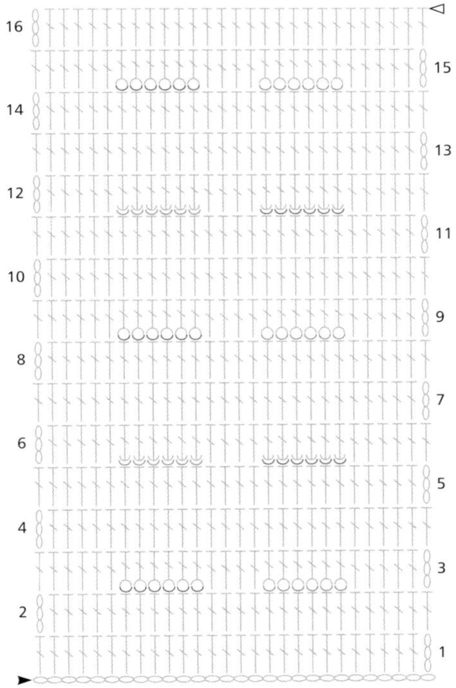

COLOURS

A

B

C

RAISED SQUARE

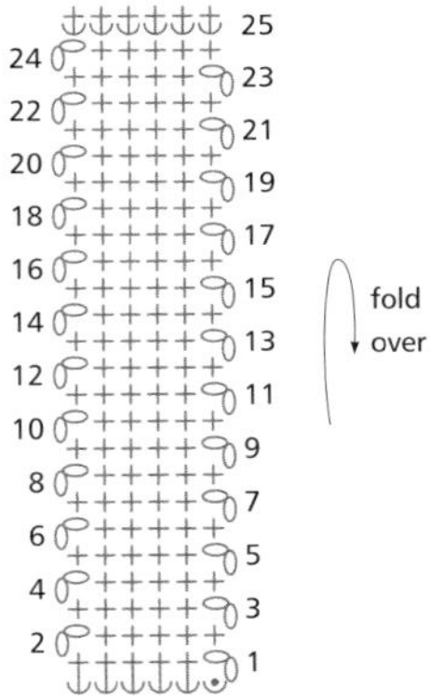

Raised squares

With RS facing, join B with ss tfl at base of row 3, on the right.

Row 1: Ch 2 (counts as first dc), 1 dc tfl in each of next 5 sts, turn. (6 sts)

Row 2: Ch 2 (counts as first dc), 1 dc in each of next 5 sts, turn.

Rep row 2, 22 times more.

Row 25: Fold over and work 1 dc tfl into corresponding st at base of row 3 and 1 dc tfl in each of next 5 sts. Note that this row is worked into the same sts on the main block as row 1 of the raised square.

Fasten off.

Work a raised square into each set of front loops indicated on chart, alternating yarns B and C.

26 Horizontal Weave

LARGE
- 15–18cm (6–7in)
- DK yarn
- 4.5mm hook

Foundation chain: Using A, ch 31.

Row 1: 1 tr in fifth ch from hook (counts as first 2 tr), 1 tr in each of next 9 ch. Join B, 1 tr in each of next 6 ch, weaving in A on reverse of each st (see page 101). Using A, 1 tr in each ch to end, turn. (28 sts)

Row 2: Ch 3 (counts as first tr), 1 tr in each of next 10 sts. Using B, BPdtr around each of next 6 sts. Using A, 1 tr in each st to end, turn.

Row 3: Ch 3 (counts as first tr), 1 tr in each of next 10 sts. Using B, FPdtr around each of next 6 sts, fasten off B. Using A, 1 tr in each st to end, turn.

Row 4: Ch 3 (counts as first tr), 1 tr in each of next 10 sts, 1 tr tfl in each of next 6 sts, 1 tr in each st to end, turn.

Row 5: Ch 3 (counts as first tr), 1 tr in each st to end, turn.

Rep row 5 twice more.

Row 8: Ch 3 (counts as first tr), 1 tr in each of next 6 sts. Join C, 1 tr tfl in each of next 14 sts, weaving in A on reverse. Using A, 1 tr in each st to end, turn.

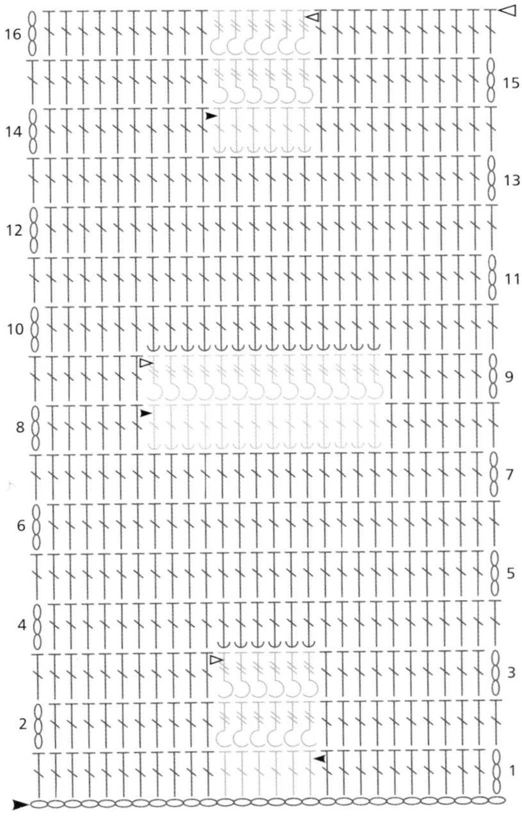

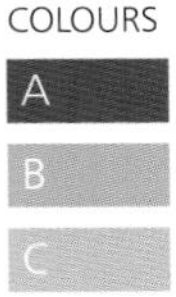

Row 9: Ch 3 (counts as first tr), 1 tr in each of next 6 sts. Using C, FPdtr around each of next 14 sts, fasten off C. Using A, 1 tr in each st to end, turn.

Row 10: Ch 3 (counts as first tr), 1 tr in each of next 6 sts, 1 tr tfl in each of next 14 sts, 1 tr in each st to end, turn.

Rep row 5, 3 times more.

Row 14: Ch 3 (counts as first tr), 1 tr in each of next 10 sts. Join B, 1 tr tfl in each of next 6 sts, weaving in A on reverse. Using A, 1 tr in each st to end, turn.

Row 15: Ch 3 (counts as first tr), 1 tr in each of next 10 sts. Using B, FPdtr around each of next 6 sts. Using A, 1 tr in each st to end, turn.

Row 16: Ch 3 (counts as first tr), 1 tr in each of next 10 sts. Using B, BPdtr around each of next 6 sts, fasten off B. Using A, 1 tr in each st to end, turn.

Fasten off.

27 Vertical Weave

LARGE
- 15–18cm (6–7in)
- DK yarn
- 4.5mm hook

Foundation chain: Ch 31.

Row 1: 1 tr in fifth ch from hook (counts as first 2 tr), 1 tr in each ch to end, turn. (28 sts)

Row 2: Ch 3 (counts as first tr), 1 tr in each of next 10 sts, BPdtr around each of next 6 sts, 1 tr in each st to end, turn.

Row 3: Ch 3 (counts as first tr), 1 tr in each of next 10 sts, FPdtr around each of next 6 sts, 1 tr in each st to end, turn.

Row 4: Ch 3 (counts as first tr), 1 tr in each of next 10 sts, 1 tr tfl in each of next 6 sts, 1 tr in each st to end, turn.

Row 5: Ch 3 (counts as first tr), 1 tr in each st to end, turn.

Row 6: Ch 3 (counts as first tr), 1 tr in each of next 10 sts, FPdtr around each of next 6 sts, 1 tr in each st to end, turn.

Row 7: Rep row 6.

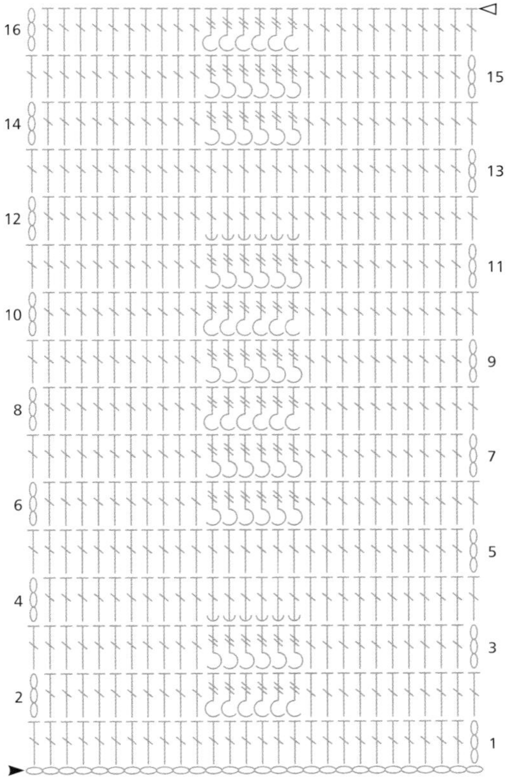

COLOUR

Row 8: Ch 3 (counts as first tr), 1 tr in each of next 10 sts, BPdtr around each of next 6 sts, 1 tr in each st to end, turn.

Rows 9–10: Rep rows 7–8.

Row 11: Rep row 6.

Rows 12–16: Rep rows 4–8.

Fasten off.

28 All in a Row

LARGE
- 15–18cm (6–7in)
- DK yarn
- 4.5mm hook

Foundation chain: Using A, ch 31.

Row 1 (WS): 1 tr in fifth ch from hook (counts as first 2 tr), 1 tr in each ch to end, turn. (28 sts)

Row 2: Ch 3 (counts as first tr), 1 tr in each st to end, turn.

To work stripe, remove hook from working loop of A, letting it hang free; do not fasten off. Join stripe colour.

Stripe: Using B, ch 2 (counts as first dc), 1 dc tfl in each st to end. Fasten off B.

Row 3: Pick up loop of A at beg of row, ch 3 (counts as first tr), 1 tr tbl in each st at base of stripe to end, turn.

Row 4: Ch 3 (counts as first tr), 1 tr in each st to end, turn.

Using C, work stripe tfl as before.

Rows 5–6: Rep rows 3–4.

Using D, work stripe tfl as before.

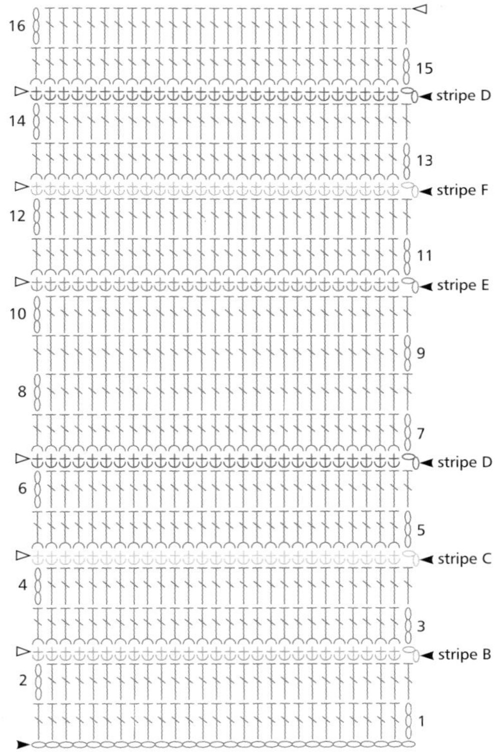

COLOURS

A

B

C

D

E

F

Rows 7–10: Rep row 3 once more and then row 4, 3 times more.

Using E, work stripe tfl as before.

Rows 11–12: Rep rows 3–4.

Using F, work stripe tfl as before.

Rows 13–14: Rep rows 3–4.

Using D, work stripe tfl as before.

Rows 15–16: Rep rows 3–4.

Fasten off.

29 Nips and Tucks

LARGE

- 15–18cm (6–7in)
- DK yarn
- 4.5mm hook

Foundation chain: Using A, ch 31.

Row 1: 1 tr in fifth ch from hook (counts as first 2 tr), 1 tr in each ch to end, turn. (28 sts)

Row 2: Ch 3 (counts as first tr), 1 tr in each st to end, turn.

Fasten off A. Join B tfl.

Row 3: Ch 3 (counts as first tr), 1 tr tfl in each st to end, turn.

Row 4: Ch 3 (counts as first tr), 1 tr in each st to end, turn.

Row 5 (tuck row): Ch 1, 1 dc tbl in each st 3 rows down to end, turn.

Fasten off B. Join A and rep row 2.

Fasten off A. Join C and rep rows 3–5.

Fasten off C. Join A and rep row 2.

Fasten off A. Join D and rep rows 3–5.

Fasten off D. Join A and rep row 2, 7 times more.

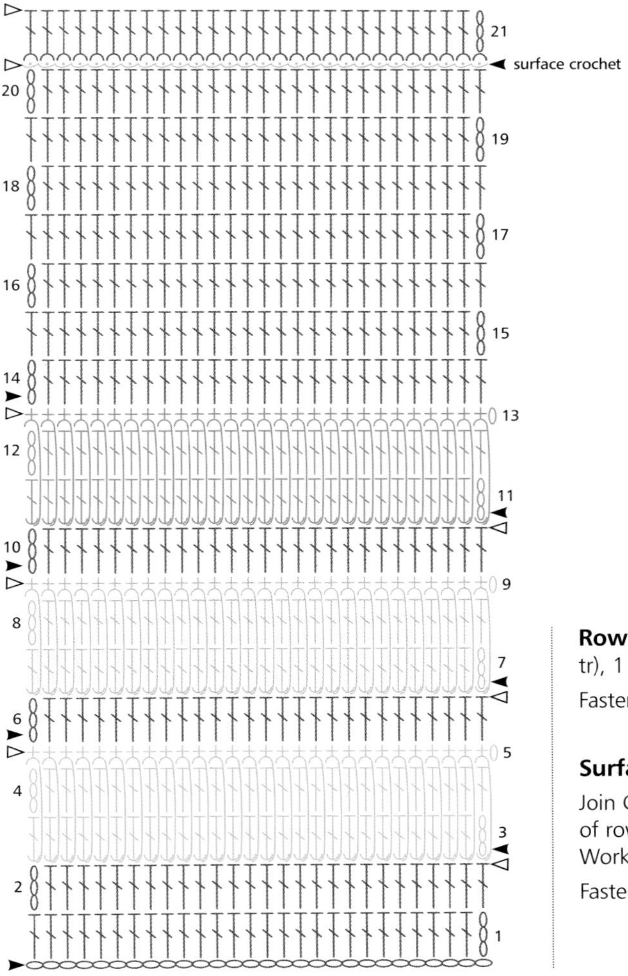

COLOURS

A

B

C

D

Row 21: Ch 3 (counts as first tr), 1 tr tbl in each st to end.

Fasten off.

Surface crochet

Join C with ss tfl to last st of row 20 (right-hand edge). Work ss tfl in each st to end.

Fasten off.

30 Beaded Star

LARGE
- 15–18cm (6–7in)
- DK yarn
- 4.5mm hook

Thread the beads on to the yarn.

Foundation chain: Ch 29.

Row 1: 1 dc in fourth ch from hook (counts as first 2 dc), 1 dc in each ch to end, turn. (27 sts)

Row 2: Ch 2 (counts as first dc), 1 dc in each st to end, turn.

BEADS

4mm silver metal beads x 236

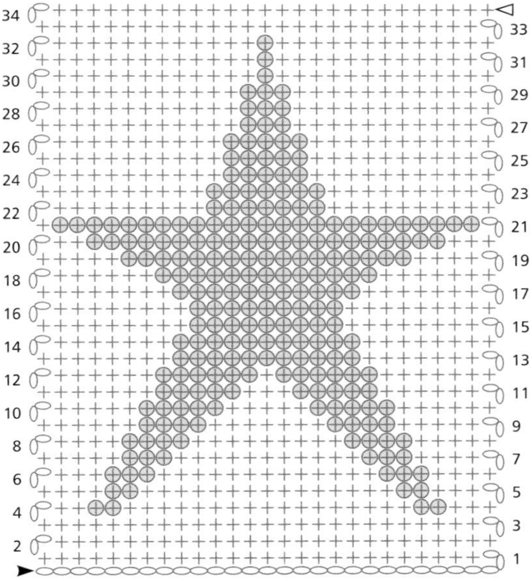

COLOUR

Continue in dc across each row for 34 rows in total, working ch 2 (counts as first dc) at beg of each row and working last dc into top of beg ch-2 before turning. Place beads as indicated on chart.

Fasten off.

SPECIAL ABBREVIATION

Place beads: On even-numbered (wrong-side) rows, slide bead along yarn to base of hook and then dc into next st. On odd-numbered (right-side) rows, slide bead along yarn to base of hook, insert hook into next st, yo, draw yarn and bead through st, and then complete the dc.

31 Lotus Flowers

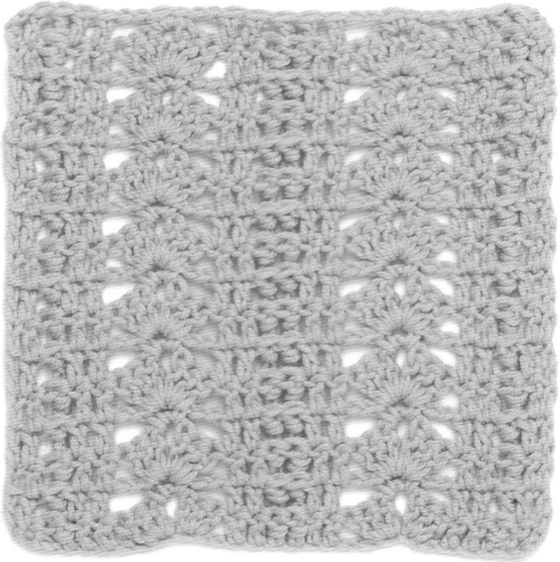

LARGE
- 15–18cm (6–7in)
- DK yarn
- 4.5mm hook

Foundation chain: Ch 31.

Row 1 (WS): 1 tr in fifth ch from hook (counts as first 2 tr), 1 tr in each of next 3 ch, skip 2 ch, 3 tr in next ch, ch 2, 3 tr in next ch, skip 2 ch, 1 tr in each of next 6 ch, skip 2 ch, 3 tr in next ch, ch 2, 3 tr in next ch, skip 2 ch, 1 tr in each ch to end, turn.

Row 2: Ch 3 (counts as first tr), 1 tr in next st, BPdtr around next st, 1 tr in each of next 2 sts, ch 2, skip 3 sts, [1 dc, ch 2, 1 dc] in next ch-2 sp, ch 2, skip 3 sts, 1 tr in each of next 2 sts, BPdtr around each of next 2 sts, 1 tr in each of next 2 sts, ch 2, skip 3 sts, [1 dc, ch 2, 1 dc] in next ch-2 sp, ch 2, skip 3 sts, 1 tr in each of next 2 sts, BPdtr around next st, 1 tr in each of next 2 sts, turn.

Row 3: Ch 3 (counts as first tr), 1 tr in next st, FPdtr around next st, 1 tr in each of next 2 sts, skip 1 dc, [3 tr, ch 2, 3 tr] in next ch-2 sp, skip 1 dc, 1 tr in each of next 2 sts, FPdtr around each of next 2 sts, 1 tr in each of next 2 sts, skip 1 dc, [3 tr, ch 2, 3 tr] in next ch-2 sp, skip 1 dc, 1 tr in each of next 2 sts, FPdtr around next st, 1 tr in each of next 2 sts, turn.

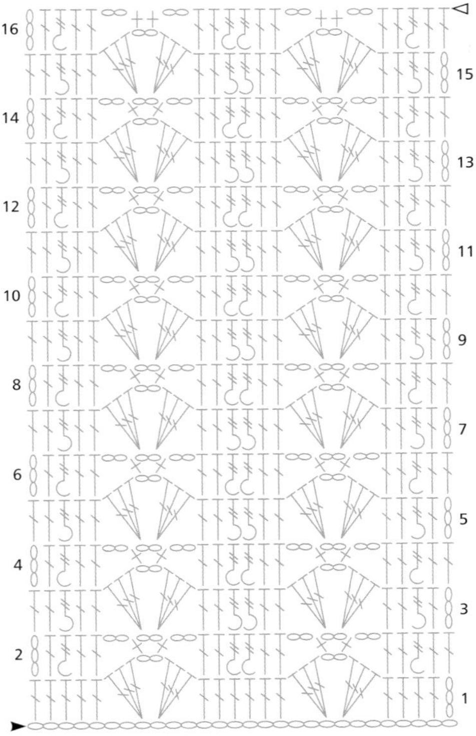

COLOUR

Rep rows 2–3, 6 times more.

Row 16: Ch 3 (counts as first tr), 1 tr in next st, BPdtr around next st, 1 tr in each of next 2 sts, ch 2, skip 3 sts, 2 dc in next ch-2 sp, ch 2, skip 3 sts, 1 tr in each of next 2 sts, BPdtr around each of next 2 sts, 1 tr in each of next 2 sts, ch 2, skip 3 sts, 2 dc in next ch-2 sp, ch 2, skip 3 sts, 1 tr in each of next 2 sts, BPdtr around next st, 1 tr in each of next 2 sts.

Fasten off.

32 Lacy Stripes

LARGE

- 15–18cm (6–7in)
- DK yarn
- 4.5mm hook

Foundation chain: Ch 30.

Row 1: 1 dc in fourth ch from hook (counts as first 2 dc), 1 dc in each ch to end, turn. (28 sts)

Row 2: Ch 2 (counts as first dc), 1 dc in each st to end, turn.

Row 3: Rep row 2.

Row 4: Ch 3 (counts as first tr), 1 tr in st at base of ch-3, *skip 2 sts, [1 tr, ch 1, 1 tr] in next st; rep from * 7 times more, skip 2 sts, 2 tr in top of beg ch-2, turn.

Row 5: Ch 3 (counts as first tr), 1 tr in next st, ch 1, skip 1 st, popcorn in next ch, ch 2, *skip 2 sts, popcorn in next ch, ch 2; rep from * 5 times more, skip 2 sts, popcorn in next ch, ch 1, skip 1 st, 1 tr in each of next 2 sts, turn.

Row 6: Ch 3 (counts as first tr), 1 tr in st at base of ch-3, skip 1 st, 1 tr in next ch, *[1 tr, ch 1, 1 tr] in next ch-2 sp; rep from * 6 times more, 1 tr in next ch-1 sp, ch 1, skip 1 st, 2 tr in last st, turn.

COLOUR

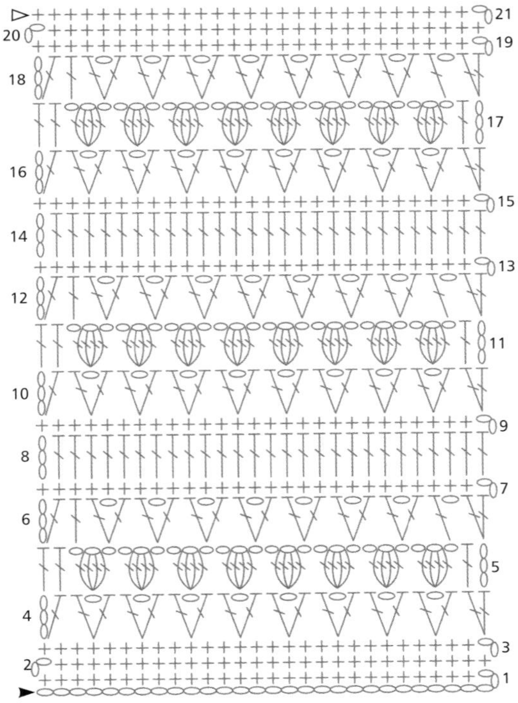

Row 7: Ch 2 (counts as first dc), 1 dc in each st and ch to end, turn.

Row 8: Ch 3 (counts as first tr), 1 tr in each st to end, turn.

Rep rows 3–8, then rows 3–7, and finally rows 2–3. Fasten off.

SPECIAL ABBREVIATION

popcorn: 4 tr in next ch, remove hook from working loop, insert hook in top of first tr of popcorn, catch working loop and draw through to close popcorn.

33 Circles and Bobbles

LARGE

- 15–18cm (6–7in)
- DK yarn
- 4.5mm hook

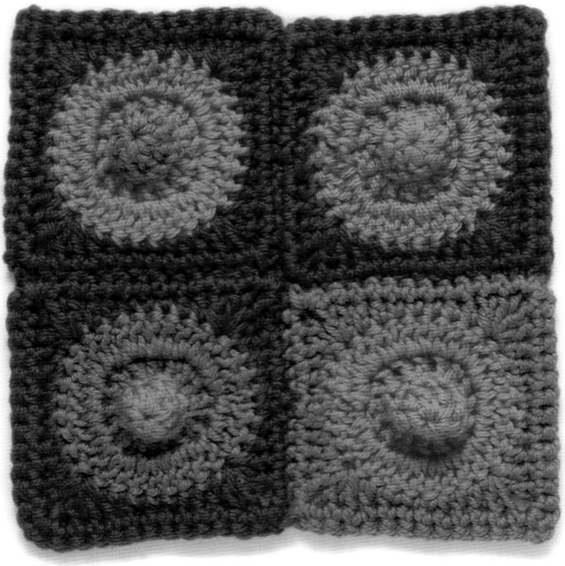

Quarter block (top right)

Foundation ring: Using A, make a magic ring.

Round 1: Ch 3 (counts as first tr), 7 tr into ring, join with ss to top of beg ch-3, turn. (8 tr)

Round 2: Ch 2 (counts as first dc), 1 dc in each st around, join with ss to top of beg ch-2, turn.

Fasten off A. Join B.

Round 3: Ch 3 (counts as first tr), 1 tr in st at base of ch-3, 2 tr in each st around, join with ss to top of beg ch-3, turn. (16 tr)

Round 4: Ch 3 (counts as first tr), 1 tr in st at base of ch-3, 2 tr in each st around, join with ss to top of beg ch-3, turn. (32 tr)

Fasten off B. Join C.

Round 5: Ch 2 (counts as first dc), 1 dc in next st, 1 htr in each of next 2 sts, [2 tr, ch 2, 2 tr] in next st, *1 htr in each of next 2 sts, 1 dc in each of next 3 sts, 1 htr in each of next 2 sts, [2 tr, ch 2, 2 tr] in next st;

QUARTER BLOCK

The colours shown are for the top right quarter

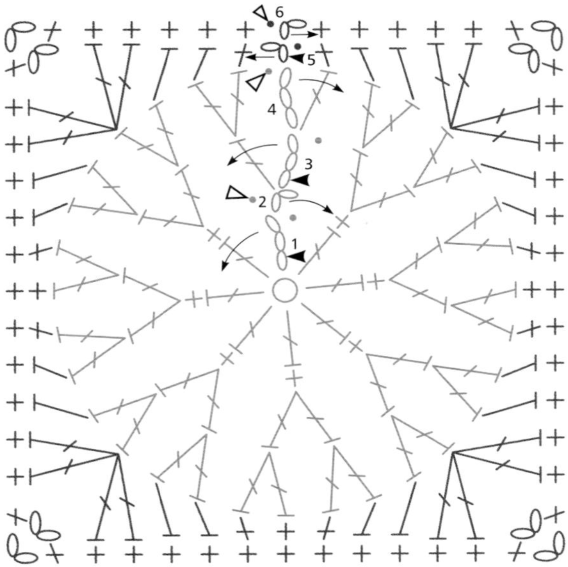

COLOURS

A

B

C

D

rep from * twice more, 1 htr in each of next 2 sts, 1 dc in next st, join with ss to top of beg ch-2, turn.

Round 6: Ch 2 (counts as first dc), 1 dc in each of next 5 sts, [1 dc, ch 2, 1 dc] in next ch-2 sp, *1 dc in each of next 11 sts, [1 dc, ch 2, 1 dc] in next ch-2 sp; rep from * twice more, 1 dc in each of next 5 sts, join with ss to top of beg ch-2.

Fasten off.

Remaining quarter blocks

Work as for top right quarter block but change colours on each round as follows:

Top left: 1–2D, 3–4A, 5–6C.

Bottom left: 1–2A, 3–4D, 5–6C.

Bottom right: 1–2B, 3–4A, 5–6D.

Join the four quarters together using the photograph as reference.

34 Circles Square

LARGE
- 15–18cm (6–7in)
- Aran yarn
- 5.5mm hook

Inner four circles

Foundation chain: Using A, ch 22.

Row 1: Starting in fourth ch from hook, *3 tr in next ch, skip 2 ch, ss in next ch (one quarter circle), skip 2 ch; rep from * twice more, 3 tr in next ch.

Remove hook from working loop, insert hook in last ch worked of foundation chain, catch working loop and draw through the ch.

Cont along other side of foundation chain, inserting hook in same chains as on row 1.

Round 2: 12 tr in same ch as last 3-tr group of row 1, insert hook through chain and last slip stitch, work ss, *11 tr in ch at base of next 3-tr group, ss in next ss; rep from * twice more, join with ss to last foundation ch. Fasten off A.

Outer 12 circles

Foundation chain: Using B, ch 70.

Row 3: Starting in fourth ch from hook, *3 tr in next ch, skip 2 ch, ss in next ch (one quarter circle), skip 2 ch, 3 tr in next ch,

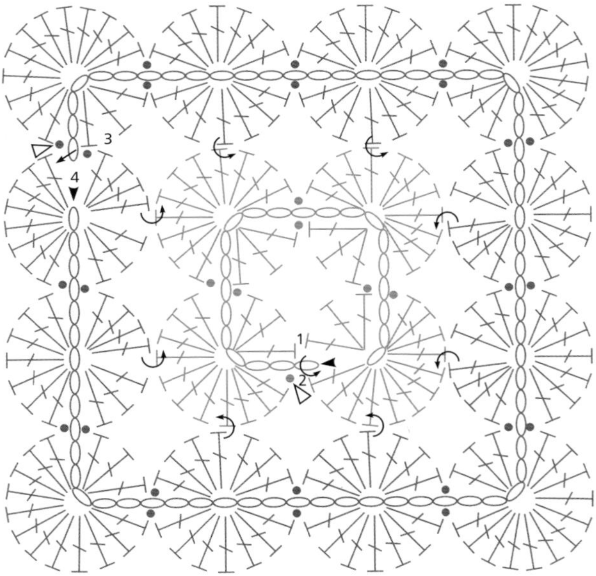

COLOURS

A

B

remove hook from working loop, insert hook in fourth tr of upper left circle of round 2, draw working loop though tr, 4 tr in ch at base of last 3-tr group worked (one half circle), skip 2 ch, ss in next ch, skip 2 ch, work another half-circle, joining it to next circle, skip 2 ch, ss, skip 2 ch; rep from * 3 times more.

Remove hook from working loop, insert hook in last ch worked of foundation chain, catch working loop and draw through the ch.

Cont along other side of foundation chain, inserting hook in same chains as on row 3.

Round 4: 8 tr in same ch as last half circle of row 3, insert hook through chain and last slip stitch, work ss, *7 tr in ch at base of next half circle, ss in next ss, 11 tr in ch at base of next 3-tr group, ss in next ss, 7 tr in ch at base of next 3-tr group, ss in next ss; rep from * twice more, 7 tr in ch at base of next half circle, ss in next ss, 11 tr in ch at base of next 3-tr group, join with ss to last ch of foundation ch.

Fasten off.

35 Multi-coloured Quatrefoil

MEDIUM
- 12–15cm ($4^3/_4$–6in)
- Aran yarn
- 5.5mm hook

Foundation ring: Using A, ch 8, join with ss to form a ring.

Round 1: Ch 4 (counts as first dtr), 5 dtr into ring, ch 3, [6 dtr into ring, ch 3] 3 times, join with ss to top of beg ch-4.

Round 2: Beg 5-dtr cl, ch 5, skip 1 ch, ss in next ch, ch 5, *6-dtr cl, ch 5, skip 1 ch, ss in next ch, ch 5; rep from * twice more, join with ss to top of beg 5-dtr cl.

Fasten off A. Join B to top of any cluster.

Round 3: Working around next 2 ch-5 sp and next ss, [3 dtr, ch 1, 3 dtr, ch 2, 3 dtr, ch 1, 3 dtr] in next ch-3 sp on round 1, *ss in top of next cl on round 2, working around next 2 ch-5 sp and next ss, [3 dtr, ch 1, 3 dtr, ch 2, 3 dtr, ch 1, 3 dtr] in next ch-3 sp on round 1; rep from * twice more, join with ss to first ss.

Fasten off B. Join C to any corner ch-2 sp.

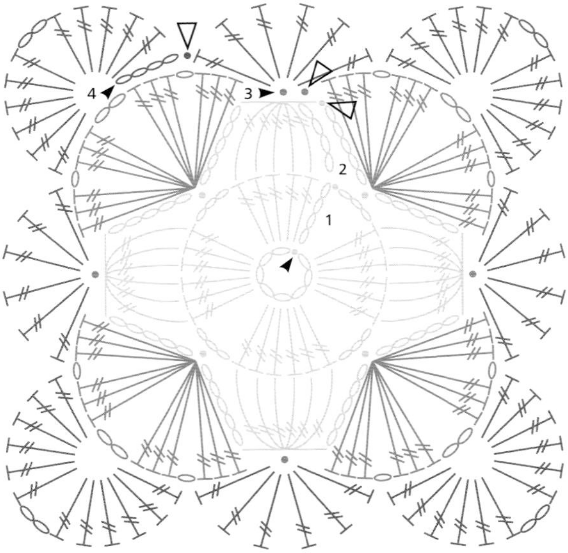

COLOURS

A

B

C

Round 4: Ch 4, [5 dtr, ch 2, 6 dtr] in sp at base of ch-4, skip 6 dtr, 6 dtr in next ss, *skip 6 dtr, [6 dtr, ch 2, 6 dtr] in next ch-2 sp, skip 6 dtr, 6 dtr in next ss; rep from * twice more, skip 6 dtr, join with ss to beg ch-4.

Fasten off.

SPECIAL ABBREVIATIONS

beg 5-dtr cl (beginning 5 double treble crochet cluster): Ch 4, *[yo] twice, insert hook in next dtr, yo, draw yarn through, [yo, draw through 2 loops on hook] twice; rep from * 4 times more, yo, draw through all 6 loops on hook.

6-dtr cl (6 double treble crochet cluster): *[Yo] twice, insert hook in next dtr, yo, draw yarn through, [yo, draw through 2 loops on hook] twice; rep from * 5 times more, yo, draw through all 7 loops on hook.

36 Concentric Circles

LARGE

- 15–18cm (6–7in)
- DK yarn
- 4.5mm hook

Foundation chain: Using A, make a magic ring.

Round 1: Ch 3 (counts as first tr), 11 tr into ring, join with ss to top of beg ch-3, turn. (12 tr)

Round 2: Ch 3 (counts as first tr), 1 tr in st at base of ch-3, 2 tr in each st around, join with ss to top of beg ch-3, turn. (24 tr)

Fasten off A. Join B.

Round 3: Ch 3 (counts as first tr), 1 tr in st at base of ch-3, *1 tr in next st, 2 tr in next st; rep from * 10 times more, 1 tr in next st, join with ss to top of beg ch-3, turn. (36 tr)

Round 4: Ch 3 (counts as first tr), 1 tr in st at base of ch-3, *1 tr in each of next 2 sts, 2 tr in next st; rep from * 10 times more, 1 tr in each of next 2 sts, join with ss to top of beg ch-3, turn. (48 tr)

Fasten off B. Join A.

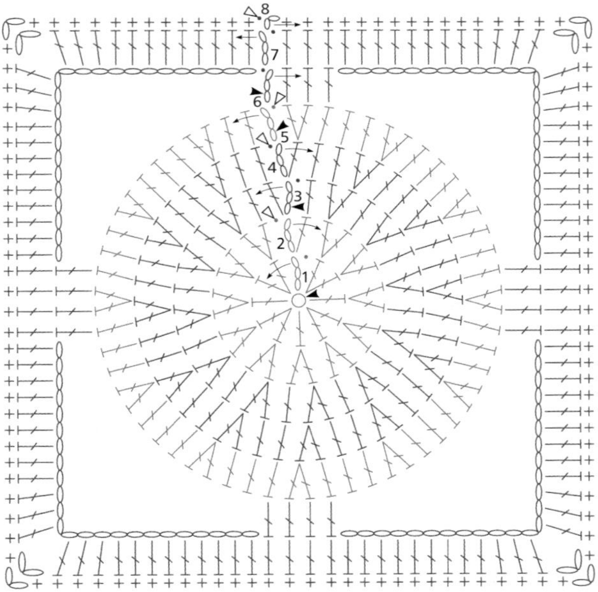

COLOURS

A

B

Round 5: Ch 3 (counts as first tr), 1 tr in each of next 2 sts, *2 tr in next st, 1 tr in each of next 3 sts; rep from * 10 times more, 2 tr in next st, join with ss to top of beg ch-3, turn. (60 tr)

Fasten off B. Join A.

Round 6: Ch 3 (counts as first tr), *1 tr in each of next 3 sts, ch 24, skip 11 sts, 1 tr in next st; rep from * twice more, 1 tr in each of next 3 sts, ch 24, skip 11 sts, join with ss to top of beg ch-3, turn.

Round 7: Ch 3 (counts as first tr), *1 tr in each of next 12 ch, ch 2, 1 tr in each of next 12 ch,1 tr in each of next 4 sts; rep from * twice more, 1 tr in each next 12 ch, ch 2, 1 tr in each of next 12 ch, 1 tr in each of next 3 sts, join with ss to top of beg ch-3, turn.

Round 8: Ch 2 (counts as first dc), 1 dc in each of next 15 sts, [1 dc, ch 2, 1 dc] in corner ch-2 sp, *1 dc in each of next 28 sts, [1 dc, ch 2, 1 dc] in corner ch-2 sp; rep from * twice more, 1 dc in each of next 12 sts, join with ss to top of beg ch-2. Fasten off.

37 Flower Trellis

LARGE
- 15–18cm (6–7in)
- DK yarn
- 4.5mm hook

Flower (make 3)

Foundation ring: Using A, make a magic ring.

Round 1: Ch 3 (counts as first tr), 7 tr into ring, join with ss to top of beg ch-3, turn.

Round 2: Ch 2 (counts as first dc), 1 dc into each st around, join with ss to top of beg ch-2, turn. Fasten off A. Join B.

Round 3: Ch 5 (counts as first trtr of petal), cont to make petal, *ch 5, make petal; rep from * 6 times more. Fasten off.

Trellis

Foundation row: Join A with ss to petal tip of flower 1, ch 6 (counts as 1 tr and ch 3), 1 dc in next petal tip of flower 1, ch 3, 1 tr in next petal tip of flower 1, ch 3, 1 tr in petal tip of flower 2, ch 3, 1 dc in next petal tip of flower 2, ch 3, 1 tr in next petal tip of flower 2, ch 3, 1 tr in petal tip of flower 3, ch 3, 1 dc in next petal tip of flower 3, ch 3, 1 tr in next petal tip of flower 3, turn.

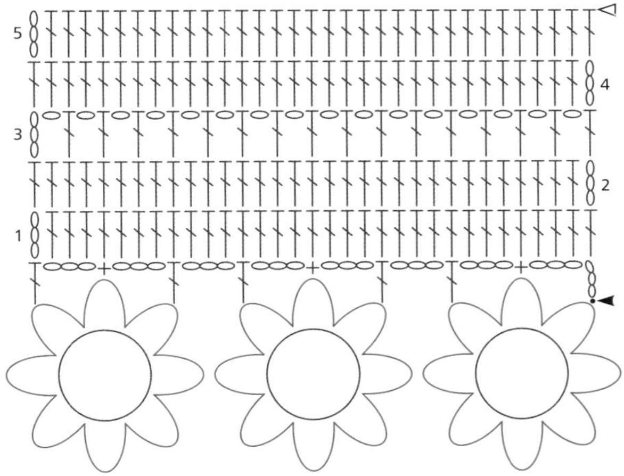

TRELLIS

COLOURS

A

B

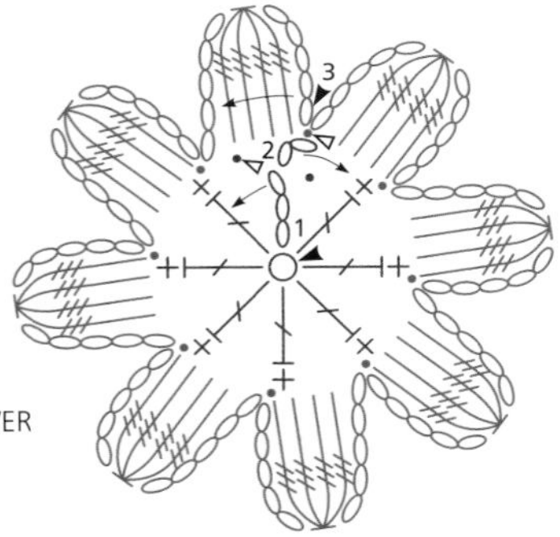

FLOWER

Row 1: Ch 3 (counts as first tr), *3 tr in next ch-3 sp, 1 tr in next st; rep from * 7 times more, turn. (33 sts)

Row 2: Ch 3 (counts as first tr), 1 tr in each st to end, turn.

Row 3: Ch 4 (counts as first tr and ch 1), skip 1 st, 1 tr in next st, *ch 1, skip 1 st, 1 tr in next st; rep from * to end, turn.

Row 4: Ch 3 (counts as first tr), *1 tr in each ch-sp and st to end, turn.

Row 5: Rep row 2. Fasten off.

Work trellis along other side of flowers in the same way.

Fasten off.

SPECIAL ABBREVIATION

Make petal: *1 trtr in st at base of ch-5, omitting final stage to leave last loop of trtr on hook; rep from * 3 times more, yo and draw through all 5 loops on hook, ch 5, ss in next st.

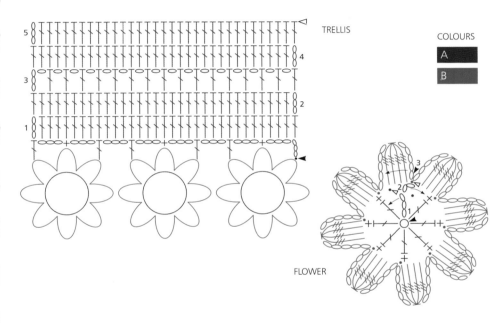

38 Multi-coloured Granny

LARGE
- 15–18cm (6–7in)
- DK yarn
- 4.5mm hook

Foundation chain: Using A, ch 6, join with ss to form a ring.

Round 1: Ch 3 (counts as first tr), 2 tr into ring, ch 3, *3 tr into ring, ch 3; rep from * twice more, join with ss to top of beg ch-3.

Fasten off A. Join B to corner ch-3 sp.

Round 2: Ch 3 (counts as first tr), [2 tr, ch 3, 3 tr] in corner sp, ch 1, *[3 tr, ch 3, 3 tr] in next corner sp, ch 1; rep from * twice more, join with ss to top of beg ch-3.

Fasten off B. Join C to corner ch-3 sp.

Round 3: Ch 3 (counts as first tr), [2 tr, ch 3, 3 tr] in corner sp, ch 1, 3 tr in next ch-1 sp, ch 1, *[3 tr, ch 3, 3 tr] in corner sp, ch 1, 3 tr in next ch-1 sp, ch 1; rep from * twice more, join with ss to top of beg ch-3.

Fasten off C. Join D to corner ch-3 sp.

Round 4: Ch 3 (counts as first tr), [2 tr, ch 3, 3 tr] in corner sp, ch 1, [3 tr, ch 1] in each ch-1 sp to corner, *[3 tr, ch 3, 3 tr] in corner sp, ch 1, [3 tr, ch 1] in each ch-1 sp to corner; rep from * twice more, join with ss to top of beg ch-3.

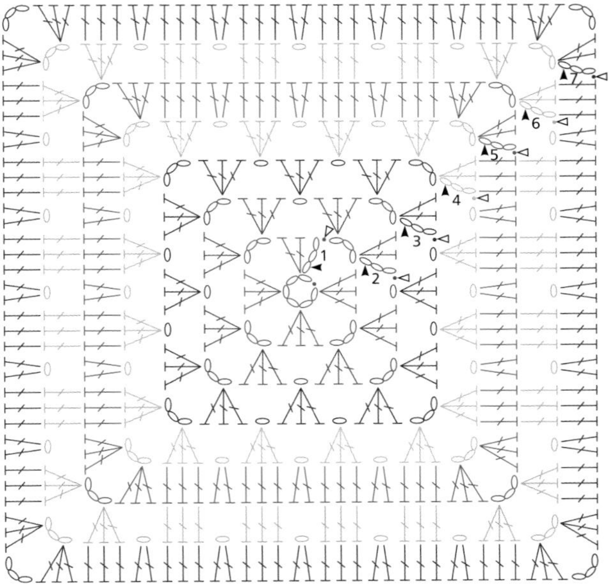

COLOURS
A
B
C
D
E

Fasten off D. Join A to corner ch-3 sp.

Round 5: Ch 3 (counts as first tr), [2 tr, ch 3, 3 tr] in corner sp, *1 tr in each of next 3 sts, 2 tr in next ch-1 sp; rep from * twice more, 1 tr in each of next 3 sts, [3 tr, ch 3, 3 tr] in corner sp; cont in patt set, working 1 tr in each st, 2 tr in each ch-1 sp, [3 tr, ch 3, 3 tr] in each corner sp, join with ss to top of beg ch-3.

Fasten off A. Join E to corner ch-3 sp.

Round 6: Ch 3 (counts as first tr) [2 tr, ch 3, 3 tr] in corner sp, ch 1, skip 3 sts, *1 tr in each of next 3 sts, ch 1, skip 2 sts; rep from * 3 times more, [3 tr, ch 3, 3 tr] in corner sp; cont in patt set, join with ss to top of beg ch-3.

Fasten off E. Join C to corner ch-3 sp.

Round 7: Ch 3 (counts as first tr) [2 tr, ch 3, 3 tr] in corner sp, *1 tr in each of next 3 sts, 2 tr in next ch-1 sp; rep from * 4 times more, 1 tr in each of next 3 sts, [3 tr, ch 3, 3 tr] in corner sp; cont in patt set, join with ss to top of beg ch-3.

Fasten off.

39 Colour Swirl Granny

MEDIUM

- 12–15cm (4¾–6in)
- Aran yarn
- 5.5mm hook

Foundation chain: Using A, ch 2.

Round 1: Starting in second ch from hook, [1 dc, 1 htr, 2 tr] in ch, remove hook from loop A, join B with dc in same ch, [1 htr, 2 tr] in same ch, remove hook from loop B, join C with dc in same ch, [1 htr, 2 tr] in same ch, remove hook from loop C, join D with dc in same ch, [1 htr, 2 tr] in same ch, remove hook from loop D, gently tighten chain into which sts have been worked.

Insert hook into working loops as required.

Round 2: Using A, *2 tr in next dc, 1 tr in next htr, 2 tr in next tr, 1 tr in next tr, remove hook from loop A; rep from * with colours B, C and D.

Round 3: Using A, *ch 2, 1 tr in next tr, skip 1 tr, 2 tr in each of next 2 tr, skip 1 tr, 1 tr in next tr, remove hook from loop A; rep from * with colours B, C and D.

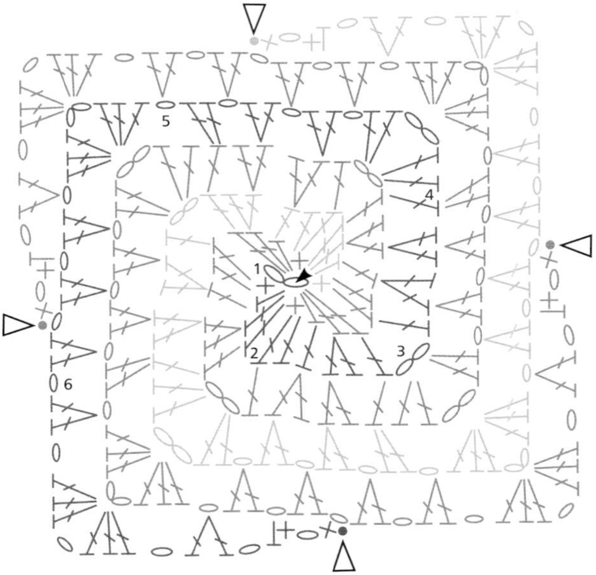

COLOURS

A

B

C

D

Round 4: Using A, *[2 tr, ch 2, 2 tr] in next ch-2 sp, [ch 1, skip 1 tr, 2 tr in next tr] 3 times, remove hook from loop A; rep from * with colours B, C and D.

Round 5: Using A, *ch 1, [3 tr, ch 2, 3 tr] in next ch-2 sp, [ch 1, skip 2 tr, 2 tr in next ch-1 sp] 3 times, remove hook from loop A; rep from * with colours B, C and D.

Round 6: Using A, *ch 1, 2 tr in next ch-1 sp, ch 1, [3 tr, ch 1, 3 tr] in next ch-2 sp, skip 3 tr, ch 1, 2 tr in next ch-1 sp, skip 2 tr, ch 1, [1 htr, 1 dc) in next ch-1 sp, skip 2 tr, ch 1, [1 dc, ss] in next ch-1 sp, fasten off A; rep from * with colours B, C and D.

NOTE

Place working loops not in use on to a split-ring marker or safety pin.

40 Scales

LARGE
- 15–18cm (6–7in)
- DK yarn
- 4.5mm hook

Foundation chain: Ch 29.

Row 1 (WS): 1 dc in fourth ch from hook (counts as first 2 dc), 1 dc in each ch to end, turn. (27 sts)

Row 2: Ch 3 (counts as first tr), 1 tr in each of next 2 sts, *make scale in next st, 1 tr in each of next 3 sts; rep from * 5 times more, turn.

Row 3: Ch 2 (counts as first dc), 1 dc in each of next 2 sts, *1 dc around ch-3 of scale, 1 dc in each of next 3 sts; rep from * 5 times more, turn.

Row 4: Ch 3 (counts as first tr), 1 tr in each of next 4 sts, *make scale in next st, 1 tr in each of next 3 sts; rep from * 4 times more, 1 tr in each of next 2 sts, turn.

Row 5: Ch 2 (counts as first dc), 1 dc in each of next 4 sts, *1 dc around ch-3 of scale, 1 dc in each of next 3 sts; rep from * 4 times more, 1 dc in each of next 2 sts, turn.

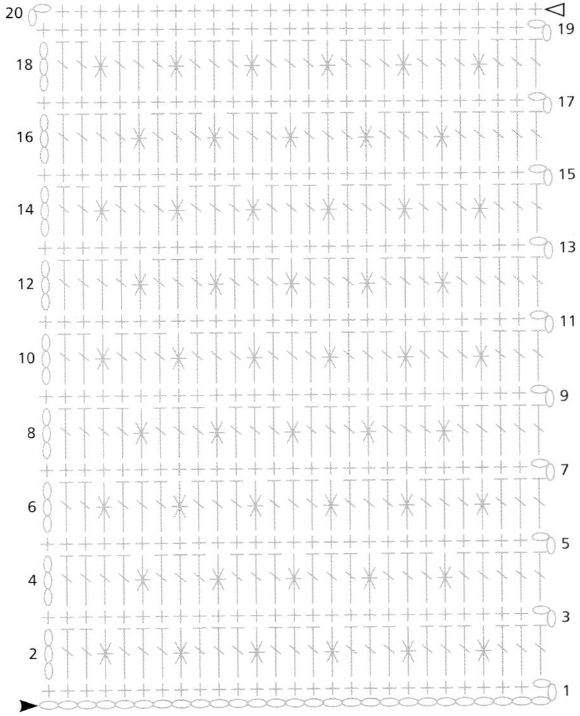

COLOUR

SCALE

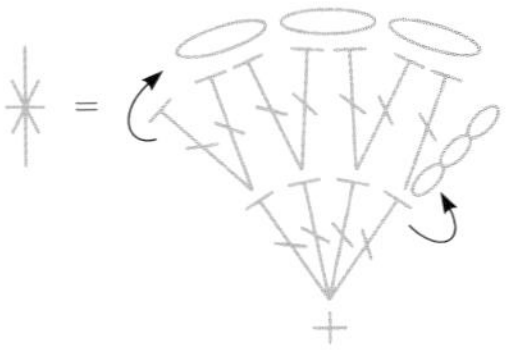

Rows 6–17: Rep rows 2–5, 3 times more.

Rows 18–19: Rep rows 2–3.

Row 20: Ch 2 (counts as first dc), 1 dc in each st to end.

Fasten off.

SPECIAL ABBREVIATION

Make scale: 4 tr in next st, turn, ch 3 (counts as 1 tr), 1 tr in st at base of ch-3, 2 tr in each st across scale, ch 3, turn.

41 Rose Garden

LARGE

- 15–18cm (6–7in)
- DK yarn
- 4.5mm hook

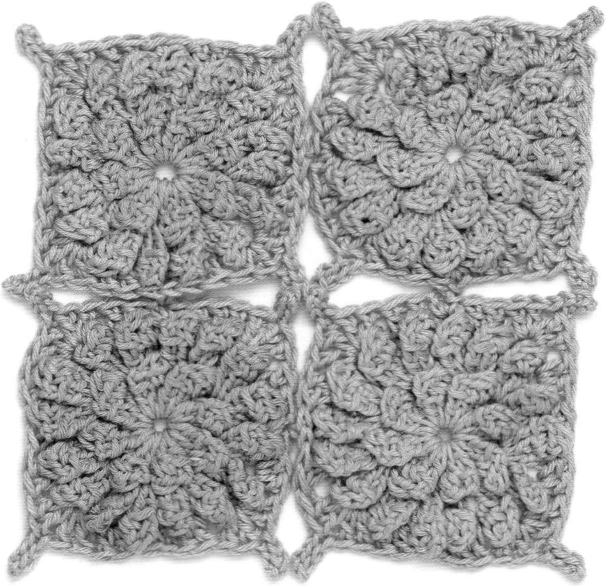

First quarter

Foundation chain: Using A, ch 6, join with ss to form a ring.

Round 1: Ch 3 (counts as first tr of petal), cont to make petal into ring; make petal 7 times more, join with ss to top of beg ch-3. (8 petals)

Round 2: Ch 3 (counts as first tr of petal), cont to make petal into ch-2 sp behind petals on round 1; make petal once more in same sp, make petal twice in each ch-2 sp around, join with ss to top of beg ch-3. (16 petals)

Fasten off A. Join B with ss to next ch-2 sp behind petal.

Round 3: Ch 3 (counts as first tr), 1 tr in sp at base of ch-3, 2 dc in next ch-2 sp, 2 tr in next ch-2 sp, *[2 tr, ch 5, join with ss to first ch of ch-5, 2 tr] in next ch-2 sp, 2 tr in next ch-2 sp, 2 dc in next ch-2 sp, 2 tr in next ch-2 sp; rep from * twice more, [2 tr, ch 5, join with ss to first ch of ch-5, 2 tr] in next ch-2 sp, join with ss to top of beg ch-3.

Fasten off.

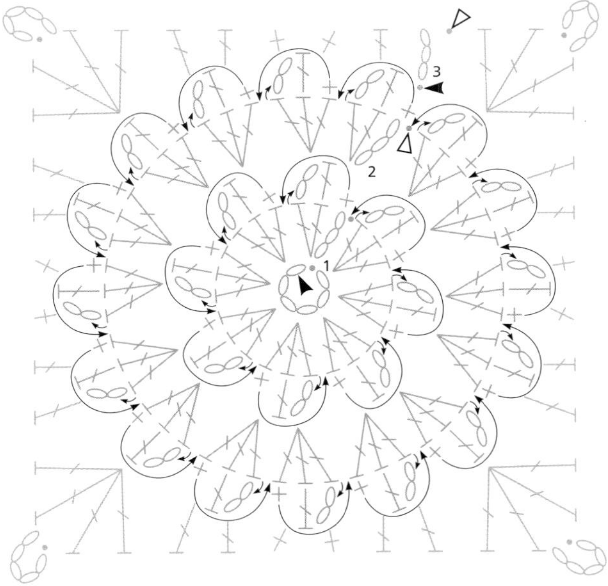

COLOURS

A

B

Remaining quarters

Work each remaining quarter in the same way, but on round 3 join to completed quarters by inserting hook between 2 dc on side edge of completed quarter before working second dc of the quarter you are making.

SPECIAL ABBREVIATION

Make petal: 3 tr around ch, turn, ch 2, 1 tr in next st, 1 dc in next st, ch 2, turn.

Note: The final ch-2 of the petal is indicated on the chart by a long curving arrow over the top of each petal. This ch-2 lies behind the petal stitches and takes you across to where you work the 3 tr to start the next petal. The petals on round 2 are worked into this ch-2 sp.

42 Large Daisy

LARGE
- 15–18cm (6–7in)
- DK yarn
- 4.5mm hook

Foundation ring: Using A, make a magic ring.

Round 1: Ch 3 (counts as first tr), 11 tr into ring, join with ss to top of beg ch-3, turn. (12 tr)

Round 2: Ch 3 (counts as first tr), 1 tr in st at base of ch-3, 2 tr in each st around, join with ss to top of beg ch-3, turn. (24 tr)

Round 3: Ch 3 (counts as first tr), 1 tr in st at base of ch-3, *1 tr in next st, 2 tr in next st; rep from * 10 times more, 1 tr in next st, join with ss to top of beg ch-3, turn. (36 tr)

Fasten off A. Join B.

Round 4: Ch 3 (counts as first tr), 1 tr in st at base of ch-3, *1 tr tbl in each of next 2 sts, 2 tr tbl in next st; rep from * 10 times more, 1 tr tbl in each of next 2 sts, join with ss to top of beg ch-3, turn. (48 tr)

Round 5: Ch 3 (counts as first tr), [1 tr, ch 2, 2 tr] in st at base of ch-3, *ch 3, skip 3 sts, 1 dc in each of next 5 sts, ch 3, skip 3 sts, [2 tr, ch 2, 2 tr] in next st; rep from * twice more, ch 3, skip 3 sts, 1 dc in each of next 5 sts, ch 3, skip 3 sts, join with ss to top of beg ch-3, turn.

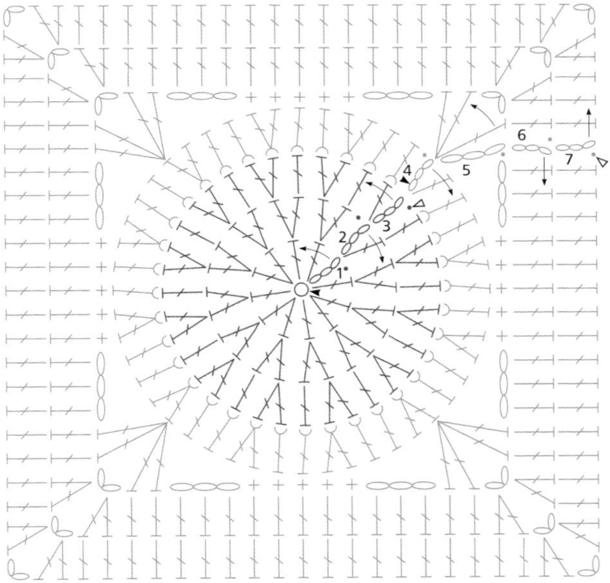

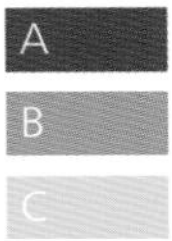

PETAL

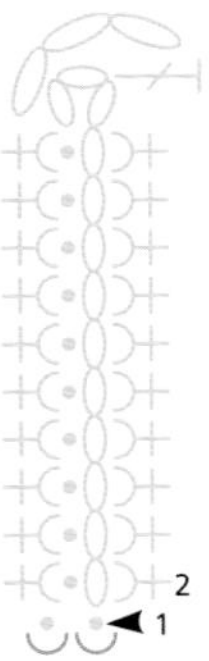

Round 6: Ch 3 (counts as first tr), *3 tr in next ch-3 sp, 1 tr in each of next 5 sts, 3 tr in next ch-3 sp, 1 tr in each of next 2 sts, [2 tr, ch 2, 2 tr] in corner ch-2 sp, 1 tr in each of next 2 sts; rep from * 3 times more ending 1 tr in last st, join with ss to top of beg ch-3, turn.

Round 7: Ch 3 (counts as first tr), 1 tr in each of next 3 sts, *[2 tr, ch 2, 2 tr] in corner ch-2 sp, 1 tr in each of next 19 sts; rep from * twice more, [2 tr, ch 2, 2 tr] in corner ch-2 sp, 1 tr in each of next 15 sts, join with ss to top of beg ch-3. Fasten off.

Petal

Join C with ss tfl at base of round 4.

Round 1: *Ch 13, skip 3 ch, ss in each loop on reverse of next 10 ch, ss in next front loop at base of round 4; rep from * 35 times more, join with ss to base of first petal.

Round 2: *1 dc tbl in each of next 10 ch, [1 tr, ch 3] in ch-3 sp at end of petal, 1 dc tbl in each of next 10 ss; rep from * 35 times more, join with ss to base of first petal.

Fasten off.

43 Square Deal

LARGE
- 15–18cm (6–7in)
- DK yarn
- 4.5mm hook

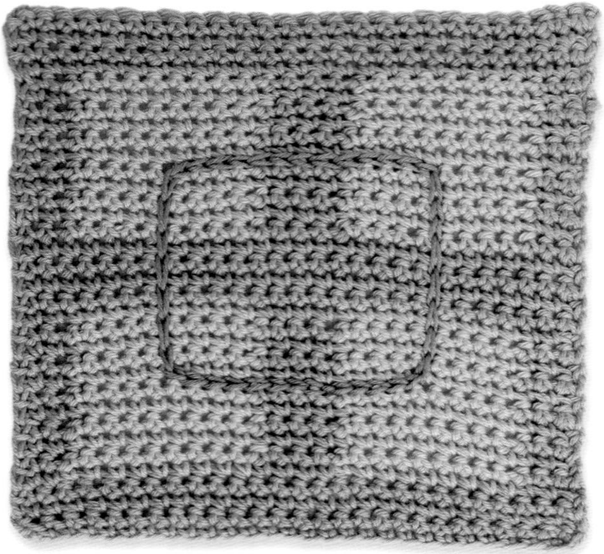

Foundation chain: Using A, ch 30.

Row 1: 1 dc in fourth ch from hook (counts as first 2 dc), 1 dc in each ch to end, turn. (28 sts)

Row 2: Ch 2 (counts as first dc), 1 dc in each st to end, turn.

Continue in dc across each row for 34 rows in total, working ch 2 (counts as first dc) at beg of each row and working last dc into top of beg ch-2 before turning.

Change colours as indicated on charts, joining in a new length of yarn for each area of colour. The main chart provides full pattern information; use the smaller chart as a guide to colour placement.

Fasten off.

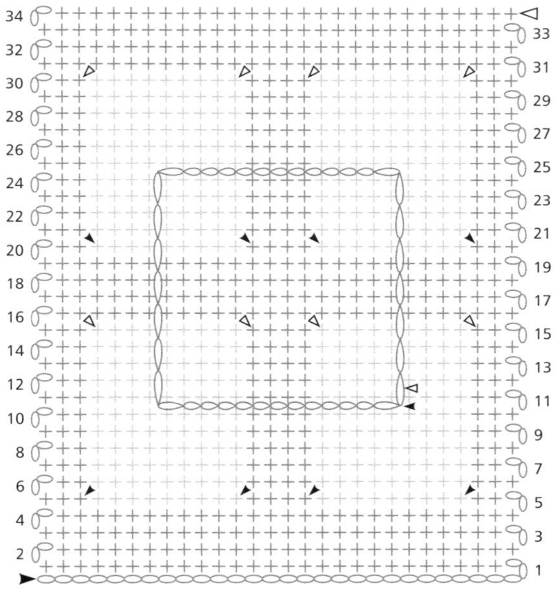

COLOURS

A

B

C

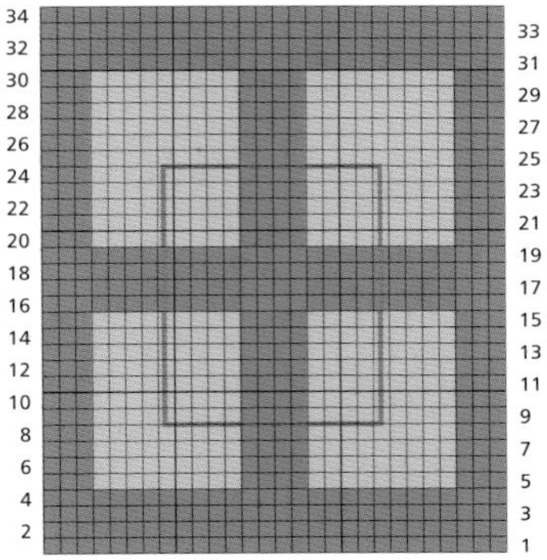

Surface crochet

Using C and referring to charts and photograph as a guide, work a square of surface chain sts around centre of block.

Fasten off.

NOTE

See page 95 for advice on working intarsia designs with multiple colour changes.

44 Pie Chart

LARGE

- 15–18cm (6–7in)
- DK yarn
- 4.5mm hook

Foundation chain: Using A, ch 30.

Row 1: 1 dc in fourth ch from hook (counts as first 2 dc), 1 dc in each ch to end, turn. (28 sts)

Row 2: Ch 2 (counts as first dc), 1 dc in each st to end, turn.

Continue in dc across each row for 34 rows in total, working ch 2 (counts as first dc) at beg of each row and working last dc into top of beg ch-2 before turning.

Change colours as indicated on charts, joining in a new length of yarn for each area of colour. The main chart provides full pattern information; use the smaller chart as a guide to colour placement.

Fasten off.

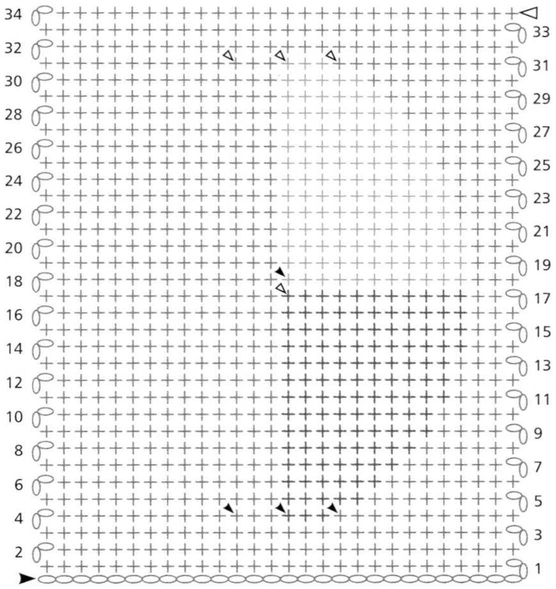

COLOURS

- A
- B
- C
- D

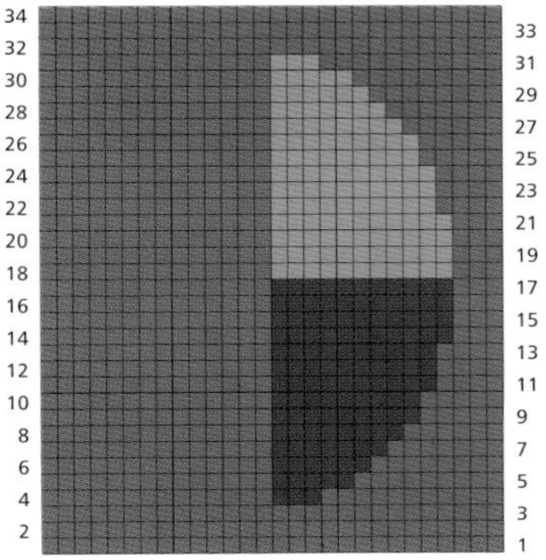

WORKING INTARSIA DESIGNS

- Work each colour area using a separate length of yarn, including for unconnected areas of the main background colour. To join a new colour, omit the final stage of the stitch before the change. Complete the stitch with the new colour.
- At each colour changeover, loop the new yarn around the old one on the wrong side of the work to prevent holes.
- Take extra care when dealing with all the yarn ends on a piece of intarsia. Carefuly weave each end into an area of crochet worked in the same colour so that it will not be visible on the right side.

45 Shoo Fly

LARGE
- 15–18cm (6–7in)
- DK yarn
- 4.5mm hook

Foundation chain: Using A, ch 31.

Row 1: 1 tr in fifth ch from hook (counts as first 2 tr), 1 tr in each of next 6 ch. Without fastening off A, join B. Using B, 1 tr in each of next 12 ch. Without fastening off B, join a new length of A. Using A, 1 tr in each ch to end, turn. (28 sts)

Row 2: Ch 3 (counts as first tr), 1 tr in each of next 5 sts. Using B, 1 tr in each of next 4 sts. Join a new length of A, 1 tr in each of next 8 sts. Join a new length of B, 1 tr in each of next 4 sts. Using A, 1 tr in each st to end, turn.

Continue in tr across each row for 16 rows in total, working ch 3 (counts as first tr) at beg of each row and working last tr into top of beg ch-3 before turning.

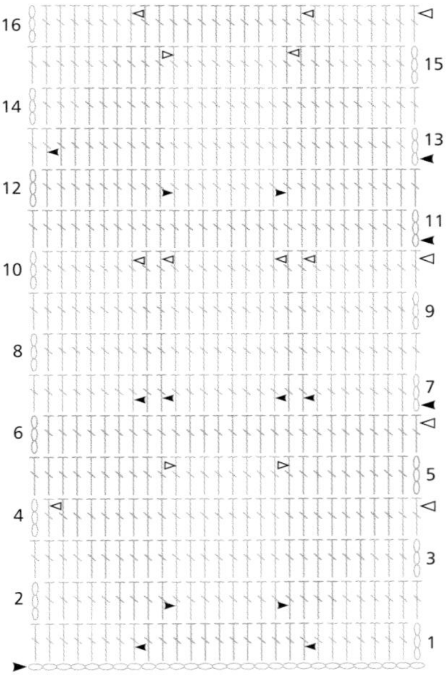

COLOURS

A

B

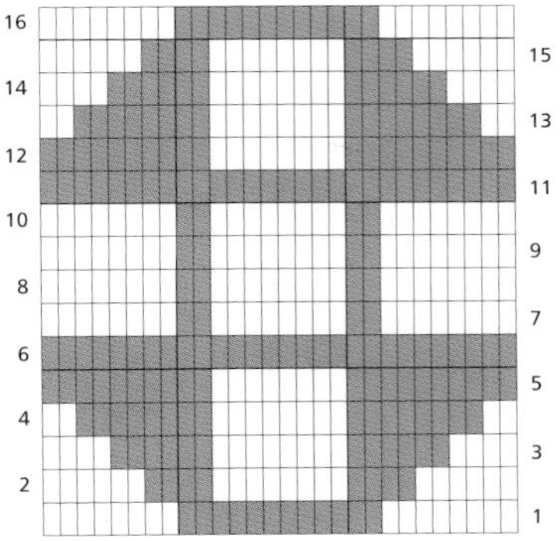

Change colours as indicated on charts, joining a new length of yarn for each area of colour. The main chart provides full pattern information; use the smaller chart as a guide to colour placement.

Fasten off.

NOTE

See page 95 for advice on working intarsia designs with multiple colour changes.

46 Homestead

LARGE

- 15–18cm (6–7in)
- DK yarn
- 4.5mm hook

Foundation chain: Using A, ch 30.

Row 1: 1 dc in fourth ch from hook (counts as first 2 dc), 1 dc in each of next 15 ch. Without fastening off A, join B. Using B and weaving in A on reverse, 1 dc in each of next 7 ch. Using A, 1 dc in each of next 4 ch, turn. (28 sts)

Row 2: Ch 2 (counts as first dc), 1 dc in each of next 3 sts. Using B and weaving in A on reverse, 1 dc in each of next 7 sts. Using A, 1 dc in each st to end, turn.

Continue in dc across each row for 34 rows in total, working ch 2 (counts as first dc) at beg of each row and working last dc into top of beg ch-2 before turning.

Change colours as indicated on charts, joining in a new length of yarn for each area of colours B, C and D, and weaving in A on reverse of door and window. The main chart provides full pattern information; use the smaller chart as a guide to colour placement.

Fasten off.

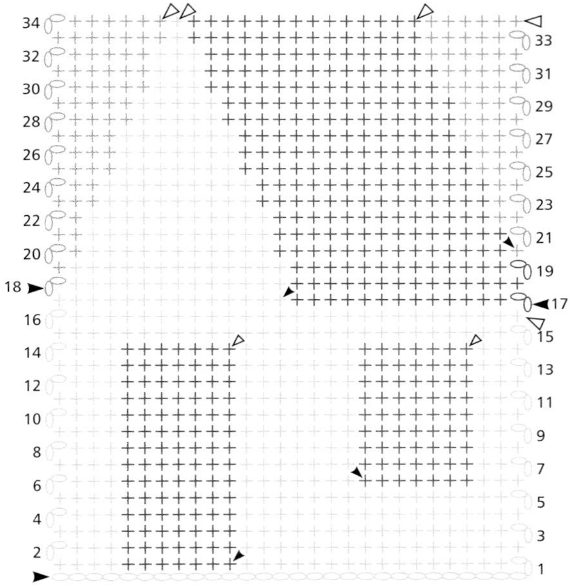

COLOURS

A

B

C

D

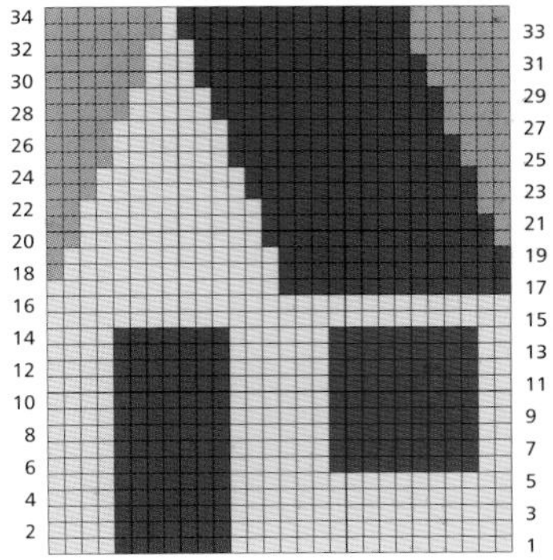

NOTE

See page 95 for advice on working intarsia designs with multiple colour changes, and page 101 for guidance on weaving in yarn on the reverse of the block.

Fair Isle

LARGE
- 15–18cm (6–7in)
- DK yarn
- 4.5mm hook

Foundation chain: Using A, ch 29.

Row 1: 1 dc in fourth ch from hook (counts as first 2 dc), 1 dc in each ch to end, turn. (27 sts)

Row 2: Ch 2 (counts as first dc), 1 dc in each st to end, turn.

Continue in dc across each row for 34 rows in total, working ch 2 (counts as first dc) at beg of each row and working last dc into top of beg ch-2 before turning.

Change colours as indicated on charts, weaving in colour not being used on reverse of block. The main chart provides full pattern information; use the smaller chart as a guide to colour placement.

Fasten off.

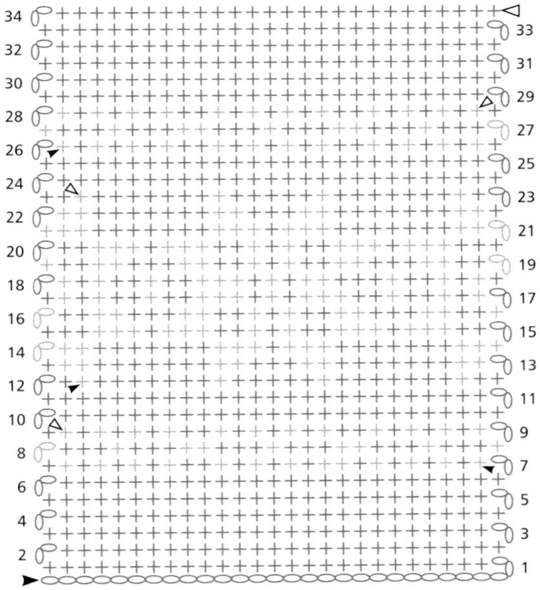

COLOURS

A

B

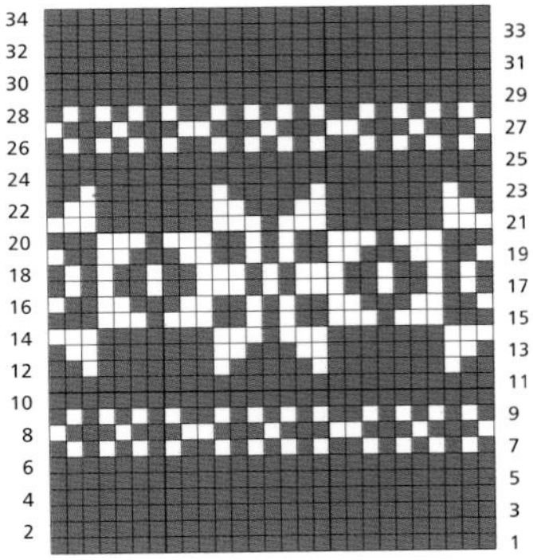

WEAVING IN YARNS

Each of the three bands of Fair Isle pattern require both yarn colours to be carried across the back of the fabric. To avoid unslightly strands of yarn on the reverse of the block, it is important to weave the colour not being used into that of the stitch being worked.

To do this, begin working into the next st in the usual way, yo, draw yarn through, wrap yarn not in use around hook from below, wrap working yarn around hook in same direction, return yarn not in use to back of work. Using working yarn, complete the st. This traps the yarn not in use into the st being worked. Repeat this process for every st.

48 Treble Crochet Triangle

MEDIUM

- 12–15cm (4¾–6in)
- Aran yarn
- 5.5mm hook

Foundation ring: Ch 8, join with ss to form a ring.

Round 1: Ch 3 (counts as first tr), 2 tr into ring, ch 3, [3 tr, ch 3] twice, join with ss to top of beg ch-3.

Round 2: Ch 3 (counts as first tr), 1 tr in each of next 2 sts, *[3 tr, ch 3, 3 tr] in next ch-3 sp, 1 tr in each of next 3 sts; rep from * once more, [3 tr, ch 3, 3 tr] in next ch-3 sp, join with ss to top of beg ch-3.

COLOUR

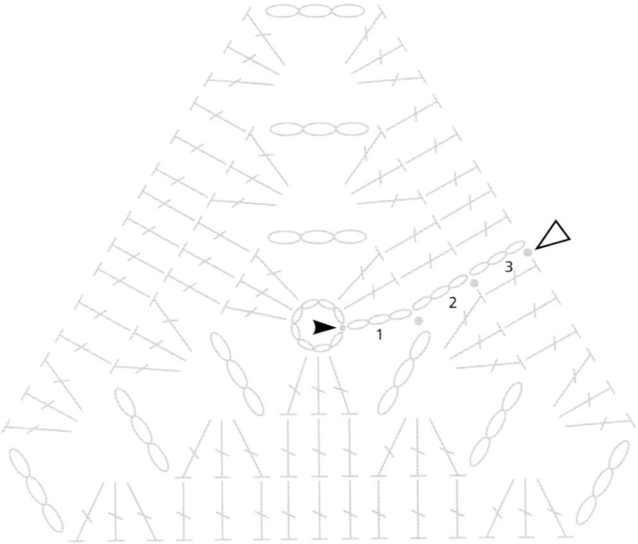

Round 3: Ch 3 (counts as first tr), 1 tr in each of next 5 sts, *[3 tr, ch 3, 3 tr] in next ch-3 sp, 1 tr in each of next 9 sts; rep from * once more, [3 tr, ch 3, 3 tr] in next ch-3 sp, 1 tr in each of next 3 sts, join with ss to top of beg ch-3.

Fasten off.

TIP: CHOOSING COLOURS

- Although pastels are perfect for making a project for a baby, any colour can be used as long as the yarn is suitable for delicate skin.
- When you have narrowed down your colour choices, place skeins of the various colour options together in natural daylight to see how well they blend together.
- When in doubt – swatch, swatch, swatch!

49 Solid Granny Triangle

SMALL
- 9–12cm (3½–4¾in)
- Aran yarn
- 5.5mm hook

Foundation ring: Ch 4, join with ss to form a ring.

Round 1: 1 dc into ring, [ch 4, 1 dc into ring] twice, ch 4, join with ss to first dc.

Round 2: Ch 4 (counts as first tr and ch 1), *[2 tr, 1 dtr, ch 3, 1 dtr, 2 tr] in next ch-4 sp, ch 1; rep from * once more, [2 tr, 1 dtr, ch 3, 1 dtr, 1 tr] in next ch-4 sp, join with ss to third ch of beg ch-4.

COLOUR

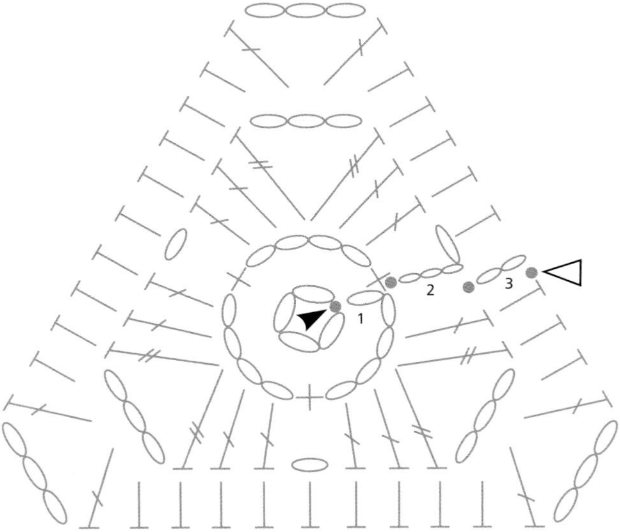

Round 3: Ch 2 (counts as first htr), 1 htr in next ch-1 sp, 1 htr in each of next 3 sts, *[1 htr, 1 tr, ch 3, 1 tr, 1 htr] in next ch-3 sp, 1 htr in each of next 3 sts, 1 htr in next ch-1 sp, 1 htr in each of next 3 sts; rep from * once more, [1 htr, 1 tr, ch 3, 1 tr, 1 htr] in next ch-3 sp, 1 htr in each of next 2 sts, join with ss to top of beg ch-2.

Fasten off.

TIP: STORING CROCHET

Apart from dirt and dust, the main enemy of crochet fabrics is direct sunlight, which can cause yarn colours to fade and fibres to weaken. Store all items in a drawer, wardrobe or other dark, dry and moth-free place. Check them regularly, refolding the larger items. It is also a good idea to make small cloth sachets filled with dried lavender flowers to tuck into your drawer or wardrobe along with your crochet, as the smell deters moths.

50 Two-tone Granny Triangle

MEDIUM

- 12–15cm (4¾–6in)
- Aran yarn
- 5.5mm hook

Foundation ring: Using A, ch 4, join with ss to form a ring.

Round 1: Ch 5 (counts as first tr and ch 3), [3 tr into ring, ch 3] twice, 2 tr, join with ss to second ch of beg ch-5.

Round 2: Ss in next ch-3 sp, ch 1 [1 dc, ch 5, 3 tr] in same sp, *ch 2, [3 tr, ch 3, 3 tr] in next ch-3 sp; rep from * once more, ch 2, 2 tr in first ch-3 sp, join with ss to second ch of beg ch-5.

Fasten off A. Join B to next ch-3 sp.

COLOURS

A

B

Round 3: Ch 1, [1 dc, ch 5, 3 tr] in sp at base of ch-1, *ch 2, 3 tr in next ch-2 sp, ch 2, [3 tr, ch 3, 3 tr] in corner ch-3 sp; rep from * once more, ch 2, 3 tr in next ch-2 sp, ch 2, 2 tr in first ch-3 sp, join with ss to second ch of ch-5.

Round 4: Ss in next ch-3 sp, ch 1, [1 dc, ch 5, 3 tr] in sp at base of ch-1, *[ch 2, 3 tr in next ch-2 sp] twice, ch 2, [3 tr, ch 3, 3 tr] in corner ch-3 sp; rep from * once more, [ch 2, 3 tr in next ch-2 sp] twice, ch 2, 2 tr in first ch-3 sp, join with ss to second ch of ch-5.

Fasten off.

51 Dainty Flower Triangle

LARGE
- 15–18cm (6–7in)
- Aran yarn
- 5.5mm hook

Foundation ring: Using A, ch 8, join with ss to form a ring.

Round 1: Beg popcorn into ring, ch 3, [popcorn into ring, ch 3] 5 times, join with ss to top of beg ch-3.

Fasten off A. Join B to any ch-3 sp.

Round 2: Ch 3 (counts as first tr), 8 tr in sp at base of ch-3, [ch 4, skip ch-3 sp, 9 tr in next ch-3 sp] twice, ch 4, join with ss to top of beg ch-3.

Round 3: Ch 3 (counts as first tr), 1 tr in st at base of ch-3, *1 tr in each of next 3 tr, [1 tr, 1 dtr, ch 3, 1 dtr, 1 tr] in next tr, 1 tr in each of next 3 tr, 2 tr in next tr, 1 dc in next ch-4 sp, 2 tr in next tr; rep from * once more, 1 tr in each of next 3 tr, [1 tr, 1 dtr, ch 3, 1 dtr, 1 tr] in next tr, 1 tr in each of next 3 tr, 2 tr in next tr, 1 dc in next ch-4 sp, join with ss to top of beg ch-3.

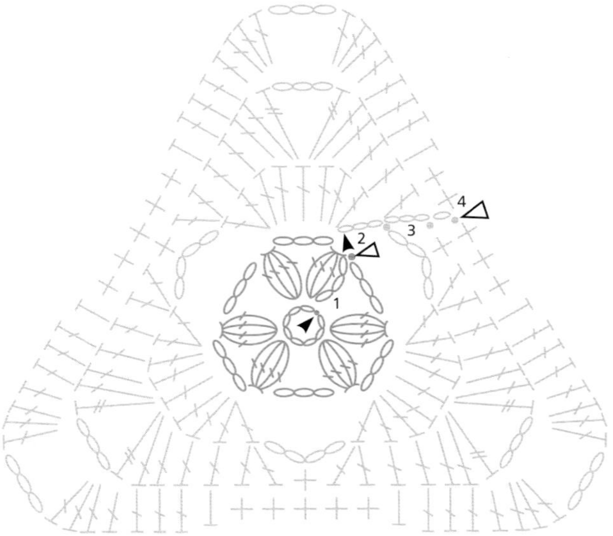

COLOURS

A

B

Round 4: Ch 1, 1 dc in st at base of ch-1, 1 dc in next st, *1 htr in next st, 1 tr in each of next 4 sts, [3 tr, ch 3, 3 tr] in next ch-3 sp, 1 tr in each of next 4 sts, 1 htr in next st, 1 dc in each of next 5 sts; rep from * once more, 1 htr in next st, 1 tr in each of next 4 sts, [3 tr, ch 3, 3 tr] in next ch-3 sp, 1 tr in each of next 4 sts, 1 htr in next st, 1 dc in each of next 3 sts, join with ss to first dc.

Fasten off.

SPECIAL ABBREVIATIONS

beg popcorn: Ch 3, 3 tr into ring, remove hook from working loop, insert hook in top of ch-3, catch working loop and draw through to close popcorn.

popcorn: 4 tr into ring, remove hook from working loop, insert hook in top of first tr of popcorn, catch working loop and draw through to close popcorn.

52 Tri-colour Triangle

SMALL

- 9–12cm ($3\frac{1}{2}$–$4\frac{3}{4}$in)
- Aran yarn
- 5.5mm hook

Foundation ring: Using A, ch 4, join with ss to form a ring.

Round 1: Ch 1, *[1 dc, 1 htr, 1 tr, 1 dtr, 1 tr, 1 htr] into ring; rep from * twice more, join with ss to first dc.

Fasten off A. Join B.

Round 2: Ch 4 (counts as first dtr), 2 tr in next htr, 1 htr in next tr, 1 dc in next dtr, 1 htr in next tr, 2 tr in next htr, *1 dtr in next dc, 2 tr in next htr, 1 htr in next tr, 1 dc in next dtr, 1 htr in next tr, 2 tr in next htr; rep from * once more, join with ss to top of beg ch-4.

Fasten off B. Join C.

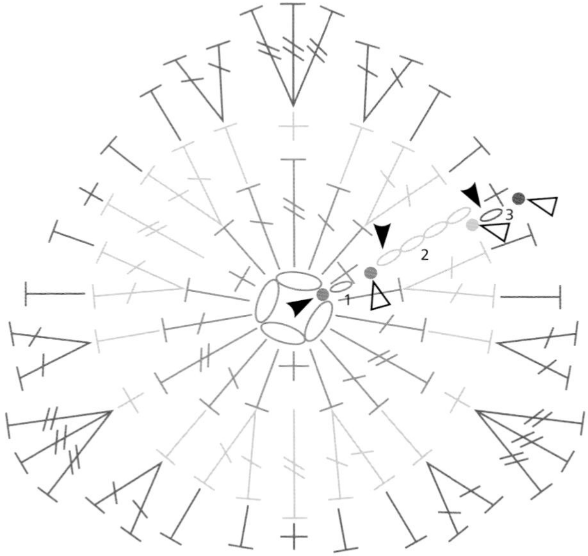

COLOURS

A

B

C

Round 3: Ch 1, 1 dc in st at base of ch-1, *1 htr in each of next 2 tr, 2 tr in next htr, 3 dtr in next dc (point made), 2 tr in next htr, 1 htr in each of next 2 tr, 1 dc in next dtr; rep from * once more, 1 htr in each of next 2 tr, 2 tr in next htr, 3 dtr in next dc, 2 tr in next htr, 1 htr in each of next 2 tr, join with ss to first dc.

Fasten off.

TIP: TURNING CORNERS

Whether you are working a triangle, square, diamond, pentagon, hexagon or octagon, pay particular attention to turning the corners. After every round, also check that you have made the correct number of stitches along each side.

53 Post Stitch Triangle

LARGE
- 15–18cm (6–7in)
- Aran yarn
- 5.5mm hook

Foundation ring: Ch 8, join with ss to form a ring.

Round 1: Ch 3 (counts as first tr), 4 tr into ring, ch 3, [5 tr into ring, ch 3] twice, join with ss to top of beg ch-3.

Round 2: Ss in next tr, ch 3 (counts as first BPtr), FPtr, BPtr, FPtr, *[2 tr, ch 3, 2 tr] in next ch-3 sp, [FPtr, BPtr] twice, FPtr; rep from * once more, [2 tr, ch 3, 2 tr] in next ch-3 sp, FPtr, join with ss to top of beg ch-3. (9 sts each side)

Round 3: Ch 3 (counts as first BPtr), [FPtr, BPtr] twice, FPtr, *[2 tr, ch 3, 2 tr] in next ch-3 sp, [FPtr, BPtr] 4 times, FPtr; rep from * once more, [2 tr, ch 3, 2 tr] in next ch-3 sp, FPtr, BPtr, FPtr, join with ss to top of beg ch-3. (13 sts each side)

COLOUR

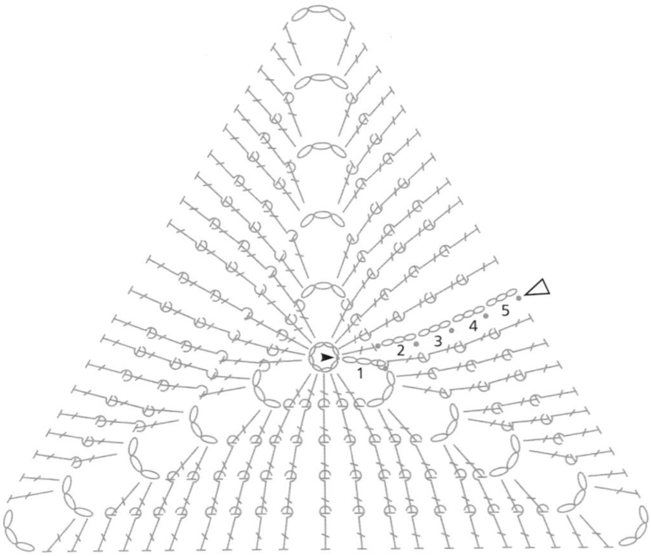

Round 4: Ch 3 (counts as first BPtr), [FPtr, BPtr] 3 times, FPtr, *[2 tr, ch 3, 2 tr] in next ch-3 sp, [FPtr, BPtr] 6 times, FPtr; rep from * once more, [2 tr, ch 3, 2 tr] in next ch-3 sp, [FPtr, BPtr] twice, FPtr, join with ss to top of beg ch-3. (17 sts each side)

Round 5: Ch 3 (counts as first BPtr), [FPtr, BPtr] 4 times, FPtr, *[2 tr, ch 3, 2 tr] in next ch-3 sp, [FPtr, BPtr] 8 times, FPtr; rep from * once more, [2 tr, ch 3, 2 tr] in next ch-3 sp, [FPtr, BPtr] 3 times, FPtr, join with ss to top of beg ch-3. (21 sts each side)

Fasten off.

54 Two-tone Trefoil

MEDIUM

- 12–15cm (4¾–6in)
- Aran yarn
- 5.5mm hook

Foundation ring: Using A, ch 4, join with ss to form a ring.

Round 1: Ch 1, 6 dc into ring, join with ss to first dc.

Round 2: Ch 1, [1 dc, ch 7, 1 dc] in first dc, *1 dc in next dc, [1 dc, ch 7, 1 dc] in next dc; rep from * once more, 1 dc in next dc, join with ss to first dc.

Round 3: Ch 1, skip first dc, [1 dc, 1 htr, 3 tr, 3 dtr, 3 tr, 1 htr, 1 dc] in next ch-7 sp (leaf made), *skip 1 dc, 1 dc in next dc, skip 1 dc, [1 dc, 1 htr, 3 tr, 3 dtr, 3 tr, 1 htr, 1 dc) in next ch-7 sp; rep from * once more, skip 1 dc, 1 dc in next dc, join with ss to first dc.

Fasten off A. Join B to second tr of any leaf.

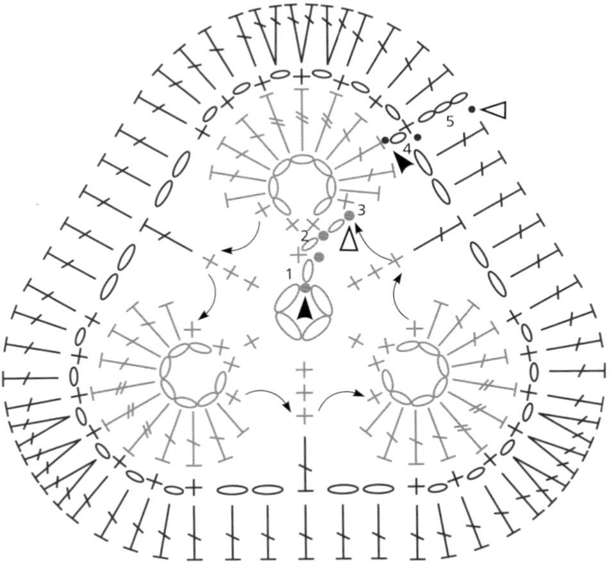

COLOURS

A

B

Round 4: Ch 1, 1 dc in st at base of ch-1, [ch 1, 1 dc in next st] 6 times, *ch 2, 1 tr in dc between leaves, ch 2, 1 dc in second tr of next leaf, [ch 1, 1 dc in next st] 6 times; rep from * once more, ch 2, 1 tr in dc between leaves, ch 2, join with ss to first dc.

Round 5: Ch 3 (counts as first tr), *[1 tr in next ch-1 sp, 1 tr in next dc] twice, 2 tr in each of next (ch-1 sp, dc, ch-1 sp), [1 tr in next dc, 1 tr in next ch-1 sp] twice, 1 tr in next dc, 2 tr in next ch-2 sp, 1 tr in next tr, 2 tr in next ch-2 sp, 1 tr in next dc; rep from * twice more, omitting last tr of last rep, join with ss to top of beg ch-3.

Fasten off.

55 Open Trefoil

EXTRA LARGE

- 18–21cm (7–8¼in)
- Aran yarn
- 5.5mm hook

Foundation ring: [Ch 16, ss in first ch] 3 times, to create 3 base loops.

Round 1: In first loop, ch 1 (counts as first dc), 23 dc into loop at base of ch-1, [24 dc into next loop] twice, join with ss to first dc.

Round 2: Ss in each of next 2 dc, ch 5 (counts as first tr and ch 2), skip 1 st, [1 tr in next st, ch 2, skip 1 st] 8 times, 1 tr in next st, skip 5 sts, *[1 tr in next st, ch 2, skip 1 st] 9 times; rep from * once more, join with ss to third ch of beg ch-5.

Round 3: Ch 1, [3 dc in next ch-2 sp] 9 times, 2 dc in sp between next 2 tr; rep from * twice more, join with ss to first dc.

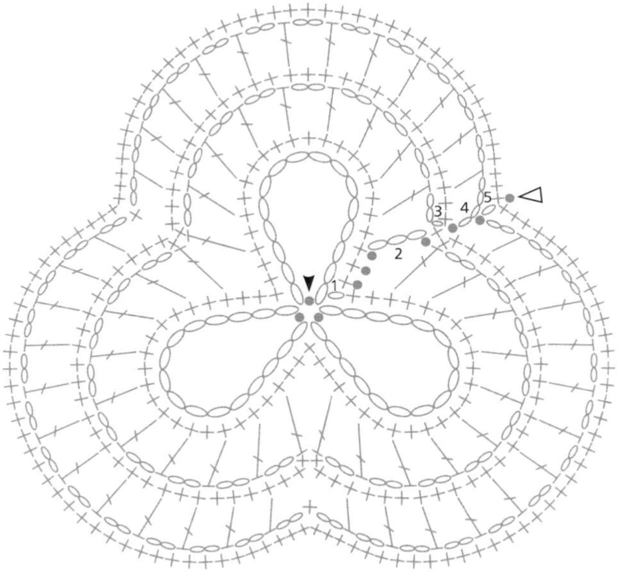

COLOUR

Round 4: Ch 4 (counts as first htr and ch 2), skip 2 sts, 1 htr in next st, *[ch 2, skip 1 st, 1 tr in next st] 10 times, ch 2, skip 1 st, 1 htr in next st, ch 2, skip 3 dc, 1 dc between sts before next dc, skip 3 sts, 1 htr in next st; rep from * once more, *[ch 2, skip 1 st, 1 tr in next st] 10 times, ch 2, skip 1 st, 1 htr in next st, ch 2, join with ss to second ch of beg ch-4.

Round 5: Ch 1, 3 dc in each ch-2 sp around, join with ss to beg ch-1.

Fasten off.

56 Tri-colour Granny Diamond

MEDIUM

- 12–15cm (4¾–6in)
- Aran yarn
- 5.5mm hook

Foundation ring: Using A, ch 4, join with ss to form a ring.

Round 1: Ch 3 (counts as first tr), 2 tr into ring, ch 2, [3 tr into ring, ch 2] 3 times, join with ss to top of beg ch-3.

Fasten off A. Join B to any ch-2 sp.

Round 2: Ch 3 (counts as first tr), [2 tr, ch 2, 3 tr] in sp at base of ch-3 (right side corner made), ch 1, [2 tr, 1 dtr, ch 2, 1 dtr, 2 tr] in next ch-2 sp (top corner made), ch 1, [3 tr, ch 2, 3 tr] in next ch-2 sp (left side corner made), ch 1, [3 tr, 1 dtr, ch 2, 1 dtr, 2 tr] in next ch-2 sp (bottom corner made), ch 1, join with ss to top of beg ch-3.

Fasten off A. Join C to ch-2 sp of right corner.

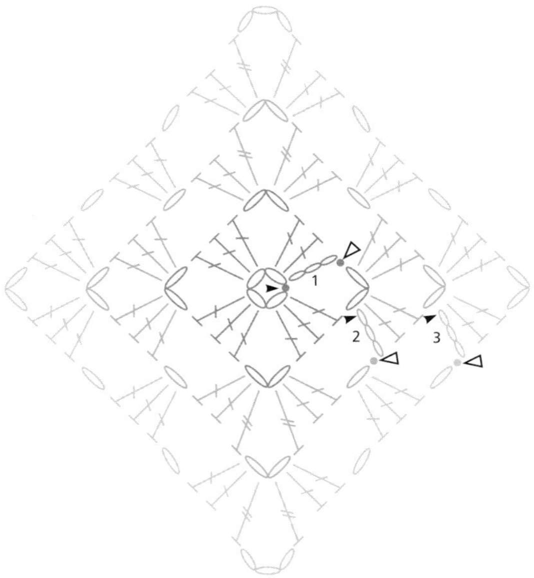

COLOURS

A

B

C

Round 3: Ch 3 (counts as first tr), [2 tr, ch 2, 3 tr] in sp at base of ch-3, ch 1, 3 tr in next ch-1 sp, ch 1, [2 tr, 1 dtr, ch 3, 1 dtr, 2 tr] in next ch-2 sp (top corner), ch 1, 3 tr in next ch-1 sp, ch 1, [3 tr, ch 2, 3 tr] in next ch-2 sp (left side), ch 1, 3 tr in next ch-1 sp, ch 1, [2 tr, 1 dtr, ch 3, 1 dtr, 2 tr] in next ch-2 sp (bottom corner), ch 1, 3 tr in next ch-1 sp, ch 1, join with ss to top of beg ch-3.

Fasten off.

TIP: DEALING WITH YARN ENDS

It is important to fasten off yarn ends securely so that they do not unravel during wear or laundering. Try to fasten off as neatly as possible so that the woven in ends do not show through to the front of the work.

57 Geometric Diamond

MEDIUM

- 12–15cm (4¾–6in)
- Aran yarn
- 5.5mm hook

Foundation ring: Ch 4, join with ss to form a ring.

Round 1: Ch 1, [1 dc, 1 htr, 1 tr, 1 dtr, ch 3, 1 dtr, 1 tr, 1 htr] twice into ring, join with ss to beg ch-1.

Round 2: Ch 5 (counts as first tr and ch 2), 1 tr in first dc, 1 tr in each of next 3 sts, [3 tr, ch 4, 3 tr] in next ch-3 sp, 1 tr in each of next 3 sts, [1 tr, ch 2, 1 tr] in next dc, 1 tr in each of next 3 sts, [3 tr, ch 4, 3 tr] in next ch-3 sp, 1 tr in each of next 3 sts, join with ss in third ch of beg ch-5.

COLOUR

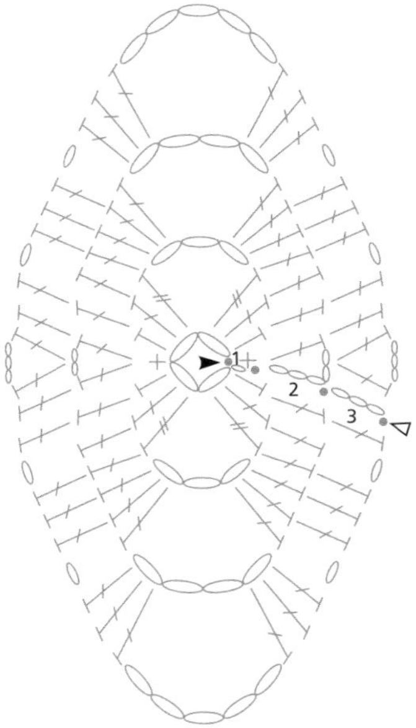

Round 3: Ch 3 (counts first tr), *[1 tr, ch 3, 1 tr] in next ch-2 sp, 1 tr in each of next 2 tr, ch 1, skip 1 tr, 1 tr in each of next 3 tr, ch 1, skip 1 tr, [3 tr, ch 5, 3 tr] in next ch-4 sp, ch 1, skip 1 tr, 1 tr in each of next 3 tr, ch 1, skip 1 tr, 1 tr in each of next 2 tr; rep from * once more, omitting last tr of last rep, join with ss to top of beg ch-3.

Fasten off.

TIP: KEEPING A RECORD

When you have finished making a crochet project, store a small amount of leftover yarn in case you need to make future repairs. Punch a hole in a piece of cardboard and knot several lengths of yarn through the hole. Make a note of the type of yarn and colour, as well as details of the project, and attach one of the ball bands to remind you of the yarn composition and any special pressing or washing instructions. File the cards away in a closed box with a lid and store in a cool, dry place.

58 Bobble Diamond

LARGE
- 15–18cm (6–7in)
- Aran yarn
- 5.5mm hook

Foundation ring: Ch 8, join with ss to form a ring.

Round 1: Ch 1, 16 dc into ring, join with ss to first dc.

Round 2: Beg popcorn in first dc, [ch 1, 1 dc in each of next 3 dc, ch 1, popcorn in next dc] 3 times, ch 1, 1 dc in each of next 3 dc, ch 1, join with ss to top of beg popcorn.

Round 3: Ss in last ch-1 sp, ch 6 (counts as first tr and ch 3), [2 tr in next ch-1 sp, 1 tr in each of next 3 dc, 2 tr in next ch-1 sp, ch 3] 3 times, 2 tr in next ch-1 sp, 1 tr in each of next 3 dc, 1 tr in next ch-1 sp, join with ss to third ch of beg ch-6.

Round 4: Beg popcorn in first st, [1 tr, ch 3, 1 tr] in next ch-3 sp, [popcorn in next tr, 1 tr in each of next 2 tr] twice, popcorn in next tr, [1 dtr, ch 3, 1 dtr] in next ch-3 sp, [popcorn in next tr, 1 tr in each of next 2 tr] twice, popcorn in next tr, [1 tr, ch 3, 1 tr] in next ch-3 sp, [popcorn in next tr, 1 tr in each of next 2 tr] twice, popcorn in next tr, [1 dtr, ch 3, 1 dtr] in next ch-3 sp, [popcorn in next tr, 1 tr in each of next 2 tr] twice, join with ss to top of beg popcorn.

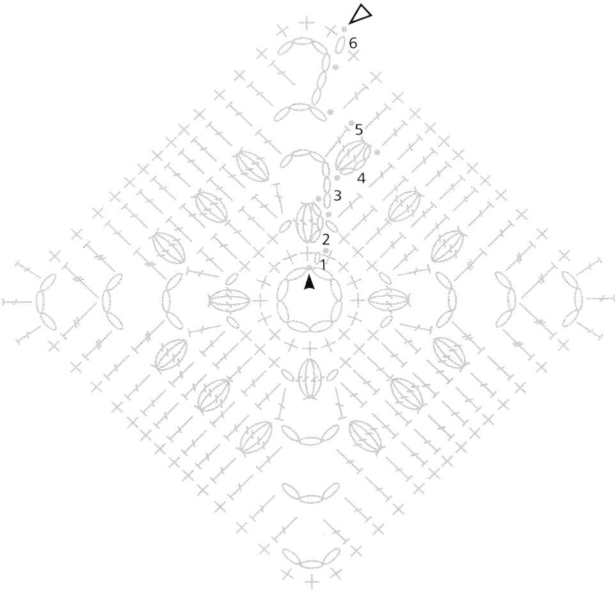

COLOUR

Round 5: Ss in first tr, [ss, ch 6 (counts as first tr and ch 3), 2 tr] in next ch-3 sp, 1 tr in each of next 9 sts, [2 dtr, ch 3, 2 dtr] in next ch-3 sp, 1 tr in each of next 9 sts, [2 tr, ch 3, 2 tr] in next ch-3 sp, 1 tr in each of next 9 sts, [2 dtr, ch 3, 2 dtr] in next ch-3 sp, 1 tr in each of next 9 sts, 1 tr in next ch-3 sp, join with ss to third ch of beg ch-6.

Round 6: Ch 1, *3 dc in next ch-3 sp, 1 dc in each of next 13 sts, 3 tr in next ch-3 sp, 1 dc in each of next 13 sts; rep from * once more, join with ss to first dc.

Fasten off.

SPECIAL ABBREVIATIONS

beg popcorn: Ch 3, 3 tr in place indicated, remove hook from working loop, insert hook in top of ch-3, catch working loop and draw through to close popcorn.

popcorn: 4 tr in place indicated, remove hook from working loop, insert hook in top of first tr of popcorn, catch working loop and draw through to close popcorn.

59 Granny Pentagon

MEDIUM

- 12–15cm (4¾–6in)
- Aran yarn
- 5.5mm hook

Foundation ring: Using A, ch 5, join with ss to form a ring.

Round 1: Ch 3 (counts as first tr), 1 tr into ring, [ch 1 (counts as corner), 2 tr into ring] 4 times, ch 1, join with ss to top of beg ch-3.

Fasten off A. Join B to any corner ch-1 sp.

Round 2: Ch 3 (counts as first tr), [1 tr, ch 1, 2 tr] in sp at base of ch-3, ch 1, *[2 tr, ch 1 (counts as corner), 2 tr] in next ch-1 sp, ch 1; rep from * 3 times more, join with ss to top of beg ch-3.

Fasten off B. Join C to any corner ch-1 sp.

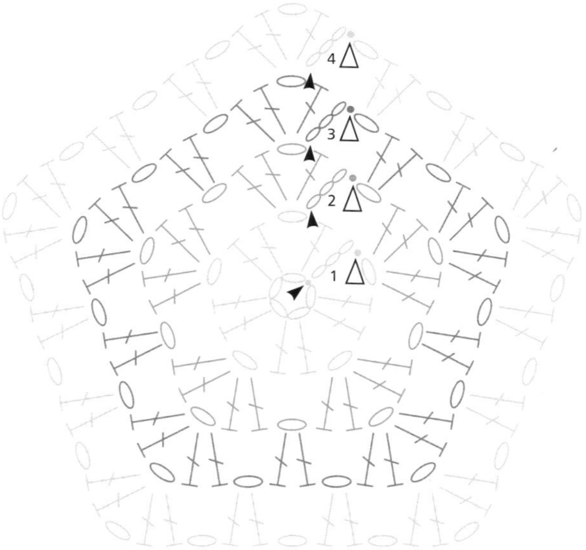

COLOURS

A

B

C

Round 3: Ch 3 (counts as first tr), [1 tr, ch 1 (counts as corner), 2 tr] in sp at base of ch-3, *ch 1, 2 tr in next ch-1 sp, ch 1, [2 tr, ch 1 (counts as corner), 2 tr] in next ch-1 sp; rep from * 3 times more, ch 1, 2 tr in next ch-1 sp, ch 1, join with ss to top of beg ch-3.

Fasten off C. Join A to any corner ch-1 sp.

Round 4: Ch 3 (counts as first tr), [1 tr, ch 1 (counts as corner), 2 tr] in sp at base of ch-3, *[ch 1, 2 tr in next ch-1 sp] twice, ch 1, [2 tr, ch 1 (counts as corner), 2 tr] in next ch-1 sp; rep from * 3 times more, [ch 1, 2 tr in next ch-1 sp] twice, ch 1, join with ss to top of beg ch-3.

Fasten off.

60 Two-tone Pentagon

SMALL
- 9–12cm (3½–4¾in)
- Aran yarn
- 5.5mm hook

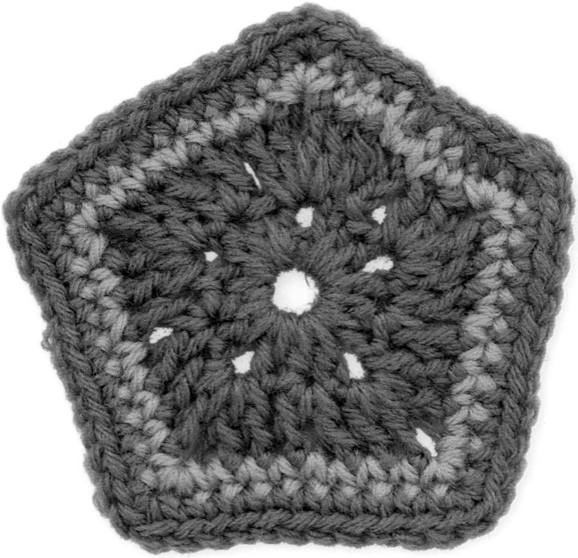

Foundation ring: Using A, ch 5, join with ss to form a ring.

Round 1: Ch 2 (counts as first htr), 2 htr into ring, [ch 2, 3 htr into ring] 4 times, ch 2, join with ss to top of beg ch-2.

Round 2: Ss in next htr, ch 4 (counts as first tr and ch 1), 1 tr in same htr, [2 tr, ch 2, 2 tr] in next ch-2 sp, skip 1 htr, *[1 tr, ch 1, 1 tr] in next htr, [2 tr, ch 2, 2 tr] in next ch-2 sp, skip 1 htr; rep from * 4 times more, join with ss to third ch of beg ch-4.

Fasten off A. Join B.

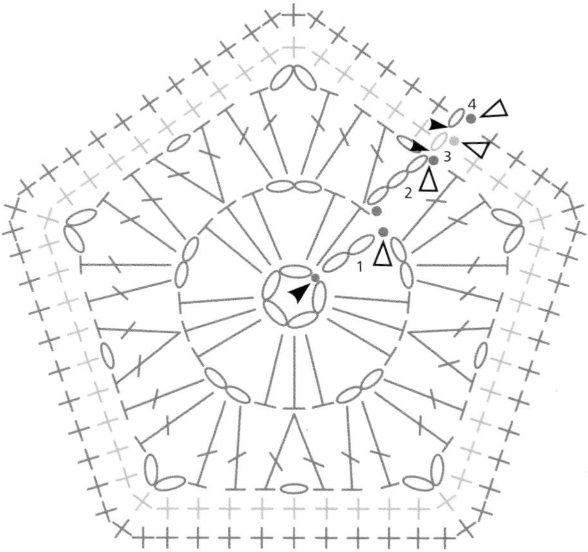

COLOURS

A

B

Round 3: Ch 1 (count as first dc), 1 dc in next ch-1 sp, *1 dc in each of next 3 sts, 3 dc into next ch-2 sp, 1 dc in each of next 3 sts, 1 dc in next ch-1 sp; rep from * 4 times more, join with ss to beg ch-1.

Fasten off B. Join A.

Round 4: Ch 1 (counts as first dc), 1 dc in each of next 5 dc, 3 dc in next dc, [1 dc in each of next 9 dc, 3 dc in next dc] 4 times, 1 dc in each of next 3 dc, join with ss to beg ch-1.

Fasten off.

61 Solid Hexagon

MEDIUM

- 12–15cm (4¾–6in)
- Aran yarn
- 5.5mm hook

Foundation ring: Ch 4, join with ss to form a ring.

Round 1: Ch 1 (counts as first dc), 11 dc into ring, join with ss to beg ch-1, turn. (12 sts)

Round 2: Ch 2 (counts as first htr), [3 htr in next dc, 1 htr in next dc] 5 times, 3 htr in next dc, join with ss to top of beg ch-2, turn. (24 sts)

Round 3: Ch 2 (counts as first htr), 1 htr in next htr, [3 htr in next htr, 1 htr in each of next 3 htr] 5 times, 3 htr in next htr, 1 htr in next htr, join with ss to top of beg ch-2, turn. (36 sts)

Round 4: Ch 2 (counts as first htr), 1 htr in each of next 2 htr, [3 htr in next htr, 1 htr in each of next 5 htr] 5 times, 3 htr in next htr, 1 htr in each of next 2 htr, join with ss to top of beg ch-2, turn. (48 sts)

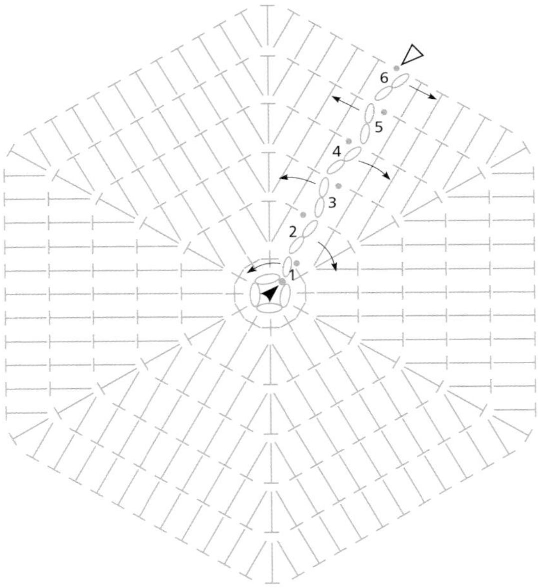

COLOUR

Round 5: Ch 2 (counts as first htr), 1 htr in each of next 3 htr, [3 htr in next htr, 1 htr in each of next 7 htr] 5 times, 3 htr in next htr, 1 htr in each of next 3 htr, join with ss to top of beg ch-2, turn. (60 sts)

Round 6: Ch 2 (counts as first htr), 1 htr in each of next 4 htr, [3 htr in next htr, 1 htr in each of next 9 htr] 5 times, 3 htr in next htr, 1 htr in each of next 4 htr, join with ss to top of beg ch-2. (72 sts)

Fasten off.

62 Colour Dot Hexagon

LARGE

- 15–18cm (6–7in)
- Aran yarn
- 5.5mm hook

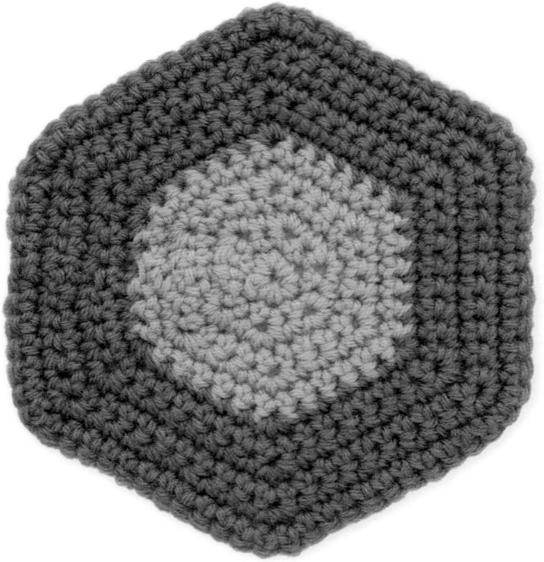

Foundation ring: Using A, ch 4, join with ss to form a ring.

Round 1: Ch 1, 6 dc into ring, join with ss to first dc, turn. (6 sts)

Round 2: Ch 1, 2 dc in each dc around, join with ss to first dc, turn. (12 sts)

Round 3: Ch 1, 1 dc in st at base of ch-1, 3 dc in next dc, [1 dc in next dc, 3 dc in next dc] 5 times, join with ss to first dc, turn. (24 sts)

Round 4: Ch 1, 1 dc in each dc around, join with ss to first dc, turn.

Round 5: Ch 1, 1 dc in st at base of ch-1, 1 dc in next dc, 3 dc in next dc, [1 dc in each of next 3 dc, 3 dc in next dc] 5 times, 1 dc in last dc, join with ss to first dc, turn. (36 sts)

Round 6: Ch 1, 1 dc in each dc around, join with ss to first dc, turn.

Fasten off A. Join B.

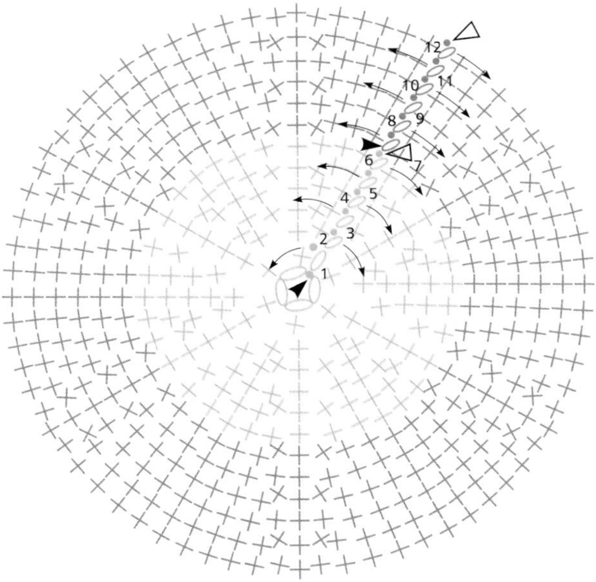

COLOURS

A

B

Round 7: Ch 1, 1 dc in st at base of ch-1, 1 dc in each of next 2 dc, 3 dc in next dc, [1 dc in each of next 5 dc, 3 dc in next dc] 5 times, 1 dc in each of next 2 dc, join with ss to first dc, turn. (48 sts)

Round 8: Ch 1, 1 dc in each dc around, join with ss to first dc, turn.

Round 9: Ch 1, 1 dc in st at base of ch-1, 1 dc in each of next 3 dc, 3 dc in next dc, [1 dc in each of next 7 dc, 3 dc in next dc] 5 times, 1 dc in each of last 3 dc, join with ss to first dc, turn. (60 sts)

Round 10: Ch 1, 1 dc in each dc around, join with ss to first dc, turn.

Round 11: Ch 1, 1 dc in each of next 5 dc, 3 dc in next dc, *1 dc in each of next 9 dc, 3 dc in next dc; rep from * 4 times more, 1 dc in each of next 4 dc, join with ss to first dc, turn. (72 sts)

Round 12: Ch 1, 1 dc in each dc around, join with ss to first dc.

Fasten off.

63 Granny Hexagon

LARGE

- 15–18cm (6–7in)
- Aran yarn
- 5.5mm hook

Foundation ring: Using A, ch 6, join with ss to form a ring.

Round 1: Ch 3 (counts as first tr), tr2tog into ring, [ch 3, tr3tog into ring] 5 times, ch 3, join with ss to top of beg ch-3.

Round 2: Ss in next ch-3 sp, ch 3 (counts as first tr), [tr2tog, ch 3, tr3tog] in sp at base of ch-3, [ch 3, (tr3tog, ch 3, tr3tog) in next ch-3 sp] 5 times, ch 3, join with ss to top of beg ch-3.

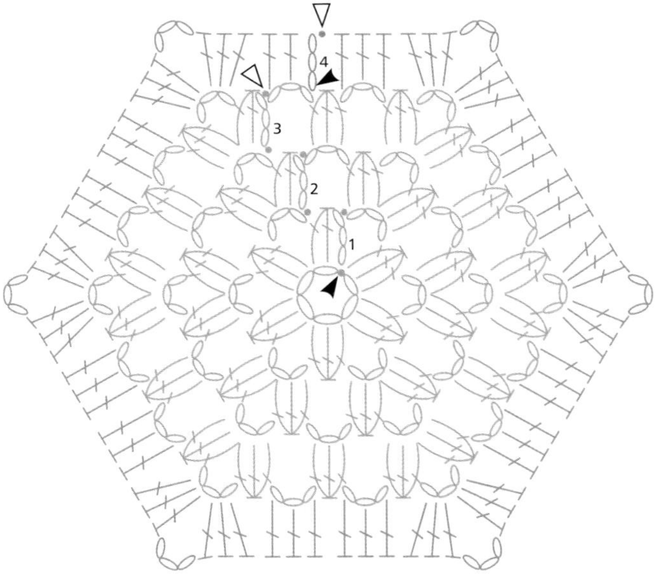

COLOURS

A

B

Round 3: Ss in next ch-3 sp, ch 3 (counts as first tr), [tr2tog, ch 3, tr3tog] in sp at base of ch-3, [ch 3, tr3tog in next ch-3 sp, ch 3, (tr3tog, ch 3, tr3tog) in next ch-3 sp] 5 times, ch 3, tr3tog in next ch-3 sp, ch 3, join with ss to top of beg ch-3.

Fasten off A. Join B to last ch-3 sp.

Round 4: Ch 3 (counts as first tr), 2 tr in sp at base of ch-3, [(3 tr, ch 2, 3 tr) in next ch-3 sp, (3 tr in next ch-3 sp) twice] 5 times, [3 tr, ch 2, 3 tr] in next ch-3 sp, 3 tr in next ch-3 sp, join with ss to top of beg ch-3.

Fasten off.

64 Classic Hexagon

EXTRA LARGE

- 18–21cm (7–8¼in)
- Aran yarn
- 5.5mm hook

Foundation ring: Using A, ch 6, join with ss to form a ring.

Round 1: Ch 4 (counts as first tr and ch 1), [1 tr into ring, ch 1] 11 times, join with ss to third ch of beg ch-4.

Round 2: Ch 3 (counts as first tr), 2 tr in next ch-1 sp, 1 tr in next tr, ch 2, [1 tr in next tr, 2 tr in next ch-1 sp, 1 tr in next tr, ch 2] 5 times, join with ss to top of beg ch-3.

Round 3: Ch 3 (counts as first tr), 1 tr in st at base of ch-3, 1 tr in each of next 2 tr, 2 tr in next tr, ch 2, [2 tr in next tr, 1 tr in each of next 2 tr, 2 tr in next tr, ch 2] 5 times, join with ss to top of beg ch-3.

Fasten off A. Join B.

Round 4: Ch 3 (counts as first tr), 1 tr in st at base of ch-3, 1 tr in each of next 4 tr, 2 tr in next tr, ch 2, [2 tr in next tr, 1 tr in each of next 4 tr, 2 tr in next tr, ch 2] 5 times, join with ss to top of beg ch-3.

Round 5: Ch 3 (counts as first tr), 1 tr in each of next 7 tr, [ch 3, 1 dc in next ch-2 sp, ch 3, 1 tr in each of next 8 tr] 5 times, ch 3,

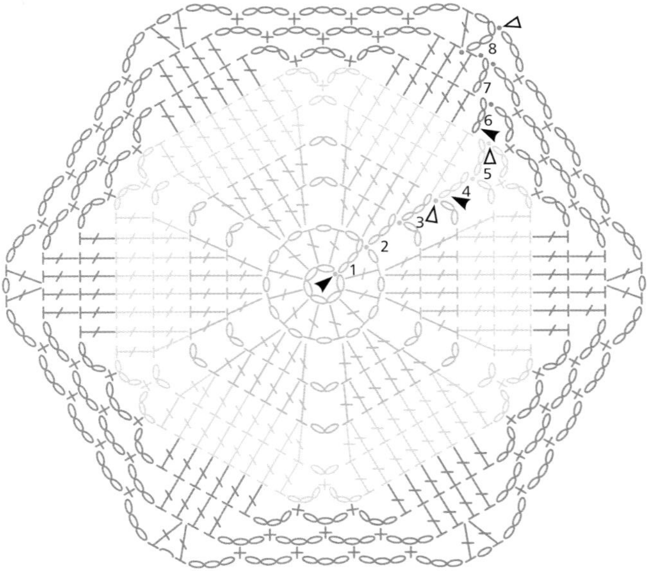

COLOURS
A
B
C

1 dc in next ch-2 sp, ch 3, join with ss to top of beg ch-3. Fasten off B. Join C.

Round 6: Ss in next tr, ch 3 (counts as first tr), 1 tr in each of next 5 tr, *ch 3, [1 dc in next ch-3 sp, ch 3] twice, skip 1 tr, 1 tr in each of next 6 tr; rep from * 4 times more, ch 3, [1 dc in next ch-3 sp, ch 3] twice, join with ss to top of beg ch-3.

Round 7: Ss in next tr, ch 3 (counts as first tr), 1 tr in each of next 3 tr, *ch 3, [1 dc in next ch-3 sp, ch 3] 3 times, skip 1 tr, 1 tr in each of next 4 tr; rep from * 4 times more, ch 3, [1 dc in next ch-3 sp, ch 3] 3 times, join with ss to top of beg ch-3.

Round 8: Ss in st-sp between second and third tr of group, ch 4 (counts as first tr and ch 1), 1 tr in st at base of ch-4, *ch 3, [1 dc in next ch-3 sp, ch 3] 4 times, [1 tr, ch 1, 1 tr] in st-sp between second and third tr of next 4-tr group; rep from * 4 times more, ch 3, [1 dc in next ch-3 sp, ch 3] 4 times, join with ss to third ch of beg ch-4.

Fasten off.

65 Swirl Hexagon

LARGE
- 15–18cm (6–7in)
- Aran yarn
- 5.5mm hook

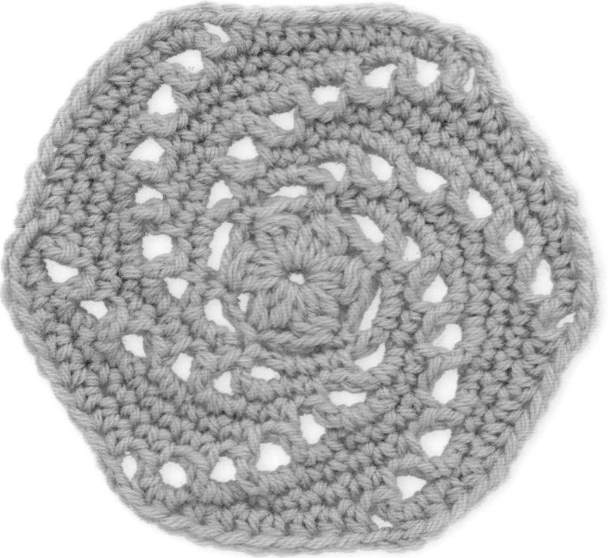

Foundation ring: Ch 4, join with ss to form a ring.

Round 1: Beg 2-tr cl into ring, [ch 2, 3-tr cl into ring] 5 times, ch 2, join with ss to top of beg 2-tr cl.

Round 2: [Ch 4, 1 dc in top of next cl] 6 times.

Round 3: [Ch 4, 2 dc in next ch-4 sp, 1 dc in next dc] 6 times.

Round 4: [Ch 4, 2 dc in next ch-4 sp, 1 dc in each of next 2 dc, skip 1 dc] 6 times.

Round 5: [Ch 4, 2 dc in next ch-4 sp, 1 dc in each of next 3 dc, skip 1 dc] 6 times.

Round 6: [Ch 4, 2 dc in next ch-4 sp, 1 dc in each of next 4 dc, skip 1 dc] 6 times.

Round 7: [Ch 4, 2 dc in next ch-4 sp, 1 dc in each of next 5 dc, skip 1 dc] 6 times.

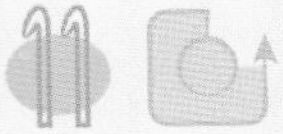

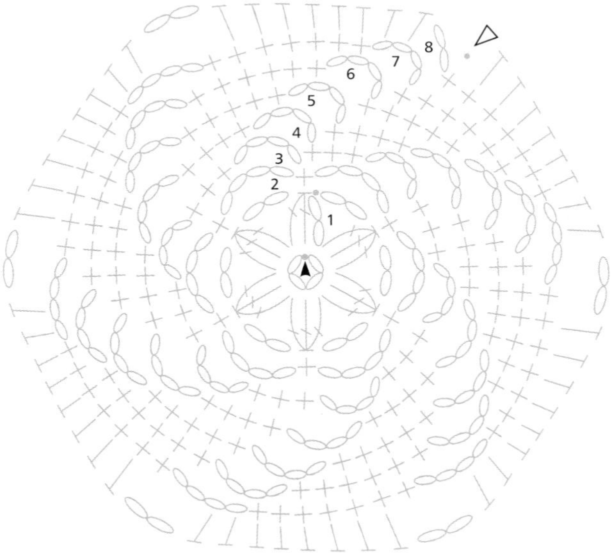

COLOUR

Round 8: [Ch 2, 2 htr in next ch-4 sp, 1 htr in each of next 6 dc, skip 1 dc] 6 times, join with ss to top of beg ch-2.

Fasten off.

NOTE

Mark beginning of round with a detachable marker or safety pin and move the marker up as you work.

SPECIAL ABBREVIATIONS

beg 2-tr cl (beginning 2 treble crochet cluster): Ch 2, [yo, insert hook into ring, yo, draw yarn through, yo, draw through 2 loops on hook] twice, yo, draw through all 3 loops on hook.

3-tr cl (3 treble crochet cluster): [Yo, insert hook into ring, yo, draw yarn through, yo, draw through 2 loops on hook] 3 times, yo, draw through all 4 loops on hook.

66 Wheel Hexagon

MEDIUM

- 12–15cm ($4^3/_4$–6in)
- Aran yarn
- 5.5mm hook

Foundation ring: Ch 6, join with ss to form a ring.

Round 1: Ch 6 (counts as first dtr and ch 2), [1 dtr into ring, ch 2] 11 times, join with ss to fourth ch of beg ch-6.

Round 2: Ss in next ch-2 sp, ch 3 (counts as first tr), [1 tr, ch 2, 2 tr] in sp at base of ch-3, [3 tr in next ch-2 sp, (2 tr, ch 2, 2 tr) in next ch-2 sp] 5 times, 3 tr in next ch-2 sp, join with ss to top of beg ch-3.

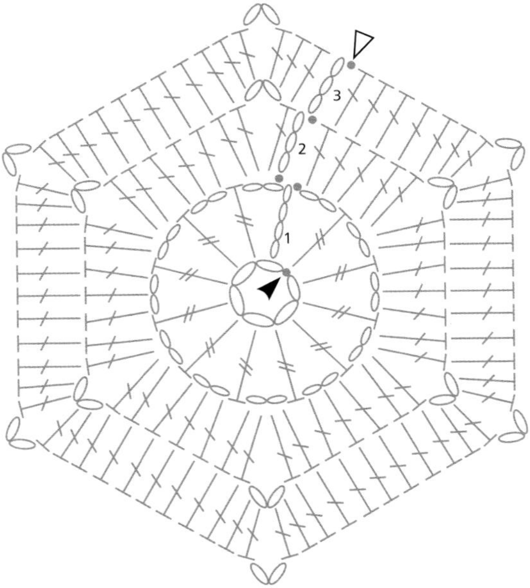

COLOUR

Round 3: Ch 3 (counts as first tr), 1 tr in next tr, [(2 tr, ch 1, 2 tr) in next ch-2 sp, 1 tr in each of next 7 tr] 5 times, [2 tr, ch 1, 2 tr] in next ch-2 sp, 1 tr in each of next 5 tr, join with ss to top of beg ch-3.

Fasten off.

TIP: LAUNDERING CROCHET

When laundering crochet, always follow the washing and pressing instructions given on the yarn ball band. If the yarn is machine washable, put the item into a zip-up mesh laundry bag to keep it from stretching and snagging during the wash cycle. For items that are not machine washable, handwash in hot water with a mild, detergent-free cleaning agent. Most purpose-made wool or fabric shampoos are ideal, but check that the one you choose does not contain optical brighteners, which will cause yarn colours to fade.

67 Treble Crochet Spoke Octagon

LARGE
- 15–18cm (6–7in)
- Aran yarn
- 5.5mm hook

Foundation ring: Ch 4, join with ss to form a ring.

Round 1: Ch 3 (counts as first tr), 23 tr into ring, join with ss to top of beg ch-3.

Round 2: Ch 3 (counts as first tr), 1 tr in each of next 2 tr, [ch 2, 1 tr in each of next 3 tr] 7 times, ch 2, join with ss to top of beg ch-3.

Round 3: Ch 3 (counts as first tr), 1 tr in st at base of ch-3, 1 tr in next tr, 2 tr in next tr, [ch 2, 2 tr in next tr, 1 tr in next tr, 2 tr in next tr] 7 times, ch 2, join with ss to top of beg ch-3.

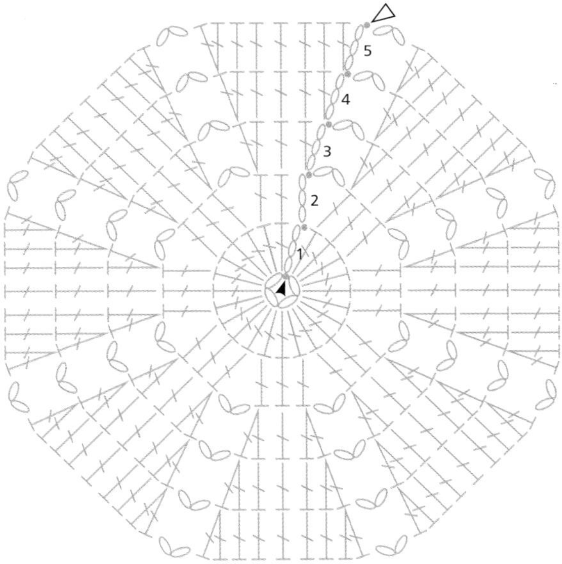

COLOUR

Round 4: Ch 3 (counts as first tr), 1 tr in st at base of ch-3, 1 tr in each of next 3 tr, 2 tr in next tr, [ch 2, 2 tr in next tr, 1 tr in each of next 3 tr, 2 tr in next tr] 7 times, ch 2, join with ss to top of beg ch-3.

Round 5: Ch 3 (counts as first tr), 1 tr in st at base of ch-3, 1 tr in each of next 5 tr, 2 tr in next tr, [ch 2, 2 tr in next tr, 1 tr in each of next 5 tr, 2 tr in next tr] 7 times, ch 2, join with ss to top of beg ch-3.

Fasten off.

68 Multi-coloured Octagon

MEDIUM

- 12–15cm (4¾–6in)
- Aran yarn
- 5.5mm hook

Foundation ring: Using A, ch 4, join with ss to form a ring.

Round 1: Ch 3 (counts as first tr), 15 tr into ring, join with ss to top of beg ch-3. (16 sts)

Fasten off A. Join B.

Round 2: Ch 3 (counts as first tr), 2 tr in st at base of ch-3, 1 tr in next tr, [3 tr in next tr, 1 tr in next tr] 7 times, join with ss to top of beg ch-3. (32 sts)

Fasten off B. Join C.

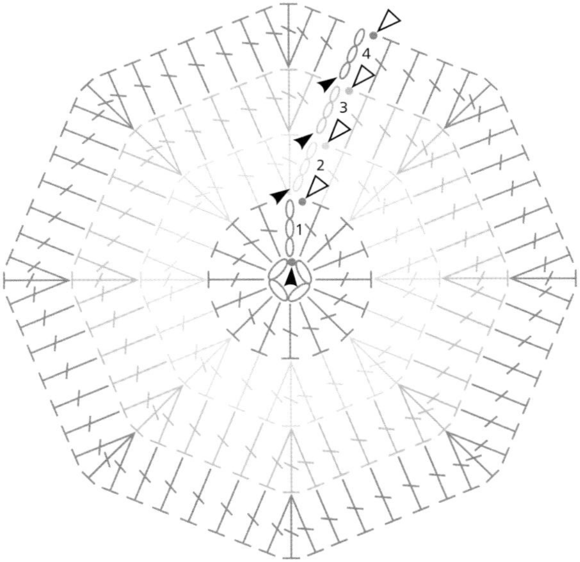

COLOURS

A

B

C

Round 3: Ch 3 (counts as first tr), [3 tr in next tr, 1 tr in each of next 3 tr] 7 times, 3 tr in next tr, 1 tr in each of next 2 tr, join with ss to top of beg ch-3. (48 sts)

Fasten off C. Join A.

Round 4: Ch 3 (counts as first tr), 1 tr in next tr, [3 tr in next tr, 1 tr in each of next 5 tr] 7 times, 3 tr in next tr, 1 tr in each of next 3 tr, join with ss to top of beg ch-3. (64 sts)

Fasten off.

69 Octagon Granny

LARGE
- 15–18cm (6–7in)
- Aran yarn
- 5.5mm hook

Foundation ring: Using A, ch 5, join with ss to form a ring.

Round 1: Ch 3 (counts as first tr), 2 tr into ring, ch 1, [3 tr into ring, ch 1] 3 times, join with ss to top of beg ch-3.

Fasten off A. Join B to any ch-1 sp.

Round 2: Ch 3 (counts as first tr), [2 tr, ch 1, 3 tr] in sp at base of ch-3, ch 1, *[3 tr, ch 1, 3 tr] in next ch-1 sp, ch 1; rep from * twice more, join with ss to top of beg ch-3.

Round 3: Ss to and into next ch-1 sp, ch 3 (counts as first tr), [1 tr, ch 1, 2 tr] in sp at base of ch-3, ch 1, *[2 tr, ch 1, 2 tr] in next ch-1 sp, ch 1; rep from * 6 times more, join with ss to top of beg ch-3.

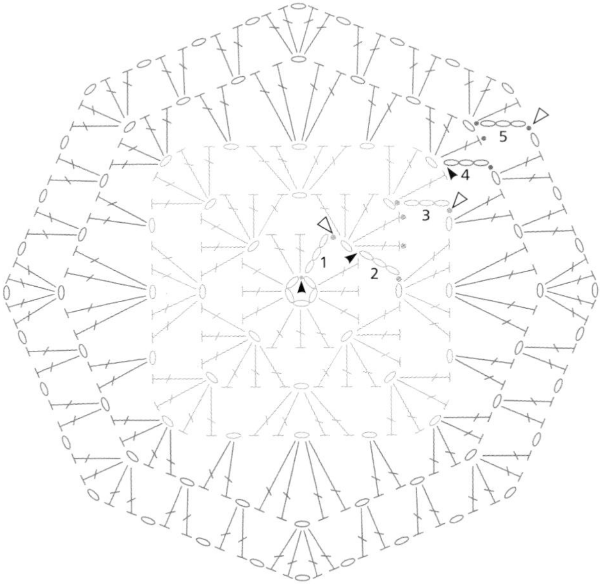

COLOURS
A
B
C

Fasten off B. Join C to next ch-1 sp.

Round 4: Ch 3 (counts as first tr), [1 tr, ch 1, 2 tr] in sp at base of ch-3, ch 1, * 2 tr in next ch-1 sp, ch 1, [2 tr, ch 1, 2 tr] in next ch-1 sp, ch 1; rep from * 7 times more, join with ss to top of beg ch-3.

Round 5: Ss to and into next ch-1 sp, ch 3 (counts as first tr), [1 tr, ch 1, 2 tr] in sp at base of ch-3, ch 1, [2 tr in next ch-1 sp, ch 1] twice, *[2 tr, ch 1, 2 tr] in next ch-1 sp, ch 1, [2 tr in next ch-1 sp, ch 1] twice; rep from * 6 times more, join with ss to top of beg ch-3.

Fasten off.

70 Octagon Wheel

MEDIUM

- 12–15cm ($4^{3}/_{4}$–6in)
- Aran yarn
- 5.5mm hook

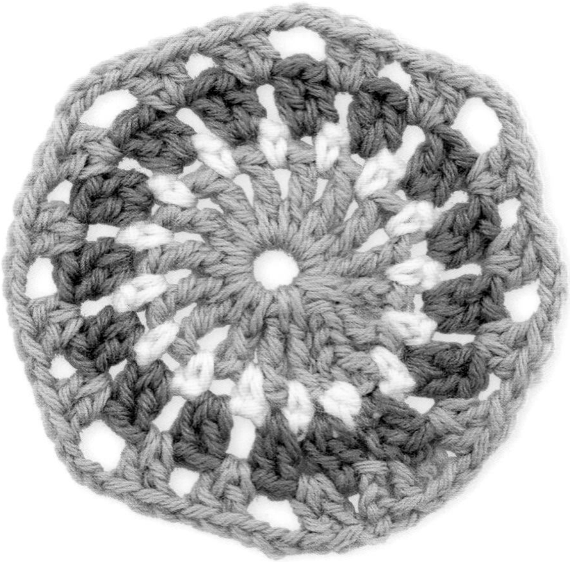

Foundation ring: Using A, ch 7, join with ss to form a ring.

Round 1: Ch 5 (counts as first dtr and ch 1), [1 dtr, ch 1] 15 times into ring, join with ss to fourth ch of beg ch-5.

Fasten off A. Join B to any ch-1 sp.

Round 2: Ch 1, 1 dc in sp at base of ch-1, ch 2, [1 dc in next ch-1 sp, ch 2] 15 times, join with ss to first dc.

Fasten off B. Join C to any ch-2 sp.

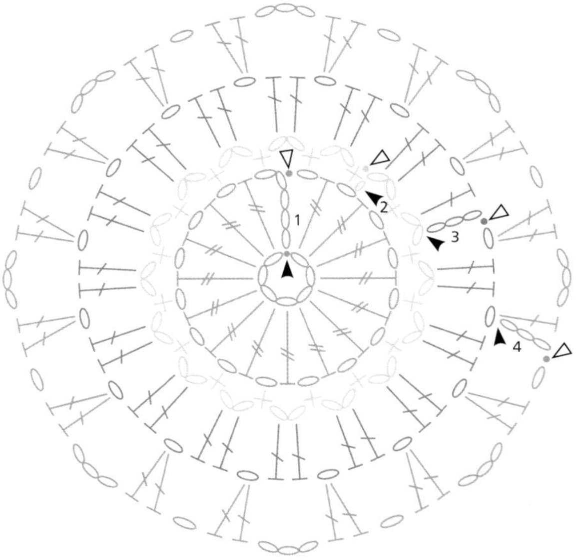

COLOURS

A

B

C

Round 3: Ch 3 (counts as first tr), 1 tr in sp at base of ch-3, ch 1, [2 tr in next ch-2 sp, ch 1] 15 times, join with ss to top of beg ch-3.

Fasten off C. Join A to any ch-1 sp.

Round 4: Ch 3 (counts as first tr), 1 tr in sp at base of ch-3, ch 3, 2 tr in next ch-1 sp, ch 1, [2 tr in next ch-1 sp, ch 3, 2 tr in next ch-1 sp, ch 1] 7 times, join with ss to top of beg ch-3.

Fasten off.

71 Octagon Frame

LARGE

- 15–18cm (6–7in)
- DK yarn
- 4.5mm hook

Foundation ring: Using A, make a magic ring.

Round 1: Ch 3 (counts as first tr), 7 tr into ring, join with ss to top of beg ch-3, turn.

Round 2: Ch 5 (counts as first tr and ch 2), [1 tr in next tr, ch 2] 7 times, join with ss to third ch of beg ch-5, turn.

Round 3: Ch 3 (counts as first tr), 2 tr in sp at base of ch-3, ch 3, [3 tr in next ch-2 sp, ch 3] 7 times, join with ss to top of beg ch-3, turn.

Round 4: Ch 3 (counts as first tr), 3 tr in sp at base of ch-3, ch 4, [4 tr in next ch-3 sp, ch 4] 7 times, join with ss to top of beg ch-3, turn.

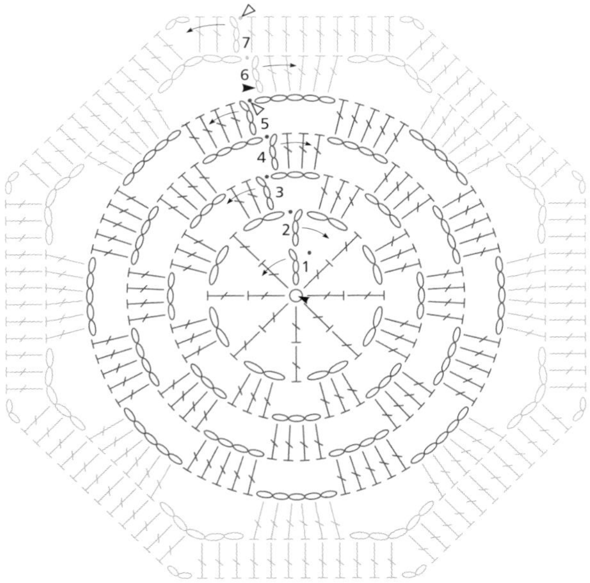

COLOURS

A

B

Round 5: Ch 3 (counts as first tr), 4 tr in sp at base of ch-3, ch 5, [5 tr in next ch-4 sp, ch 5] 7 times, join with ss to top of beg ch-3, turn.

Fasten off A. Join B.

Round 6: Ch 3 (counts as first tr), 5 tr in sp at base of ch-3, ch 5, [6 tr in next ch-5 sp, ch 5] 7 times, join with ss to top of beg ch-3, turn.

Round 7: Ch 3 (counts as first tr), [2 tr, ch 2, 3 tr] in sp at base of ch-3, 1 tr in each of next 6 tr, [(3 tr, ch 2, 3 tr) in next ch-5 sp, 1 tr in each of next 6 tr] 7 times, join with ss to top of beg ch-3.

Fasten off.

72 Two-tone Bobble Octagon

LARGE

- 15–18cm (6–7in)
- Aran yarn
- 5.5mm hook

Foundation ring: Using A, ch 4, join with ss to form a ring.

Round 1: Ch 5 (counts as first tr and ch 2), [1 tr into ring, ch 2] 7 times, join with ss to third ch of beg ch-5.

Round 2: Ch 3 (counts as first tr), 2 tr in st at base of ch-3, ch 2, [3 tr in next tr, ch 2] 7 times, join with ss to top of beg ch-3.

Round 3: Ch 3 (counts as first tr), 1 tr in st at base of ch-3, 1 tr in next tr, 2 tr in next tr, ch 2, [2 tr in next tr, 1 tr in next tr, 2 tr in next tr, ch 2) 7 times, join with ss to top of beg ch-3.

Fasten off A. Join B.

Round 4: Ch 5 (counts as first tr and ch 2), skip 1 tr, MB in next tr, ch 2, skip 1 tr, 1 tr in next tr, ch 2, [1 tr in next tr, ch 2, skip 1 tr, MB in next tr, ch 2, skip 1 tr, 1 tr in next tr, ch 2] 7 times, join with ss to third ch of beg ch-5. Fasten off B. Join A.

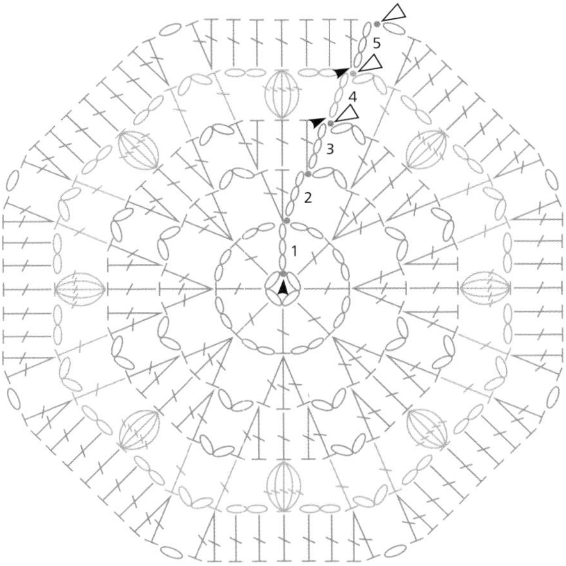

COLOURS

A

B

Round 5: Ch 3 (counts as first tr), 1 tr in st at base of ch-3, 2 tr in next ch-2 sp, 1 tr in top of next bobble, 2 tr in next ch-2 sp, 2 tr in next tr, ch 1, [2 tr in next tr, 2 tr in next ch-2 sp, 1 tr in top of next bobble, 2 tr in next ch-2 sp, 2 tr in next tr, ch 1] 7 times, join with ss to top of beg ch-3.

Fasten off.

SPECIAL ABBREVIATION

MB (make bobble): [Yo, insert hook in st, yo, draw yarn through, yo, draw through 2 loops on hook] 5 times in same st, yo, draw through all 6 loops on hook.

73 Celtic Octagon

MEDIUM

- 12–15cm (4¾–6in)
- Aran yarn
- 5.5mm hook

Foundation ring: Using A, ch 6, join with ss to form a ring.

Round 1: [Ch 4, 3 dtr into ring, ch 4, ss into ring] 4 times.

Fasten off A. Join B.

Round 2: Ch 6 (counts as first tr and ch 3), skip (ch-4 sp, 3 dtr, ch-4 sp), *[1 tr, ch 3, 1 tr] in next ss, ch 3, skip (ch-4 sp, 3 dtr, ch-4 sp); rep from * twice more, 1 tr in next ss, ch 3, join with ss to third ch of beg ch-6.

Round 3: Ch 5, *3 dtr in sp at base of ch-5, ch 4, 1 dc in next tr, ch 4; rep from * 6 times more, 3 dtr in next ch-3 sp, ch 4, join with ss to first ch of beg ch-5.

Fasten off B. Join C.

Round 4: Ch 5, *skip (ch-4 sp, 3 dtr, ch-4 sp), 1 dc in next dc, ch 4; rep from * 6 times more, skip (ch-4 sp, 3 dtr, ch-4 sp), join with ss to first ch of beg ch-5.

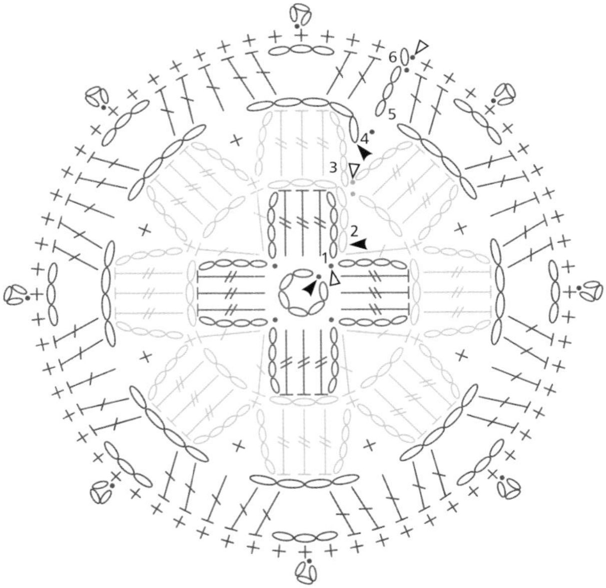

COLOURS

- A
- B
- C

Round 5: Ch 3 (counts as first tr), [2 tr, ch 3, 2 tr] in sp at base of ch-3, [1 tr in next dc, (2 tr, ch 3, 2 tr) in next ch-4 sp] 7 times, join with ss to top of beg ch-3.

Round 6: Ch 1, 1 dc in each of next 2 tr, *2 dc in next ch-3 sp, ch 3, ss in last dc made, 1 dc in same ch-3 sp, 1 dc in each of next 5 tr; rep from * 6 times more, 2 dc in next ch-3 sp, ch 3, ss in last dc made, 1 dc in same ch-3 sp, 1 dc in each of next 2 tr, join with ss to beg ch-1.

Fasten off.

Arrange petals of round 3 in front of round 4, and petals of round 1 in front of round 2.

74 Tri-colour Bullseye

LARGE

- 15–18cm (6–7in)
- Aran yarn
- 5.5mm hook

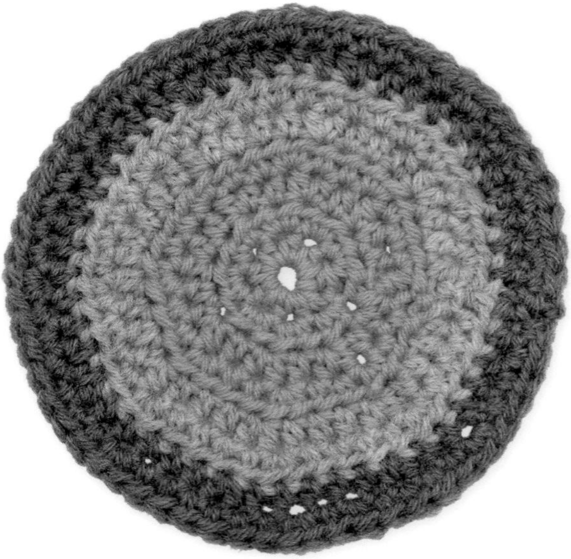

Foundation ring: Using A, ch 4, join with ss to form a ring.

Round 1: Ch 2, 8 htr into ring, join with ss to top of beg ch-2, turn. (8 sts)

Round 2: Ch 2, 2 htr in each htr around, join with ss to top of beg ch-2, turn. (16 sts)

Round 3: Ch 2, [1 htr in next htr, 2 htr in next htr] 8 times, join with ss to top of beg ch-2, turn. (24 sts)

Round 4: Ch 2, [1 htr in each of next 2 htr, 2 htr in next htr] 8 times, join with ss to top of beg ch-2, turn. (32 sts)

Fasten off A. Join B.

Round 5: Ch 2, [1 htr in each of next 3 htr, 2 htr in next htr] 8 times, join with ss to top of beg ch-2, turn. (40 sts)

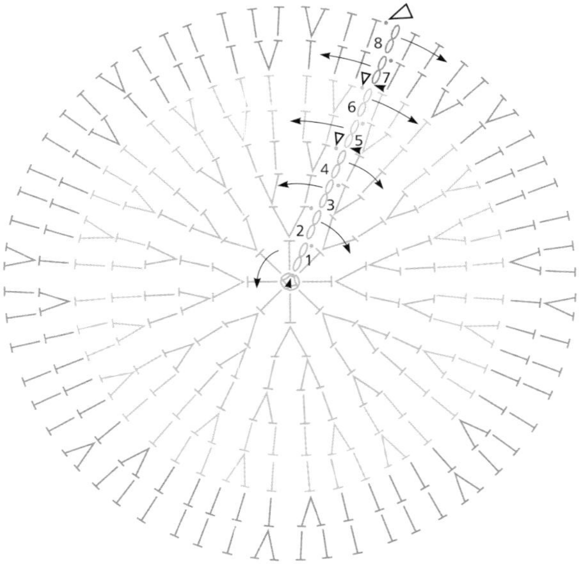

COLOURS
A
B
C

Round 6: Ch 2, [1 htr in each of next 4 htr, 2 htr in next htr] 8 times, join with ss to top of beg ch-2, turn. (48 sts)

Fasten off B. Join C.

Round 7: Ch 2, 1 htr in each of next 3 htr, 2 htr in next htr, [1 htr in each of next 5 htr, 2 htr in next htr] 7 times, 1 htr in each of next 2 htr, join with ss to top of beg ch-2, turn. (56 sts)

Round 8: Ch 2, 1 htr in each of next 4 htr, 2 htr in next htr, [1 htr in each of next 6 htr, 2 htr in next htr] 7 times, 1 htr in each of next 2 htr, join with ss to top of beg ch-2, turn. (64 sts)

Fasten off.

75 Picot Spiral

LARGE
- 15–18cm (6–7in)
- Aran yarn
- 5.5mm hook

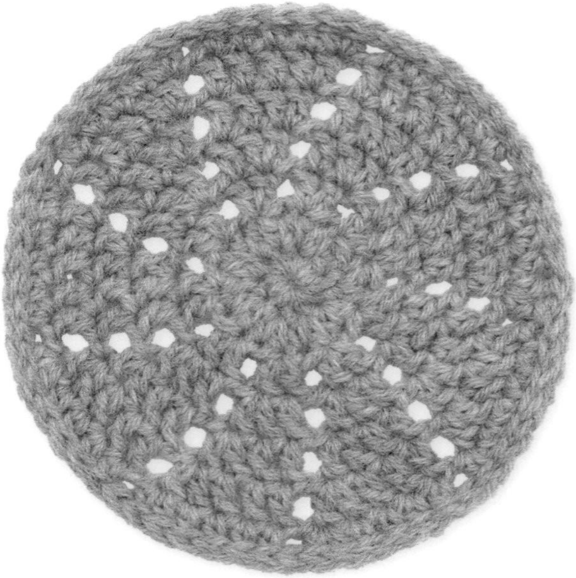

Foundation ring: Ch 4, join with ss to form a ring.

Round 1: Ch 1, 9 dc into ring, do not join.

Round 2: [2 htr in next dc] 9 times.

Round 3: [2 tr in next htr, ch 1, skip 1 htr] 9 times.

Round 4: [2 tr in next tr, 1 tr in next tr, ch 1, skip ch-1 sp] 9 times.

Round 5: [2 tr in next tr, 1 tr in each of next 2 tr, ch 1, skip ch-1 sp] 9 times.

Round 6: [2 tr in next tr, 1 tr in each of next 3 tr, ch 1, skip ch-1 sp] 9 times.

COLOUR

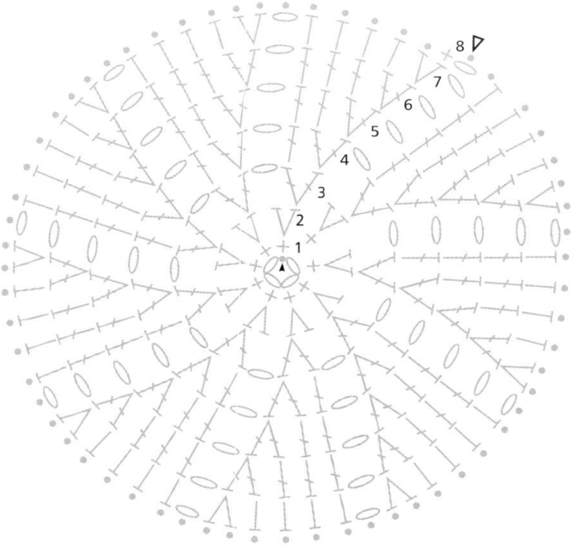

Round 7: [2 htr in next tr, 1 htr in each of next 4 tr, ch 1, skip ch-1 sp] 9 times.

Round 8: 1 dc in next htr, ss in each htr and ch-1 sp around.

Fasten off.

NOTE

Mark beginning of round with a detachable marker or safety pin and move the marker up as you work.

76 Tri-colour Granny Circle

LARGE
- 15–18cm (6–7in)
- Aran yarn
- 5.5mm hook

Foundation ring: Using A, ch 4, join with ss to form a ring.

Round 1: Ch 3, 1 htr into ring (counts as first puff st), ch 1, [puff st into ring, ch 1] 7 times, join with ss to top of first puff st.

Round 2: Ss in next ch-1 sp, ch 3 (counts as first tr), 1 tr in sp at base of ch-3, ch 2, [2 tr in next ch-1 sp, ch 2] 7 times, join with ss to top of beg ch-3.

Round 3: Ss in next ch-2 sp, ch 3 (counts as first tr), [1 tr, ch 1, 2 tr] in sp at base of ch-3, ch 1, *[2 tr in next ch-2 sp, ch 1] twice; rep from * 6 times more, join with ss to top of beg ch-3.

Fasten off A. Join B to next ch-1 sp.

Round 4: Ch 3 (counts as first tr), 2 tr in sp at base of ch-3, ch 1, [3 tr in next ch-1 sp, ch 1] 15 times, join with ss to top of beg ch-3.

Fasten off B. Join C to next ch-1 sp.

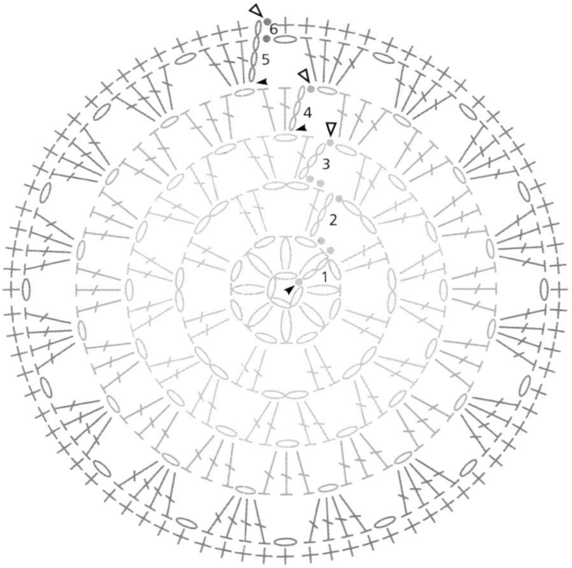

COLOURS

A

B

C

Round 5: Ch 3 (counts as first tr), 3 tr in sp at base of ch-3, ch 1, [4 tr in next ch-1 sp, ch 1] 15 times, join with ss to top of beg ch-3.

Round 6: Ch 1 (counts as first dc), 1 dc in each tr and ch-1 sp around, join with ss to beg ch-1.

Fasten off.

SPECIAL ABBREVIATION

puff st: [Yo, insert hook into foundation ring, draw yarn through] twice, yo, draw through all 5 loops on hook.

77 Water Wheel

LARGE
- 15–18cm (6–7in)
- Aran yarn
- 5.5mm hook

Foundation ring: Ch 4, join with ss to form a ring.

Round 1: Ch 3 (counts as first tr), 1 tr into ring, [ch 2, 2 tr into ring] 5 times, ch 2, join with ss to top of beg ch-3.

Round 2: Ch 3 (counts as first tr), 2 tr in st at base of ch-3, 1 tr in next tr, *ch 3, skip 2 ch, 3 tr in next tr, 1 tr in next tr; rep from * 4 times more, ch 3, skip 2 ch, join with ss to top of beg ch-3.

Round 3: Ch 3 (counts as first tr), 2 tr in st at base of ch-3, 1 tr in next tr, tr2tog over next 2 tr, *ch 4, skip 3 ch, 3 tr in next tr, 1 tr in next tr, tr2tog over next 2 tr; rep from * 4 times more, ch 4, skip 3 ch, join with ss to top of beg ch-3.

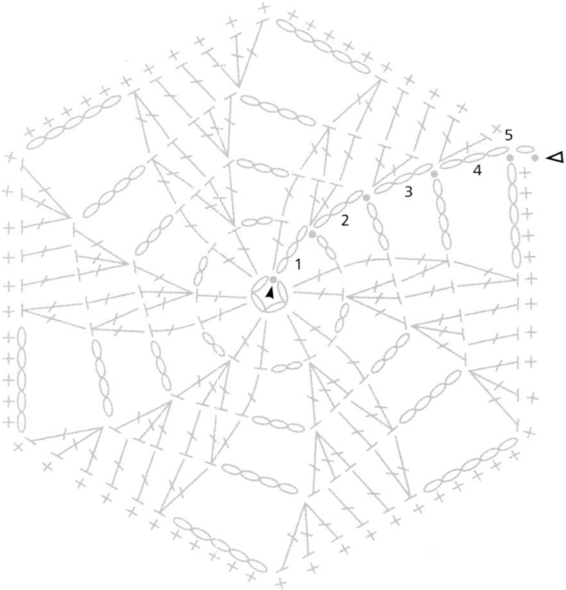

COLOUR

Round 4: Ch 3 (counts as first tr), 2 tr in st at base of ch-3, 1 tr in each of next 2 tr, tr2tog over next 2 tr, *ch 5, skip 4 ch, 3 tr in next tr, 1 tr in each of next 2 tr, tr2tog over next 2 tr; rep from * 4 times more, ch 5, skip 4 ch, join with ss to top of beg ch-3.

Round 5: Ch 1 (counts as first dc), 1 dc in each tr and ch around, join with ss to beg ch-1.

Fasten off.

78 Colour Swirl Circle

LARGE
- 15–18cm (6–7in)
- Aran yarn
- 5.5mm hook

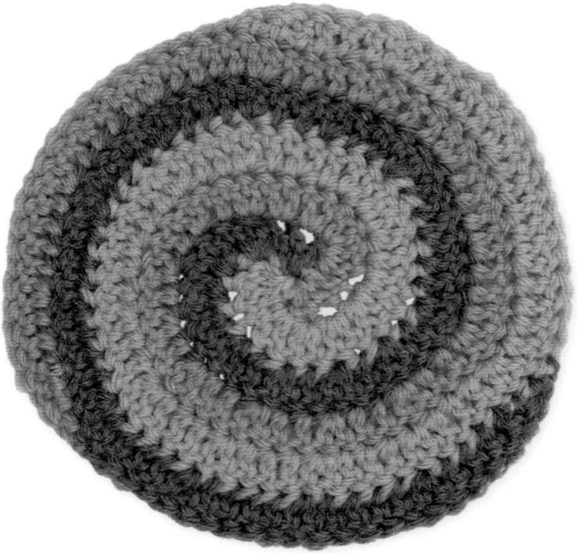

Foundation chain: Using A, ch 2.

Round 1: Working into second ch from hook, [1 dc, 1 htr, 2 tr] in ch, remove hook from loop A, join B with dc in same ch, [1 htr, 2 tr] in same ch, remove hook from loop B, join C with dc in same ch, [1 htr, 2 tr] in same ch, remove hook from loop C, gently tighten chain into which sts have been worked. (4 sts in each colour)

Round 2: Using A, *2 tr in each of next 4 sts, remove hook from loop A; rep from * with colours B and C. (8 sts in each colour)

Round 3: Using A, *[2 tr in next st, 1 tr in next st] 4 times, remove hook from loop A; rep from * with colours B and C. (12 sts in each colour)

Round 4: Using A, *[2 tr in next st, 1 tr in each of next 2 sts] 4 times, remove hook from loop A; rep from * with colours B and C. (16 sts in each colour)

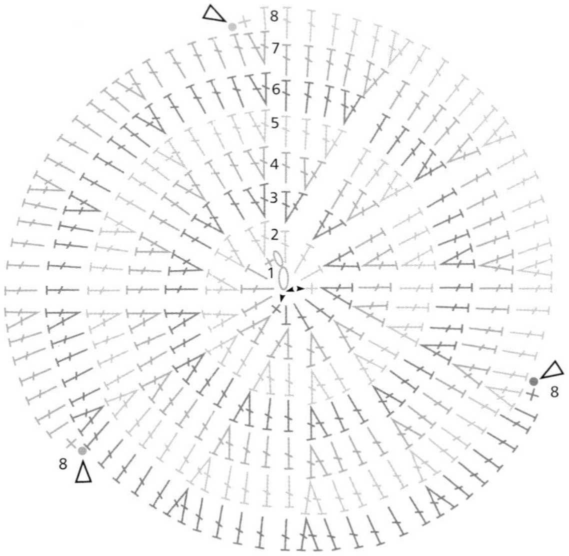

COLOURS
A
B
C

Round 5: Using A, *[2 tr in next st, 1 tr in each of next 3 sts] 4 times, remove hook from loop A; rep from * with colours B and C. (20 sts in each colour)

Round 6: Using A, *[2 tr in next st, 1 tr in each of next 4 sts] 4 times, remove hook from loop A; rep from * with colours B and C. (24 sts in each colour)

Round 7: Using A, *[2 tr in next st, 1 tr in each of next 5 sts] 4 times, remove hook from loop A; rep from * with colours B and C. (28 sts in each colour)

Round 8: Using A, *1 htr in next st, 1 dc in next st, ss in next st, fasten off A; rep from * with B and C.

NOTE

Place working loops not in use on to a split-ring marker or safety pin.

79 Geometric Wheel

LARGE
- 15–18cm (6–7in)
- Aran yarn
- 5.5mm hook

Foundation ring: Ch 10, join with ss to form a ring.

Round 1: Ch 3 (counts as first tr), 29 tr into ring, join with ss to top of beg ch-3. (30 tr)

Round 2: Ch 6 (counts as first tr and ch 3), skip 2 tr, [1 tr in next tr, ch 3, skip 2 tr] 9 times, join with ss to third ch of beg ch-6.

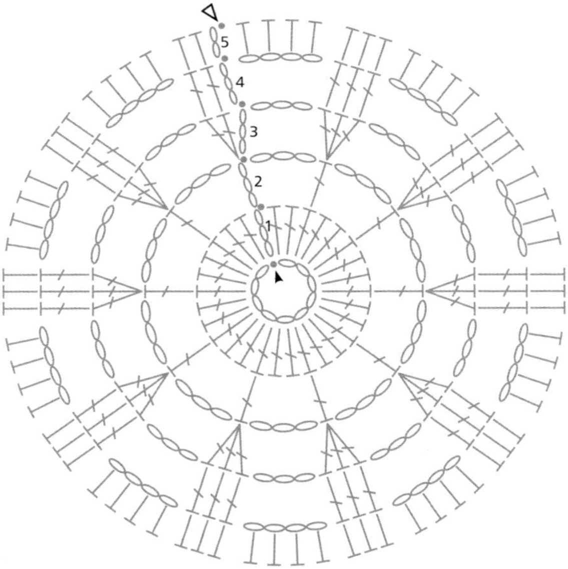

COLOUR

Round 3: Ch 3 (counts as first tr), 2 tr in st at base of ch-3, ch 3, [3 tr in next tr, ch 3] 9 times, join with ss to top of beg ch-3.

Round 4: Ch 3 (counts as first tr), 1 tr in each of next 2 tr, ch 4, [1 tr in each of next 3 tr, ch 4] 9 times, join with ss to top of beg ch-3.

Round 5: Ch 2 (counts as first htr), 1 htr in each tr and ch around, join with ss to top of beg ch-2.

Fasten off.

80 Tri-colour Medallion

SMALL

- 9–12cm (3½–4¾in)
- Aran yarn
- 5.5mm hook

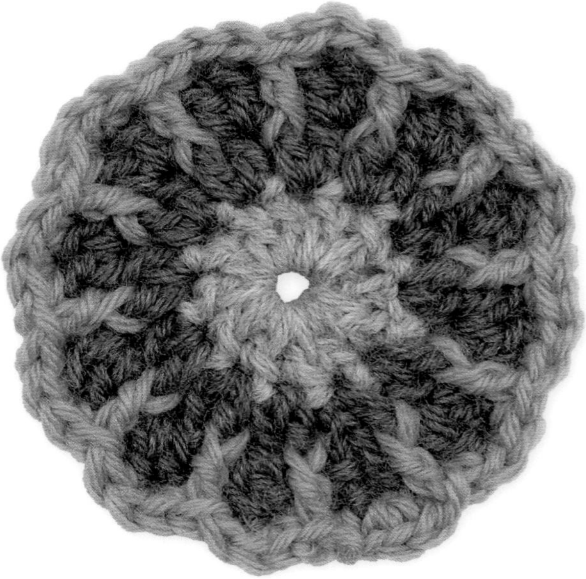

Foundation ring: Using A, ch 4, join with ss to form a ring.

Round 1: Ch 3 (counts as first tr), 11 tr into ring, join with ss to top of beg ch-3.

Fasten off A. Join B.

Round 2: Ch 3 (counts as first tr), 1 tr in st at base of ch-3, 2 tr in each st around, join with ss to top of beg ch-3.

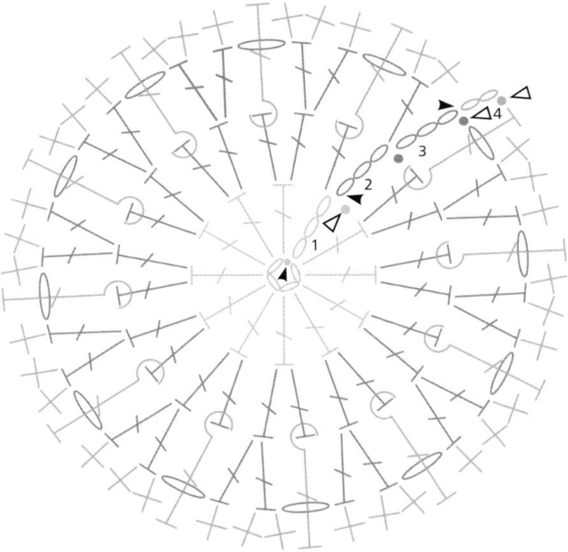

COLOURS

A

B

C

Round 3: Ch 3 (counts as first tr), 1 tr in st at base of ch-3, ch 1, skip 1 st, *2 tr in next st, ch 1, skip 1 st; rep from * 10 times more, join with ss to top of beg ch-3.

Fasten off B. Join C.

Round 4: Ch 2 (counts as first dc), 2 dc in next tr, working in front of next ch-1 sp FPtr around skipped st of round 2, *1 dc in next tr, 2 dc in next tr, working in front of next ch-1 sp FPtr around skipped st of round 2; rep from * 10 times more, join with ss to top of beg ch-2.

Fasten off.

81 Popcorn Circle

MEDIUM

- 12–15cm (4¾–6in)
- Aran yarn
- 5.5mm hook

Foundation ring: Using A, make a magic ring.

Round 1: Ch 3 (counts as first tr), 15 tr into ring, join with ss to top of beg ch-3.

Round 2: Beg popcorn, 2 tr in next tr, [popcorn in next tr, 2 tr in next tr] 7 times, join with ss to top of beg popcorn.

Round 3: Ch 3 (counts as first tr), 2 tr in top of popcorn at base of ch-3, 1 tr in next tr, [2 tr in next st or popcorn, 2 tr in next st or popcorn] 11 times, join with ss to top of beg ch-3.

Fasten off A. Join B.

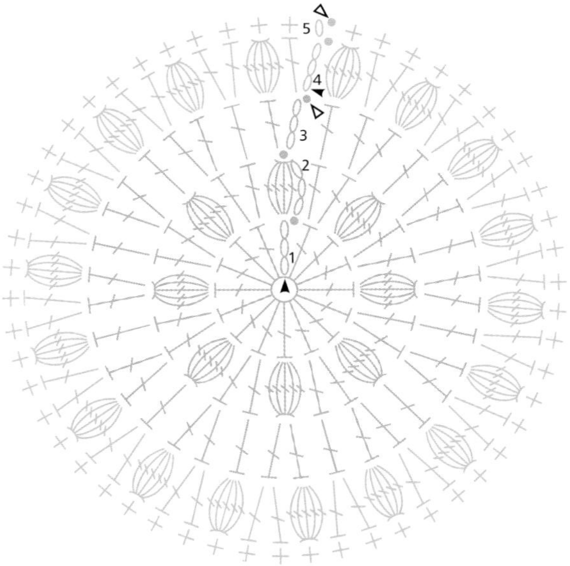

COLOURS

A

B

Round 4: Ch 3 (counts as first tr), 1 tr in st at base of ch-3, popcorn in next tr, [2 tr in next tr, popcorn in next tr] 17 times, join with ss to top of beg ch-3.

Round 5: Ch 1 (counts as first dc), 1 dc in each st or popcorn around, join with ss to beg ch-1.

Fasten off.

SPECIAL ABBREVIATIONS

beg popcorn: Ch 3, 4 tr in st at base of ch-3, remove hook from working loop, insert hook in top of first tr of popcorn, catch working loop, yo, draw through loop and st.

popcorn: 5 tr in next st, remove hook from working loop, insert hook in top of first tr of popcorn, catch working loop, yo, draw through loop and st.

82 Post Stitch Spoke Wheel

LARGE

- 15–18cm (6–7in)
- Aran yarn
- 5.5mm hook

Foundation ring: Ch 4, join with ss to form a ring.

Round 1: Ch 3 (counts as first tr), 11 tr into ring, join with ss to top of beg ch-3. (12 sts)

Round 2: Ch 3 (counts as first tr), FPtr around beg ch-3 of round 1, [1 tr in next tr, FPtr around tr at base of last tr worked] 11 times, join with ss to top of beg ch-3. (24 sts)

Round 3: Ch 3 (counts as first tr), 1 tr in next st, FPtr around FPtr at base of last tr worked, [1 tr in each of next 2 sts, FPtr around FPtr at base of last tr worked] 11 times, join with ss to top of beg ch-3. (36 sts)

Round 4: Ch 3 (counts as first tr), 1 tr in each of next 2 sts, FPtr around FPtr at base of last tr worked, [1 tr in each of next 3 sts, FPtr around FPtr at base of last tr worked] 11 times, join with ss to top of beg ch-3. (48 sts)

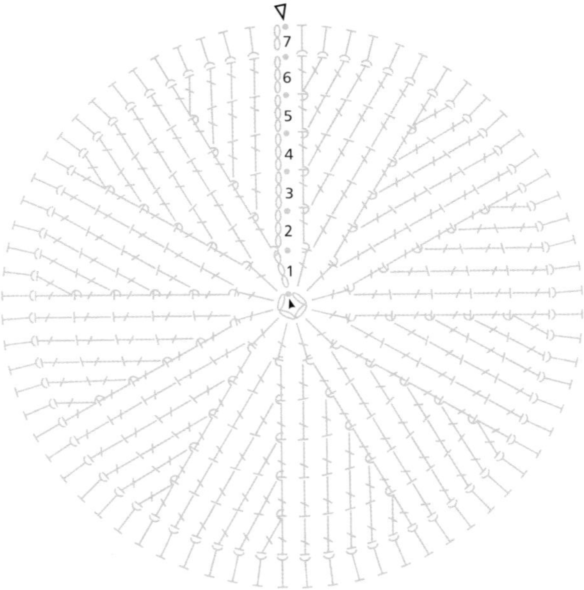

COLOUR

Round 5: Ch 3 (counts as first tr), 1 tr in each of next 3 sts, FPtr around FPtr at base of last tr worked, [1 tr in each of next 4 sts, FPtr around FPtr at base of last tr worked] 11 times, join with ss to top of beg ch-3. (60 sts)

Round 6: Ch 3 (counts as first tr), 1 tr in each of next 4 sts, FPtr around FPtr at base of last tr worked, [1 tr in each of next 5 sts, FPtr around FPtr at base of last tr worked] 11 times, join with ss to top of beg ch-3. (72 sts)

Round 7: Ch 2 (counts as first htr), 1 htr tbl in each st around, join with ss to top of beg ch-2. (72 sts)

Fasten off.

83 Flower Medallion

MEDIUM

- 12–15cm (4¾–6in)
- Aran yarn
- 5.5mm hook

Foundation ring: Using A, ch 6, join with ss to form a ring.

Round 1: Ch 4 (counts as first dtr), 2 dtr into ring, [ch 1, 3 dtr into ring] 5 times, ch 1, join with ss to top of beg ch-4, turn.

Fasten off A. Join B.

Round 2: Ss in next ch-1 sp, ch 7 (counts as 1 dc and ch 6), [1 dc in next ch-1 sp, ch 6] 5 times, join with ss to first ch of beg ch-7, do not turn.

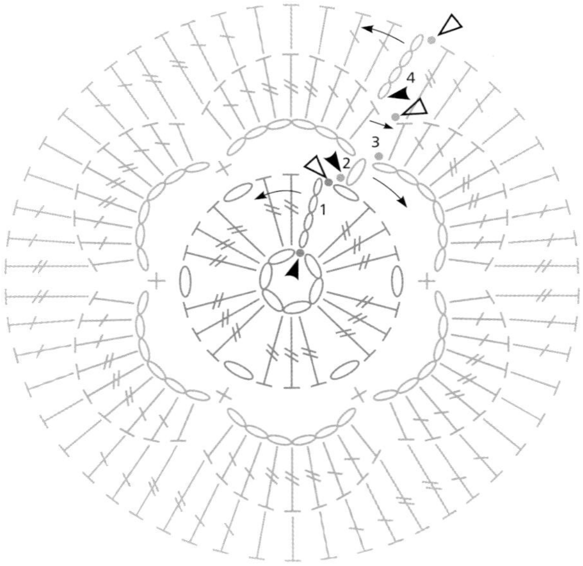

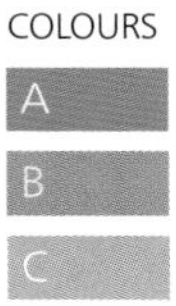

Round 3: Ss in next ch-6 sp, [1 htr, 2 tr, 3 dtr, 2 tr, 1 htr] in each ch-6 sp around, join with ss to first htr, turn. (6 petals)

Fasten off. Join C to first htr of any petal.

Round 4: Ch 4 (counts as first dtr), *1 tr in each of next 2 tr, 1 htr in each of next 3 dtr, 1 tr in each of next 2 tr, 1 dtr in each of next 2 htr; rep from * 5 times more, omitting last dtr of last rep, join with ss to top of beg ch-4.

Fasten off.

84 Bobble Border Wheel

LARGE
- 15–18cm (6–7in)
- Aran yarn
- 5.5mm hook

Foundation ring: Ch 4, join with ss to form a ring.

Round 1: Ch 5 (counts as first tr and ch 2), [1 tr into ring, ch 2] 7 times, join with ss to the third ch of beg ch-5.

Round 2: Ch 3 (counts as first tr), 2 tr in st at base of ch-3, ch 2, [3 tr in next tr, ch 2] 7 times, join with ss to top of beg ch-3.

Round 3: Ch 3 (counts as 1 tr), 1 tr in st at base of ch-3, 1 tr in next tr, 2 tr in next tr, ch 2, [2 tr in next tr, 1 tr in next tr, 2 tr in next tr, ch 2] 7 times, join with ss to top of beg ch-3.

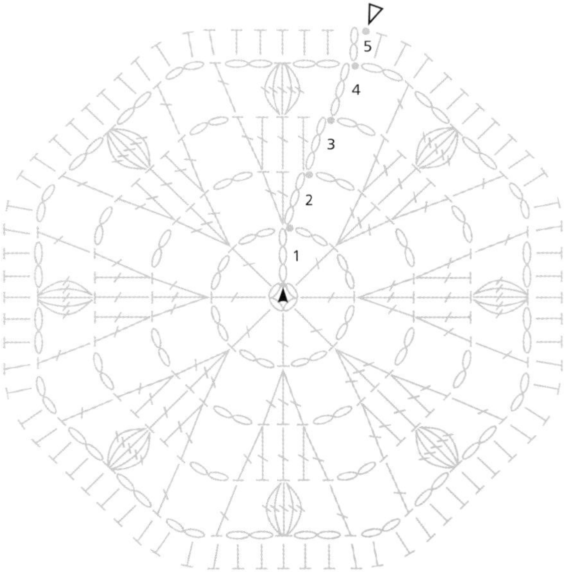

COLOUR

Round 4: Ch 5 (counts as first tr and ch 2), skip 1 tr, MB in next tr, ch 2, skip 1 tr, 1 tr in next tr, ch 2, [1 tr in next tr, ch 2, skip 1 tr, MB in next tr, ch 2, skip 1 tr, 1 tr in next tr, ch 2] 7 times, join with ss to third ch of beg ch-5.

Round 5: Ch 2 (counts as first htr), 1 htr in each stitch and ch around, join with ss to top of beg ch-2.

Fasten off.

SPECIAL ABBREVIATION

MB (make bobble): Work 5 tr in next st, omitting final stage so that 1 loop of each remains on hook, yo, draw through all 6 loops on hook.

85 Spoke Wheel

EXTRA LARGE

- 18–21cm (7–8¼in)
- Aran yarn
- 5.5mm hook

Foundation ring: Using A, ch 4, join with ss to form a ring.

Round 1: Ch 3 (counts as first tr), 9 tr into ring, join with ss to top of beg ch-3.

Fasten off A. Join B.

Round 2: Ch 4 (counts as first tr and ch 1), [1 tr in next tr, ch 1] 9 times, join with ss to third ch of beg ch-4.

Round 3: Ch 3, 1 tr in st at base of ch-3, ch 2, [2 tr in next tr, ch 2] 9 times, join with ss to top of beg ch-3.

Fasten off B. Join C.

Round 4: Ch 3, 1 tr in st at base of ch-3, 1 tr in next tr, ch 2, [2 tr in next tr, 1 tr in next tr, ch 2] 9 times, join with ss to top of beg ch-3.

Fasten off C. Join A.

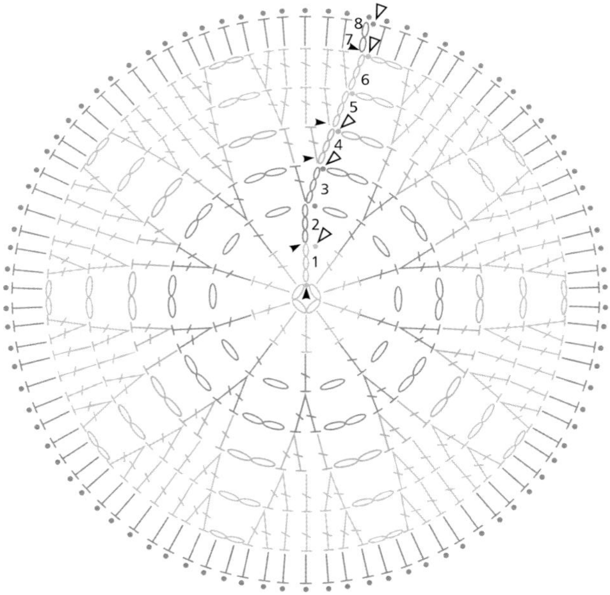

COLOURS

A

B

C

Round 5: Ch 3, 1 tr in st at base of ch-3, 1 tr in next tr, 2 tr in next tr, ch 2, [2 tr in next tr, 1 tr in next tr, 2 tr in next tr, ch 2] 9 times, join with ss to top of beg ch-3.

Round 6: Ch 3 (counts as first tr), 1 tr in st at base of ch-3, 1 tr in each of next 3 tr, 2 tr next tr, ch 2, [2 tr in next tr, 1 tr in each of next 3 tr, 2 tr in next tr, ch 2] 9 times, join with ss to top of beg ch-3.

Fasten off A. Join B.

Round 7: Ch 2 (counts as first htr), 1 htr in each st and 2 htr in each ch-2 sp around, join with ss to top of beg ch-2.

Round 8: Ss in each st around.

Fasten off.

86 Two-tone Lazy Wheel

LARGE
- 15–18cm (6–7in)
- Aran yarn
- 5.5mm hook

Foundation ring: Using A, ch 17, join with ss to eighth ch.

Row 1: Working into ch-9 tail, 1 dc in second ch from hook, 1 htr in next ch, 1 tr in next ch, 2 tr in next ch, 1 tr in next ch, 2 dtr in next ch, 1 dtr in next ch, 2 trtr in next ch, 1 trtr in next ch, do not turn.

Row 2: Working from left to right along row 1, reverse dc tfl in each st to end, ss into centre ring, do not turn.

Remove hook from working loop. Join B to centre ring.

Row 3: Working through back loop only of each st 2 rows below (behind reverse dc row), 1 dc in next st, 1 htr in next st, 1 tr in next st, 2 tr in next st, 1 tr in next st, 2 dtr in next st, 1 dtr in next st, 2 trtr in next st, 1 trtr in next st.

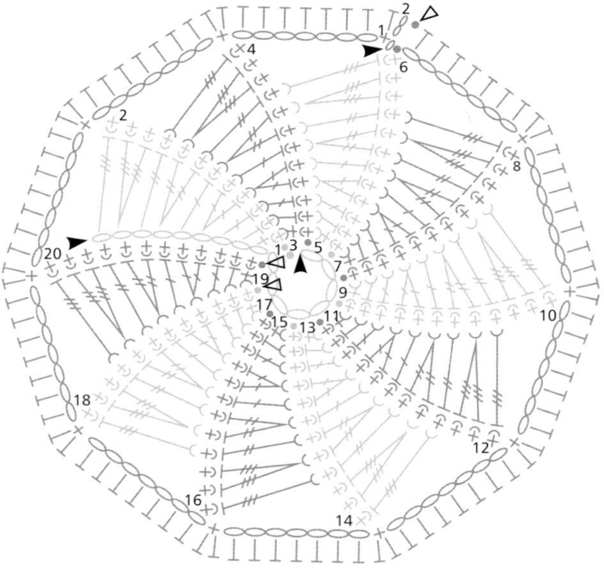

COLOURS

A

B

Rep rows 2–3, alternating A and B, until 10 repeats have been completed.

Fasten off, leaving a 30cm (12in) tail. Sew first and tenth repeats together through back loops of sts in row 19.

Join B to trtr at point of any repeat.

Round 1: Ch 1, 1 dc in trtr at base of ch-1, ch 7, [1 dc in next trtr, ch 7] 9 times, join with ss to first dc.

Round 2: Ch 2 (counts as first htr), 1 htr in st at base of ch-2, 7 htr in next ch-7 sp, [2 htr in next dc, 7 htr in next ch-7 sp] 9 times, join with ss to top of beg ch-2.

Fasten off.

87 Bobble Swirl Motif

LARGE

- 15–18cm (6–7in)
- Aran yarn
- 5.5mm hook

Foundation ring: Ch 6, join with ss to form a ring.

Round 1: 12 dc into ring, join with ss to first dc.

Round 2: Ch 4 (counts as first tr and ch 1), [1 tr in next dc, ch 1] 11 times, join with ss to third ch of beg ch-4.

Round 3: FPpuff st around beg ch-4 of round 2, *[ch 1, 1 tr, ch 1, 1 tr] in next ch-1 sp, FPpuff st around next tr; rep from * 10 times more, [ch 1, 1 tr, ch 1, 1 tr] in next ch-1 sp, join with ss to top of first FPpuff st.

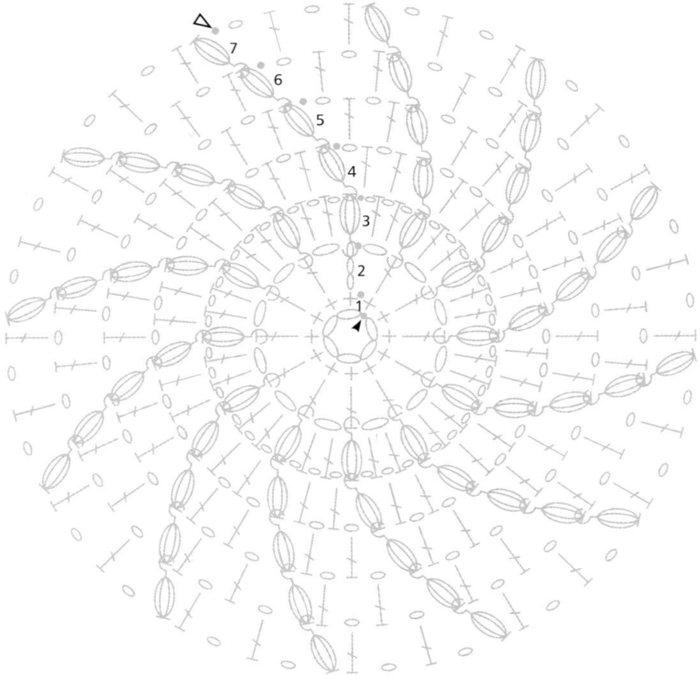

COLOUR

Round 4: *FPpuff st around next FPpuff st, 1 tr between next 2 tr, ch 1, 1 tr between second tr and next FPpuff st, ch 1; rep from * 11 times more, join with ss to top of first FPpuff st.

Rep round 4, 3 times more.

Fasten off.

SPECIAL ABBREVIATION

FPpuff st (front post puff stitch): [Yo, insert hook from front to back to front around post of indicated stitch, draw yarn through] 4 times in same st, yo, draw through all 9 loops on hook.

88 Six-pointed Snowflake

MEDIUM

- 12–15cm (4¾–6in)
- Aran yarn
- 5.5mm hook

Foundation ring: Ch 4, join with ss to form a ring.

Round 1: 6 dc into ring, join with ss to first dc.

Round 2: Ch 5 (counts as first tr and ch 2), 1 tr in first dc, *[1 tr, ch 2, 1 tr] in next dc; rep from * 4 times more, join with ss to third ch of beg ch-5.

Round 3: Ss in next ch-2 sp, ch 3 (counts as first tr), [1 tr, ch 3, 2 tr] in sp at base of ch-3, *[2 tr, ch 3, 2 tr] in next ch-2 sp; rep from * 4 times more, join with ss to top of beg ch-3.

COLOUR

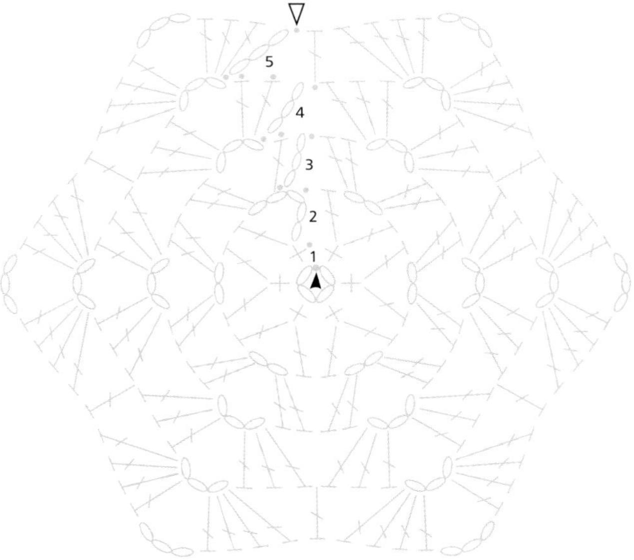

Round 4: Ss to and into next ch-3 sp, ch 3 (counts as first tr), [2 tr, ch 3, 3 tr] in sp at base of ch-3, *[3 tr, ch 3, 3 tr] in next ch-3 sp; rep from * 4 times more, join with ss to top of beg ch-3.

Round 5: Ss to and into ch-3 sp, ch 3 (counts as first tr), [3 tr, ch 3, 4 tr] in sp at base of ch-3, *1 tr between 2 groups of tr, [4 tr, ch 3, 4 tr] in next ch-3 sp; rep from * 4 times more, 1 tr between 2 groups of tr, join with ss to top of beg ch-3.

Fasten off.

89 Two-tone Crystal Snowflake

MEDIUM

- 12–15cm (4¾–6in)
- Aran yarn
- 5.5mm hook

Foundation ring: Using A, ch 4, join with ss to form a ring.

Round 1 (RS): Ch 3 (counts as first tr), 1 tr into ring, ch 1, [2 tr into ring, ch 1] 5 times, join with ss to top of beg ch-3.

Fasten off A. Join B to next ch-1 sp.

Round 2: Ch 3 (counts as first tr), [1 tr, ch 1, 2 tr] in sp at base of ch-3, *[2 tr, ch 1, 2 tr] in next ch-1 sp; rep from * 4 times more, join with ss to top of beg ch-3.

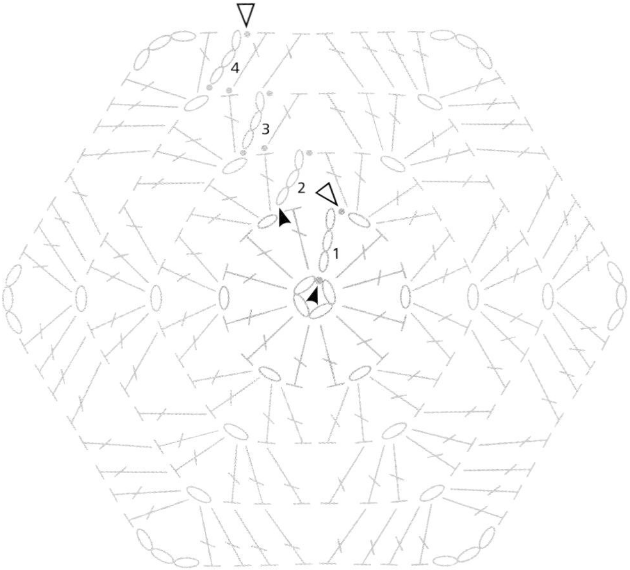

COLOURS

A

B

Round 3: Ss to and into next ch-1 sp, ch 3 (counts as first tr), [1 tr, ch 1, 2 tr] in sp at base of ch-3, 1 tr in next tr, skip 2 tr, 1 tr in next tr, *[2 tr, ch 1, 2 tr) in next ch-1 sp, 1 tr in next tr, skip 2 tr, 1 tr in next tr; rep from * 4 times more, join with ss to top of beg ch-3.

Round 4: Ss to and into next ch-1 sp, ch 3 (counts as first tr), [1 tr, ch 3, 2 tr] in sp at base of ch-3, 1 tr in each of next 2 tr, skip 2 tr, 1 tr in each of next 2 tr, *[2 tr, ch 3, 2 tr] in next ch-1 sp, 1 tr in each of next 2 tr, skip 2 tr, 1 tr in each of next 2 tr; rep from * 4 times more, join with ss to top of beg ch-3.

Fasten off.

90 Pretty Snowflake

LARGE
- 15–18cm (6–7in)
- Aran yarn
- 5.5mm hook

Foundation ring: Ch 9, join with ss to form a ring.

Round 1: Ch 8 (counts as first tr and ch 5), 3 tr into ring, [ch 5, 3 tr into ring] 4 times, ch 5, 2 tr into ring, join with ss to third ch of beg ch-8.

Round 2: Ss in each of next 2 ch, ch 7 (counts as first tr and ch 4), 4 tr in sp at base of ch-7, *ch 1, [4 tr, ch 4, 4 tr] in next ch-5 sp; rep from * 4 times more, ch 1, 3 tr in next ch-5 sp, join with ss to third ch of beg ch-7.

COLOUR

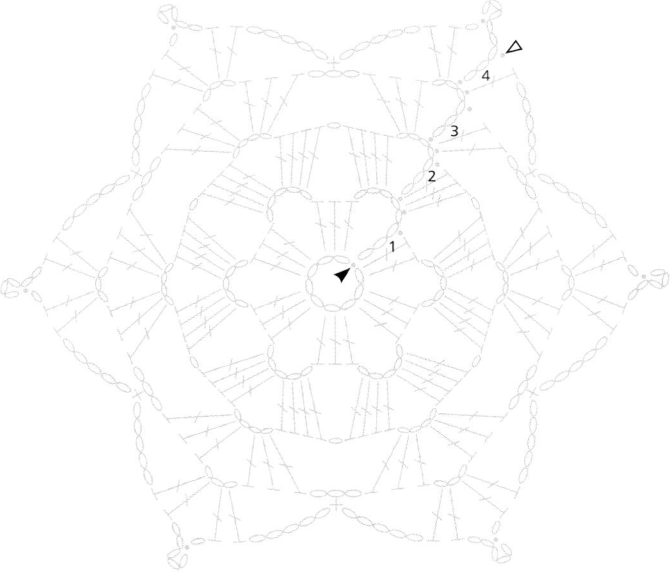

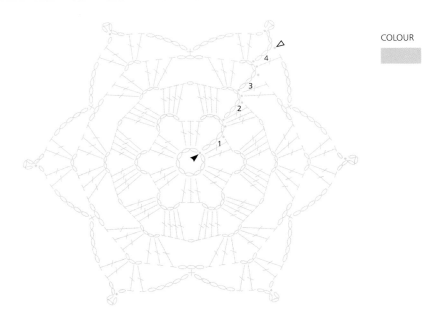

Round 3: Ss in each of next 2 ch, ch 6 (counts as first tr and ch 3), 3 tr in sp at base of ch-6, *ch 3, [3 tr, ch 3, 3 tr] in next ch-4 sp; rep from * 4 times more, ch 3, 2 tr in next ch-3 sp, join with ss to third ch of beg ch-6.

Round 4: Ss in each of next 2 ch, ch 8, ss in fourth ch from hook, ch 1, 2 tr in sp at base of ch-8, ch 5, 1 dc in next ch-3 sp, *ch 5, [2 tr, ch 5, ss in fourth ch from hook, ch 1, 2 tr] in next ch-3 sp, ch 5, 1 dc in next ch-3 sp; rep from * 4 times more, ch 5, 1 tr in next ch-3 sp, join with ss to third ch of beg ch-8.

Fasten off.

91 Large Double Snowflake

EXTRA LARGE
- 18–21cm (7–8¼in)
- Aran yarn
- 5.5mm hook

Foundation ring: Using A, ch 6, join with ss to form a ring.

Round 1: Ch 3 (count as first tr), 1 tr into ring, [ch 2, 2 tr into ring] 5 times, ch 2, join with ss to top of beg ch-3.

Round 2: Ch 3 (counts as first tr), 1 tr in st at base of ch-3, 2 tr in next tr, *[1 tr, 1 dtr, picot, 1 tr] in next ch-2 sp, 2 tr in each of next 2 tr; rep from * 4 times more, [1 tr, 1 dtr, picot, 1 tr] in next ch-2 sp, join with ss to top of beg ch-3.

Fasten off A. Join B with ss to top of last picot.

Round 3: *Ch 5, ss in picot sp at base of ch-5, ch 9, ss in top of next picot; rep from * 5 times more, join with ss to base of beg ch-5.

Round 4: *Ss in next ch-5 sp, ch 6, ss in sp at base of ch-6, 9 dc in next ch-9 sp; rep from * 5 times more, join with ss to beg ch-5 sp.

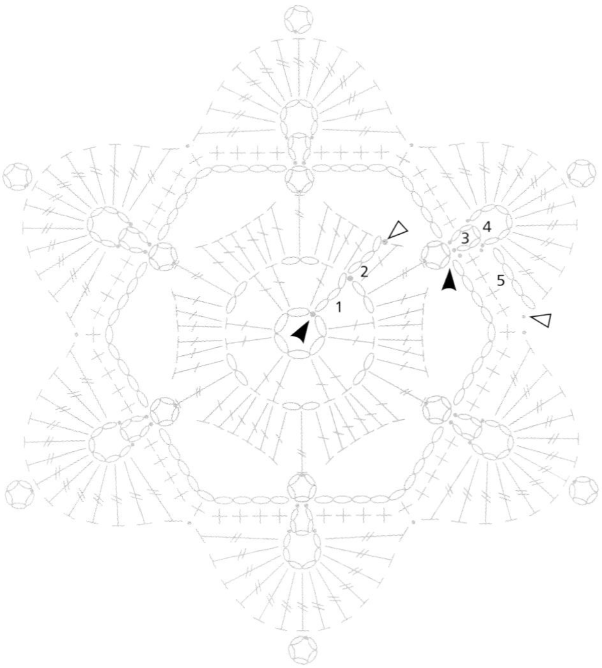

COLOURS

A

B

Round 5: Ch 4 (counts as first dtr), 6 dtr in next ch-6 sp, picot, 6 dtr in same ch-6 sp, *skip 4 dc, ss in next dc, skip 4 dc, 7 dtr in next ch-6 sp, picot, 6 dtr in same ch-6 sp; rep from * 4 times more, skip 4 dc, ss in next dc, skip 4 dc, join with ss to top of beg ch-4.

Fasten off.

SPECIAL ABBREVIATION

Picot: Ch 5, ss in st at base of ch-5.

92 Treble Crochet Star

MEDIUM
- 12–15cm (4¾–6in)
- Aran yarn
- 5.5mm hook

Foundation ring: Ch 5, join with ss to form a ring.

Round 1: Beg 2-tr cl into ring, ch 3, [3-tr cl into ring, ch 3] 4 times, join with ss to top of beg 2-tr cl.

Round 2: Ss in next ch-3 sp, ch 3 (counts as first tr), [2 tr, ch 2, 3 tr] in sp at base of ch-3, *[3 tr, ch 2, 3 tr] in next ch-3 sp; rep from * 3 times more, join with ss to top of beg ch-3.

Round 3: Ss in next st, ch 3 (counts as first tr), 1 tr in next st, [3 tr, ch 2, 3 tr] in next ch-2 sp, 1 tr in each of next 2 sts, skip 2 sts, *1 tr in each of next 2 sts, [3 tr, ch 2, 3 tr] in next ch-2 sp, 1 tr in each of next 2 sts, skip 2 sts; rep from * 3 times more, join with ss to top of beg ch-3.

COLOUR

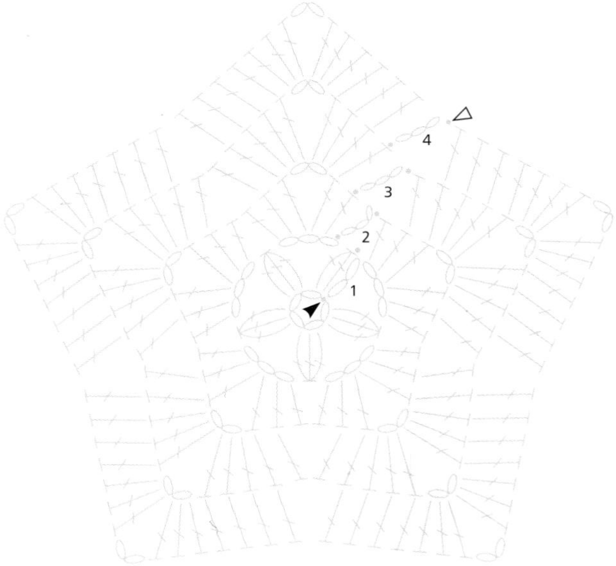

Round 4: Ss in next st, ch 3 (counts as first tr), 1 tr in each of next 3 sts, [3 tr, ch 2, 3 tr] in next ch-2 sp, 1 tr in each of next 4 sts, skip 2 sts, *1 tr in each of next 4 sts, [3 tr, ch 2, 3 tr] in next ch-2 sp, 1 tr in each of next 4 sts, skip 2 sts; rep from * 3 times more, join with ss to top of beg ch-3.

Fasten off.

SPECIAL ABBREVIATIONS

beg 2-tr cl (beginning 2 treble crochet cluster): Ch 2, [yo, insert hook into ring, yo, draw yarn through, yo, draw through 2 loops on hook] twice, yo, draw through all 3 loops on hook.

3-tr cl (3 treble crochet cluster): [Yo, insert hook into ring, yo, draw yarn through, yo, draw through 2 loops on hook] 3 times, yo, draw through all 4 loops on hook.

93 Large Five-pointed Star

MEDIUM
- 12–15cm ($4^3/_4$–6in)
- Aran yarn
- 5.5mm hook

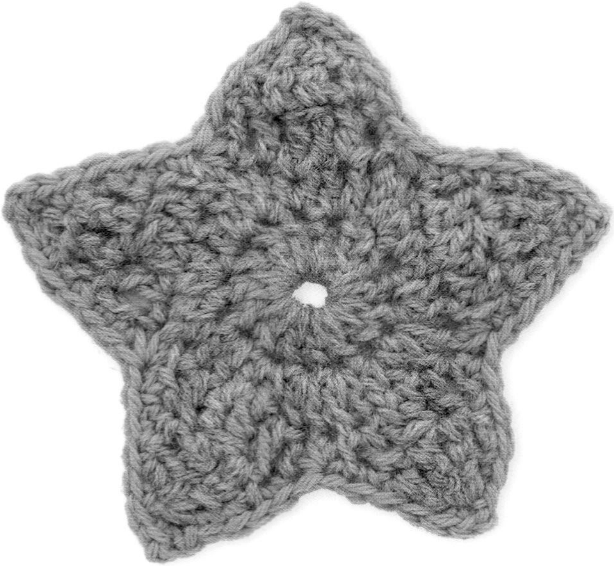

Foundation ring: Using A, ch 4, join with ss to form a ring.

Round 1: Ch 3 (counts as first tr), 14 tr into ring, join with ss to top of beg ch-3.

Round 2: Ch 3 (counts as first tr), [2 tr in next tr, 2 htr in next tr, 2 tr in next tr] 5 times, ending 1 tr in st at base of beg ch-3, join with ss to top of beg ch-3.

First point

Row 3: Ch 3 (counts as first tr), 1 tr in next tr, tr2tog over next 2 htr, 1 tr in each of next 2 tr, turn.

Row 4: Ch 2 (counts as first tr), tr4tog over next 3 sts and third ch of beg ch-3, ch 1.

Fasten off.

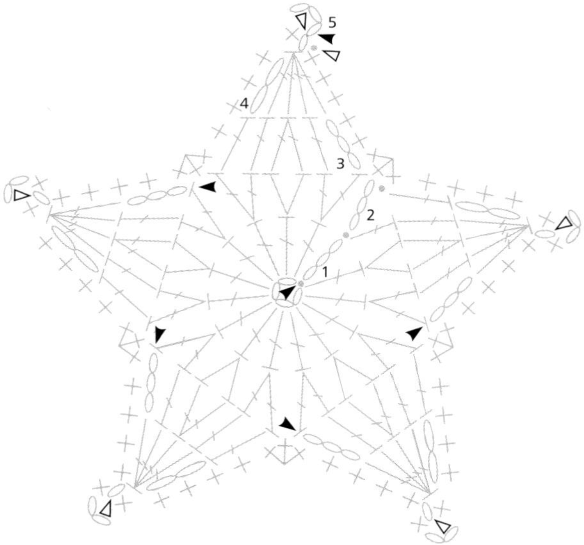

COLOURS

A

B

Remaining four points

Rejoin A to next unworked tr of round 2 and work second point as for first point.

Work three more points in the same way.

Join B to any point.

Round 5: Ch 3, 1 dc in st at base of ch-3, *4 dc down side edge of point, dc3tog at inner corner, 4 dc up side edge of next point, [1 dc, ch 2, 1 dc] at outer point; rep from * 4 times more, 4 dc down side edge of point, dc3tog at inner corner, 5 dc up side edge of next point, join with ss to first ch of beg ch-3.

Fasten off.

94 Lacy Five-pointed Star

MEDIUM

- 12–15cm (4¾–6in)
- Aran yarn
- 5.5mm hook

Foundation ring: Ch 3, join with ss to form a ring.

Round 1: Ch 2 (counts as first htr), 9 htr into ring, join with ss to top of beg ch-2, turn.

Round 2: Ch 1, *[2 htr, ch 2, 2 htr] in next htr, skip 1 htr; rep from * 4 times more, join with ss to first htr, turn.

Round 3: Ch 1, skip 1 htr, *1 dc in next htr, [2 dc, ch 2, 2 dc] in next ch-2 sp, 1 dc in next htr, skip 2 htr; rep from * to end of round, join with ss to first dc, turn.

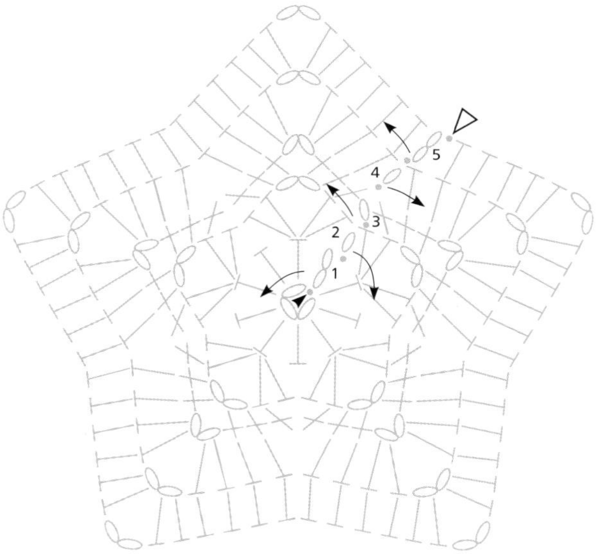

COLOUR

Round 4: Ch 1, skip first dc, *1 htr in each of next 2 dc, [(2 htr, ch 2, 2 htr) in next ch-2 sp, 1 htr in each of next 2 dc, skip 2 dc; rep from * to end of round, join with ss to first htr, turn.

Round 5: Ch 2 (counts as first htr), 1 htr in each of next 4 htr, *[2 htr, ch 2, 2 htr] in next ch-2 sp, 1 htr in each of next 8 htr; rep from * 3 times more, [2 htr, ch 2, 2 htr] in next ch-2 sp, 1 htr in each of next 3 htr, join with ss to first htr.

Fasten off.

95 Six-pointed Star

SMALL
- 9–12cm ($3\frac{1}{2}$–$4\frac{3}{4}$in)
- Aran yarn
- 5.5mm hook

Foundation chain: Using A, ch 2.

Row 1: 1 dc in second ch from hook, turn. (1 st)

Row 2: Ch 1, 2 dc in dc, turn. (2 sts)

Row 3: Ch 1, 2 dc in first dc, 1 dc in next dc, turn. (3 sts)

Row 4: Ch 1, 2 dc in first dc, 1 dc in each of next 2 dc, turn. (4 sts)

Row 5: Ch 5, dc2tog over second and third chs from hook, 1 dc in each of next 2 ch, 1 dc in each of next 4 dc, 4 xdc, turn. (11 sts)

Row 6: Ch 1, dc2tog over first and second xdc, 1 dc in each st to end, turn. (10 sts)

Rep row 6, twice more. (8 sts)

Row 9: Ch 1, 2 dc in first dc, 1 dc in each dc to end, turn. (9 sts)

Rep row 9, 3 times more. (12 sts)

Row 13: Ch 1, ss in each of next 5 dc, ch 1, 1 dc in st at base of ch-1, 1 dc in each of next 3 dc, turn leaving last 4 dc unworked.

COLOURS

A

B

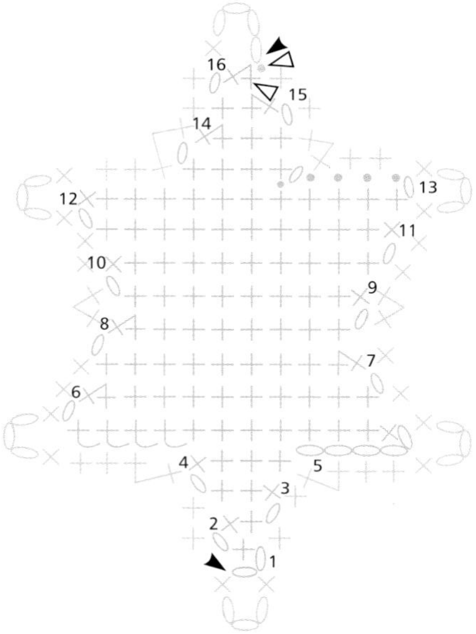

Row 14: Ch 1, dc2tog over first and second dc, 1 dc in each of next 2 dc, turn.

Row 15: Ch 1, dc2tog over first and second dc, 1 dc in next dc, turn.

Row 16: Ch 1, dc2tog over remaining 2 dc, turn.

Fasten off A. Join B to any point.

Edging round: Ch 4, 1 dc in st at base of ch-4, *2 dc down side edge of point, dc2tog at inner corner, 2 dc up side edge of next point, [1 dc, ch 3, 1 dc] at outer point; rep from * 4 times more, 2 dc down side edge of point, dc2tog at inner corner, 2 dc up side edge of next point, join with ss to first ch of beg ch-4. Fasten off.

SPECIAL ABBREVIATION

xdc (extended double crochet): Insert hook into base of last st, yo, draw yarn through, yo, draw through 1 loop on hook, yo, draw through both loops on hook.

96 Starburst Flower

LARGE

- 15–18cm (6–7in)
- Aran yarn
- 5.5mm hook

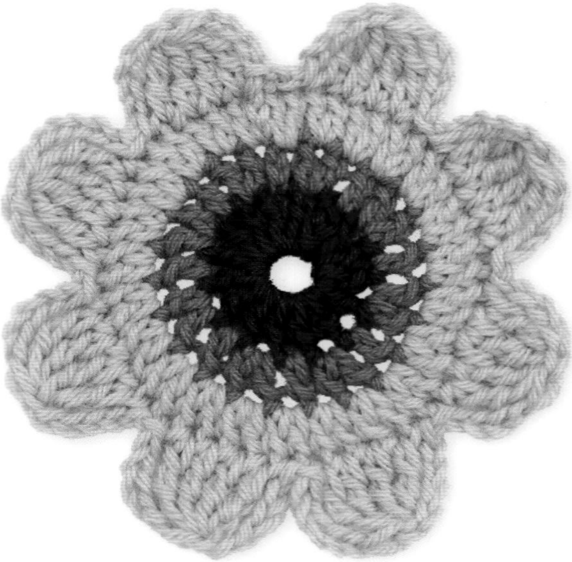

Foundation ring: Using A, ch 6, join with ss to form a ring.

Round 1: Ch 3 (counts as first tr), 15 tr into ring, join with ss to top of beg ch-3. (16 sts)

Fasten off A. Join B.

Round 2: Ch 3 (counts as first tr), 2 tr in next tr, [1 tr in next tr, 2 tr in next tr] 7 times, join with ss to top of beg ch-3. (24 sts)

Fasten off B. Join C.

Round 3: Ch 3 (counts as first tr), 1 tr in st at base of ch-3, 2 tr in each of next 23 tr, join with ss to top of beg ch-3. (48 sts)

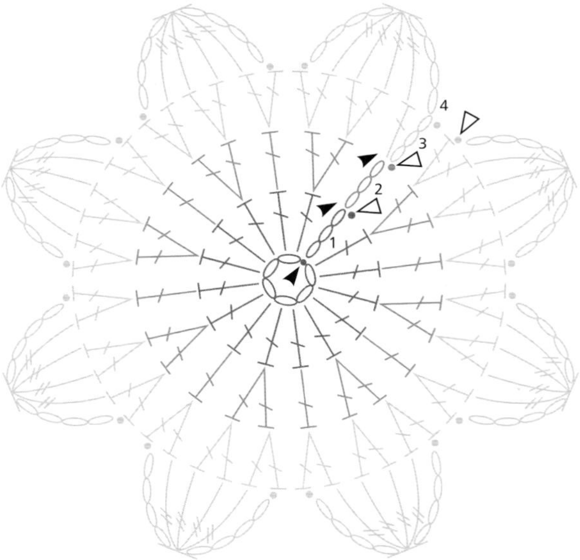

COLOURS

A

B

C

Round 4: *Ch 4 (counts as first dtr), dtr4tog, ch 4, ss in next tr (petal made), ss in next tr; rep from * 6 times more, ch 4, dtr4tog, ch 4, ss in next tr.

Fasten off.

SPECIAL ABBREVIATION

dtr4tog (double treble 4 stitches together): [(Yo) twice, insert hook in next st, draw yarn through, (yo, draw through 2 loops on hook) twice] 4 times, yo, draw through all 5 loops on hook.

97 Primrose

EXTRA LARGE

- 18–21cm (7–8¼in)
- Aran yarn
- 5.5mm hook

Foundation ring: Using A, ch 6, join with ss to form a ring.

Round 1: Ch 6 (counts as first tr and ch 3), [1 tr into ring, ch 3] 6 times, join with ss to third ch of beg ch-6.

Round 2: [(1 dc, ch 4, 1 dc) in next ch-3 sp, (ss, ch 3, ss) in next tr] 6 times, [1 dc, ch 4, 1 dc] in next ch-3 sp, [ss, ch 3, ss] in third ch of beg ch-6.

Fasten off A. Join B to any ch-4 sp.

Round 3: Ch 3 (counts as first tr), [2 tr, ch 2, 3 tr] in sp at base of ch-3, *[3 tr, ch 2, 3 tr] in next ch-4 sp: rep from * 5 times more, join with ss to top of beg ch-3.

Round 4: Ss in next tr (centre tr of 3-tr group), ch 3 (counts as first tr), 1 tr in next tr, *[2 tr, ch 2, 2 tr] in next ch-2 sp, 1 tr in each of next 2 tr, skip 2 tr, 1 tr in each of next 2 tr; rep from * 5 times more, [2 tr, ch 2, 2 tr] in next ch-2 sp, 1 tr in each of next 2 tr, skip last tr, join with ss to top of beg ch-3.

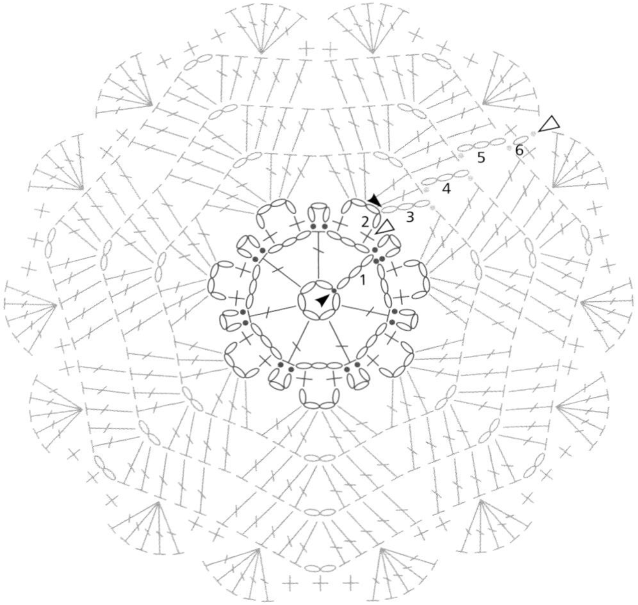

COLOURS

A

B

Round 5: Ss in next tr, ch 3 (counts as first tr), 1 tr in each of next 2 tr, *[2 tr, ch 2, 2 tr] in next ch-2 sp, 1 tr in each of next 3 tr, skip 2 tr, 1 tr in each of next 3 tr; rep from * 5 times more, [2 tr, ch 2, 2 tr] in next ch-2 sp, 1 tr in each of next 3 tr, skip last tr, join with ss to top of beg ch-3.

Round 6: Ch 1, 1 dc in st at base of ch-1, *skip 1 tr, 5 tr in next tr (shell made), skip 1 tr, 1 dc in next tr, 1 dc in next ch-2 sp, 1 dc in next tr, skip 1 tr, 5 tr in next tr, skip 1 tr, 1 dc in each of next 2 tr; rep from * 5 times more, skip 1 tr, 5 tr in next tr, skip 1 tr, 1 dc in next tr, 1 dc in next ch-2 sp, 1 dc in next tr, skip 1 tr, 5 tr in next tr, skip 1 tr, 1 dc in next tr, join with ss to first dc.

Fasten off.

98 Sunflower

MEDIUM

- 12–15cm (4¾–6in)
- Aran yarn
- 5.5mm hook

Foundation ring: Using A, ch 5, join with ss to form a ring.

Round 1: Ch 3 (counts as first tr), 15 tr into ring, join with ss to top of beg ch-3.

Fasten off A. Join B.

Round 2: Ch 1, 2 dc in st-sp between ch-3 and next tr, [2 dc in st-sp before next tr] 14 times, 2 dc in st-sp before ch-3, join with ss to beg ch-1.

Fasten off B. Join C.

Round 3: Ch 5 (counts as first trtr), skip first dc, trtr4tog tbl over next 4 dc, [ch 9, trtr5tog tbl over last st and next 4 sts] 7 times, ch 9, join with ss to top of beg trtr4tog.

Round 4: Ch 1, 9 dc in next ch-9 sp, [skip trtr5tog, 9 dc in next ch-9 sp] 7 times, join with ss to beg ch-1.

Fasten off.

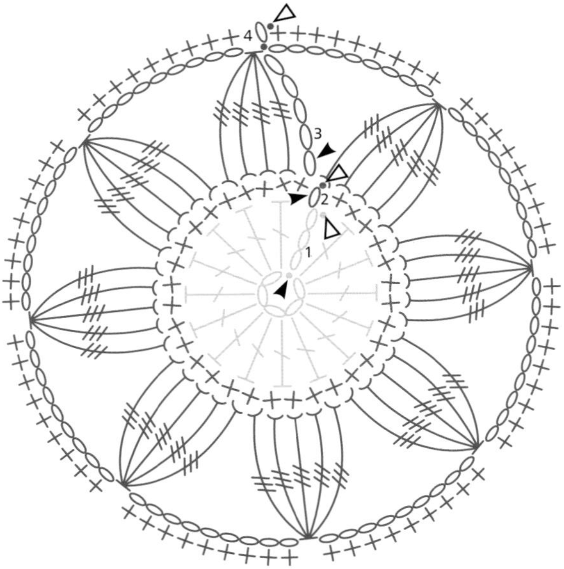

COLOURS

A

B

C

SPECIAL ABBREVIATIONS

trtr4tog tbl (triple treble 4 stitches together through back loops): Working tbl of sts, *[yo] 3 times, insert hook in next st, yo, draw yarn through, [yo, draw through 2 loops on hook] 3 times; rep from * 3 times more, yo, draw through all 5 loops on hook.

trtr5tog tbl (triple treble 5 stitches together through back loops): Working tbl of sts, [yo] 3 times, insert hook in same st as last st of previous cluster, yo, draw yarn through, [yo, draw through 2 loops on hook] 3 times, *[yo] 3 times, insert hook in next st, yo, draw yarn through, [yo, draw through 2 loops on hook] 3 times; rep from * 3 times more, yo, draw through all 6 loops on hook.

99 Two-tone Anemone

MEDIUM

- 12–15cm (4¾–6in)
- Aran yarn
- 5.5mm hook

Foundation ring: Using A, ch 6, join with ss to form a ring.

Round 1: Ch 1, 24 dc into ring, join with ss to first dc.

Round 2: Ch 5 (counts as first tr and ch 2), 1 tr in next dc, [ch 1, skip 1 dc, 1 tr in next dc, ch 2, 1 tr in next dc] 7 times, ch 1, skip 1 dc, join with ss to third ch of beg ch-5.

Fasten off A. Join B to next ch-2 sp.

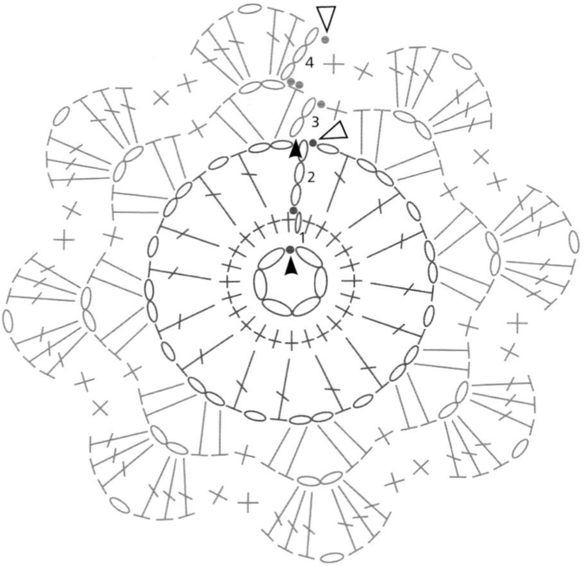

COLOURS

A

B

Round 3: Ch 2 (counts as first htr), [1 htr, ch 2, 2 htr] in sp at base of ch-2, 1 dc in next ch-1 sp, *[2 htr, ch 2, 2 htr] in next ch-2 sp, 1 dc in next ch-1 sp; rep from * 6 times more, join with ss to top of beg ch-2.

Round 4: Ss to and into next ch-2 sp, ch 3 (counts as first tr), [2 tr, ch 1, 3 tr] in sp at base of ch-3, 1 dc in st-sp before next dc, 1 dc in st-sp after next dc, *[3 tr, ch 1, 3 tr] in next ch-2 sp, 1 dc in st-sp before next dc, 1 dc in st-sp after next dc; rep from * 6 times more, join with ss to top of beg ch-3.

Fasten off.

100 Dogwood

MEDIUM
- 12–15cm (4¾–6in)
- Aran yarn
- 5.5mm hook

Foundation ring: Make a magic ring.

Round 1: Ch 1, 7 dc into ring, join with ss to beg ch-1.

Round 2: Ch 5, [skip 1 dc, 1 dc in next dc, ch 4] 3 times, join with ss to first ch of beg ch-5.

Round 3: Ss in next ch, ch 3 (counts as first tr), 6 tr in sp at base of ch-3, ch 2, skip 1 dc, [7 tr in next ch-4 sp, ch 2, skip 1 dc] 3 times, join with ss to top of beg ch-3.

Round 4: Ch 1, 1 dc in st at base of ch-1, [1 dc in each of next 2 tr, 2 dc in next tr] twice, skip 2 ch, *2 dc in next tr, [1 dc in each of next 2 tr, 2 dc in next tr] twice, skip 2 ch; rep from * twice more, join with ss to beg ch-1.

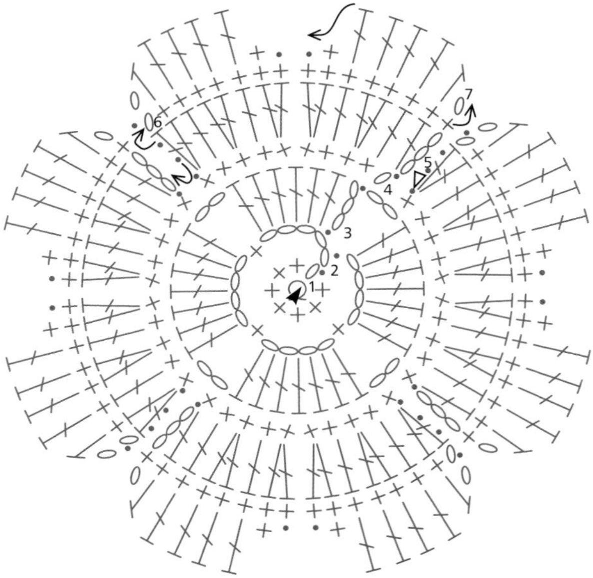

COLOUR

Complete the first petal in rows as follows.

Row 5: Ch 3 (counts as first tr), 1 tr in st at base of ch-3, [1 tr in next dc, 2 tr in next dc] twice, 2 tr in next dc, [1 tr in next dc, 2 tr in next dc] twice, turn. (16 sts)

Row 6: Ch 1, skip first tr, 1 dc in each of 14 tr, 1 dc in top of beg ch-3, turn.

Row 7: Ch 1, skip first dc, 1 htr in next dc, 1 tr in each of next 4 dc, 1 dc in next dc, ss in each of next 2 dc, 1 dc in next dc, 1 tr in each of next 4 dc, 1 htr in last dc, ch 1, ss in beg ch-1 of row 6, 2 ss in side edge of tr below, 1 ss in side edge of dc below tr, 1 ss in next dc of round 4.

Rep rows 5–7, 3 times more, to complete each remaining petal.

Fasten off.

Techniques

Choosing Yarn

The blocks in this book are worked in DK- or Aran-weight yarn, but they can all be made with whatever yarn will work best for your project.

Questions to consider

As well as colour, the fibre composition and the drape potential of a yarn are vital to the success of a project. Consider carefully the characteristics you require of the finished crocheted fabric.

- Would it be better if the fabric had some elasticity or not?
- Would a fabric with a good drape be better or one with a firm tension and no drape?

Fit for purpose

If your proposed project is an afghan, then perhaps a soft, cosy fabric with good drape would be most suitable. Some people consider pure wool yarns preferable when crocheting an afghan or large project because wool is lighter than cotton and improves the drape of the crochet fabric; but there are times when synthetic yarns are better – particularly for baby items that may require frequent washing. For a bag, a firm, resilient fabric would be ideal, and for a cushion, well, the choice is up to you.

Test it out

Select a range of single balls or hanks of yarn and work a few sample blocks. With experience you will be able to gauge how a yarn may perform, but there are always surprises. Remember that the hook size and the block being worked will influence the final result – so experiment with yarns, hook sizes and block patterns with more or less texture or loft.

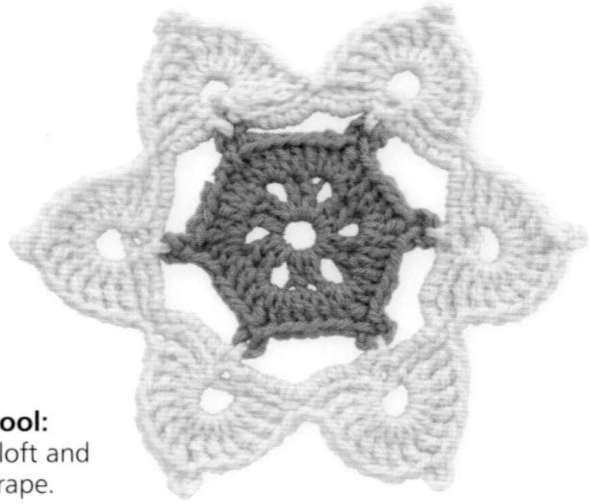

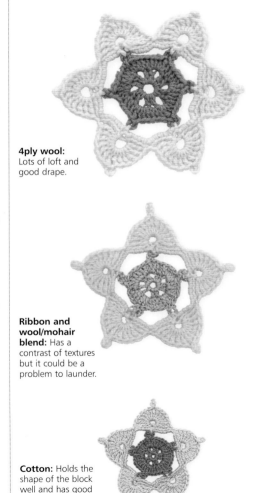

4ply wool: Lots of loft and good drape.

Ribbon and wool/mohair blend: Has a contrast of textures but it could be a problem to launder.

Cotton: Holds the shape of the block well and has good stitch definition.

Getting Started

All of the blocks begin with a foundation chain (when working in rows) or a foundation ring or magic ring (when working in rounds). See page 212 for a reminder of how to work particular crochet stitches.

Slip knot
Wrap yarn into a loop, insert hook into loop, catch yarn with hook and pull it through. Tighten loop on hook to form slip knot; this secures the yarn to the hook.

Foundation chain
Make the number of chain stitches specified in the pattern. Each V-shaped loop on the front is one chain stitch. The loop on the hook (the working loop) is not counted as a stitch. The first row of crochet stitches are worked into these chain stitches.

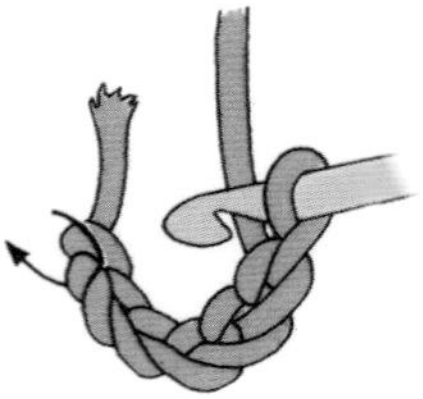

Foundation ring
Make a short length of foundation chain as specified in the pattern. Join the chains into a ring by working a slip stitch into the first chain. The first round of crochet stitches are worked into the centre of the ring, not into the chain stitches.

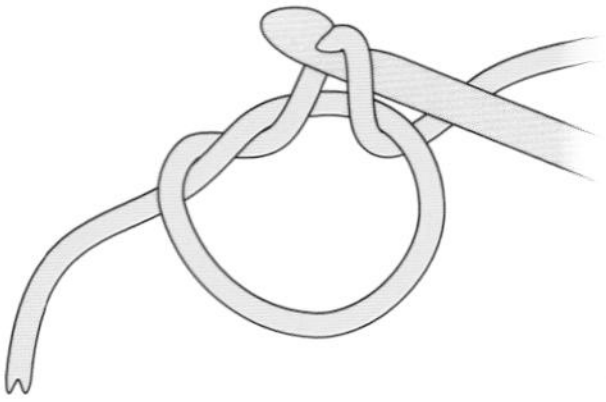

Magic ring
Use this alternative to a foundation ring for working in the round when you want to avoid a hole in the centre of your work. Wrap the yarn into a ring, insert the hook, and draw a loop through. Work the first round of crochet stitches into this ring, then pull the yarn tail tightly to close the ring.

Turning and starting chains

Extra chains are worked at the beginning of a row (turning chains) or round (starting chains) to bring the hook up to the correct height for the stitch you will be working next. Usually these chains count as the first stitch of the row or round, except for double crochet where the turning chain is ignored. Some blocks vary from the standard number of chains, and some count the turning chain as the first double crochet stitch. The pattern will always tell you when this is the case. A chain may also be longer than the number required for the stitch, and in that case counts as one stitch plus a number of chains. Again, the pattern will always explain this.

At the end of the row, the final stitch is usually worked into the turning chain of the previous row, either into the top chain of the turning chain or into another specified stitch of the chain. At the end of a round, the final stitch is usually joined to the starting chain with a slip stitch.

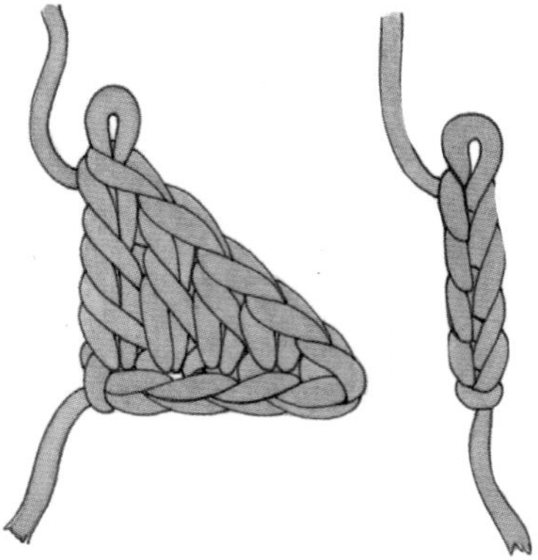

STANDARD NUMBER OF TURNING CHAINS

Double crochet (dc): 1 turning chain
Half treble crochet (htr): 2 turning chains
Treble crochet (tr): 3 turning chains
Double treble crochet (dtr): 4 turning chains
Triple treble crochet (trtr): 5 turning chains

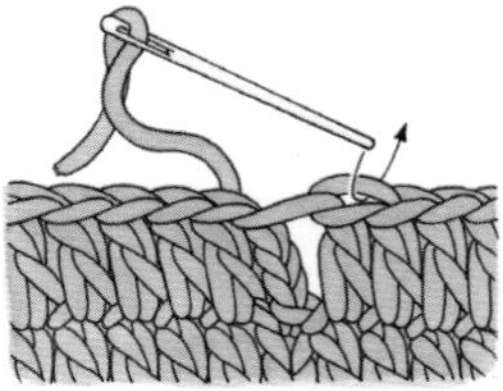

Finishing the last round

For a neater finish, don't use a slip stitch to join the last stitch of the final round to the first stitch of the round. Instead, fasten off the yarn after the last stitch, thread a tapestry needle and pass it under the top loops of the first stitch of the round and back through the centre of the last stitch.

TIPS FOR NEAT EDGES WHEN WORKING IN ROWS

- Turn your work and take the working yarn around the outside to its new position and not over the top between the hook and the crochet edge.
- If you work the last stitch into the top of the turning chain and the edge bulges, pull out the last stitch and work it tightly into the chain below the top chain, to take in the slack.
- Rather than working into the top loops, work around the stem of the stitch, inserting the hook from back to front, around the post and to the back again.
- If your chain stitches are tight, work an extra turning chain to stop the edges of the block from becoming too tight. If your chains are loose, work one less turning chain than specified.

Stitch Reminder

Here is a concise guide to the basic crochet stitches used to make the blocks.

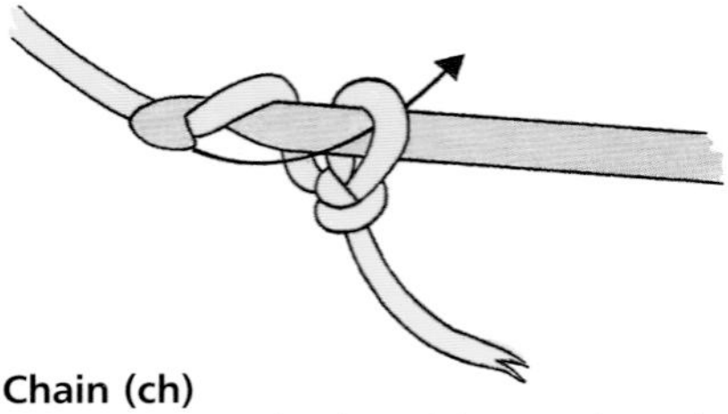

Chain (ch)
Wrap yarn over hook and draw it through loop on hook to form a new loop on hook.

Slip stitch (ss)
Insert hook into next stitch, wrap yarn over hook and draw through stitch and loop on hook.

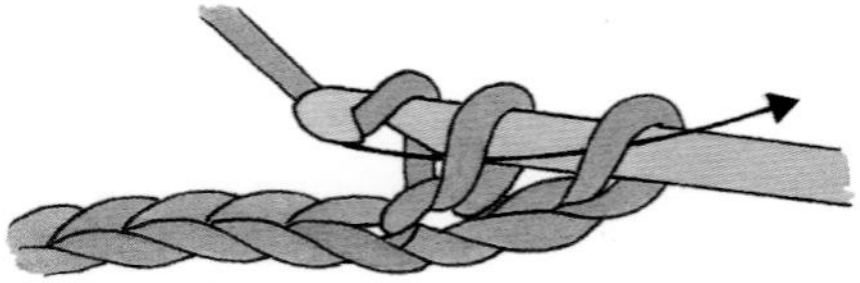

Double crochet (dc)
Insert hook into next stitch, yarn over hook and draw through stitch (2 loops on hook). Yarn over hook and draw through both loops.

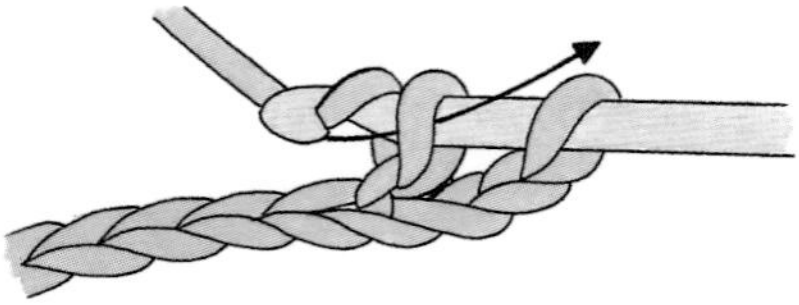

Extended double crochet (xdc)
Insert hook into next stitch, yarn over hook and draw through stitch (2 loops on hook). Yarn over hook and draw through first loop (2 loops on hook). Yarn over hook and draw through both loops.

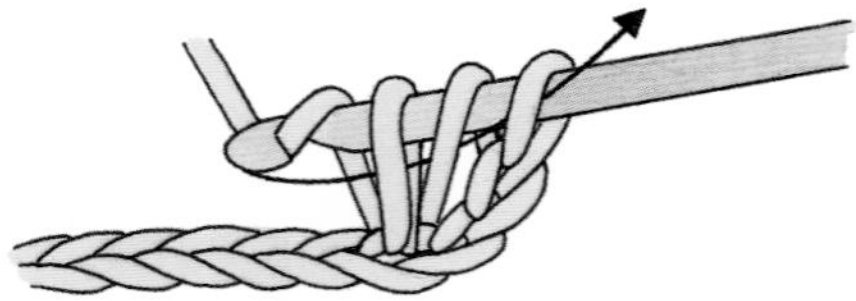

Half treble crochet (htr)
Yarn over hook, insert hook into next stitch, yarn over hook and draw through stitch (3 loops on hook). Yarn over hook and draw through all three loops.

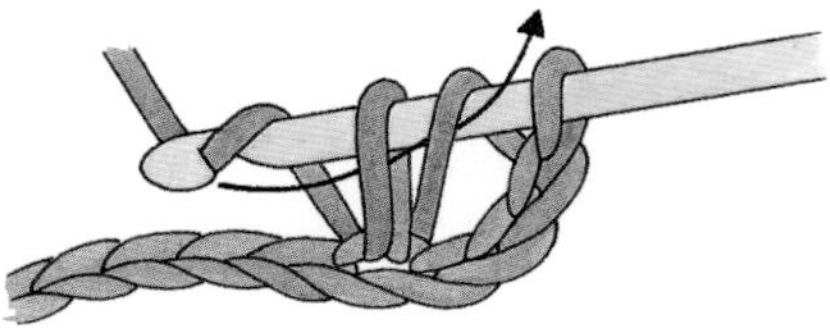

Treble crochet (tr)
Yarn over hook, insert hook into next stitch, yarn over hook and draw through stitch (3 loops on hook). *Yarn over hook and draw through two loops; repeat from * once more.

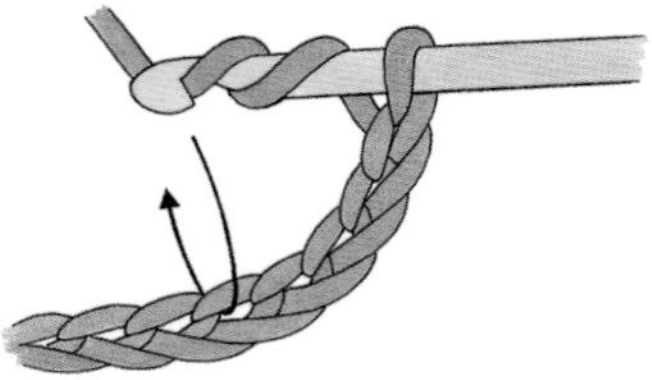

Double treble crochet (dtr)
Yarn over hook twice, insert hook into next stitch, yarn over hook and draw through stitch (4 loops on hook). *Yarn over hook and draw through two loops; repeat from * twice more.

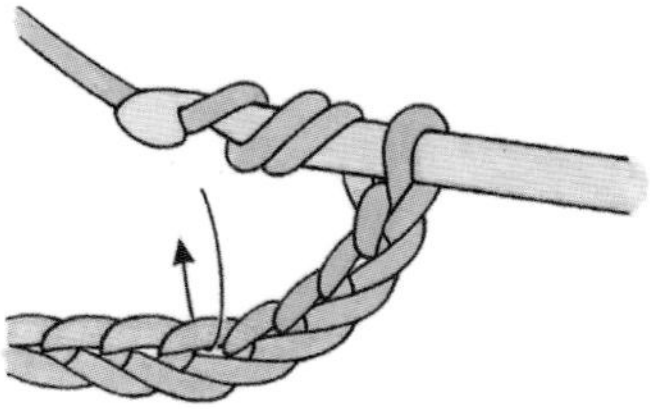

Triple treble crochet (trtr)
Yarn over hook three times, insert hook into next stitch, yarn over hook and draw through stitch (5 loops on hook). *Yarn over hook and draw yarn through two loops; repeat from * three times more.

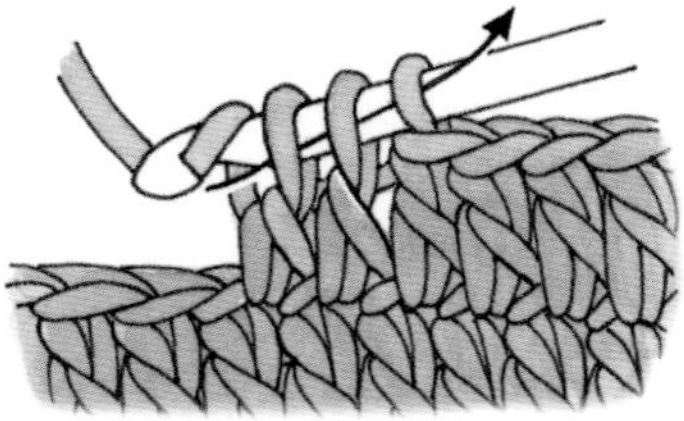

Decrease (e.g. dc2tog, tr3tog)
Work specified number of stitches, omitting final stage of each stitch so that last loop of each stitch remains on hook. Wrap yarn over hook and draw through all loops on hook.

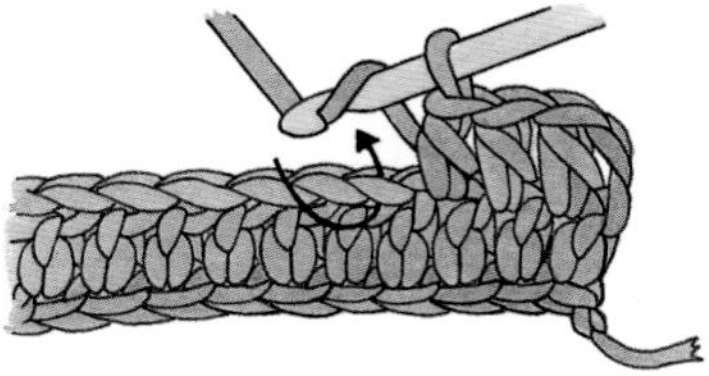

Through front loop (tfl)
Rather than inserting hook under both top loops to work the next stitch, insert it only under the front loop.

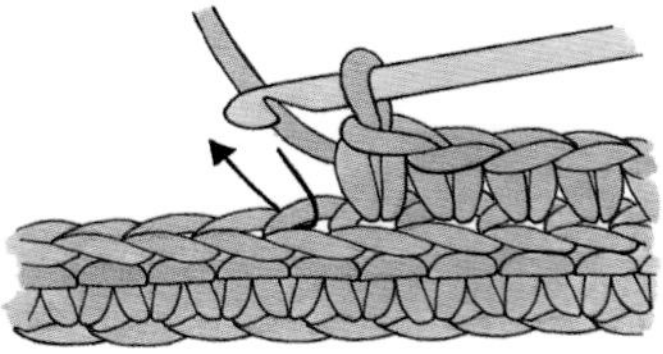

Through back loop (tbl)
Rather than inserting hook under both top loops to work the next stitch, insert it only under the back loop.

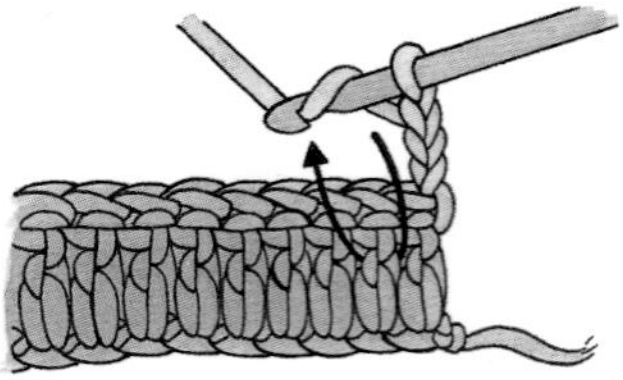

Front post (FP)
Work around the stem of the stitch, inserting hook from front to back, around the post and to front again.

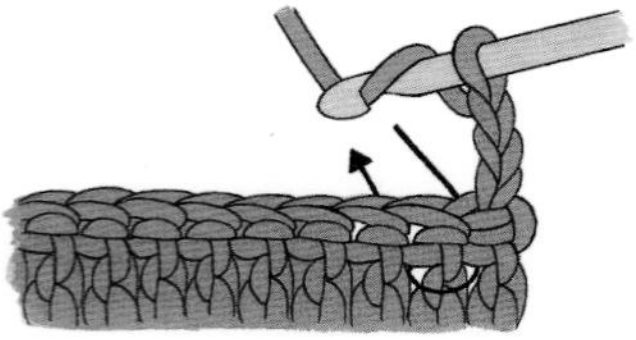

Back post (BP)
Work around the stem of the stitch, inserting hook from back to front, around the post and to back again.

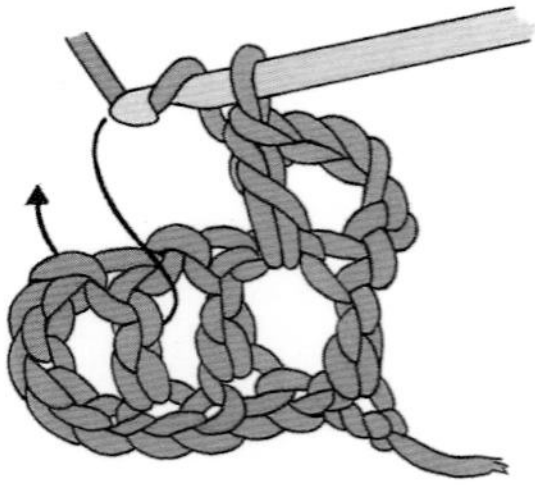

Chain space (ch sp)
Insert hook into space below chains. Here, a double treble crochet stitch is being worked into a chain-1 space.

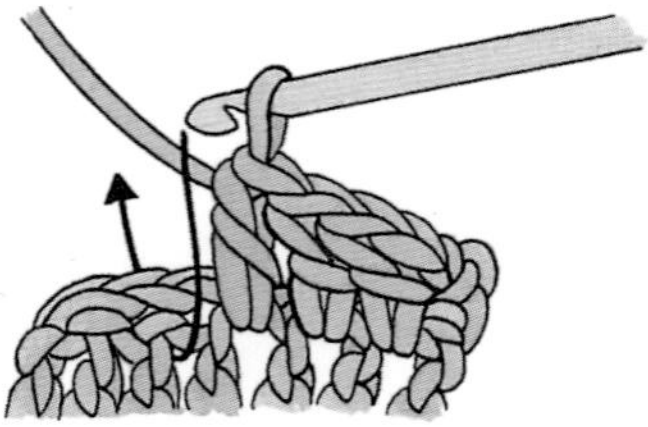

Stitch space (st-sp)
Insert hook between stitches of the previous row, instead of into top of stitch.

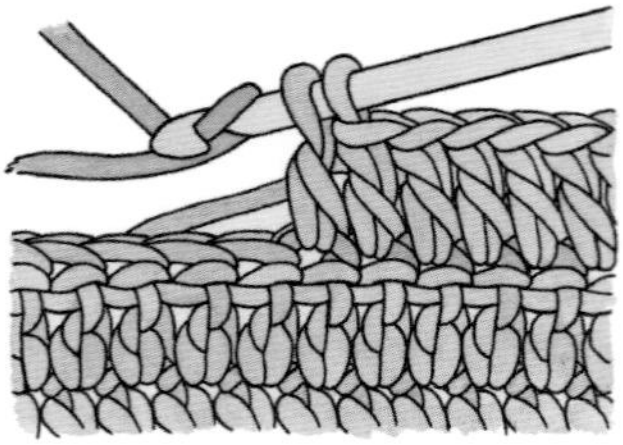

Joining yarn on a row
Work last stitch with old yarn, omitting final stage. Wrap new yarn over hook and draw through all loops on hook. The new yarn will form the top loops of the next stitch in the new colour.

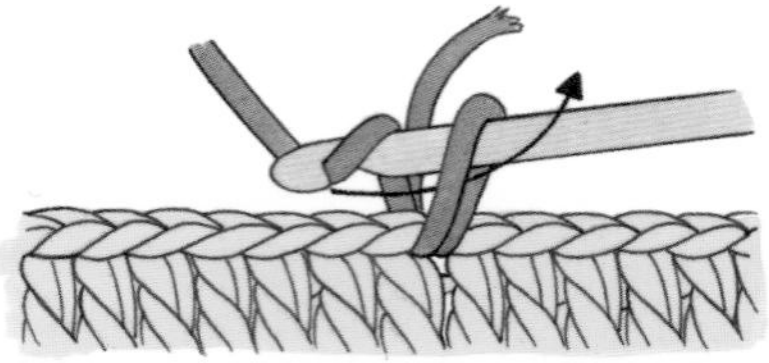

Joining yarn on a round
Method 1: Work joining slip stitch at end of round using new colour. Method 2 (above): Insert hook where required, draw up a loop of new colour, leaving a 10cm (4in) tail, and work specified number of starting chains. Continue with new yarn.

Cluster (cl)
Work specified number of stitches in places indicated in pattern, omitting final stage of each stitch so that last loop of each stitch remains on hook. Wrap yarn over hook and draw through all loops on hook.

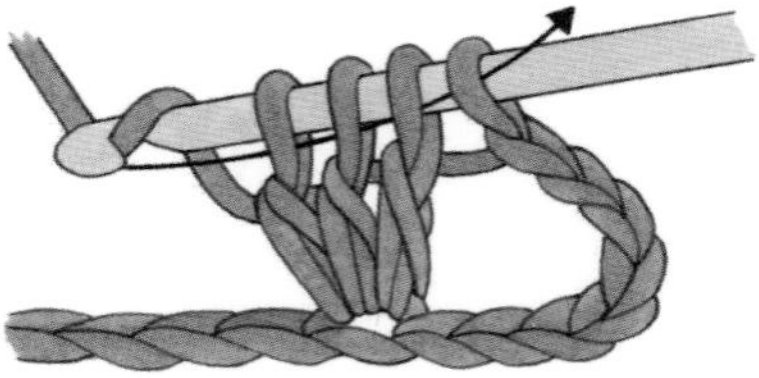

Bobble
Work specified number of stitches into same place, omitting final stage of each stitch so that last loop of each stitch remains on hook. Wrap yarn over hook and draw through all loops on hook.

Popcorn
Work specified number of stitches into same place. Take hook out of working loop and insert it under both top loops of first stitch of popcorn. Pick up working loop with hook and draw it through to fold the group of stitches and close the popcorn at the top.

Puff stitch
Work specified number of half treble crochet stitches into same place, omitting final stage of each stitch so that two loops of each one remain on hook. Wrap yarn over hook and draw through all loops on hook.

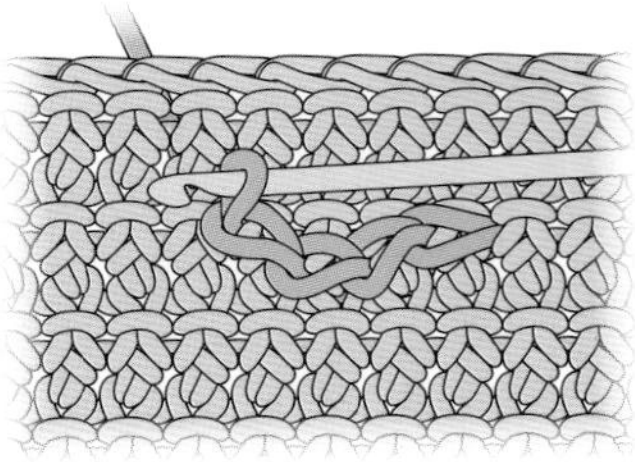

Surface crochet
Hold working yarn at back of finished block, insert hook from front to back through fabric in a space between two stitches, and pull through a loop. Insert hook between next two stitches and pull another loop through fabric and first loop on hook (like working a chain or slip stitch). Work around the posts of stitches, through gaps between stitches or as specified in pattern.

Fitting Blocks Together

Some block shapes fit together easily to make a continuous surface with no gaps. Other types of blocks will not interlock exactly; the spaces between them can be left empty for a lighter, more lacy effect. Alternatively, the spaces between blocks can be filled with small connector pieces.

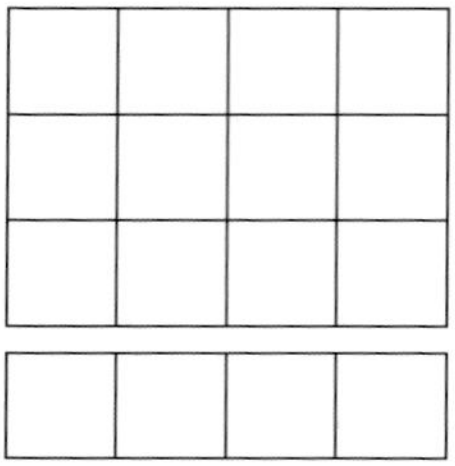

Squares
Join squares into strips, then join the strips to make the size and shape you want.

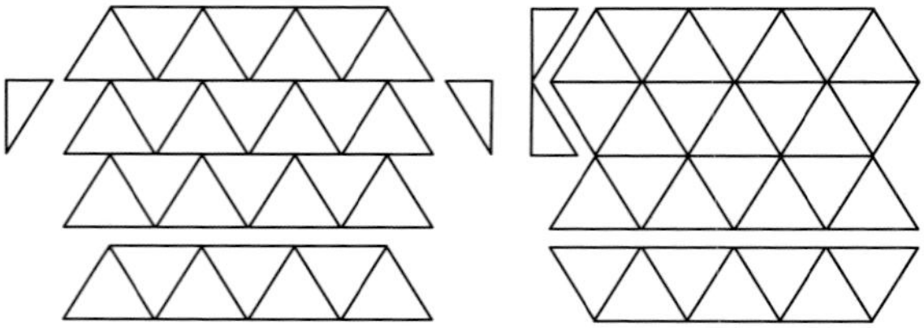

Triangles
Join triangles into strips, alternating the direction as required, then join the strips. Add half-triangles to the side edges if desired.

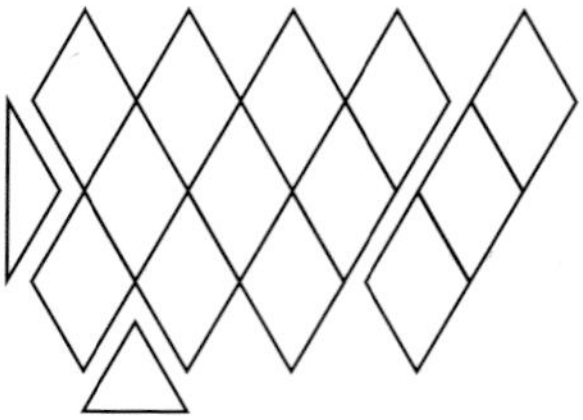

Diamonds
Assemble into diagonal strips, then join the strips. If you wish, work half-diamonds (triangles) to fit the gaps on the side edges.

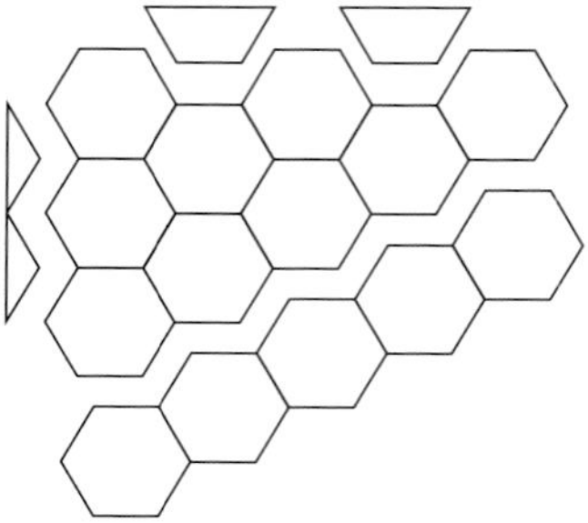

Hexagons
Join hexagons into diagonal strips, then join the strips to make the whole. Shallow triangles can fill the spaces on the side edges. The gaps on the top and bottom edges can be filled with half-hexagons.

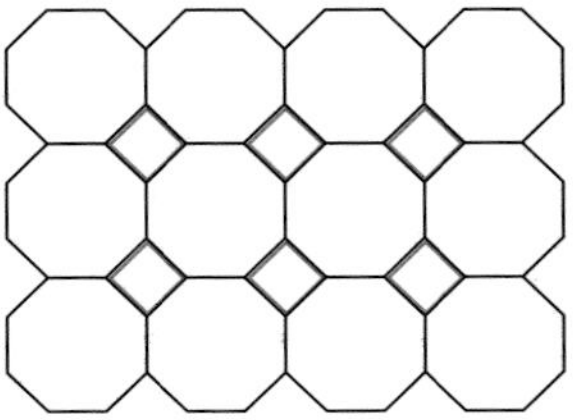

Octagons

Octagons can be joined with small square connectors set 'on point' if required. Join one strip of octagons, matching opposite faces. Join the square connectors between them. Then add the octagons of the row below, one at a time. Repeat as required. Triangles may be used to fill the gaps around the edges.

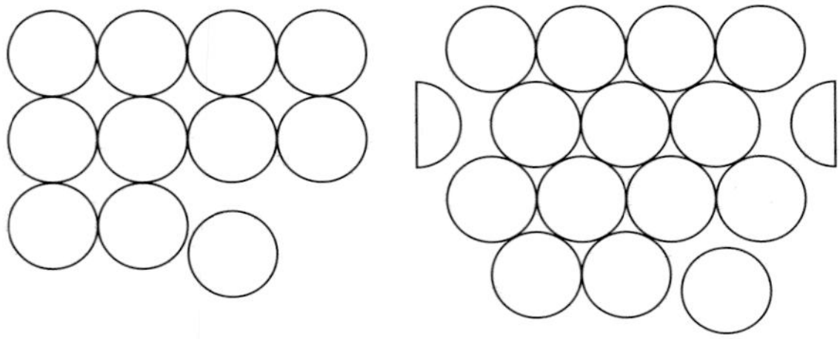

Circles with spaces

Circles may be joined where they touch on four sides for an open, lacy effect. Join each circle in place in turn. For a firmer result, add connector pieces between the circles, as below. For smaller spaces without the use of connectors, join the circles in offset rows, and fill side edges with half-circles if desired.

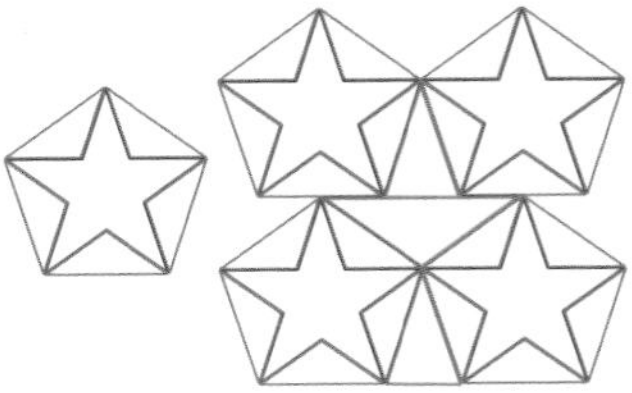

Stars and pentagons

Triangles added to a five-pointed star make a solid five-sided pentagon. Pentagons may be arranged in rows and the spaces filled with more triangles.

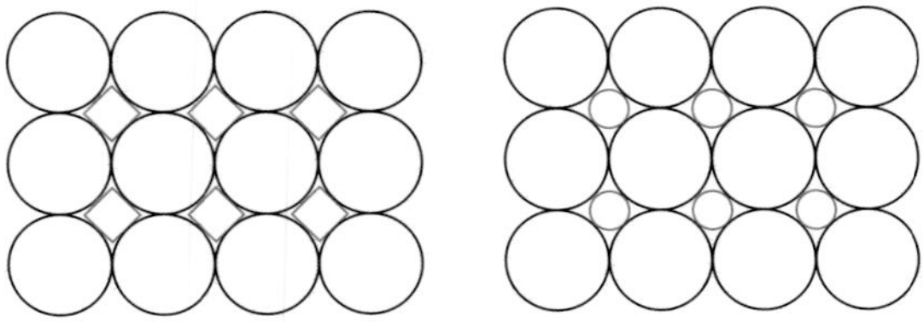

Circles with connectors

For a solid arrangement of circles, the gaps may be filled with small square connectors, stretched slightly to fit. Alternatively, using smaller circles as connectors leaves only small gaps between the shapes.

SNOWFLAKES AND FLOWERS

Shapes such as snowflakes have six points, and may therefore be treated as hexagons. Flowers may be treated as circles.

Planning Your Design

Make a visual plan of your design in order to check the final size and appearance, and to count how many blocks of each type and/or colour you will need.

Planning stages

1 Measure your sample block(s), and decide on the finished size required. How many blocks will be required in each direction?

2 Draw each block to about 2.5 x 2.5cm (1 x 1in), or as appropriate (don't draw too small). Large sheets of graph paper are helpful when drawing shapes such as squares, diamonds and triangles. Other shapes are trickier to draw – if you have access to a computer with appropriate software, you can draw one shape such as a circle, then copy and paste it to make the arrangement you need. Otherwise, draw the shape of your sample block on to thin cardstock, then cut out the outline to make a template. Draw around the template, fitting the outlines closely together.

3 Roughly colour in the plan to indicate the patterns and colours of your chosen blocks.

4 At the side of the plan, write a list of each block and colourway, and count how many blocks of each design will be needed.

5 Calculate the amount of yarn required of each colour (see opposite).

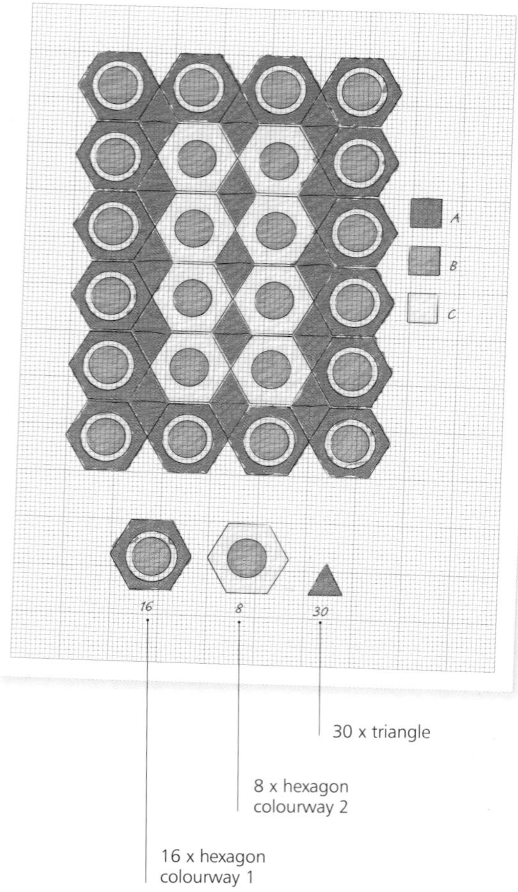

Sketch for a hexagon blanket design

Tension

Tension refers to the number of stitches and rows to a given width and length of crochet fabric. It's important to crochet a test block before you start your project to establish what your tension is.

If you want to match the size of the blocks shown in this book, work a sample block using the same yarn weight and hook size, and then block (see page 220) and measure your sample. As a rule, if your block is smaller than required, work another sample using a hook one size larger. If your block is larger, make another using a hook one size smaller.

Tension can be affected by the colour and fibre composition of the yarn and the size and brand of the crochet hook, so you may need to make several sample blocks using different hooks until you match the block size required.

When designing your own project, you need to establish the tension that you want for the project. Work a sample block using your chosen yarn and the hook size that is recommended for that particular yarn, and then block the motif. If your block is smaller than required, make another sample using a hook one size larger. If your block fabric feels tight and hard, make another sample using a hook one size larger. If your block fabric feels loose and floppy, make another using a hook one size smaller. Continue to work sample blocks until you are happy with the size and feel of your crochet fabric.

A WORD OF CAUTION

Your tension may vary depending on the stitch that dominates the block. For instance, you may need a larger hook for a block of double crochet, a slightly smaller hook for treble crochet and an even smaller hook for filet designs.

Calculating yarn amounts

The most reliable way to calculate how much yarn you need to buy for a specific project is to buy a ball of each yarn you are going to use for the project and then make some sample blocks.

The amount of yarn per ball or skein can vary considerably between colours of the same yarn because of the different dyes that have been used, so it's a good idea to make the samples using the actual colours you intend to use.

1. Using the yarn and a suitable size of hook, work three samples of each block you intend to use, making sure that you allow at least 8cm (3in) of spare yarn at every colour change. This will compensate for the extra yarn you will need for weaving in the ends.

2. Unravel the three blocks and carefully measure the amount of yarn used for each colour in each block.

3. Take the average length of yarn and multiply it by the number of blocks you intend to make. Don't forget to add extra yarn to your calculations for joining the blocks together and for working any edgings.

4. Compare this figure to the length of yarn in a whole ball (this information is usually printed on the ball band) and use this to calculate the number of balls to buy. If in doubt, always buy extra yarn.

Blocking and Joining

Always block your crochet before joining pieces together. This involves pinning blocks out to the correct size and then either steaming them with an iron or moistening them with cold water and allowing them to dry. Blocks can be joined by sewing or crocheting them together. Use the same yarn for joining as you used for working the blocks or a matching stronger yarn.

Blocking guidelines

Always be guided by the information given on the ball band of your yarn and, when in doubt, choose the cold water blocking method below.

1 Make a blocking board by securing one or two layers of quilter's wadding, covered with a sheet of cotton fabric, over a 60 x 90cm (24 x 36in) piece of flat board. Checked fabric is ideal because you can use the regular grid of checks to help with alignment of edges and points.

2 Pin out several blocks at the same time, using plenty of short metal pins. Gently ease the block into shape before inserting each pin.

3 To block woollen yarns with warm steam, hold a steam iron set at the correct temperature for the yarn about 2cm (¾in) above the surface of the block and allow the steam to penetrate for several seconds.

4 Lay the board flat and allow the blocks to dry completely before removing the pins.

5 To block acrylic and wool/acrylic blend yarns, pin out the pieces as above, then use a spray bottle to mist the crochet with cold water until it is moist, but not saturated.

6 Gently pat the fabric to help the moisture penetrate more easily. Lay the board flat and allow the blocks to dry completely before removing the pins.

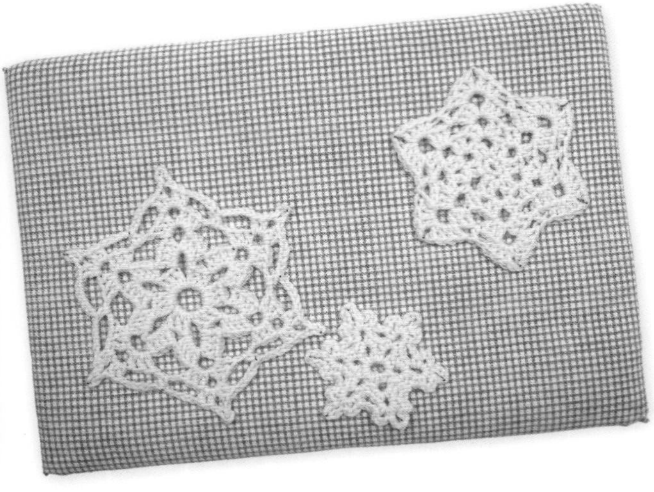

Blocking motifs with the right side up allows you to adjust the picots, bobbles and other textured stitches so that they look their best.

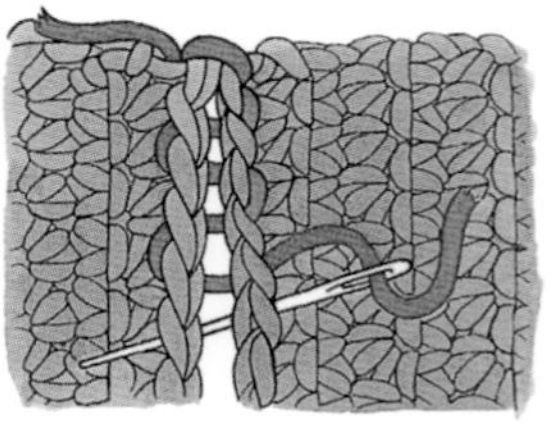

Woven seam
Lay the blocks with the edges touching and wrong sides facing upwards. Using a tapestry needle, weave back and forth around the centres of the stitches, without pulling the stitches too tightly.

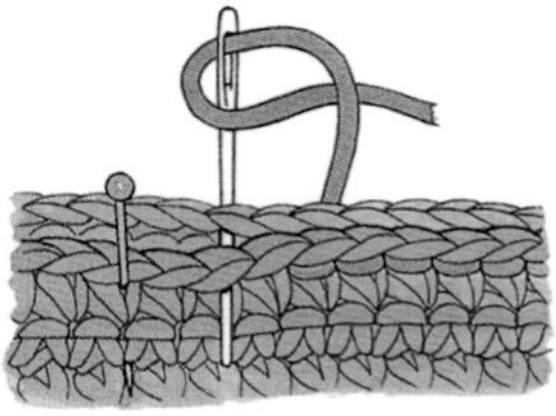

Backstitch seam
Hold the blocks to be joined with right sides together, pinning if necessary. Using a tapestry needle, work a line of backstitches along the edge.

Overcast seam
Using a tapestry needle, insert the needle into the back loops of corresponding stitches. For extra strength, work two stitches into the end loops.

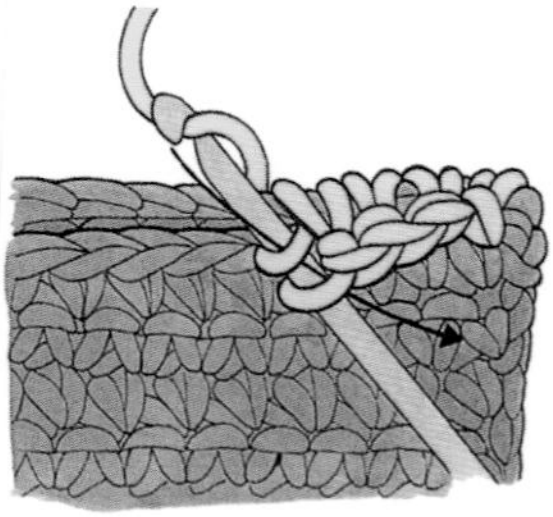

Double crochet seam
Work as for the slip stitch seam below, but work a row of double crochet stitch from the right or wrong side, depending on your preference.

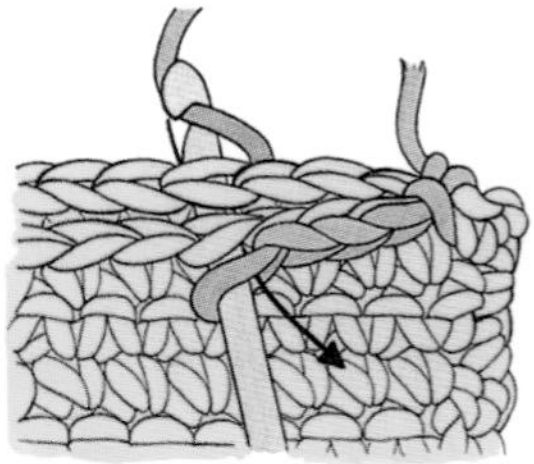

Slip stitch seam
Joining blocks with wrong sides together gives a firm seam with an attractive ridge on the right side. If you prefer the ridge not to be visible, join the blocks with right sides together so the ridge is on the wrong side. Work a row of slip stitch through both top loops of each block. When working this method along the side edges of blocks worked in rows, work enough evenly spaced stitches so that the seam is not too tight.

Reading Patterns and Charts

Block patterns are worked using a combination of stitches. In order to save space as well as make them easier to follow, abbreviations are used. Charts are visual representations of the written pattern and, once mastered, are quicker and easier to follow. All charts show the right side of the block.

Stitch symbol charts (all blocks)

All of the blocks in this book are accompanied by a stitch symbol chart. These show each type of stitch used in the block and where it is worked in relation to the other stitches. The stitches are coloured to match the yarn colours used. A solid arrowhead indicates where a new yarn is joined; an outline arrowhead indicates where a yarn is fastened off.

Filet charts (blocks 1–12)

Filet patterns are very long when written out in full, making them appear far more complicated than they really are, so they are always worked from a chart. Filet designs are simply a sequence of 'open mesh' spaces and 'solid mesh' blocks. Each square on the chart represents two stitches, forming an open space or a solid block. Work the foundation chain as instructed in the written pattern, then follow the chart from row 1.

Colourwork charts (blocks 43–47)

Colourwork designs include a coloured chart on a grid. It is easier to see the placement of colours on this type of chart. One square on the chart represents one stitch. Work the foundation chain as instructed in the written pattern, then follow the chart from row 1.

Charts in rows

All rows are numbered. Right-side rows start at the right, and are read from right to left. Wrong-side rows start at the left, and are read from left to right.

Charts in rounds

These begin at the centre, and each round is usually read anticlockwise (the direction of working). When working blocks in the round, you will usually have the right side of the crochet facing you. Some blocks require you to turn the work, and this is indicated on the charts with an arrow pointing in the direction in which you should read the chart for that round. Each round is numbered near the beginning of the round.

Abbreviations and symbols

The list opposite includes the common crochet abbreviations and symbols. Any special abbreviations and instructions are explained with the relevant pattern.

ABBREVIATION AND SYMBOL VARIATIONS

Always read the list of abbreviations and symbols provided with the pattern you are using before starting a project. The abbreviations and symbols for the main stitches are standardised, but different pattern publishers and designers may use different ones for others, such as 'flo' (front loop only) rather than 'tfl' (through front loop).

Abbreviations

alt	alternate
beg	beginning
BP	back post
ch	chain
cl	cluster
cont	continue
dc	double crochet
dec	decrease
dtr	double treble crochet
foll	follow(ing)
FP	front post
htr	half treble crochet
inc	increase
MB	make bobble
patt	pattern
rep	repeat
RS	right side
sp	space
ss	slip stitch
st(s)	stitch(es)
tbl	through back loop
tfl	through front loop
tog	together
tr	treble crochet
trtr	triple treble
WS	wrong side
xdc	extended double crochet
yo	yarn over

Chart symbols

- join yarn
- fasten off yarn
- direction of working
- magic ring
- chain
- slip stitch
- double crochet
- extended double crochet
- half treble crochet
- treble crochet
- double treble crochet
- triple treble crochet
- cluster (e.g. cluster of 3 tr)
- bobble (e.g. bobble of 3 xdc)
- puff stitch (e.g. puff of 5 htr)
- popcorn (e.g. popcorn of 4 tr)
- through back loop (e.g. dc tbl)
- through front loop (e.g. dc tfl)
- front post (e.g. FPtr)
- back post (e.g. BPdtr)

Arrangement of symbols

JOINED AT TOP
A group of symbols joined at the top indicates that these stitches should be worked together at the top, as in cluster stitches, and for decreasing the number of stitches (e.g. dc2tog, tr3tog).

JOINED AT BASE
Symbols joined at the base should all be worked into the same stitch below.

JOINED AT TOP AND BASE
Sometimes a group of stitches are joined at both top and bottom, making a bobble, puff or popcorn.

ON AN ANGLE
Symbols may be drawn at an angle, depending on the construction of the stitch pattern.

DISTORTED SYMBOLS
Some symbols may be lengthened, curved or spiked, to indicate where the hook is inserted below.

Index

Credits

Quarto would like to thank the following for providing yarns used to make the blocks:

Lion Brand Yarns
www.lionbrand.com

Rowan Yarns
www.knitrowan.com